RAC
FOOD
ROUTES

The motorist's guide to seeing, tasting and buying Britain's best local food

edited by Henrietta Green

George Philip & Son Limited
London

First published in Great Britain in 1988 by
George Philip & Son Limited, 27a Floral Street,
London WC2E 9DP

and

Jarrold and Sons Limited, Norwich

© Jarrold and Sons Ltd, Norwich/Rich and Green Ltd, London 1988

Editor: Henrietta Green

Design Consultants: Geoff Staff BA, ASTD; Bernard Higton

British Library Cataloguing in Publication Data

RAC Food Routes

The motorist's guide to seeing, tasting and buying Britain's
best local food

1. Food industry and trade—Great Britain
—Directories   2. Beverage industry—
Great Britain—Directories
I. Green, Henrietta   II. Royal Automobile Club
338.4'76413'002541   HD9011.3
ISBN 0-540-01172-X

Typesetting by Taylor Jackson Designs Ltd, Lowestoft
Printed and bound by Jarrold and Sons Ltd, Norwich

CONTENTS

FOREWORD

Several years ago the family visited an old working mill in the middle of a steep, sheltered valley in Wales.

As the car bumped up the drive we could hear the pitching of a huge iron wheel as it turned, powered by the flow of the mill stream. Once inside there was the constant grind of the stones as they crushed wheat to flour; outside, children shrieked with laughter as they played with the farm animals and from the adjacent barn came the hearty applause of an appreciative audience watching a cookery demonstration.

Everyone was having fun — there was so much to see and do. Later on, after a superb tea with piles of Welsh cakes generously spread with farmhouse butter and Welsh honey, we piled into the car clutching our trophies — a sack of freshly milled flour and a bundle of farmhouse recipes with which to experiment.

We had learnt a lot and had come to understand how flour was made, its different qualities and properties. Suitably inspired, we wanted to start cooking immediately!

As we drove off we felt like Marco Polo drinking his first cup of tea in China — we had discovered something exciting and interesting which could be enjoyed and shared by everyone. So, RAC FOOD ROUTES was born.

RAC FOOD ROUTES tells you about all the interesting places with food connections that you can visit, so you can plan your own Food Route. With 42 regional maps, each one clearly marked with the food sites, you can choose the places to visit. From pick your own to fish your own, whisky distilleries, vineyards, breweries, cider presses and farmhouse dairies where you can watch the cheese-making and taste the cheese — I've included them all.

There are specialist food and farm shops; museums where you learn about our food heritage, farm trails and farm museums which teach you the history of agriculture and land cultivation; country houses, ·and their kitchens filled with ranks of shining copper pans, which show you how the other half lived and kitchen gardens which required an army of gardeners to tend them. There's even a museum, dedicated to the history of tea drinking, which has over a thousand teacups, and a rock factory where you can poke your own name through the stick.

There really is so much to discover, watch, catch, see, learn, taste and buy. With over 1100 places to visit listed in RAC FOOD ROUTES, I've tried to tell you exactly what you'll find and how to get there. I've mentioned details on the main exhibits, the produce on sale and all the vital details, such as the price of admission and the opening hours. You'll notice that each site is marked with a symbol e.g. ≋ = smokery, but remember that some places may also cover a full range of other food activities as well. For a fuller explanation and a key to the listings, please turn to page 16.

I've included shopping tips — specialities to look out for — and regional recipes which provide all sorts of ideas on how to prepare local produce. Each region has an introduction written by a chef, hotelier or cookery writer who really knows that area and its food.

When you go off on a food foray, particularly if you're planning to visit a pick your own — you may need to take containers in which you can pack the food. If the weather is hot and your journey is long, it's always a good idea to take an insulated container or, failing that, damp newspaper will keep food cool.

I hope you'll have as good a time following food routes as I did discovering them. Drive carefully and have fun.

7

MILLING IN THE TRADITIONAL WAY

W A Jordan

● **The mill house and flour mill on the River Ivel**

Over 100 years ago there were more than 400 independent flour mills in Bedfordshire. By the 1950s only a handful of these original mills were left and Jordans' Holme Mill, on the River Ivel near Biggleswade, was one of them. There has been a mill on the River Ivel since the Domesday Book when, together with its sister mill, it was valued at 47 shillings.

One hundred years ago, all these Bedfordshire mills were producing white flour, which is made from the starchy endosperm of the wheat grain. During the milling process the outer layers of bran and much of the wheatgerm content is removed, leaving only 71% of the grain remaining; this is then bleached with chlorine dioxide, a tasteless disinfectant.

White flour has been popular for producing white bread since the Middle Ages when white was associated with purity. Bakers were known to have whitened the grain with chalk, alum and, in extreme cases, with arsenic powder and ground-up bones. Even in the Dark Ages, quality was being sacrificed for 'purity'.

As recently as the last century, white flour and bread were served only to the gentry, while the working classes ate brown bread and only the animals were given the bran and wheatgerm. The government did recognise, however, that white flour had all its natural goodness removed and imposed the regulation that all flours which contained less than 100% of the whole wheat grain would include some kind of vitamin and mineral supplement — and this requirement is still recognised today.

During the 1970s it was realised that this artificial enriching of the flour could not replace the natural goodness of 100% wholemeal flour. The natural enzymes which are essential to our health, because they help the body's natural bacteria to prosper, are only present in 100% wholemeal flour. Consequently such flour became popular, both for its taste and its health-giving properties.

Most of the mills producing 100% wholemeal flour — both watermills and windmills — use traditional mill-stones to grind the grain, working relatively slowly without allowing the grain to overheat; this means the wheat germ is not destroyed and its full nutritional quality is retained.

The mills work in the following way. On arriving at the mill the sacks of corn are hoisted to the 'lucam' on the top floor by the 'sack hoist', either from inside the mill or direct from the cart or lorry, though nowadays grain is often delivered in bulk and blown through pipes to the top of the mill. The grain is then stored in wooden bins which today are usually lined with galvanised sheet steel to keep out rats and mice. These bins are positioned over each pair of millstones and a chute from each one leads to a hopper above the stones. The grain is then shaken into the 'eye' of the millstones. The bottom millstone — the bedstone — stays still while the upper stone — the runner, revolves at about 100 rpm. Each stone has a set of furrows cut in it. The grain passes through the eye of the runnerstone and is forced through the gap between the stones. The action of the furrows crossing each other breaks the grain and scrapes out the wholemeal flour which then falls out of the perimeter of the stones, down the 'meal spout' and into the 'meal sack' on the floor below. The miller is able to regulate the fineness or coarseness of the meal by either screwing down the runnerstone so that the stones grind more closely and produce a finer meal, or by raising the runnerstone for a coarser meal. The amount of grain fed into the stones is regulated by the 'twist peg' positioned next to the chute.

Most stoneground mills now produce 100% wholemeal flour. In those that still make white flour, the sack of meal must be hoisted again to the top of the mill, and put through a 'wire machine' on the first floor. In this machine rotating brushes in a wire gauze cylinder brush the flour through the gauze and the bran falls out of the end.

After a devastating fire, Holme mill was rebuilt in 1896 with 'Carter's Roller System' and was the most progressive mill of the time. Today it still

● **The flour mill turbine**

uses the original applewood water wheel installed in 1896, and is the county's leading producer of 100% wholemeal flour.

The five feet fall of the river water ensures a steady 25hp to power the rollers and other machinery. Rollers work in a similar manner to stones and, for us, provide the most efficient system, retaining all the goodness and enzymes in the grain, unlike modern high-speed rollers which run at 800 rpm and burn away the natural goodness. We prefer to sacrifice the 'advantages' of high speed production in favour of the quality obtained by milling in the traditional way.

● **A wholemeal loaf**

GRAINS AND THEIR USES

Grains have been farmed since the Stone Age and used for baking bread — 'The Staff of Life'. In Roman times grains were thought to have been provided by the goddess Ceres, which is why they became known as cereals.

Some grains fare better in some climates than in others. Traditionally wheat and rye thrive in the temperate zones of Europe and North America, rice and millet flourish in the Eastern tropics, and maize is prevalent in Central and Southern America as well as in parts of Africa. Today, by changing the soil with chemicals and fertilizers, and using new strains of seeds, different types of cereals are grown all over the world.

In the past, grain was used as a trading currency, and today its value is still enormous. The countries that produce the largest quantities have a great deal of bargaining power in world markets.

Barley

Barley was the most important bread grain in ancient times and is thought to be native to Iraq, where it was originally milled to make bread and fermented to make beer. It is still used to make beer today — the grains are sprouted as part of the malting process, which increases the vitamin and enzyme content of the beer. Whole barley grains can be cooked as a rice substitute, and

can also be mixed with other grains. When the barley grain has been hulled and polished it is known as Pearl Barley and this is a traditional ingredient of soups and stews in Britain. Barley flour can be used to make bread, but as the flour is weak in gluten, it produces a flattish loaf.

Maize

Maize corn was originally found in Mexico and has been cultivated for thousands of years. There are many different types of maize, all with different uses: some are used to make corn oil — a light cooking oil; 'flour corn' is used for breakfast cereals such as cornflakes; 'pop corn' which is 'popped' to make the popular snack; and, the most well known, 'sweet corn' — delicious when picked fresh from one of the many pick your own farms, boiled until tender and spread with melted butter.

Millet

Millet was once the principal grain of Europe and was grown in China long before rice was introduced. We are all familiar with millet from seeing it hanging in bird cages, but it is not used only for this. The small grains, with their high protein content, can be used as a thickening agent in soups and stews, or can be boiled like rice and used in the Middle Eastern dish 'couscous'.

Oats

Oats are traditionally the staple grain of Scotland and are featured widely in Scottish cooking although they were originally farmed in Central Europe. They are best known as the main ingredient of porridge — traditionally served with salt in Scotland, and with sugar in England — and are high in fibre and vitamin B.

They are also used in traditional English dishes such as parkin and for coating foods such as fish. Oats are either kept whole, or milled to produce flaked oats and various types of oatmeal.

Rye is thought to come from Asia and has many uses — the Scandinavians use it to make crispbreads, the Americans to make whisky, the Dutch to make gin and the Russians to make beer. It is very low in gluten and is often mixed with wheat when baking to make tasty rye bread. The Germans make excellent pumpernickel — a dark flat bread, high in fibre and with a distinctive flavour — from pure rye. Rye is generally thought to have been responsible for the mystery of the 'Marie Celeste', a ship which was found floating totally intact but with no crew on board; modern science has a theory that the crew could have been suffering from horrific hallucinations and walked off the ship. The hallucinations could have been caused by eating rye grains affected by a type of parasitic fungus!

============ Wheat ============

Wheat is probably the most important grain on earth today — half of the population relies on it as a staple food. It originated around the Mediterranean but is so versatile that it will grow on almost any ground. There are many different types of wheat, these include: Durum, which is used for pasta products; Bulgar, which remains whole throughout the milling process — it is eaten instead of rice in North America and is becoming increasingly popular in Britain; and Triticale, a new grain with a high protein content which is a cross between wheat and rye — it is used commercially for breadmaking. The strength of the wheat grain is affected by where it grows — hard 'strong' wheat originates from the Americas and 'soft' wheats are grown in England and Europe. 'Strong' wheat is higher in protein and has a stronger

gluten content which makes it better for bread baking. 'Soft' wheats have a better flavour and are more suitable for baking cakes and biscuits. Flour for making bread is usually a mixture, or 'grist', of 60% strong flour and 40% soft flour. Wholemeal flour contains 100% wheat and wheatmeal flour contains 80-90% wheat including all the germ and some bran.

FRUIT

	MAY	JUNE	JULY	AUG	SEP	OCT	NOV	DEC
Apples				●——	——	—●		
Blackberries				●——	——	—●		
Blackcurrants		●——	——	—●				
Cherries		●——	——	—●				
Damsons				●——	——	—●		
Elderberries					●			
Gooseberries		●——	——	—●				
Greengages			●—	—●				
Loganberries			●—	—●				
Medlars							●	
Pears				●——	—●			
Plums			●—	—●				
Raspberries		●——	——	——	—●			
Red Currants		●——	——	—●				
Strawberries		●——	——	——	—●			
Tayberries			●——	——	—●			
Whitecurrants			●—	—●				

This chart is a guide to the seasonal availability of fruit and vegetables in Britain. However, any guide can only be approximate, bearing in mind how changeable the summers in Britain can be and how much later the crops are in the north than in the south. We would advise you to telephone the Pick Your Own farm before setting out to check on availability in order to avoid disappointment.

VEGETABLES IN SEASON — VEGETABLES

	JAN	FEB	MAR	APR	MAY	JUN	JUL	AUG	SEP	OCT	NOV	DEC
Artichokes												
Globe						●——————————●						
Asparagus					●————————●							
Beans												
Broad						●———●						
Green						●——————————●						
Runner							●——————————●					
Beetroot	●———————————————————————————————————————●											
Brussel Sprouts	●———————————●						●——————————————●					
Cabbage												
Primo						●————————●						
Red	●———●											●
Spring Greens	●———————●									●———●		
Carrots	●———————————●					●——————————————●						
Cauliflower and	●———————————————————————————————————————●											
Broccoli							●———●					
Celeriac	●———————●				●——————————————————●							
Celery	●———●											
Courgettes						●——————————●						
Mangetout						●————————●						
Marrows							●——————————●					
Peas					●————————————————●							
Potatoes					●————————————————●							
New						●———●						
Pumpkins							●——————————●					
Spinach					●————————————————————●							
Sweetcorn								●———●				
Tomatoes							●————————●					

PLANNING YOUR FOOD ROUTE

Britain has been divided into eight main regions (below), and each region has been sub-divided into several smaller areas (opposite). To plan your food route, identify the area you want to explore, and turn to the appropriate map. You can then move around the region by following the colour-coded bands at the top of each page.

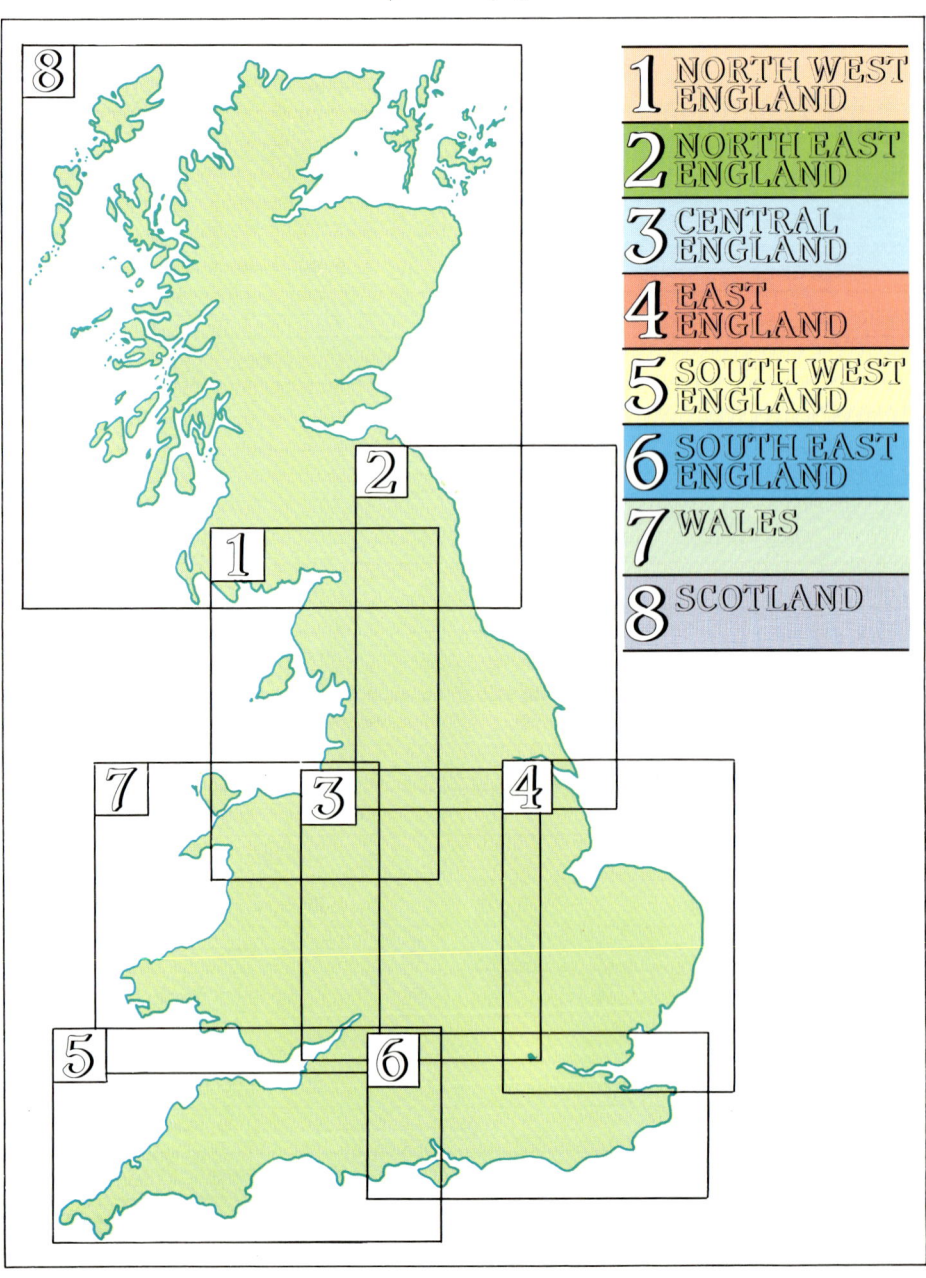

1 NORTH WEST ENGLAND
2 NORTH EAST ENGLAND
3 CENTRAL ENGLAND
4 EAST ENGLAND
5 SOUTH WEST ENGLAND
6 SOUTH EAST ENGLAND
7 WALES
8 SCOTLAND

NORTH WEST ENGLAND

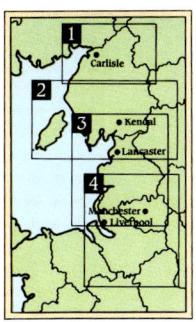

NORTH EAST ENGLAND

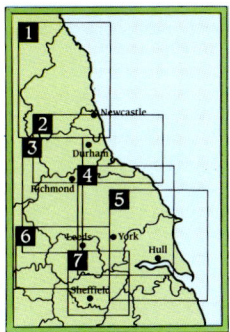

CENTRAL ENGLAND

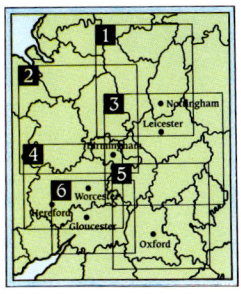

EAST ENGLAND

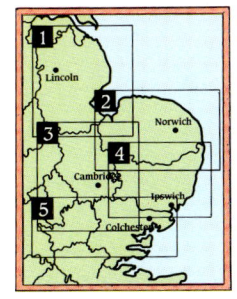

SOUTH WEST ENGLAND

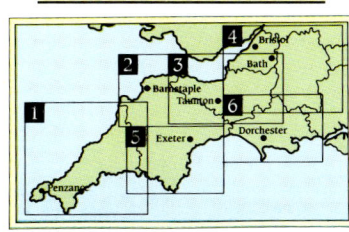

SOUTH EAST ENGLAND

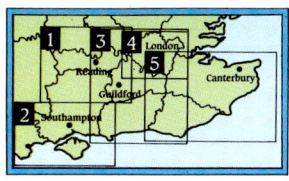

WALES

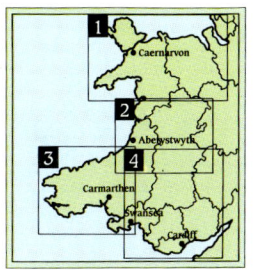

SCOTLAND

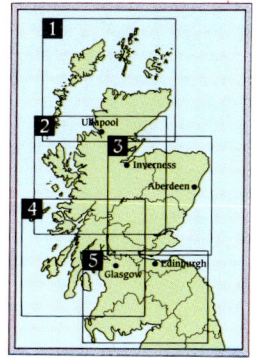

Continued overleaf

THE LISTINGS

The area maps mark every entry in the listings, which are ordered alphabetically. Each entry has its own map reference, plus detailed, coded information. The symbols are explained below, using fictitious examples.

MAP SCALE
England and Wales 8½ miles to inch
Scotland 16½ miles to inch
Greater London 2½ miles to inch

☐ Area featured on this map
☐ Area not featured on this map
(turn to appropriate map)

SYMBOLS

✳ Mill
〰 Smokery
▱ Cheese-maker
◇ Any other visitable food producer
✎ Vineyard
🍷 Any other visitable drink producer
🎣 Fish farm
🌿 Herb farm or kitchen garden
🏛 Historic house or estate
🏢 Museum with special food interest
♈ Farm
🍖 Specialist food shop
☺ Farm shop or Pick your Own
♈ Restaurant with featured recipe

Each site is marked according to its main interest but very often they offer more than one activity

LISTINGS FACILITIES

🍴 Snacks only available
🍴 Full meals i.e. lunch, tea and dinner
♿ Disabled facilities see below
🆆🅲 Toilets
🚗 Car park
⛱ Picnic area
🛝 Children's playground

MINIMUM REQUIREMENTS FOR DISABLED VISITORS
At least one entrance must have no steps or be equipped with a ramp whose gradient does not exceed 1:12.
All doors must be at least 75cm (29½ ins) clear opening width, with a head-on approach.
Lifts must have gate opening of at least 75cm (29½ ins); lifts must be at least 122cm (48 ins) deep and 91cm (36 ins) wide.
Toilet facilities must have a door width of 75cm (29½ ins) and be able to close behind wheelchair.

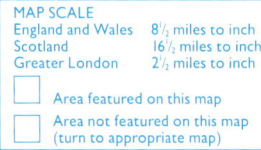

MAP 1 SOUTH WEST ENGLAND

St. Ives — HAYLE MUSEUM OF BREWING
Camb
Hayle
St. Just — Penzance — 30 — Marazion — Breage
3071 — 394
30 — Helston
Land's End — Sennen — Mount's Bay
3083

CORNWALL
A — B

🍺 Map 1 B2
Hayle Museum of Brewing
The Street, Hayle,
Cornwall PL14 6PZ
Tel. Hayle (0872) 51770

From Penzance follow A3 eastwards, after 3 miles turn left onto B1191. Signposted.

This museum specialises in the history of brewing and visitors may see how the business has developed over the years.

☞ museum only: adults £1.50, senior citizens & children 60p
◐ all year Mon-Fri 10-4.30, Sat-Sun 11-4.30
Facilities: 🍴🍴🆆🅲🚗☺

★ summer 'brew-ups' on Bank Hols Mar-Oct
🍴 restaurant serves lunches and teas

RESTAURANT RECIPE

♈ Map 1 D2
ABBOTS HOTEL
Whitechurch Road, Penryn,
Cornwall PL13 5QL
Tel: Penryn (0288) 332121
From Penryn follow A39 eastwards, hotel on right after 1 mile.
A large, nicely furnished hotel and restaurant, well known for its regional speciality menu
◐ Mon-Sun Meals: 12.30-2, 7-10
Price range £2.50-10 Set L £7.50 Set D £11.75
Seats 110
Cards: Access, Amex, Diners
Facilities: ♈🍴♿🚗

Entries are listed alphabetically within the map region.

Postal address.

Directions are taken from the nearest town or village marked on the map. Whilst every effort has been taken to ensure their accuracy, motorists should also consult their route-finder or, in London, a street gazetteer.

Admission prices given where applicable. For obvious reasons the symbol does not appear on listings for shops.

All establishments are closed on Christmas and New Year's Day and Good Friday. Some are open only by appointment whilst others, particularly Pick your Own, will vary according to the weather, so check in advance to avoid disappointment.

Details of any special events.

Details of catering facilities featuring regional specialities.

Restaurants with a reputation for serving local produce; one of their recipes follows

RESTAURANT FACILITIES
🍷 Licensed
🍴 Childrens' meals
♿ Disabled facilities see bottom left
🚗 Car park

Days and times when meals are served.

Average price per person of set meal — L-lunch, D-dinner — otherwise average price per person to eat à la carte.

Number of seats.

Credit cards accepted.

NORTH WEST ENGLAND

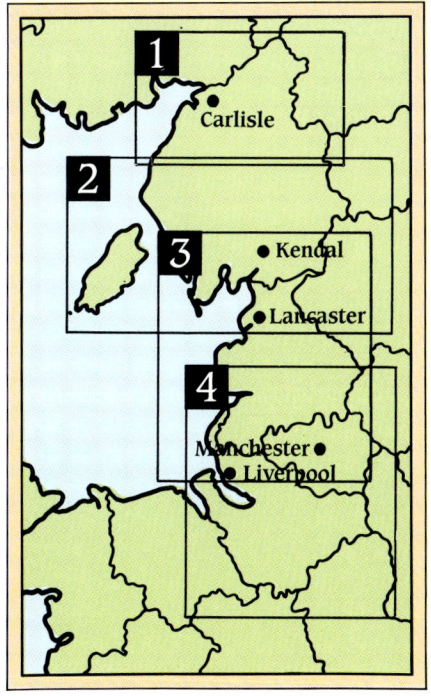

NORTH WEST ENGLAND

● **Peele Castle, Isle of Man**

by Russell Harty
JOURNALIST & BROADCASTER

Let us, at this stage, suppose that you are making your first hesitant trip to the North West. All that you have heard, so far, indicates that the staples of your diet will be fish and chips, tripe and black pudding.

You slide into the North West somewhere near the Cheshire Plain. This part of the world should, strictly speaking, carry a government health warning. If you lower the windows of a speeding car, you can catch great gulps of fresh air that have blown across the water from Ireland and dropped some of its native fatness on this green part of the earth. Cream oozes out of the pastures and the fields are full of the fat kine of Joseph's dream. I don't suppose many of the wealthy landowners and the comfortable farmers get much satisfaction from the fact that, because of the distressing EEC policy, they have to pour a lot of milk down the local drains. But, rules or not, we live in unequal times and there is plenty of rich cream left on the top of their vats and that is why such glorious Cheshire cheeses roll out of this particular landscape. They

do say that the reason why the Cheshire cat is grinning is because it's been at the cream.

The word cheese has a powerful ring: round, fat, full, creamy, satisfying. And within a small stone's throw there is the County Palatine of Lancashire, where they make something called Lancashire Cheese; and here the whole process of praise and justification starts again.

We are moving, though, to huge conurbations which, in all honesty, have seen better days. Imagine the Adelphi in Liverpool and the Midland Hotel in Manchester in the great days of this region's high prosperity. If you were preparing to embark to the New World, you would stay at the Adelphi and you would be expected, nay, required, to dress for dinner. And if you had spent August in Scotland you would break your comfortable railway journey in Manchester, check into the Midland and live in splendour. One did not, and one needed not, enquire into the state of the less privileged. They would be eating chips, fish and mushy peas, paying less, sweating less and, perhaps, in the deepness of our mythology, enjoying it more.

But the huge change which took place after the war and after our reasonable withdrawal from Empire, brought the Indians, the Pakistanis, the Chinese, the Thais, the Greeks, the Italians — the lot — pouring into this starved region. And haven't they done well, thank you. I would take a straight bet that there is more good Chinese food to be found in Manchester than in any other comparable British city. And when I'm working in Liverpool I find it much more interesting to investigate the delicacies of dal and Korma than to chicken out at a chicken inn and have some helpless battery pullet dolled up in a plastic box.

Travel now beyond the big cities and into one of the most unspoiled and natural wastelands of Britain. Once you move further north, you will find hidden valleys and tentative villages, each with a pub or a farmhouse that will furnish you with as good a pub lunch or cream tea as anywhere else in this large land. There's Cumberland sausage, Lancashire hotpot, homemade pies, seafoods, and chip 'butties'. Eccles, Goosnargh or Chorley cakes, and cream teas.

By the time you reach the Lake District, all sensible resolutions will have disappeared through the sun roof. Some few years ago a handful of energetic and enterprising restaurateurs laid down their culinary roots in this blessed plot. They taught by example. Others were quick to learn. The area is not large, but if you look at any sensible guide to good eating you will see that the Lake District is peppered with congratulatory black dots, stars, rosettes, goblets, the lot. The weather can be hellish and spoil your day, but at night the restaurants spoil your choice. I have dined in Tokyo, Rome, Los Angeles and Paris and I have heard, in all these far away places, strong recommendations for friends of mine who supervise the luxurious eating houses of what Wordsworth called 'these savage parts'.

You will have noticed that I have not mentioned any individual place by name. Two reasons for this. One is that I have a lot of friends in this eating business and there is no space to list them all. The other reason is that they are a fierce and jealous breed and I should be ostracised by them all.

Good heavens, I have not mentioned the kippers from the Isle of Man, the sausages from Clitheroe, the smoked trout from Lancaster, the Morecambe Bay shrimps, the damson pies from the Lyth valley.

But I have to stop this. I am making myself hungry and I am writing this in the middle of London, from whence the nearest chip shop is 217 miles.

Russell Harty

MAP 1 NORTH WEST ENGLAND

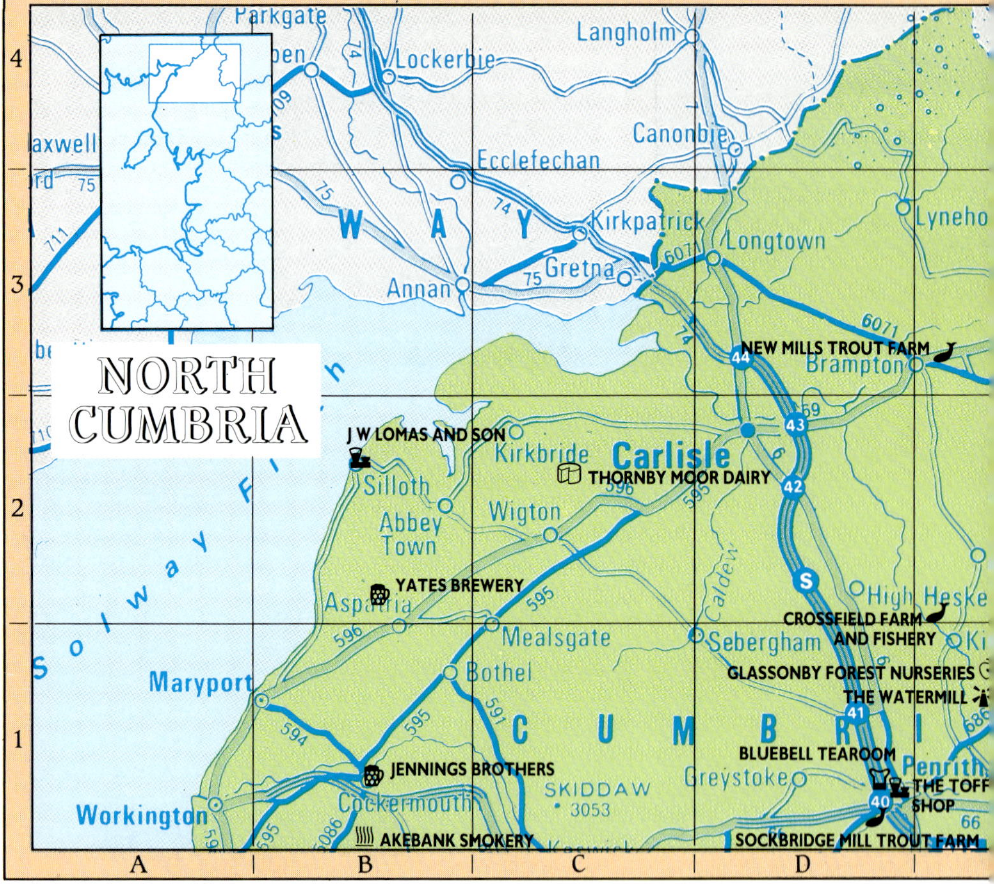

This area boasts spectacular countryside which most visitors neglect in favour of the Lakes. It is here that butchers make the best Cumberland sausage which looks like a curled rope and is filled with coarsely chopped pork. A good place to buy it is in Carlisle, at the Kitchen Market Hall or around the central square. Other specialities to look out for from local butchers are Herdwick Lamb with a good gamey flavour and Westmorland Pie, a delightful old-fashioned treat made from minced lamb, currants and sugar wrapped in a crusty pastry.

Map 1 E1
Acorn Bank Garden
Temple Sowerby, Penrith,
Cumbria CA10 1SP

From Penrith follow A66 eastwards, after 5 miles turn left onto B6412 for ¼ mile, then turn right onto unclassified road for ½ mile to garden on left. Signposted.

These extensive gardens owned by the National Trust include the finest herb garden in the north of England. It is the Trust's most comprehensive collection of culinary and medicinal herbs and among the 250 varieties growing are many rare plants. Visitors may also see the 2 walled orchards and a number of wild fruit trees like crab apple and bird cherry. The gardens are full of daffodils and narcissi in spring.

☞ adults 80p, children (5-17) 40p
◐ Apr-Oct daily 10-5.30
Facilities: ♿ WC 🚗

Map 1 B1
Akebank Smokery
The Manor, Mosser,
Cockermouth,
Cumbria CA13 0RB
Tel. Cockermouth (0900) 826517

From Cockermouth follow A5086 southwards, after 2 miles turn left onto unclassified road for 1 mile to Mosser.

As well as selling its own produce, this smokery is happy to smoke customers' own food brought into the shop. Specialities include local cheese, garlic sausage, Cumberland sausage and smoked pike pâté.

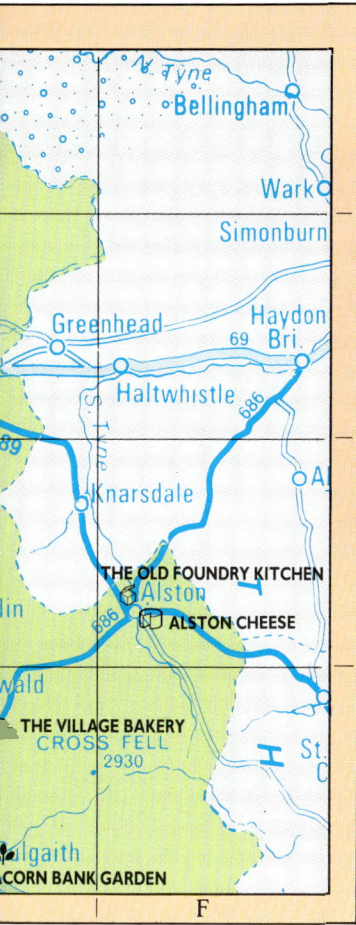

also available and short courses in cheese-making can be arranged.

◗ 31 Mar-Oct Mon-Fri 10.30-5; Nov-30 Mar Mon-Fri 11-3; weekends by appointment
Facilities: ♿

♪ Map 1 E2
Crossfield Farm and Fishery
Crossfield, Nr Kirkoswald, Cumbria CA10 1EU
Tel. Lazonby (076883) 711

From Kirkoswald follow unclassified road north westwards towards Armathwaite, after 1½ miles turn right in Staffield to farm. Signposted.

At this trout fishery, situated in the beautiful Eden Valley, visitors can catch their own fish and then cook and eat them using the farm's barbecue and picnicking facilities.

☞ rod £9.00 per day, £5.00 half-day, £1.25 an hour
◗ all year daily any reasonable time
Facilities: 🍽️ ♿ 🚾 🚗 🛏️

😋 Map 1 E1
Glassonby Forest Nurseries
Glassonby Lodge, Penrith, Cumbria CA10 1DT
Tel. Lazonby (076883) 382

From Penrith follow A686 north eastwards, after 6½ miles turn left onto unclassified road for 2 miles to Glassonby.

Pick your own raspberries here from a 3-acre field.
◗ in season daily 10-7.30
Facilities: 🚗

🍇 Map 1 B1
Jennings Brothers
Castle Brewery, Brewery Lane, Cockermouth, Cumbria CA13 9NE
Tel. Cockermouth (0900) 823214

In town centre.

Jennings have been brewing traditional Cumbrian ales in Cockermouth since 1828. Visitors are welcome to tour the brewery which has been on its present site since 1880 and see the brewing process before tasting the cask-conditioned bitter. A fine maltings building has recently been converted to house the museum of brewing. The brewery offers information on a 'real ale' trail and the bitter can be bought at any of Jennings' pubs in the town and throughout Cumbria.

☞ free
◗ tours: all year evenings by appointment
Facilities: 🚾 🚗

🎣 Map 1 B2
J W Lomas and Son
4 Wampool Street, Silloth, Cumbria CA5 4AA
Tel. Silloth (0965) 31334

In town centre.

This family-run fishmonger was established in 1904 and is

☞ free
◗ by appointment
Facilities: 🍽️ 🚗
🍽️ homemade cream teas

⛪ Map 1 F2
Alston Cheese
The Butts, Alston, Cumbria CA9 3JU
Tel. Alston (0498) 81931

In village.

This working dairy and shop are divided by glass partitions so visitors can see the cheese-making processes throughout the day. They are welcome to taste and buy the products. The staff are well-informed on cheese-making and are happy to answer any questions. As well as its own cheese, the shop sells a range of 10 to 12 cheeses from the north of England and the Borders, all made by small scale cheese-makers. Locally produced jams and pickles are

● **Cumberland sausage and spiced apple sauce**

MAP 1   NORTH WEST ENGLAND

the best place to buy Silloth shrimps, which are similar in size, colour and taste to the better known Morecambe Bay shrimps. It also sells local salmon and sea trout, fresh fish from Aberdeen such as cod, hake and halibut and free-range poultry and eggs.
◐ all year Mon-Fri 8.30-6, Sat 8.30-1

NETTLE HAGGIS

Always choose young, flowering, hairy-stalked nettles for this dish as they are much more tender.

bunch of nettles
salt & pepper
2 tbsp oatmeal
rashers of bacon

Boil a pint of water, put in the nettles, cover and simmer for 10 minutes. Strain and reserve the water. Cut the rind from the bacon and fry. Pour the bacon fat over the nettles and chop finely. Put ½ pint of the nettle water in the frying pan and when it boils toss in the oatmeal, stirring constantly. Season with pepper and boil until it resembles properly cooked porridge. Stir in the chopped nettles and check seasoning. Serve hot with the fried bacon.

♪ Map 1 E3
New Mills Trout Farm
Brampton, Cumbria CA8 2QS
Tel. Brampton (06977) 2384
From Brampton follow A69 eastwards for 1 mile to farm. Signposted.

One of the joys of visiting New Mills Trout Farm is feeding the fish. Floating walk-ways have been constructed so that visitors can view the fish in their natural surroundings. Millions of gallons of water pass through the farm daily on their way to the River Irthing, helping to produce high quality, pink-fleshed rainbow trout. Rods

and bait can be hired and a small shop sells fresh and smoked trout, game in season, preserves and Cumberland sausage.
☞ rod & bait £1.00 per day
◐ Oct-Jun Wed-Sun 10-5.30; Jul-Sep daily 10-5.30
Facilities: 🍽 🔧 ♿ 🚾 🚗 🏕

♦ Map 1 F2
The Old Foundry Kitchen
Tyne Willows, Alston, Cumbria
Tel. Alston (0498) 81135
In village.

The Old Foundry Kitchen is situated next to Alston's narrow-gauge railway and makes a range of coarsely ground mustards. Visitors can watch a demonstration of mustard making and taste the finished product. Four varieties of mustard are made and can be bought on the premises.
☞ free
◐ by appointment
Facilities: 🚾 🏕

♪ Map 1 D1
Sockbridge Mill Trout Farm
Tirril, Penrith,
Cumbria CA10 2JT
Tel. Penrith (0768) 65338

From Penrith follow A6 southwards, after 1 mile turn right onto B5320 for 2 miles to Tirril. Signposted.

Visitors can fish their own at this attractive and secluded trout farm. The farm has its own smokery and sells smoked trout and smoked trout pâté as well as fresh fish.
☞ rod & bait £1
◐ all year daily 7-6 or dusk
Facilities: 🍽 🔧 🚾 🚗 🏕
🍽 teas served with smoked trout sandwiches, homemade scones, cakes; also cream teas Easter-Oct

🏠 Map 1 C2
Thornby Moor Dairy
Thornby Moor House, Aikton, Wigton, Cumbria CA7 0JZ
Tel. Wigton (0965) 43160
From Wigton follow A596 north eastwards, after 2 miles turn left onto unclassified road for 2 miles to Aikton.

All aspects of open-vat cheese-making may be seen at the Thornby Moor Dairy which uses cows', goats' and ewes' milk. Visitors can see the animals, watch demonstrations of cheese-making and taste the cheeses. A selection of 13 varieties and flavours of cheese, including home-smoked, is on sale.
☞ adults £1.00, children (under 16) free
◐ all year Mon-Sat 10-3

🍬 Map 1 D1
The Toffee Shop
7 Brunswick Road, Penrith,
Cumbria CA11 7LU
Tel. Penrith (0768) 62008
In town centre.

This shop sells its handmade fudge in 3 varieties — plain, chocolate and mint; they also make treacle and butter toffees. Fudge and toffee are available loose in quantities from ¼lb or boxed from ½lb to 3lb. Sadly, it is not possible for visitors to see the production process because of the secret recipe used.
◐ all year Mon-Fri 9.30-5, Sat 9-5, closed Bank Hols

🍬 Map 1 E1
The Village Bakery
Melmerby, Penrith,
Cumbria CA10 1HE
Tel. Langwathby (076881) 515
From Penrith follow A686 north eastwards for 9 miles to Melmerby. Signposted.

Situated at the foot of the Melmerby Fell on the Northern Pennines this family-run bakery

MAP 1

and restaurant is dedicated to the simple enjoyment of good food. Housed in a converted 18thC barn, the Village Bakery specialises in quality bread and confectionery made from locally milled wholemeal and wheatmeal flour and baked in a wood-fired brick oven. The oven, believed to be unique, also provides heat for a small greenhouse of herbs and vegetables which has been built on top of it. Bread, rolls, pies, biscuits and cakes are on sale daily in the shop as well as stoneground flour, fruit juices and herb plants.

◑ 26 Mar-24 Dec Tue-Sat 8.30-5, Sun, Bank Hols 9.30-5
Facilities: 🍴 📷 wc 🚗

🍴 homemade meals served with organically grown fruit & vegetables from small-holding behind bakery

---

✣ Map 1 E1
The Watermill
Little Salkeld, Penrith, Cumbria CA10 1NN
Tel. Langwathby (076881) 523
From Penrith follow A686 north eastwards, after 4¹/₂ miles turn left at Langwathby onto unclassified road for 1¹/₂ miles to Little Salkeld.

This is one of the few working watermills in the country still producing stoneground flours in the old-fashioned way. Organic British grain, specially grown for the mill by farmers in Yorkshire and Cumbria, is ground using a traditional method of production. The wheat is dried, cleaned and then milled through granite burr stones with nothing added or taken away. The shop sells the whole range of flours produced at the mill along with organic oat products such as muesli. Flour is available for sale in 500g to 32Kg sacks.

☞ adults 75p, senior citizens & children 50p
◑ all year by appointment
Facilities: 🍴 wc 🚗 🥢

🐝 Map 1 B2
Yates Brewery
Ghyll Farm, Westnewton, Cumbria CA5 3NX
Tel. Aspatria (0965) 21081
From Aspatria follow B5301 northwards, after 2 miles turn left at Westnewton onto unclassified road for 1 mile to farm.

A small traditional brewery situated on a farm which also keeps a herd of dairy goats. Visitors are welcome to tour the brewery by appointment and to buy the beer produced in 4¹/₂ gallon containers. Goats' milk is also sold and sometimes cream and meat.

☞ free
◑ by appointment
Facilities: wc 🚗

🍴 Map 1 D1
BLUEBELL TEAROOM
Three Crowns Yard, Penrith, Cumbria
Tel: Penrith (0768) 66660
In town centre.

A pretty, cosy restaurant on the first floor of a bookshop, serving homemade cakes, good teas and coffees and light lunches. As well as this Honey and Sesame Seed Cake, everything is made with wholefood ingredients and local produce where possible.

◑ Mon-Sat Meals: 9.30-5.00
Price range £1.50-4.00
Seats 24
Facilities: 🍴 🚗

HONEY AND SESAME SEED CAKE

5oz butter
4oz demerara sugar
3 tbsp honey
1 tbsp water
2 large eggs
7oz wholewheat flour
¹/₂ tsp baking powder
1 tbsp sesame seeds

Heat the oven to gas 2 (300F, 160C). Melt the butter, sugar and honey over a low heat. Add the water and cool slightly. Beat in the eggs, flour and baking powder. Beat well. Pour into a greased and lined 2lb loaf tin. Sprinkle sesame seeds over the top and bake for 1¹/₂ hours until just firm.

● **The Village Bakery, Melmerby**

MAP 2   NORTH WEST ENGLAND

SOUTH
CUMBRIA
& ISLE
OF MAN

5

Workington
Cockermouth
SKIDDAW
3053
595
596
595
5086
66
Keswick
Whitehaven
Derwent Water
591
Cumbrian
St. Bees Hd
595
5086
Buttermere
595
5086
Borrowdale
4
Egremont
Mountains
SCA FELL
595
THE GINGERBREAD SHOP
Grasmere
Gosforth
ROTHAY MANOR
Seascale
MUNCASTER WATERMILL
Conis
HAWKSHEAD TROUT FARM
3
Bride
RICHARD WOODALL
Torver
Win
me
593
ASHDOWN SMOKERS
Bootle
Broughton in
Furness
5084
New
B
595
590
14
10
Ramsey
COUNTRY MATTERS
5092
Greenodd
5093
Ballaugh
Sulby 3
2
Ulverston
10
14
18
595
Milom
HOLKER HALL
AND GARDENS
2
SNAEFELL
2036
590
Peel
Laxey
LAXEY GLEN MILLS
Dalton
in Furness
Bards
27
ISLE OF MAN MILK MARKETING
ASSOCIATION
590
5087
Dalby
Barrow
in Furness
Morecam
Douglas
BUSHY'S BREW PUB
I. of Walney
Mo
5
3
He
1
Erin
CROIT-E-CALEY FRUIT FARM
RONALDSWAY
Castletown

| | A | B | C | D |

Whatever time of year you visit the Lake District — whether it's during spring when the valleys are awash with Wordsworth's daffodils, summer when the lakes glisten in the sun, autumn when the damsons are ripe for picking, or winter when the land is wrapped in snow — it never fails to enchant. Now a thriving tourist centre, this area once had a flourishing trade in spices with the West Indies. Rum, brandy, ginger and many other spices were imported through Whitehaven — and smuggled from the Isle of Man. Needless to say many of this area's traditional dishes — Cumberland sauce and Rum Nicky to name but two — are laden with spices.

Map 2 F3
Abbot Hall Art Gallery and Museum of Lakeland Life and Industry
Kirkland, Kendal,
Cumbria LA9 5AL
Tel. Kendal (0539) 22464

In town centre. Signposted.

The Museum of Lakeland Life and Industry contains reconstructed workshops full of hand-worn tools and farmhouse rooms which capture the flavour of everyday life in the Lake District. The museum has a farming display

Stoke · Culgaith · M6 · 40 · 66 · 66 · 6091 · 592 · 66 · Eden · Middleton in Teesdale · Bisho · W. A

Ullswater · Appleby · Barnard Castle · 688 · 61

Patterdale · Shap · 39 · 592 · Hawes Water · Brough · 685 · 66 · Bowes

S · ombleside · 38 · **SLACK'S FARM SHOP** · Tebay · Kirkby Stephen · 685 · HIGH SEAT 2328 · Reeth

Windermere · 591 · 685 · 683 · P · Muker

ABBOT HALL ART GALLERY AND MUSEUM OF LAKELAND LIFE AND INDUSTRY · 684 · 37 · Kenda · Sedbergh · 684 · Leyburn · 684

Levens · 592 · 5074 · 683 · Hawes · Aysgarth · Middle

590 · **SILLFIELD FARM TRADITIONAL CHEESES** · WHERNSIDE 2419

36 · **HERON CORN MILL** · Kirkby Lonsdale · N · Buckden

HIGGINSON BUTCHERS · ton · INGLEBOROUGH 2373

OOKBURGH SHERMEN · Grange over Sands · A35 · 683 · Ingleton · 65 · N

Carnforth · 35 · 687

ay · 5105 · M6 · Hornby · Clapham · Grassington

nbe · 34 · 683 · Settle

n · 589 · 683 · **Lancaster** · L · Long Preston · 65 · Blub

33 · A · 59

F · G · H · I

and a farm kitchen where visitors can see agricultural implements, cheese-making equipment and farm food production exhibits. Char — similar to trout — is a local delicacy found in the Lakes and the Gallery has a unique collection of char pots and plates dating from the 18thC. These are shallow round bowls, originally made from delftware and decorated with hand painted fish. Kendal mint cake is for sale.

adults £1.00, senior citizens & children 50p, family ticket (2 adults & up to 4 children) £2.50
Spring Bank Hol-Oct Mon-Fri 10.30-5, Sun 2-5; Nov-Spring Bank Hol Mon-Fri 10.30-5, Sat 2-5
Facilities:

MAP 2   NORTH WEST ENGLAND

Map 2 C3
Ashdown Smokers
Skellerah Farm, Corney, Millom,
Cumbria LA19 5TW
Tel. Bootle (06578) 324

*From Bootle follow A595
northwards, after ½ mile turn
right onto unclassified road for
1½ miles to Corney.*

One of the few remaining
traditional dry-curers and oak-
smokers, they use no
chemicals, additives or artificial
substances. Their oak comes
from Eskdale, their juniper
from Coniston and their salt
from Cheshire. More than 40
products are smoked, including
their speciality Herdwick
Macon, a unique Cumbrian
delicacy — a mutton ham is
smoked over oak and juniper
and sold whole or sliced.
Cumberland and venison
sausages, Buttermere eels,
Windermere char as well as
fresh poultry, game, fish,
shellfish and farmhouse
cheeses are available in season.
Demonstration tours of work
in progress and limited tastings
are available.
☞ free
● all year Mon-Sat 9-5, tours by
appointment
Facilities: 🚻 🚌

Map 2 B1
Bushy's Brew Pub
1 Victoria Street, Douglas,
Isle of Man
Tel. Douglas (0624) 75139
In town centre.
A small, informal and
welcoming brewery and pub.
The brewery produces 2

types of beer: a normal bitter
called Bushy's Bitter and a 'best'
known as Bushy Tail. Both are
served in the adjoining pub or
can be bought in bottles to
enjoy at home.
● pub: during licensing hours;
brewery: by appointment
Facilities: 🚌 🍴 🚻 🚌 /🏠
🍴 homemade traditional &
vegetarian meals served in pub

Map 2 D2
Country Matters
The Old Bull Pen, Hallthwaites,
Millom, Cumbria LA18 5HP
*From Broughton in Furness follow
A595 westwards, after 3½ miles
turn left onto unclassified road
for ¼ mile to Hallthwaites.
Signposted.*
This unusual herb farm
produces herbs for health.
Visitors will be taken on a tour
of 'herbs through the ages', on
which the still room equipment
of a traditional herbalist can be
seen, including cauldrons,
ladles, pestles and mortars and
drying beams. The herb garden,
where medicinal and culinary

herbs are grown, is situated on
the edge of a trout stream.
Herb plants and dried herbs are
for sale and also a range of
herbal preserves, herbs for
marinades and stuffings.
☞ free
● all year daily 10-6 or dusk in
winter, or by appointment

Map 2 A1
Croit-E-Caley Fruit Farm
The Level, Colby, Isle of Man
Tel. Port Erin (0624) 833218
*From Port Erin follow A5
eastwards, after 2½ miles turn
left onto B33 for ½ mile to farm.
Signposted.*
A pick your own farm and a
farm shop offering
strawberries, raspberries,
gooseberries, rhubarb, broccoli
and runner beans in season.
Produce is also available ready-
picked and the shop sells goats'
and ewes' milk yoghurt.
● mid Jun-early Sep daily 9.30-6
Facilities: 🚌 🚻 🚌 🍽

Map 2 E2
Flookburgh Fishermen
Moor Lane, Flookburgh,
Nr Grange-over-Sands,
Cumbria LA11 7LS
Tel. Flookburgh (044853) 353
*From Grange-over-Sands follow
B5277 south westwards for 4
miles to Flookburgh. Signposted.*
This fish processor is well-
known for its local Morecambe
Bay shrimps, sold either fresh
or potted, for its cockles which
are gathered from the sands
and for its selection of local fish
like 'flukes' — flounders, as well
as whitebait and salmon.
Visitors are welcome to watch
the shrimp-potting. A range of
frozen foods and ice cream is
also on sale.
● all year Mon-Fri 8-5; Sat in
summer telephone for details

MAP 2

🏪 Map 2 E4
The Gingerbread Shop
Church Cottage, Grasmere,
Cumbria LA22 9SW
Tel. Grasmere (09665) 428

In village centre.

For the past 130 years the
famous original Grasmere
gingerbread has been baked
daily from a secret recipe and it
is only obtainable here in
Grasmere from the
Gingerbread Shop. Visitors to
the shop, which has changed
very little since the days when it
was a village school from 1660
to 1854, can also buy

homemade rum butter, fudge,
truffles and jams.
🕐 mid Feb-mid Nov daily 9.30-
4.30

🎣 Map 2 E3
Hawkshead Trout Farm
The Boathouse, Hawkshead,
Cumbria LA22 OQF
Tel. Hawkshead (09666) 541

*From Ambleside follow A593
south westwards, after ½ mile
turn left onto B5286 for 3 miles,
then turn right into Newby
Bridge Road for 1½ miles to farm
on left. Signposted.*

At this trout farm, set in the
peaceful surroundings of

Esthwaite Water, visitors can
feed the trout or catch their
own. The farm smokes its own
rainbow trout. These and fresh
trout are for sale in the shop.
🎣 rod & bait £2.50, fish caught
£1.35 per lb
🕐 farm: 2 Apr-Oct daily 9-6;
shop: Nov-Apr daily 10-2
Facilities: ♿ 🚗 🍴

⚙️ Map 2 F2
Heron Corn Mill
c/o Waterhouse Mills,
Milnthorpe, Cumbria LA7 7AR
Tel. Morecambe (0524) 734858

*From Carnforth follow A6
northwards, after 7 miles turn
left to mill. Signposted.*

This restored 18thC water-
powered corn mill stands on
the site of an ancient heronry
on the west bank of the River
Bela. It is remarkable for its 4
pairs of stones driven from a
single 14 foot diameter water
wheel. Visitors can follow the
entire milling process and
guided tours are available.
Interesting displays explain the
history of the mill. Stoneground
flour and oatmeal can be
bought from the small shop.
🎟️ adults £1.00
🕐 31 Mar-Sep Tue-Sun, Bank
Hols 11-5
Facilities: ♿ 🚻 🚗 🍴

🏪 Map 2 E2
Higginson Butchers
Main Street, Grange-over-
Sands, Cumbria LA11 6AB
Tel. Grange-over-Sands (04484)
4367

In town centre.

● **The Gingerbread Shop, Grasmere**

27

MAP 2   NORTH WEST ENGLAND

This butchers' shop sells well-hung local fresh meat and game in season. It also stocks home-cooked meats, cured bacon, Cumberland sausage, homemade pies, haggis, venison and a variety of cooked dishes.

◗ all year Mon-Sat 7-6, closed Bank Hols
Facilities: ♿

🛏 Map 2 E2
Holker Hall and Gardens
Cark-in-Cartmel, Grange-over-Sands, Cumbria LA11 7PL
Tel. Flookburgh (044853) 328

From Grange-over-Sands follow B5277 westwards, after 4 miles turn left to Hall. Signposted.

Holker Hall, the former home of the Dukes of Devonshire, has a 120-acre deer park and a fascinating kitchen exhibition from the Zanussi Collection. This contains antique household appliances from the Victorian, Edwardian and wartime periods. A baby animal house, with a collection of domestic and farm animals, will keep the children amused. The gift shop sells a variety of preserves including lemon cheese, jellies, jams and mustards.

☞ adults £1.65, children (over 6) £1.00
◖ 3 Apr-1 Nov Mon-Fri, Sun 10.30-6
Facilities: ☕ 🚾 🚗 ♿ ⚙
☕ Clock Tower cafeteria serves homemade snacks including apple pies & a selection of cakes

---

🏠 Map 2 B1
Isle of Man Milk Marketing Association
Central Creamery, Cronkbourne, Tromode, Douglas, Isle of Man
Tel. Douglas (0624) 73731

From Douglas follow A22 westwards, after 1 mile turn left

● **Muncaster Mill, Ravenglass**

at Tromode onto unclassified road for ¼ mile to Cronkbourne.

At this modern milk processing establishment, which receives milk from 130 farms, milk cartoning, cream, butter and cheese production takes place. It produces 1,500 tonnes of cheese a year including Cheddar, Cheshire, Leicester, Double Gloucester, Caerphilly and also small smoked cheeses. Visitors can buy milk, cream, butter and some of the cheeses.

☞ free
◖ all year by appointment
Facilities: 🚾 🚗

MORECAMBE BAY SHRIMPS

Don't miss these famous sweet brown shrimps. There is also the excellent local Solway salmon which is usually served either plainly poached or with a shrimp sauce.

🌾 Map 2 B2
Laxey Glen Mills
Laxey, Isle of Man
Tel. Douglas (0624) 781202

In town centre. Signposted.

Part of a heritage trail, this old-fashioned mill with a wheel and pulley system was established

in 1860 and produces most types of flour.

☞ 50p
◖ all year Mon-Fri 9-4
Facilities: 🚗

🌾 Map 2 C3
Muncaster Watermill
Ravenglass, Cumbria CA18 1ST
Tel. Ravenglass (06577) 232

From Ravenglass follow A595 north eastwards, after 1 mile turn left to mill. Signposted.

Muncaster Watermill is one of the few surviving water-powered corn mills in the country. The mill building, dating from about 1700, houses original 19thC machinery still in perfect working order. It produces a range of stoneground flours and oatmeal from organically grown English cereals. Visitors are free to wander about the mill where frequent demonstrations of milling take place and see the water wheel, the mill race and the kiln. A variety of stoneground flours in packs ranging from 500g to 32Kg are for sale.

☞ adults 70p, children (5-16) 35p, family ticket (2 adults & 2 children or 3 adults) £1.75
◖ Apr, May, Sep Sun-Fri 11-5; Jun-Aug Sun-Fri 10-6
Facilities: 🚾 🚗 ♿

MAP 2

RESTAURANT RECIPE

🍴 Map 2 E4

ROTHAY MANOR

Rothay Bridge, Ambleside,
Cumbria LA22 0EH
Tel: Ambleside (05394)
33605

*From Ambleside follow
Langdale Road south
westwards towards A593 for
¹/₄ mile to Manor on left just
before Rothay Bridge.
Signposted.*

A beautiful Georgian manor
house set in its own grounds.
The restaurant features
polished wood tables and has
a genuinely inviting
atmosphere.
● Mon-Sun Meals: 12.30-2,
8-9; closed 4 Jan-12 Feb
Price range £6-20 Set D £18
Seats 65
Cards: Access, Amex, Diners,
Visa
Facilities: 🍴🛏️♿🚗

CUMBERLAND RUM NICKY

pastry:
12oz flour sifted
3oz lard
3oz butter
1 egg
2oz sugar
filling:
*1¹/₂lb dates - stoned, roughly
chopped and soaked for ¹/₂
hour in ¹/₄ pint boiling water*
4 knobs stem ginger chopped
2oz butter
2oz brown sugar
3 tbsp rum

Heat oven to gas 3 (325F,
170C). Rub the lard and
butter into the flour. Dissolve
the sugar in the egg and add
to the flour and fat mixture.
Line two flan cases. Add the
dates to the ginger and
spread on top of the pastry.
Cream the butter and sugar
and dot on the dates and
ginger. Cover with strips of
pastry in a lattice effect. Bake
for 30-45 minutes. Allow the
pies to cool and, just before
serving, pour over the rum.

🧀 Map 2 F2

Sillfield Farm Traditional Cheeses

Sillfield Farm, Endmoor,
Nr Kendal, Cumbria LA8 0HZ
Tel. Crooklands (04487) 328

*From Kendal follow A65
southwards for 5 miles to
Endmoor. Signposted.*

Sillfield Farm is the storage
centre for Peter Gott's thriving
business selling British
farmhouse cheeses. Cheeses
are selected from all over the
country and brought here
where they are kept under
prime conditions and turned
weekly by hand to ensure
perfect maturing. Peter Gott
stocks a wide range with an
emphasis on local cheeses such
as Alston, Allerdale and
Cumberland Farmhouse. Also
on sale are free-range duck and
hens' eggs, bacon and sausages.
Visitors can buy from the farm
or visit their stall at Kendal
Market on Wednesday and
Saturday between 5.30 and
2.00, Milnthorpe Market all day
Friday, Barrow Market Hall on
Wednesday, Friday and
Saturday between 8.00 and 5.00
or The Cheese and Bacon Shop
in Windermere, Tuesday-
Saturday between 9.00 and
5.00.
● by appointment

🧀 Map 2 F4

Slack's Farm Shop

Tebay, Penrith,
Cumbria CA10 3SG
Tel. Orton (05874) 446

In village.

All the pigs used for pork
products sold in this farm shop
are raised either on the farm
itself or locally on additive and
antibiotic-free feed. Bacon is
cured on the premises in the
traditional manner and
specialities include home-cured
farmhouse Cumbrian bacon in
vacuum packs and traditional
Cumberland sausage. Visitors

are welcome in the shop and
working butchery and a large
selection of fresh meats —
various burgers by the lb, fresh
or frozen, farmed venison
joints, chops, steaks, casserole
cuts — and cheese are for sale.
Specialist mixed packs are
available on request for
customers with allergies.
● all year Mon-Fri 9-5, Sat
9-12.30

🧀 Map 2 C3

Richard Woodall

Lane End, Waberthwaite,
Millom, Cumbria LA19 5YJ
Tel. Ravenglass (06577) 386

*From Bootle follow A595
northwards, after 4 miles turn
left onto unclassified road for 1
mile to Waberthwaite.*

The Woodalls have been
producing home-cured hams
and bacon since 1828. They still
use the same recipes today and
their specialities include: dry
salt-cured Cumberland ham
and bacon; Cumbria Royal ham,
a sweet ham cured in brown
ale, brown sugar, treacle and
salt; an air-dried ham — similar
to the Italian Parma ham —
which is matured for 12 months
and then thinly sliced and eaten
raw; and Cumberland sausage.
Visitors are welcome to see the
curing and also to watch
Cumberland sausage being
made. All produce is for sale at
the shop.
☞ free
● all year Mon-Fri 8.30-12.15,
1.15-5.30, Sat 8.30-12
Facilities: 🚗

MAP 3 NORTH WEST ENGLAND

LANCASHIRE

SELLET HALL HERB GARDEN

FERROCRETE FARM

J ATKINSON AND COMPANY

LUNE SMOKED FOODS

HEANINGBROOK TROUT FARM

FARM MAID FOO

CORONATION ROCK COMPANY

THE CHOCOLATE HOUSE

BENNETT'S BISTRO

LANCASHIRE FRUIT GROWERS

Everyone has heard of Lancashire Hot Pot — but how many people have tasted the real thing? Each Lancashire family had their own recipe but it was generally agreed that the main ingredients were scrag or neck chops of lamb, onions and — of course — potatoes. Traditionally it was stewed slowly in a tall earthenware pot but nowadays any casserole will do. Another treat is the local Lancashire cheese which toasts like a dream — even Ben Gunn dreamt about it when he was abandoned on Treasure Island.

Map 3 C5
J Atkinson and Company
China Street, Lancaster,
Lancashire LA1 1EX
Tel. Lancaster (0524) 65470

In town centre.

Established in 1837 and still run as a family business, these tea and coffee merchants deal in both wholesale and retail trade. Coffee beans are roasted daily to both their own and customers' special requirements.
● all year Mon-Sat 8.30-5, Wed 8.30-12.30

Map 3 E3
The Chocolate House
1 Glenfield Park, Philips Road, Blackburn, Lancashire BB1 5PF
Tel. Blackburn (0254) 581019

From Blackburn follow A677 eastwards, after 1½ miles turn left onto A6119 for 1 mile to Glenfield Park on left.

This small family-run business offers an interesting range of handmade chocolates, fudge and confectionery from sugar mice to marzipan pigs. They are all made from the finest Swiss chocolate, cream and liqueurs to their own recipes with no artificial colouring, flavouring or preservatives. Visitors are welcome to watch the chocolates being hand-rolled and dipped and can inspect the kitchen and taste the fudge at any time. The chocolates, including a selection of truffles and all-in-one rum, raisin and orange sticks are on sale in the shop, either loose or in boxes or baskets, together with the confectionery.

free
● all year Mon-Fri 9-5.30, Sat 9.30-5; demonstrations by appointment
Facilities: & ♿ 🚗

ECCLES CAKES
These rich pastry cakes stuffed with fruit come from this area and are widely available throughout Lancashire. According to Michael Smith, an expert on British teas, Eccles cakes should always be served warm with clotted cream or rum butter.

Map 3 B3
Coronation Rock Company
11 Cherry Tree Road North, Marton, Blackpool, Lancashire FY4 4NY
Tel. Blackpool (0253) 62366

From Blackpool town centre follow A583 eastwards for 2 miles to factory.

Established in 1927, this sugar confectionery manufacturer produces an extensive range of traditional lettered rock. Here visitors can see the famous Blackpool rock being made by hand and discover the magic of the words in the middle. There is a special viewing area where many of the hand skills in confectionery-making are demonstrated. Sticks of rock and other confectionery can be bought at the factory shop.

free
● all year Mon-Thur 9-3, Fri 9-2.30, closed Bank Hols
Facilities: ♿ 🚗

MAP 3   NORTH WEST ENGLAND

Map 3 D4
Farm Maid Foods
Singletons Dairies, Mill Farm,
Preston Road, Longridge,
Preston, Lancashire PR3 3AN
Tel. Longridge (077478) 2112

*From Preston follow B6243 north
eastwards for 7½ miles to
Longridge. Signposted.*

This cheese factory makes all its
cheeses in the traditional way
to an old recipe using
vegetarian rennet only. There is
a display of old cheese-making
equipment and visitors are
encouraged to taste and buy
the cheeses made. These
include Lancashire, Cheshire,
Cheddar, Double Gloucester,
Red Leicester, Caerphilly,
Wensleydale and Bleasdale.

free
all year Mon-Fri 9-5 by
appointment, closed Bank Hols
Facilities:

Map 3 D6
Ferrocrete Farm
Arkholme, Carnforth,
Lancashire LA6 1AU
Tel. Hornby (0468) 21965

*From Carnforth follow B6254
eastwards for 6 miles to
Arkholme.*

The owners of Ferrocrete Farm
produce only good, wholesome
food. A working dairy, goat and
sheep farm, making cheese and
yoghurt on the premises. The
cheeses contain no animal
rennet and all products are free
of additives and artificial
ingredients. Herbs and
vegetables are grown to the
Soil Association's organic
farming standards and all the
produce is for sale. Visitors can
be shown around the farm,
watch demonstrations and
taste the products.

free
by appointment any
reasonable time
Facilities:

RESTAURANT RECIPE

Map 3 C3
BENNETT'S BISTRO
15 Park Street, Lytham St
Annes, Lancashire FY8 5LU
Tel: Lytham (0253) 739265
In town centre.

A terraced Victorian house in
which 3 rooms have been
turned into a restaurant. In
the winter there are open, log-
burning fires.
Tue-Sat Meals: 12-2.30,
7-9.30
Price range £5-10
Seats 51
Facilities:

POACHED HALIBUT in white wine sauce

6 halibut steaks
1 large onion chopped
¼ pint white wine
flour
butter
1 pint milk
1 onion studded with cloves
¼ pint single cream

Poach the halibut steaks for 5
minutes. Remove the bones
and keep warm. To make the
sauce: sweat the onion in a
little butter, add the wine and
reduce until half. Add a
bechamel sauce made from a
roux of flour and butter, a
pint of milk and the clove-
studded onion to taste.
Simmer for 30 minutes and
strain. Combine the 2 sauces,
add the cream and serve with
the fish.

Map 3 E4
Heaningbrook Trout Farm
The Heaning,
Newton-in-Bowland,
Clitheroe,
Lancashire BB7 3ED
Tel. Dunsop Bridge (02008) 274

*From Clitheroe follow B6478
northwards, after 5 miles turn
left into Dunsop Bridge Road for
½ mile to farm. Signposted.*

A freshwater spring from the
Bowland Hills provides a
natural environment for
breeding rainbow trout.
Visitors can fish their own, feed
the fish or look around the
farm which has a number of
farm animals, including goats,
ducks, geese and horses. The
shop sells a wide selection of
frozen fish as well as its own
fresh trout and homemade
pâté.

rod £1.50, £1.50 to fish
all year daily 9.30-7.30 or dusk
Facilities:

Map 3 C2
Lancashire Fruit Growers
Mere Brow Fruit Farm, The
Gravel, Mere Brow, Tarleton,
Nr Preston, Lancashire
Tel. Preston (0772) 814804

*From Preston follow A59
southwards, after 6 miles turn
right at Tarleton onto A565 for 1
mile, then turn left to farm.
Signposted.*

In the middle of a leisure
complex with various facilities,
Lancashire Fruit Growers have
60 acres of strawberries,
blackcurrants and gooseberries.
Visitors may pick their own or
buy at the farm shop which also
sells cream, eggs, vegetables,
jam, fruit wine and fruit pies.
1 Jul-14 Aug daily 10-8
Facilities:

Map 3 C5
Lune Smoked Foods
Duke Street, St George's Quay,
Lancaster, Lancashire LA1 1RB
Tel. Lancaster (0524) 69563

In town centre. Signposted.

This smokery produces a wide
range of preservative-free
smoked foods using a
combination of traditional
methods and modern kilns.
Smoked products include
Scotch salmon and smoked
salmon pâté; rainbow trout,
hot-smoked over a mixture of

MAP 3

● **Sellet Hall Herb Garden**

oak and beech chippings; chicken, marinaded for 48 hours in a sweet pickle before being hot-smoked; and St George smoked ham, slowly matured and cold-smoked. Unsmoked products include a selection of poultry and game. Tours of the smokery are available by arrangement.

☞ free
● all year Mon-Fri 9-5; closed Bank Hols
Facilities: 🚗

🌿 Map 3 E4
Sabden Treacle Mines
Lower House Mill, The Holme, Sabden, Nr Blackburn, Lancashire BB6 9DZ
Tel. Burnley (0282) 79392

From Whalley follow A671 southwards, after ¹/₂ mile turn left onto unclassified road for 2¹/₂ miles to Sabden.

Visitors to Sabden Treacle Mines will see an exhibition on the local legend — the Valley of the Treacle Mines. The exhibition includes Higher House Mill where raw treacle

rock is refined and woven into parkin cake by the parkin weavers. It is then sold from the Parkin Parlour together with ginger beer, a by-product of treacle rock. Treacle Miner toys are on sale in the shop.
● all year Mon-Fri 9-6, Sat 9-1
Facilities: 🚾

🌼 Map 3 D6
Sellet Hall Herb Garden
Sellet Hall, Whittington, Via Carnforth, Lancashire LA6 2QF
Tel. Kirkby Lonsdale (0468) 71865

From Kirkby Lonsdale follow A65 westwards, after ³/₄ mile turn left onto unclassified road for ¹/₄ mile to garden.

This is the largest display garden of specialised herbs in the north of England. The beautiful formal setting of the gardens complements the demonstration beds of unusual herbs and wild plants. Guided tours are available by arrangement. Herb plants in pots or planted in terracotta containers are for sale in the

garden shop as well as herb jellies, vinegars, butters and oils.
☞ free
● garden: 31 Mar-Oct daily 9-4; shop: all year
Facilities: 🚗

MAP 4   NORTH WEST ENGLAND

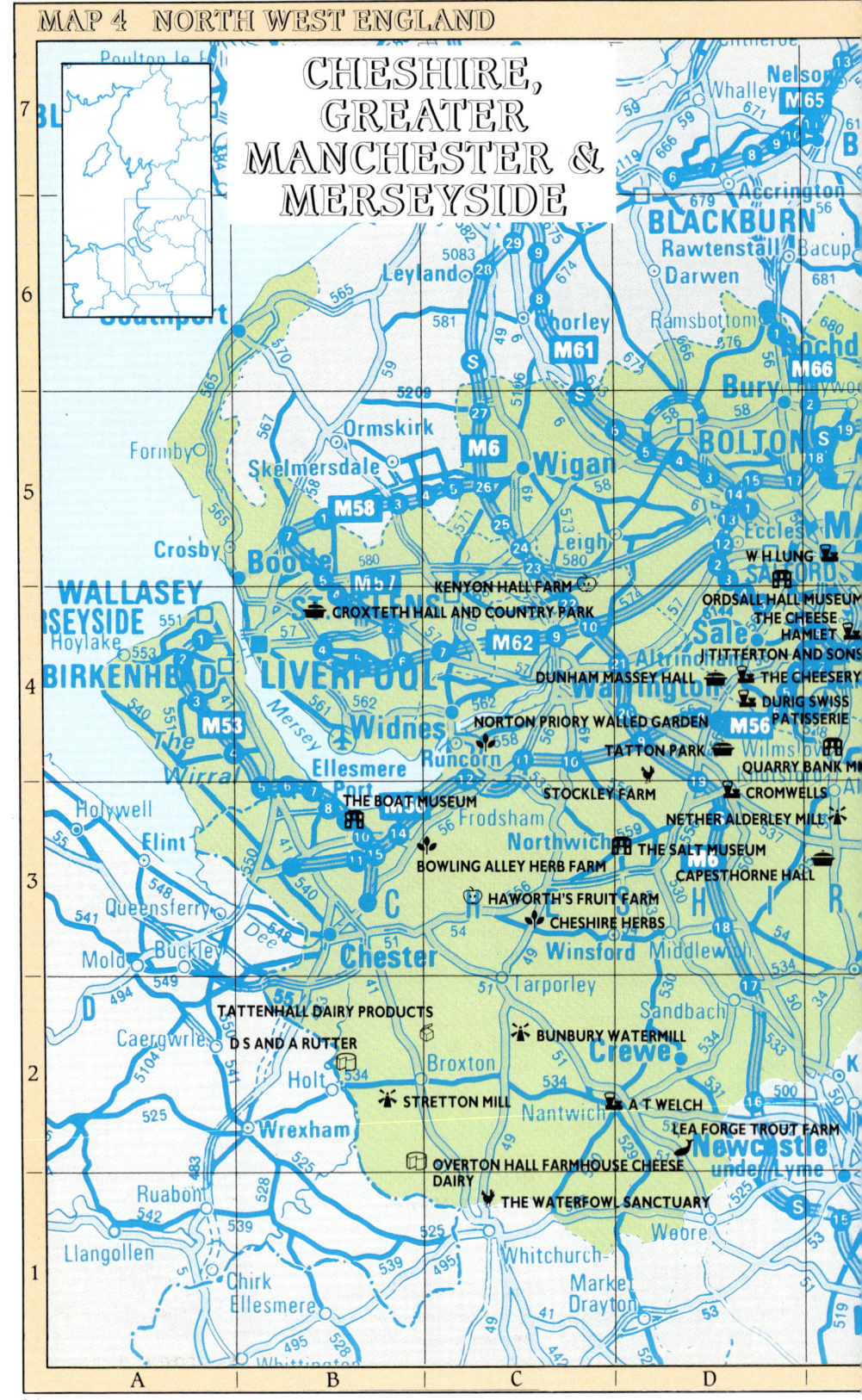

CHESHIRE, GREATER MANCHESTER & MERSEYSIDE

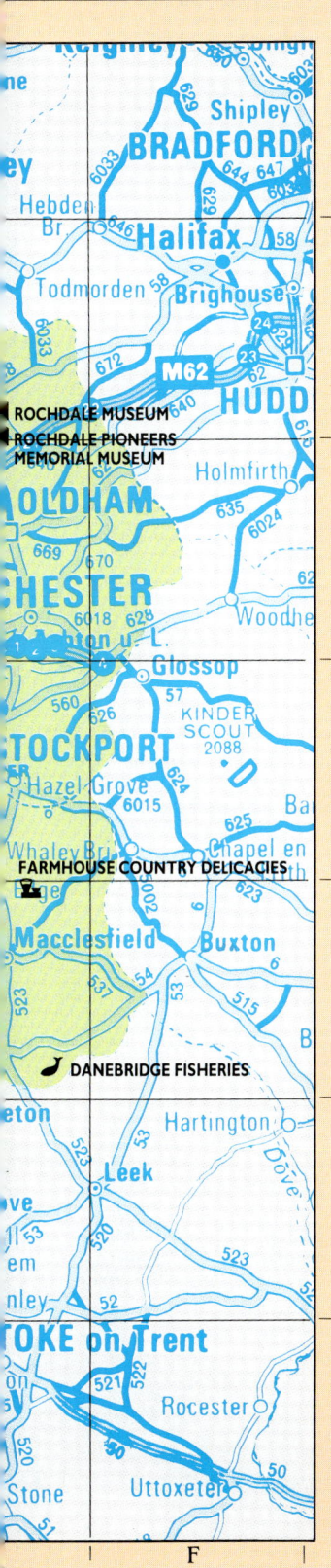

Cheese has been made in Cheshire for centuries — even before the Romans arrived. It has always been made with cows' milk and its characteristic flavour comes from the underlying rock salt in Cheshire's plains. Once there were six cheese fairs in the area; today only one remains. This is held each summer in Nantwich and draws cheeses from all over the world. Magnificent truckles compete alongside smallholders' goats' cheeses — it's a sight well worth seeing.

Map 4 B3
The Boat Museum
Dockyard Road, Ellesmere Port, Cheshire L65 4EF
Tel. Liverpool (051) 3555017
In town centre. Signposted.

This is a working museum situated in the old docks at the junction of the Shropshire Union and the Manchester Ship Canals. Visitors can see over 50 historic canal boats. The narrow boats dating from the early 20thC have ranges and utensils specially designed for life afloat. There are also reconstructions of canalside cottages with fully equipped kitchens of 1840, 1900, 1930 and 1950.

☞ free
◐ Apr-Oct daily 10-5; Nov-Mar Sat-Thur 11-4
Facilities: 🛋 🍴 ♿ 🚻 🚗 🎪
🍴 boatman's & ferryman's lunches served

Map 4 C3
Bowling Alley Herb Farm
Commonside, Alvanley,
Via Warrington,
Cheshire WA6 9DH
Tel. Manley (09284) 285

From Frodsham follow A56 south westwards, after 1 mile turn left onto B5393 for 1½ miles to Alvanley.

A small family-run herb farm which grows and sells over 70 varieties of common and unusual herbs, either as plants, fresh-cut or dried. The plants are grown organically and naturally in a knot garden and a herb rockery. Farm produce can be purchased from the shop; this includes the farm's own low fat spiced or herb soft cheeses in 3 varieties: Gourmet, a mild flavoured cheese with mustard, garlic and parsley; Triple Herb with parsley, garlic and chervil; and Eastern Spice with paprika, basil, chillies and oregano. Other produce includes farmhouse Cheshire cheeses, home-cured bacon, sausages, a selection of farm-baked goods, spices, herb teas and homemade ice cream.

☞ free
◐ all year daily 11-6
Facilities: 🚻 🚗 🎪

Map 4 C2
Bunbury Watermill
Mill Lane, Bunbury, Tarporley, Cheshire
Tel. Liverpool (051) 9227260
From Tarporley follow A51 southwards, after 2 miles turn right onto unclassified road for 1 mile to Bunbury.

This restored working 19thC watermill, which supplied

MAP 4 NORTH WEST ENGLAND

markets with fine quality flour, provides a realistic glimpse of the past. Today visitors can watch stoneground flour being milled and afterwards buy a pack along with some printed recipes.

🎟 adults 50p, senior citizens & children 30p
◐ Easter-Sep Sat, Sun, Bank Hols 2-5 or by appointment
Facilities: 🚾 🚗 😋

REGIONAL RECIPE

CHESHIRE SOUP

A practical, warming quick dish using local Cheshire cheese.

4 pints chicken stock
1lb potatoes diced
1/2lb leeks chopped
salt & pepper
6oz carrots grated
2oz oatmeal
2oz Cheshire cheese grated

Put the stock, potatoes and leeks in a large pan. Season, bring to the boil and simmer gently for 15 minutes. Add the carrots and the oatmeal and simmer for a further 10 minutes. Just before serving add the cheese.

🚢 Map 4 E3
Capesthorne Hall
Macclesfield, Cheshire SK11 9JY
Tel. Macclesfield (0625) 861221
From Wilmslow follow A34 southwards, after 5 miles turn right to Hall. Signposted.

Capesthorne has been the home of the Bromley-Davenport family and their ancestors since Domesday times. Here, amongst other rooms, visitors can see the hall, the state dining room laid for a banquet with the family silver and china, and the kitchen with a display of old kitchen ranges and utensils. The gardens include a herb and kitchen garden and there is an enjoyable walk to follow which

takes you past an old ice house and a watermill. Farm produce including preserves, herbs and special packs of confectionery can be bought from the shop.

🎟 adults £2.00, children (over 5) £1.00, family ticket (2 adults & any children travelling in the same car) £5.00.
◐ Apr Sun; May, Sep Wed, Sat, Sun; Jun-Aug Tue-Thur, Sat, Sun, Bank Hols; park, gardens & chapel: 12-6, hall: 2-5
Facilities: 🚌 🍴 ♿ 🚾 🚗 😋 🗑 🏛
★ barbecues & garden parties
🍴 the garden restaurant serves 3-course lunches, afternoon & high teas with homemade cakes & scones

🧀 Map 4 E4
The Cheese Hamlet
706 Wilmslow Road, Didsbury, Greater Manchester M20 0DW
Tel. Manchester (061) 4344781
From Manchester follow A34 Wilmslow Road southwards for 3 miles to Didsbury.

This shop specialises in English farmhouse cheeses and stocks over 120 varieties, as well as some from the continent. They have won the National Retail Cheese Award 3 times and have now been banned from entering for 3 years in order to give other retailers a chance.
◐ all year Mon-Sat 9.30-5.30

🧀 Map 4 D4
The Cheesery
1 Regent Road, Altrincham, Cheshire WA14 1RY
Tel. Manchester (061) 9280537
In town centre.

Cheeses to suit all tastes — matured English farmhouse, a wide range of specialist English and a variety of continental examples — are sold here. The Cheesery also has its own cooked hams, boiled or honey roast, as well as a wide selection of specialist grocery lines

including quality coffee beans and teas.
◐ all year Mon, Tue, Thur-Sat 9-5, Wed 9-3; closed Bank Hols

🌿 Map 4 C3
Cheshire Herbs
Fourfields, Forest Road, Little Budworth, Nr Tarporley, Cheshire CW6 9ES
Tel. Little Budworth (082921) 578
From Tarporley follow A49 northwards for 3 1/2 miles to farm on right.

This herb nursery specialises in the more unusual herbs that produce a delicate and delicious flavour. Help is always at hand to advise visitors on the best methods of growing and cooking herbs. Plants are available for sale in 9cm or larger pots. A small shop sells herb related products such as pot-pourri made to the nursery's own recipe, mustards, teas and dried herbs.

🎟 free
◐ Apr-24 Dec daily 10-5
Facilities: ♿ 🚾 🚗

🧀 Map 4 D3
Cromwells
15 King Street, Knutsford, Cheshire WA16 6DW
Tel. Knutsford (0565) 54832
In town centre.

Cromwells make luxury handmade English chocolates from natural ingredients. The range includes dark, milk and white chocolates and truffles with unusual flavours such as passion fruit, orange curacao or banana. They are available either loose by weight or wrapped in boxes. Customers can choose their own chocolates and wrappings. Prices range from 65p for 2 chocolates in a box to £15.50. Special products and packaging are made for Christmas including chocolate Santas; Easter products include

MAP 4

• **The kitchen, Croxteth Hall**

chocolate eggs and rabbits. A short talk with tastings is available by prior arrangement.
◐ all year Tue-Sat 9.30-5; 6 weeks before Christmas & Easter Mon-Sat 9-6; closed 3 weeks after Christmas, 2 weeks after Easter & all Bank Hols

---

🚢 Map 4 B4
Croxteth Hall and Country Park
Liverpool, Merseyside LI2 OHB
Tel. Liverpool (051) 2285311
From Liverpool follow A5049 north eastwards for 3 miles to junction with A5058, then continue straight over onto unclassified road for 2 miles to park. Signposted.

A unique historic working country estate where visitors can sample an Edwardian lifestyle. The centrepiece of the park is the Hall, in which the above and below stairs life of 'Croxteth 1905' is recreated with character figures in furnished room settings including the kitchens. Outside, Croxteth Home Farm is an approved Rare Breeds centre where traditional farm animals are housed in original buildings. There are displays to inform and guide the visitor. The walled garden contains old fruit trees trained into curious

shapes, peaches and figs growing in greenhouses and a herb garden. There is also an original mushroom house and a set of beehives. Plants and home produce are on sale when available, including fruit, vegetables, mushrooms, eggs and honey.
☞ adults £2.00, children & senior citizens £1.00
◐ Easter-Sep Mon-Sun 11-5
Facilities: 🚌 🍴 ♿ 🚻 🚗 🍽
★ various farm & garden events throughout the year
🍴 café in 'The Old Riding School' provides snacks, lunches & teas

---

🎣 Map 4 E3
Danebridge Fisheries
Pingle Cottage, Danebridge, Wincle, Macclesfield, Cheshire SKII OQE
Tel. Wincle (02607) 293
From Macclesfield follow A523 southwards, after 4 miles turn left onto A54 for 2 miles, then turn right onto unclassified road for 2 miles to Danebridge. Signposted.

This family-run trout farm and fishing lake are located in the beautiful Dane Valley which is fed by spring water from the same hills which feed the springs at Buxton Spa. The well-stocked lake, fed by 2 clear

water springs, is a popular fly fishing trout lake, with specimens of up to 16lb. Day or part-day tickets can be booked and rods can be hired. Visitors can buy pink-fleshed Dane Valley rainbow trout which are kept alive in a holding tank until required. The fishery is also licensed to deal in game which is available in season.
☞ rod £6.00 for 5 hours including 2 fish to take away, £10.00 per day including 3 fish
◐ all year daily 9.30-4.30
Facilities: ♿ 🚻 🚗

🚢 Map 4 D4
Dunham Massey Hall
Altrincham, Cheshire WA14 4SJ
Tel. Manchester (061) 9411025
From Altrincham follow A56 south westwards, after 2 miles turn right onto B5160 for 1 mile to Dunham. Signposted.

This 18thC house, owned by the National Trust, is set in over 230 acres of ancient parkland which has a herd of 150 fallow deer. There is also the old slaughterhouse, formerly the game larder, which now contains a display on the park's natural history. In the Hall over 30 rooms are on show to visitors including a vast kitchen. The moat from the original Tudor building still provides water for an Elizabethan mill which is in working order.
☞ adults £2.50, children £1.00, family ticket £6.00
◐ house: Apr-1 Nov Mon-Wed, Fri-Sat 1-5, Sun, Bank Hols 12-5; garden & shop: Apr-1 Nov Fri-Sat 12-5.30, Sun, Bank Hols 11-5.30
Facilities: 🚌 🍴 🚻 🚗 🍽
★ 9-10 Jun Edwardian Extravaganza
🍴 lunches & teas served in the licensed self-service restaurant — homemade soups, savouries, cakes, pastries & scones

MAP 4   NORTH WEST ENGLAND

Map 4 D4
Durig Swiss Patisserie
2-4 Broomfield Lane,
Hale, Altrincham,
Cheshire WA15 9AQ
Tel. Manchester (061) 9281143

From Altrincham follow A538 southwards, after 1 mile turn right at Hale into Broomfield Lane to shop.

All the products at the Durig Swiss Patisserie are made on the premises and are free from artificial colours, preservatives and flavourings. Specialities include patisserie, handmade chocolates, preserves, chutneys, ice creams and sorbets. A selection of breads including rye, oat and other brown breads is also on sale. Seasonal items are available for Mothers' Day, Valentine's Day, Easter and Christmas.
◗ all year Tue-Sat 9-5; closed Good Friday & Easter week, first 3 weeks Aug

Map 4 E3
Farmhouse Country Delicacies
The Homestead Farm,
Pott Shrigley, Macclesfield,
Cheshire SK10 5RU
Tel. Macclesfield (0625) 72381

● **Goats' milk cheeses at Farmhouse Country Delicacies**

From Macclesfield follow A523 northwards, after 2 miles turn right onto B5091 for 2½ miles to Pott Shrigley. Signposted.

All the produce for sale at Farmhouse Country Delicacies is homemade and contains no preservatives, additives or colourings of any kind. Eighteen varieties of cheese are made from the goat herds and there are 10 types of sausage, many from recipes over 100 years old, as well as bacon and ham from the rare herd of Tamworth Pigs. Some meats are rubbed with honey and molasses and smoked over apple wood, whilst others are sweet-cured with honey or cured with salt rubbed in by hand every day for a month.
◗ all year daily 10.30-9
Facilities: ▥ ▭

SOUL MASS CAKE
Similar to parkin, this cake was traditionally made for All Soul's Day when children went from house to house singing for a 'soul'. Look out for it at the beginning of November.

Map 4 C3
Haworth's Fruit Farm
Eddisbury Fruit Farm, Yeld Lane, Kelsall, Nr Tarporley, Cheshire CW6 OTE
Tel. Tarporley (0829) 51188/ 51300

From Chester follow A51 eastwards, after 5 miles turn left onto A54 for 2 miles, then turn left just after Kelsall into Yeld Lane for 1 mile to farm. Signposted.

This 50-acre farm offers a wide variety of fruit on a pick your own or ready-picked basis. Depending on the month there are gooseberries, strawberries, raspberries, red and blackcurrants, rhubarb, tayberries, loganberries, plums,

blackberries, 15 varieties of apples and 4 of pears.
◗ 2 Jul-21 Aug daily 10-6; 3 Sep-23 Dec daily 10-4.30
Facilities: ▥ ▭ ▱

Map 4 C5
Kenyon Hall Farm
Winwick Lane,
Croft, Warrington,
Cheshire WA3 7ED
Tel. Culcheth (092576) 3646/ 3161

From Leigh follow A572 southwards, after 3½ miles turn left onto A579 for 1 mile to farm on left. Signposted.

At Kenyon Hall you can pick your own strawberries, gooseberries, raspberries, red and blackcurrants, peas and beans. A tea shop is open on fine afternoons and other farm produce is also available, including cream, local honey, asparagus, tayberries, rhubarb, courgettes, beetroot, turnips, carrots, onions, mangetout, kohlrabi, salad crops and pot herbs.
◗ late Jun-mid Aug 9.30-8
Facilities: ▥ ▭ ▱

Map 4 D2
Lea Forge Trout Farm
Walgherton, Nantwich,
Cheshire CW5 7LF
Tel. Crewe (0270) 841108

From Nantwich follow A51 southwards for 4 miles to farm. Signposted.

Set in pleasant rural surroundings, this trout farm and fishery invites visitors to fish their own trout or purchase them ready-caught. A shop sells fresh and frozen trout products, fresh and

MAP 4

frozen salmon and a wide range of frozen food including game. Tours around the farm are available by arrangement when visitors may feed the fish.

☞ rod £1, fish caught £1.40 per lb

◑ all year daily 10-7.30 or dusk
Facilities: ⑩ ♿ ⓦⓒ 🚗 ♨

🗿 Map 4 E5
W H Lung
83-97 Upper Brook Street, Greater Manchester
Tel. Manchester (061) 2366675

In city centre.

Manchester has a large Chinese community and the biggest 'Chinatown' in England outside London. This popular Chinese supermarket, although situated outside the main Chinatown area of Princes Street, sells the full range of Chinese food including rice and noodles, pickles and sauces, prawns, fresh vegetables and frozen dim-sum. It also sells Chinese kitchen utensils such as woks, ladles and bamboo steaming trays.

◑ all year daily 10-7

🕊 Map 4 E3
Nether Alderley Mill
Congleton Road, Nether Alderley, Cheshire

From Alderley Edge follow A34 southwards, after 1 mile turn left to mill. Signposted.

This 15thC watermill has 2 overshot water wheels working in tandem and a stone-tiled low-pitched roof. Derelict for 30 years, it has now been fully restored by the National Trust and there are occasional demonstrations of flour grinding. Stoneground flour is sold in souvenir bags according to availability.

☞ adults £1.10
◑ Apr-Jun, Oct Wed, Sun, Bank Hols 2-5.30 or dusk; Jul-Sep Tue-Sun, Bank Hols 2-5.30
Facilities: 🚗

🍀 Map 4 C4
Norton Priory Walled Garden
Warrington Road, Runcorn, Cheshire WA7 1RE
Tel. Runcorn (09285) 65029

From Runcorn follow A558 eastwards, after 1 mile turn left into Warrington Road for 1/4 mile to garden. Signposted.

Walled gardens became popular in this country with the Georgian aristocracy. This restored walled garden, built between 1757 and 1770 by Sir Richard Brooke, was the source of fresh garden produce for the manor house close by. A head gardener and 8 under-gardeners were employed here. The garden was opened to visitors in May 1987 and offers something for both the keen amateur gardener and those who just want a stroll in pleasant surroundings. In high summer the soft fruits can be seen ripening and in autumn the orchard trees will be bearing their fruits. There are extensive herb gardens of both culinary and medicinal herbs, along with many varieties of old fruits, a fruit arch and cordon fruit. An exhibition on the history of the garden can be seen at the gardener's cottage.

☞ adults 40p, senior citizens & children 20p, family ticket (2 adults & 3 children) £1.00
◑ Mar-Oct Mon-Fri 12-5, Sat, Sun, Bank Hols 12-6
Facilities: ⓦⓒ 🚗 ♨

🏛 Map 4 D5
Ordsall Hall Museum
Taylorson Street, Salford, Greater Manchester M5 3EX
Tel. Manchester (061) 8720251

From Manchester follow A57 westwards, after bridge turn left onto A5066 for 1/2 mile to museum on right. Signposted.

One of the finest period houses in the region and dating back over 600 years, this museum has an historic kitchen with a 19thC display including oatcake-making and dairy equipment and a kitchen table laid out ready for the cook. There is also a 'daily shopping' exhibit which includes antique food containers and advertisements. Other rooms include the Great Hall and Star Chamber bedroom.

☞ free
◑ all year Mon-Fri 10-12.30, 1.30-5, Sun 2-5
Facilities: ⓦⓒ

● **Black pudding stall, Bury open market**

MAP 4   NORTH WEST ENGLAND

⊞ Map 4 B2
Overton Hall Farmhouse Cheese Dairy
Overton Hall, Malpas, Cheshire
SY14 7DG
Tel. Malpas (0948) 860519

From Broxton follow A41 southwards, after 4 miles turn right at Hampton Heath roundabout onto B5069 for 1½ miles to Malpas, then turn right onto unclassified road for ½ mile to dairy on left. Signposted.

Overton Hall makes Cheshire cheese, the oldest recorded cheese in Britain, in the same way that it has always been made, by hand. Both coloured and white Cheshire are sold at the shop, either as mini-cheeses weighing 1lb and 2½lb or cut to size. Blue Cheshire is sometimes available. Iced Jersey Cream, a superior ice cream and the farm's other speciality, is sold in various flavours.

☞ free
◑ all year daily 9.30-5.30
Facilities: ♿ 🚐

● **Working the spinning mole at Quarry Bank Mill**

🏠 Map 4 E4
Quarry Bank Mill
Styal, Cheshire SK9 4LA
Tel. Wilmslow (0625) 527468

From Wilmslow follow B5166 northwards for 2 miles to museum. Signposted.

This working museum of the cotton industry has weaving and spinning demonstrations as well as an historic kitchen and garden. The 250-acre estate is now a country park.

☞ adults £2.50, children £1.75, family ticket £7.00
◑ Oct-Mar Tue-Sun 11-4; Apr, May Tue-Sun 11-5; Jun-Sep daily 11-5; open Bank Hols
Facilities: 🍺 🍴 ♿ 🚽 🚐 ☕
🍴 mill kitchen serves regional hot dishes including Cheshire fidget pie, tripe & onions, meat & tatty pie, steak & kidney pie; also daily vegetarian dishes & homebaked cakes

🏠 Map 4 E6
Rochdale Museum
Sparrow Hill, Rochdale,
Greater Manchester OL16 1QT
Tel. Rochdale (0706) 47474

In town centre. Signposted.

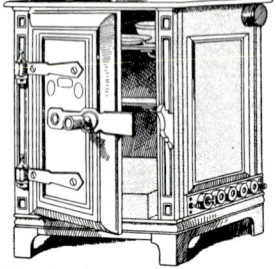

This local museum has an interesting folk-life collection, including a selection of domestic implements and utensils.

● **The cheese dairy, Overton Hall**

MAP 4

☞ free
◑ Jan-Nov Mon-Fri 12-5, Sat 10-1, 2-5, closed Bank Hols except Aug
Facilities: 🚻 🚗

🏛 Map 4 E6
Rochdale Pioneers Memorial Museum
31 Toad Lane, Rochdale, Greater Manchester
Tel. Rochdale (0706) 47474
In town centre. Signposted.
The Rochdale Equitable Pioneers Society opened their first small shop in the ground floor of this building on 21 December 1844. At first only a few basic commodities were sold, such as butter, sugar, flour, oatmeal and candles. However, after their early success, the Rochdale Principles of Co-operation were evolved and provided the pattern for Consumer Co-operation — Co-ops — in Britain and throughout the world. Visitors can see the original shop with its rudimentary furniture and scales.

☞ adults 25p, senior citizens free, children 10p
◑ all year Tue-Sat 10-12, 2-4, Sun 2-4; closed Bank Hols
Facilities: 🚻 🚗 ♿

🏚 Map 4 B2
D S and A Rutter
Old Beachin Farm, Churton, Chester, Cheshire CH3 6LU
Tel. Broxton (082925) 268
From Holt follow A534 eastwards, after ½ mile turn left at Farndon onto B5130 for 1½ miles to Churton. Signposted.
Of interest on this farm is the dairy where visitors are free to wander around and watch cheese being made. Spècialities include farmhouse Cheshire, Wensleydale and Double Gloucester. All are made from unpasteurised milk and are available for sale, in a range of sizes from 6oz to 5lb, from the farmshop. Also on sale are 1, 2

● **Salt Museum, Northwich**

or 4 litre cartons of ice cream and butter in 500g packs.
☞ free
◑ farm: all year daily 10.30-1 by appointment; shop: all year daily 9-5

🏛 Map 4 D3
The Salt Museum
162 London Road, Northwich, Cheshire CW9 8AB
Tel. Northwich (0606) 41331
In town centre. Signposted.
This industrial history museum has lively and informative displays on Cheshire's salt industry, from Roman times to the present day. The displays, which include models, photographs, maps and diagrams, give a wealth of information on salt, its chemistry, world resources, formation, methods of extraction and traditional uses. Visitors can also see a film on the story of salt. The souvenir shop is well stocked with a wide range of information sheets, postcards and souvenirs.

☞ adults 60p, children 30p
◑ Jan-Jun, Sep-Dec Tue-Sun 2-5; Jul-Aug Tue-Sat 10-5, Sun, 2-5; open Bank Hols
Facilities: 🚻 🚗

🐄 Map 4 D4
Stockley Farm
Smithy Farm House, Arley Estate, Arley, Northwich, Cheshire CW9 6LZ
Tel. Arley (056585) 323
From Northwich follow B5075 north eastwards, after 1½ miles turn left onto A559 for 1½ miles, then turn right onto unclassified road for 2 miles to Arley.
At this family-run farm visitors can see just how a dairy farm works. They will be picked up from the car park by a tractor-trailer and taken around the farm. From the viewing gallery in the farm's fully automatic modern milking parlour they will see the cows being milked and then taste the milk in the milk bar. Stockley Farm has 230 dairy cows and rears its own heifers. Visitors are welcome to handle and to feed the farm animals including pigs and sheep. The farm grows various cereals including wheat and barley.

☞ adults £1.00, children (over 3) 50p
◑ Easter-2 Oct Wed, Sat, Sun, Bank Hols 2-6
Facilities: 🍴 🚻 ♿
🍴 snacks include the farm's own milk & homemade cakes

MAP 4

NORTH WEST ENGLAND

⚒ Map 4 B2
Stretton Mill
Stretton, Nr Farndon, Cheshire
Tel. Northwich (0606) 41331
From Broxton follow A534 westwards, after 2 miles turn left onto unclassified road for 1 mile to Stretton. Signposted.

There has been a mill at Stretton since at least the 14thC. In 1978 the mill was restored to working order and the miller now takes visitors on a guided tour of his working watermill. They can watch the centuries' old process of grinding flour with millstones driven by water wheels. The old stable block, originally used as a farmer's workshop, now houses displays which tell the story of the millers, the mill and its restoration. No produce is for sale as corn is milled for animal consumption only.

☞ adults 60p, children 30p
● Apr-Oct Tue-Sun, Bank Hols 2-6
Facilities: 🚾 🚗 🍽

⑤ Map 4 C2
Tattenhall Dairy Products
Drumlan Hall, Newton Lane,
Tattenhall, Nr Chester,
Cheshire CH3 9NE
Tel. Tattenhall (0829) 70995

From Chester follow A41 southwards, after 6 miles turn left onto unclassified road for 1 mile to Tattenhall. Signposted.

A large, modern dairy farm which makes real dairy ice cream from home-produced milk and double cream. Visitors can see where the ice cream is made and then taste for free the 20 flavours of ice cream and 6 flavours of sorbets. Cornets or tubs of ice cream and sorbets can be purchased from the farm shop, or the family's favourite flavour can be taken home in $\frac{1}{2}$, 1 and 4 litre packs.

☞ free
● May-Sep daily 11-6; Oct-Apr Thur-Sun 1-5
Facilities: 🍽 🚾 🚗 🍽
🍽 teas served with homemade scones, jam & clotted cream

🍲 Map 4 D4
Tatton Park
Knutsford,
Cheshire WA16 6QN
Tel. Knutsford (0565) 54822

From Knutsford follow A50 northwards, after 2 miles turn right onto A5034 for $\frac{1}{2}$ mile to Park. Signposted.

Tatton Park is unique in England — a complete historic country estate. Visitors are welcome to the magnificent mansion, the Old Hall, the 1930s working Home Farm, beautiful gardens including an orangery, and 1,000 acres of deer park and meres. There is an historic Victorian kitchen and cellars — including wine cellar, brewhouse and beer cellar — and a splendid Georgian dining room. The Home Farm is working as it was in the 1930s with livestock yards, mill, workshops, stores and offices. A wide variety of produce is on sale at the farm shop including the estate's own venison (Sep-Mar), ice cream (Jun-Sep), yoghurt (Apr-Oct), cheese and vegetables, as well as turkey, lamb, pork and fresh eggs.

☞ mansion: adults £1.25, senior citizens 90p, children 55p; farm: adults & senior citizens 90p, children 45p; all-in ticket to mansion, garden, Old Hall and farm: adults £3.40, senior citizens £2.80, children £1.60
● all year daily; farm closed Nov-Mar Mon-Sat
Facilities: 🍲 🍽 ♿ 🚾 🚗 🍽 /Ⱥ

🥾 Map 4 E4
J Titterton and Sons
24 Princes Street, Stockport,
Greater Manchester
Tel. Manchester (061) 4806905
In town centre.

James Titterton started selling pork in 1875 and 5 generations later the family are still carrying on the tradition. Amongst a wide range of products are traditional sausages made from pork steaks and shoulder and rich pork pies make with belly pork and bacon. All products

● **The kitchen at Tatton Park, Knutsford**

MAP 4

● The Waterfowl Sanctuary, Whitchurch

can be bought in standard pack sizes but larger packs can be supplied by prior arrangement.
◐ all year Mon-Sat 8.30-5.30

✿ Map 4 C1

The Waterfowl Sanctuary

Bradeley Green Farm, Tarporley Road, Whitchurch, Shropshire SY13 4HD
Tel. Whitchurch (0948) 3442

From Whitchurch follow A49 northwards for 2 miles to farm on right. Signposted.

As well as having a Waterfowl Sanctuary, this dairy farm also

offers visitors a chance to see the fish farm and walk the nature trail.

☞ adults £1.00, children (under 14) 50p
◐ Apr-Oct daily 9-9; Nov-Mar daily 9-5
Facilities: 🚻 🚗

🏪 Map 4 C2

A T Welch

45 Hospital Street, Nantwich, Cheshire CW5 5RL
Tel. Nantwich (0270) 625491

In town centre.

This is a replica of an old grocer's shop, where items from the bygone days of the grocery trade and farming industry are displayed. All of the items are in full working order and span the years from 1900 to 1950. The old shop takes visitors back to a time when self-service and pre-packed foods were unheard of. Visitors can see pork sausages being made from local pork, containing no preservatives,

colouring or mixed meats. Specialities include fresh local pork, home-cured bacon, over 60 varieties of cheese including local farmhouse Cheshire and continental examples, cooked meats, pâtés, fresh dairy produce and fresh ground coffee. At Christmas there is a large range of specialist foods to choose from and hampers can be made up.

◐ shop: all year Tue, Thur, Fri 9-5.30, Wed 9-1, Sat 9-5; Yesteryear Shoppe & coffee shop: Tue, Thur- Sat 10-3.30, Wed 10-12 (coffee only)
Facilities: ☕ 🍴 ♿ 🚻
🍴 coffee shop selling snacks & lunches including a Cheshire cheese lunch with farmhouse Cheshire, own pork sausages with plum tomatoes & brown sauce

·CALENDAR OF EVENTS·

APRIL

Egg Rolling
5 April
An old custom - brightly coloured eggs are rolled down a slope at Avenham Park, Preston, Lancashire

JULY

Nantwich Cheese Show
27 July
An annual cheese show at Nantwich, Cheshire.

AUGUST

Lowther Driving Trials and Country Show
5-7 August
An annual country show at Lowther, near Penrith, Cumbria.

SEPTEMBER

Egremont Crab Fair
17 September
A traditional fair established in 1267 which includes a distribution of free apples (originally crab apples) to visitors.

OCTOBER

North Western Dairy Show
20 October
An annual show held in Nantwich, Cheshire.

AGRICULTURAL SHOWS

A number of annual agricultural shows are held in the North West of England — they are normally a good source of local produce. The following are a selection:

JUNE

Cheshire County Show
21-22 June at Tatton Park, Knutsford, Cheshire.

JULY

Cumberland County Show
21 July at Bitts Park, Carlisle, Cumbria.

Royal Lancashire Show
26-28 July at Astley Park, Chorley, Lancashire.

AUGUST

Lunesdale Show
9 August at Kirkby Lonsdale, Lancashire.

Lancaster and Morecambe Show
13 August at Morecambe, Lancashire.

Skelton Show
20 August at Hutton-in-the-Forest, near Penrith, Cumbria.

Millom and Broughton Show
27 August at Broughton, Cumbria.

SEPTEMBER

Westmorland County Show
8 September at Kendal, Cumbria.

NORTH EAST ENGLAND

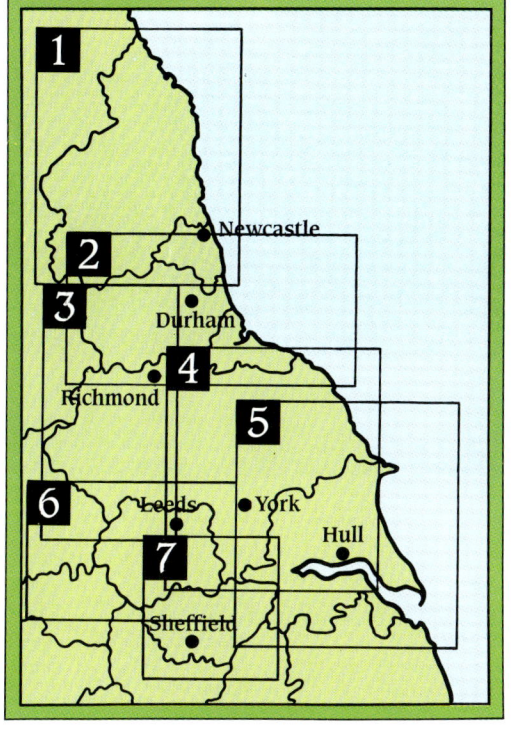

NORTH EAST ENGLAND

● **Scarborough**

by Alan Porter
SPECIALIST FOOD MERCHANT

I am a Yorkshireman but I can speak for Durham and Northumberland — we like our food here and plenty of it. That's not to say that quality does not count, but value for money is the key!

Although there are large industrial centres in the North East, the heart of the region is its countryside — farming communities set in their ways and eating habits.

There is a particular fondness for beer; nowhere else in England are there so many outstanding inns and pubs selling the locally-made beer from Sam Smith's, Theakston's, Tetley's, Taylor's or Thwaite's. Otley is a fairly typical market town although it does have more pubs per capita than any other town in the country! Each one is unique and the beer tastes different in them all.

There are only slightly fewer butchers and it always amazes me how so small a town can eat so many

pies, sausages, black puddings, faggots and hams. Market days are ideal for visitors, with the butchers' windows full of newly baked pies and sizzling spare ribs and the pubs full to overflowing with deals being struck, old friends being greeted and everyone enjoying the humming activity.

The average Yorkshireman also likes simple food; ham and eggs, fish and chips, pork pie and black pudding are the staple diet. Years ago I used to buy real hams and bacon from Messrs Richardson who unfortunately don't even cure them any more. When I visited them there was always a spare rib or some real lard to take home. I will never forget that spare rib, you could cut it with the back of a fork and the flavour was positively delightful.

In my opinion the best food in the North East, or anywhere else for that matter, is always found at the farmer's table. There is nothing like a potato just pulled or a tomato just picked from the plant. My daughter's godparents' farm at Harewood grows all sorts of wonderful exotic vegetables for us and whenever we visit there are huge bowls of delights such as Romanesco — a cross between cauliflower and broccoli — and pink fir apple potatoes dug just before our arrival and prepared to perfection.

The farm's crops are for sale at Ingles in Harrogate, a fabulous shop offering the best produce from all over the world. Roy Ingle encourages his local growers to develop more interesting varieties and his customers can experience everything from tiny bunch carrots to nasturtium leaves and flowers.

Another interesting place to visit is Botton Village in Danby Dale on the North Yorkshire Moors. Botton is part of the Camphill Village Trust where they continue to practise traditional crafts. The village has its own creamery producing 6 different flavours of cheese and also makes cheese for other farmers in the area. The mill produces organic wheat which is made into bread, cakes and biscuits which are eaten in the village and also delivered to local health food shops.

My favourite recipes — Kidneys on Toast, Kippers on Brown Bread — are breakfast dishes, simply because breakfast is my favourite meal. And when made with superb local ingredients it is unbeatable. Kidneys from the dales, wholemeal bread from Gillygate Wholefood Bakery in York, made from flour they mill themselves, and kippers from Whitby which should be jugged for 7 minutes exactly — just enough time to make a pot of real coffee. Louis, my son, shows signs of following in the family tradition. At 10 years old he is positively neurotic about not eating colourings or preservatives. I tease him but am secretly proud that he cares. Let us hope that his generation will revive that quality of life so quickly disappearing even in Yorkshire, one of its last remaining strongholds.

MAP 1 NORTH EAST ENGLAND

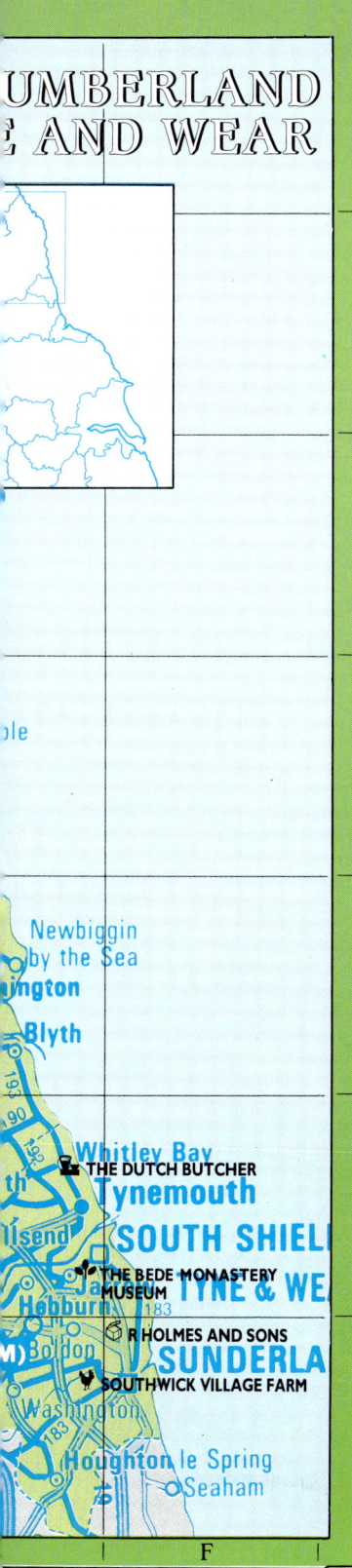

UMBERLAND AND WEAR

(map labels:) ole · Newbiggin by the Sea · ington · Blyth · Whitley Bay · THE DUTCH BUTCHER · Tynemouth · lsend · SOUTH SHIEL · THE BEDE MONASTERY MUSEUM · TYNE & WE · Hebburn · th · Jarrow · R HOLMES AND SONS · SUNDERLA · Boldon · SOUTHWICK VILLAGE FARM · Washington · Houghton le Spring · Seaham

F

A magnificent wild area, this is the big country of England. The people are straightforward and as down-to-earth as their food. The main industry along the coast was herring fishing and curing and the coastline, with its stunning beaches scattered with tiny fishing villages, was covered with hundreds of smokehouses. Now they are reduced to a handful and the most famous is at Craster, where the kippers have been cured in exactly the same way for 150 years.

🌿 Map 1 E2

The Bede Monastery Museum

Jarrow Hall,
Church Bank, Jarrow,
Tyne and Wear NE32 3DY
Tel. Tyneside (091) 4892106

From Jarrow follow A185 eastwards, after ¼ mile turn left onto unclassified road to St Paul's Church and Jarrow Hall. Signposted.

This museum covers the history of the Anglo-Saxon and medieval monastery of St Paul's, specialising in recipes from those periods. It also has a well-established herb garden. Herb plants, vinegars and dried flowers can be purchased.

☞ adults 45p, senior citizens & children 20p
◑ Apr-Oct Tue-Sat 10-5.30, Sun 2.30-5.30; Nov-Mar Tue-Sat 11-4.30, Sun 2.30-5.30; open Bank Hols
Facilities: 🍽 🍴 ♿ 🚗 ♨ /⚠\
🍴 lunches &.teas served featuring homemade soups & cakes

🕊 Map 1 D4

Brinkburn Fruits

Brinkburn High House,
Longframlington, Morpeth,
Northumberland NE65 8AR
Tel. Longframlington (066570) 274

From Longhorsley follow A697 northwards, after 2½ miles turn left onto B6344 for 1 mile to farm. Signposted.

Here there are 12 acres of pick your own fields, with fruits such as strawberries, raspberries, gooseberries and red and blackcurrants. Refreshments are available at weekends.
◑ early Jul-mid Aug daily 10-7
Facilities: ♿ 🚗 ♨

🌷 Map 1 E2

City Farm

Stepney Bank, Byker,
Newcastle upon Tyne,
Tyne and Wear NE1 2PW
Tel. Tyneside (091) 2323698

In city centre.

A well-established city farm right in the middle of

● **Lindisfarne Castle, Holy Island**

MAP 1   NORTH EAST ENGLAND

Newcastle. Animals living here include 2 breeding cows, a mixed herd of goats, a small flock of sheep and 4 breeding sows as well as chickens and ducks. The goats provide about 150 pints of milk a week which are made into cheese and yoghurt. Visitors can watch goat milking demonstrations and buy produce including milk, cheese, yoghurt, duck and goose eggs and organically grown vegetables.

☞ free
◐ May-Oct Tue-Sun 10-7; Nov-Apr Tue-Sun 10-4.30
Facilities: ▨ ⛟ ☺
★ Jul summer fayre

🦐 Map 1 C2
The Corbridge Larder
Hill Street, Corbridge, Northumberland NE45 5AA
Tel. Corbridge (043471) 2948
In town centre.

This delicatessen specialises in wholefoods and unusual groceries but is best known for its cheeses. It stocks over 60 varieties including 15 local ones

from Northumberland, Cumbria and Yorkshire and traditional farmhouse cheeses from all over Britain bought directly from the producers and stored until in peak condition. It also sells a range of locally-baked cakes, pies, quiches and pâtés.
◐ all year Mon-Sat 9-5.30

🏛 Map 1 C2
Corbridge Roman Site
Corbridge, Northumberland
Tel. Corbridge (043471) 2349
From Corbridge follow A69 north westwards, after ¼ mile turn left onto unclassified road for ½ mile to site. Signposted.

Corbridge was a prosperous town and supply depot for the garrisons of Hadrian's Wall in the 3rd and 4thC. It is now owned by English Heritage and its remains include an imposing storehouse and 2 large granaries which are the best preserved in England. The museum contains Roman farming tools and domestic implements.
☞ adults £1.25, senior citizens 95p, children 60p
◐ Apr-Sep Mon-Sat 9.30-6.30, Sun 2-6.30; Oct-Mar 9.30-4, Sun 2-4
Facilities: ▤ ♿ ▨ ⛟

🍎 Map 1 C2
Corbridge Soft Fruit
Brocksbushes Farm, Stocksfield, Northumberland NE43 7UB
Tel. Corbridge (043471) 3400
From Corbridge follow A69 eastwards for 2 miles to farm at junction with A68.

A 60-acre pick your own fruit farm with strawberries, raspberries, gooseberries, red and blackcurrants. A wide range of vegetables, local cheese, cream, eggs and butter is also available.
◐ end Jun-Aug Sat-Thur 9.30-6.30, Fri 9.30-8
Facilities: ▨ ⛟ ☺ ⚠

🍲 Map 1 D4
Cragside
Rothbury, Morpeth, Northumberland NE65 7PX
Tel. Rothbury (0669) 20333
From Rothbury follow B6341 north eastwards, after 1½ miles turn right to Cragside. Signposted.

Cragside, owned by the National Trust, is a magnificent Victorian mansion set in 900 acres of parkland. It was built as a country retreat by the first Lord Armstrong and was the first house in the world to be lit by hydro-electricity.

● **The kitchen, Cragside, Morpeth**

MAP 1

The house was designed by Richard Norman Shaw and visitors can see the original kitchen, built in about 1870, with its extensive range of utensils used for catering on a grand scale and its unusual hydraulic spit. A range of National Trust goods is on sale in the shop. Fishing is available.

☞ adults £2.80, children £1.40
◑ Apr-Sep Tue-Sun, Bank Hols 1-5.30; Oct Wed, Sat, Sun 1-5.30
Facilities: ☕ ¶ ♿ ♿ 🚗 ♨ /⌂\
¶ restaurant serves lunches, teas & dinners — selection of 19thC dishes include venison pie, Lord Armstrong's soup, Northumbrian hodge podge & Tumbleton Trout with Gilnockie sauce

---

❦ Map 1 E5
Dunstan Steads Farm Park
Dunstan Steads, Embleton, Alnwick, Northumberland NE66 3DT
Tel. Embleton (066576) 221

From Embleton follow unclassified road south eastwards for 1 mile to Dunstan Steads.

A mixed farm in an area of outstanding natural beauty where children can stroke and feed many of the animals, most

of which are kept under cover. They include hens — any eggs found can be taken home — pigs and piglets, rabbits and baby chicks as well as a number of rare breeds. The farm trail gives explanations of the features and activities of the farm. In the Old Steading, used for lambing in March and April, there are often pet lambs and young calves to feed. There are trailer rides around the farm on most days.

☞ full park: adults £1.20, children (under 15) 80p; animals only: adults 90p, children 60p
◑ full park: 3-8 Apr, 29 May-3 Jun, 25 Jul-31 Aug daily 1.30-5.30; animals only: 9 Apr-28 May, 4 Jun-25 Jul, 1-16 Sep daily 4-5.30; other times by appointment
Facilities: ¶ ♿ 🚗 ♨ /⌂\

⚒ Map 1 E2
The Dutch Butcher
4 Park Avenue, Whitley Bay, Tyne and Wear
Tel. Tyneside (091) 2522047
In town centre.

The Dutch Butcher is a marvellous centre for fresh

meats, cut and displayed in the continental style. Apart from sandwiches, pies and cooked meats, this butcher and delicatessen offers a wide range of unusual products which visitors can sample before buying. Amongst its specialities are veal olives, pepper burgers and marinaded turkey fillet with garlic, brandy and cream.
◑ all year Mon-Fri 8-5.30, Sat 8-4.30; closed most Bank Hols
Facilities: ☕
☕ prize winning Northumberland sausage is served

☀ Map 1 C6
Heatherslaw Mill
Ford Forge, Cornhill-on-Tweed, Northumberland TD12 4TJ
Tel. Crookham (089082) 338

From Cornhill-on-Tweed follow A697 eastwards, after 4 miles turn left onto B6354 for 2 miles to mill. Signposted.

Heatherslaw Mill is England's most northerly water driven undershot working cornmill and the only one in Northumberland. Dating from the 1830s it is built on 3 floors and has enclosed water wheels.

● **The Dutch Butcher, Whitley Bay**

MAP 1   NORTH EAST ENGLAND

There has been a mill on this site since at least 1280. Visitors can follow a self-guided tour on which they will see all the milling machinery and also the museum with its milling and rural life exhibits. The mill sells its own wholemeal stoneground wheat flour in packs from 500g to 30Kg and pearl barley in 500g packs. Muesli, bran, wheat germ, oat flakes, oatmeal and barley flour are also sold.

☞ adults 60p, senior citizens & children (over 5) 30p
● Apr-25 Sep daily 11-6; Oct Sat, Sun 10-5; or by appointment
Facilities: 🚐 🍴 🚻

🍴 cafe with a changing menu of homebaked food using its own flour serves light lunches & teas as well as snacks; specialities include Border tart, wholemeal scones & vegetarian quiches

☘ Map 1 C2
Hexham Herbs
The Chesters Walled Garden, Chollerford, Nr Hexham, Northumberland
Tel. Humshaugh (043481) 483

From Hexham follow A6079 northwards, after 4 miles turn left onto B6318 for ¼ mile, then at roundabout take 1st exit for ½ mile to Chesters. Signposted.

This 200-year-old walled garden situated on the line of Hadrian's Wall next door to Chesters Roman Fort is a specialist herb nursery growing herbs that can be used for culinary and medicinal purposes, dyes and bee plants. The garden is laid out with specimen herb beds and mature herbaceous borders. All plants are clearly labelled. The history of herbs can be seen in a Roman garden which contains herbs the Romans used, an Elizabethan knot garden, a gold and silver garden and a thyme bank.
Over 300 different herbs are

sold in pots and freshly cut for cooking, plus dried herbs and pot pourris.

☞ adults 40p, children free
● 31 Mar-Oct Wed-Sun, Bank Hols 10-5; Nov-Mar by appointment
Facilities: ♿

★ courses in herb cookery are run jointly with the Hexham School of Cookery

♟ Map 1 B2
GENERAL HAVELOCK INN
Radcliffe Road, Haydon Bridge, Northumberland NE46 1JF
Tel: Haydon Bridge (043484) 376

In town centre.

A converted stable block dating from 1825 and backing onto the River Tyne. The cooking is all done on the premises with nothing bought in except the bread. Their North Shields Smokies are a spicy, quick first course.

● Wed-Sun Meals: Wed-Sun 12-1.30, Wed-Sat 7.30-8.30
Price range £5 upwards
Set D £12.50
Seats 28
Facilities: ♟ 🅿 ♿

NORTH SHIELDS SMOKIES

4oz smoked cod
5fl oz white wine
2-3 black peppercorns
1 bayleaf
4oz Cheddar cheese
French mustard
Parmesan

Heat oven to gas 6 (400F, 200C). Poach the fish in the white wine, bayleaf and peppercorns. Take out the fish, add the cheese and a good dollop of mustard. Return the fish to the sauce, divide into ramekins, grate a little parmesan on top of each one and bake for 10 minutes.

⑤ Map 1 F1
R Holmes and Sons
Whitburn Moors Farm, Sunderland Road, Cleadon, Tyne and Wear SR6 7UN
Tel. Tyneside (091) 5293127

From Sunderland follow A1018 northwards for 2 miles to farm on right.

This dairy farm has been worked by the Holmes family for over 150 years. In 1984 they started producing yoghurt, made in the churn, in 4 flavours — strawberry, raspberry, peach melba and black cherry — using whole fruit with no artificial flavours or colourings. They also sell pasteurised, unpasteurised, skimmed and semi-skimmed milk.

☞ free
● all year Mon-Fri 9-5, Sat 9-12
Facilities: 🚻 🚐

🏪 Map 1 E2
W G Lough and Son
1,2 and 5 Holly Avenue West, Jesmond, Newcastle upon Tyne, Tyne and Wear NE2 BH
Tel. Tyneside (091) 2811351

From Newcastle follow B1309 north eastwards for 1½ miles to Jesmond.

Prominently displayed in this local butchers' shop is the 'Q' symbol, the Mark of Quality awarded by the Q Guild of Butchers. There are always display cuts of lean meat in the shop including cooked hams, Dutch veal, poultry and game. Also on display are Crowns of Lamb and Guards of Honour. All beef in the shop is hung for 14 days before sale and sausages are made on the premises including a gluten and preservative-free Cumberland sausage. This is an old-fashioned butcher in the best tradition selling only quality meats.

● all year Mon-Fri 8-1, 2-5.30, Sat 8-1

MAP 1

🏨 Map 1 E6
Marine Life Centre and Fishing Museum
4 Main Street, Seahouses,
Northumberland NE68 5RG
Tel. Seahouses (0665) 721257

From Bamburgh follow B1340 south eastwards for 3 miles to Seahouses.

This museum follows the history of the fishing industry in Seahouses from its most prosperous days in the 1880s to the present. Visitors can enjoy a walk through time and see a typical fisherman's cottage with the fisherman baiting his lines and his wife 'sceinning' mussels for bait. In the yard women are hanging herrings on tenterhooks before racking them in the smokehouse to produce kippers. In the cooper's shop herring barrels are made — this was an important local industry and at one time there were 40 coopers in Seahouses making over 4,000 barrels a year. A video tells the story of the local fishing industry including trawling, lobster catching and salmon fishing. Also on display are 2 cobles, local fishing boats — a sailing one and the last motorised example with models of lobster pots and line fishing. A new sailing coble is actually being built in the museum. The biggest seawater aquarium in the North East is also housed here and it includes every type of local marine fish — all landed and donated by the local fishermen.
☞ adults £1.20, senior citizens £1.00, children (5-16) 80p
◐ Apr-Sep daily 10-6, Oct daily 10-4
Facilities: 🍽 ❙❂❙ 🆆🅲 🚗 ⛺
❙❂❙ lunches, teas & dinners served in fish & chip restaurant with fish bought directly from boat in harbour

☺ Map 1 D2
Milbourne Fruit Farm
East Town Farm, Milbourne,
Ponteland, Newcastle upon
Tyne, Tyne and Wear NE20 0EE
Tel. Belsay (066181) 278

From Belsay follow A696 southwards for 4 miles to farm. Signposted.

Twenty acres of this 200-acre farm are devoted to pick your own fruit including 7 varieties of strawberries, raspberries, gooseberries, red and blackcurrants, tayberries, apples, plums and a full range of vegetables in season. The shop sells local cream, eggs and bulb onions for winter storage.
◐ Jul-Sep daily 10-7
Facilities: ❙❂❙ 🆆🅲 🚗 ⛺ /⅍\
❙❂❙ farmhouse teas are served

☺ Map 1 D2
North Acomb Farm Shop
North Acomb Farm,
Stocksfield-on-Tyne,
Northumberland NE43 7UF
Tel. Stocksfield (0661) 843181

From Corbridge follow A69 eastwards for 4 miles to farm. Signposted.

Set in 270 acres of the Tyne Valley, this farm produces milk, double cream, free-range eggs and meat. The farm shop sells butter, cheese, yoghurt, dairy ice cream, fruit, vegetables, game, poultry, farmhouse Cumberland sausages and preserves.
◐ Apr-Oct daily 9-6; Nov-Mar daily 10-5
Facilities: 🍽 🆆🅲 🚗 ⛺ /⅍\
🍽 coffee shop serves homebaked food

🎁 Map 1 C3
Redesdale Sheep Dairy
Soppitt Farm, Otterburn,
Newcastle upon Tyne,
Tyne and Wear NE19 1AF
Tel. Otterburn (0830) 20276

From Otterburn follow A696 south eastwards, after 1 mile turn left onto B6341 for 2 miles to dairy. Signposted.

This organic sheep dairy farm makes a range of cheeses from cows' and sheep's milk, including Redesdale cheese. Visitors are welcome to walk around the farm, watch the cheese and other dairy produce being made and sample the results. There is also an apiary and visitors can watch a bee-keeping and honey production video and see a daily demonstration which includes viewing the inside of a beehive. The farm's shop, in a converted byre, sells various cheeses, cheesecake, yoghurts, Quarg, whey drinks, biscuits and ice lollies as well as home-fed pork and lamb in season. Specialist pickles, local marmalades, fudge and chocolate truffles are also available along with a range of beeswax products and honey.
☞ adults 80p, children 40p
◐ farm shop: all year daily 10-6; apiary: 31 Mar-1 Oct daily 11-5
Facilities: 🍽 ❙❂❙ ♿ 🆆🅲 🚗 ⛺ /⅍\
❙❂❙ shepherd's lunches served with cheese, local farmhouse pâtés & home-cured ham & teas with homemade cakes

〰 Map 1 E5
L Robson and Son
Fish Curers, Craster, Alnwick
Northumberland NE66 3TR
Tel. Embleton (066576) 223

From Embleton follow unclassified road south eastwards for 2 miles to Craster.

This is a traditional smokery where kippers have been cured since 1856. Visitors can see herring and salmon being

MAP 1   NORTH EAST ENGLAND

prepared, cured and smoked. Kippers smoked on the premises are available for sale.

☞ free

◐ Jun-Sep Mon-Fri 8-1, 2-3.30, Sat 8-1, closed Bank Hols

Facilities: ⚈

⚈ restaurant where visitors can try the oak-smoked kippers

Map 1 D6
St Aidan's Winery

Lindisfarne Liqueur Company, Holy Island, Northumberland TD15 2RX
Tel. Berwick-upon-Tweed (0289) 89230

From Berwick-upon-Tweed follow A1 southwards, after 9 miles turn left onto unclassified road for 1 mile to Beal. Holy Island is reached by the causeway at low tide and tide tables are posted at each end.

Lindisfarne Mead, valued in Northumberland for its restorative properties, is reputed to be the finest mead in the world. The monks from Lindisfarne Priory started production in the 7thC with a brewhouse twice the size of their kitchen. The secret recipe has been jealously guarded for over 1,000 years but the basics are fermented grape juice, water from an artesian well on

the island, finest honeys and locally gathered herbs. Visitors can sample Lindisfarne Mead in the winery showroom. Other products made using mead are sold and these include preserves like marmalade and strawberry preserve, honey and fudge. Also sold is orange and lemon curd with advocaat.

☞ free

◐ Mar-Oct daily 9-5.30; Nov-Feb Mon-Fri 9-5.30

Facilities: 🚗

Map 1 E1
Southwick Village Farm

271 Southwick Road, Sunderland, Tyne and Wear SR5 2AB
Tel. Tyneside (091) 5489002

From Sunderland follow A1231 westwards towards Southwick, after 1 mile turn left to farm.

A working city farm containing various livestock including Jersey cows, sheep, goats, pigs, ponies, a variety of poultry and a donkey. Fruit and vegetables are also grown. Visitors can watch the video which demonstrates lambing and calving and professional instruction is given in milking goats and cows. Guided tours are available.

☞ free

◐ all year Mon-Fri 8.30-4.30 (8.30-7 in summer), Sat, Sun, Bank Hols 9-4

Facilities: 🚻 ⚈ 🛆

Map 1 E1
Stenhouse

211-215 Coatsworth Road, Gateshead, Tyne and Wear
Tel. Tyneside (091) 4772001

In town centre.

Producing only strictly kosher foods, this specialist Jewish bakery and delicatessen makes its own bread and cakes on the premises including cholla and a selection of interesting seed breads. A large assortment of patisserie is also sold in the shop.

◐ all year Mon-Thur 8.30-6, Fri 8.30-2, Sun 9-1

Map 1 C2
Straker and Leatham

2 Market Street, Hexham, Northumberland NE46 3NU
Tel. Hexham (0434) 602929

In town centre.

This delicatessen sells fine foods from around the world including fresh pasta and sauces, salamis and cured meats such as smoked venison, smoked salmon, trout and eel from Scotland, locally-made pâtés, puddings and bread. It also stocks a wide range of cheeses including a number of local examples like Redesdale and Alston and Browngill goats' cheeses.

◐ all year Mon-Sat 9-5

Map 1 D3
Temple Thornton Fruit Farm

Meldon Park, Morpeth, Northumberland NE61 3SW
Tel. Morpeth (067072) 635/661

From Morpeth follow B6343 westwards, after 7 miles turn right to farm. Signposted.

● 'Materna's kitchen' in the Vindolanda Trust

MAP 1

A 10-acre pick your own fruit farm with strawberries, raspberries and blackcurrants.
◗ Jun-Sep daily 10-6
Facilities: 🚾 🚗 ⛺

🏠 Map 1 B2
Vindolanda Trust
Chesterholm Museum, Bardon Mill, Hexham, Northumberland NE47 7NJ
Tel. Bardon Mill (04984) 277

From Haydon Bridge follow A69 westwards, after 4 miles turn right after Bardon Mill onto unclassified road for 1 mile to Vindolanda on left. Signposted.

Vindolanda was a 4thC Roman fort and civilian settlement which has been excavated over the last 20 years. 'Materna's kitchen' is a full-scale reconstruction of a Roman frontier kitchen where visitors can learn about Roman cooking methods and utensils. Finds from the excavation are displayed in museum cases. A taped commentary explains Materna's life style in AD200. The museum's shop sells 'Roman' recipe cards and herbs. A butcher's shop can be seen in the main street.

☞ adults £1.50, senior citizens £1.25, children 80p

◗ Jan, Feb, Nov, Dec daily 10-4; Mar, Oct daily 10-5; Apr-Sep daily 10-5.30; May, Jun daily 10-6; Jul, Aug daily 10-6.30
Facilities: 🍽 ⅃ 🚾 🚗 ⛺

🚢 Map 1 C3
Wallington
Cambo, Morpeth, Northumberland NE61 4AR
Tel. Scots' Gap (067074) 283

From Cambo follow B6342 southwards for 1 mile to house on right. Signposted.

Situated in 13,000 acres of lakes and woodland, this country house was built in 1688 on the site of medieval Fenwick Castle. Eighteen rooms are open to the public including the Edwardian kitchen which was in use until 1967 and is now arranged as it was in 1900. The house has exceptionally fine porcelain and there are also good collections of dolls' houses and coaches. In the extensive grounds there is an interesting ice house which is where the Victorians stored

their ice during the summer. A range of National Trust goods is on sale in the shop.

☞ adults £2.50, children (under 17) £1.25; garden & grounds only: adults £1, children (under 17) 50p
◗ house: Apr-Sep Wed-Mon 1-5.30; Oct Wed, Sat, Sun 1-5.30; garden: Apr-Sep daily 10-7; Oct daily 10-6; Nov-Mar daily 10-4
Facilities: 🍽 ⅃ ⅃ 🚾 🚗 ⛺

🏠 Map 1 C7
Wine and Spirit Museum
Palace Street, Berwick-upon-Tweed, Northumberland TD15 1HR
Tel. Berwick-upon-Tweed (0289) 305153

In town centre. Signposted.

This museum contains hundreds of artefacts covering 300 years of the wine and spirit trade. These include the Northumberland County Council's official 'peck' and 'bushel' brass weights, hydrometers and glassware. Lindisfarne Mead products can be bought from the shop.

☞ free
◗ Apr-Sep Mon-Sat 10-5
Facilities: ⅃ 🚾 🚗

● **The kitchen, Wallington, Morpeth**

MAP 2 · NORTH EAST ENGLAND

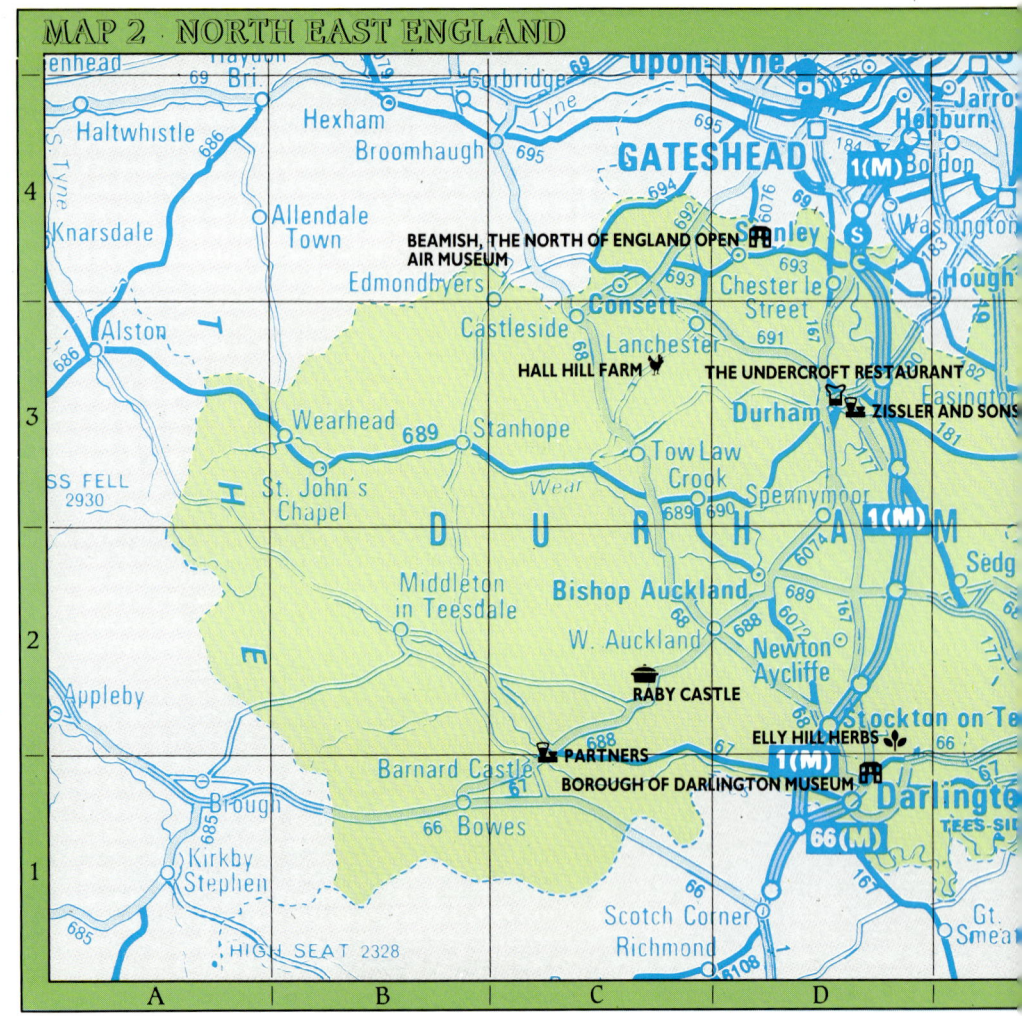

The industrial North is a land of contrasts. It covers the sensational unspoilt scenery in the Pennines to the industrial mining and ship building communities in the foothills and along the coast. Conditions were hard; hearty, satisfying food — including sweet and savoury puddings and pies — were the order of the day. Some are still popular today: Newcastle pudding, like a bread and butter pudding; and singin' hinnies, griddle-baked fruit scones which are so called because they sing and sizzle while cooking.

Map 2 D4
Beamish, The North of England Open Air Museum
Beamish,
Co, Durham DH9 0RG
Tel. Stanley (0207) 231811

From Chester-le-Street follow A693 westwards for 3 miles to Beamish on right. Signposted.

The 1987 European Museum of the Year, Beamish is a recreation of Northern life showing how people in the North of England lived and worked over 50 years ago. Many of the buildings have been moved here and re-erected. The Old Town with shops and houses includes a 1920's Co-op with a grocery department and a full range of 1920's goods. Dry goods were weighed here and wrapped in different coloured papers, butter was sold from large beechwood casks and cut to size with butter pats, bacon was cut to order and coffee was ground by hand. The Sun Inn, a working Victorian pub, was moved from Bishop Auckland and re-erected; a pint of ale can be enjoyed here in the summer. Newcastle Breweries' heavy Clydesdale horses are stabled at the rear with drays and

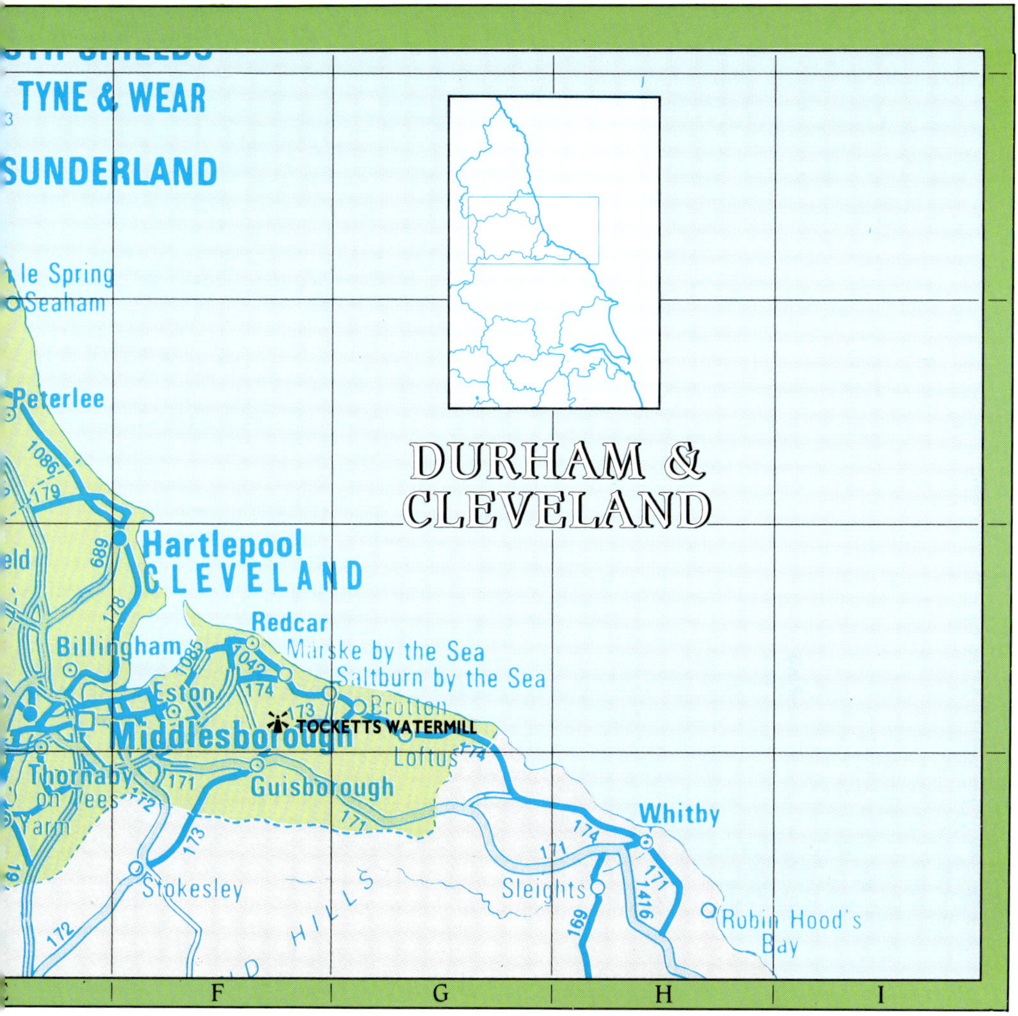

le Spring
Seaham

Peterlee

1086

179

689

Hartlepool
CLEVELAND

128

Redcar
Billingham
Marske by the Sea
1089
Saltburn by the Sea
Eston
174
Brotton
173
Middlesborough TOCKETTS WATERMILL
Loftus 174
Thornaby
171
Guisborough
on Tees
72
171
173
Stokesley
171
Whitby
174
171
169
1416
172
Sleights
D HILLS
Robin Hood's
Bay

F   G   H   I

DURHAM & CLEVELAND

delivery vehicles. In a 1920's house there is a kitchen with its original range and gas cooker and a Maling dinner service displayed on the large Welsh dresser. The colliery community includes furnished pit cottages and kitchens from 1890, 1910 and 1930. In the 1910 cottage the 'pitman's wife' demonstrates baking in a coal-fired oven. Home Farm is an early 20thC working farm with a traditional farmhouse where the 'farmer's wife' goes about her daily chores in the farmhouse kitchen with its magnificent kitchen range of around 1910, and its pantry and dairy. The farm's livestock includes several rare breeds including Durham Shorthorn cattle, British Saddleback pigs,

Teeswater sheep and various breeds of hens, ducks and geese. There is also a farm machinery and farming life exhibition. Demonstrations take place daily.

☞ Apr-Oct: adults £3.30, senior citizens & children £2.30;

Nov-Mar: adults £1.95, senior citizens & children £1.25

◑ Apr-Oct daily 10-6; Nov-Mar Tue-Sun 10-4

Facilities: ☕ ⑩ WC 🚗 ♿ /🔥

⑩ salads, sandwiches, sweets & drinks in Dainty Dinah tea rooms over Co-op

MAP 2 — NORTH EAST ENGLAND

☕ Map 2 D3

THE UNDERCROFT RESTAURANT

The College, Durham
Cathedral, Durham,
Co Durham DH1 3EQ
Tel: Durham (091) 3863721

In city centre.

The restaurant and kitchen
are open-plan, with the high
arched ceiling a particular
feature.

● Mon-Sat 9.30-5, Sun 11-5
Meals: 12-2.30, Sun 12-2
Price range from 70p
Seats 80
Facilities: ♨ ♿ 🚗

BRAISED BEEF with beer

*2¹/₂lb stewing beef
seasoned flour
oil
12 shallots
¹/₂ pint Guinness
¹/₂ pint Newcastle Brown
1lb young carrots
1lb young turnips halved
¹/₄lb mushrooms
¹/₄lb black olives stoned
zest of ¹/₂ orange grated
bouquet garni*

Trim the meat, cut into bite-
sized pieces, roll in the flour
and brown in oil in a
casserole. Add the onions
and deglaze with the
Guinness and Newcastle
Brown and add the bouquet
garni and the orange zest.
Simmer until almost tender
then add the remaining
vegetables and cook for a
further 20 minutes.

🏠 Map 2 D1
Borough of Darlington Museum

Tubwell Row, Darlington,
Co Durham DL1 1PD
Tel. Darlington (0325) 463795

In town centre.

This museum features a bee-
keeping display with an
observation beehive in the
summer months. There is also
an exhibition on early cattle
including the bones of the prize
1,000 guinea shorthorn bull
'Comet' who was bred in the
Darlington area at the
beginning of the 19thC.

☞ free
● all year Mon, Tue, Wed, Fri
10-1, 2-6, Thur 10-1, Sat 10-1,
2-5.30

🌿 Map 2 D2
Elly Hill Herbs

Elly Hill House,
Barmpton, Darlington,
Co Durham DL1 3JF
Tel. Darlington (0325) 464682

*From Darlington follow A66
north eastwards for 2 miles to
junction with A1150, then
continue northwards on
unclassified road for ¹/₂ mile to
Elly Hill House on right.*

This herb farm could not be in
a more attractive setting.
Situated in a 17thC farmhouse
and surrounded by fields, Elly
Hill Herbs offers a pleasant and
informative visit. Nina Pagan,
owner and manager of the
garden, has studied herbs for
years and offers interesting
guided tours. Herb plants are
on sale along with a variety of
herb products such as pot
pourri, herb pillows, candles
and books.

☞ free
● May-Sep by appointment
Facilities: 🍴 📶 🚗 ⛺

🌿 Map 2 C3
Hall Hill Farm

Lanchester, Durham,
Co Durham DH7 0TA
Tel. Bishop Auckland (0388)
730300

*From Lanchester follow B6296
southwards for 3 miles to farm.
Signposted.*

The best time to visit this
beautiful 750-acre farm is at
Easter, when there is the
opportunity to watch the
lambing. Sheep are the main
product at Hall Hill, with 900
breeding ewes producing over
1,400 lambs each April. Beef
cattle are fattened here too and
wheat is grown. Visitors can see
a modern farm at work.

☞ free
● Easter, May-Sep Sun, Bank
Hols 1-5

🗝 Map 2 C1
Partners

26 Horsemarket, Barnard
Castle, Co Durham DL12 8LZ
Tel. Teesdale (0833) 38072

In town centre.

This delicatessen stocks a wide
range of food. There are several
local farmhouse cheeses from
cows', sheep's and goats' milk,
local honey, chocolates, crême
fraiche and, when available,
Yorkshire and Bradenham
hams. They also sell organically
grown vegetables and a
selection of their own prepared
dishes.

● Jul-Christmas Mon-Sat 9.30-5

SOUTH TYNE YEAST CAKE

*¹/₂lb butter
¹/₂lb caster sugar
2 eggs
1lb plain flour
1oz fresh yeast or ¹/₂oz dried
yeast dissolved in 5fl oz of
sour milk
¹/₂ tsp bicarbonate of soda
¹/₂lb currants
¹/₂lb sultanas
4oz chopped mixed peel*

Heat oven to gas 4 (350F,
180C). Cream the butter and
sugar, beat in the eggs and
add the dried fruits. Fold in
the flour alternately with the
yeast and bicarbonate of soda
mixtures. Knead to a smooth,
soft dough and put this into 2
1lb greased bread tins. Prove
until doubled in size and
bake for about 2 hours. Keep
at least a week before eating.

MAP 2

🏰 Map 2 C2
Raby Castle
Staindrop, Darlington,
Co Durham DL2 3AH
Tel. Staindrop (0833) 60202

From Barnard Castle follow A688 north eastwards for 7 miles to castle. Signposted.

Historic Raby Castle in its 200-acre deer park has a magnificent medieval kitchen which was used daily from 1370 to 1954, first by its builders the Nevilles, one of the area's most powerful families, and then by the Lords Barnard who lived here for 350 years. Thirty-six foot square, the kitchen has Victorian ranges and a good collection of copper cooking utensils, all in superb condition. Visitors can see the adjoining sculleries and the 14thC servants' hall where the servants had their meals and where old recipe books are on display. The gardens have a 200-year-old fig tree. The Castle's shop sells the estate's venison and other game and also soft fruits in season. Other food sold includes Kendal Mint Cake and Lakeland Products preserves.

☞ castle & gardens: adults £2.00, senior citizens & children (5-15) £1.20
◑ 2-6 Apr, May-Jun Wed, Sun 1-5; Jul-Sep Sun-Fri 1-5
Facilities: 🍲 🚻 🚗 ♨

🏭 Map 2 F2
Tocketts Watermill
Tocketts, Skelton Road,
Guisborough, Cleveland
Tel. Middlesbrough (0642) 39285

From Guisborough follow A173 north eastwards for 1½ miles to mill on left. Signposted.

This working watermill, the only one in Cleveland, produces stoneground wholemeal flour which can be bought in 1½Kg bags. Visitors can see the milling and farming exhibits and the collection of agricultural implements. On Sundays bread made from the mill's flour is available for tasting.

☞ adults 60p, senior citizens 30p, children 25p
◑ Easter-Oct Mon, Wed, Thur, Sun 10-5.30
Facilities: 🍲 🚻 🚗 ♨ 🛗

STOTTIE CAKES

This is the land of the 'cake' sandwich – a large flat loaf cut into segments which can be filled with savoury or sweet fillings.

🏪 Map 2 D3
Zissler and Sons
104 Bondgate, Darlington,
Co Durham DL3 7LB
Tel. Darlington (0325) 462590

In town centre.

Here, visitors can buy Zissler's wide range of pork products including pork pies, sausages, polony and black pudding which are all famous throughout the county. They also sell home baked bread, English cheeses and pease pudding, a local speciality.
◑ all year Mon, Tue, Thur, Fri 8.30-5.30, Wed 8.30-4, Sat 8.30-5

● **Raby Castle**

MAP 3 NORTH EAST ENGLAND

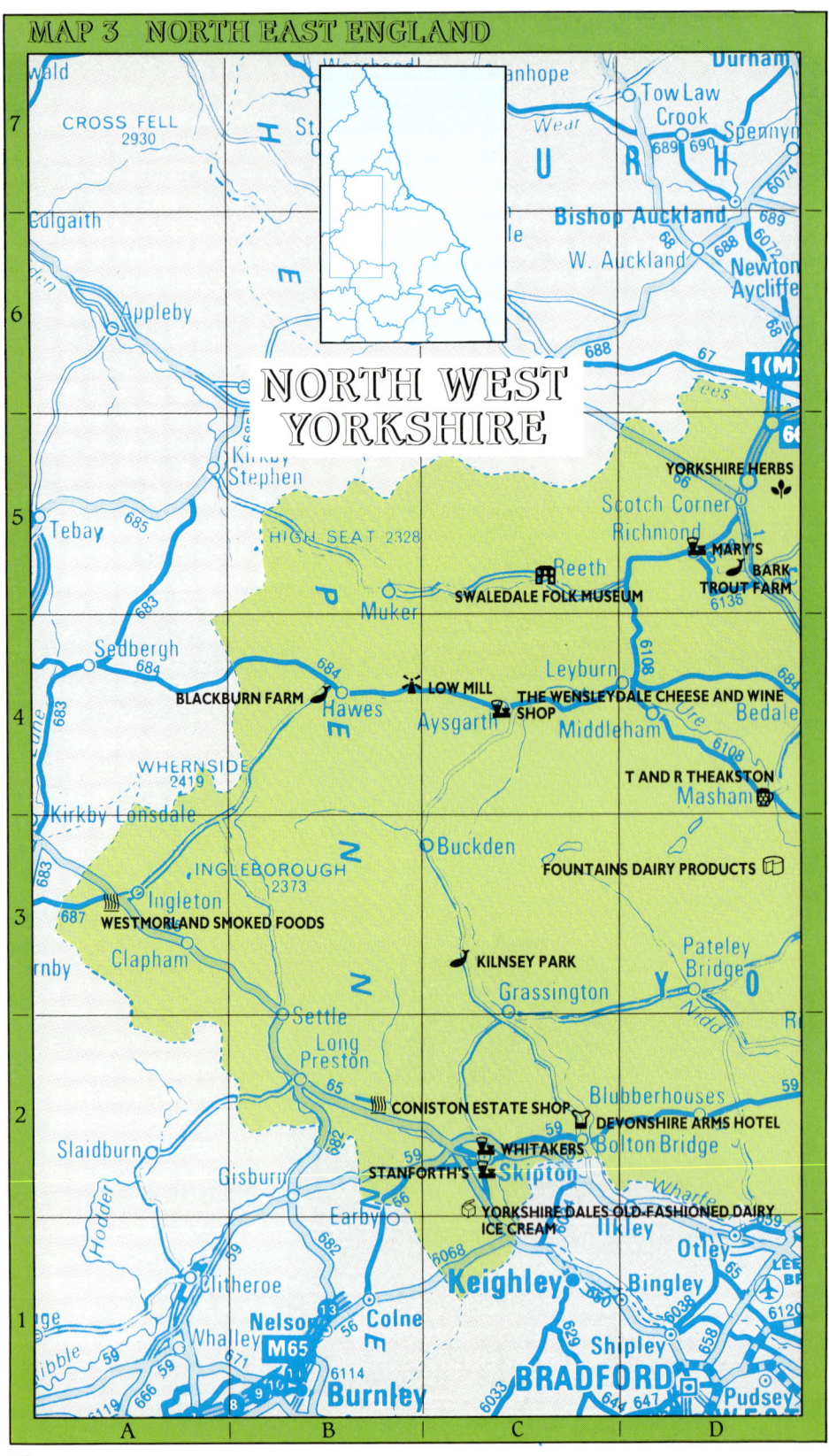

NORTH WEST YORKSHIRE

Durham
Tow Law
Crook
Spennym
Wear
689 690
6074

Bishop Auckland
W. Auckland
Newton
Aycliffe
688
67 1(M)
Tees

CROSS FELL
2930

wald
Woodhead
anhope
St.

HE
E

UR
H

Culgaith
Appleby

YORKSHIRE HERBS
66
Scotch Corner
Richmond
MARY'S
BARK
TROUT FARM

Kirkby Stephen

HIGH SEAT 2328

Reeth
SWALEDALE FOLK MUSEUM
6136

Tebay
685
683

Muker

P

E
N
N
I
N
E

WHERNSIDE
2419

Sedbergh
684
683

BLACKBURN FARM
Hawes
LOW MILL
Aysgarth
Leyburn
THE WENSLEYDALE CHEESE AND WINE
SHOP
Middleham
6108
Bedale
684
6108

Kirkby Lonsdale

Kirkby Lonsdale

T AND R THEAKSTON
Masham

INGLEBOROUGH
2373

Buckden

FOUNTAINS DAIRY PRODUCTS

Ingleton
687
WESTMORLAND SMOKED FOODS

rnby
Clapham

KILNSEY PARK

Pateley
Bridge

Y

O

Grassington
Nidd

Settle
Long
Preston
65

Slaidburn

CONISTON ESTATE SHOP
Blubberhouses
59
DEVONSHIRE ARMS HOTEL
Bolton Bridge
WHITAKERS
Gisburn
STANFORTH'S
Skipton
Wharfe
Earby
66
YORKSHIRE DALES OLD-FASHIONED DAIRY
ICE CREAM
Ilkley
Otley
59
65
LEE
BR

Hodder
682
6068
Keighley
Bingley
6120

Clitheroe
13
Colne
629
Shipley
658

Whalley
M65
671
Nelson
56
BRADFORD
Pudsey

ibble
59
666 59
6114
8
6033
641 647
WEST
Burnley
7

7

6

5

4

3

2

1

A   B   C   D

The Yorkshire Dales have long been valued as rich and fertile pastureland. Even now the area is peppered with markets — at Ripon or Richmond, for example — offering local produce. Cheese has been made in Wensleydale for centuries. The monks from Jervaulx Abbey started the tradition. When the Abbey was dissolved they handed on the recipe to a local inkeeper who in turn passed it to the neighbouring farmers' wives. It is a mild crumbly cheese often eaten with apples and according to a local saying 'An apple pie without cheese is a like kiss without a squeeze!".

🎣 Map 3 D5
Bark Trout Farm
Park Gate Lane,
Brompton-on-Swale,
North Yorkshire DLT 7HA
Tel. Richmond (0748) 818499

From Richmond follow B6271 eastwards, after 2 miles turn left to farm. Signposted.

Tours, demonstrations and fish your own facilities are available on this trout farm. Fish can be bought in any quantity.

☞ rod & bait £3.00 per day
◐ all year daily 8-dusk
Facilities: 🚗 🍽

🎣 Map 3 B4
Blackburn Farm
Gayle, Hawes,
North Yorkshire DL8 3NX
Tel. Hawes (09697) 524

From Hawes follow B6255 southwards for ½ mile to farm. Signposted.

This fish your own trout farm has a 3-fish limit, but ready-cleaned trout are sold by the pound as well as free-range eggs, jams and jellies.

☞ rod £9.00 per day
◐ all year daily 8.30-5
Facilities: 🍴 🚾 🚗 🍽

〰 Map 3 B2
Coniston Estate Shop
Coniston Hall,
Coniston Cold, Skipton,
North Yorkshire BD23 4EB
Tel. Gargrave (075678) 8136

From Skipton follow A65 north westwards for 7 miles to estate on right. Signposted.

Situated by a 24-acre lake in the parkland estate of nearby Coniston Hall, this fish farm offers fish your own trout from the lake or 2½ miles of river, with fly-fishing only and a limit of a 2-fish catch. Visitors may wander on the woodland trail around the lake, see the oak-smoking on the premises and visit the shop housed in a 17thC barn where ready-caught fresh or smoked trout are sold as well as game, cheese, fresh and frozen meat, herbs, homemade biscuits, jams, jellies, pâté, pickles and marmalade.

☞ lake & woodland trail: 25p; lake fishing: £10 per day; river fishing: £8 per day
◐ all year daily 10-6
Facilities: ♿ 🚾 🚗

REGIONAL RECIPE

YORKSHIRE TREACLE TART

12oz shortcrust pastry
6oz mixed dried fruit
2oz grated apples
½ lemon, juice and grated rind
3oz golden syrup
1½oz brown breadcrumbs

Heat oven to gas 7 (425F, 210C). Butter an 8-inch pie dish and line with half the pastry. Mix the dried fruit with the apples, lemon juice and rind, syrup and breadcrumbs and spread the mixture over the pastry base. Cover with the remaining pastry. Bake for 45 minutes, lowering the heat after the first 15 minutes.

🏠 Map 3 D3
Fountains Dairy Products
Kirkby Malzeard, Ripon,
North Yorkshire HG4 3QD
Tel. Kirkby Malzeard (076583) 212/495

From Ripon follow B6265 westwards, after 1 mile turn right onto unclassified road for 5 miles to Kirkby Malzeard.

This dairy has revived the production of Coverdale cheese, a mild white cows' milk cheese which was made in Coverdale up to 1935. It also makes Wensleydale and other English varieties. Visitors are welcome to watch the cheese-making process and to see the storeroom. Cheese can be bought from 1lb to 12lb.

☞ free
◐ by appointment
Facilities: 🚾 🚗

🎣 Map 3 C3
Kilnsey Park
Kilnsey, Skipton,
North Yorkshire BD23 5PS
Tel. Grassington (0756) 752150

From Skipton follow B6265 northwards, after 8½ miles turn left onto B6160 for 3 miles to Kilnsey. Signposted.

The Yorkshire Dales provide a beautiful setting for this trout farm and Daleslife Centre. Visitors can feed or catch fish in their natural surroundings and buy trout smoked on the premises. The farm shop also sells pheasant, grouse and duck. The Daleslife Visitor Centre, housed in a magnificent converted barn, contains a freshwater aquarium and a display of Dales life. This includes a fascinating interpretation of the River Wharfe and Wharfedale using models, samples and videos. There is also a graphic presentation of a year in the life of a shepherd and fly-fishing in Wharfedale.

☞ adults 95p, senior citizens & children 65p
◐ all year daily 9-5.30
Facilities: 🥪 🚾 🚗 🍽
🥪 sandwiches made from smoked trout or Wensleydale cheese

MAP 3   **NORTH EAST ENGLAND**

✛ Map 3 B4
Low Mill
Bainbridge, Leyburn,
North Yorkshire DL8 3EF
Tel. Wensleydale (0969) 50416

*From Hawes follow A684
eastwards for 4 miles to
Bainbridge.*

This 17thC watermill, restored
to working order, is now a
museum with a collection of
agricultural implements.
Visitors can see the original mill
interior.

☞ adults 75p, children 25p
◗ Jul-16 Sep, daily 2-5, Bank Hol
weekends
Facilities: 🚻 🚗 ⛺

🏪 Map 3 D5
Mary's
5-6 Trinity Church Square,
Richmond,
North Yorkshire DL10 4HY
Tel. Richmond (0748) 4052

In town centre.

Situated in the middle of the
Market Square, this delicatessen
is thought of by locals as a mini
'Fortnum and Mason'. As well
as general provisions it stocks a
good range of English and
continental cooked meats,
sausages and over 70 different
cheeses, many of which are
handmade locally. Other
specialities include hand-baked

biscuits and hand-dipped
chocolates.
◗ Feb-Dec daily 8-6; Jan daily
8-5.30
Facilities: 🍽 🚻
🍽 light lunches & afternoon
teas served in upstairs tea
room; home-baked cakes
including Yorkshire curd tarts

🏪 Map 3 C2
Stanforth's
9 Millbridge, Skipton,
North Yorkshire BD23 1NJ
Tel. Skipton (0756) 3477

In town centre.

Stanforth's is a family butcher
established over 60 years ago
and run today by the grand-
daughter of the original Mr
Stanforth. This 'celebrated pork
butcher' is famous for its pork
pies, still made from the original
recipe, and its own polony,
black puddings, sausages and
cooked meats.
◗ Mon, Wed, Thur 7-5, Tue
7-12.30, Fri 6-5, Sat 6-4, closed
Bank Hols

🏛 Map 3 C5
Swaledale Folk Museum
Reeth, Nr Richmond,
North Yorkshire DL11 6QT
Tel. Richmond (0748) 84373

*From Richmond follow A6108
Swaledale Road westwards, after
5½ miles turn right onto B6270
for 5 miles to Reeth. Signposted.*

Swaledale Folk Museum shows
the rural life of the inhabitants
of this remote hill farming area.
On display is every facet of their
lives from farming implements
and lead mining tools to
pastimes and domestic items.
One exhibit shows a typical
Swaledale housewife making
cheese and butter in a 19thC
kitchen.

☞ adults 50p, children (5-14)
25p
◗ 1 Apr-Oct daily 10-6 or by
appointment
Facilities: ♿ 🚗

RESTAURANT RECIPE

🍴 Map 3 C2
DEVONSHIRE ARMS HOTEL
Bolton Abbey, Nr Skipton,
North Yorkshire BD23 6AJ
Tel: Skipton (0756) 71441

*From Bolton Bridge follow
B6160 northwards for ½ mile
to Bolton Abbey.*

A country house hotel with
cheery open log fires. There is
a notable cheese board with
at least 10 regional cheeses
from within a 25-mile radius.
Other specialities include a
clear Beef Consommé topped
with a Stilton soufflé and a
traditional Rabbit Terrine
which is cheap and easy to
make.

◗ Mon-Sun Meals: 12-2,
7-9.30
Price range Set L £9.75 Set D
£16.50 A la carte from £16.50
Seats 60
Cards: Access, Amex, Diners
and Visa
Facilities: 🍷 🎵 ♿ 🚗

RABBIT TERRINE
*2 rabbits weighing together
5½lb
1lb lean pork
2lb pork fat
2 eggs
1 orange zest and juice
2 tbsp brandy
1oz butter
2 bayleaves
2 sprigs rosemary
2 sprigs thyme
2 shallots
salt & pepper*

Heat the oven to gas 3 (325F,
160C). Joint and bone the
rabbits setting the fillets
aside. Cut the remaining
meat into strips and place in
a bowl with the pork and
12oz of the pork fat. Season,
add the orange, bayleaves,
shallots and herbs, cover and
leave to marinade for 2-3
hours. Heat the butter in a
pan and lightly fry the rabbit
fillets and allow to cool.
Mince the meat twice through
a mincer, beat in the eggs and
brandy and season. Line a
terrine with the remaining
pork fat, spoon in a layer of
the mixture, lay the fillets on
top and cover with the
remaining mixture. Cook in a
water bath for 1 hour. Serve
cold with a Cumberland
sauce.

MAP 3

🍺 Map 3 D4
T and R Theakston

The Brewery, Masham, Ripon,
North Yorkshire HG4 4DX
Tel. Ripon (0765) 89544

From Ripon follow A6108 north westwards for 10 miles to Masham.

Theakston is a family-run brewery which uses traditional beer-making processes to produce its famous 'Old Peculier' and 'XB' beers. The visitor centre has exhibitions on old brewing methods and the history of the Theakston family. Visitors can also watch 2 coopers servicing wooden casks. Tours of the brewery run each day for the first 15 people to arrive.

☞ visitor centre: free; brewery tours: £1.00
◑ visitor centre: Jun-Sep Wed-Sun 10-4.30; brewery tour: 4.30
Facilities: 🚾

🦪 Map 3 C4
The Wensleydale Cheese and Wine Shop

Main Street, Aysgarth,
North Yorkshire
Tel. Aysgarth (09693) 413

In village.

This shop, situated in the beautiful Wensleydale, sells a variety of local cheeses which are displayed and can be cut to size. These include Wensleydale — both blue and white — and cheese from a local farmhouse in Swaledale. It also sells Yorkshire Dales Ice Cream from Keighley in West Yorkshire.
◑ Apr-Sep Mon-Sat 9-6; Oct-Mar Mon-Tue, Thur-Sat 9-6

〰️ Map 3 A3
Westmorland Smoked Foods

Unit 5D, Ingleton Industrial Estate, Ingleton, Via Carnforth, Lancashire
Tel. Ingleton (0468) 41906

From Kirkby Lonsdale follow A65 southwards, after 5½ miles turn right into Ingleton Industrial Estate. Signposted.

A pioneer in the field of cheese smoking, this company is probably the largest producer of traditionally smoked cheese in England. It also smokes Scotch salmon which is packaged under the Debrett name. Visitors can go on a guided tour of the shop to see the traditional methods of smoking.
☞ free
◑ all year Mon-Fri 8-5 or by appointment, closed Bank Hols
Facilities: 🚗

RICHMOND MARKET

Visit the large local market in Richmond on Saturdays. The cobbled market place is the biggest of its type in England. Skipton market, on Mondays, Fridays and Saturdays, is excellent for cheese and ham.

🦪 Map 3 C2
Whitakers

25 High Street, Skipton,
North Yorkshire
Tel. Skipton (0756) 2531

In town centre.

This shop specialises in chocolates and confectionery, particularly after-dinner mints, fudge and truffles.
◑ Oct-May Mon-Sat 9-6; Jun-Sep daily 9-6

🍦 Map 3 C2
Yorkshire Dales Old-Fashioned Dairy Ice Cream

Aireside Mills,
Cononley, Keighley,
West Yorkshire BD20 8LW
Tel. Crosshills (0535) 36644

From Skipton follow A629 southwards, after 2 miles turn right onto unclassified road for 1 mile to Cononley.

Visitors are welcome to tour this ice cream manufacturer and to sample the ice cream which is made from natural ingredients with no artificial colour or preservatives. Amongst the many flavours are natural, strawberry, chocolate, hazelnut, coffee, orange and passion fruit. Other products include natural fruit sorbets, milk shakes, milk ice lollies and a speciality ice cream bombe with a liqueur centre.
☞ free
◑ all year Mon-Fri 9.30-4.30
Facilities: 🚾 🚗 ☕

🌿 Map 3 D5
Yorkshire Herbs

The Herb Centre, Croft,
Middleton Tyas, Richmond,
North Yorkshire
Tel. Barton (0325) 77686

From Scotch Corner follow unclassified road eastwards for 2 miles towards Croft. Signposted.

This specialist herb farm has herb display areas and grows a wide variety of culinary, aromatic, decorative and medicinal herbs. It sells potted and cut herbs from its own greenhouses.
☞ free
◑ Apr-Oct daily 9-5; Nov-Mar Mon-Fri 9-5
Facilities: ♿ 🚾 🚗

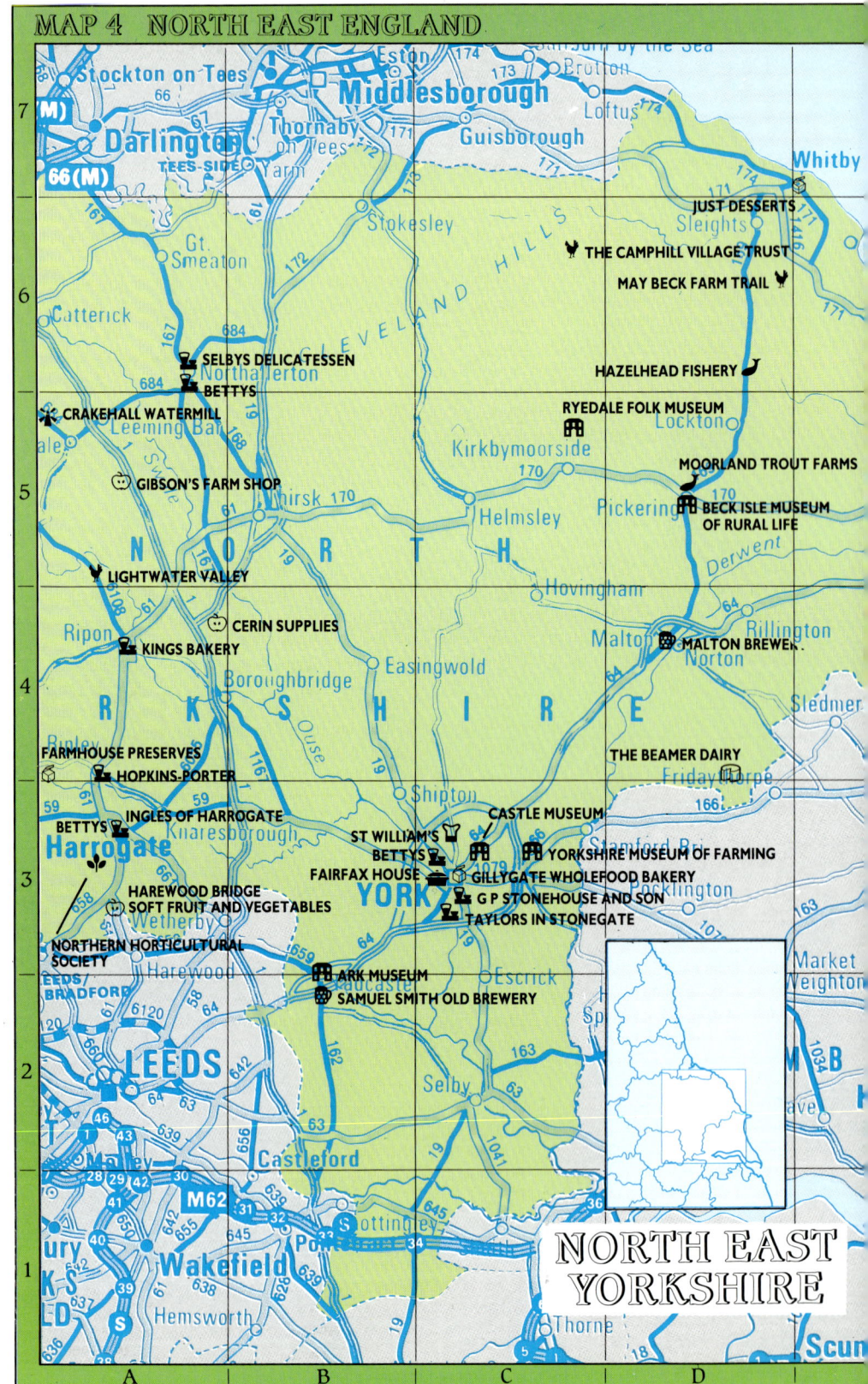

MAP 4 NORTH EAST ENGLAND

NORTH EAST YORKSHIRE

JUST DESSERTS
THE CAMPHILL VILLAGE TRUST
MAY BECK FARM TRAIL
HAZELHEAD FISHERY
RYEDALE FOLK MUSEUM
MOORLAND TROUT FARMS
BECK ISLE MUSEUM OF RURAL LIFE

SELBYS DELICATESSEN
BETTYS
CRAKEHALL WATERMILL
GIBSON'S FARM SHOP
LIGHTWATER VALLEY
CERIN SUPPLIES
KINGS BAKERY
MALTON BREWERY

THE BEAMER DAIRY
FARMHOUSE PRESERVES
HOPKINS-PORTER
INGLES OF HARROGATE
BETTYS
CASTLE MUSEUM
ST WILLIAM'S
BETTYS
FAIRFAX HOUSE
YORKSHIRE MUSEUM OF FARMING
GILLYGATE WHOLEFOOD BAKERY
G P STONEHOUSE AND SON
TAYLORS IN STONEGATE
HAREWOOD BRIDGE
SOFT FRUIT AND VEGETABLES
NORTHERN HORTICULTURAL SOCIETY
ARK MUSEUM
SAMUEL SMITH OLD BREWERY

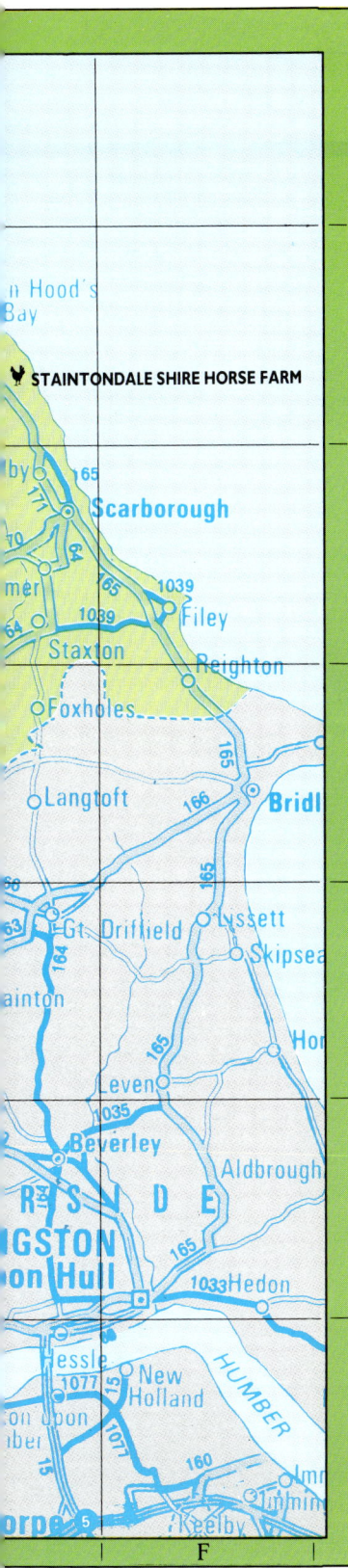

STAINTONDALE SHIRE HORSE FARM

This is James Herriot country. As if this was not enough to tempt the visitor there is York Minster, ruined abbeys galore and fine country houses — not to mention plenty of fine Yorkshire foods. The farming is mixed with particular emphasis on sheep and pigs. The area offers an interesting range of pork products from homemade sausages to York ham, the most famous of England's regional hams. It is dry-cured and said to have first been smoked with oak sawdust left by the carpenters during the building of York Minster.

🏠 Map 4 B3
Ark Museum
Kirkgate, Tadcaster,
North Yorkshire
Tel. Tadcaster (0937) 835778

In town centre.

Housed in a unique timber-framed building with possible Pilgrim Fathers associations, this museum of brewing and local history holds constantly changing exhibitions with brewing and coopering artefacts on display.

☞ adults 50p, senior citizens & children 10p
● all year Thur, Sat, Sun 10-4
Facilities: 🚾 🚗

🏠 Map 4 D4
The Beamer Dairy
Chapel Farm,
Thixendale, Malton,
North Yorkshire YO17 9TG
Tel. Driffield (0377) 88340

From York follow A166 eastwards, after 15 miles turn left onto unclassified road for 3 miles to Thixendale.

This goat dairy farm with its herd of British Toggenberg goats makes 3 different vegetarian goats' cheeses, all free from artificial colouring, additives and preservatives. They can be tasted and purchased from the dairy's own shop. The cheeses are sold whole or cut to size.

☞ free
● all year daily 10-5
Facilities: 🚗

🏠 Map 4 D5
Beck Isle Museum of Rural Life
Pickering,
North Yorkshire YO18 8DU
Tel. Pickering (0751) 73653

In town centre. Signposted.

There is something for everyone in this museum of rural life. Housed in a handsome stone-built Regency residence, exhibits span 2 centuries with collections of domestic and social items

displayed in reproductions of their original settings. The Dairy displays cream separators, butter churns and an interesting arch-backed 'butter worker' for removing the whey. Bottles and jugs are on display in the Victorian Pub while the Village Shop stocks all the necessities: sugar, flour, salt and tea. The Cottage Kitchen has a variety of authentic utensils and is dominated by a charming black-leaded range.
☞ adults 70p, children (5-16) 35p
● Apr-Jul, Oct daily 10.30- 12.30, 2-5; Aug-Sep daily 10-7
Facilities: 🍴

MAP 4   NORTH EAST ENGLAND

♨ Map 4 A3
Bettys
1 Parliament Street, Harrogate,
North Yorkshire HG1 2QU
Tel. Harrogate (0423) 64659

In town centre.

Bettys, overlooking the town's
Montpelier Gardens, was
established in Harrogate in 1919
by Frederick Belmont, a young
Swiss confectioner who settled
in North Yorkshire. It specialises
in Yorkshire cookery and sells
an amazing selection of cakes
— over 400 different lines — all
of which are handmade in
Bettys' own bakery using a
unique combination of Swiss
and Yorkshire recipes. Cakes
include fat rascals, spiced tea
cakes, Ripon spiced bread, curd
tarts and spiced fruit cake
served in the Yorkshire
tradition with Wensleydale
cheese. There is also a selection
of rare teas and coffees,
blended and roasted by Bettys,
such as Sumatra Mandheling
and Cuban Extra Turquino
Lavado.
◑ all year Mon-Sat 9-5.30; Sun,
Bank Hols 10-6
Facilities: ☕ ⦿ wc
⦿ a snack at Bettys includes an
interesting selection of rare
coffees & teas, traditional
Yorkshire cakes & pastries as
well as specialities such as
Rarebits made with farmhouse
Cheddar & Yorkshire ale served
with chutney; scrambled eggs
with smoked salmon &
Yorkshire cheese lunches. The
Children's Menu includes real
ice cream milk shakes, Bettys
clown & double decker
sandwiches

TOFFEES

The famous Harrogate toffee
in those distinctive blue and
silver tins can be bought at
several places in the area,
including John Farrah's,
Royal Parade, Harrogate.

♨ Map 4 C3
Bettys
St Helen's Square, York,
North Yorkshire YO1 2QP
Tel. York (0904) 59142

In city centre.

A sister shop and tea-room to
the original Bettys in Harrogate
selling the same marvellous
variety of Yorkshire food.
◑ all year daily 9-9
Facilities: ☕ ⦿ wc
⦿ dinner served in addition to
lunches & teas

♨ Map 4 A6
Bettys
188 High Street, Northallerton,
North Yorkshire DL7 8LF
Tel. Northallerton (0609)
775154

In town centre.

A sister shop and tea-room to
the original Bettys in Harrogate
selling the same marvellous
variety of Yorkshire food.
◑ all year Mon-Sat 9-5.30, Sun
10-5.30
Facilities: ☕ wc

♥ Map 4 C6
The Camphill Village Trust
Botton Village, Danby, Whitby,
North Yorkshire YO21 2NJ
Tel. Castleton (0287) 60871

*From Whitby follow A171
westwards, after 14 miles turn
left onto unclassified road for 4
miles to Castleton, then turn left
onto unclassified road for 3 miles
to village. Signposted.*

Camphill Village Trust at Botton
Village, nestling in Danby Dale
in the North Yorkshire Moors,
is a community of mentally
handicapped adults who work
in the village's 400 acres of
farms and workshops. The
workshops include a new
creamery, where Botton cheese
is made, and a bakery. There is
also a herb garden and a
wholefood centre. The entire

farm is open to visitors who are
welcome to walk around the
estate — a free map is
provided. Botton cheese,
yoghurt and cream are made in
the creamery and sold from the
shop. Other produce for sale
includes herbs, Botton peanut
butter and gifts.
🎫 free
◑ all year daily 9-12.15, 2-5.30;
workshops closed Bank Hols;
guided tours by appointment
Facilities: ☕ ⦿ & ⛽ ⛺
★ 5 Jul open day 1-6
⦿ teas served including
homemade cakes

🏛 Map 4 C3
Castle Museum
York, North Yorkshire YO1 1RY
Tel. York (0904) 53611

In city centre. Signposted.

The collection that now
constitutes England's largest
folk museum was begun by Dr
John Kirk of Pickering and has
been housed since 1938 in the
old prison buildings within the
bailey of York Castle, built by
William the Conqueror in 1069.
As well as many artefacts from
Yorkshire life in bygone days,
there are reconstructions of a
dairy, farmhouse kitchen,
Moorland cottage, sweetshop,
hotel/pub, period rooms and
the Hearth Gallery tracing the
history of ovens from antiquity
to the microwave. The
Raindale Mill was added to the
site in 1966.
🎫 adults £2.25, senior citizens
& children £1.15, York residents
free
◑ Apr-Sep Mon-Sat 9.30-6.30,
Sun 10-6; Oct-Mar Mon-Sat
9.30-5, Sun 10-5
Facilities: wc ⛺ ♿
⦿ tea room serves a wide
selection of food including
homemade soups & quiches,
Yorkshire curd tart, Yorkshire
parkin, Wensleydale cheese
sandwiches & fresh cream
scones

MAP 4

● The bar, King William IV Hotel, Castle Museum, York

MAP 4 **NORTH EAST ENGLAND**

• **Terry's sweet shop, Castle Museum, York**

☺ Map 4 A4
Cerin Supplies
Cerin House,
Back Lane, Dishforth,
North Yorkshire YO7 3LH
Tel. Thirsk (0845) 578002

*From Boroughbridge follow A1
northwards, after 3 miles turn
right onto A168 for 1 mile to
Dishforth.*

This farm shop sells all manner
of goats' milk products,
including yoghurt, ice cream
and cheese, as well as free-
range eggs and home-grown
vegetables. Visitors may also
see the farm animals.
◗ all year daily by appointment
Facilities: ▨

🏃 Map 4 A5
Crakehall Watermill
Little Crakehall, Bedale,
North Yorkshire DL8 1HU
Tel. Bedale (0677) 23240

*From Leeming Bar follow A684
westwards for 3 miles through
Bedale to Crakehall and mill
near bridge over Crakehall Beck.*

This ancient mill, which has
been restored to working
order after lying derelict for 50
years, is an excellent example of
a country corn mill. It was in
existence at the time of the
Domesday Book survey of
1086, although the present

building dates from the 17thC
and the machinery from the
18thC. The mill now produces
wholemeal flour, ground by 2
pairs of millstones driven by a
15 foot diameter breastshot
water wheel. Milling can be
seen by visitors on most days.
Stoneground wholemeal flour
is for sale in 500g and 1.5Kg
sacks.
☞ adults 50p, senior citizens &
children (5-16) 25p
◗ Easter-Oct Tue-Thur, Sat 10-5,
Sun, Bank Hols 11-5
Facilities: ▯ ▨ 🚗
▯ teas served including cakes &
scones made from mill's own
wholemeal flour

🍲 Map 4 C3
Fairfax House
Castlegate, York,
North Yorkshire YO1 1RN
Tel. York (0904) 55543

In city centre. Signposted.

This Georgian town house
features an historic kitchen and
sells preserves and chocolates
in the shop.
☞ adults £1.75, senior citizens
£1.50, children 75p
◗ Mar-1 Jan Mon-Thur 11-4.30,
Sun 1.30-4.30

📦 Map 4 A4
Farmhouse Preserves
Stumps Lane,
Darley, Harrogate,
North Yorkshire HG3 2RR
Tel. Harrogate (0423) 7809961/
74578

*From Harrogate follow A59
westwards, after 7 miles turn
right onto unclassified road
towards Darley for 2 miles to
shop on left.*

Farmhouse Preserves are
experts on jam — the 3-letter
word embracing quality
preserves, marmalades and
curds. They make and sell a
wide variety of jam which
visitors are welcome to taste.
Their more exotic varieties

• **Crakehall Watermill**

MAP 4

include 3-fruit and brandy marmalade, Worcesterberry jam — a cross between a gooseberry and blackcurrant — plum jam with walnuts and brandy and strawberry and Cointreau jam. No artificial preservatives or additives are used and the jams are sold in 12, 8 and 1oz jars.

☞ free
◗ all year Mon-Fri 9-5 or by appointment, closed Bank Hols
Facilities: 🚻 🚗

☺ Map 4 A5
Gibson's Farm Shop
Hopetown House, Burneston, Bedale, North Yorkshire DL8 2JN
Tel. Thirsk (0845) 567252

From Leeming Bar follow A1 southwards, after 5 miles turn right onto B6285 for ½ mile to Burneston. Signposted.

A specialist farm shop with a reputation throughout Britain for its quality meat products at reasonable prices. Its specialities are Hopetown House Sausage,

a Cumberland-type sausage made to an old family recipe, Hopetown House Black Pudding and whole carcasses or joints of pork selected from the farm's own pigs. Game is sold in season, including grouse, partridge, duck, venison, hare and rabbit. Beef, lamb, poultry, eggs and vegetables are also sold. Visitors can see the farm's pigs, hens, geese, ducks and guinea fowl.
◗ all year Mon-Thur 8-6.30, Fri 8-6, Sat 8-5, closed Bank Hols
Facilities: ♿ 🚻 🚗

🍞 Map 4 C3
Gillygate Wholefood Bakery
Millers Yard, Gillygate, York, North Yorkshire YO3 7EB
Tel. York (0904) 610676

In city centre.

This bakery in the centre of York is run by a workers co-operative. All its products are made from organically-grown ingredients and are free from additives. The mill bakery shop sells its own stoneground Yorkshire flour in 1.5Kg, 3.5Kg and bulk packs, and wholewheat bread with the Soil Association's symbol of organic purity. More unusual lines include cheese and thyme and cheese and garlic loaves; traditional Yorkshire parkin, apple cider, carob flapjacks and Karl's scrunchy bars.
☞ free
◗ shop: all year Mon-Sat 9-6; mill & bakery: by appointment
Facilities: 🍽 🍴 🚻
🍴 vegetarian & wholefood lunches, teas & snacks in bakery's café

☺ Map 4 A3
Harewood Bridge Soft Fruit and Vegetables
Wharfedale Grange, Harewood, Nr Leeds, West Yorkshire LS17 9LW
Tel. Leeds (0532) 886320

From Harewood follow A61 northwards for 2 miles to farm.

This 200-acre arable farm has 12 acres of pick your own fruit and vegetables, including strawberries, gooseberries, tayberries, raspberries, red and blackcurrants, broad beans, garden peas, calabrese, onions and courgettes. The shop also sells potatoes, spinach, beetroot, lettuce, cabbage and pot herbs.
◗ end Jun-beg Aug daily 9-6
Facilities: 🚗

🎣 Map 4 D6
Hazelhead Fishery
Newgate Foot Farm, Saltergate, Lockton, Nr Pickering, North Yorkshire YO18 7NR
Tel. Pickering (0751) 60215

From Pickering follow A169 northwards for 9 miles to fishery. Signposted.

A fish your own trout farm which also offers fly-fishing tuition and has occasional horse-driving demonstrations. Customer-caught trout is sold by the brace with a 2 brace limit.

☞ rod £10 per day, £5 per ½ day (1 brace limit)
◗ Apr-1 Oct 8-6 by appointment
Facilities: 🚗 🛶

🧀 Map 4 A4
Hopkins-Porter
Old Stable Shop, Ripley Castle, Ripley, North Yorkshire HG3 3RN
Tel. Harrogate (0423) 771466

In village.

Stocking one of the largest ranges of English and continental cheeses in the country, this high-quality establishment set in the grounds of Ripley Castle also carries many delicacies and wines from all over the world. Typical products for sale include

MAP 4　NORTH EAST ENGLAND

homemade pâtés, pastries, bread, preserves, fish, continental meats, chocolate, biscuits and organic wines and beers. There are also regular wine and cheese tastings.

◐ all year Tue-Sun & Bank Hols 8.30-5
Facilities: 🚌 ᴡᴄ 🚗 ♨ ⚠
★ regular wine & cheese tastings, telephone for details

RESTAURANT RECIPE

♈ Map 4 C3
ST WILLIAM'S
3 College Street, York, North Yorkshire YO1 2JF
Tel: York (0904) 34830
In city centre.

This self-service restaurant situated in a medieval building features old English dishes and also serves the famous local Theakston's beer.

◐ Mon-Sat 10-5, Sun 12-5
Price range £4-8
Seats 140
Facilities: ᴡᴄ

YORKSHIRE CURD CHEESECAKE

8oz butter
4oz sugar
pinch of salt
pinch of nutmeg
grated rind of ¹/₂ lemon
2oz currants
1lb curd cheese
6 eggs beaten
drop of milk
splash of port

Heat oven to gas 4 (350F, 180C). Cream butter and sugar then mix in the lemon rind, nutmeg, salt and currants. Add the curd cheese, mix well and add the beaten eggs, port and milk. Pour into a 10-inch flan dish and bake for 45 minutes or until set.

🔨 Map 4 A3
Ingles of Harrogate
59 Leeds Road, Harrogate, North Yorkshire HG2 8BE
Tel. Harrogate (0423) 872421
In town centre.

Three generations of the Ingles family have run this shop which stocks a wide range of food and specialises in supplying the restaurant trade. Produce includes about 30 varieties of fruit and vegetables with salad leaves flown in once a week from Paris. Local smoked products like trout and salmon, local game and poultry, wet fish and fresh herbs are sold throughout the year.

◐ all year daily 7-5.30

🍮 Map 4 E7
Just Desserts
97-98 Church Street, Whitby, North Yorkshire YO22 4DE
Tel. Whitby (0947) 603361
In town centre.

A far cry from the average seaside ice cream parlour, Just Desserts is more like a French-style 'glacier', a 'patisserie' and a tea room all in one and produces and sells top-quality dairy ices made with fresh milk, cream and butter as well as real fruit sorbets with such flavours as plum, rhubarb and mango. Also available are continental style ice cream cakes made with real liqueurs, fresh cream cheesecakes, treacle tarts, Christmas cakes and Christmas puddings, all made on the premises. Ice cream and sorbets may be purchased in 1 and 4 litre packs.

◐ Apr-30 Oct daily 10.30-5.30, 31 Oct-Mar Sat, Sun 10.30-4.30
Facilities: 🍴 ᴡᴄ

🔨 Map 4 A4
Kings Bakery
2 Old Market Place, Ripon, North Yorkshire HG4 1EQ
Tel. Ripon (0765) 3408

In city centre.

A specialist bakery in the centre of the historic market city of Ripon which bakes an excellent range of breads, scones, teacakes, pastries and cakes. Visitors can see a small collection of antique baking implements hanging on the walls.

◐ all year Mon 8.30-5, Tue, Fri 8.30-5.30, Wed 8.30-4.30, Thur 8-5.30, Sat 8-4

♈ Map 4 A5
Lightwater Valley
North Stainley, Ripon, North Yorkshire HG4 3HT
Tel. Ripon (0765) 85321
From Ripon follow A6108 northwards for 4 miles to park. Signposted.

This 125-acre family action park and visitor farm is possibly the largest in Britain. Lightwater Valley has a huge variety of attractions including working farms where visitors can see exactly how farm animals are kept commercially today. A pig farm shows each stage of the pig's development, a poultry unit houses over 5,000 chickens and the calf unit rears calves from 6 days to 12 weeks old. There is also a trout farm and a farm museum with modern agricultural implements on show. The shop sells Lightwater Valley's own eggs and meat.

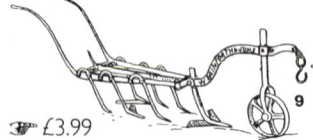

🚜 £3.99
◐ Easter-May Wed, Thur, Sat, Sun, Bank Hols 10.30-3.30; 23 May-6 Sep daily 10.30-3.30; Sep Sat-Sun 10.30-3.30
Facilities: 🚌 🍴 ♿ ᴡᴄ 🚗 ♨
🍴 full range of tasty wholesome meals served daily in licensed Farmyard Restaurant with carvery, cold table & special menu for children under 11

MAP 4

⬢ Map 4 D4
Malton Brewery
Crown Hotel,
Wheelgate, Malton,
North Yorkshire YO17 OHP
Tel. Malton (0653) 697580

In town centre.

In an industry dominated by national giant corporations, this brewery prides itself on brewing beers by traditional methods and using only traditional ingredients. Visitors are invited to tour the small premises and see the brewing process, then sample the beers in the adjoining pub, which also serves bar meals. Visitors may also buy beer in $4\frac{1}{2}$ gallon polypins.

☞ free
◗ brewery: mornings only, if staff available, otherwise by appointment; pub: normal licensing hours
Facilities: 🍺 🍴 ♿ 🚻 🚗
🍴 meals served in pub

⚘ Map 4 D6
May Beck Farm Trail
Nr Ruswarp, North Yorkshire
Tel. Helmsley (0439) 70657

From Whitby follow B1416 southwards, after 4 miles turn right onto unclassified road for $\frac{1}{2}$ mile to farm. Signposted.

A self-guided farm trail around a typical moorland sheep farm with 300 Swaledale sheep and 50 cows. The trail demonstrates ways in which the farmer has made use of the land resources of the area and includes the farm buildings and barns, sheep handling pens and dipping trough, examples of crop rotation and grouse breeding.

☞ free; guide booklet 45p from Tourist Information Centres in the area
◗ all year daily any reasonable time
Facilities: 🚗 🛊

🎣 Map 4 D5
Moorland Trout Farms
Newbridge,
Newton Road, Pickering,
North Yorkshire YO18 8JJ
Tel. Pickering (0751) 73101

From Pickering follow A170 westwards, after $\frac{1}{4}$ mile turn right onto unclassified road for $\frac{1}{2}$ mile to New Bridge.

Visitors can fish for their own trout — tackle provided — tour the premises and visit the smokery at this Yorkshire trout farm. There are regular demonstrations and several farm trails. Fresh and smoked trout are for sale as well as frozen salmon and scampi.

☞ 25p including fish food & leaflet; fishing licence: £3; rod 50p
◗ Apr-Sep daily 8-6; Oct-Mar daily 8-4.30
Facilities: 🍺 🍴 🚻 🚗 🛊
🍴 snacks & all kinds of meals served including scones, sausage rolls & other homebaked produce

🌿 Map 4 A3
Northern Horticultural Society
Harlow Car Gardens,
Crag Lane, Harrogate,
North Yorkshire HG3 1QB
Tel. Harrogate (0423) 68515

From Harrogate follow B6162 south westwards for 1 mile to gardens on right. Signposted.

Harlow Car Gardens is the home of the Northern Horticultural Society and is one of the finest gardens in the north of England. There are almost 70 acres of landscaped gardens and woodland with vegetable and fruit plots giving a year-round panorama of colour. A well equipped study centre is based in the garden where information is provided about plants and how to grow them. A wide selection of more unusual plants for the garden and home are on sale. A shop supplies gardening books as well as gifts and souvenirs. Trained staff are on hand to advise and help with information and give practical demonstrations in gardening.

☞ adults £2.00, senior citizens £1.50, accompanied children free
◗ all year daily 9-7.30 or dusk
Facilities: 🍺 🍴 ♿ 🚻 🚗 🛊
★ many shows & demonstrations throughout the year

● **May Beck Farm**

MAP 4 **NORTH EAST ENGLAND**

● **Ryedale Folk Museum**

🏠 Map 4 C5
Ryedale Folk Museum
Hutton-le-Hole,
North Yorkshire YO6 6UA
Tel. Lastingham (07515) 367

From Kirbymoorside follow A170 eastwards, after ½ mile turn left onto unclassified road for 2 miles to Hutton-le-Hole.

This museum concentrates on the past living and working conditions of ordinary people in North East Yorkshire. Exhibits include a rebuilt medieval cruck-framed longhouse with a salt box and spice cupboard built into the chimney wall of the inglenook. There is also a fine collection of household and agricultural implements.

☞ adults £1.20, senior citizens 90p, children 60p, family ticket £3.00
● 27 Mar-Oct daily 11-6
Facilities: ♿ WC 🚗 ☕

💾 Map 4 B2
Samuel Smith Old Brewery
The Old Brewery, Tadcaster,
North Yorkshire LS24 9SB
Tel. Tadcaster (0937) 832225

In town centre.

This brewery was established in 1758 and has been producing traditional ales ever since. Visitors are taken on a guided tour of the brewery which includes seeing the traditional brewing process with Yorkshire slate fermenting squares still in use, the cooper's shop and the brewery's Shire horses and stables. The tour concludes with a sample of beer in the cellar bar.

☞ adults £1.50, children 50p
● all year Mon-Thur, tours at 11, 2 & 7 by appointment
Facilities: WC 🚗

🍴 Map 4 A6
Selbys Delicatessen
6 Market Row, Northallerton,
North Yorkshire
Tel. Northallerton (0609) 3928

In town centre.

This small delicatessen aims to provide a personal and helpful service and specialises in British and continental cheeses — particularly from Yorkshire, with some unusual ewes' milk varieties. Also for sale are home-cooked foods, using wholemeal flour and fresh ingredients, such as game pies and English hams. Customers may sample the cheeses and special order dishes can be made up.
● all year Mon-Sat 9-5
Facilities: ☕ ♿ 🚗

🐓 Map 4 E6
Staintondale Shire Horse Farm
Staintondale, Nr Scarborough,
North Yorkshire YO13 0EY
Tel. Scarborough (0723) 870458

From Scarborough follow A171 northwards, after 4½ miles turn right at Cloughton onto unclassified road for 3 miles to Staintondale.

Set in the North York Moors National Park, this small mixed sheep and poultry farm also specialises in Shire horses. Visitors are invited to twice-daily talks about the horses and to try the cart rides. There is an interesting collection of stables, carts and farm implements

MAP 4

which give a picture of how life used to be on the farm. There is also a cottage museum and an old dairy with butter and milk churns, a cooler and a cream separator. Weekend courses in driving and working horses are available.

☞ adults £1.50, senior citizens £1.00, children 75p
◐ May-mid Sep Tue-Fri, Sun, Bank Hols 10.30-4.30
Facilities: 🍽 wc 🚗 🚼 ♿
🍽 tea shop serves farm-baked & other homemade produce including cakes, salads, sandwiches & ploughman's lunches; tea & coffee made from fresh spring water

G P Stonehouse and Son
Map 4 C3
1A Stamford Street East, Leeman Road, York, North Yorkshire YP2 4YD
Tel. York (0904) 55061
From York follow A59 north westwards, after 1 mile turn left for shop, 550 yards past the National Railways Museum.

Stonehouse and Son is a family-run specialist butchers famous for their prize-winning sausages — over 14 varieties are made. The shop has a display of home produced meats and meat products such as black puddings.
◐ all year Mon, Tue, Thur, Fri 8-5.30; Wed, Sat 8-1; closed Bank Hols

Taylors in Stonegate
Map 4 C3
46 Stonegate, York, North Yorkshire YO1 2AS
Tel. York (0904) 22865
In city centre.

A specialist family-run shop selling over 30 different teas and coffees. Founded in 1886 by the Taylor family, the shop imports and blends fine teas and coffees from all over the world. Teas for sale include Mango Blossom, Japanese Cherry and Cinnamon; coffees include Ethiopean Mocha, Nicaraguan and a Swiss water-process decaffeinated variety. Taylors also has an interesting display of 100 antique teapots.
◐ all year Mon-Sat 9-5.30, Sun 9-6; open most Bank Hols
Facilities: 🍽 🍴 wc

light lunches & teas are served as well as snacks — specialities include Yorkshire rarebit, mushroom & Blue Wensleydale cheese omelette, Yorkshire ham salad, Yorkshire cheese lunch. Cakes & pastries include Yorkshire curd tart, speciality fruit cake with Wensleydale cheese & spiced Yorkshire teacakes

Yorkshire Museum of Farming
Map 4 C3
Murton, York, North Yorkshire YO1 3UF
Tel. York (0904) 489966
From York follow A1079 eastwards, after 2½ miles turn left onto A166 for ¼ mile, then turn left onto unclassified road for ¼ mile to Murton. Signposted.

This museum of farming is set in 8 acres of attractive parkland. The visitor can experience the complete process of food production, from sowing to harvesting. Eggs, honey and stoneground flour are for sale in the shop.

☞ adults £2.00, senior citizens £1.25, children £1.00, family ticket (2 adults & 4 children) £5.00
◐ May-Sep daily 10.30-5.30; Mar, Apr, Oct Tue-Sun 10.30-5.30 or by appointment
Facilities: 🍽 🍴 ♿ wc 🚗 🚼
🍴 home-cooked meals served using farm produce & Yorkshire recipes; vegetarian dishes available

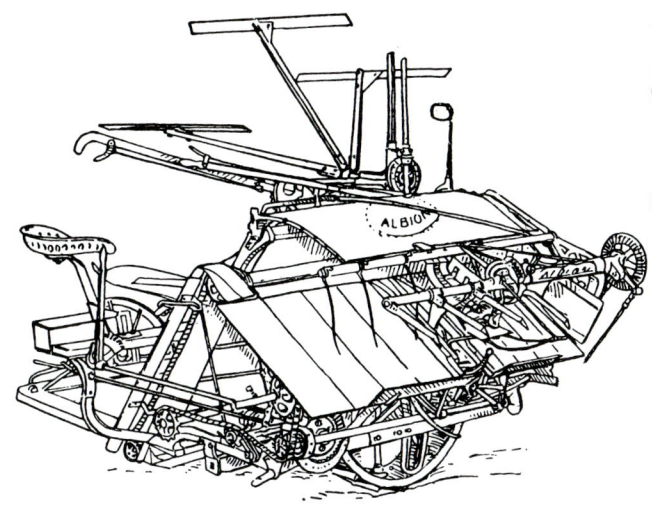

● **Self-binding reaping machine**

MAP 5   NORTH EAST ENGLAND

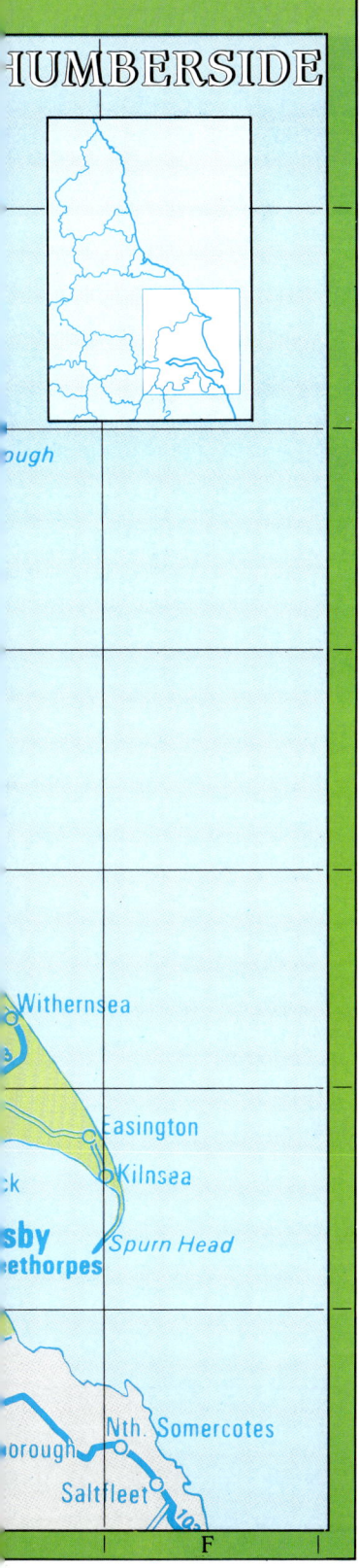

The Humber Estuary was once packed with trawlers on their way to fish in the plentiful waters of the North Sea. They would return laden with their catches and Grimsby still handles most of the cod eaten in Britain. Other varieties which pass through Humberside's major ports of Hull, Grimsby and Bridlington are lemon sole, skate, whiting, haddock, coley, dogfish and witches. There are fewer boats now but you can still watch them unloading throughout the day. To catch the dockside markets, be sure to get there early in the morning.

🏠 Map 5 D5

Bridlington Harbour History Room and Aquarium

Harbour Road, Bridlington, Humberside YO15 2NR
Tel. Bridlington (0262) 670148

In town centre.

This general fishing museum has exhibits on trawling and photographs and models of fishing boats. Its aquarium contains specimen fish from the North Sea, some of which have been donated by local fishermen, and include cod, wrasse, sole, eel, lesser spotted dogfish, plaice and dabs as well as crabs, lobsters and sea urchins.

☞ adults 30p, children (5-14) 15p
◐ Apr-Oct daily 9-9, Nov-Mar daily depending on weather conditions — telephone for details

📷 Map 5 D5

John Bull's World of Rock

Carnaby, Nr Bridlington, Humberside
Tel. Bridlington (0262) 678525

From Bridlington follow A166 south westwards, after 2 miles turn left in Carnaby into Moor Lane for ¼ mile to factory on right.

Established in 1911, John Bull's makes traditional rock and confectionery. Visitors are welcome to tour the factory, see the skilled craftspeople at work creating a range of handmade rock and then have a go at putting their own initial into a stick of rock. Old-fashioned fudge and toffee are also made to recipes over 100 years old. Aniseed, lemon and lime-flavoured rock as well as the traditional peppermint can be bought in the factory shop along with other sweets, fudge and toffee.

☞ free
◐ Apr-Sep daily 10.30-5; Oct-Mar Mon-Fri 10.30-4
Facilities: 🚻 🚌

FISH AND CHIPS

The Gainsborough in Hull rivals Harry Ramsden in Leeds as the largest fish and chip shop in the world. It's worth a visit.

🍴 Map 5 B3

Hasholme Carr Farm

Holme upon Spalding, Market Weighton, Humberside
Tel. Market Weighton (0696) 60393

From Holme upon Spalding follow A614 southwards, after 2½ miles turn left onto unclassified road for 2 miles to farm. Signposted.

This working farm uses heavy horses instead of mechanical machinery and visitors can see them at work. Some of the horses are quite famous and have appeared on television in plays and commercials. There is also a tour of the farm available.

☞ adults £1.00, children 50p
◐ Apr-Sep daily 10.30-5
Facilities: 🚻 🚌 🍽️

MAP 5　　NORTH EAST ENGLAND

• **Hornsea Museum**

🏛 Map 5 D4
Hornsea Museum
11 Newbegin, Hornsea,
Humberside HU18 1AB
Tel. Hornsea (04012) 3443

In town centre. Signposted.

"A museum of great charm with an excellent collection mostly relating to domestic life and social and agricultural history." This is how Sir Hugh Casson described the museum in 1980 when he made the Award of Small Museum of the Year. Based in an 18thC farmhouse, displays include a 19thC farmhouse kitchen complete with inglenook fireplace and oat-cake dryer. There are also drawing room, bedroom and authentic dairy displays.

☞ adults 50p, senior citizens & children (over 5) 40p, family ticket £1.50
◐ 1 Apr-Oct daily 2-5; 20 Jul-10 Sep Mon-Sat 11-5, Sun 2-5
Facilities: 🚻 ⛺

🏛 Map 5 C3
Northern Shire Horse Centre
Flower Hill Farm,
North Newbald,
Humberside YO4 3TG
Tel. North Newbald (06965) 270

From Beverley follow A1079 westwards, after 5 miles turn left onto unclassified road for 2½ miles to farm on left. Signposted.

Here visitors can see a Victorian farmhouse kitchen with its old range, brick floor and display of utensils and artefacts. Seventeen Shire horses are kept on the farm for showing at agricultural shows. There is also a collection of horse-drawn vehicles. The Loft Museum houses a collection of bygone tools and implements. Visitors are welcome to walk around the farm and see the pheasants, bantams, peacocks and chicks and enjoy a vintage tractor ride.

☞ adults 1.00, senior citizens 60p, children (5-16) 50p
◐ May-Sep Mon-Thur, Sun 10-5
Facilities: 🚌 🍴 🚻 🚗 ⛺ ⚠
🍴 teas served including homemade cakes, sandwiches & pies

RESTAURANT RECIPE

🍽 Map 5 E2
The Granary
Haven Mill, Garth Lane,
Grimsby, Humberside
Tel: Grimsby (0472) 46338

In town centre.

Part of a converted grain mill complete with its original features and equipment such as grain hoppers and crushers. Their recipe for Jugged Pigeon makes a succulent bird.

◐ Mon-Sat Meals: 10.30-2.30; Tue-Sat 7.30-10.30
Price range £4-12
Seats 100
Cards: Access, Visa
Facilities: 🍽 ♿ 🚗

GRANARY JUGGED PIGEON

4 wood pigeons
3oz butter
4 bacon rashers
½ onion chopped
2 cloves garlic chopped
¼lb mushrooms sliced
1 glass port
2oz double cream
Worcestershire sauce
1 tbsp redcurrant jelly

In a heavy pan brown the wood pigeons in butter. Wrap each pigeon in a rasher of bacon and add the onion, garlic, mushrooms and port. Cover and cook gently for about 50 minutes. Take out and keep warm. Stir the cream into the pan juices and add a dash of Worcestershire sauce and the redcurrant jelly and simmer for 5 minutes. Pour the sauce over the pigeons and serve on French bread croutons.

MAP 5

☺ Map 5 C4
Park House Farm
Malton Road, Beverley,
Humberside HU17 7RA
Tel. Leconfield (0401) 50374

*From Beverley follow A164 north
westwards, after 1 mile turn left
onto B1248 for 1 mile, then turn
right to farm.*

32 acres of this 441-acre farm
are given over to soft fruit
growing. Pick your own fruit
includes strawberries,
gooseberries, raspberries,
tayberries, red, black and
whitecurrants, blackberries,
blueberries and loganberries.
Bunched carrots, red beet,
cabbage, cauliflowers, new
potatoes, salads, eggs, cream
and ice cream are also for sale.
● end Jun-mid Aug daily 10-6
Facilities: ☕ ♿ 🚗 ☺

🏠 Map 5 C3
Skidby Windmill
Skidby, Nr Beverley,
Humberside
Tel. Hull (0482) 882255

*From Beverley follow A164
southwards for 3½ miles to mill
on right. Signposted.*

An interesting windmill which
has been restored to working
order. It contains a museum of
milling and corn production
which includes exhibits of
horse-powered grain
production. The mill sells its
own wholemeal flour in 500g
and 1.5Kg bags.
☞ adults 65p, senior citizens &
children 30p
● May-Sep Tue-Sat 10-4.30, Sun
2-4.30, closed Bank Hols
Facilities: ☕ ♿ 🚗 ☺

🦞 Map 5 D5
Taste o'the Sea
Langdale's Wharf, Bridlington,
Humberside YO15 3AN
Tel. Bridlington (0262) 678987

In town centre.

A subsidiary of a company
operating fishing boats in the
North Sea, this fishmonger sells
mostly locally-caught fish
including cod, haddock, ling,
plaice, lemon sole, mackerel
and herring. It has its own
holding tanks, both on the pier
and in the shop, for keeping live
lobsters, oysters and crabs.
Smoked salmon is produced in
its own smoking kiln.
● end May-Oct Mon-Sat
8.30-5.30, Sun 10-5; Nov-Apr
Mon-Sat 8.30-5, Sun 10-5

🏛 Map 5 D3
Town Docks Museum
Queen Victoria Square,
Kingston-upon-Hull,
Humberside HU1 3DY
Tel. Hull (0482) 222737

In city centre.

One of the most prominent
Victorian buildings in the city,
once the offices of the Hull
Dock Company, houses this
maritime museum which
opened in 1975. Its main
collections relate to the harvest
of the sea, Hull's former main
industry. The exhibits on fishing
and trawling include paintings
and models of local fishing
boats including Yorkshire
cobles, a North Sea herring
drifter, a Paull shrimper and the
later sailing and steam trawlers.
A mural shows the different
types of fish caught.
☞ free
● all year Mon-Sat 10-5, Sun
1.30-4.30
Facilities: ☕ ♿

🏠 Map 5 C2
Wrawby Windmill
Mill Lane, Wrawby, Brigg,
Humberside DN20 8RL
Tel. Brigg (0652) 53699

*From Brigg follow A18 north
eastwards for 1 mile to Wrawby.*

This is the last working postmill
in the north of England and one
of the best preserved in the
country. Wrawby Mill was built
in the late 18thC and restored
in the 1960s. Once again it is
producing stoneground flour
which is available in bags from
2lb upwards.
☞ adults 40p, children 25p
● 2 Apr, 2 & 30 May, 26 Jun, 31
Jul, 29 Aug telephone for details

MAP 6 NORTH EAST ENGLAND

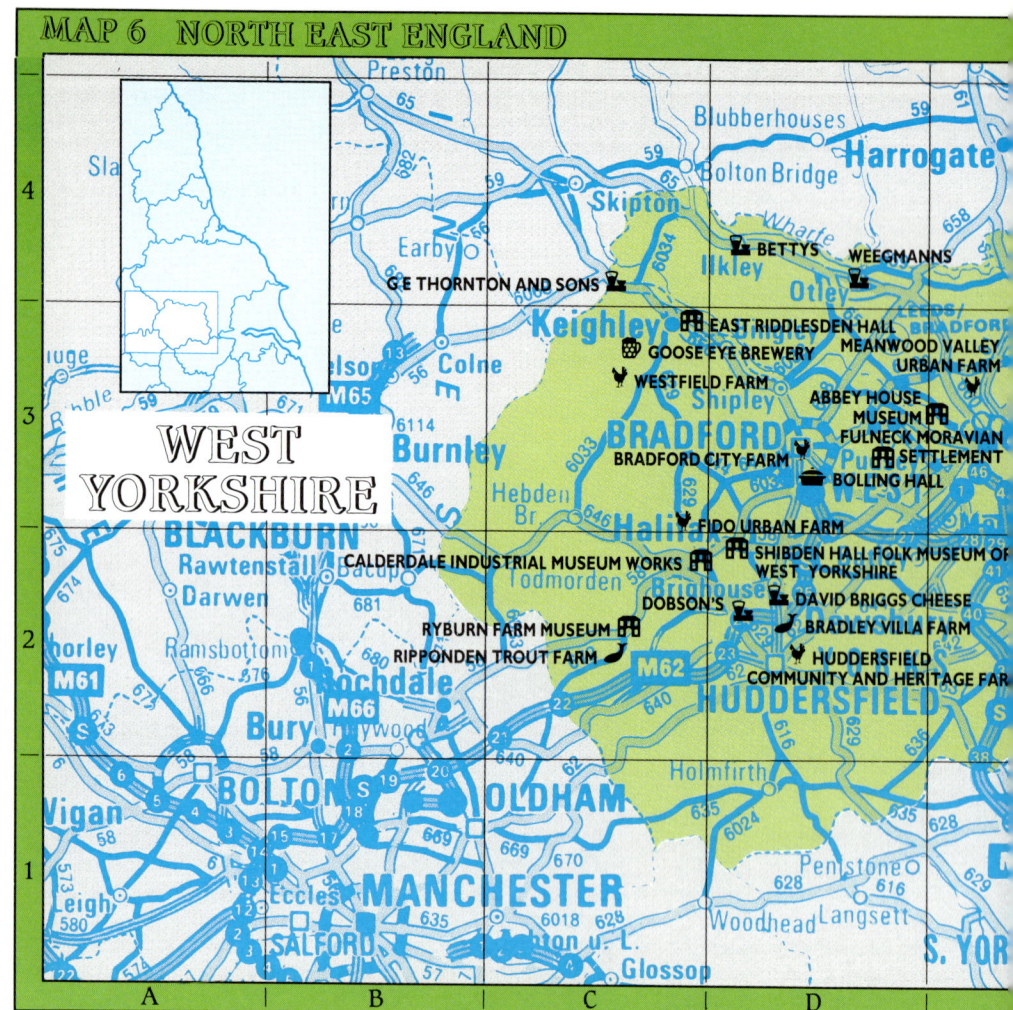

Bronte Liqueur — a mixture of honey, orange, brandy, herbs and spices — is named after the famous Bronte sisters who lived and wrote in Haworth. It is on sale throughout the area and is used in a number of local recipes including a delicious sticky cake on sale at Bettys. A short journey across the windswept moors will take you to Hebden Bridge where in the spring you may be lucky to catch the world's Dock Pudding Championship.

Abbey House Museum

🏠 Map 6 E3
Abbey House Museum
Kirkstall, Leeds,
West Yorkshire LS5 3EH
Tel. Leeds (0532) 755821
From Leeds follow A65 westwards for 3 miles to museum.

The former gatehouse of the 12thC Cistercian Abbey at Kirkstall was sold to Leeds Corporation in 1925 and converted into a museum. This includes Folk Galleries which illustrate life in the region and replica shops containing authentic goods. Amongst these is a Victorian pub, a grocer's shop, a tobacconist's, an artisan's cottage and a gallery devoted to fireplaces and large exhibits of cooking implements, tableware and drinking vessels.

☞ adults 60p, senior citizens & children 25p
◐ Apr-Sep Mon-Sat 10-6, Sun 2-6; Oct-Mar Mon-Sat 10-5, Sun 2-5
Facilities: ♿ 🚻 🚗 👶 ⚠

Bettys

🏪 Map 6 D4
Bettys
The Grove, Ilkley,
West Yorkshire LS29 9EE
Tel. Ilkley (0943) 608029
In town centre.

A sister shop and tea room to the original Bettys in Harrogate, selling the same marvellous variety of Yorkshire food. (See Bettys, Harrogate)
◐ all year Mon-Fri 9-5.30, Sat, Sun 9-7; open most Bank Hols
Facilities: 🍽

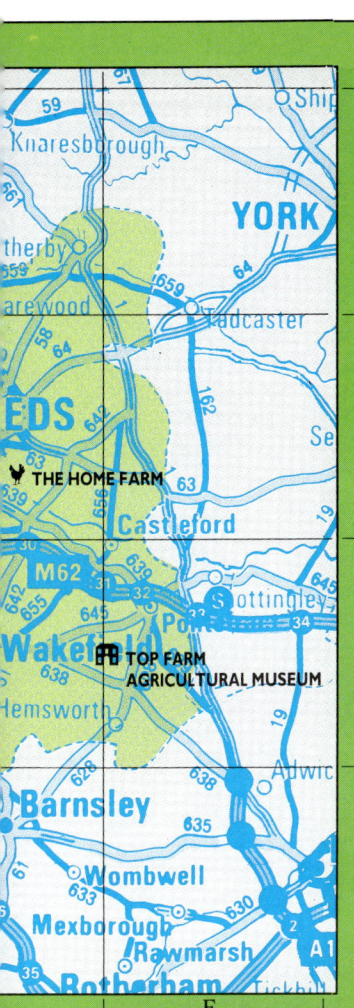

🏛 Map 6 D3
Bolling Hall

Bolling Hall Road, Bradford,
West Yorkshire BD4 7LP
Tel. Bradford (0274) 723051

*From city centre follow A650
southwards, after 1 mile turn
right at roundabout into
Flockdon Road for 150 yards,
then turn left into Brompton
Avenue for 50 yards to hall.
Signposted.*

Bolling Hall is a fine example of
West Yorkshire domestic
architecture with appropriately
furnished rooms and a 17thC
kitchen. In the grounds visitors
can see the culinary herb
garden which has been based
on an original design.

🎟 free
◗ Apr-Sep Tue-Sun 10-6;
Oct-Mar Tue-Sun 10-5
Facilities: 🚻 🚗 🍽

🐦 Map 6 D3
Bradford City Farm

Illingworth Fields,
Walker Drive, Bradford,
West Yorkshire BD8 9ES
Tel. Bradford (0274) 43500

In city centre.

This charity-run inner-city farm
gives children a chance to see
farm animals at work. Organic
vegetables and eggs are for sale.

🎟 free
◗ Apr-Oct daily 9.30-8;
Nov-Mar daily 9.30-6
Facilities: 🍽 ♿ 🚻 🚗 🍽 🏛

🎣 Map 6 D2
Bradley Villa Farm

Bradford Road, Huddersfield,
West Yorkshire HD2 2JY
Tel. Huddersfield (0484) 21782

*From Huddersfield follow A641
northwards for 3 miles to farm at
junction with A6107.*

This 120-acre trout farm has
'choose your own' pink
rainbow trout in easy-to-see
tanks. Also available are
homemade ice cream, dairy
products, eggs, chickens, game,
local honey, cheese and cream.

🎟 free
◗ all year Mon-Fri 9-5.30,
Sat 9-5
Facilities: 🚗

🧀 Map 6 D2
David Briggs Cheese

82 Commercial Street,
Brighouse,
West Yorkshire HD6 1AQ
Tel. Brighouse (0484) 720912

In town centre.

This specialist cheese shop
carries a large range of English,
Welsh and Irish farmhouse
cheeses plus an extensive range
from the continent. It also

● **The Grocer's Shop, Abbey House Museum**

MAP 6

NORTH EAST ENGLAND

stocks a large number of single malt whiskies and specialist beers.

◑ all year Mon-Sat 9-5

🏠 Map 6 C2
Calderdale Industrial Museum Works

Winding Road, Halifax, West Yorkshire
Tel. Halifax (0422) 59031

In town centre.

Winner of one of the 1987 Museum of the Year Awards, this museum clatters, thumps, smells and even speaks as it portrays 150 years of the lives of Halifax workers and industries. One of its exhibits is a display of Rowntree MacIntosh's toffees — the smell is so authentic visitors just follow their noses. Locally made sweets and toffees are for sale in the shop.

☞ adults 50p, senior citizens & children 25p
◑ all year Tue-Sat, Bank Hols 10-5, Sun 2-5
Facilities: 🚽 ♿

🍬 Map 6 D2
Dobson's

70 Southgate, Elland, West Yorkshire
Tel. Elland (0422) 77365

From Halifax follow A629 southwards for 3 miles to Elland.

A traditional sweet shop with antique jars and mahogany fittings which sells old-fashioned boiled sweets made locally in Dobson's factory. Specialities include Yorkshire mixtures with 18 different flavours, pear drops, cough candy, humbugs, mint imperials

and herbal voice tablets, as well as good quality traditional fudge.

◑ all year Mon-Thur 9-12, 12.30-5.30, Fri 9-5.30, Sat 9-4.30

🏠 Map 6 C3
East Riddlesden Hall

Bradford Road, Keighley, West Yorkshire BD20 5EL
Tel. Keighley (0535) 607075

From Keighley follow A650 eastwards for 1 mile to house on right. Signposted.

This traditional 17thC West Yorkshire manor house, owned by the National Trust, has a great medieval barn, 120 feet long, which contains a collection of traditional agricultural machinery and a formal walled garden with a kitchen garden. In 1180 the Hall was the grange of Bolton Abbey and visitors can see the monastic fishponds which were mentioned in the Domesday Book. These ponds would have originally been stocked with trout for the monks but now contain brown trout, perch, tench and roach.

☞ adults £1.30, children 60p
◑ Apr Sat, Sun & Easter week 2-6; May, Jun, Sep, Oct Wed-Sun 2-6; Jul, Aug Wed-Sun 12-6
Facilities: 🚌 🍴 ♿ 🚗 😋

🐾 Map 6 C3
Fido Urban Farm

Furness Avenue, Illingworth, Halifax, West Yorkshire
Tel. Halifax (0422) 240054

From Halifax follow A629 northwards for 3 miles to Illingworth. Signposted.

This urban farm has lots of friendly sheep, pigs, goats, ducks, horses, rabbits, hens and geese who love to see children. It is run by Furness Improvement Development Organisation, an independent community association and registered charity. Fresh eggs are sold every day and

sometimes vegetables grown on the farm are available.

☞ free
◑ all year daily 8.30-4.30
Facilities: ♿ ♿ 😋 🅿

🏠 Map 6 D3
Fulneck Moravian Settlement

Fulneck, Nr Pudsey, West Yorkshire LS28 8NT
Tel. Pudsey (0532) 564862

From Leeds follow A647 westwards, after 5 miles turn left onto B6156 for 1/2 mile to Pudsey. Signposted.

One of only 3 such settlements in Britain, this Moravian and Folk Museum has displays of kitchen equipment and agricultural implements. A pottery produces pierced porcelain dishes and ornaments which, as well as baked goods, meats, cheeses and sweets, may be purchased from the shop.

☞ museum: adults 35p, children 10p; pottery: free
◑ museum: Apr-Sep Wed, Sat 2-5; shop & pottery: all year Tue-Sun 9.30-5

MAP 6

Facilities: 🍽️ ♨ wc 🚗
🍽️ restaurant serves local fare all day using fresh produce

🍺 Map 6 C3
Goose Eye Brewery
Goose Eye Hotel,
Goose Eye, Keighley,
West Yorkshire BD22 0PD
Tel. Keighley (0535) 605807

From Keighley follow B6143 south westwards, after 2 miles turn right at Oakworth onto unclassified road for 1½ miles to Goose Eye. Signposted.

A traditional bitter 'Pommes Revenge' is brewed in this 300-year-old converted paper mill. Visitors can tour the brewery and taste the beer.

☎ telephone for details
◑ tours by appointment
Facilities: 🍽️ ♨ & wc 🚗 ⚠
🍽️ licensed restaurant specialising in steaks

🐓 Map 6 E3
The Home Farm
Temple Newsam Estate, Leeds,
West Yorkshire LS15 0AD
Tel. Leeds (0532) 645535

From city centre follow A63 eastwards for 1 mile to estate on right.

The Home Farm on Temple Newsam Estate is a working farm which plays an important part in the national conservation of rare breeds of farm animals. An approved centre of the Rare Breeds Survival Trust, it has over 600 animals including 10 rare breeds of cattle and pigs, 4 breeds of sheep and working heavy horses as well as hens, geese, ducks and turkeys. The museum has a farm history exhibition which contains restored agricultural carts, implements and displays of old farming methods. The farm trail leads visitors around the

● **The Home Farm**

MAP 6   **NORTH EAST ENGLAND**

● **The Home Farm**

animal paddocks and a herb garden can be seen near Temple Newsam House. The estate shop sells farm produce including goats' milk.

☞ farm & gardens: free; house: adults 65p, senior citizens & children 30p
◑ farm: Apr-Oct daily 10-5; Nov- Mar Tue-Sun 10-4; gardens: all year daily any reasonable time
Facilities: ⬛ ⬛ ⬛ ⬛ ⬛ ⬛
★ Oct harvesting day with working threshing machines
⬛ teas served, homemade scones a speciality

🐦 Map 6 D2
Huddersfield Community and Heritage Farm
Peace Pit Lane, Leeds Road, Huddersfield, West Yorkshire
Tel. Huddersfield (0484) 536239
From Huddersfield follow A62 north eastwards for 1 mile to farm. Signposted.

This community farm, built on reclaimed wasteland, was created as a result of a partnership between the Manpower Services Commission, community volunteers, local schools and the Probation and Social Services departments. Visitors may watch demonstrations of milking, see the rare breeds and learn about wildlife habitats on information boards. Organic

vegetables, free-range eggs and goats' milk are for sale. There is a nature trail and mooring space for boats on the adjoining canal.

☞ free; donations welcome
◑ all year Mon-Fri 9.30-4.30, Sat, Sun by appointment
Facilities: ⬛ ⬛ ⬛ ⬛

🐦 Map 6 E3
Meanwood Valley Urban Farm
Sugarwell Road, Meanwood, Leeds, West Yorkshire LS7 2QG
Tel. Leeds (0532) 629759
From city centre follow A61 northwards for 1 mile to farm on left. Signposted.

Part of a community project to regenerate derelict land, train the unemployed and provide inner-city children with farm experience, this urban farm has a wide range of animals, including rare breeds. Visitors may watch goat milking demonstrations and the cultivation of plants. The shop sells organically grown vegetables, deep-litter eggs, herbs, goats' milk and cheese.

☞ adults 30p, children 15p; annual membership £3
◑ Apr-Oct daily 8-8; Nov-Mar daily 9-6 or dusk
Facilities: ⬛ ⬛ ⬛ ⬛ ⬛

🎣 Map 6 C2
Ripponden Trout Farm
Bar Lane, Ripponden, Nr Halifax, West Yorkshire HX6 4EX
Tel. Halifax (0422) 822151
From Halifax follow A58 south westwards, after 5 miles turn left onto A672 for ½ mile, then turn right onto unclassified road for ¼ mile to farm on left. Signposted.

A small working trout farm and fishery situated in the picturesque Ryburn valley. The farm has a hatchery, a lake and a

small river. Visitors can see all stages of the farming of rainbow, brown and brook trout including demonstrations of smoking. All sizes of fresh and smoked trout can be bought from the shop.

☞ charge for conducted tour, telephone for details
◑ all year daily 10-5, tours by appointment
Facilities: ♿ ⬛

🏠 Map 6 C2
Ryburn Farm Museum
Ripponden, Nr Halifax, West Yorkshire
Tel. Halifax (0422) 54823
From Halifax follow A58 south westwards for 5 miles to Ripponden.

This small farmhouse with an adjoining barn has displays of a typical Pennine hill farm which include a cosy farm kitchen, a dairy and a collection of agricultural implements.

☞ 10p
◑ Mar-Oct Sat, Sun, Bank Hols 2-5

🏠 Map 6 D2
Shibden Hall Folk Museum of West Yorkshire
Godley Lane, Halifax, West Yorkshire
Tel. Halifax (0422) 52246
From Halifax follow A58 eastwards, after 1½ miles turn right to museum. Signposted.

Step back in time at this magnificent black and white timbered 15thC home with its homely and welcoming atmosphere. Here visitors can see the Hall's 17thC kitchen and dining room as well as a dairy and brewhouse. The original farm buildings have been transformed into an early 19thC village centre and include an estate worker's cottage, pub and various workshops — all with period furniture and

MAP 6

household objects. Locally made sweets and toffees are for sale.

☞ May-Aug: adults 60p, senior citizens & children 30p; Mar & Apr: adults 50p, senior citizens & children 25p

◉ Apr-Sep Mon-Sat 10-6, Sun 2-5; Mar, Oct, Nov Mon-Sat 10-5, Sun 2-5; Feb Sun 2-5

Facilities: 🍺 🚽 🚗 ♨

★ 4 craft weekends held each year; these include baking and Havercake — local oat-cake making

G E Thornton and Sons
Map 6 C4

39 Main Street,
Crosshills, Keighley,
West Yorkshire BD22 0NJ
Tel. Crosshills (0535) 33108

From Keighley follow A629 north westwards for 5 miles to Crosshills.

This family butchers' shop was established in 1884 by the great-grandfather of Peter Whitaker, the present partner, and is well-known for its champion sausages. As well as these the shop sells a wide range of cooked meats and pâtés, all made daily on the premises, homemade preserves, cheeses and bacon.

◉ all year Mon-Fri 8.30-12, 2-3.30, Sat 8.30-12

Top Farm Agricultural Museum
Map 6 F2

West Hardwick, Wakefield,
West Yorkshire WF4 1RG
Tel. Hemsworth (0977) 611165

From Hemsworth follow B6273 north westwards, after 2 miles turn right onto B6428 for 2 miles, then turn left onto unclassified road for 1/2 mile to West Hardwick.

One thousand articles are on display at this agricultural museum including old tractors, carts and threshing machines. Visitors can also see the small dairy which still has its original equipment.

☞ adults £1.00, senior citizens & children 50p

◉ Apr-Jul, Sep-Oct Sat, Sun, Bank Hols 10.30-5; Aug Tue-Sun 10.30-5

Facilities: 🍺 🚽 🚗 ♨ ⚠

★ weekend programme of special events, telephone for details

Weegmanns
Map 6 D4

6 Market Place, Otley,
West Yorkshire
Tel. Otley (0943) 462327

In town centre.

Established over 100 years ago, this pork butcher sells a wide range of pork products including pies, sausages and dry-cured hams made on the premises.

◉ all year Mon-Sat 8-5.30

Westfield Farm
Map 6 C3

Tim Lane, Haworth,
West Yorkshire BD22 7SA
Tel. Haworth (0535) 44568

From Keighley follow B6143 south westwards, after 2 miles turn left in Oakworth into Tim Lane for 1/4 mile to farm on right.

A traditional Yorkshire hill farm with sheep and suckler cows which are bred for the table. 'Mules' — Swaledale sheep crossed with Blueface Leicester ewes — are bred and mated with Suffolk rams to produce fat lambs for the autumn. The highlight of the year is in April when visitors can watch the sheep lambing. Visitors can also follow the 2-mile-long Westfield farm trail on which they can see the farmyard and sheep grazing the same land which would have been grazed hundreds of years ago.

☞ free

◉ all year daily any reasonable time

Facilities: 🚗

● **Hay tedder**

MAP 7   NORTH EAST ENGLAND

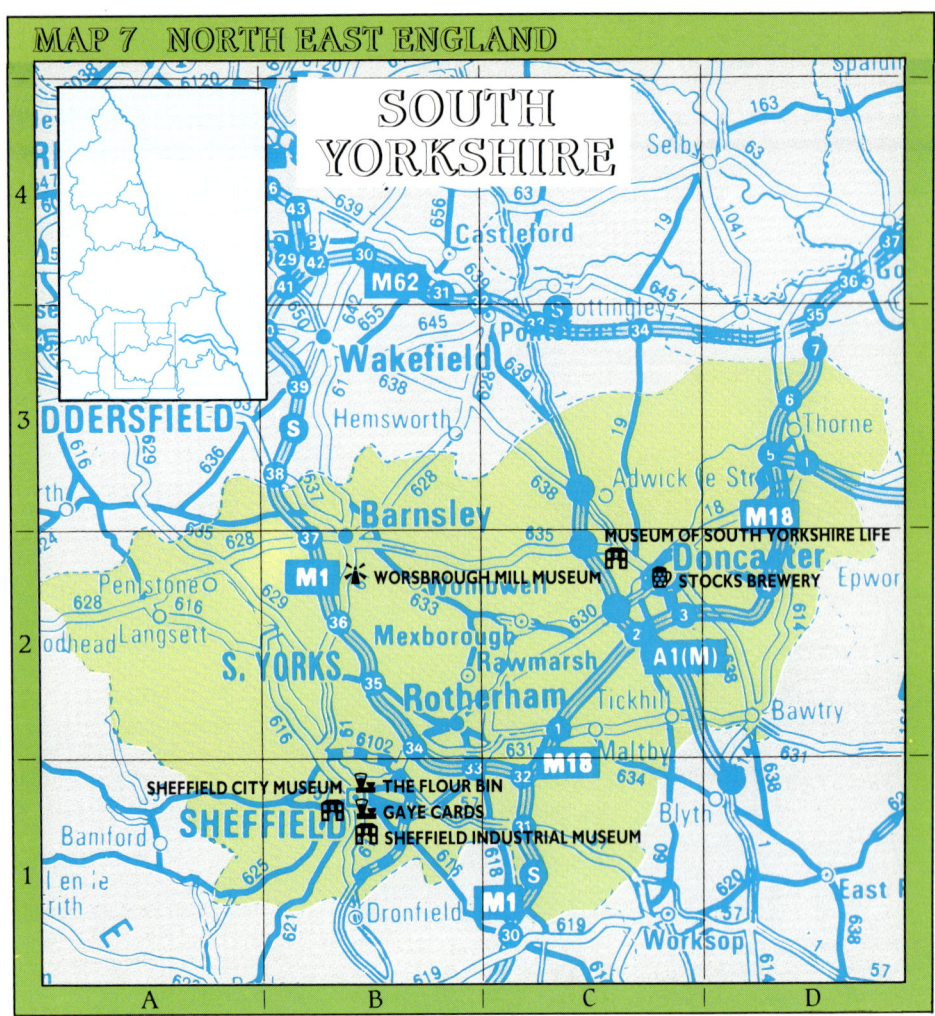

SOUTH YORKSHIRE

Sheffield, famous for its expert cutlery-making, popularised the art of elegant eating. In 1988 it celebrates the bicentenary of Thomas Bolsover who invented Sheffield Plate. This was a method of plating silver onto copper which became the mass-produced substitute of silver and Sheffield's main industry.

Map 7 B1
The Flour Bin
36 Exchange Street, Sheffield,
South Yorkshire S2 5TS
Tel. Sheffield (0742) 724842
In city centre.

The Flour Bin supplies the home baker with about 40 different types of bread, biscuit and cake flour including chapatti flour, 'Caudwells' flour from an old water-powered mill at Rowsley, and Turos, a smooth dark brown malted flour re-introduced after an absence of 25 years. It also sells grains, yeast, dried fruits, nuts, seeds and pulses.

◗ all year Mon-Wed, Fri, Sat 8.30-5, closed Bank Hols; & Moorfoot Market, Sheffield Tue, Wed, Fri, Sat; & Mansfield Market Thur
Facilities: &

Map 7 B1
Gaye Cards
7-8 North Gallery,
Exchange Street, Sheffield,
South Yorkshire S1 2AJ
Tel. Sheffield (0742) 729842

In city centre.

The full range of the famous Robin Hood Cakes are sold here including speciality cakes for Easter and Valentine's Day. These cakes, baked from an old traditional family recipe at the bakery in Ranskill in Sherwood Forest, are all rich in brandy-soaked fruit and free from preservatives, additives, artificial colouring or flavouring. Cake decorations are also on sale.

◗ all year Mon-Sat 9-5.30

MAP 7

Map 7 C2
Museum of South Yorkshire Life
Cusworth Hall,
Cusworth, Doncaster,
South Yorkshire DN5 7TU
Tel. Doncaster (0302) 782342

From Doncaster follow A638 northwards, after 2 miles turn left at junction with A635 onto unclassified road for 1 mile to museum. Signposted.

This family-orientated museum, housed in a beautiful Georgian mansion, specialises in the social history of South Yorkshire. It contains displays of kitchen utensils and agricultural equipment and has a small display on the servants of the 1920s and 30s. A book containing their reminiscences is on sale in the shop together with toffee and fudge in museum-labelled boxes.

☞ free
◑ Mar-Oct Mon-Thur, Sat 11-5, Sun 1-5; Nov-Feb Mon-Thur, Sat 11-4, Sun 1-4
Facilities: ▥ ➡ ☺
★ 31 Mar Easter egg decorating; 22-24 Dec Victorian Christmas evenings with supper in the Great Kitchen

Map 7 B1
Sheffield City Museum
Weston Park, Sheffield,
South Yorkshire S10 2TP
Tel. Sheffield (0742) 768588

From city centre follow A57 westwards for 1 mile to museum. Signposted.

A general museum with an interesting collection of cutlery displayed as table settings. The exhibits are mostly locally-made but include examples from all over the world. The museum has a fine collection of old Sheffield Plate and porcelain including ceramics from local factories such as Rockingham near Rotherham and Pinxtone in Nottinghamshire. Thomas Bolsover, the inventor of

Sheffield Plate, will be the subject of a major exhibition in 1988. The museum shop sells a selection of books on cutlery including 'Is it Silver?', the story of Sheffield Plate.

☞ free
◑ all year Mon-Sat 10-5, Sun 11-5
Facilities: ▥ ▯◖ ੬ ᴡᴄ ☺

THE BARNSLEY CHOP
This huge lamb chop, weighing over a pound, is best when cooked on a very hot grill until almost black on the outside yet still pink in the middle. Sold at butchers throughout South Yorkshire, but remember to insist on a single-sided chop. It's far superior to the butterfly cut which poses as the real thing in the south.

Map 7 B1
Sheffield Industrial Museum
Kelham Island,
Off Alma Street, Sheffield,
South Yorkshire S3 8RY
Tel. Sheffield (0742) 722106

In city centre. Signposted.

Situated on an island in the River Don this museum includes displays on a range of modern Sheffield manufacturers including Bassetts sweets and Thorntons chocolates. Visitors will also see traditional craftsmen at work including a cutler in a cutler's workshop demonstrating the techniques for cutlery-making. To commemorate the bicentenary of the death of Thomas Bolsover, the museum will be staging a major exhibition, including a magnificent array of 18thC Sheffield Plate, from 7 Sep to 1 Jan 1989.

☞ adults £1.00, senior citizens & children 50p
◑ all year Wed-Sat 10-5, Sun 11-5
Facilities: ▥ ੬ ᴡᴄ ➡

Map 7 C2
Stocks Brewery
The Hallcross, 33-34 Hallgate, Doncaster, South Yorkshire
Tel. Doncaster (0302) 328213

In town centre.

Traditional brewing from malted barley and best quality hops may be seen by request at this brewery.

☞ free
◑ all year daily during normal working hours
Facilities: ▥ ▯◖ ੬ ᴡᴄ ➡
▯◖ pub, with beer garden adjoining, serves beer & bar meals & 3 different brews available for off-sales

Map 7 B2
Worsbrough Mill Museum
Worsbrough, Barnsley,
South Yorkshire S70 5LJ
Tel. Barnsley (0226) 203961

From Barnsley follow A61 southwards for 2 miles to mill.

A corn mill at Worsbrough is mentioned in the Domesday Book but the present watermill dates from 1625, with a steam-powered extension added in the 19thC. Though the advent of rolling mills took much of the trade away, Worsbrough was still operating commercially in the 1960s. It is now an industrial museum set in a 130-acre country park. The mill is open for visitors to see the water wheel, bagging and drive floor, engine room and stone floor. Actual milling of stoneground wholemeal flour can be seen on milling days. Preserves and 1½Kg bags of flour are for sale and during the many special events throughout the year homebaked produce may be bought.

☞ 25p (voluntary charge)
◑ all year Wed-Sun, Bank Hols 10-5.30
Facilities: ੬ ᴡᴄ ➡
★ milling & steam threshing days

· CALENDAR OF EVENTS ·

FEBRUARY

Shrovetide Skipping Festival
Shrove Tuesday
An old custom - local housewives cook pancakes when the Pancake Bell is rung at noon in Foreshore Street, Scarborough, North Yorkshire.

Pancake Race
Shrove Tuesday
Annual pancake race on Whitby Pier, North Yorkshire

MARCH

Carlins Sunday
27 March — 5th Sunday in Lent
'Carlins' or grey peas (a traditional Lent dish) are eaten throughout North East England - look out for them on pub menus.

Morpeth Northumbrian Gathering
8-10 April
An annual gathering with traditional food available at Morpeth, Northumberland.

MAY

Gawthorpe Feast
1 May
A celebration that dates back many centuries at Gawthorpe, near Ossett, West Yorkshire.

JUNE

Cottingham and District Show
4-5 June
An annual agricultural show at Cottingham, Hull, Humberside.

North Yorkshire Show
25 June
An annual agricultural show at Northallerton, North Yorkshire.

JULY

English Civil War Garrison
2-3 July
A Civil War re-enactment by the English Civil War Society who cook period food at Prudhoe Castle, Prudhoe, Northumberland.

Great Yorkshire Show
12-14 July
The biggest annual agricultural show in the north of England at Harrogate, North Yorkshire.

Cleveland County Show
23 July
An annual agricultural show at Middlesbrough, Cleveland.

Nostell Priory Country Fair
24 July
An annual country fair at Nostell Priory, near Wakefield, West Yorkshire.

AUGUST

Egton Bridge Gooseberry Show
2 August — 1st Tuesday in August
Held for over 150 years - many varieties and very large gooseberries are exhibited, some as big as table tennis balls.

Great British Beer Festival
2-6 August
An annual beer festival at Queens Hall, Leeds, West Yorkshire.

Leeds Show
5-7 August
An annual horticultural show with wines and honey at Roundhay Park, Leeds, West Yorkshire.

English Civil War Garrison
13-14 August
A Civil War re-enactment by the English Civil War Society which includes cooking period food at Helmsley Castle, Helmsley, North Yorkshire.

Kilnsey Show
30 August
An annual local agricultural show at Kilnsey in North Yorkshire.

SEPTEMBER

Denby Dale Pie
3 September
The legendary Denby Dale giant pie will be baked in 1988 - the first time since 1964 - to celebrate 200 years of piemaking - the dish is 18 feet long by 6 feet wide and 18 inches deep - in Denby Dale, West Yorkshire.

First Fruits of the Harvest Ceremony
A Saturday in September
A harvest festival tradition with a colourful procession from the town hall to the base of Trinity Tower in Richmond, North Yorkshire.

OCTOBER

Harvest of the Sea
October — Sunday of 2nd week
A fishermen's thanksgiving service in St Oswald's Church, Flamborough, North Humberside - the church is decorated with crab pots and nets.

CENTRAL ENGLAND

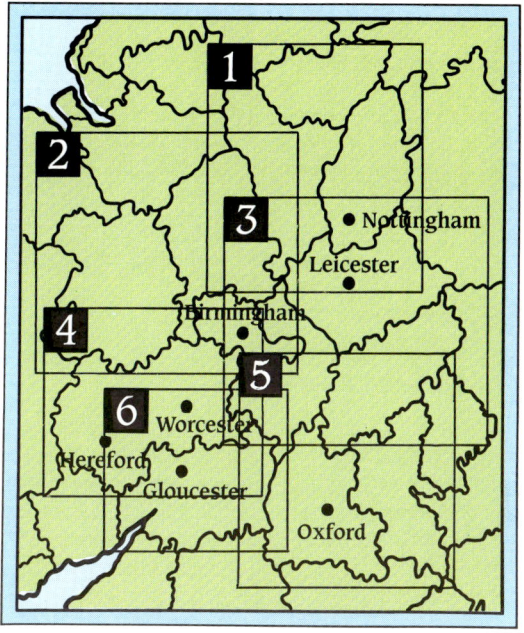

CENTRAL ENGLAND

● **The Market Place, Shrewsbury**

by Warren and Judy Knock

HOTELIERS

The Midland Shires have for centuries been the home of the country gentleman's sports of hunting, shooting and fishing, centred on the great estates and manor houses, which have existed, often, since medieval times. It has always been a prosperous area, its wealth coming from farming the rich soils of the great river valleys of the Severn, Avon and Trent, and, especially in early times, from the wool trade based on sheep grazing the golden limestone uplands of the Cotswolds.

The food of the region reflects this diversity and richness, from the hearty raised pork pies of Leicestershire, originating from the Roman habit of wrapping meat in flour and oil paste (today, Melton Mowbray's pork pies are especially notable), to Shropshire's poor man's dish, Haddock and Bacon Pot, a kind of savoury bread and butter pudding.

Some of England's finest beef comes from Herefordshire, whose stocky red-coated cattle almost match the dark red earth of the county, while spring lamb from the Cotswolds or the Shropshire hills is especially tender. As befits hunting country, game also features in local recipes such as 'Venison Role' from Warwickshire and 'Smothered Rabbit', in which the meat is simmered in cider and stock, then coated in a spicy onion sauce and browned under the grill. In our restaurant, on the Cotswold edge above Gloucester, we apply this method to pork fillet and it has become very popular. Although some way from the sea, the Midlands have a strong tradition of fish-eating, often of river fish from the many streams, but in the past fish was reared in special fish-ponds. A Lady Blencowe of Northamptonshire in 1694 used a recipe for broiled carp. Today you mainly find farmed trout for sale, either fresh or smoked on the spot, as at Winston in the pretty Coln Valley near Cirencester. But before road transport developed, sea fish was brought to the ancient river port of Gloucester, while salmon from the Severn and Wye have always been justly renowned. Nowadays Gloucester's old market has excellent fish-stalls and the long-established food markets in Leicester, Oxford and Northampton also have fine displays of fresh fish, though the main accent is on local produce; meat and poultry, fruit and vegetables.

Much of the fruit comes from perhaps the lushest part of all the Midlands, the Vale of Evesham, watered by the Avon, with its own small market towns, Evesham and Pershore. The air of the Vale in spring is fragrant with the scent of apple and plum blossom, and a little later the delicate green asparagus appears. An early summer treat, you will find it in local markets and restaurants.

Fruit is widely used in local cooking, in mousses and fools — gooseberry fool is a particular favourite — puddings and pies. The different varieties of plum are gorgeous and can be used in all sorts of ways. In one recipe, for 'Pershore Plums', from a country house in Worcestershire, they are baked with almonds and served cold.

We have too our special cakes and pastries, such as well-known 'Bakewell Tart' (properly 'Bakewell Pie') and 'Banbury Cakes', but look out for Shrewsbury Cakes — really a spicy biscuit — and Staffordshire oatcakes.

Such rich farming country naturally produces cheeses, including Leicestershire's famous blue Stilton and Red Leicester, and Double Gloucester. This cheese and its relation, Single Gloucester — made only on a few farms — uses the milk of Old Gloucester cows. Its continued existence may be due to an eighteenth-century Duke of Beaufort, master of the Beaufort Hunt, who ordered his tenants to keep only Old Gloucester cows, not for the quality of their milk, but because they were not afraid of his hounds!

When thirst strikes, you have a wide choice of drinks. Many pubs display the signs of one of the several traditional local breweries, whose ales all have their own distinctive flavour. Names to look out for include Horne Ales in Nottinghamshire and Hook Norton in Oxfordshire, and Burton-on-Trent in the north of the region is Britain's most famous brewing town, the home of Marston and Bass, among others.

Old-fashioned, non-fizzy cider can be found, especially around Herefordshire and Gloucestershire, with their large orchards, while on good restaurant wine lists you should see the fine white table wines from our vineyards. Natural mineral water is not lacking either, whether you choose widely-distributed Malvern Water or the spring water of Derbyshire's Buxton or Ashbourne.

To find around you evidence that the Midland Shires offer a wide choice of food and drink derived from the local soil and people, explore the great medieval market towns — Warwick, Oxford, Northampton, Gloucester — but then get off the A roads and follow those wandering lanes through tucked-away villages. You will enjoy yourself.

MAP 1   CENTRAL ENGLAND

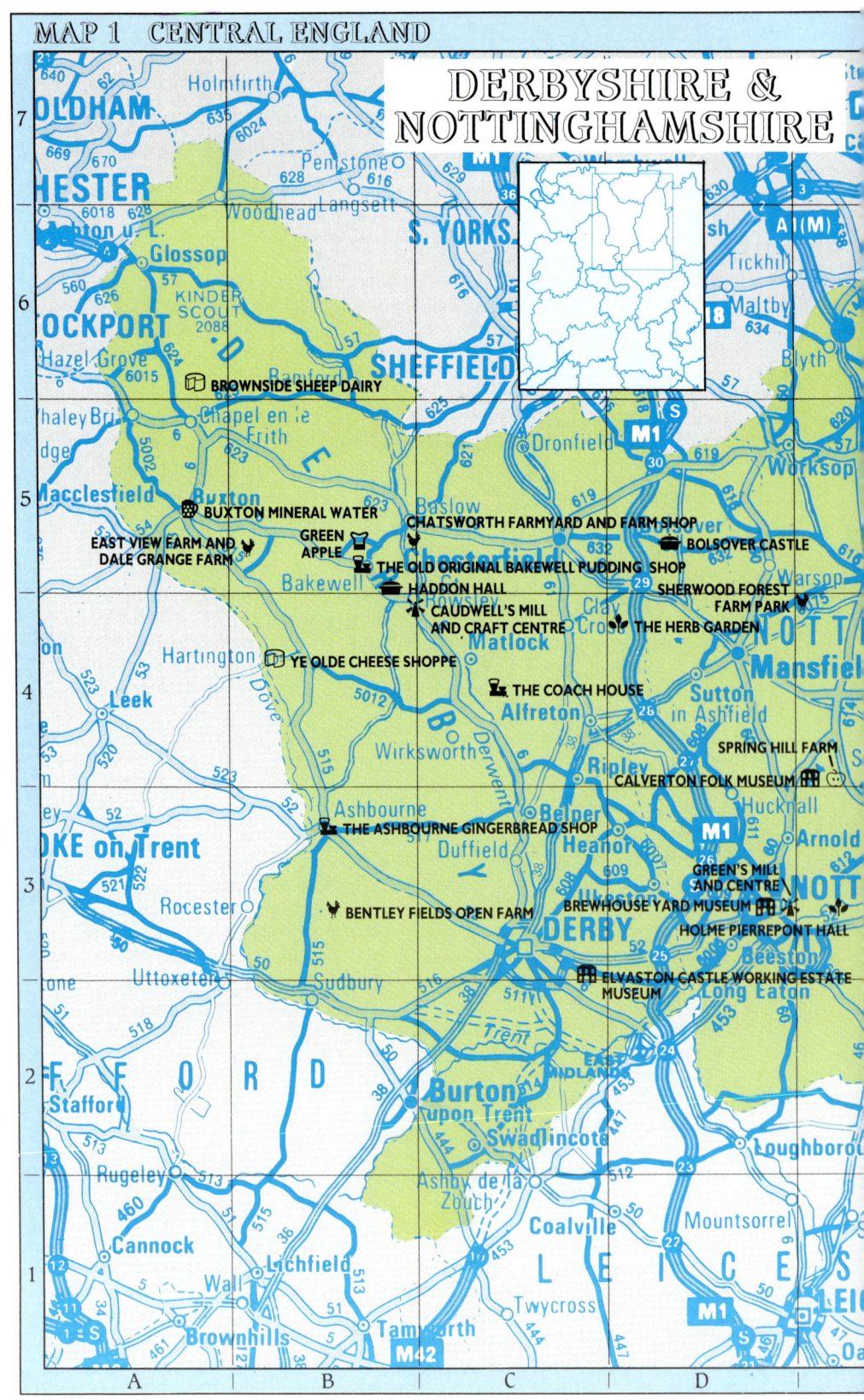

DERBYSHIRE & NOTTINGHAMSHIRE

BROWNSIDE SHEEP DAIRY

BUXTON MINERAL WATER

CHATSWORTH FARMYARD AND FARM SHOP

GREEN APPLE

EAST VIEW FARM AND DALE GRANGE FARM

BOLSOVER CASTLE

THE OLD ORIGINAL BAKEWELL PUDDING SHOP

HADDON HALL

SHERWOOD FOREST FARM PARK

CAUDWELL'S MILL AND CRAFT CENTRE

THE HERB GARDEN

YE OLDE CHEESE SHOPPE

THE COACH HOUSE

SPRING HILL FARM

CALVERTON FOLK MUSEUM

THE ASHBOURNE GINGERBREAD SHOP

GREEN'S MILL AND CENTRE

BREWHOUSE YARD MUSEUM

BENTLEY FIELDS OPEN FARM

HOLME PIERREPONT HALL

ELVASTON CASTLE WORKING ESTATE MUSEUM

Nottingham boasts a Goose Fair which dates back to the 13thC. It may not have been the oldest fair in the country but it certainly was the biggest. Now an enormous funfair, it was once the market where farmers from all over England brought their Michaelmas geese. North east of Nottingham is Southwell where Bramley apples were first grown over 180 years ago; the parent tree can still be seen at Bramley Cottage.

 Map 1 B3
The Ashbourne Gingerbread Shop
26 St John Street, Ashbourne, Derbyshire
Tel. Ashbourne (0335) 43227
In town centre.

Ashbourne Gingerbread, a ginger shortbread biscuit, is a local delicacy. It is believed to have been created by the chef to French officers held prisoner in Ashbourne during the Napoleonic Wars in 1805 and subsequently passed to a local baker. His descendants are still in business at the same shop making and selling the Gingerbread.
● all year Mon-Sat 8-5.30

♥ Map 1 B3
Bentley Fields Open Farm
Alkmonton, Longford, Derby, Derbyshire DE6 3DJ
Tel. Great Cubley (033523) 240
From Ashbourne follow A515 southwards, after 6 miles turn left onto unclassified road for 2 miles to Alkmonton. Signposted.

Visitors to this dairy and sheep farm may watch the cows being milked at 1 o'clock and see over 60 breeds of livestock, including poultry and lambs.

Eggs are for sale and there is a farm trail.
☞ adults £1.00, senior citizens & children 50p
● Easter, May, Aug Sun, Mon, Bank Hols 11-6; Jul-Aug Sun 11-6
Facilities: ⊩ ⌨ 🚗 ⌂ ⌷
⊩ tea room serves farmhouse teas with homemade cakes

🍲 Map 1 D5
Bolsover Castle
Castle Street, Bolsover, Nr Chesterfield, Derbyshire S44 6PR
Tel. Chesterfield (0246) 823349
In town centre. Signposted.

This early 17thC country house owned by English Heritage is perched on a wooded hill above the town of Bolsover. In the kitchens of the 'Little Castle' visitors can see the stone floor channelled for drainage, the bread ovens which occupy the whole of one wall, plus the larder, servery and bakery. Also on display is a model, based on a drawing in the Smithson Collection, of how the kitchen would have looked in the 17thC.
☞ adults £1.25, senior citizens 95p, children 60p
● Apr-Sep daily 9.30-6.30; Oct-Mar Mon-Sat 9.30-4, Sun 2-6, closed for lunch Oct-Mar Mon, Thu, Fri
Facilities: ⌨ 🚗

⌷ Map 1 D3
Brewhouse Yard Museum
Castle Boulevard, Nottingham, Nottinghamshire NG7 1FB
Tel. Nottingham (0602) 411881
In city centre. Signposted.

Many aspects of daily life in Nottingham are shown in these

MAP 1   CENTRAL ENGLAND

five 17thC houses. Almost all the material in the museum was either made or used in the area which gives a local flavour to the displays. Changes in domestic life are shown through a series of period rooms. Nottingham's rural domestic economy is shown in the down-hearth kitchen of the 17th and the 18thC, whilst the urban economy is shown in the range kitchen of the later 19thC. Both kitchens contain local cooking equipment and recipes. The range kitchen and its living room are set out as the living accommodation of the proprietors of a newly opened general store, with each room reflecting the changing seasons and the appropriate holidays. Recreated shops show a range of small local traders dating between 1919 and 1939. A culinary and medicinal herb garden can also be viewed.

☞ free
● all year daily 10-12, 1-5
Facilities: ♿ 🚻 ♨

🏠 Map 1 A6
Brownside Sheep Dairy
New House Farm,
Chapel-en-le-Frith,
via Stockport,
Derbyshire SK12 6QL
Tel. Chinley (0663) 50647
From Chapel-en-le-Frith follow A624 northwards, after 1 mile turn right past the railway bridge onto unclassified road for 1 mile to farm.

This small working farm which is found high up in the Peak District, aims to teach visitors about sheep dairy farming. The owner is on hand to answer visitors' questions as they are invited to watch the milking and walk around the farm. On sale are 1 pint packs of sheep's milk as well as hard and soft cheeses and yoghurt.

☞ adults £1.50, children £1.00
● all year by appointment
Facilities: 🚌

🍶 Map 1 A5
Buxton Mineral Water
The Natural Baths,
The Crescent, Buxton,
Derbyshire SK17 6BQ
Tel. Buxton (0298) 5106
In town centre. Signposted.
Buxton Spring Water, a natural mineral water, is bottled here and visitors can see the water emerging from its protected source 5,000 feet below the Derbyshire Peaks, inside the Victorian natural baths building. Bottled Buxton Spring Water, either natural or flavoured with orange, lemon or lime, can be bought from the Tourist Information Centre in the same building. Across the road is St Ann's Well where the same water runs freely and can be tasted and collected.

☞ free
● Apr-Oct daily 9.30-5; Nov-Mar Mon-Sat 10-12.30, 1.30-4, Sun 12-4

🎪 Map 1 E4
Calverton Folk Museum
Main Street, Calverton,
Nottingham, Nottinghamshire
Tel. Nottingham (0602) 652836
From Nottingham follow A60 northwards, after 5 miles turn right onto A614 for 1 mile, then turn right onto B6386 for 1 mile, then turn right onto unclassified road for 1 mile to Calverton.

The museum is housed in a 200-year-old cottage which has a fascinating kitchen, retained and furnished in Victorian style.

☞ free
● all year by appointment

🌳 Map 1 B4
Caudwell's Mill and Craft Centre
Rowsley, Matlock,
Derbyshire DE4 2EB
Tel. Matlock (0629) 734374
In village.
This well-preserved water-powered 19thC roller mill has

much of its original machinery still in working order. It illustrates the change in milling technology from stones to rolls, heralding the modern age of milling. Both strong wholemeal and strong white flour milled here is for sale, in 32, 6.5, 3 and 1.5Kg packs. Guided tours are available throughout the year by arrangement.

☞ adults 70p, senior citizens & children 30p; guided tours: adults £1.00, senior citizens & children 50p
● Jan-Feb Sat-Sun 10-4; Mar-Oct Mon-Sun 10-6; Nov-Dec Mon-Sun 10-4
Facilities: 🚌 🍴 🚻 🚌 ♨
🍴 wholefood homebaked lunches & teas including vegetarian dishes served in Excelsior Country Parlour, also take-away

🐂 Map 1 B5
Chatsworth Farmyard and Farm Shop
Stud Farm, Pilsley, Nr Bakewell,
Derbyshire DE4 1UH
Tel. Baslow (024688) 3392
From Rowsley follow B6012 northwards, after 3 miles turn right at Edensor to Chatsworth. Signposted.
In the farmyard there are dairy and beef cows, a bull, sheep, goats, pigs, poultry and their offspring. A daily milking demonstration and commentary start at 3.30 each afternoon. The shop sells farm-produced meat, poultry, game and dairy products as well as sausages, cooked meats, pâtés, bread and cakes — which are prepared in the shop's kitchen. The Duchess of Devonshire has masterminded a new range of preserves, sauces, mustards, biscuits, jams and pickles which are for sale alongside a wide variety of English farmhouse cheeses and selected wines, fruit and vegetables. Presentation hampers of all shapes and sizes are available.

MAP 1

● Labels representing the range of food products available from the Chatsworth Farm Shop

🐾 adults £1.50, children 80p, family ticket £4.00
◑ farmyard: Apr-4 Oct daily 10.30-4.30; farm shop: Apr-Oct Mon-Sat, Bank Hols 9-5.30; Nov-Mar Mon-Sat 9-5
Facilities: ▥ 🚗 ♨ ⌂

🐾 Map 1 C4
The Coach House
Lea, Nr Matlock, Derbyshire DE4 5QJ
Tel. Matlock (0629) 84346
From Matlock follow A615 eastwards, after 3 miles turn right onto unclassified road for 2 miles to Lea.

This shop sells homemade Jersey ice cream in 15 flavours, homemade cheese made from Jersey milk and also yoghurt. Customers are welcome to taste the ice cream. Pâté, bread and homemade cakes are also on sale.

◑ Jan-Easter Tue-Sun 10.30-6.00; Easter-Dec daily 10.30-6.00
Facilities: ▥ 🍴 ♿ ▥ 🚗
🍴 ice cream parlour & restaurant have a good selection of dishes including vegetarian & steak & kidney pies

---

🌾 Map 1 B5
East View Farm and Dale Grange Farm
Chelmorton, Buxton, Derbyshire SK17 9SL
Tel. Buxton (0298) 85345
From Buxton follow A515 south eastwards, after 3 miles turn left onto A5270 for 1 mile, then turn right onto unclassified road for $\frac{1}{2}$ mile, then turn left onto unclassified road for $\frac{1}{4}$ mile to Chelmorton.

Chelmorton is one of England's oldest villages and these 2 farms, set in a beautiful and historical dale in the Peak National Park, together cover 300 acres including an extensive conservation area containing many rare plants and wildlife. Visitors are welcome to follow the trail around the working farm where all livestock, such as the 190 Friesian and Hereford cattle and 50 crossbred ewes, are reared without hormone injections or sprays. Wool, milk, beef and lamb are sold commercially.

🐾 free; tours: £1
◑ all year Mon-Fri telephone for details
Facilities: ▥ 🚗 ♨

🏛 Map 1 C3
Elvaston Castle Working Estate Museum
Borrowash Road, Elvaston, Derby, Derbyshire DE7 3EP
Tel. Derby (0332) 73799

MAP 1   CENTRAL ENGLAND

From Derby follow A6 south eastwards, after 4 miles turn left onto B5010 for 1 mile, then turn left onto unclassified road for $\frac{1}{2}$ mile to estate. Signposted.

A working agricultural museum housed in the estate's original workers' cottages. The gardener's cottage, alongside a dairy, wash house and potting shed, has a cottage garden where vegetables and herbs are grown. Visitors can watch regular demonstrations of baking and food processing in the reconstructed and fully equipped 1910 kitchen and can watch a number of craftsmen at work in the original craft workshops. These include a blacksmith, a saddler and a cobbler. Traditional machinery and heavy horses are used to cultivate arable crops and hay in a 30-acre field and a working cornmill mills flour and animal feed. The flour, together with free-range eggs, home-produced honey and a book of local Derbyshire recipes, can be bought in the shop.

☞ adults 60p, senior citizens & children (5-16) 30p
◑ Apr-Oct Wed-Sat 1-5, Sun, Bank Hols 10-6
Facilities: ≋ ⦿ ⛫ ⓦ 🚗 🐾 ⚗
★ demonstrations include horse ploughing, haymaking, butter & cheese-making
⦿ homemade lunches & teas served in Elvaston Country Park

🌬 Map 1 D3
Green's Mill and Centre
Belvoir Hill, Sneinton, Nottingham, Nottinghamshire NG2 4LF
Tel. Nottingham (0602) 503635

From city centre follow A612 Southwell Road eastwards, after $\frac{1}{2}$ mile turn right into Sneinton Road for $\frac{1}{4}$ mile to Belvoir Hill on left.

A restored 19thC tower windmill which produces wholemeal stoneground flour

● **Green's Mill, Sneinton**

that is for sale. Visitors are given a demonstration by the miller himself and they can also visit the science centre to watch an audio-visual presentation on the mill's past history. It was once owned and worked by George Green (1793-1841) a famous scientist and mathematician. The flour is sold in 1.5, 3, 12 and 25Kg bags.

☞ free
◑ all year Wed-Sun, Bank Hols 10-12, 1-5
Facilities: ⓦ 🚗 ⚗

● **The kitchen, Haddon Hall**

 Map 1 B5
Haddon Hall
Bakewell, Derbyshire DE4 1LA
Tel. Bakewell (062981) 2855

From Bakewell follow A6 south eastwards for 2 miles to house on left. Signposted.

The 14thC kitchen at Haddon Hall is remarkably unchanged and is a perfect example of a medieval kitchen with bread ovens, chopping block, oak work surfaces, large cooking fires and a butchers 'shop' where meat was hung and prepared. Visitors can also see the old banqueting hall with its original table dating from 1480 and the dining room which is

● **Haddon Hall design china in situ in the Great Chamber**

MAP 1

still used by the Duke of Rutland and his family. Minton China's 'Haddon Hall' design is based on a tapestry in the Hall. A dinner service is on display and the china is on sale in the shop. Elderflower cordial made by the Duke of Rutland's brother, Lord John Manners, is on sale and also Ashbourne Gingerbread. The restaurant is situated in the Hall's early 20thC kitchen and here visitors can see the unusual pulley system which operates a dumb waiter that transports food to the dining room by rail.

☞ adults £2.50, senior citizens £1.90, children (5-16) £1.40
● Apr-Jun, Sep-2 Oct Tue-Sun 11-6; Jul-Aug Tue-Sat 11-6; open Bank Hols
Facilities: 🍽️ 🚻 🚗 ⛺
🍽️ licensed restaurant serves lunches & teas, specialities include homemade Bakewell pudding

🌷 Map 1 E6
Hayton Castle Farm Trail
Hayton Castle Farm, Retford, Nottinghamshire DN22 9BB
Tel. Retford (0777) 817683
From East Retford follow A620 north eastwards, after 5 miles turn left at North Wheatley onto unclassified road towards Clayworth for 1 mile to farm on left.

This 270-acre family farm with arable fields, meadows, woods and livestock has an excellent 2-mile farm trail which visitors can wander around using their printed guide or the directional signs. The trail follows meadows beside the Chesterfield canal, a wildlife area, fields of cereals and oil seed rape and 3 small ancient woodlands. There are picnic areas in the woods and on the site of a 12thC moated farmstead. The family is always on hand to answer any questions.

🍽️ Map 1 B5
GREEN APPLE
Diamond Court, Water Street, Bakewell, Derbyshire DE4 1WL
Tel: Bakewell (062981) 4404
In town centre. Signposted.
A quiet, informal restaurant with a self-service lunch and a waitress-served dinner. The menu changes frequently with Bakewell Pudding a firm favourite.
● Nov-Easter: L – Mon, Wed-Sat, D – Thur-Sat; Easter-Oct: L – daily, D – Wed-Sat;
Meals: 12-2, 7-10
Price range Set L £4.00-6.00, Set D £8.00-10.00
Seats 55
Cards: Access, Diners, Visa
Facilities: 🍷 🚻 ♿

BAKEWELL PUDDING
*puff pastry
strawberry or raspberry jam
12 egg yolks
3 egg whites
12oz butter melted
12oz caster sugar
12oz ground almonds
½oz almond essence
(optional)*
Heat oven to gas 4 (350F, 180C). Line 2 shallow 14-inch oven dishes with the puff pastry. Cover with a thick layer of jam. Mix the remaining ingredients together and spread over the jam. Bake for 30 minutes.

☞ free
● all year daily any reasonable time
Facilities: 🚗 ⛺

🌿 Map 1 D4
The Herb Garden
Hall View Cottage, Hardstoft, Pilsley, Nr Chesterfield, Derbyshire S45 8AH
Tel. Chesterfield (0246) 854268
From Chesterfield follow B6039 south eastwards for 6 miles to Hardstoft.

A cottage herb garden and nursery where over 150 different kinds of culinary, medicinal and aromatic herb plants are grown and sold, mostly in 3½-inch square pots. Guided parties can be taken around the gardens, by prior arrangement. Each herb is clearly labelled so that visitors can get an idea of exactly what a mature specimen looks like. An informal talk with hints and information on cooking with herbs, herbs in salads and herbs used medicinally as well as ideas on drying your own herbs will be given while on the tour.

☞ free
● Apr-Oct Fri-Wed 10-6
Facilities: 🚻 🚗

🌿 Map 1 E3
Holme Pierrepont Hall
Holme Pierrepont, Nr Nottingham, Nottinghamshire NG12 2LD
Tel. Radcliffe on Trent (06073) 2371
From Bingham follow A52 westwards, after 4 miles turn right onto unclassified road for ½ mile to Holme Pierrepont. Signposted.

Dating from Tudor times, this family home has a beautiful Victorian courtyard garden and Jacob sheep grazing in the park.
☞ adults £2.00, children £1.00
● Easter, Jun-Aug Tue-Fri, Sun, Bank Hols 2-6
Facilities: 🍽️ 🚻 🚗 ⛺
🍽️ homemade teas served in the Long Bakery overlooking spectacular countryside

🌷 Map 1 E4
Manor Farm Tea Shoppe
Manor Farm, Bleasby, Nottingham, Nottinghamshire NG14 7FX
Tel. Newark (0636) 830241
From Southwell follow A612 southwards, after 2 miles turn left onto unclassified road for 1 mile to Bleasby.

Walk across the orchard past the pond and manor house garden to the tea shop which is situated in a cowshed on this working farm. Pigs, cows and calves can be seen in the adjoining stable. There is also a dovecote with nesting boxes which dates back to 1763 and contains a small collection of old farm tools.

◐ all year daily 10.30-6

Facilities: ☕ 🍽 ♿ WC 🚗

🍽 light lunches & teas served including cakes, cream teas & ploughmans

---

Map 1 E3

Meadowcraft Herbs

The Bungalow, Gibsmere, Nottinghamshire NG14 7FS

Tel. Newark (0636) 830072

From Southwell follow A612 southwards, after 2 miles turn left onto unclassified road for 2 miles through Bleasby to Gibsmere.

Situated in a conservation area with a lakeside setting,

Regional Recipe

Sage and Onion Dumplings

This mixture can also be baked by itself as a pudding or used to stuff a loin of pork.

2 large onions
1lb white breadcrumbs
3 tbsp sage chopped
salt & pepper
2oz butter melted
1 egg beaten
flour

Parboil the onions and chop finely. Mix with the breadcrumbs and sage, season and stir in the butter and egg. Shape them into balls between the palms of your hands and roll them in flour. Arrange them around a joint about half an hour before it is cooked. Turn once or twice to crispen.

Meadowcraft gives visitors a new insight into the fascinating subject of herbs. There are talks and tours around the organically grown herbs which are divided into culinary, fragrant, medicinal and historical beds and advice is given on their use and cultivation. Organically grown individual herb plants or selections in patio or kitchen pots, dried herbs and spices are on sale.

☞ free

◐ all year daily 10-dusk

Map 1 F6

North Leverton Windmill

West View, Sturton Road, North Leverton, East Retford, Nottinghamshire DN22 0AB

Tel. Gainsborough (0427) 880662

From East Retford follow unclassified road eastwards, after 4 miles turn left for ½ mile to North Leverton. Signposted.

This is one of the last working windmills in Nottinghamshire with a tower mill which was built in 1813. Wheat is milled into wholemeal flour which can be bought in 1½, 3½, 7, 14, 28 and 56lb quantities.

• **The Old Original Bakewell Pudding Shop**

MAP 1

☞ adults 50p, children 25p
◐ all year daily 2-5
Facilities: ⓦ 🚗 ☺

🐝 Map 1 B5
The Old Original Bakewell Pudding Shop
The Square, Bakewell,
Derbyshire DE4 1BT
Tel. Bakewell (062981) 2193
In town centre.

This bakery shop, dating back to the late 17thC, specialises in the famous Bakewell Puddings. These were first made by accident at a local inn around 1860 as a result of a misunderstanding between the mistress and her cook. Visiting noblemen ordered strawberry tart but the cook, instead of stirring the egg mixture into the pastry, spread it on top of the jam. The result was so successful that a lady living in this shop, then a cottage, obtained the recipe and started her own business. Bakewell puddings are still handmade here from the secret 120-year-old recipe. The puddings are available in 3 sizes: small 35p each, medium £1.75 each and large £2.50 each. Homemade bread, confectionery and preserves are also available.
◐ 31 Mar-Oct daily 9-6; Nov-30 Mar Mon-Fri 9-5, Sat, Sun 9-6
Facilities: ☕ ⑩ ⓦ
⑩ large restaurant caters for all tastes & specialises in local trout & Bakewell Pudding, hot with custard or cream; open Nov-30 Mar Mon-Fri 10-4.30, Sat, Sun 9-6; 31 Mar-Oct daily 9-6.

🌷 Map 1 E4
Sherwood Forest Farm Park
Lamb Pens Farm,
Edwinstowe, Mansfield,
Nottinghamshire NG21 9HL
Tel. Mansfield (0623) 822255/823558
From Ollerton follow A6075 westwards, after 4 miles turn left

onto unclassified road towards Clipstone for ½ mile to farm park. Signposted.

Set in the heart of Sherwood Forest, this farm park keeps 30 of the rarest breeds of cattle, sheep, pigs and goats in small paddocks for visitors to walk around. Animals include Middle White and Tamworth pigs, Hebridean, Soay and Herdwick sheep, Highland, Dexter and South Devon cattle, black swans, geese and 25 breeds of duck. Red and white potatoes in 25Kg bags are for sale in the shop. Visitors can see the display of vintage tractors, the farm museum, the pets' corner and the gift shop.
☞ adults £1.25, senior citizens £1.00, children (over 2) 75p
◐ Apr-19 Oct daily 10.30-5.30
Facilities: ☕ ♿ ⓦ 🚗 ☺ ⚠
☕ tea room serves homemade cakes & snacks

ASHBOURNE

Originally famous for its gingerbread, Ashbourne has now achieved additional fame for its pure spring water.

☺ Map 1 E4
Spring Hill Farm
Moor Lane,
Calverton, Nottingham,
Nottinghamshire NG14 6FZ
Tel. Nottingham (0602) 652129
From Bingham follow B687, then A6097 northwards, after 7 miles turn left onto unclassified road towards Calverton for 1 mile to farm. Signposted.

A pick your own farm with 120 acres of strawberries, gooseberries, raspberries, red and blackcurrants, tayberries, loganberries, rhubarb, blackberries and 7 kinds of apple. The shop sells local vegetables, honey, preserves, chutney, juices, free-range eggs and flowers as well as ready-picked fruit.

◐ PYO: Jul-Oct daily 9-7.30; shop: all year daily 9-7.30
Facilities: ⓦ 🚗 ☺ ⚠

🧀 Map 1 B4
Ye Olde Cheese Shoppe
Dairy Crest Foods, Dove Dairy, Hartington,
Derbyshire SK17 0AN
Tel. Hartington (029884) 496
In village.

This Cheesery was established in the 1870s and now has a 12,000 gallon capacity and cheese stores which can hold 90,000 cheeses. One of only 6 dairies in the world making Stilton cheese, its speciality is Hartington Stilton cheese — both blue and white — and the dairy produces more than 250,000 Stilton cheeses a year. The range includes the 16lb variety, 8lb halves, 5lb smalls, 6oz, 9oz and 16oz stone pots and wrapped wedges. Hartingtons produce about a quarter of all Stilton cheese made. In blue Stilton a mould belonging to the penicillium type is allowed to grow naturally in the cheese while white Stilton is sold young, before the veining has had time to develop. Most traditional English cheeses, hand cut and wrapped, locally made butter and 3 flavours of whole milk yoghurt are for sale.
◐ Jan-Mar Wed-Fri 9-5, Sat 9-4; Apr-Dec Mon-Fri 9-5, Sat, Sun 9-4

MAP 2   CENTRAL ENGLAND

WEST MIDLANDS, SHROPSHIRE & STAFFORDSHIRE

STAFFORDSHIRE ORGANIC CHEESE

THE BREAD BIN

THE KRUSTY LOAF

BROWNS OF DRAYTON — TERN FISHERIES

FORDHALL FARM

THE MILL AT WORST

WACKLEY FARM

THE SETT

PIMHILL FARM AND MILL

THE STRAWBERRY FARM

OLD POLICE HOUSE

CHADWE MILL

HADLEY PARK FARM

HAYFORD FARM FRUIT AND VEG

BOSCOBEL HOUSE

CRESSAGE BAKERY

THE LAWNS

MOORS FARM AND COUNTRY RESTAURANT

REG MAY BUTCHERS

ACTON SCOTT WORKING FARM MUSEUM

THE WOOD BREWERY

THE WERNLAS COLLECTION

CLAYBURY MILL

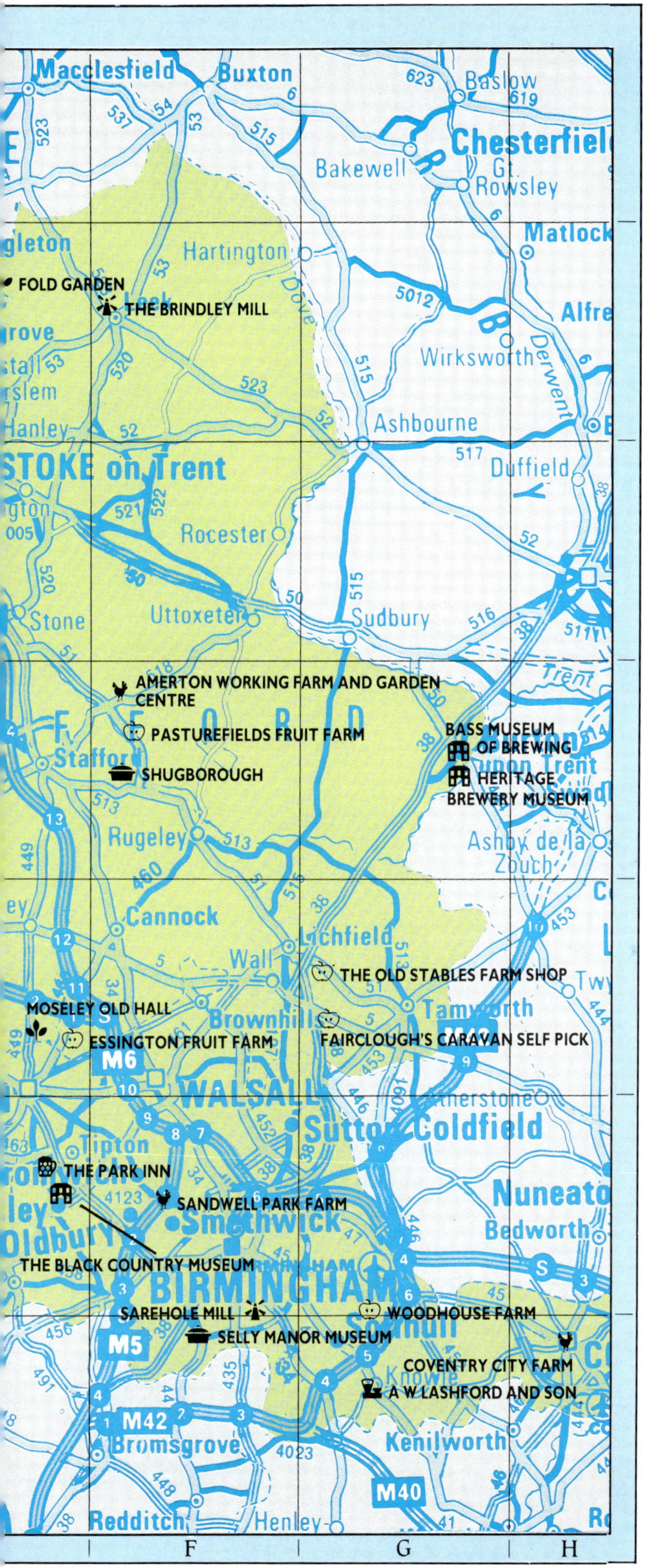

This is an area of contrasts as it stretches from Birmingham, Britain's second largest city, to the wilds of Shropshire where you can wander for miles without seeing a soul. Oatcakes — thin oatmeal pancakes — are eaten morning, noon and night in Staffordshire. You will find them in almost every shop you visit, together with pikelets which are similar to a crumpet. Washed down with a pint of good local ale they make a superb snack.

Map 2 B2
Acton Scott Working Farm Museum

Wenlock Lodge, Acton Scott, Nr Church Stretton, Shropshire SY6 6QN
Tel. Marshbrook (06946) 306

From Church Stretton follow A49 southwards, after 3 miles turn left onto unclassified road for 1 mile to Acton Scott. Signposted.

This farm museum is stocked and run as it was in the 19thC. Crops are grown and animals reared on land where chemicals and tractors have never been used. Working with Shire horses and skilled manpower the farm demonstrates 19thC arable techniques and implements. The stock includes horses, cows, sheep, pigs and poultry of breeds rarely seen today. Throughout the season

● **Shire horses ploughing at Acton Scott Working Farm Museum**

MAP 2   CENTRAL ENGLAND

visitors can watch butter being made and a number of traditional crafts are demonstrated in a period setting. Cheese-making takes place 3 times a week and hand milking each day in the main cowshed. There is also a reconstructed cottage and a full display of restored implements. Farm-produced butter in ¹/₂lb packs is available from Apr-Oct; potatoes from Sep-Oct; free-range eggs from Apr-Oct and honey all year round. Farm-produced ice cream, locally produced flour, confectionery and preserves can also be bought.

☞ Mar-May, Sep-Oct adults £1.20, senior citizens & children (over 5) 60p; Jun-Aug adults £1.50, senior citizens & children 75p, family ticket (2 adults & 3 children) £4.00, season ticket adult £4.00, children £2.00

● 28 Mar-Oct Mon-Sat 10-5, Sun, Bank Hols 10-6
Facilities: ♿ ⫟ ⬤ 🚻 🚗 ⛺
⫟ homemade soups, salads, quiches, vegetable stews, shepherds pie, fidget pie made to a local recipe & homemade cakes available

---

♥ Map 2 F4
Amerton Working Farm and Garden Centre
Amerton Farm,
Stowe-by-Chartley, Stafford,
Staffordshire ST18 0LA
Tel. Weston (0889) 270294
From Stafford follow A518 north eastwards, after 6 miles turn left to farm.

This dairy farm and garden centre has its own bakery selling a wide range of fresh produce including cream, ice cream and cheeses. Visitors

may watch the pedigree Jersey cows being milked between 4-5.30pm, see the manufacture of cream, ice cream and cheese on the premises and feed the hens. The farm shop sells Jersey cream in 5 and 10oz cartons, dairy ice cream in cones and ¹/₂, 1, 2, and 4-litre packs as well as bakery produce and small cheeses. The garden centre offers a large selection of dry goods, plants and fish. There is a farm trail.

☞ free
● all year daily 9-7
Facilities: ♿ ⫟ ⬤ 🚻 🚗 ⛺ ⛰
⫟ converted cowshed with seating for 120 serves cream teas & traditional farmhouse cooking including steak & kidney pudding, roast beef, apple pie, ice cream specialities & homemade sweets; vegetarian food available on request

● **Bass Museum**

MAP 2

🏠 Map 2 G4
Bass Museum of Brewing
Horninglow Street,
Burton-upon-Trent,
Staffordshire DE14 1JZ
Tel. Burton-upon-Trent (0283)
45301

In town centre. Signposted.

This museum specialises in the
history of brewing and visitors
may see how the business has
developed over the years.
There are displays of brewery
tools and transport, including
steam and horse — the stable
houses Shire horses. The Bass
brewery itself is open to visitors
and tours are available by prior
arrangement.

☞ museum: adults £1.50,
senior citizens & children 60p;
brewery tour: extra charge
◑ all year Mon-Fri 10-4.30,
Sat-Sun 11-4.30
Facilities: 🚌 🍴 🅆🅲 🚗 ♨
★ Mar-Oct summer 'steam-ups'
on Bank Hols
🍴 restaurant serves lunches &
teas & has a wide selection of
food; beer & lager on sale in bar

• **The kitchen at the Black Country Museum**

🏠 Map 2 E2
**The Black Country
Museum**
Tipton Road, Dudley,
West Midlands DY1 4SQ
Tel. Birmingham (021) 5579643

*From Dudley follow A4037
northwards for 1 mile to
museum on right. Signposted.*

This open-air museum,
recreating life in industrial
Britain, first started taking
shape in 1975 and now covers
26 acres. Many authentic
buildings have been re-
assembled here and staff wear
19thC costume. Exhibits
include a farm, mill, pub, coal-
fired bakery, a grocer's shop, a
colliery and 5 domestic kitchens
in period houses. Also planned
are a brewery, sweet shop, fish
and chip shop and a baker's.
There are also narrow-boat
rides, trams and the world's
first steam engine.

☞ adults £3.00, senior citizens
£2.50, children £2.00, family
ticket (2 adults & 3 children)
£8.50

◑ all year daily 10-5 or dusk
Facilities: 🚌 🍴 ♿ 🅆🅲 🚗 ♨ 🅰
🍴 variety of food, including
regional specialities like faggots
& peas, is available in Stables
Restaurant; local real ale sold in
pub

🛏 Map 2 E3
Boscobel House
Brewood, Staffordshire
Tel. Brewood (0902) 850244

*From Wolverhampton follow A41
north westwards, after 9 miles
turn right at Tong Norton onto
unclassified road for 4 miles to
house. Signposted.*

This timber-framed hunting
lodge was built in the 17thC
and later turned into a
farmhouse. English Heritage
has reconstructed the building
and visitors can see the dairy
and cheese room with
equipment on display.

☞ adults £1.25, senior citizens
95p, children 60p
◑ Apr-Sep daily 9.30-6.30; Oct-
Mar Mon-Sat 9.30-4, Sun 2-4
Facilities: 🅆🅲 🚗 ♨

MAP 2 — CENTRAL ENGLAND

Map 2 D5
The Bread Bin
72 Shropshire Street, Market Drayton, Shropshire TF9 3DG
Tel. Market Drayton (0630) 2795

In town centre.

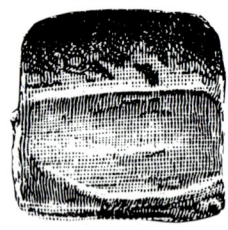

This specialist food shop and bakery draws its inspiration from a number of sources, both continental and British. As well as bread pudding, butter buns, Robert Clive cakes, biscuits and novelty interpretations of traditional gingerbread, they also bake a wide range of European, especially German-style, pastries.
● all year daily 8.30-5.30; closed Mon, Tue 1-2 & Bank Hols

Map 2 F6
The Brindley Mill
Mill Street, Leek, Staffordshire
Tel. Leek (0538) 381446

From Leek follow A523 north westwards for 1 mile to mill on right. Signposted.

A fully operational water-powered corn mill dating from 1752 which stands in a garden by the River Churnet. The mill houses the James Brindley Centre, which contains information concerning the life and work of the famous canal builder whose workshop was nearby. Displays and artefacts illustrate the history of milling and small quantities of flour are ground from wheat and barley.

☞ adults 70p, senior citizens & children 30p
● Easter-Oct Sat, Sun, Bank Hols 2-5; Jul-Aug Mon, Tue, Thur 2-5; or by appointment
Facilities: 🚌

Map 2 D5
Browns of Drayton
23 High Street, Market Drayton, Shropshire TF9 4NR
Tel. Market Drayton (0630) 2264

In town centre.

No pre-packed goods are sold in this traditionally run grocery shop; emphasis is laid on personal customer service. As well as being the principal stockists of Market Drayton Gingerbread they also sell most groceries, specialities being bacon, coffee and cheese — including Appleby's Hawkstone Cheshire.
● Tue-Sat 8.30-5.30, ½ day Mon & Thur
Facilities: 🚌

Map 2 D3
Chadwell Mill
Chadwell, Nr Newport, Shropshire TF10 9BG
Tel. Newport (0952) 70578

From Newport follow A41 southwards, after 3½ miles turn left onto unclassified road for ½ mile to Chadwell. Signposted.

This red brick mill has been carefully restored by its owner

to working order and now produces stoneground wholemeal flour. It is unusual in that it uses natural spring water from St Chad's Well instead of water from a stream. Visitors are welcome to look round the mill and to attend demonstrations. Stoneground flour is sold in 1.5 and 32Kg bags.

☞ adults 80p, senior citizens & children (over 5) 40p
● Mar-Oct Sun, Bank Hols & School Hols 11-5.30
Facilities: 🚌 🍴 📷 📶 🚗 🐕
🍴 teas served with generous portions of homemade food including cakes & biscuits using mill's own flour & spring water

Map 2 D1
Claybury Mill
Cleobury Mortimer, Shropshire DY14 8QG
Tel. Cleobury Mortimer (0299) 270034

In town centre.

Restoration of Claybury Mill should be finished by March 1988 when it will be in full working order as part of a museum of milling and arable farm implements. Stoneground flour will be for sale to visitors.

☞ adults £1.00, senior citizens & children 50p
● see local press for details
Facilities: 📶

Map 2 H1
Coventry City Farm
1 Clarence Street, Hillfields, Coventry, West Midlands CV1 4SS
Tel. Coventry (0203) 25323

From city centre follow Trinity Street north eastwards for ¼ mile into White Street and Victoria Street, then turn left into Clifton Street, then right into Albert Street to farm on right.

This lively and interesting farm is situated in the middle of Coventry. Visitors are welcome to visit the farm and to buy the

MAP 2

organic vegetables grown here and the free-range eggs, goats' milk and cheese that are produced.

☞ free — donations welcome
◗ all year daily 10-4
Facilities: ☕ ♿ 🚻 🚗 🍽 ⚠

⊙ Map 2 C3
Cressage Bakery
Shrewsbury Road, Cressage,
Shropshire SY5 6DS
Tel. Cressage (095289) 239

From Shrewsbury follow A458 south eastwards for 8 miles to Cressage.

All bread and cakes are made in the original 'homebaked' style. Visitors can view the bakehouse and see the traditional methods and equipment including 'peel' ovens. The bakery was highly commended in a Rank Hovis competition for its wholemeal bread. A full range of breads, confectionery and cream cakes are on sale.

☞ free
◗ all year Mon-Sat 6.30-8.00
Facilities: ☕ 🚻 🚗

⊙ Map 2 E3
Essington Fruit Farm
Bognop Road, Essington,
Staffordshire WV11 2BA
Tel. Wolverhampton (0902) 735724

From Wolverhampton follow A460 northwards, after 3 miles turn right into Bognop Road for 1 mile to farm on left. Signposted.

This 35-acre pick your own farm has a wide range of fruit and vegetables including most varieties of berries and their hybrids — tayberries, marionberries and tummelberries. A good selection of vegetables is also available, specialities being courgettes, mangetout and spinach. Free-range eggs are for sale.

◗ Jul-Aug daily 9-9; Sep-Jun Fri-Sun 9-9
Facilities: 🚻 🚗 🍽

⊙ Map 2 G3
Fairclough's Caravan Self Pick
Watling Street, Hints,
Nr Tamworth,
Staffordshire B78 3DW
Tel. Shenstone (0543) 480984

From Tamworth follow A453 westwards, after 1 mile turn right onto A5 for 3 miles to Hints. Signposted.

250 acres of pick your own featuring strawberries, raspberries, gooseberries, loganberries, tayberries, black and redcurrants, beans, onions, calabrese, peas, cauliflowers and potatoes. Soft drinks are also sold.

◗ end Jun-Jul telephone for times
Facilities: 🚗 🍽

❧ Map 2 E6
Fold Garden
26 Fold Lane, Biddulph,
Staffordshire ST8 7SG
Tel. Stoke-on-Trent (0782) 513028

From Tunstall follow A527 northwards for 3 miles to Biddulph, continue for 1 mile then turn right into Fold Lane for ¼ mile to gardens on left.

An introductory talk prepares visitors for the guided tour of the gardens, taking in over 200 varieties of culinary, medicinal and old-fashioned scented herbs. A shop on the premises sells all the garden's herb plants as well as 5oz jars of mustard and 1lb jars of jam made from traditional recipes.

☞ free
◗ all year daily by appointment
Facilities: 🚻 🚗

🐓 Map 2 D5
Fordhall Farm
Tern Hill, Market Drayton,
Shropshire TF9 3PS
Tel. Tern Hill (063083) 255

From Market Drayton follow A53 westwards, after 2½ miles turn left to farm. Signposted.

This has been an organic grassland farm for over 40 years. All the animals are reared and fed to comply with the standards set by the Soil Association's organic symbol. The fully organic permanent pastures consist of a large mixture of grasses, herbs, meadow flowers and wild plants which help to produce the flavour of the beef, lamb, pork, veal, chicken and goose, all of which can be bought here. A fresh spring supplies the needs of the house, stock and dairy. There is also a farm walk and a nature trail where flowers and wildlife can be seen.

☞ free
◗ all year daily during daylight hours
Facilities: ♿ 🚻 🚗 🍽 ⚠

🐓 Map 2 D3
Hadley Park Farm
Leegomery, Telford,
Shropshire TF1 4QE
Tel. Telford (0952) 3677

From Wellington follow A442 northwards, after 1 mile turn right onto unclassified road for 1½ miles to Leegomery. Signposted.

A dairy farm which gives milking demonstrations in the summer and also has a farm trail. Visitors will see the farmyard animals — goats, pigs, calves, chickens and ducks. The farm shop sells milk products made from the farm's own pedigree herd of Friesian cows. On offer are 15 flavours of ice cream, 6 varieties of yoghurt, cream, milk, ice cream cakes, jam, goats' milk and sauces as well as locally made honey, organic flour, cheeses and apple juice.

☞ free
◗ shop: May-Oct daily 10-7; Oct-May daily 10-6; milking: May-Oct daily 3.30-4.30; trail: May-Oct daily 10-5
Facilities: 🍴 🚻 🚗 🍽
🍴 cream teas & ice cream

MAP 2   CENTRAL ENGLAND

☺ Map 2 B3
Hayford Farm Fruit and Veg
Birch Grove, Westbury,
Nr Shrewsbury,
Shropshire SY5 9PE
Tel. Shrewsbury (0743) 884859

From Shrewsbury follow B4386 westwards for 8½ miles to farm. Signposted.

Set in the Shropshire countryside this 20-acre pick your own fruit and vegetable farm also has a herd of pedigree Ayrshire cattle producing fresh cream. Pick your own includes strawberries, raspberries, gooseberries, red and blackcurrants, peas, broad and runner beans and mangetout. Also available are carrots, cauliflowers, cabbages, potatoes and calabrese.
◗ all year daily 10-8
Facilities: 🚻 🚗 ☕

🏠 Map 2 G4
Heritage Brewery Museum
Anglesey Road, Burton-upon-Trent, Staffordshire DE14 3PF
Tel. Burton-on-Trent (0283) 69226

In town centre.

Built in 1881 this brewery, now a museum, still produces Burton ale in the traditional manner. Organised tours of the working exhibits show a very open process of brewing with old coppers and wooden vats. A recently restored original brewery steam engine drives the old malt mill. A blacksmith and cooper can be seen at work on selected days. For a souvenir, buy a pint of beer in the brewery's specially moulded Victorian bottles, cork-topped to allow the beer to mature.
☞ £2.50 including a pint of beer
◗ all year by appointment
Facilities: 🍵 🚻 🚗

● **The Heritage Brewery Museum**

💰 Map 2 D5
The Krusty Loaf
3 High Street, Market Drayton, Shropshire TF9 1DY
Tel. Market Drayton (0630) 2924

In town centre.

"If we can't make it ourselves we don't sell it" boast the owners of the Krusty Loaf, a bread and cake shop. At the rear of their small shop is a bakery which turns out high quality bread — white, 100% wholemeal, granary and German rye. Small groups can be shown around the premises and watch the baker at work.
◗ all year Fri-Tue 7.30-5, Thur 7.30-1.30; tours by appointment
Facilities: 🍵

🍖 Map 2 G1
A W Lashford and Son
18 St John's Way, Shopping Precinct, Knowle, Nr Solihull, West Midlands B93 0LE
Tel. Knowle (05645) 4989

From Solihull follow A41 southwards for 3 miles to Knowle.

This family butcher, established in 1889, has received 38 awards in the last 7 years for its 14 varieties of sausage. These include the Gloucester sausage — a fresh prime English pork sausage flavoured with a mixture of spices and herbs; the royal sausage — produced to commemorate the Royal Wedding and accepted as a wedding gift by their Royal

MAP 2

Highnesses the Prince and Princess of Wales; beef and horseradish — a prime English beef sausage seasoned with 6 spices including ground horseradish root and a gluten-free sausage made using only prime English pork and rice bran. Fresh meats, home-cooked meats and pies are also available.

● all year Mon-Sat 7-5.30, Fri 7-6.00
Facilities: 🚗

🏠 Map 2 D3
The Lawns
Church Street, Broseley, Shropshire TF12 5DG
Tel. Telford (0952) 882557

From Much Wenlock follow B4376 eastwards, after 3 miles turn left onto B4373 for 1/4 mile, then turn left into Church Street for 1/4 mile to house on left. Signposted.

The Lawns, now the private home of the Berthoud family, houses one of the largest collections of English pottery and porcelain on permanent display in a private house. The collections are shown in the setting of a fine 18thC house which was once the home of John Rose, the founder of the Coalport china works. Many examples of china may be seen in the house including a collection of over 1,000 teacups. An exhibition, 'Tea for Three', traces the history of tea and tea drinking in England from the 17thC to the present day. It features a 19thC room setting in which a Victorian lady presides over the tea table. In the Great Kitchen visitors may view the open bar grate fitted with smoke-jack, period furniture, a laundry and a dairy.

☞ tour: £2.00
● Apr-Oct Thur-Sun, Bank Hols 11-5 or by appointment
Facilities: 🚾 🚗
★ illustrated talks, study sessions & seminars

🐄 Map 2 C2
Reg May Butchers
South Road, Ditton Priors, Nr Bridgnorth, Shropshire WV16 6SH
Tel. Ditton Priors (074634) 628

From Shipton follow unclassified road south eastwards for 3 miles to Ditton Priors.

This well-established butcher cures his own bacon and hams and makes his own hand-raised pork pies, game pies and faggots. Visitors are welcome to tour the bakehouse.

● all year Mon-Fri 8-5.30, Sat 8-1.30
Facilities: 🚾

SHREWSBURY BISCUITS

Found in many local bakeries these biscuits were traditionally made with a little rose water. Nowadays this is usually left out, but the flavours of caraway seeds and dry sherry make Shrewsbury biscuits a delicious local speciality.

🏠 Map 2 E4
The Mill at Worston
Great Bridgeford, Stafford, Staffordshire ST18 9QA
Tel. Stafford (078575) 710/711

From Stafford follow A5013 north westwards, after 4 miles turn right onto unclassified road for 1/4 mile to Worston. Signposted.

This pub and restaurant incorporates a milling museum which features the mill wheel and machinery as well as agricultural implements.

☞ free
● 9-midnight by appointment
Facilities: 🍽 🚾 🚗 /🏠
🍽 licensed restaurant serving lunches, teas & dinners with the accent on homemade fish, game & vegetarian dishes

☺ Map 2 E3
Moors Farm and Country Restaurant
Chillington Lane, Codsall, Nr Wolverhampton, Staffordshire WV8 1QH
Tel. Codsall (09074) 2330

From Wolverhampton follow A41 north westwards, after 4 miles turn right onto unclassified road through Codsall towards Chillington Hall for 2 miles to Moors Farm.

A mixed farm selling fruit, potatoes, poultry, eggs, homemade preserves, cakes, chutney and Christmas puddings from its shop.

● all year by appointment
Facilities: 🍽 & 🚾 🚗 🐂 /🏠
🍽 restaurant serves freshly cooked meals from food produced on farm & also provides vegan & vegetarian menus

🌿 Map 2 E3
Moseley Old Hall
Moseley Old Hall Lane, Fordhouses, Wolverhampton, Staffordshire WV10 7HY
Tel. Wolverhampton (0902) 782808

From Wolverhampton follow A449 northwards, after 4 miles turn right onto unclassified road for 1 mile to hall. Signposted.

This historic house, once a refuge for Charles II after the Battle of Worcester, has an original herb and knot garden in which only 17thC plants are grown. The room containing the bed in which King Charles slept is also open to the public.

☞ adults £1.80, children 90p, family ticket £5
● 12 Mar-26 Jun, 17 Sep-30 Oct Sat, Sun 2-6; 29 Jun-11 Sep Wed, Sun 2-6, Bank Hols & following Tues 2-6 (except 3 May)
Facilities: 🍽 & 🚾 🚗 🐂

MAP 2   CENTRAL ENGLAND

⌣ Map 2 G3
The Old Stables Farm Shop
Packington Moor Farm, Packington, Lichfield, Staffordshire WS14 9QA
Tel. Shenstone (0543) 481223/ 481259

From Tamworth follow A51 north westwards for 4½ miles to Packington. Signposted.

This pick your own farm has vegetables, fruit and eggs all year round. The shop sells local farmhouse cheeses, free-range eggs, cream and pâtés as well as homebaked farm kitchen fare.
● PYO: end Jun-early Aug daily 10-8; shop: summer Tue-Sun 9.30- 6; winter Tue-Sat 9.30-6, Sun 9.30-12.30
Facilities: 🍺 🚾 🚐 ⛺ ⛰

🍺 Map 2 E2
The Park Inn
Holdens Brewery, George Street, Woodsetton, Nr Dudley, West Midlands DY1 4LW
Tel. Wolverhampton (0902) 880051

From Wolverhampton follow A4123 southwards, after 4 miles turn right onto A457 for ¼ mile, then turn left into George Street to pub on right, with brewery behind.

One of the few remaining traditional family breweries in the Midlands, this company started as a single brewery pub in 1915 and now has 18 pubs and a brewery. The inn can be visited during normal licensing hours and beer unique to the Midlands, as well as lager and spirits, can be bought. Visitors can also tour the brewery.
☞ by arrangement
● tours by appointment
Facilities: 🍺 🚾 🚐

⌣ Map 2 F4
Pasturefields Fruit Farm
c/o Green Farm, Weston, Stafford, Staffordshire ST18 0JA
Tel. Weston (0889) 270760

From Stafford follow A518 north eastwards, after 5 miles turn right onto A51 for 1½ miles to farm on left. Signposted.

A wide variety of strawberries and raspberries is available here for pick your own enthusiasts. Organic manures are preferred to chemicals and the crops are laid out to make picking as easy as possible. The shop also sells many other fruits and vegetables as well as local cream and free-range eggs.
● end Jun-mid Aug daily 9.30-8.30
Facilities: 🍺 🚾 🚐 ⛺

RESTAURANT RECIPE

♟ Map 2 C3
OLD POLICE HOUSE
Castle Court, off Castle Street, Shrewsbury, Shropshire SY1 2BG
Tel: Shrewsbury (0743) 236200

In town centre.

A converted Victorian police station and jail which is surprisingly cosy and comfortable. One of the features of this restaurant is its wide selection of English cheeses.
● Mon-Fri Meals: 12-1.45, 7-9.45.
Price range £2.00-12.00, Set L £5.00, £9.00, Set D £11.95
Seats 35
Cards: Access, Visa
Facilities: ♟ ♨

HARE AND PHEASANT PIE

1 saddle of hare cut into 1 inch cubes
breasts of a pheasant
1 glass dry white wine
¼ tsp nutmeg grated
measure of brandy
2oz butter
4 tbsps veal or game stock (from bones of hare and pheasant)
bouquet garni
4 sticks celery cut into 4-inch strips
10 juniper berries
pastry:
4oz wholemeal flour
2oz butter
2oz lard or vegetable fat
pinch of salt
egg to glaze

Heat oven to gas 2 (300F, 150C). Brown the hare in 1oz butter, add the white wine and 2tbsp stock and simmer for 15 minutes. In another pan, brown the pheasant breasts in the remainder of the butter, pour on the brandy and flame. Add 2tbsp stock and herbs and poach gently for 10 minutes. Cut the pheasant into cubes and mix with the hare in a pie dish. Reduce the juices from the game by half and pour over. Add the juniper berries and celery. Meanwhile make the pastry in the usual way and roll it out to cover the pie, decorating with the trimmings. Brush the surface with beaten egg and bake for 1½ hours.

MAP 2

Map 2 C4
Pimhill Farm and Mill
Lea Hall, Harmer Hill,
Shrewsbury,
Shropshire SY4 3DY
Tel. Bomere Heath (0939)
290342

From Shrewsbury follow A528 northwards for 5 miles to Lea Hall on right. Signposted.

A family-run organic farm set around an Elizabethan manor house in the heart of the Shropshire countryside. Alarmed at the increasing use of chemicals, the family turned to organic farming more than 30 years ago. They have since built up a thriving herd of pedigree Ayrshire cattle as well as sheep and pigs and grow wheat and oats of the best quality. The mill is modern but traditional millstones are used for grinding the organic wheat. Visitors to the farm are able to buy from a wide variety of organic flour and cereals, as well as a range of farm produce such as jams, biscuits, free-range eggs, chickens and ice cream.

☞ free
◗ all year Mon-Fri, Bank Hols 9-6, Sat 9-12.30
Facilities: ⬛ ⛐ ⛾

Map 2 F2
Sandwell Park Farm
Salters Lane, West Bromwich,
West Midlands B71 4BG
Tel. Birmingham (021) 5530220

From West Bromwich town centre take Reform Street north into Lloyd Street for ¹/₂ mile, turn right into Salters Lane to farm on right. Signposted.

This working farm and museum dates back to the beginning of the century. Visitors can see demonstrations of rural crafts and inspect historic farming equipment. A tea room has been built into the old farmhouse, which retains its original features.

☞ free
◗ all year daily 10-4.30
Facilities: ⛲ ♿ ⬛ ⛐ ⛾ ⛧
⛲ teas served with homemade cakes

Map 2 F2
Sarehole Mill
Cole Bank Road, Hall Green,
Birmingham, West Midlands
Tel. Birmingham (021) 7776612

From Birmingham follow A34 southwards, after 5 miles turn right into Cole Bank Road for ¹/₄ mile to mill on right.

Sarehole is an outstanding example of an 18thC water-powered mill and was restored to full working order in the 1960s. One of the 2 water wheels is regularly operated when there is enough water in the millpond. The process of corn grinding can be followed on all 3 floors of the mill and in an adjoining building there is a reconstruction of a blade grinding workshop. The granary contains displays of local agriculture and rural life and across the yard is a 19thC bakehouse. Stoneground flour from another mill is sold on the premises.

☞ free
◗ 19 Mar-30 Oct daily 2-5

Map 2 F1
Selly Manor Museum
Sycamore Road, Bournville,
Birmingham,
West Midlands B30 1UB
Tel. Birmingham (021) 4720199

From Birmingham follow A38 southwards, after 2 miles turn left towards Bournville on A4040 for ¹/₂ mile, then turn left into Sycamore Road for 100 yards to museum on left at corner with Maple Road.

This fascinating 14th to 16thC half-timbered house has a 17thC kitchen and dining room, complete with an excellent collection of furniture and implements. Outside there is a garden containing herbs and plants introduced into Britain before 1800 as well as a number of native species.

☞ free
◗ mid Jan-mid Dec Tue-Fri 10-5; closed Bank Hols
Facilities: ⛐ ⛾

● **Selly Manor**

MAP 2   CENTRAL ENGLAND

♥ Map 2 C4
The Sett
Village Farm, Stanton upon
Hine Heath, Shrewsbury,
Shropshire SY4 4LR
Tel. Shrewsbury (0939) 250391

*From Shrewsbury follow A49
northwards, after 3 miles take
right fork onto A53 for 6 miles
then turn left onto unclassified
road for 1 mile to Stanton upon
Hine Heath. Signposted.*

Visitors are assured of a warm
welcome when they arrive at
Village Farm, situated in the
centre of Stanton upon Hine
Heath, a village mentioned in
the Domesday Book and
situated in one of the most
beautiful areas of Shropshire.
Over the years the farm's
attractions have proved to be
extremely popular, in particular
the children's activities and the
Ministry of Agriculture-devised
farm trail with small animals
which visitors can handle.
Potatoes in 55Kg bags are for
sale in season.

☞ adults £1.00, children (under
14) 50p
● Easter-Sep Fri-Sun, Bank Hols
2-5 or by appointment
Facilities: ⬤ ⬤ ⬤ ⬤ ⬤ ⬤
⬤ cream teas served

● **Tamworth pigs at Shugborough Park Farm**

🍲 Map 2 F4
Shugborough
Milford, Nr Stafford,
Staffordshire ST17 0XB
Tel. Little Haywood (0889)
881388

*From Stafford follow A34
eastwards, after 1½ miles turn
left onto A513 for 3 miles to
house entrance on left.
Signposted.*

Shugborough's 900-acre estate,
the ancestral home of Lord
Lichfield, offers visitors a chance
to see the Mansion,
Staffordshire County Museum,
Park Farm with its 19thC
farmhouse and working corn
mill and beautiful parklands and
gardens including a herb
garden. Of particular interest
are the fully restored working
kitchens which have been
returned to the time of the
1880s complete with copper
sinks, brass taps, pine tables
and dressers and a gigantic
polished black range. At Park
Farm, a working museum,
traditional recipes and methods
of farmhouse cooking, butter
and cheese-making and bread-
baking are all demonstrated
using the original equipment in
authentic surroundings.
'Shugborough Gold' cheese,
made with milk from the
estate's livestock, is on sale.

☞ mansion, museum & farm:
adults £4.00, senior citizens &
children (over 5) £2.00, family
ticket (2 adults & 2 children)
£8.00
● Apr-Sep daily 11-5; Oct-Dec
daily 11-4; open Bank Hols
Facilities: ⬤ ⬤ ⬤ ⬤ ⬤ ⬤
★ demonstrations from the
Farmhouse Cookbook. Dec:
Christmas at Shugborough —
evenings of seasonal festivities
& traditional food
⬤ lunches, teas & dinners are
served in licensed restaurant
with emphasis on traditional
homebaking & cooking

🏠 Map 2 E5
**Staffordshire Organic
Cheese**
New House Farm, Acton,
Newcastle-under-Lyme,
Staffordshire ST5 4EE

*From Newcastle-under-Lyme
follow A53 southwards, after 3
miles turn left onto A5182 and
immediately right onto
unclassified road for ¼ mile to
Acton.*

● **Longhorn cattle, Shugborough Park Farm**

MAP 2

Cheese-making began on this 86-acre farm in 1984 using unpasteurised milk from cows fed on naturally grown pastures. The cheese is made by traditional methods using no chemicals and contains non-animal rennet for the benefit of vegetarian customers. Ice cream is also made on the premises, again with natural ingredients only. Visitors can buy cheese, plain or with herbs, yoghurt, ice cream, vegetables and free-range eggs. Farm tours by arrangement. All produce is weighed to customers' requirements except the ice cream which comes in cones, tubs, 0.5 and 1 litre packs.

🍓 free
● all year Tue, Thur, Fri, Sat 9-6
Facilities: 🚾 🚗

😊 Map 2 D4
The Strawberry Farm
Lubstree Park, Wellington,
Telford, Shropshire TF2 8LW
Tel. Telford (0952) 607975

From Newport follow A518 south westwards, after 4 miles turn right at roundabout in Donnington onto unclassified road for 1½ miles to Lubstree Park. Signposted.

A pick your own farm selling strawberries, raspberries, potatoes and more unusual vegetables such as mangetout and dwarf beans. The shop sells speciality ice cream and dried flowers.
● all year daily 9-7
Facilities: 🚾 🚗 🛝

🗡 Map 2 D5
Tern Fisheries
Broomhall Grange, Peatswood,
Market Drayton,
Shropshire TF9 2PA
Tel. Market Drayton (0630) 3222

From Market Drayton follow A53 eastwards for ½ mile to fisheries on right. Signposted.

This is the largest fish farm in Shropshire and Staffordshire, situated on the county boundary and using the high quality water from the River Tern. The farm produces rainbow trout for visitors to fish or buy. Fish are also smoked on the premises over oak sawdust and no artificial colouring or preservatives are used. The shop sells fresh and smoked rainbow trout and salmon all year round.

🍽 adults £1.50, children 50p
● May-Oct daily 10-5
Facilities: ♿ 🚾 🚗 🛝 🏧

📖 Map 2 B4
Wackley Farm
Burlton, Shrewsbury,
Shropshire SY4 5TD
Tel. Cockshutt (093922) 660

From Burlton follow A528 north westwards for 1 mile to Wackley. Signposted.

This sheep, dairy and arable farm produces ewes' milk, cheese and potatoes which are all for sale to visitors.
🍽 free
● all year daily 9-5
Facilities: 🚗

🐓 Map 2 B1
The Wernlas Collection
Green Lane, Onibury,
Nr Craven Arms,
Shropshire SY7 9BL
Tel. Bromfield (058477) 318

From Ludlow follow A49 north westwards, after 5 miles turn right onto unclassified road for ¼ mile to Onibury. Signposted.

A living museum of rare breeds of poultry set in a 10-acre site overlooking some of the most spectacular scenery in Shropshire. More than 50 pure breeds of large fowl are on display, as well as other rare breeds of farm animals. Fresh eggs are for sale.
🍽 adults £1.35, children (over 4) 60p
● 2 Apr-Oct Tue-Sun, Bank Hols 10.30-5.30
Facilities: 🚾 🚗 🛝

🍺 Map 2 B2
The Wood Brewery
The Plough Inn, Wistanstow,
Craven Arms,
Shropshire SY7 8DG
Tel. Craven Arms (05882) 2523

From Craven Arms follow A49 northwards, after 1½ miles turn left onto unclassified road for ¼ mile to Wistanstow. Signposted.

A small independent brewery which brews a range of traditional beers from Herefordshire hops. These include cask-hopped Parish Bitter, Wood's Wonderful Warmer for the winter and Christmas Cracker, a full bodied bitter, as well as their popular Special Bitter. Visitors are welcome to tour the brewery by appointment. Beer is on sale in the Inn or can be bought in 2 gallon polypins to take away.
🍺 telephone for details
● by appointment
Facilities: ♿ 🚾 🚗

😊 Map 2 G2
Woodhouse Farm
Catherine-de-Barnes Lane,
Solihull,
West Midlands B92 0DJ
Tel. Birmingham (021) 7043096

From Solihull follow B4102 eastwards, after 2½ miles turn left onto B4438 for ½ mile to farm on left.

A pick your own farm covering 400 acres with strawberries — including a freezer variety — gooseberries, raspberries, blackcurrants, broad and stick beans, calabrese, new potatoes, cabbage, salads, cauliflower and mangetout. Free-range eggs, ready-picked produce and frozen cream are also available from the shop.
● PYO: end Jun-early Aug daily 10-7; shop only: Aug-mid Feb Wed, Thur 9.30-2, Fri, Sat 9.30-4, Sun 10-2
Facilities: 🚾 🚗

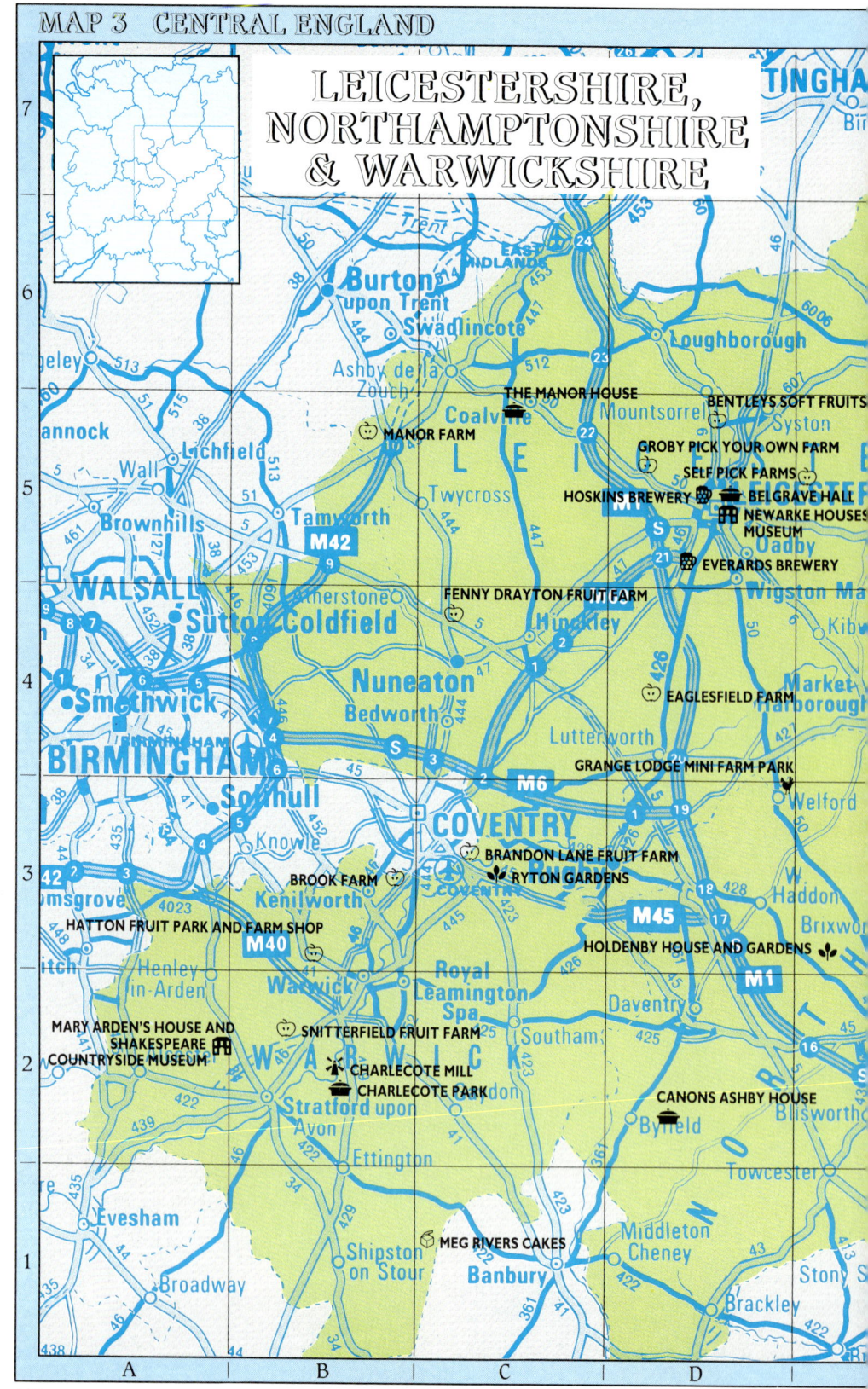

MAP 3   CENTRAL ENGLAND

LEICESTERSHIRE, NORTHAMPTONSHIRE & WARWICKSHIRE

TINGHA

Burton upon Trent
Swadlincote
Ashby de la Zouch
Coalville
MANOR FARM
THE MANOR HOUSE
Loughborough
Mountsorrel
BENTLEYS SOFT FRUITS
Syston
GROBY PICK YOUR OWN FARM
SELF PICK FARMS
Twycross
HOSKINS BREWERY
BELGRAVE HALL
NEWARKE HOUSES MUSEUM
Oadby
EVERARDS BREWERY
Wigston Ma
Lichfield
Wall
Brownhills
Tamworth
FENNY DRAYTON FRUIT FARM
Hinckley
Market Harborough
Kibw
Nuneaton
Bedworth
EAGLESFIELD FARM
Lutterworth
GRANGE LODGE MINI FARM PARK
Welford
Solihull
Knowle
COVENTRY
BRANDON LANE FRUIT FARM
RYTON GARDENS
Haddon
Brixwor
Brook Farm
Kenilworth
HATTON FRUIT PARK AND FARM SHOP
HOLDENBY HOUSE AND GARDENS
Henley-in-Arden
Warwick
Royal Leamington Spa
Daventry
MARY ARDEN'S HOUSE AND SHAKESPEARE COUNTRYSIDE MUSEUM
SNITTERFIELD FRUIT FARM
Southam
CHARLECOTE MILL
CHARLECOTE PARK
CANONS ASHBY HOUSE
Stratford upon Avon
Byfield
Blisworth
Ettington
Towcester
Evesham
MEG RIVERS CAKES
Middleton Cheney
Shipston on Stour
Banbury
Stony S
Broadway
Brackley

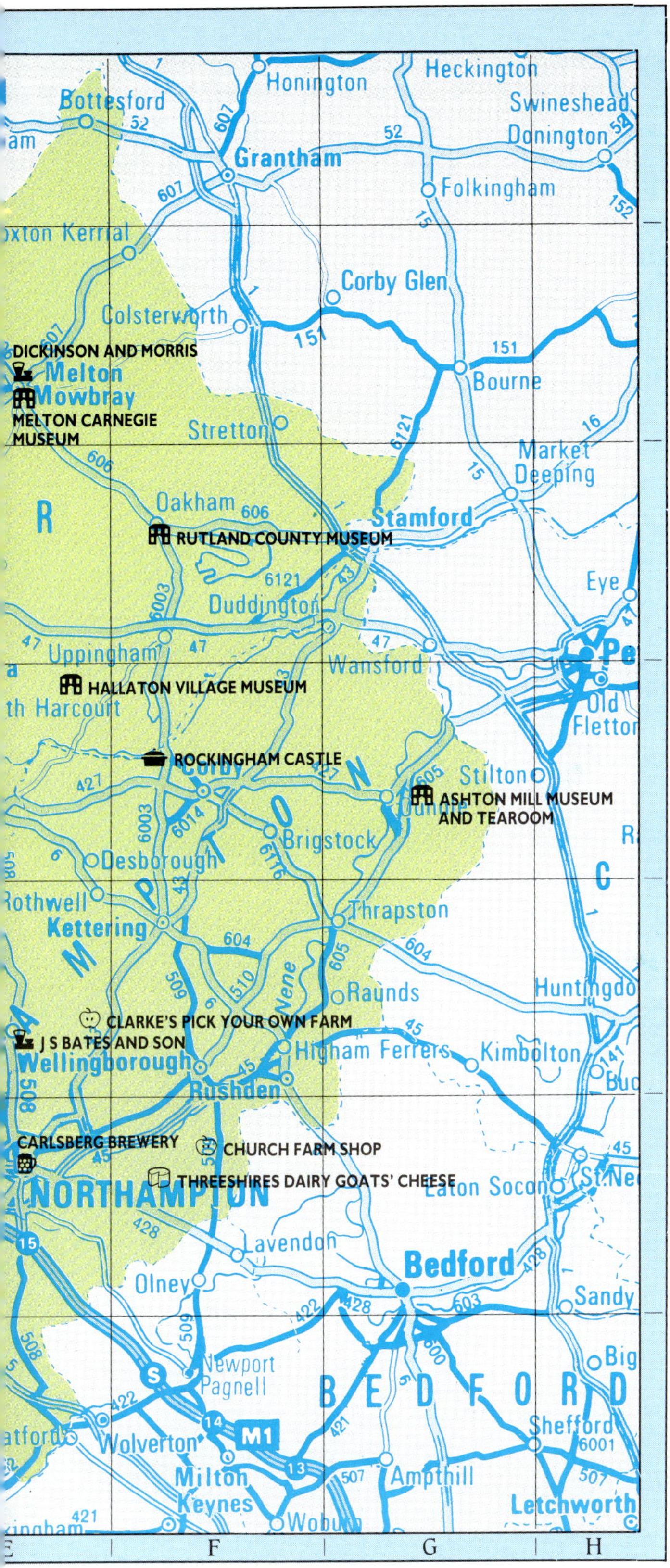

Map

Honington · Heckington · Swineshead
Bottesford · 52 · 52 · Donington · 54
Grantham · Folkingham · 152
607 · 15
xton Kerrial · Corby Glen
Colsterworth · 151

DICKINSON AND MORRIS
Melton · 151 · Bourne · 16
Mowbray · Stretton · Market
MELTON CARNEGIE · 6121 · Deeping
MUSEUM · 606 · 15
R · Oakham 606 · Stamford · Eye
RUTLAND COUNTY MUSEUM · 6121
Duddington
5003 · 6121
47 · Uppingham · 47 · 47 · Wansford · Pe
a · 47
th Harcourt · **HALLATON VILLAGE MUSEUM** · Old
Fletton
427 · **ROCKINGHAM CASTLE** · N
Corby · Stilton · R
6014 · 6003 · **ASHTON MILL MUSEUM** · C
508 · 6 · Brigstock · 6116 · **AND TEAROOM**
Desborough · 6
Rothwell
Kettering · Thrapston
604
509 · 510 · 605 · 604 · Huntingdo
M · Raunds · 45
CLARKE'S PICK YOUR OWN FARM · 45
J S BATES AND SON · **Higham Ferrers** · Kimbolton · Buc
Wellingborough · 45
508 · **Rushden**
CARLSBERG BREWERY · 45 · **CHURCH FARM SHOP**
THREESHIRES DAIRY GOATS' CHEESE · Eaton Socon · St Ne
NORTHAMPTON · 45
15 · 428 · Lavendon
Bedford
Olney · Sandy
422 · 428 · 603 · Big
508 · 500
Newport · S
Pagnell
422 · 14 · M1 · 421 · Shefford · 6001
Wolverton · 13 · 507
Milton · 507 · 507
Keynes · Woburn · **Letchworth**
421

E · F · G · H

Apparently Blue Stilton cheese was first made at Quenby Hall in Leicestershire. But it was sent by the housekeeper to a relation who ran the Bell Inn at Stilton in Cambridgeshire, a famous coaching inn. He served it to his customers who liked it so much that they promptly called it after the local village and the name stuck. Daniel Defoe, when he first tasted it, wrote that it was "brought to table with the mites and maggots round it so thick, that they bring a spoon for you to eat the mites with, as you do the cheese". Nowadays production is tightly controlled and Stilton is only made at certain creameries in Leicestershire, Nottinghamshire and Derbyshire.

Map 3 G4
Ashton Mill Museum and Tearoom
Ashton, Peterborough, Cambridgeshire PE8 5LD
Tel. Oundle (0832) 72264

From Oundle follow A605 north eastwards, after ½ mile turn right onto unclassified road for 1 mile to Ashton. Signposted.

Part of a conservation village within an estate, the museum contains mill and farming machinery from the turn of the century to the present day. A display of mounted fish caught locally and an old forge give a fascinating glimpse of the area's rural life.

free
all year by appointment
Facilities:
small tea room offers fresh, homemade fare including cream teas, cakes & sandwiches

MAP 3　　　CENTRAL ENGLAND

Map 3 E3
J S Bates and Son
105 Northampton Road,
Brixworth, Northamptonshire
Tel. Northampton (0604)
880226

In village.

These butchers specialise in
making Brixworth pâté to their
own recipe using chicken livers,
garlic and sherry. They cook
their own hams and make pork
sausages to a family recipe.
They also make game pies and
a range of fish pâtés including
crab, smoked mackerel and
smoked salmon. A selection of
cheeses is on sale and includes a
local goats' cheese and
farmhouse Stilton and Cheddar.
There is also a branch of Bates
in Market Harborough,
Leicestershire.
● all year Mon-Fri 7-5.30,
Sat 7-2

Map 3 D5
Belgrave Hall
Church Road, Belgrave,
Leicester, Leicestershire
Tel. Leicester (0533) 666590

*From Leicester follow A46
northwards, after 1½ miles turn
left onto A6 for ½ mile to
Belgrave.*

This Queen Anne house was
built in 1709-13 and, as well as
containing much period
furniture, also possesses an
early 19thC kitchen. There is a
dairy in the stable block, a herb
and water garden and displays
of agricultural implements and
coaches. A wide selection of
herbs are for sale.
☞ free
● all year Mon-Sat 10-5.30,
Sun 2-5.30

Map 3 D5
Bentleys Soft Fruits
Loughborough Road, Wanlip,
Leicester, Leicestershire
Tel. Leicester (0533) 673702

*From Mountsorrel follow A6
southwards for 2½ miles to farm.*

All soft fruits are sold on a pick
your own basis or ready-picked
on this 15-acre farm. Cream
and ice cream are also available
in the shop.
● end Jun-early Aug daily 10-7
Facilities: WC 🚗 ☕

Map 3 C3
Brandon Lane Fruit Farm
Brandon Lane, Coventry,
Warwickshire CV3 3GW
Tel. Coventry (0203) 305782

*From Coventry follow A423 south
eastwards, after 3 miles join A45
at Tollbar End roundabout, then
turn immediately left at Shell
petrol station onto unclassified
road for 200 yards to farm on
left. Signposted.*

A pick your own farm with
strawberries, raspberries, red
and blackcurrants, tayberries,
gooseberries, plums, apples,
pears, blackberries and a large
selection of field vegetables and
asparagus. Eggs, tomatoes, fruit
juices and honey are for sale in
the shop.
● May, Sep-Christmas daily
10-6; Jun-Aug daily 10-8;
late night opening Thur
Facilities: ♿ WC ☕

Map 3 B3
Brook Farm
Stoneleigh Road,
Gibbet Hill, Coventry,
Warwickshire CV4 7AB
Tel. Coventry (0203) 410292

*From Coventry follow A46
southwards, after 3 miles turn
right and follow signs to
University of Warwick onto
unclassified road to farm on left
immediately after Westley
Bridge.*

A 20-acre pick your own farm
selling strawberries,
raspberries, gooseberries, red
and blackcurrants, tayberries
and blackberries. The farm
shop also has vegetables, herb
plants, free-range eggs, cream,
ice cream, honey, apples, plums,
pears, house plants, apple
juices, salads and preserves.

● end Jun-mid Aug daily 10-8;
mid Aug-end Jun 10-5.30
Facilities: WC 🚗 ☕

Map 3 D2
Canons Ashby House
Canons Ashby, Nr Daventry,
Northamptonshire NN11 6SD
Tel. Blakesley (0327) 860044

*From Weedon Bec follow A5
southwards for 3 miles, turn right
onto B4525 for 6½ miles to
Canons Ashby. Signposted.*

This 16thC manor house is
owned by the National Trust
and set in a 70-acre park. It has
a number of treasures including
a fine historic kitchen.
☞ adults £2.00, children £1.00
● Apr-Oct Wed-Sun, Bank Hols
1-5
Facilities: 🍴 WC 🚗 ☕
🍴 teas served with homemade
scones, tea-breads, biscuits,
tarts & cakes

Map 3 E2
Carlsberg Brewery
140 Bridge Street,
Northampton,
Northamptonshire NN1 1PZ
Tel. Northampton (0604)
234333

In town centre.

Special one-hour tours of the
brewery take place twice a day
and guests may refresh
themselves afterwards by
tasting the Carlsberg lager.
☞ free; minimum age 10 years
● all year Mon-Fri 9.15 & 2.15 by
appointment; closed Bank Hols
Facilities: WC 🚗

Map 3 B2
Charlecote Mill
Hampton Lucy, Warwick, Warwickshire CV35 8BB
Tel. Stratford-upon-Avon (0789) 842072

From Stratford-upon-Avon follow A46 northwards, after 2 miles turn right onto unclassified road for 2 miles to Hampton Lucy.

This 18thC mill is situated on the site of an earlier mill — which was originally mentioned in the Domesday Book and valued at 6s 8d. In 1978 John Bedington started restoring the mill with the help of numerous friends and Birmingham millwright Bob Atkins who repaired the west water wheel at the expense of the BBC for their film of 'The Mill on the Floss'. The mill is now in use for the production of wholemeal flour, principally from high quality, organically grown English wheat.

☞ mill: adults 80p, children (5-16) 30p; shop: free
◐ by appointment

Map 3 B2
Charlecote Park
Wellesbourne, Warwickshire CV35 9ER
Tel. Stratford-upon-Avon (0789) 840277

From Stratford-upon-Avon follow B4086 eastwards, after 4 miles turn left onto B4088 for 1 mile to Charlecote. Signposted.

Charlecote Park, an Elizabethan house with 19thC Elizabethan revival interiors, is owned by the National Trust. It has a fully-equipped Victorian kitchen and an historic brewhouse, as well as a landscaped park where William Shakespeare was caught poaching deer. Visitors can follow the park trail and look out for the flock of Jacob sheep and herds of red and fallow deer. The shop sells the National Trust's own fudge, honey, conserves, mustard, teas and a range of local foods.

☞ adults £2.50, children (5-17) £1.25, family ticket (2 adults & 3 children) £7.00
◐ 2 Apr-Oct Tue-Wed, Fri-Sun, Bank Hols 11-6
Facilities:
coffees, lunches & teas served in Orangery include homemade soups & salads, homebaked cakes & cream teas

Map 3 F2
Church Farm Shop
Strixton, Wellingborough, Northamptonshire NN9 7PA
Tel. Wellingborough (0933) 664378

From Wellingborough follow A509 southwards for 5 miles to Strixton. Signposted.

The shop belonging to this 1,000-acre farm sells a complete range of organically

• **Baking Day, Warwickshire, 1872**

MAP 3   **CENTRAL ENGLAND**

grown vegetables as well as beef, lamb, pork and poultry reared without any harmful chemicals. Game, farmhouse cookery, jams, cakes, pickles, mushrooms, honey, cheeses, collect your own eggs and hampers filled with fresh produce are also for sale. Visitors can see the livestock and baby animals and watch educational videos.
● all year Mon-Fri 9-6, Sat 9-5
Facilities: 🚾 🚗

☺ Map 3 E3
Clarke's Pick Your Own Farm
Hanington, Nr Northampton, Northamptonshire
Tel. Northampton (0604) 781256

From Kettering follow A43 southwards, after 5 miles turn right at Oasis Inn onto unclassified road for 1 mile to Hannington. Signposted.

A pick your own farm with strawberries, raspberries, blackcurrants, gooseberries, broad beans, runner beans, potatoes, onions, carrots, beetroot, swedes and courgettes. Fishing facilities are also available.
● Jul-end Aug daily 10-8; end Aug-1 Oct Sat, Sun
Facilities: 🚾 🚗 🍽 🏧

🐖 Map 3 E6
Dickinson and Morris
10 Nottingham Street, Melton Mowbray, Leicestershire LE13 1NW
Tel. Melton Mowbray (0664) 62341

In town centre.

The famous hand-raised Melton Mowbray pork pies have been baked and sold on these premises for over 100 years. The shop also sells homemade sausages, bread and cakes including the world-famous Melton Hunt Cake.
● all year Mon-Sat 8.30-5

☺ Map 3 D4
Eaglesfield Farm
Main Street, Leire, Lutterworth, Leicestershire LE17 5HF
Tel. Leire (0455) 209647

From Lutterworth follow A426 northwards, after 4 miles turn left onto unclassified road for 1½ miles to Leire. Signposted.

This farm was first established as a poultry business in 1914 and has pick your own fruit and vegetables including raspberries, strawberries, red and blackcurrants, broad beans and sweet corn. The shop sells ready-picked fruit, vegetables, eggs, cream, poultry, venison, rabbits and trout from a trout farm 400 yards away.
● shop: May-Oct Mon-Fri 9-1, 2-5.30, Sat 9-12, Sun 10-12.30; PYO: Jun-Sep daily 9-8
Facilities: 🚾 🚗 🍽

REGIONAL RECIPE

TOMATO CHUTNEY

An excellent regional chutney to accompany the local pork pies.

4lb ripe tomatoes sliced
3 large onions sliced
1lb brown sugar
¼lb salt
1oz mixed whole cloves, cinnamon and peppercorns tied in a muslin bag
½ tsp cayenne
½ pint vinegar

Put the tomatoes, onions, sugar, salt, pickling spice and cayenne into a large saucepan. Pour over the vinegar and bring to the boil. Simmer gently for 1½ hours, stirring to prevent burning. Pour into sterilised jars and cover.

🍺 Map 3 D5
Everards Brewery
Castle Acres, Narborough, Leicester, Leicestershire LE9 5BY
Tel. Leicester (0533) 891010

From Leicester follow A46 southwards for 3 miles to Castle Acres Industrial Estate. Signposted.

A traditional family-owned brewery with one of the most up to date production and processing plants in Europe. Visitors are welcome to tour the brewery and watch a video on beer production. The shop sells draught ales, bottled and canned beers and also wines and spirits.
🚌 tour: £2.00 including souvenir pot of 'old original' mustard & 2 pints of Everards ale to be sampled in one of their local pubs
● all year Mon-Thur tours at 10.45 by appointment, closed Bank Hols
Facilities: 🚾 🚗

☺ Map 3 C4
Fenny Drayton Fruit Farm
Lodge Farm,
Fenny Drayton, Nuneaton, Warwickshire CV13 6BH
Tel. Atherstone (0827) 712172

From Nuneaton follow A444 northwards, after 3 miles turn right immediately after crossing A5 to farm. Signposted.

Fifty acres of this 300-acre farm have been turned over to pick your own produce, including gooseberries, raspberries, strawberries, red and blackcurrants, tayberries, blackberries, rhubarb, loganberries, mangetout, beans, peas and plums. The shop sells ready-picked fruit and vegetables, fresh or frozen. There is also a farm trail.
● all year daily 9-8.30; 1-29 Sep daily 9-6
Facilities: 🍴 🚾 🚗 🍽 🏧

🌾 Map 3 D3
Grange Lodge Mini Farm Park
Naseby Road, Welford, Northamptonshire NN6 7HZ
Tel. Welford (085881) 625

MAP 3

From Welford follow A50 northwards, after 1/4 mile at edge of village turn right into Naseby Road for 400 yards to farm. Signposted.

A 7½-acre farm of small paddocks and pens dedicated to the preservation of rare breeds. Animals, all of which visitors may touch and feed, include Shetland ponies, Dexter and Jersey cows, sheep, pigs, goats, rabbits, guinea pigs and 18 types of poultry. An old walled garden has organically grown fruit and vegetables and fishing is available on the reservoir. Visitors may tour the farm, see the production of clotted cream and, during the season, between March and July, watch chicks and ducklings hatch in the incubator. Free-range eggs are for sale.

☞ adults 90p, senior citizens & children (2-14) 50p
◑ Mar-Oct daily 10.30-6; Nov-Feb Sat, Sun 10.30-6 or dusk
Facilities: ⊞ ⅃ 🆆🅲 🚗 ⛺ ⯑
⅃ teas with organically grown homecooked food: scones, jams & cakes with lashings of clotted cream

---

☺ Map 3 D5
Groby Pick Your Own Farm
The Old Hall, Groby, Leicestershire LE6 0FL
Tel. Leicester (0533) 876626

From Leicester follow A50 north westwards, after 4 miles turn right in Groby into Newton Linford Lane to farm. Signposted.

Situated on the edge of Charnwood Forest and near Bradgate Park, the stately home of Lady Jane Grey, this pick your own farm has a wide range of

fruit and vegetables. The specialities are mangetout, blueberries, tayberries, calabrese and courgettes. Frozen vegetables, honey, jams, eggs, cream and dried flowers are also available. A reservoir has fishing facilities for carp and tench, pony rides are available and there is also an Iron Age farmstead where visitors can experience life as it was 2,000 years ago.
◑ Jul-Aug daily 10-8; Sep Mon-Fri 2-6, Sat, Sun 10-6
Facilities: ⊞ ⅃ 🆆🅲 🚗 ⛺ ⯑
★ Jul Shire horses Jul-Aug Iron Age farmstead
⅃ tea barn serves homemade cakes, scones, biscuits & ice cream

---

🏠 Map 3 E4
Hallaton Village Museum
Hog Lane, Hallaton, Market Harborough, Leicestershire LE16 8UE
Tel. Hallaton (085889) 216

From Uppingham follow B664 south westwards, after 2 miles turn right onto unclassified road for 3 miles to Hallaton.

A small village rural life museum with displays of dairy and butcher's equipment and baking and home cooking items all of which were once used in and around the village.
☞ free
◑ 2 May-24 Oct Sat, Sun 2.30-5 or by appointment
Facilities: ⅃ ⯑

☺ Map 3 B3
Hatton Fruit Park and Farm Shop
Stud Farm, Hatton, Warwickshire CV35 8XB
Tel. Warwick (0926) 843411

From Warwick follow A41 north westwards for 3 miles to Hatton. Signposted.

Built by the descendants of Sir Richard Arkwright, inventor of the Spinning Jenny, this farm now has 16 acres turned over

to pick your own, with strawberries, white, red and blackcurrants, gooseberries, loganberries, tayberries, rhubarb, peas, broad beans, mangetout, spinach, carrots and beetroot. The shop also sells exotic fruit, coffee beans, teas, English and continental cheeses, handmade pork pies, local honey and preserves. There is a craft centre and 2 farm trails.
◑ shop & cafe: Feb-Dec daily 9-5.30; PYO: late Jun daily 10-7
Facilities: ⊞ ⅃ 🆆🅲 🚗 ⛺ ⯑
⅃ cafe offers lunch & light refreshments

PORK PIES

Real, old-fashioned pork pies may still be found at Dickinson & Morris in Melton Mowbray. The distinctive taste may be traced to the pigs which are fed on whey, a by-product of the locally produced Stilton.

🍀 Map 3 E3
Holdenby House and Gardens
Holdenby, Northampton, Northamptonshire NN6 8DJ
Tel. Northampton (0604) 770241

From Northampton follow A50 northwards, after 4 miles turn left onto unclassified road through Church Brampton to Holdenby. Signposted.

This historic house has herb and kitchen gardens and rare breeds of farm animals. Refreshments can be taken in the original Victorian kitchen which still has the old range and other period equipment. The shop sells herb plants and locally made fudge and preserves.
☞ house: adults £2.50, children £1.00; grounds: adults £1.50, children 75p
◑ 3 Apr-Jun, Sep Sun 2-6; Jul-Aug Thur, Sun 2-6; open Bank Hols, or by appointment
Facilities: ⊞ 🆆🅲 🚗 ⛺ ⯑

MAP 3

CENTRAL ENGLAND

🍇 Map 3 D5

Hoskins Brewery

Beaumanor Brewery,
Beaumanor Road, Leicester,
Leicestershire LE4 5QE
Tel. Leicester (0533) 661122

*From city centre follow A5131
Abbey Lane northwards
(following A6 signs), after 1 mile
turn right at Mann Egerton
Garage into Corporation Road,
then left into Beaumanor Road
to brewery on right.*

At the end of the last century
Hoskins Brewery was started at
Hope Cottage, Beaumanor

Road in a brewhouse that was
not much larger than a modern
day living room. From the start
it prospered and soon their
beers became known all over
the country, winning medals at
4 of the Brewers' Exhibitions
between 1922 and 1926. The
Beaumanor Brewery is still in
existence and is operated as a
working museum. Visitors are
welcome to view the brewing
process in one of the country's
last traditional cottage
breweries. Many items are on
display such as 18th and 19thC
coopers' tools, cask branding

irons and a bottle plant from
the 1930s which is still in
working order. A guided tour
also includes a slide
presentation and a meal
accompanied by a pint of
Hoskins bitter.

☞ free to tap room and grist
room

◑ normal licensing hours or by
appointment; tours 11.30 & 7.15
booking essential
Facilities: 🍺 🍴 ♿ 🚻 🚗

● **The Tap Room**

● **The Masking Tun**

● **Fermentation**

🍎 Map 3 B5

Manor Farm

Chilcote, Nr Burton-upon-
Trent, Staffordshire DE12 8DL
Tel. Clifton Campville (082786)
282

*From Tamworth follow A453
north eastwards for 6 miles to No
Man's Heath, then turn left onto
unclassified road for 1½ miles to
Chilcote.*

● **Hoskins Brewery**

MAP 3

A pick your own farm with strawberries, raspberries, gooseberries, blackcurrants and potatoes. Eggs and cream are also for sale.
◐ Jul-Aug daily 10-8
Facilities: 🚾 🚗 ♨ ⚠

🚢 Map 3 C5
The Manor House
Donington-le-Heath,
Nr Coalville, Leicestershire
Tel. Coalville (0530) 31259

From Leicester follow A50 north westwards, after 8 miles turn left at Bardon onto unclassified road for 2 miles to Donington. Signposted.

The Manor House dates from 1280 and is a good example of a first floor hall house, furnished mainly with pieces from the 16th and 17thC. The historic kitchen is particularly interesting and there is also a herb garden.
☞ free

◐ 30 Mar-2 Oct Wed-Sun, Bank Hols & following Tue 2-6
Facilities: 🍽 🚾 🚗

🏠 Map 3 A2
Mary Arden's House and Shakespeare Countryside Museum
Wilmcote, Stratford-upon-Avon, Warwickshire
Tel. Stratford-upon-Avon (0789) 293455

From Stratford-upon-Avon follow A34 northwards, after 2½ miles turn left onto unclassified road for 1 mile to Wilmcote. Signposted.

This is a farmhouse and countryside museum, the centre of which is the carefully restored Tudor farmstead, home of Shakespeare's mother, with its dovecote, cider press and other outbuildings. Neighbouring Glebe Farm has a fully equipped Victorian kitchen, scullery and dairy, a kitchen garden under cultivation and a wide range of farming implements and other equipment associated with country life in the past.
☞ adults £1.40, children 50p
◐ Nov-Mar Mon-Sat 9-4.30; Apr-Sep Mon-Sat 9-6, Sun 10-6; Oct Mon-Sat 9-5, Sun 10-5
Facilities: 🍽 ♿ 🚾 🚗 ♨
🍽 light lunches & teas with homemade cakes served Apr-Oct

🏠 Map 3 E6
Melton Carnegie Museum
Thorpe End, Melton Mowbray, Leicestershire LE13 1RB
Tel. Melton Mowbray (0664) 69946

In town centre. Signposted.

A general museum with interesting displays on two of the famous local delicacies — Stilton cheese and Melton Mowbray pork pies.
☞ free
◐ Easter-Sep Mon-Sat 10-5, Sun 2-5; Oct-Easter Mon-Fri 10-4.30, Sat 10.30-4
Facilities: ♿

● **The kitchen at Mary Arden's House**

117

MAP 3   **CENTRAL ENGLAND**

🏠 Map 3 D5
Newarke Houses Museum
The Newarke, Leicester,
Leicestershire
Tel. Leicester (0533) 554100
In city centre.

One of the attractions in this
social history museum is a
reconstruction of a 1930's
village grocer's shop which had
been run by the same family for
100 years. The shop has its
original fittings, Victorian brass
scales and a large number of
interesting containers, tins,
cartons and flour barrels.

☞ free
◗ all year Mon-Sat 10-5.30, Sun
2-5.30

🕯 Map 3 C1
Meg Rivers Cakes
Main Street, Middle Tysoe,
Warwickshire CV35 0SE
Tel. Tysoe (029588) 799
*From Ettington follow A422
eastwards, after 5 miles turn
right onto unclassified road for 2
miles to Middle Tysoe.*

A small retail bakery known for
its fruit cakes which are cooked
only with ingredients free from
preservatives, colouring or
artificial flavourings. Customers
are welcome to come and taste
the product, meet the famous
cakemaker, Meg Rivers, and
discuss recipes and baking

methods. Six varieties of cake
are sold, ranging in size from 2
to 4lb and varying in price from
£7 to £15. Customers can
arrange to have a cake sent
anywhere in the world. Other
products for sale include
Christmas puddings,
shortbread, mincemeat and
mince pies.

☞ free
◗ all year Mon-Fri 10-4 or by
appointment

🏰 Map 3 F4
Rockingham Castle
Market Harborough,
Leicestershire LE16 8TH
Tel. Rockingham (0536) 770240
*From Corby follow A6116 north
westwards, after 2 miles turn*

*right onto A6003 for ½ mile to
castle on left. Signposted.*

This historic family home
situated in the centre of an
agricultural village and estate
welcomes visitors both to the
house and its grounds. There is
an historic kitchen dating from
the Tudor period and a shop
which sells Rockingham's own
fruit and vegetables and also
jams and preserves.

☞ adults £2.50, senior citizens
£1.80, children £1.10
◗ Easter-Jul, Sep Thur, Sun 2-6;
Aug Tue, Thur, Sun 2-6; Bank
Hols & following Tue 2-6; or by
appointment
Facilities: 🍴 🚻 🚗 🎈
🍴 teas served with special
homemade scones & cakes
baked in village

Bee Garden

● **Ryton Gardens**

MAP 3

⚏ Map 3 F5
Rutland County Museum
Catmos Street, Oakham,
Leicestershire LE15 6HW
Tel. Oakham (0572) 3654

*From Oakham follow A6003
southwards for ¼ mile to
museum. Signposted.*

This museum aims to recreate
the rural life of Rutland during
the 19th and early 20thC. It has
a wide range of agricultural
displays which emphasise
population change, food
production and supply and
food processing. Also on view
are various kitchen and
domestic items.

☞ free
◗ Nov-Mar Tue-Sat 10-1, 2-5;
Apr-Oct Tue-Sun 2-5
Facilities: ⅃ ⅏ ☎

❧ Map 3 C3
Ryton Gardens
The National Centre for
Organic Gardening, Ryton on
Dunsmore, Coventry,
Warwickshire CV8 3LG
Tel. Coventry (0203) 303517

*From Coventry follow A423 south
eastwards, after 2 miles turn left
onto A45 for 2 miles, then turn
left onto B4029 at Ryton for ½
mile to gardens on right.
Signposted.*

"Unique in Britain and possibly
the world" claims Ryton
Gardens. This centre for
organic gardening has 22 acres
which cover every conceivable
subject from herbs, bush and
soft fruit, allotments and
unusual vegetables to wild
flowers, pest control, bee
pollination and much much
more. The shop sells organically
produced vegetables, fruit,
wholefoods, freshly made
bread, scones, quiches and a
wide range of dairy produce
and frozen meat from free-
range organically fed stock. It
also sells unusual seeds.

☞ adults £2.00, senior citizens
& children £1.00, family ticket
(2 adults & children) £4.50 —
tickets can be re-used for free
entry for 1 year
◗ Apr-Sep daily 10-6; Oct-Mar
daily 10-4
Facilities: ☕ ⅃⅃ ⅏ ☎ ☎ ↻ ⚠
★ organic cheese & wine
evening and barbecues
⅃⅃ award winning specialist café
which uses only additive-free
ingredients; vegetarian cooking
plus occasional free-range
organic meat barbecues are
available; special diets catered
for

☺ Map 3 E5
Self Pick Farms
South Croxton Road, Beeby,
Nr Leicester,
Leicestershire LE7 8BH
Tel. Hungarton (053750) 667

*From Leicester follow A47
eastwards, after 3½ miles turn
left onto unclassified road
through Scraptoft and Beeby for
3 miles to farm. Signposted.*

A pick your own farm with all
varieties of soft fruit plus
Worcesterberries, loganberries
and boysenberries. New
potatoes, calabrese, onions,
broad beans and peas are also
for sale and there is a tractor
train.
◗ Jul-mid Aug daily 10-8; mid
Aug-mid Oct Mon-Fri 2-7, Sat,
Sun 10-7
Facilities: ☕ ⚆ ☎ ↻

☺ Map 3 B2
Snitterfield Fruit Farm
Kings Lane, Snitterfield,
Nr Stratford-upon-Avon,
Warwickshire CV37 0QA
Tel. Stratford-upon-Avon
(0789) 731711

*From Stratford-upon-Avon follow
A46 northwards, after 3 miles
turn left onto unclassified road
for 1 mile to Snitterfield.
Signposted.*

A 240-acre pick your own farm
specialising in tayberries,
tummelberries, raspberries,
strawberries, plums, many
varieties of apples, pears, red
and blackcurrants and many
vegetables.
◗ Jun-Jul daily 10-8; Aug-Oct
daily 10-6; Nov-Dec daily 10-4
Facilities: ⚆ ☎ ↻

⚏ Map 3 F2
Threeshires Dairy Goats'
Cheese
The Woodyard,
Castle Ashby, Northampton,
Northamptonshire NN7 1LG
Tel. Yardley Hastings (0933)
664762

*From Northampton follow A428
south eastwards, after 6 miles
turn left onto unclassified road
for 1½ miles to Castle Ashby.*

This flourishing dairy has been
making cheese since 1984. Jill
Woodford, the cheese-maker,
learnt to make goats' milk
cheese as they do in France; the
result is a delicious full-
flavoured creamy cheese. She
sells a wide variety of cheeses,
each one named after a local
village. The most famous is
Castle Ashby, a semi-soft
pyramid, dusted in charcoal and
ripened to form a natural rind.
Visitors are welcome to see the
cheese-making and pick out a
selection. Jillian suggests that
visitors bring their own bread
and wine so that they can picnic
in the Castle Ashby House
grounds.

☞ free
◗ all year Mon-Fri 2.30-5.30,
Sun 10-1 or by appointment
Facilities: ⚆ ☎ ↻

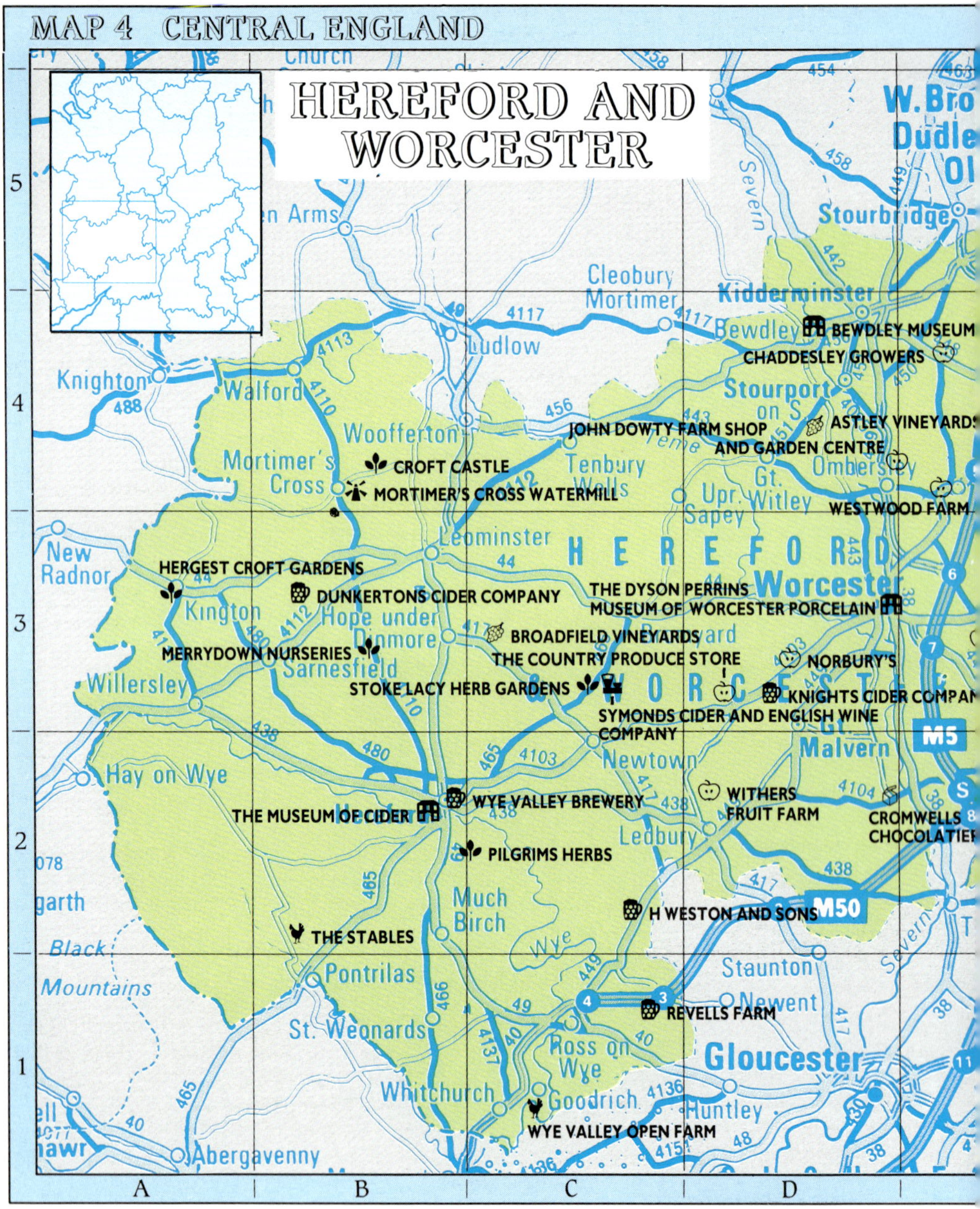

MAP 4 CENTRAL ENGLAND

HEREFORD AND WORCESTER

Church
W. Bro
Dudle
Ol
Stourbridge
n Arms
Cleobury
Mortimer
Kidderminster
4117
Bewdley
BEWDLEY MUSEUM
Ludlow
CHADDESLEY GROWERS
4113
Stourport
on S
Knighton
488
Walford
Woofferton
JOHN DOWTY FARM SHOP
ASTLEY VINEYARDS
AND GARDEN CENTRE
Ombersley
Mortimer's
Cross
CROFT CASTLE
Tenbury
Wells
MORTIMER'S CROSS WATERMILL
Upr. Witley
Gt.
Sapey
WESTWOOD FARM
New
Radnor
Leominster
44
HEREFOR
Worceste
HERGEST CROFT GARDENS
THE DYSON PERRINS
MUSEUM OF WORCESTER PORCELAIN
DUNKERTONS CIDER COMPANY
Kington
Hope under
Dinmore
BROADFIELD VINEYARDS
MERRYDOWN NURSERIES
THE COUNTRY PRODUCE STORE
NORBURY'S
Sarnesfield
Willersley
STOKE LACY HERB GARDENS
KNIGHTS CIDER COMPAN
SYMONDS CIDER AND ENGLISH WINE
COMPANY
Malvern
M5
Hay on Wye
WYE VALLEY BREWERY
WITHERS
FRUIT FARM
4104
THE MUSEUM OF CIDER
CROMWELLS
CHOCOLATIER
Ledbury
PILGRIMS HERBS
078
Much
Birch
H WESTON AND SONS
M50
garth
THE STABLES
Black
Mountains
Pontrilas
Staunton
Newent
St. Weonards
REVELLS FARM
Ross on
Wye
Gloucester
Whitchurch
Goodrich
4136
Huntley
Abergavenny
WYE VALLEY OPEN FARM

A | B | C | D

Here we are in the 'core' of apple country. Every lane you turn down leads to another orchard and every barn you explore houses at least one cider press, even if its cogs no longer turn. You can follow a cider trail throughout the area which will take you to everything from a small family business operating traditional machinery to a large modern commercial unit; details can be found in the local Tourist Information Centres. There is fierce rivalry between this area and the South West as to whose cider — or scrumpy — is superior. Long may the battle continue.

which show how the land has been cultivated and which crops were grown over the centuries. Publications and souvenirs are available.

☞ adults 40p, senior citizens 25p, accompanied children free
● Mar-Nov Tue, Thur-Sat, Bank Hols 10-5, Sun 2-5

☺ Map 4 E4
Ashboroughs Fruit Farm
Burcot Lane, Bromsgrove, Worcestershire B60 1PH
Tel. Bromsgrove (0527) 32318

From Bromsgrove follow A38 northwards, after ½ mile turn right into Burcot Lane for ¼ mile to farm on left. Signposted.

This pick your own farm has 25 acres of strawberries, 15 acres of apples — including Discovery, Cox, Russet, Laxton and Bramley, 5 acres of raspberries and 2 acres of gooseberries, red and blackcurrants. Vegetables are also grown.
● Jul Mon-Fri 10-7.30, Sat, Sun 10-6.30; Sep-Oct Mon-Fri 10-4, Sun 10-5
Facilities: ☕ 🚻 🚗 ♨
☕ charity refreshment stall during strawberry season & at weekends, reduced prices for jam-making at end of season

● **Avoncroft Mill**

✺ Map 4 D4
Astley Vineyards
Astley, Stourport-on-Severn, Worcestershire DY13 0RU
Tel. Stourport (02993) 2907

From Stourport follow A451 southwards, after 3 miles turn left onto unclassified road for ¼ mile to vineyards. Signposted.

This small family-run 4½-acre vineyard produces 4 wines of character from Madeleine Angevine, Kerner, Huxelrebe and Müller-Thurgau grapes. The grapes are pressed and the juice fermented and bottled at the Three Choirs Vineyard in Gloucestershire. Customers are welcome to look around the vineyard and buy the wine by the bottle or case, with discounts for case sales.

☞ free
● shop: all year Mon-Sat 9-5.30, Sun by appointment
Facilities: 🚻 🚗 ♨

🏠 Map 4 E4
Avoncroft Museum of Buildings
Stoke Heath, Bromsgrove, Worcestershire B60 4JR
Tel. Bromsgrove (0527) 31886/ 31363

● **Collecting the flour**

🏠 Map 4 F2
Almonry Museum
Abbey Gate, Evesham, Worcestershire WR11 4BG
Tel. Evesham (0386) 6944

In town centre. Signposted.

This museum contains a varied collection of exhibits from prehistoric times to the present day including Romano-British, Anglo-Saxon, Medieval and monastic remains. There are also agricultural implements

MAP 4

CENTRAL ENGLAND

From Bromsgrove follow A38 southwards, after 1½ miles turn left onto B4091 for ¼ mile to Stoke Heath. Signposted.

Set in 15 acres of Worcestershire countryside, this is a museum where visitors are invited to stroll around the old buildings painstakingly restored by craftsmen. Exhibits include a working windmill producing stoneground flour, a 16thC thatched barn, an 18thC granary, a 17thC dovecote, a sawmill and an icehouse. Stoneground wholemeal flour is for sale in 3.3lb bags. There are wagon rides, a gift shop and a miniature railway nearby.

☞ adults £1.90, senior citizens £1.10, children 95p, family ticket (2 adults & 2 children) £4.95
◗ Jun-Aug daily 11-5.30; Apr, May, Sep, Oct Tue-Sun, Bank Hols 11-5.30; Mar, Nov Tue-Thur, Sat, Sun 11-4.30
Facilities: ♨ ⑩& ⑳ 🚗 ☕ ⛽
⑩ tea-room serves snacks, light lunches & ice cream

🏠 Map 4 D4
Bewdley Museum
Load Street, Bewdley, Worcestershire DY12 2AE
Tel. Bewdley (0299) 403573
In town centre.

● **The hydraulic ram pump at Bewdley**

This museum, housed in a converted 18thC butchers' shambles, has exhibits on the folk-life, crafts and industries of the Wyre Forest. Visitors can see displays of local agriculture and butchery, and a working 18thC brass foundry that made brass jam kettles called maslin pans.

☞ adults 35p, senior citizens & children 15p
◗ Mar-Nov Mon-Sat 10-5.30, Sun 2-5.30

REGIONAL RECIPE

PEAR AND ORANGE CARAMEL

Although this is principally an apple area other fruit - particularly pears - are grown.

2lb firm pears, peeled, cored and quartered
4 large oranges
½ pint water
5oz sugar

Add 3oz sugar to the water and poach the pears gently over a low heat until tender. Place in a serving dish. Peel the rind thinly from two oranges and cut into strips. Cook the rind until tender, drain and set aside. Remove the pith from all the oranges, divide them into segments, mix with the pears and chill. Boil the remaining sugar with 1 tbsp water to make a caramel. Allow to set on an oiled plate then crush into small pieces. Sprinkle over the pears and oranges and garnish with the orange peel.

▭ Map 4 E2
Bredons Norton Dairy Goats
Brookfield Farm, Bredons Norton, Tewkesbury, Gloucestershire GL20 7EZ
Tel. Bredon (0684) 72209/72704
From Tewkesbury follow B4080 northwards, after 5 miles turn right onto unclassified road for ¼ mile to farm. Signposted.

Set in the picturesque village of Bredons Norton, this dairy goat farm, with over 200 goats, produces milk, cheese and yoghurt without additives or preservatives. Visitors may walk around the farm and see cheese-making, the milking plant and the young kids. There are guided tours by arrangement. Products for sale in the farm shop include soft and semi-soft goats' milk cheeses with and without herbs, yoghurt and fresh or frozen goats' milk.

☞ free, small charge for guided tours
◗ by appointment
Facilities: 🚻 🚗 ☕

🍷 Map 4 C3
Broadfield Vineyards
Broadfield Court Estate, Bodenham, Herefordshire HR1 3LG
Tel. Bodenham (056884) 483
From Leominster follow A49 southwards, after 4 miles turn left onto A417 for 2 miles, then turn left onto unclassified road for 1 mile to vineyards.

In 1085 Broadfield was mentioned in the Domesday Book. Successive occupants have added to this large country house and 50 vines were planted in 1972. Reichensteiner is the leading vine grown here — it makes a white wine with real body and local character. Huxelrebe is also grown — although the vines suffered badly during the cold winter of 1982 — along with Müller-Thurgau and Seyve Villard. Broadfield also has old English gardens and 2 dairy farms with 350 cows. Wines are sold in cases of 12 bottles.

☞ £1.50 including tour and winetasting
◗ by appointment
Facilities: ⑩& 🚻 🚗 ☕

MAP 4

Map 4 E4
Chaddesley Growers
1 Potters Park, Chaddesley
Corbett, Kidderminster,
Worcestershire DY10 4QA
Tel. Kidderminster (056283) 461

*From Kidderminster follow A448
southwards for 3½ miles to farm
on left in Chaddesley Corbett.
Signposted.*

Two fields covering 12 acres are
available for pick your own
including strawberries,
gooseberries, raspberries, red
and blackcurrants, tayberries,
rhubarb and broad beans. A
large range of pot-grown
culinary herbs and ready-
picked blueberries are also for
sale.
● mid Jun-early Aug daily 10-8
Facilities: 🚻 🚗 ♨

Map 4 D3
**The Country Produce
Store**
Pullens Farm,
Ridgeway Cross, Nr Malvern,
Worcestershire WR13 5JW
Tel. Ridgeway Cross (088684)
232/599

*From Worcester follow A4103
south westwards, after 12 miles
turn right onto B4220 for ½ mile
to farm on right. Signposted.*

This farm shop sells over 20
varieties of apples and pears as
well as its home-produced
cider and apple juice in 3
varieties: Apple Dew Original
(Cox and Bramley), Bramley
and Egremont made from
Golden Russet apples. Also
available are raspberries,
strawberries, organic herbs,
stoneground flour, country
wines and a wide range of
vegetables. The farm sells
homebaked fruit pies, honey,
preserves and dried flowers.
● all year Mon-Fri 9-5.30, Sat 10-
4, Sun 10-1
Facilities: 🚻 🚗
★ regular demonstrations of
cider & wine-making, complete
with tastings

Map 4 F3
Court House Farm
Atch Lench, Evesham,
Worcestershire WR11 5SP
Tel. Evesham (0386) 870225

*From Evesham follow A435
northwards, after 4 miles turn
left at Harvington Cross onto
unclassified road for 1½ miles to
Atch Lench.*

Customers are welcome to
look around this small goat
dairy farm which sells its own
milk and soft cheese, plain or
herb and garlic.
☞ free
● by appointment

Map 4 B4
Croft Castle
Nr Leominster,
Herefordshire HR6 9PW
Tel. Yarpole (056885) 246

*From Mortimer's Cross follow
B4362 north eastwards, after 2
miles turn left onto unclassified
road for ¼ mile to castle.
Signposted.*

This Welsh border castle is
now owned by the National
Trust. It has a lovely walled
garden containing a vineyard
and a herb garden. A stall sells
fruit, plants and herbs from the
garden. Wine is sold when
available. Visitors can also see
the splendid avenue of
350-year-old Spanish chestnut
trees.
☞ £1.60
● Apr, Oct Sat, Sun, Bank Hols
2-5; May-Sep Wed-Sun, Bank
Hols 2-6
Facilities: ♿ 🚻 🚗 ♨

Map 4 D2
Cromwells Chocolatiers
20 Church Street,
Upton upon Severn,
Worcestershire WR8 0HT
Tel. Evesham (06846) 3926

*From Great Malvern follow A449
southwards, after 3 miles turn
left onto A4104 for 6 miles to
Upton upon Severn.*

Cromwells chocolates have
been made by hand in the
workshop at the rear of this
shop since 1984. Using
imported Belgian couverture,
their range includes mostly
dark chocolates with a few milk
and white and a selection of
cream centres and truffles. Solid
chocolate animals are also on
sale and these include frogs,
mice, cats and dogs and a range
of Christmas gifts. Customers
are invited to visit the
workshop. The shop's
namesake, Oliver Cromwell, is
credited with bringing
chocolate to Great Britain after
he captured the cocoa
plantations in the West Indies
from the Spaniards. Cromwells
have branches in Bath,
Farnham, Waterloo Station and
Glasgow Station.
☞ shop:free; tours: telephone
for details
● Oct-May Mon-Sat 9-1, 2-5.30;
Jun, Jul, Aug daily 9-1, 2-5.30,
tours by appointment

Map 4 F2
The Domestic Fowl Trust
Honeybourne Pastures,
Honeybourne, Evesham,
Worcestershire WR11 5QJ
Tel. Evesham (0386) 833083

*From Broadway follow A46 north
eastwards, after 3½ miles turn
left into Ryknild Street for 2 miles
to Honeybourne. Signposted.*

This living museum of poultry is
an outstanding conservation
centre for all rare breeds of
domestic fowl. The Trust has
about 130 different breeds.
There is also a children's farm
with chicks and young animals,
an adventure playground, tea
room, giftshop and wild
waterfowl. Visitors are able to
buy free-range eggs and
homemade cakes.
☞ adults £1.00, children 50p
● all year Sat-Thur 10.30-5
Facilities: 🍴 ♿ 🚻 🚗 ♨ ⛰

123

MAP 4　　　　　　　　**CENTRAL ENGLAND**

☺ Map 4 D4
John Dowty Farm Shop and Garden Centre
Ombersley, Droitwich,
Worcestershire WR9 OJH
Tel. Worcester (0905) 620230

From Ombersley follow A449 northwards for 1 mile to shop on right. Signposted.

This is Britain's oldest established farm shop, founded in 1921 as part of a 300-acre farm selling direct to the public. All varieties of fruit and vegetable, both home-grown and imported are for sale. Eggs, pot plants, flowers, seeds and Christmas trees are also available.

● all year Mon-Sat 8.30-5.30, Sun 10-5
Facilities: 🚻 🚗 ⛺

🍓 Map 4 B3
Dunkertons Cider Company
Luntley, Pembridge,
Nr Leominster,
Herefordshire HR6 9ED
Tel. Pembridge (05447) 653

From Leominster follow A44 westwards, after 9 miles turn left at Pembridge onto unclassified road for 1½ miles to Luntley. Signposted.

Deep in the Herefordshire countryside is one of the few farms still making their own cider. Here individual varieties of cider apples such as Foxwhelp, Yarlington Mill, Medaille D'or, Sherrington Norman and Goddard are

pressed and fermented separately. No water, preservatives, artificial flavouring or colouring are added. Ciders from single varieties are also produced such as the unique Kingston Black, Court Royal and Breakwells Seedling, as well as a delicious dry perry made from pears. Visitors can taste the products straight from oak casks. On sale are litre bottles of cider and perry, gallon and 1¼ pint stone jars for draught cider, or visitors may bring their own containers.

☞ free
● Apr-Dec Mon-Sat 10-6, Sun 12-2; Jan-Mar Mon-Fri 4-6, Sat 10-6
Facilities: 🚗

🏛 Map 4 D3
The Dyson Perrins Museum of Worcester Porcelain
Severn Street, Worcester,
Worcestershire WR1 2NE
Tel. Worcester (0905) 23221

In city centre.

Worcester porcelain was founded in 1751 by Dr John Wall and this museum houses the largest collection of Worcester porcelain in the world. The collection shows both everyday pieces including a selection of 18thC teabowls and saucers and examples from some of the dinner services made for the Royal Family and European monarchs. The Royal Worcester Porcelain Works is adjacent and a tour offers visitors a fascinating glimpse of the working life of this world famous factory. China and porcelain are on sale in the retail shop and also in the 'seconds' shop.

☞ free
● museum: all year Mon-Fri 9.30-5, Sat 10-5; factory tour: all year Mon-Fri 9.55 & 2; shops: all year Mon-Sat 9-5
Facilities: ⬛ 🍴 🚻 🚗

🍴 restaurant serves buffet lunches & teas with homemade cakes & pastries

---

🍃 Map 4 A3
Hergest Croft Gardens
Kington,
Herefordshire HR5 3EG
Tel. Kington (0544) 230160/ 230218

From Kington follow A44 westwards and turn left immediately onto unclassified road for ½ mile to gardens. Signposted.

An old-fashioned kitchen garden growing a wide range of fruit and vegetables is one of the features here, along with an apple avenue and double herbaceous borders.

☞ adults £1.30, children 60p
● 24 Apr-11 Sep daily 1.30-6.30; 12 Sep-30 Oct Sun 1.30-6.30
Facilities: ⬛ 🍴 🚻 🚗 ⛺
🍴 teas, including scones & Welsh cakes, served on Sun & Bank Hols; set price lunch £3.50, teas £1.40

🍓 Map 4 D3
Knights Cider Company
Crumpton Oaks Farm,
Storridge, Nr Malvern,
Worcestershire WR13 5HP
Tel. Malvern (06845) 4594

From Worcester follow A4103 south westwards for 10 miles to Storridge. Signposted.

Knights make traditional ciders of a high standard and during the autumn cider-making demonstrations are available to all, as well as tastings in the farm shop every day of the week. During the spring there is a stunning blossom walk and visitors can see apple trees in full flower. Cider is sold in ½ and 1 gallon containers. Other produce is pick your own or ready-picked, including strawberries, raspberries, gooseberries, red and

MAP 4

There is a giant herb wheel at Merrydown Nurseries, specialists in growing herbs and cottage garden flowers. The log cabin shop sells container-grown herbs, flowers and vegetable plants as well as a large selection of wholefoods, fruit, vegetables and organically produced bacon.

☞ free
◑ all year daily 10-6; Nov-Feb closed Sun pm
Facilities: ᕃ ⊟

• Knights Cider Company

blackcurrants and tayberries, as well as vegetables, honey, eggs and jams.

☞ free
◑ Apr-Oct daily 10-6.30; Nov-Mar daily 11-5
Facilities: ᵂᶜ ⊟ ♨
★ (spring) blossom walk & (autumn) cider pressing open day

❧ Map 4 B3
Merrydown Nurseries
Bush Bank, Canon Pyon, Herefordshire HR4 8EJ
Tel. Canon Pyon (043271) 688/9

From Hereford follow A438 westwards for 1 mile, then turn right onto A4110 for 8 miles to nurseries behind the Bush Inn in Bush Bank.

❦ Map 4 B4
Mortimer's Cross Watermill
Mortimer's Cross, Nr Leominster, Herefordshire
Tel. Wolverhampton (0902) 765105

From Leominster follow A44 westwards, after 4 miles turn right onto A4110 for 3 miles, then turn right onto B4362 to mill on left. Signposted.

• A 19th century cider mill

MAP 4   CENTRAL ENGLAND

An 18thC sandstone watermill which was grinding animal feed until the 1940s. It has recently been restored by English Heritage to working condition.

☞ adults £1.00, senior citizens 75p, children 50p

◖ Apr-Sep Thur, Sun, Bank Hols 2-6

🏠 Map 4 B2
The Museum of Cider
The Cider Mills, Pomona Place, Whitecross Road, Hereford, Herefordshire HR4 0LW
Tel. Hereford (0432) 54207

From city centre follow A438 westwards, after 1/4 mile turn left into Grimmer Road for 1/4 mile to Pomona Place. Signposted.

The Museum of Cider is housed in a former cider works and tells the story of traditional cider-making through the ages: from how the apples were harvested, milled and pressed on the farm right through to the mechanical production of cider in factories. On display is a 350-year-old French beam press, an old farm cider house with all its equipment in working order and a complete set of travelling cider maker's 'tack' which used to be taken from farm to farm during the

autumn cider-making season. Visitors can watch the resident master cooper making and repairing wooden casks. The original champagne cider cellars have been restored and can be seen with their tiers of bottles where Methode Champenoise was first applied to cider in 1905. The cellars also contain a display of cider production in the late 1920s, complete with presses and machinery for washing, filling, corking and labelling. In the vat-house visitors can see the great oak vats, many dating back to Napoleonic times. In the distillery cider brandy is produced in a 40 gallon pot — this is the first producer of cider brandy in Britain for over 200 years. Royal Cider — the wine of England — and an all apple aperitif and new cider apple liqueur are also produced. These along with cider brandy marmalade and locally made cider and perry are sold in the museum shop which also stocks a wide range of gifts.

☞ adults £1.20, senior citizens & children 90p

◖ Apr-Oct Mon-Sun 10-5.30; Nov- Dec Mon-Fri 1-5; Jan-Mar by appointment
Facilities: 🍽️ 👤 🚻 🚗 🥄

😊 Map 4 D3
Norbury's
Crowcroft, Leigh Sinton, Nr Malvern, Worcestershire WR13 5ED
Tel. Leigh Sinton (0886) 32206/ 33391

From Worcester follow A4103 south westwards for 7 1/2 miles to farm on right.

During July Norbury's Fruit Farm runs a pick your own cherry unit. Then from mid-August to end-October all the most popular varieties of apples are on offer, including Kidd's Orange Red, a good late eating apple which is picked in October and keeps until March. Pears are available for picking mid-September to mid-October. Norbury's also has a reputation for making its own prize-winning cider, perry and fruit wines which visitors are able to see being made during October by appointment. However, there are tastings for passing callers all year round. The farm shop is open during normal licensing hours and sells draught cider and draught perry in 1/2, 1 and 5 gallon containers, bottled cider and perry in 1 litre bottles and apple and white cherry wine in 70cl bottles.

☞ free

◖ cider: all year Mon-Fri 9-1, 2-5; shop: Wed-Fri 2-5.30, Sat, Sun 10-5.30
Facilities: 🚻 🚗 🥄

🌿 Map 4 C2
Pilgrims Herbs
Gate House Farm, Dinedor, Hereford, Herefordshire HR2 6PF
Tel. Hereford (0432) 73382

From Hereford follow A49 southwards, after 1 mile turn left onto B4399, then after 1/4 mile turn right onto unclassified road for 2 miles to Dinedor Cross. Signposted.

MAP 4

This herb nursery grows many varieties of herbs and flowers, for sale either fresh-cut or dried. Produce available at the shop also includes hop shoots, April-May, hop bines in September and homemade herb jellies and relishes.

☞ free
◐ Apr-Oct Tue 10-6
Facilities: 🚻 🚗

🍎 Map 4 C1
Revells Farm
Linton, Ross-on-Wye, Herefordshire HR9 7SD
Tel. Ross-on-Wye (0989) 82270

From Ross-on-Wye follow A449 north eastwards, after 2 miles turn right at roundabout onto B4221 for 3 miles, then turn right onto unclassified road for 1 mile to Linton.

The non-alcoholic apple and fruit juices produced on this farm are made in the traditional way with no preservatives, colouring or sugar added. Their own and locally grown fruit is pressed and bottled immediately. Varieties include Golden Russet (from Egremont Russet apples), Cloudy Apple and Clear Apple (from Cox and Bramley apples), Apple and Blackcurrant, Apple and Blackberry and Apple and Plum. All products carry the

Food From Britain Quality mark. All types of juice are for sale in 680ml green-glass bottles, either singly or in cases of 6. Cider is also produced.

☞ free
◐ by appointment
Facilities: 🚗

ASPARAGUS

Prize asparagus grow in the Vale of Evesham. Look out for them during the season at Evesham market.

😋 Map 4 E3
Spetchley Fruit Farm
Spetchley, Nr Worcester, Worcestershire WR7 4QL
Tel. Spetchley (090565) 639

From Worcester follow A422 eastwards, after 3½ miles turn right onto B4084 for 1 mile to farm on right. Signposted.

A 45-acre pick your own fruit farm selling strawberries, gooseberries, loganberries, raspberries, red and blackcurrants, tayberries, blackberries, plums, apples and damsons. Potatoes and broad beans are also available.
◐ PYO: end Jun-mid Aug; shop: May-Oct telephone for opening times
Facilities: 🍴 🚾 🚗 🍽

🌱 Map 4 B2
The Stables
Abbey Dore Court, Nr Hereford, Herefordshire HR2 0AD
Tel. Golden Valley (0981) 240279

From Pontrilas follow B4347 northwards for 2½ miles to Abbey Dore.

This family-run dairy farm was started in 1967 and now comprises a pedigree Jersey herd and a many-faceted ornamental walled garden. Visitors are welcome to view the Jersey herd and the calves in the stables. Plants, apples,

● **Norbury's cider**

MAP 4   CENTRAL ENGLAND

pears and plums from the
orchard, cream, milk and butter
are for sale.

☞ adults £1.00, children 50p
◑ mid Mar-23 Oct Thur-Tue
11-6; 24 Nov-24 Dec Thur-Tue
11-4
Facilities: ⊪ & ⓌⒸ ☎
⊪ morning coffee, light lunches
& cream teas with Jersey cream,
homemade bread, scones,
cakes & pâté; suppers by
arrangement

5. Cherry Pearmain

6. South Quining

7. Knotted Kernel

❧ **Map 4 C3**
Stoke Lacy Herb Gardens
Stoke Lacy, Bromyard,
Herefordshire HR7 4JH
Tel. Hereford (0432) 820232

*From Hereford follow A465 north
eastwards, after 10 miles turn
right onto unclassified road for ¼
mile to Stoke Lacy. Signposted.*

A herb garden and nursery
with a variety of produce on
offer — all made from home-
grown ingredients. Herb jellies,
vinegars and a variety of herb
teas are on sale, as well as
ointments and lotions, pot-
pourri, dried culinary herbs,
herb plants and seeds. Stoke
Lacy also runs courses on
growing, cooking and using
herbs.

☞ free
◑ all year Mon-Fri 10-4.30
Facilities: ⓌⒸ ☎

🍶 **Map 4 C3**
Symonds Cider and
English Wine Company
The Cider Mill,
Stoke Lacy, Bromyard,
Herefordshire HR7 4HG
Tel. Munderfield (08353) 411

*From Hereford follow A465 north
eastwards, after 10 miles turn
right onto unclassified road for ¼
mile to Stoke Lacy. Signposted.*

Cider has been produced by
the Symonds family at Stoke
Lacy since 1939. All their ciders
are made from genuine

Herefordshire cider apples and
are matured in traditional oak
vats. Cider and perry can be
tasted and are on sale at the
shop.
◑ all year Mon-Sat 9-7

🐓 **Map 4 F3**
Twyford Country Centre
Twyford Farm, Evesham,
Worcestershire WR11 4TP
Tel. Evesham (0386) 6108/2278

*From Evesham follow A435
northwards for 2 miles to farm
on right. Signposted.*

A good day out for the family at
this fruit farm and garden
centre where the attractions
include farm trails, a carp pool
and fishing from the banks of
the River Avon. The farm shop
provides a superb selection of
its own fresh fruit and
vegetables, also preserves,
mustard, biscuits and eggs.

☞ free
◑ Apr-Oct daily 9-6; Nov-Mar
daily 10-5
Facilities: ☕ ⊪ & ⓌⒸ ☎ ♨ ⚠
⊪ country cafe prides itself on
homemade lunches & teas; all
food is grown on farm

🍇 **Map 4 C2**
H Weston and Sons
The Bounds, Much Marcle,
Herefordshire
Tel. Much Marcle (053184) 233

*From Ledbury follow A449
south westwards, after 5 miles
turn right at Much Marcle
onto unclassified road for ½
mile to The Bounds.
Signposted.*

Westons have been making a
traditional cider and perry for
over 100 years and, although
their methods may have
changed, they still remain an
independent family business
whose policy is to offer their
customers a choice of products
of the highest quality. Perry
pear trees, from which the
perry is produced, have been
grown in this part of
Herefordshire since the
Norman Conquest, and are
different from dessert pear
trees. All ciders and perry,
which are matured in old oak
vats, are produced on the
premises and are on sale in the
shop. Tours and tastings take
place twice a week.

MAP 4

free
● tours: Tue, Thur 2-3 by appointment; shop: open longer hours
Facilities: 🚗

☺ Map 4 E4
Westwood Farm
Westwood Park, Droitwich, Worcestershire WR9 0A2
Tel. Droitwich (0905) 774769

From Droitwich follow A4133 westwards, after ¼ mile turn right to farm. Signposted.

Seven acres of this 200-acre farm are turned over to pick your own featuring strawberries, raspberries, gooseberries, courgettes, broad beans and rhubarb.
● Jul daily 10-5
Facilities: 🚗 ♨

☺ Map 4 D2
Withers Fruit Farm
Wellington Heath, Ledbury, Herefordshire HR8 1NF
Tel. Ledbury (0531) 2017

From Ledbury follow A438 northwards, after ½ mile turn right onto B4214 for 1 mile, then turn right onto unclassified road for ½ mile to Wellington Heath. Signposted.

All types of hard and soft fruit are available on this 84-acre pick your own farm. The farm shop also sells ready-picked produce.
● late Jun-Nov daily 9-7
Facilities: ♿ 🚗 ♨

🍺 Map 4 B2
Wye Valley Brewery
The Barrels,
69 St Owen Street, Hereford, Herefordshire HR1 2JQ
Tel. Hereford (0432) 274968

In city centre.

Traditional ales are brewed here in Herefordshire's only brewery. Visitors are welcome to tour the brewery, to taste the beer in the pub attached and to take it home in 4 pint and 1 gallon containers.
free
● by appointment
Facilities: 🍴 ♿ 🚗

♥ Map 4 C1
Wye Valley Open Farm
Goodrich, Ross-on-Wye, Herefordshire
Tel. Monmouth (0600) 892296

From Goodrich follow unclassified road southwards towards Symonds Yat East, after ½ mile turn left onto unclassified road for ¼ mile to farm. Signposted.

An open farm where visitors are encouraged to browse in the traditional farm buildings, see the large collection of rare breeds of chickens, ducks and geese and perhaps enjoy a picnic beside the River Wye. The farm also has a cider press and makes homemade cider, as well as selling jams, cakes, local chutney and honey in the shop.
adults £1.60, children 90p
● Easter-Oct daily 11-6
Facilities: 🍴 ♿ 🚗 ♨

RESTAURANT RECIPE

♥ Map 4 F2
THE HUNTER'S LODGE
High Street, Broadway, Worcestershire WR12 7DT
Tel: Broadway (0386) 853247

In town centre.

A large house famous for its excellent regional cooking, set in a picturesque town.
● Tue-Sun Meals: 12.30-2, 7.30-9.45; closed two weeks in Feb & Aug
Price range £12.00-22.00, Set L £8.50
Seats 55
Cards: Access, Amex, Diners, Visa
Facilities: 🍷 ♿ 🚗

WYE SALMON
FINGERS in dill cream with cucumber puffs

1 lb fresh salmon
juice of a lemon
butter
1 glass dry white wine
fresh dill chopped
salt & pepper

cayenne pepper
1 cup double cream
1 small cucumber deseeded and finely chopped
celery salt
fresh breadcrumbs
puff pastry
1 egg beaten

Heat oven to gas 4 (350F, 180C). Skin and bone the salmon, cut into thin fingers and sprinkle with the lemon juice. Melt a knob of butter in a sauté pan, add the wine, dill, salt, pepper and a pinch of cayenne. Bring to the boil, remove from the heat, add the salmon fingers, cover and poach for about 7 minutes. Drain and place on individual dishes and keep warm. Reduce stock, add the cream, reduce again and pour over the fish. Meanwhile, sauté the cucumber, celery salt and breadcrumbs in a little butter. Roll out the pastry, cut small rounds and place the cucumber mixture in the middle. Cover with a second round of pastry. Brush with egg and bake in a moderate oven until golden.

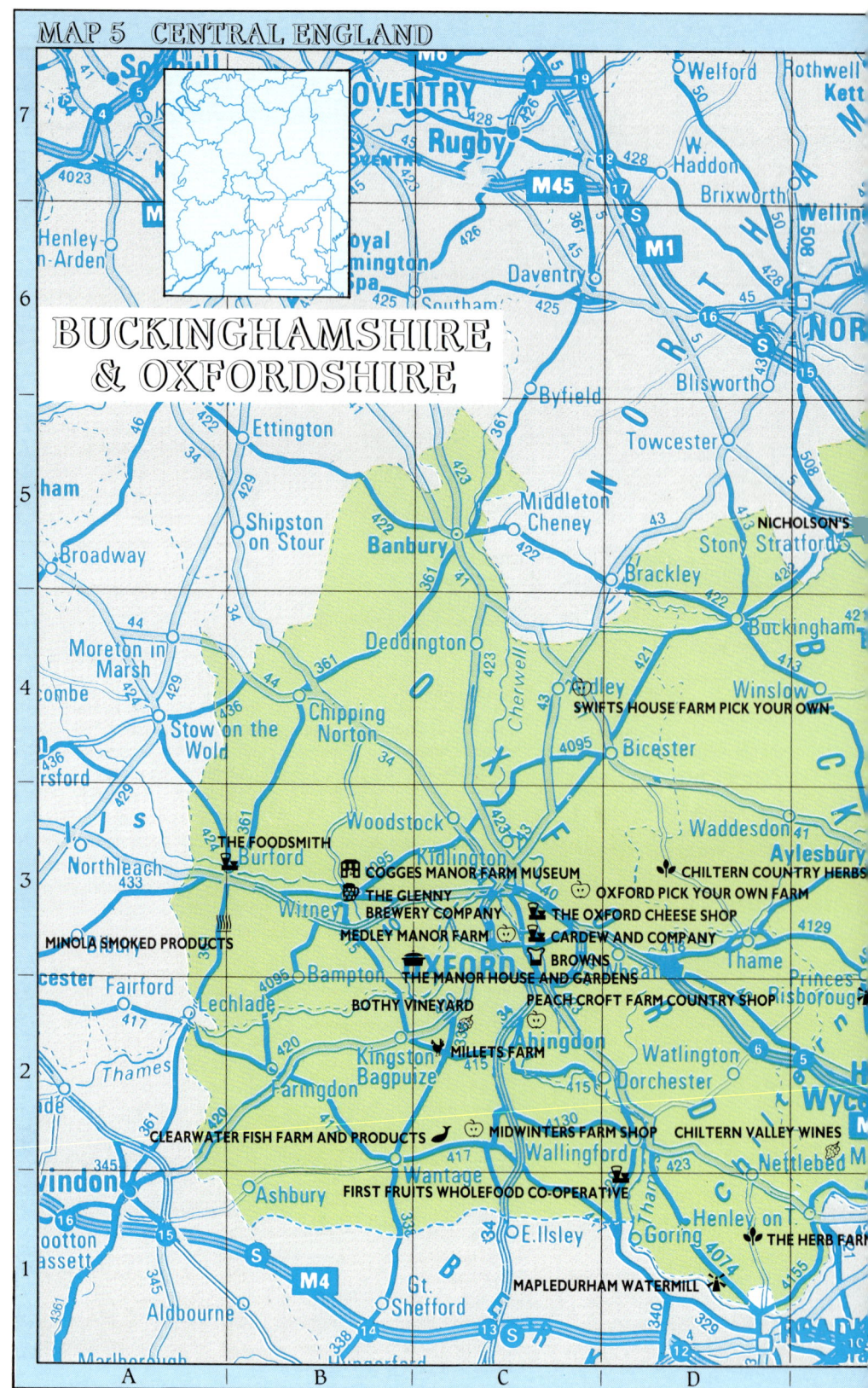

MAP 5 CENTRAL ENGLAND

BUCKINGHAMSHIRE & OXFORDSHIRE

THE FOODSMITH
COGGES MANOR FARM MUSEUM
THE GLENNY BREWERY COMPANY
MEDLEY MANOR FARM
MINOLA SMOKED PRODUCTS
CHILTERN COUNTRY HERBS
OXFORD PICK YOUR OWN FARM
THE OXFORD CHEESE SHOP
CARDEW AND COMPANY
BROWNS
THE MANOR HOUSE AND GARDENS
SWIFTS HOUSE FARM PICK YOUR OWN
NICHOLSON'S
BOTHY VINEYARD
PEACH CROFT FARM COUNTRY SHOP
MILLETS FARM
CLEARWATER FISH FARM AND PRODUCTS
MIDWINTERS FARM SHOP
CHILTERN VALLEY WINES
FIRST FRUITS WHOLEFOOD CO-OPERATIVE
THE HERB FARM
MAPLEDURHAM WATERMILL

Watered by the Thames, this is lush and rolling countryside. It has everything you could possibly want — green pastures, winding rivers, Cotswold stone cottages and, of course, Oxford, 'the city of dreaming spires'. Further north, in Banbury you will find Banbury cakes, one of Britain's oldest sweetmeats. Described in great detail by Gervase Markham in 1615 as oval rough puff pastries filled with butter, nutmeg, currants, peel and minced lamb, they are still made and sold near Banbury Cross.

Map 5 C2
Bothy Vineyard
Bothy Cottage, Frilford Heath, Abingdon, Oxfordshire

From Abingdon follow A415 westwards, after 2 miles turn right at Marcham onto unclassified road for 1 mile, then turn left onto unclassified road for ¼ mile to vineyard on right.

There were vineyards on the Abingdon Abbey estate, which included the parish of Marcham, as long ago as the Middle Ages. The present 3-acre vineyard was planted in 1978 and contains 4,000 vines of 4 different varieties trained on the Guyot system. Exactly which wines are produced depends on the vintage. Visitors are welcome to look around the vineyard and winery and taste the wines. A market garden also grows asparagus, red and blackcurrants, gooseberries and raspberries. Wine is for sale by the bottle or case. Fruit is also on sale.

free
Sat, Sun by appointment
Facilities:

Map 5 E3
Buckinghamshire County Museum
Church Street, Aylesbury, Buckinghamshire HP20 2QP
Tel. Aylesbury(0296) 82158/ 88849

In town centre.

This museum covers a wide variety of subjects and it has a special gallery on Buckinghamshire rural life which includes a display of kitchen equipment, farm tools and machinery. Visitors can also see a collection of Roman and Medieval cooking vessels and equipment.

free
all year Mon-Fri 10-5, Sat 10-12.30, 1.30-5
Facilities:

Map 5 C3
Cardew and Company
131-134 The Covered Market, Oxford, Oxfordshire OX1 3DZ
Tel. Oxford (0865) 242315

In city centre.

Cardew is the only specialist tea and coffee merchant in Oxford. It sells freshly roasted coffee and pure original teas straight from the tea-chests. Tea and coffee-making equipment is also for sale.
all year Mon-Sat 8.45-5; closed Bank Hols

● **Olney pancake race**

MAP 5   CENTRAL ENGLAND

❧ Map 5 F2

Chenies Manor

Chenies, Buckinghamshire
Tel. Little Chalfont (02404) 2888

From Chesham follow B485 eastwards for 4 miles to Chenies.

This is a magnificent manor house, parts of which date back to 1460 although there are some even earlier remains in the form of a 13thC stone crypt. There is a special physic garden containing many hundreds of medicinal, fragrant and culinary herbs. Some of these are for sale.

☞ adults £2.00, children £1.00
● Apr-Oct Wed, Thur 2-5 or by appointment
Facilities: ▮❙ & WC 🚗 ♨
▮❙ homemade teas in the garden room

🍺 Map 5 E3

The Chiltern Brewery

Nash Lee Road,
Terrick, Aylesbury,
Buckinghamshire HP17 0TQ
Tel. Stoke Mandeville (029661) 3647

From Aylesbury follow A413 south eastwards, after 3 miles turn right onto B4009 for 1½ miles to brewery. Signposted.

This is the only working traditional brewery in Buckinghamshire and was the first brewery to be established in the county this century. It is situated on a small farm which keeps cows, sheep and hens. Visitors can tour the brewery and buy the draught beer, a speciality bottled beer to take away and also a beer flavoured mustard.

☞ free
● all year Mon-Fri 9-5
Facilities: WC 🚗

❧ Map 5 D3

Chiltern Country Herbs

Trinity Farm House,
49 Worminghall Road, Oakley,
Nr Aylesbury,
Buckinghamshire HP18 9QU
Tel. Brill (0844) 238020

From Thame follow B4011 northwards, after 6 miles turn left into Worminghall Road for ¼ mile to farm.

An Elizabethan-style herb display garden with special herb seats and also more than 100 varieties of herb plants for sale in 3½ and 5-inch pots, and in decorative terracotta pots. Herb books, posters, seeds and dried herbs are also sold.

☞ free
● all year Mon-Sat 9.30-5.30, Apr-Aug Sun 11-5.30
Facilities: 🚗 ♨

🏛 Map 5 F2

Chiltern Open Air Museum

Newland Park, Gorelands Lane,
Chalfont St Giles,
Buckinghamshire HP8 4AD
Tel. Chalfont St Giles (02407) 71117

● The herb garden, Chiltern Country Herbs

MAP 5

From Chesham follow A416 southwards, after 2½ miles turn left onto A413 for 3 miles, then turn left onto B4442 for ¼ mile, then turn right onto unclassified road for 1 mile to museum.

The museum's motto is 'rebuilding the past for the future', and it features various historic farm buildings from the surrounding area that have been rebuilt on site, including an unusual baker's granary which was used to store flour. Information about food production is provided, while the 'Farming Year' exhibition explains how the land was prepared and sown and the grain harvested both by hand and later by mechanical methods.

☞ adults £1.40, senior citizens £1.00, children 70p
◐ 3 Apr-Oct Wed, Sun, Bank Hols 2-6; Aug Wed-Sun 2-6
Facilities: 📶 🗑 🚗 ♨ ⚠
★ 3 Jul Anglo-American Day with traditional American food & drink
📶 teas with homemade cakes

🐚 Map 5 E2
Chiltern Valley Wines
Hambleden,
Henley-on-Thames,
Oxfordshire RG9 6JW
Tel. Turville Heath (049163) 330

From Henley-on-Thames follow A4155 eastwards, after 3 miles turn left onto unclassified road for 2 miles to vineyard.

Here at the old Luxters vineyard the ancient tradition of vine growing is revived on the slopes of the Hambleden Valley, where some 2,000 years ago the Romans grew vines. The vineyard's winery and bottling facilities are amongst the most modern in Europe. The style of the wine is explained by the ability to achieve a unique quality in the fruit during the cool, temperate English summers. These allow

for slow, steady ripening of the grapes during the longer days of the northern latitude. The milder autumns also contribute to the ultimate quality and ripeness. Natural sugar levels are monitored daily so that the grapes are harvested at their optimum. They are crushed, then pressed immediately but the fermentation is kept cool and slow to preserve the fruitiness. Their aim is to use the latest technology to prevent spoilage but not to interfere with the natural wine-making process. Producer of the English Vineyards Association's 'English Wine of the Year, 1987', this vineyard produces 4 varieties of white wine: dry, reserve, medium dry and a special cuvée, blended from their grapes which include Madeleine Angevine, Bacchus, Reichensteiner and Müller-Thurgau. It is available in bottles and cases. Tours and tastings are available by prior arrangement.

☞ free
◐ all year by appointment
Facilities: ♿ 🗑 🚗

🐟 Map 5 C2
Clearwater Fish Farm and Products
Ludbridge Mill,
East Hendred, Oxford,
Oxfordshire OX12 8LN
Tel. Abingdon (0235) 833732

From Wantage follow A417 eastwards for 3 miles to farm on left.

Visitors can fish for their own trout at this fish farm. There is a smokery which gives tastings on certain days and a shop that offers superb smoked products and champagne. Customers are able to buy fresh and smoked trout, smoked trout pâté — 4oz and 8oz, best Scotch salmon from 4oz to 3lbs and

smoked Scottish wild venison — 8oz and 1lb. Also handmade fresh cream truffle chocolates.

☞ rod & bait 50p
◐ Nov-Mar Tue-Sun 10-5; Apr-Oct Tue-Sun, Bank Hols 10-6
Facilities: 🗑 🚗 ♨ ⚠
★ Spring Bank Hol village enterprise open week

🏠 Map 5 B3
Cogges Manor Farm Museum
Church Lane, Witney,
Oxfordshire OX8 6LA
Tel. Witney (0993) 72602

In town centre. Signposted.

This farming and country life museum is housed in attractive Cotswold stone farm buildings and a manor house dating from the 13th to the 17thC. The house, which has been restored to show how life was lived there 80 years ago, contains 2 working kitchens: a large stone-flagged kitchen with a cast iron range which is used regularly for cooking demonstrations and the back kitchen which has a working bread oven and an open fire for down hearth cooking. Butter is made in the nearby dairy, and vegetables are grown in a walled garden next to a productive apple orchard. The farm buildings have displays and demonstrations of agricultural implements and machinery, as well as a variety of livestock including Berkshire pigs, Shorthorn cattle and sheep which can also be seen grazing in the fields.

☞ adults £1.50, senior citizens & children 80p
◐ 29 Mar-Sep daily 10.30-5.30; Oct-6 Nov daily 10.30-4.30
Facilities: 🍴 📶 ♿ 🗑 🚗 ♨
★ regular cooking demonstrations on farm range, butter-making, sheep-shearing, steam threshing — telephone for details
📶 lunches & teas served with homemade produce

MAP 5 **CENTRAL ENGLAND**

☺ Map 5 F1
Copas Bros
Calves Lane Farm, Billet Lane,
Langley Park, Iver,
Buckinghamshire SLO OLX
Tel. Iver (0753) 651175

*From Slough follow A412 north
eastwards, after 3 miles turn
right into Billet Lane for ½ mile to
farm. Signposted.*

A pick your own farm offering
gooseberries, strawberries,
cherries, raspberries, red and
blackcurrants, plums and broad
beans. The shop sells potatoes,
eggs, apples and Christmas
poultry.
◐ PYO: end Jun-Oct Wed-Sat
2-7, Sun 10-5; shop: Sun 10-1
Facilities: ☕

☺ Map 5 E4
Critchleys
Kings Farm, Stoke Hammond,
Milton Keynes,
Buckinghamshire MK17 9DD
Tel. Critchley (052527) 470

*From Bletchley follow A4146
southwards for 2 miles to Stoke
Hammond. Signposted.*

A 30-acre pick your own farm
with most vegetables and soft
fruits. Ready-picked varieties
include beans, peas, potatoes,
sprouts, onions, beetroot,
sweet corn, raspberries,
strawberries and gooseberries.
Visitors can also see the farm
animals.
◐ all year daily 10-6
Facilities: ♨ ⚏ ☕ ⛺ /⋀

☺ Map 5 F1
Denham Pick Your Own Farm
Hollybush Lane, Denham,
Buckinghamshire
Tel. Denham (0895) 834707

*From Uxbridge follow A4020
northwards, after 1 mile join A40
and follow north westwards for 1
mile through Denham, then turn
left into Hollybush Lane for 1
mile to farm. Signposted.*

A pick your own farm offering a
variety of fruit and vegetables
including mangetout, coriander
and parsley. A selection is also
sold from a shop.
◐ Jun-Aug daily 9.30-7
Facilities: ⚏ ☕ ⛺

OXFORD MARMALADE
Coarse cut with a bitter tang,
Oxford marmalade is famous
throughout the world. Buy it
from Frank Cooper's in the
High.

🍎 Map 5 D1
First Fruits Wholefood Co-operative
2b Honey Lane, Cholsey,
Wallingford, Oxfordshire
Tel. Cholsey (0491) 652444

*From Wallingford follow A329
southwards, after 2 miles turn
right onto unclassified road for
½ mile to Cholsey.*

● **Shrove Tuesday, tossing the pancake**

MAP 5

This wholefood shop run by local Christians helps provide employment for physically and mentally handicapped people. It specialises in mueslies and nuts and stocks a wide variety of other wholefoods, herbs and spices, non-alcoholic drinks and vegetarian pâtés.

● all year Mon-Tue, Thur-Sat 9-5, closed Bank Hols

🐾 Map 5 B3
The Foodsmith
High Street, Burford,
Oxfordshire OX8 4RR
Tel. Burford (0993) 823594

In town centre.

This shop, set in one of the most picturesque villages in the Cotswolds, specialises in high quality Cordon Bleu and vegetarian food. The dishes — many of which are suitable for picnics — are made daily and include vegetarian pâtés, samosas, baked hams, roast beef, chicken dishes, moussaka and a variety of sweets. Local cheeses are also sold.

● all year Mon-Sat 8.30-6, Sun 8.30-1.30
Facilities: 🍽

🐝 Map 5 B3
The Glenny Brewery Company
The Two Rivers Brewery,
Station Lane, Witney,
Oxfordshire OX8 6BH
Tel. Witney (0993) 2574

In town centre.

The Glenny Brewery brews prize-winning traditional draught beers using English malt and hops. Visitors are welcome to tour the brewery and taste the beer. Beer is sold in 4½ gallon polypins.

☞ free
● all year daily 8-4
Facilities: 📶 🚗

OXFORD SAUSAGES

The mixture of veal and pork is not stuffed into skins but simply into a sausage shape.

1 lb lean shoulder pork
1 lb shoulder of veal
1 lb beef suet
½ lb white breadcrumbs
½ lemon, grated rind only
1 tsp nutmeg grated
1 tsp dried sage chopped
pinch each of thyme, savory, and marjoram, chopped
salt & pepper
2 egg yolks
2½ oz butter

Mince or finely chop the pork, veal and beef suet, add the breadcrumbs, lemon rind, nutmeg, sage, thyme, savory, marjoram, salt and pepper. Bind the mixture with the egg yolks. Mix thoroughly and roll into sausage shapes with floured hands. Fry in butter for about 10 minutes, turning to prevent burning.

🌿 Map 5 D1
The Herb Farm
Peppard Road, Sonning Common, Nr Reading,
Berkshire RG9 4NJ
Tel. Kidmore End (0734) 724220

From Reading follow B481 northwards for 4 miles to farm.

This herb nursery has a large display garden including a traditional formal knot garden. Over 200 varieties of culinary and cosmetic herbs are available either ready-cut or in pots and selections can be planted up while visitors wait, according to their requirements. There is also a small collection of antique farm machinery. A shop sells a range of herb products — teas, chutneys, mustards, jellies and vinegars as well as a wide range of kitchen accessories.

☞ free

● 20 Mar-Sep Tue-Sun, Bank Hols 10-5 or by appointment
Facilities: ♿ 🚗 ☕
★ 3rd Sun in Jul Herb Farm Country Fayre

😊 Map 5 F1
Home Cottage Farm
Bangors Road South,
Iver Heath,
Buckinghamshire SLO OBB
Tel. Iver (0703) 653064

From Uxbridge follow A4007 westwards, after 1½ miles turn left at Black Horse Inn in Iver Heath onto unclassified road for ¼ mile to farm. Signposted.

A pick your own farm covering 21 acres with all the usual apple varieties — including Egremont, Blenheim and Lanes Prince Albert — pears, red and blackcurrants, tayberries, raspberries, loganberries and occasional vegetables. Hens, turkeys, guinea fowl, bantams, geese, muscovy ducks, doves and sheep may also be seen.

● all year Mon-Sat 9-4
Facilities: 🚗

🎐 Map 5 E2
Lacey Green Windmill
Windmill Farm, Lacey Green,
Aylesbury, Buckinghamshire

From Princes Risborough follow A4010 southwards, after 1 mile turn left onto unclassified road for ½ mile to Lacey Green. Signposted.

This is the oldest surviving 'smock-mill' and one of the oldest windmills in Britain. Built in 1650, it is possible that the machinery is original. Designed to produce white flour from wheatmeal, it was restored in the early 1970s and is now in working order again.

☞ nominal charge
● May-25 Sep Sun, Bank Hols 3-6

MAP 5   CENTRAL ENGLAND

Map 5 C3
The Manor House and Gardens
Stanton Harcourt, Oxfordshire
Tel. Oxford (0865) 881928

From Kingston Bagpuize follow A415 northwards, after 3 miles turn right onto B4449 for 3 miles to house on right in Stanton Harcourt. Signposted.

A magnificent feudal manor house of which the Great Kitchen, Pope's Tower and the Gate House are the only original buildings now remaining. The Old Kitchen was built in the 14thC and has been described by Pevsner as the most spectacular and complete medieval kitchen surviving in England. It is essentially one big oven with open fires in bays against the wall. A smoke vent in the octagonal roof is reached by the corner stair turret and covered with wooden shutters which may be individually opened according to the direction of the wind. Centuries of black smoke can be seen high above the fire bays. Home-grown plants and eggs are for sale.

☞ adults £2.00, children £1.00
◑ Apr-Sep Thur, Sun & Bank Hols 2-6
Facilities: 🍽 🚻 ♿ 🅿 ☕

Map 5 D1
Mapledurham Watermill
Mapledurham, Reading, Berkshire RG4 7TR
Tel. Reading (0734) 723350

From Reading follow A4074 northwards, after 2½ miles turn left onto B4526 for ½ mile, then turn left onto unclassified road for 1 mile to house. Signposted.

This watermill is situated in the grounds of Mapledurham House, an Elizabethan mansion by the River Thames. It is the last working watermill on the Thames still producing stoneground wholewheat flour. Visitors are welcome to tour the mill and buy the flour, bran and semolina in the shop. A launch leaves from Caversham Promenade in Reading at 2pm on open days if visitors prefer to come by river.

● **The smokery at Minola**

MAP 5

adults 90p, children 40p
● Easter Sun-Sep Sat, Sun, Bank Hols 1.30-5; Oct-Mar Sun 2-4
Facilities: 🍴 🚻 🚗 🏕 ⚠
★ May National Mills Day — telephone for details
🍴 cream & afternoon teas served with homemade cakes & scones

☺ Map 5 C3
Medley Manor Farm
Binsey Lane, Oxford, Oxfordshire OX2 0NJ
Tel. Oxford (0865) 241251
From Oxford follow A420 westwards, after 1/2 mile turn right into Binsey Lane for 1/4 mile to farm. Signposted.
Visitors to this 25-acre farm may pick their own strawberries, gooseberries, raspberries, red and blackcurrants, tayberries, rhubarb, potatoes, carrots, spinach, onions, beetroot, broad beans, runner beans, mangetout and sweet corn. Parsley is also sold.
● end Jun-Aug daily 9.30-7
Facilities: 🚗

☺ Map 5 C2
Midwinters Farm Shop
Little Croft,
Milton Hill, Abingdon,
Oxfordshire OX14 4DP
Tel. Abingdon (0235) 831247
From Abingdon follow B4017 southwards, after 3 miles turn right onto A4130 to shop on right.
Midwinters have been growing fruit for over 50 years and specialise in 18 varieties of apple. Pick your own on the estate is offered for raspberries and strawberries only, but apples, cherries, plums, a wide range of vegetables and free-range eggs may be bought in the farm shop.
● all year daily 9.30-5.30
Facilities: 🚻 🚗

🌱 Map 5 C2
Millets Farm
Kingston Bagpuize Road, Frilford, Nr Abingdon, Oxfordshire OX13 5PD
Tel. Frilford Heath (0865) 391266
From Kingston Bagpuize follow A415 eastwards for 2 miles to Frilford.
This pick your own farm set in the Vale of the White Horse grows a wide variety of fruit and vegetables including apples, pears, plums, strawberries, raspberries, gooseberries, tayberries, red and blackcurrants, peas, runner beans, courgettes and sprouts. There is also a herb garden and a garden centre. Fly fishing for rainbow trout (up to 10lb) is available on the spring fed lakes. A farm shop sells fruit, vegetables, dairy produce, freshly baked bread, pies, jams, wholefood items, game and eggs.
● shop: all year daily 9-6; PYO: 29 Mar-30 Nov daily 9-6 telephone for details; trout farm: 29 Mar-30 Nov daily 9-dusk
Facilities: 🛒 🍴 ♿ 🚻 🚗 🏕 ⚠
🍴 Millet's Munchery serves morning coffee, lunch & teas with strawberries & cream in season

〰 Map 5 A3
Minola Smoked Products
Kencot Hill Farmhouse, Filkins, Lechlade, Gloucestershire GL7 3QY
Tel. Filkins (036786) 391
From Burford follow A361 southwards for 3 1/2 miles to smokery on left. Signposted.
For one of the widest ranges of smoked foods in the country a visit to Minola is a memorable experience. The smokery is one of the few in Britain to cure food in the traditional way using whole oak logs. One newspaper voted their smoked

salmon the best in Europe. There is an interesting variety of smoked foods for sale: trout, mackerel, eel, kippers, oysters, quails' eggs, prawns, duck breasts and hams. Visitors are able to see the smoke houses and the preparation of various foods including the slicing of smoked salmon.
free
● all year Mon-Fri 8-6, Sat 9-5, Sun 9.30-12
Facilities: 🚻 🚗

🐟 Map 5 E5
Nicholson's
71 Church Street, Wolverton, Milton Keynes, Buckinghamshire MK12 5LD
Tel. Milton Keynes (0908) 312872
In town centre.
An enormous variety of both fresh and frozen fish can be found at this fishmonger. Most of the fish is British-caught and comes from all over the country — from Milford Haven in Wales, Aberdeen in Scotland, North and South Shields, Scarborough, Whitby, Hull, Grimsby, Lowestoft and Brixham in England. Their salmon comes from Scotland and their trout from North Yorkshire. Naturally cured smoked fish includes eel, cod's roe and salmon. They also make their own fish cakes and dress crabs and lobsters. Fresh farm eggs are also sold and sometimes duck and guinea fowl eggs.
● all year Mon, Sat 9-1, Tue, Thur, Fri 8.30-6, Wed 8.30-1

🐟 Map 5 C3
The Oxford Cheese Shop
17 The Covered Market, Oxford, Oxfordshire
Tel. Oxford (0865) 721420
In city centre.
One of the widest selections of cheeses in the county is stocked

MAP 5

CENTRAL ENGLAND

here and includes English and French farmhouse cheeses. A wide range of vegetarian foods is sold such as pâtés, houmous, samosas and other snacks.
● all year Mon-Sat 8.30-5, closed Bank Hols
Facilities: 🚻 ♿

RESTAURANT RECIPE

🍴 Map 5 C3
BROWNS
5-9 Woodstock Road, Oxford, Oxfordshire OX2 6HA
Tel: Oxford (0865) 511995
In city centre.
A large busy restaurant popular with both town and gown.
● Mon-Sat 11-11.30,
Sun 12-11.30
Price range £8-13
Seats 220
Facilities: ♿ 🚻

OXFORD SAUCE
1¼lb redcurrant jelly
glass of port
zest & juice of 2 oranges
zest & juice of 1 lemon
½ onion finely chopped
pinch cayenne
pinch ginger
½ tsp mustard
Melt the redcurrant jelly with the port, orange and lemon juice. Blanch the onion, orange and lemon zest, strain, add to the pan and bring to the boil. Remove from heat, stir in the spices and leave to cool. Serve with cold ham or turkey.

😊 Map 5 C3
Oxford Pick Your Own Farm
Elsfield, Oxford, Oxfordshire OX3 9SW
Tel. Stanton St John (086735) 873
From Wheatley follow B4027 north westwards for 4 miles to farm on left. Signposted.

A very large selection of fruit and vegetables is available for pick your own on this 70-acre farm. There are also less common items such as peppers, pumpkins, radishes, leeks, celery and marrows. Speciality vegetables include mangetout, fennel, seakale, asparagus, kohlrabi and garlic. Farm animals are on display.
● Jun-Nov daily 9.30-7
Facilities: ☕ 🚻 🅿️ 🧺

😊 Map 5 C2
Peach Croft Farm Country Shop
Peach Croft Farm, Radley, Abingdon, Oxfordshire OX14 2HP
Tel. Abingdon (0235) 20094
From Abingdon follow A4183 northwards, after 1½ miles turn right onto unclassified road for 1½ miles to farm on left. Signposted.
This 650-acre farm has pick your own soft fruit and vegetables. Free-range chickens, bronze turkeys and geese are also available and the farm shop sells local free-range eggs, bread and pastries.
● all year daily 9-6
Facilities: ☕ 🚻 🅿️ 🧺 ⛺

😊 Map 5 E2
Peterley Manor Farm
Peterley Lane, Prestwood, Great Missenden, Buckinghamshire HP16 0HH
Tel. Great Missenden (02446) 2959

From High Wycombe follow A4128 northwards, after 3 miles turn right onto unclassified road for 1 mile to farm on left.

This farm has pick your own strawberries, raspberries and other soft fruits including whitecurrants as well as a good selection of vegetables. All are also for sale ready-picked at the farm shop, along with salads, cream, eggs and more unusual items such as chilli peppers, aubergines and pumpkins.
● May-Dec Tue-Fri 9-5.30, Sat 9-5, Sun 10-1
Facilities: 🅿️ 🧺

🏚 Map 5 F3
Pitstone Green Farm Museum
Vicarage Road, Pitstone Green, Leighton Buzzard, Bedfordshire
Tel. Cheddington (0296) 668152
From Tring follow B488 northwards, after 3 miles turn left onto unclassified road for ¼

● **Wickenden Vineyard**

MAP 5

mile to Pitstone Green. Signposted.

This farm and local history museum is situated in the buildings of a working arable farm and is run by volunteers from the Pitstone Local History Society. Visitors can see a Victorian kitchen and a dairy as well as exhibitions on rural life and displays of farming implements.

☞ adults £1.00, senior citizens & children (5-16) 50p
◑ Jun, Jul, Sep 2nd Sun 11-5 or by appointment
Facilities: 🆆🅲 🚗

☺ Map 5 C4
Swifts House Farm Pick Your Own
Swifts House, Stoke Lyne, Bicester, Oxfordshire OX6 9RR
Tel. Fritwell (08696) 440

From Bicester follow A41 northwards for 3 miles to farm on left. Signposted.

Pick your own fruit and vegetables in 8 acres of farmland. Crops available include strawberries, raspberries, broad beans, peas, new potatoes, mangetout,

courgettes and spring onions.
◑ end Jun-early Aug Tue-Sun 10-7
Facilities: 🚗 ☕

🍇 Map 5 F1
Wickenden Vineyard
Cliveden Road, Taplow, Buckinghamshire SL6 0EP
Tel. Maidenhead (0628) 29455

From Maidenhead follow A4 eastwards, after 1 mile turn left into Cliveden Road for 1½ miles to vineyard on right.

In 1976 the Lock family planted their first 400 vines to establish this English vineyard. Today it spreads over nearly 4 acres and nurtures some 5,000 vines producing grapes for Wickenden English white table wine. The grape harvest is pressed, crushed and filtered in the traditional way before being left to mature in oak casks or vats which hold up to 4,000 gallons of wine. After maturing the wine is bottled on the vineyard's 'Anjou' automatic bottling and labelling plant. Two types of English white table wine are produced: 'popular', a dry wine and 'oak matured', a medium dry wine. A selection of French wines is also on sale.

☞ shop: free
◑ all year Mon-Sat 10-2, 6-9
Facilities: 🍽 🆆🅲

MAP 6 CENTRAL ENGLAND

GLOUCESTERSHIRE

Map 6 C1

Alderley Trout Farm

Wotton-under-Edge,
Gloucestershire GL12 7QT
Tel. Dursley (0453) 842540

From Nailsworth follow A46 southwards, after 6 miles turn right onto unclassified road for 2½ miles to Alderley. Signposted.

A family-run trout farm producing trout and a wide range of trout products. Part of the farm can be viewed by visitors. Fresh whole and filleted trout, frozen gutted trout, smoked whole and

The River Severn and its many tributaries rush through the county of Gloucester. Along the banks wild life flourishes, in the waters swim many species of fish: chad, salmon, trout and, of course, elvers — tiny, baby eels which are caught from March to May and sold around Gloucester and Stroud. It is certainly worth visiting the display on eels and elvers at the Gloucester Folk Museum.

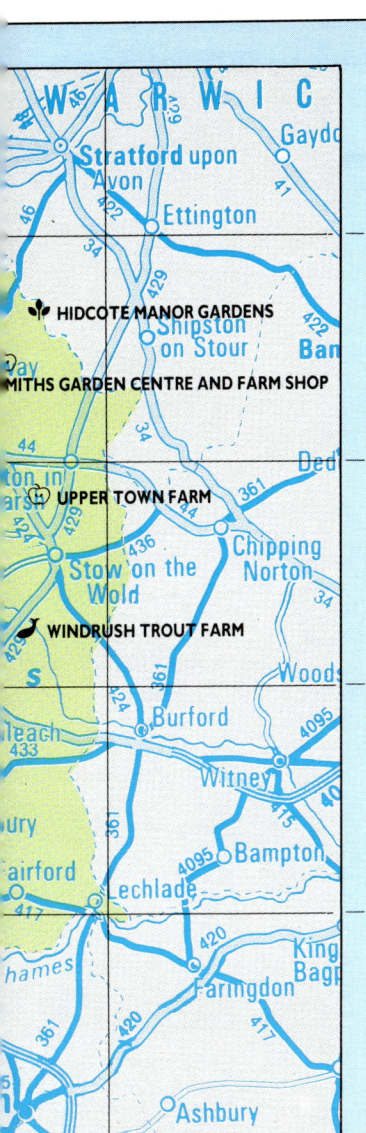

In village. Signposted.

A farming and rural life museum set in an old corn mill in a pretty Cotswold village. Visitors can see the old corn mill machinery, agricultural implements, domestic bygones and china.

☞ adults £1.00, senior citizens 80p, children 50p
◐ 9 Mar-Oct daily 10.30-7; Nov-Feb Sat-Sun 10.30-dusk
Facilities: 🚻 🚗 ⛄

❧ Map 6 E2
Barnsley House Garden
Barnsley, Nr Cirencester, Gloucestershire GL7 5EE
Tel. Bibury (028574) 281

From Cirencester follow A433 north eastwards for 4 miles to Barnsley, then turn left onto unclassified road for ½ mile to house. Signposted.

This attractive 4-acre garden includes an unusual vegetable section which was laid out as a decorative 'potager' in 1975 using designs from the 17thC. The paths are arranged in an intricate pattern which allows picking without treading on the soil. There is also a small formal herbal garden.

☞ adults £1.50, senior citizens £1.00, children free; admission free Dec-Feb
◐ all year daily 10-6 or dusk
Facilities: 🚻 🚗 ⛄

🥄 Map 6 E2
Bibury Trout Farm
Bibury, Nr Cirencester, Gloucestershire GL7 5NL
Tel. Bibury (028574) 215/212

In village.

Set in the attractive village of Bibury near the Arlington Mill Museum, this fish farm keeps its trout in natural ponds. Visitors can see the fish in all stages of development and either catch or feed them. Produce for sale includes fresh and smoked rainbow trout, smoked trout and salmon pâté, herb plants and wine.

☞ adults 75p, senior citizens 50p, children 25p; rod 75p
◐ all year Mon-Sat 9-6 or dusk, Sun 11-6 or dusk
Facilities: 🍴 ♿ 🚗 ⛄

🍯 Map 6 D2
Clare's Kitchen
Aycote Farm, Rendcomb, Cirencester, Gloucestershire GL7 7EP
Tel. North Cerney (028583) 463

From Cirencester follow A417 north westwards, after 1 mile turn right onto A435 for 4 miles, then turn right onto unclassified road for ¼ mile to Rendcomb.

A preserve workshop situated on a farm which produces a wide range of unusual marmalades, jams, chutneys, mustards and nut spreads for the wholefood trade. All the products are made to the owner's own recipes and are additive and preservative-free, many being made from organically grown fruits and vegetables. Varieties include tangerine and brandy marmalade, made with raw sugar, wild plum jam made with apple juice instead of sugar, banana chutney, houmous, white wine and tarragon mustard, cashew and carob spread and vegetarian mincemeat with brandy. Sizes and packs vary according to the product. Fresh fruit and vegetables are also for sale in season.

☞ free
◐ all year by appointment

〰 Map 6 E2
Coln Valley Fish and Game
The Smokery, Winson, Cirencester, Gloucestershire GL7 5ER
Tel. Fossebridge (028572) 400

From Bibury follow unclassified road north westwards for 2 miles to Winson.

A traditional smokery using the original 'London Smokeholes'. This is one of the very few established businesses still using methods that produce smoked foods with a distinct and smokey flavour. The small

filleted trout and a smoked trout pâté are available from the shop. Shellfish, seafish, game, pâtés, and dairy ice cream are also sold.

☞ free
◐ all year Mon-Sat 10-5.30; closed Bank Hols
Facilities: 🚗

🏨 Map 6 E2
Arlington Mill and Cotswold Country Museum
Bibury, Cirencester, Gloucestershire GL7 5NL
Tel. Bibury (028574) 368

MAP 6   CENTRAL ENGLAND

shop offers a full range of their products — smoked salmon, trout, eel, chicken and gravadlax — dilled salmon — as well as a variety of luxury seafoods and game in season. Customers' own fish can also be smoked.

☞ free
● all year Mon-Fri 8-12.30, 1.30-4.30; closed Bank Hols
Facilities: 🚻 🚗

Map 6 E3
Cotswold Countryside Collection
Fosseway,
Northleach, Cheltenham,
Gloucestershire GL54 3JH
Tel. Northleach (0451) 60715

From Northleach follow A429 Fosseway northwards for ¼ mile to museum on left. Signposted.

This award-winning museum tells the fascinating story of rural life in the Cotswolds. Two of the attractions are the Lloyd-Baker Collection which represents the whole range of agricultural methods and techniques in the time of horse

power, and a purpose-built gallery of Cotswold farm buildings displaying the seasons of the agricultural year and the skills of both the carter and wheelwright. There is also the 'Below Stairs' gallery which re-creates the atmosphere of a laundry, kitchen and dairy.

☞ adults 60p, senior citizens 40p, children 30p
● Apr-Oct daily, Bank Hols 10-5.30, Sun 2-5.30
Facilities: 🚌 🍴 🚻 🚗 🖐

Map 6 E3
Cotswold Farm Park
Guiting Power, Cheltenham,
Gloucestershire GL54 5UG
Tel. Guiting Power (04515) 307

From Stow on the Wold follow B4077 westwards, after 5 miles turn left onto unclassified road for 1 mile to farm park. Signposted.

Visitors to Cotswold Farm Park have the opportunity of seeing the most comprehensive collection of rare breeds of British farm animals in the country. There is something for

all age groups at this Rare Breeds Survival Centre. In order to provide a full service there is a café, quality gift shop, pets' corner, an education centre, farm trail, picnic site and adventure playground.

☞ adults £2.00, senior citizens £1.50, children £1.00
● Apr-Sep daily 10.30-6
Facilities: 🚌 🍴 🚻 🚗 🖐 ⛰
🍴 lunches & teas with pies, pasties, quiches, sandwiches, cakes & biscuits

---

Map 6 D2
Cowcombe Farm Herbs
Gipsy Lane, Chalford, Stroud,
Gloucesteshire GL6 8HP
Tel. Frampton Mansell (028576) 544

From Cirencester follow A419 westwards, after 8 miles turn left onto unclassified road for ½ mile to farm. Signposted.

Set above the Stroudwater Valley, this small, family-run herb nursery has demonstration gardens of over 100 species of wild and garden herbs and over 60 species of

---

RESTAURANT RECIPE

Map 6 D2
KINGSHEAD HOUSE
Birdlip,
Gloucestershire GL4 8JH
Tel: Gloucester (0452) 862299

From Gloucester follow A417 eastwards for 8 miles to Birdlip.

A comfortable, small, oak-beamed restaurant in a 17thC stone building. The menu is well priced and interesting, with dishes such as brochette of fresh salmon with a lobster sauce, and hot smoked fillet of trout with horseradish cream. This recipe for black and white mushrooms combines two 18thC dishes to make a pretty starter.

● Tue-Sun, closed Sat L, Sun D, Meals: 12.15-2.15, Sun 12.15-1.45; 7.15-10

Price range Set L £9.50,
Set D £12.95
Seats 32
Cards: Access, Amex, Diners, Visa
Facilities: 🍷 🚻 🚗

BLACK AND WHITE MUSHROOMS
Fricassée of white mushrooms:

½ pint of whipping cream
12oz button mushrooms
juice of half a lemon
salt & pepper
nutmeg
arrowroot

Heat the cream, add the mushrooms, lemon juice and seasonings and simmer. When cooked, remove the mushrooms, add the arrowroot and thicken to

double cream consistency. Return mushrooms to the sauce and keep warm.

Ragout of field mushrooms:

12oz flat mushrooms
sunflower oil
salt & pepper
fresh rosemary
½ pint red wine
knob of butter

Heat the oil and toss the mushrooms with the seasoning and rosemary. Add the red wine and cook until some of the liquid is absorbed. Remove mushrooms, reduce sauce slightly, thicken with butter and pour over the mushrooms. Serve in individual dishes, the white mushrooms on one side with the dark alongside.

MAP 6

wildflower plants. It is also the home of the Seed Bank and Exchange for herb and wildflower seed. Free-range eggs are available from the rare breed poultry and ducks and honey is produced from the farm's own bees. All varieties of herbs and wildflowers may be purchased, either in pots or dried. Seeds are also for sale.

☞ free
● Easter-Sep Wed-Sun 10-5 or by appointment
Facilities: |●| 🚗 🚻
|●| lunches & teas by arrangement

☺ Map 6 C4
The Glasshouse Shop
Church End Nurseries, Twyning, Tewkesbury, Gloucestershire GL20 6DA
Tel. Tewkesbury (0684) 292288

From Tewkesbury follow A38 northwards for 2½ miles to shop.

This farm, completely under glass, grows and sells salad crops such as tomatoes, cucumbers, green peppers and lettuce and visitors can see the crops growing in the glasshouses. Its specialities are Beefsteak and Cherry tomatoes. All produce is grown naturally without pesticides as, they claim, pests are controlled by their natural enemies.
● Mar-Aug daily 9-5; Sep-Dec Mon-Sat 9-5.
Facilities: 🚗

🏠 Map 6 C3
Gloucester Folk Museum
99-103 Westgate Street, Gloucester, Gloucestershire GL1 2PG
Tel. Gloucester (0452) 26467

In city centre.

Set partly in 3 timber-framed buildings dating from the 15th and early 17thC, this delightful museum provides a fascinating look into the social history, crafts, industries and folklore of the city and county of Gloucester. Displays include a Severn fishing gallery with a section on salmon, eels, and elvers — a great local delicacy. There is also a dairy which features the famous double and single Gloucester cheese, an ironmonger's shop, kitchen range and equipment and an agricultural gallery housing a number of machines made for food production.

☞ free
● all year Mon-Sat, Bank Hols 10-5
Facilities: 🚾 🚻

❧ Map 6 E4
Hidcote Manor Gardens
Hidcote Bartrim, Chipping Campden, Gloucestershire GL55 6LR
Tel. Mickleton (038677) 333

From Broadway follow A46 north eastwards, after 6 miles turn right onto unclassified road for 2 miles to gardens. Signposted.

One of the most famous gardens in England, the 10-acre site was created this century by the great horticulturalist Major Lawrence Johnston. It is now owned by the National Trust. As well as a wide variety of plants, shrubs and trees, there is an extensive kitchen garden and an apple and pear orchard is being established. Visitors can buy herb plants and the shop sells the National Trust's own fudge, conserves, mustard, teas and honey.

☞ adults £2.70, children £1.35
● Apr-Oct Mon, Wed-Thur, Sat-Sun 11-8 (last admission 7)
Facilities: 🍽 |●| ♿ 🚾 🚗
|●| homebaked light lunches served in licensed restaurant including some vegetarian dishes

● **Grocer's shop sign, Gloucester Folk Museum**

MAP 6

CENTRAL ENGLAND

Map 6 C1
House of Cheese
13 Church Street, Tetbury,
Gloucestershire GL8 8JG
Tel. Tetbury (0666) 52865

In town centre.

This is, as its name implies, a specialist cheese shop which stocks a wide selection of British and continental cheeses. It specialises in cheeses from the smaller British farmhouse producers which include local varieties: Berkeley, Single Gloucester and Nuns of Caen from Charles Martell; Lanock Blue, a ewes' milk cheese from Scotland; and Pantyllyn and Llanboidy cheeses from Wales. They also have a cheese stall in Cirencester Market on Monday and Friday and in Ledbury Market on Saturday.
● all year Mon-Wed, Fri 9-5, Thur 9-1, Sat 9-4

Map 6 C3
Norton Fruit Farm
Tewkesbury Road,
Norton, Gloucester,
Gloucestershire GL2 9LH
Tel. Norton (0452) 731203

From Gloucester follow A38 northwards for 4 miles to Norton.
This 20-acre pick your own farm has strawberries, raspberries, tayberries and red and blackcurrants. The shop also sells cut flowers and a wide selection of vegetables including mangetout, peppers, aubergines, celery, cucumbers and tomatoes. The farm also has fishing facilities and farm animals.
● all year daily 9-5.30
Facilities: 🍽 🚾 🚌 🛁

Map 6 C3
Over Farm Market
Over, Gloucester,
Gloucestershire GL2 8DB
Tel. Gloucester (0452) 21014

From Gloucester follow A40 westwards, after 2 miles turn right at Dog Inn in Over onto unclassified road for 1/4 mile to farm. Signposted.

A full range of fruit and vegetables is available on this pick your own farm. Specialities include several varieties of squash, bunching carrots, sweet corn and courgettes. Single and double Gloucester

cheese, free-range eggs, dairy products, herbs, ice cream, condiments and preserves are also for sale. The farm has its own goats.
● all year daily Mon-Sat 9-6, Sun 10-5
Facilities: 🚌

Map 6 C3
The Robert Opie Collection
Albert Warehouse,
Gloucester Docks,
Gloucestershire GL1 2EH
Tel. Gloucester (0452) 302309

In city centre.

This colourful exhibition can be described as a century of shopping basket history. There are 200,000 items on display relating to the history of our consumer society. Here are the packs, tins and bottles which have filled the larder and crowded the shelves of Britain's grocers since Victorian times. It is possible to follow the development of brands which

● **Selection of grocery goods from the Robert Opie Collection**

MAP 6

have remained family favourites for generations and be reminded of others which have quietly disappeared. Even the commercial television era is given coverage with the continual screening of advertisements which for the last 30 years have informed, amused, influenced and often exasperated us.

☞ adults £1.50, senior citizens £1.00, children 75p, family ticket (2 adults & up to 4 children) £3.95

◑ all year Tue-Sun 10-6
Facilities: ☕ ♿ 🚻

---

§ Map 6 B3
St Anne's Vineyard
Oxenhall, Nr Newent,
Gloucestershire GL18 1RW
Tel. Gorsley (098982) 313

From Newent follow B4221 westwards, after 1 mile turn right onto unclassified road for 1 mile to Oxenhall. Signposted.

A family-run vineyard which came into production in 1984 and now grows over 100 varieties of vine, many of them on an experimental basis. All the wines are made on the premises and there is an interesting range of English examples as well as traditional country fruit wines made with English fruit — gooseberry, raspberry, tayberry, redcurrant and plum — with no

concentrates or flavourings. The wines are sold in 70cl bottles with a 10% reduction for a case of 12. Visitors can tour the vineyard and are always welcome to taste before buying. Homemade preserves are also for sale.

☞ free
◑ all year Tue-Fri 2-7, Sat, Sun, Bank Hols 10-7
Facilities: 🚗

REGIONAL RECIPE

POTTED CHEESE

This recipe may be made with any good hard cheese.

3lb double Gloucester cheese
½lb butter
¼ pint of sherry
½ oz mace

Pound the cheese and butter together with a pestle and mortar. Gradually stir in the sherry and add the mace. Mix thoroughly, put into small pots and top with clarified butter.

✸ Map 6 D1
Shipton Mill
Long Newnton, Tetbury,
Gloucestershire GL8 8RP
Tel. Tetbury (0666) 53620

From Tetbury follow B4014 south eastwards for 1 mile to Long Newnton. Signposted.

A small Cotswold flour mill producing stoneground flour for sale to master bakers and retail outlets. The first mill on this site was recorded in the Domesday Book and flour has been produced here ever since. In 1980 it was completely overhauled and visitors are now able to see this beautifully restored mill in full working order.

☞ £1.00
◑ all year Mon-Fri 9.30-4 by appointment
Facilities: 🚻 🚗

☺ Map 6 E4
Smiths Garden Centre and Farm Shop
Station Road,
Chipping Campden,
Gloucestershire GL55 6JD
Tel. Evesham (0386) 840367

From Shipston-on-Stour follow B4035 westwards for 6½ miles to Chipping Camden. Signposted.

Pick your own strawberries and flowers on this 4-acre site. The shop also sells free-range eggs, soft fruit, apples, homemade cider and preserves. There is a garden centre with display gardens adjacent.

◑ Apr-Oct daily 9-6; Nov-Mar daily 9-4.30
Facilities: ☕ 🚗 ♿

145

MAP 6 — CENTRAL ENGLAND

♪ **Map 6 D1**

Somerford Lakes Reserve
Somerford Keynes,
Nr Cirencester,
Gloucestershire GL7 6ED
Tel. Kemble (028577) 226

From Cirencester follow A419 south eastwards, after 4 miles turn right onto unclassified road for 3 miles to Somerford Keynes.

This nature reserve gives one-hour guided tours around a beautiful 120-acre lake aboard an Edwardian-style electric launch and offers visitors the chance to see the spectacular wildlife collection and also to visit the famous eel farm, one of only two in the whole of England. Visitors can buy fresh and smoked eel and rainbow trout, goats' milk and ice cream.
☞ adults £2.50, children £1.50
◗ all year 10-7 by appointment
Facilities: 🚗 ⛺

❧ **Map 6 D3**

Sudeley Castle
Winchcombe,
Gloucestershire GL54 5JD
Tel. Cheltenham (0242) 602308

From Cheltenham follow A46 north eastwards for 7 miles to Winchcombe. Signposted.

● **Sudeley Castle**

A working country home set in the heart of the Cotswolds offering falconry, crafts and home produce. Visitors walking around the 1,000-year-old estate can see the herb garden and buy plants, homemade jams and honey from the shop. There is an adventure playground for children.

☞ adults £3.25, senior citizens £2.75, children £1.75, family ticket (2 adults & 2 children) £8.00
◗ castle: Apr-Oct daily 12-5; grounds: Apr-Oct daily 11-5.30
Facilities: 🍽 WC 🚗 ⛺ ⚠

🍇 **Map 6 B3**

Three Choirs Vineyards
Rhyle House,
Welsh House Lane,
Nr Newent,
Gloucestershire GL18 1LR
Tel. Dymock (053185) 233/555

From Newent follow B4215 northwards, after 2 miles turn right into Welsh House Lane for 1 mile to vineyards on right. Signposted.

Three Choirs
ENGLISH ROSÉ TABLE WINE   70cl.

In the 12thC William of Malmesbury wrote about Gloucestershire wines 'no county in England has so many or so good vineyards'. This vineyard, one of the largest in England, has grown from half an acre in 1973 to over 20 acres today, with a potential output of 100,000 bottles. Its wines are produced from the Müller-Thurgau and Reichensteiner grapes, but they are experimenting with other varieties including Pinot Noir, the champagne variety, which has produced a very interesting rosé. Visitors can wander unaccompanied around the vineyards and a free map is provided. Free tastings are available and wine and cider made on the premises are for sale.

● **Tasting the Three Choirs vintage**

● **Three Choirs wines**

MAP 6

☞ free
● Easter-Dec Mon-Fri 9-5, Sat-Sun 10-5; or by appointment
Facilities: ⛺ ♿ 🚻 🚗 ☕
★ first Sunday of month tastings of vineyard's more unusual wines
🍴 ploughman's lunches serving local single & double Gloucester cheese

☺ Map 6 E3
Upper Town Farm
Longborough,
Moreton-in-Marsh,
Gloucestershire GL56 0QQ
Tel. Cotswold (0451) 30413

From Stow on the Wold follow A424 northwards, after 2 miles turn right onto unclassified road for ½ mile to Longborough. Signposted.

A 30-acre pick your own farm with gooseberries, raspberries, red and blackcurrants and plums. The farm shop also sells 6 varieties of apples, potatoes, cabbages, beans, cauliflowers and pears.
● soft fruit: end Jun-Aug daily 9-8; orchard fruit: mid Aug-early Nov daily 9-dusk
Facilities: 🚻 🚗

⊞ Map 6 E2
Waterton Farm
Ampney Crucis, Cirencester,
Gloucestershire GL7 5RR
Tel. Cirencester (0285) 67976/67863

From Cirencester follow A417 eastwards for 2 miles to Ampney Crucis.

In 1986 this farm set up a sheep dairy following the increasing popularity of the unique flavour of sheep dairy products. Visitors can watch the sheep being milked and also join in the yoghurt tasting. A special attraction for children is the children's farm. There is a beautiful herb garden where expert advice is on hand for any questions. Raspberries and strawberries can be picked

from a field close by when in season. All the produce — herb plants, soft fruit and, from April to September, sheep's milk yoghurt and milk can be bought at the farm shop.
☞ herb garden & fruit field: free; dairy: adults 75p, senior citizens & children 25p
● May-Sep Wed, Sun 3-5 (milking at 3)
Facilities: ♿ 🚗

SINGLE GLOUCESTER

Seek out the wonderful white single Gloucester cheese made by Charles Martell at the Cirencester market on Friday. The cheese is made from the milk of the Martell's Old Gloucester cows.

❀ Map 6 B2
Westbury Court Garden
Westbury-on-Severn,
Gloucestershire GL14 1PD
Tel. Westbury-on-Severn (045276) 461

From Gloucester follow A48 south westwards for 9 miles to garden. Signposted.

This Dutch-style water garden, owned by the National Trust, dates from 1700 and has been planted with authentic plants of the period including a selection of herbs. Visitors can also see some varieties of fruit trees which were grown in the 18thC including plums, pears and apples.
☞ £1.10
● Apr-Oct Wed-Sun, Bank Hols 11-6
Facilities: ♿ 🚗 ☕

🐟 Map 6 E3
Windrush Trout Farm
Rissington Road,
Bourton on the Water,
Cheltenham, Gloucestershire
Tel. Cotswold (0451) 20541

From Stow on the Wold follow A429 southwards, after 4½ miles turn left onto unclassified road for ½ mile to Bourton on the Water.

● **Windrush Trout Farm**

A family-run trout farm situated on the River Windrush in the heart of the Cotswolds. This was one of the first trout farms and was often used as the blueprint for others throughout the country. Here visitors can watch or feed the fish at various stages of their development. Fresh trout and salmon can be bought from the farm shop each day and rods can be hired to fish your own.
☞ adults 70p, senior citizens 50p, children 35p
● Apr-Oct daily 10.30-5
Facilities: ☕

· CALENDAR OF EVENTS ·

FEBRUARY

Lichfield Old Fair and Pancake Race
Shrove Tuesday
Held for over 300 years - wine and simnel cake are served in the Guildhall in Lichfield, Staffordshire.

Olney Pancake Race
Shrove Tuesday
This annual pancake race has taken place since 1445 between the housewives of Olney in Buckinghamshire.

APRIL

Bottle Kicking and Hare Pie Scrambling
4 April — Easter Monday
An ancient custom - two hare pies are cut up and scattered to the crowd to 'scramble' for. 'Bottle-kicking' follows - a game which involves two teams kicking three casks filled with beer, at Hallaton, near Market Harborough, Leicestershire.

Annual Elver Eating Contest
4 April — Easter Monday
An annual tradition when elvers - baby eels - are eaten in Epney, Gloucestershire.

MAY

Cheese Rolling Ceremony
1st Sunday in May
Three decorated cheeses are blessed and rolled anti-clockwise around the church in Randwick, near Stroud, Gloucestershire.

Wicken Love Feast
12 May —Ascension Day
A typical village custom with a procession to the County Hotel where parishioners share a feast of Thursday Cake and ale (now usually wine), in Wicken, Northamptonshire.

Bread and Cheese Throwing
29 May
A traditional custom - after Evensong, baskets of bread and cheese are thrown from a wall near the castle and scrambled for in the lane below, at St Briavels, Forest of Dean, Gloucestershire.

AUGUST

English Civil War Battle
6-7 August
A Civil War re-enactment by the English Civil War Society which includes cooking period food at Kirby Hall, near Corby, Northamptonshire.

SEPTEMBER

Rare Breeds Survival Trust Show and Sale
9-10 September
Held at the National Agricultural Centre, Kenilworth, Warwickshire.

Burton-on-Trent Beer Festival
22-24 September
An opportunity to sample beers from all over the country at Burton-upon-Trent, Staffordshire.

Dr Johnson Supper
24 September
This annual supper is held in the Guildhall, Lichfield, Staffordshire - tickets from Dr Johnson Museum.

OCTOBER

Warwick Ox Roast and Mop
15 October
An old custom held annually in Warwick, Warwickshire - the first slice of the beast is offered by auction in aid of the Mayor's Charity Fund.

AGRICULTURAL SHOWS

A number of annual agricultural shows are held in Central England — they are normally a good source of local produce. The following are a selection:

MAY

Nottinghamshire Agricultural Show
6-7 May at Winthorpe, Newark, Nottinghamshire.

Shropshire and West Midlands Agricultural Show
18-19 May at Shrewsbury, Shropshire.

Stafford County Show
25-26 May at Stafford, Staffordshire.

Rutland Agricultural Show
29-30 May at Oakham, Rutland.

JUNE

Three Counties Show
14-16 June at Malvern, Worcestershire.

JULY

Royal International Agricultural Show
4-7 July
The largest annual agricultural show in the Midlands at the National Agricultural Centre in Stoneleigh, Warwickshire.

EAST ENGLAND

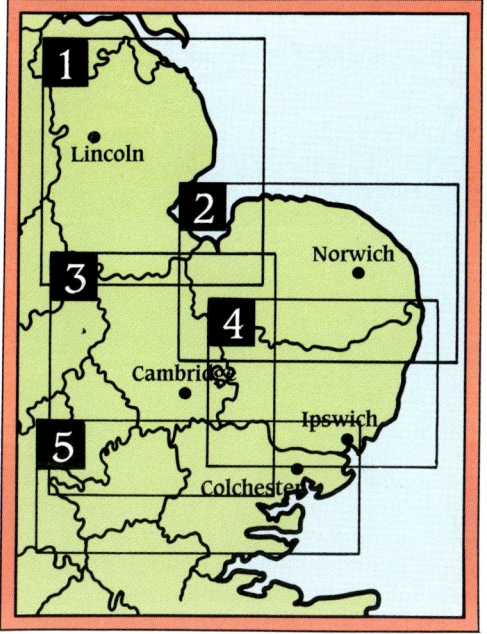

EAST ENGLAND

● **The Market Place, Great Yarmouth**

by Brigitte Tilleray

COOKERY WRITER

A 'food treasure hunt' was the theme of a mini car rally recently organised with friends as part of a long weekend entertainment. It took place in East Anglia and the results were amazing: by the time the last car reached us my cottage kitchen looked like 5 a.m. at Covent Garden, Billingsgate and Smithfield put together. The men sang the praises of local wines, beer and cider and a few guilty looks were exchanged when we started counting how many locally made chocolates we had eaten. A pregnant friend assured me that her baby would be born with rosy cheeks now she had discovered the delectable local apple juice and the children joined in with a game of spot the preserve; they blindfolded each other, stuck their fingers in pots of locally made preserves and tried to guess the flavour.

The recollection of this particular weekend illustrates the pleasure which can be found along the gastronomic routes of East Anglia.

The abundance of local specialities has been praised for centuries. The Romans were already sampling the local oysters while settling around Colchester and the 350 miles of coastline stretching from Leigh-on-Sea to the Wash still provides one of the major food resources of the region. The variety to be found on fish market stalls is of a kind normally associated with the continent: lobsters from the Norfolk coast, crabs from Cromer, sweet pink shrimps from the Wash as well as mussels, whelks and cockles. Take an early trip to Leigh-on-Sea, the major source for cockles in Britain, and take them direct from the sheds where they are boiled daily, or drive to the Suffolk or Norfolk coast and enjoy fresh Pacific oysters all year round. Armed with buckets and rakes you can gather the Stiffkey blue-shelled cockles or, from early June, pick samphire — the asparagus of the sea which is acquiring such a reputation in the culinary world.

Fresh fish is just as prolific as shellfish and whether it is herrings from Lowestoft, sprats from Aldeburgh, whitebait from Southend or dabs and lemon soles from the Suffolk coast, the resulting dish will be delicious. From the East Anglian smoke houses you can purchase lightly coloured oak-smoked kippers, bloaters or red herrings, a speciality the Great Yarmouth fishermen inherited from their forefathers.

In fact, the traditions of yesteryear seem to govern the food industry here. Modern machinery may have turned East Anglia into the granary of Britain, but it is still possible to find much traditionally prepared fare. There is ground flour from the numerous windmills and watermills and hams cured or smoked from ancient recipes, each one a family secret and distinctive in taste and colour. Speciality sausages are sold at every butcher, all slightly meatier than the normal breakfast sausage and many of them prize winners in local shows and markets. They are often surprisingly spiced, with apples, tomatoes or nuts added to the sausage meat.

Traditional breeds of geese and turkey are being reared once more, although modern traffic will never again allow the farmers to walk their flocks to London as they used to. But East Anglian poultry farmers take early orders and it is well worth trying the Christmas Bronze or Black turkey, the Norfolk goose and the farm cockerel which is fed on the gleanings from harvest time onwards.

Game of all kinds abounds in the area. Pheasant, venison, partridge, pigeon, hare and rabbit as well as wild fowl have been part of the staple diet of Brecklanders and Flanders — the people of the Fens — for centuries.

A third of the vegetables consumed in Great Britain are grown in East Anglia, especially peas, carrots, potatoes, root vegetables and brassicas which are grown on a very large scale. Market gardeners abound and vegetables sold on cottage doorsteps or outside farm gates are part of the local scene. Some are very seasonal, like the fine green Norfolk asparagus, probably the nearest species to the original 16thC wild asparagus; its distinctive taste has no equal. Other vegetables are very ancient like the Oakey onion, the Painted Lady runner bean or the Cottager's kale, one of England's oldest vegetables.

To conclude the culinary tour of this vast area it is essential to mention the wide range of hand-prepared jams, preserves, conserves and condiments. Motivated by the success of ancient family businesses such as Colmans and Tiptree and encouraged by the large number of herb farms scattered around, many housewives have turned a kitchen hobby into a profitable business. The number of brand names appearing on the British market and abroad highlight the fact that East Anglians are now at the forefront in the promotion of regional food.

Brigitte Tillexay

MAP 1   EAST ENGLAND

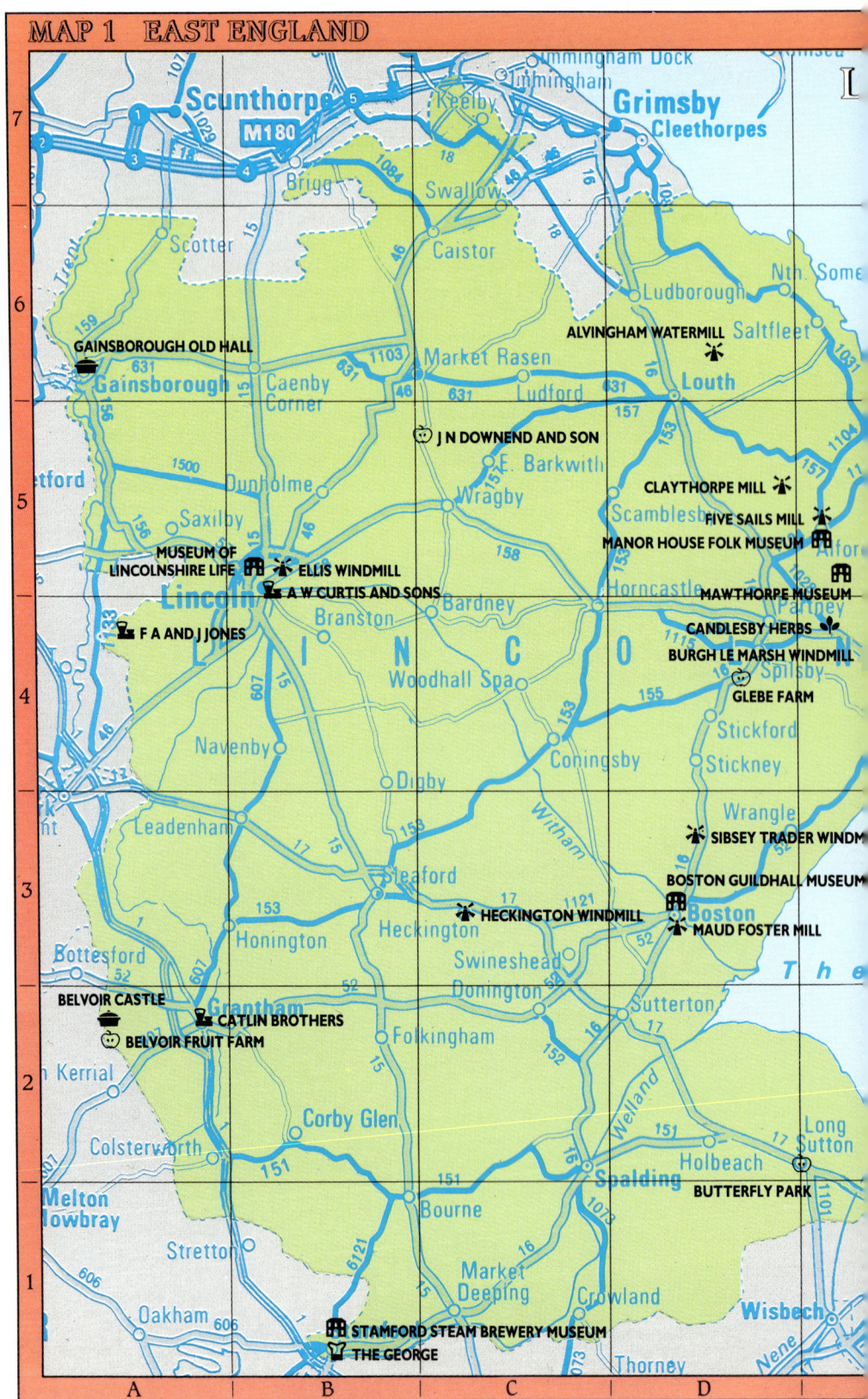

NCOLNSHIRE

Mablethorpe
Sutton on Sea

Skegness
CHURCH FARM MUSEUM

Hunstanton   149 Bra
W a s h   Doc
                    Snettisha
        Sandring
              Hillin
King's Lynn
47
Narborough

F

The flat countryside and rich fertile soil combine to make this an interesting agricultural area. Grains and potatoes are grown and there are some superb pork products. Just about every part of the pig is used, as you will see when you visit any of the local pork butchers. Stuffed chine — neck of pig stuffed with parsley, thyme, marjoram, lettuce and spring onions; haslet — a savoury minced pork loaf; sausages — particularly Lincolnshire flavoured with tomato; brawn; faggots; polony and stuffed trotters — all are on sale.

Map 1 D6
Alvingham Watermill
Church Lane, Alvingham,
Louth, Lincolnshire LN11 OQD
Tel. South Cockerington
(050782) 544

From Louth follow A16 northwards, after 3½ miles turn right onto unclassified road for 1 mile, then turn right onto unclassified road for ½ mile, then turn left onto unclassified road for 1 mile to mill. Signposted.

There has been a watermill here for at least 900 years, grinding corn for bread and animal feed right up to the 1960s. Alvingham is now the only complete, working mill of the 13 mills which once drew their power from the River Lud. Most of the machinery has been restored to working order and visitors can see the mill at work on open days.

adults 50p, children 40p
Jul-Aug Mon, Thur 2-5, every 2nd & 4th Sun 2-5.30; Easter-Aug Bank Hol 11-5.30; or by appointment
Facilities:

Map 1 A2
Belvoir Castle
Belvoir, Grantham,
Lincolnshire NG32 1PD
Tel. Grantham (0476) 870262

From Grantham follow A607 south westwards, after 4 miles turn right onto unclassified road for 3 miles to castle. Signposted.

Belvoir Castle, home of the Duke and Duchess of Rutland, dates back to Norman times. In its historic kitchen and bakehouse visitors may see a collection of brass and pewter cooking implements. Inside the castle are some amazing treasures, including paintings, tapestries, Chinese silks, furniture, porcelain and sculpture. The terraced gardens

MAP 1　　　EAST ENGLAND

were ingeniously planned so that there is something in flower virtually throughout the year. Elderflower cordial, a refreshing drink made from elderflowers, is on sale. (See also Belvoir Fruit Farms below)

☞ adults £2.50, children £1.40
◑ 19 Mar-2 Oct Tue-Thur, Sat 12-6, Sun 12-7, Bank Hols 11-7 or by appointment
Facilities: ⬛ ⬛ ⬛ 🚗 ⬛ ⬛
★ 17 Jul teddy bears' picnic
⬛ specialities include homemade steak & kidney pie, cakes & scones

---

☺ Map 1 A2
Belvoir Fruit Farm
Belvoir, Grantham,
Lincolnshire NG32 1PB
Tel. Grantham (0476) 870286
From Grantham follow A607 south westwards, after 4 miles turn right onto unclassified road for 3 miles to farm. Signposted.
A pick your own farm selling asparagus and seasonal soft fruits including raspberries, strawberries, gooseberries, blackberries and blackcurrants. Also on sale are local cream and elderflower and raspberry cordials.
◑ end Jul-Aug daily 10-8
Facilities: ⬛ ⬛ 🚗 ⬛

⬛ Map 1 D3
Boston Guildhall Museum
South Street, Boston,
Lincolnshire PE21 6HT
Tel. Boston (0205) 65954
In town centre. Signposted.
The 15thC guildhall, now the borough museum, contains a large kitchen dating back to 1552. Equipped as it would have been in the early 17thC, there are 3 original fireplaces and roasting spits which were ingeniously turned by hot air. Here cooks used to prepare the lavish feasts the city fathers frequently enjoyed before municipal reform in the 1830s. During World War II the

kitchen was used as a restaurant.
☞ adults 30p, children (under 16) free
◑ Apr-Oct Mon-Sat 10-5, Sun 1.30-5; Nov-Mar Mon-Sat 10-5

⬛ Map 1 E4
Burgh le Marsh Windmill
Burgh le Marsh, Lincolnshire
Tel. Lincoln (0522) 552222
In village. Signposted.
One of 3 surviving 5-sailed windmills in the county, Burgh le Marsh windmill is a typical 19thC Lincolnshire tower mill and has been restored to full working order. It produces stoneground flour which visitors can buy. They can also visit the milling museum.
☞ adults 50p, children 25p
◑ Easter-Oct 2nd & last Sun of month, Banks Hols 11-5
Facilities: 🚗

☺ Map 1 E2
Butterfly Park
Long Sutton, Spalding,
Lincolnshire PE12 9LE
Tel. Holbeach (0406) 363833
In village. Signposted.
A farm shop selling an extensive range of fruit and vegetables including some exotic varieties. Plums and 8 varieties of apples are a speciality as are early and late strawberries. Butterfly Park has the largest indoor tropical butterfly house in the U.K. Other attractions include the butterfly garden, farm walk and adventure playground.
◑ all year daily 10-6
Facilities: ⬛ 🚗 ⬛ ⬛

🌿 Map 1 E4
Candlesby Herbs
Cross Keys Cottage,
Candlesby, Nr Spilsby,
Lincolnshire PE23 5SF
Tel. Scremby (075485) 211

From Skegness follow A158 westwards, after 7 miles turn right onto A1028 for ½ mile to garden. Signposted.
Candlesby Herbs specialise in growing herbs for the modern small garden. Visitors can look round the herb garden and workshop where there is extensive information on all aspects of herbs: how to grow them, preserve them and use them in cooking, beauty and pot-pourri. Plants, dried herbs and a range of products including herbal and flower teas are on sale.
☞ free
◑ all year Tue-Sun, Bank Hols 10-5

⬛ Map 1 A2
Catlin Brothers
11 High Street, Grantham,
Lincolnshire NG31 6PN
Tel. Grantham (0476) 65428
In town centre. Signposted.

Grantham Gingerbread was first made in 1750 in the bakery behind Catlin's. The original recipe has been handed down through the firm and is still used today. The bakery also produces 250-300 prize-winning breads, cakes and savoury meat products. Visitors can also buy other specialities including Lincolnshire sausage.
◑ all year Mon, Tue, Thur, Fri 7.30-5, Wed 7.30-2.30, Sat 7.30-5.30
Facilities: ⬛ ⬛ ⬛ ⬛
★ demonstrations & lectures by arrangement

MAP 1

• **The grounds of Church Farm Museum, Skegness**

Map 1 E4
Church Farm Museum
Church Road South, Skegness,
Lincolnshire
Tel. Skegness (0754) 66658

*From Skegness follow A158
westwards, after ½ mile turn left
into Queen's Road and left again
into Church Road to museum.
Signposted.*

This farm museum depicts life
in Lincolnshire at the turn of
the century and features a
farmhouse furnished with
period artefacts. The kitchen
has a traditional range,
scrubbed top table and a pantry
stocked with farm produce
which shows the self-sufficiency
of country households before
modern technology. There is
bacon from home-killed pigs,
wholemeal flour ground by the
local windmill, home-produced
eggs, home-brewed beer and
jams and pickles using the
farm's own apples and
vegetables. A barn has a display
of typical farm machinery
including a locally made
winnower, a carrot washer and
a potato sorter. Another
outbuilding is devoted to dairy
produce, with cows and milking
equipment on display. There
are regular dairy and baking
demonstrations.

adults 60p, children (over 5)
40p
Apr-Oct daily 10.30-5.30
Facilities:
★ 4-10 Jul craft week with
baking, buttermaking & other
craft demonstrations —
telephone for details
on special baking days
scones baked on museum's cast
iron range for sale

Map 1 D5
Claythorpe Mill
Claythorpe, Nr Alford,
Lincolnshire LN13 0DU
Tel. Withern (0521) 50687
*From Alford follow A1104
northwards, after 2 miles turn
left onto B1373 for 2 miles, then
turn left onto unclassified road
for 1½ miles to Claythorpe.
Signposted.*
Visitors to this mill and
smokery are welcome to tour
the premises and purchase the
home-smoked produce
including trout, salmon, eels,
chicken and pepper mackerel.
free
3 Apr-mid Dec Tue-Sun, Bank
Hols 10-5, Fri, Sat 7-9; by
appointment to see mill
working
Facilities:
tea room's summer menu
has cold dishes of smoked fish,
shellfish & poultry with

homemade salads; winter
menu comprises selection of
hot & cold dishes

Map 1 B5
A W Curtis and Sons
164 High Street, Lincoln,
Lincolnshire
Tel. Lincoln (0522) 27212
In city centre.
This is one of several branches
of a well-established chain of
butchers in the area. Apart
from meat and meat products
they also run a bakery which
makes superb traditional meat
pies. All their produce is made
in the company's Lincoln
butchery and bakery and
includes a number of local
specialities like stuffed chine,
roast chaps, haslet, Lincolnshire
sausage, cooked ham and cured
bacon. Bakery specialities
include Lincolnshire plum
bread. Other branches in
Lincoln are at 2 Silver Street
and 25 Simcil Street and there
are also branches in Scunthorpe
and Newark.
all year Mon-Sat 8-5.30

**GRANTHAM
GINGERBREAD**

Apart from Prime Ministers,
Grantham produces other
specialities.
*4oz butter
4oz caster sugar
3 eggs
½lb plain flour
³/₄oz ground ginger
1½ tsp baking powder
milk*
Heat oven to gas 4 (350F,
180C). Cream the butter and
sugar until light and fluffy
and beat in the eggs. Sift in
the flour, ginger and baking
powder and stir to a soft
consistency, adding milk if
necessary. Spoon into a well-
greased 1lb loaf tin and bake
for 1½ hours, or until firm.

MAP 1　　　　　　　　　　　　　**EAST ENGLAND**

☺ Map 1 C5
J N Downend and Son
Top Farm, Lissington,
Lincolnshire LN3 5AF
Tel. Wickenby (06735) 351

*From Market Rasen follow B1202
southwards for 4 miles to
Lissington. Signposted.*

A pick your own farm selling a
range of soft fruits including
gooseberries, strawberries,
blackcurrants and blackberries.
Sweet corn grown in the
glasshouse is a speciality and
cauliflowers and beans are
available ready-picked.
◗ Jul-Sep daily 10-8
Facilities: 🚻 🚗

🏵 Map 1 B5
Ellis Windmill
Mill Road, Off Burton Road,
Lincoln, Lincolnshire LN2 2JH
Tel. Lincoln (0522) 41824

In city centre.

Ellis Windmill is a working flour
mill producing stoneground
wholemeal flour milled on
French or Burr stones. Guided
tours are available. The flour,
made on the premises, is for
sale in 1lb and 3½lb bags.

☞ adults 30p, children 15p
◗ May-Sep Sat, Sun 2-6; Oct-
Apr 2nd & 4th Sat & Sun 2-dusk
Facilities: 🚗 🍽

🏵 Map 1 E5
Five Sails Mill
East Street, Alford, Lincolnshire
Tel. Boston (0205) 52188

In town centre.

This 5-sailed windmill is one of
the last 3 of its kind and has
been in continuous use for
over 170 years. Visitors are able
to see it in operation and can
buy stoneground flour, muesli,
oats and other products.

☞ adults 50p, children 30p
◗ all year Sat 11-5
Facilities: 🚗

156

● **The kitchen at Gainsborough Old Hall**

🏠 Map 1 A6
Gainsborough Old Hall
Parnell Street, Gainsborough,
Lincolnshire DN21 2NB
Tel. Gainsborough (0427) 2669

In town centre. Signposted.

This is one of the best
preserved late-medieval manor
houses in the country. The
Great Hall has a buttery,
servery and spectacular kitchen
— probably the most complete
of its kind in England. It
comprises 2 great hearths, 2
bread ovens and 3 store rooms
with sleeping quarters above.
The displays, using replicas,
sounds and smells, show the
kitchen in 1483 preparing a
feast for King Richard III.

☞ adults 60p, senior citizens &
children (under 16) 30p
◗ Easter-Oct Mon-Sat 10-5, Sun
2-5; Nov-Easter Mon-Sat 10-5
Facilities: 🍴 🚻 🍽

☺ Map 1 D4
Glebe Farm
East Keal, Spilsby,
Lincolnshire PE23 4BB
Tel. Spilsby (0790) 53300

*From Spilsby follow A16 south
westwards for 3 miles to farm.
Signposted.*

A smallholding selling pick your
own seasonal soft fruit
including strawberries,

raspberries and blackcurrants.
There is a rural walk by the fish
ponds but no fishing is allowed.
◗ Jul-Aug daily 10-7
Facilities: 🚻 🚗 🍽

🏵 Map 1 C3
Heckington Windmill
c/o Pearoom Craft and Heritage
Centre, Station Road,
Heckington, Sleaford,
Lincolnshire NG34 9JJ
Tel. Sleaford (0529) 60765

In village. Signposted.

Visitors can explore all the
floors and the galley of this
unique 8-sailed windmill. Still in
full working order, the mill
produces stoneground
wholemeal flour from the
highest quality organically
grown English wheat. Produce
is sold from a small shop on the
premises.

☞ adults 40p, children 20p
◗ Apr-mid Sep Sat, Sun, Bank
Hols 2-4.30; mid Sep-Mar Sun
2-4; key available from craft
centre during office hours
Facilities: 🚻 🚗

🎣 Map 1 A4
F A and J Jones
Red House Farm, North Scarle,
Lincoln, Lincolnshire LN6 9HB
Tel. Spalford (052277) 224

MAP 1

● **Heckington Windmill**

MAP 1   EAST ENGLAND

From Lincoln follow A46 south westwards, after 4 miles turn right onto unclassified road for 5 miles through Eagle to North Scarle.

The main specialities of Red House Farm are traditional Lincolnshire sausages and raised pork pies, but they also supply sausage rolls, Cornish pasties, Lincolnshire haslet, potted beef and many other products which are all made on the premises. They use no artificial preservatives, flavourings or colourings and the meat is from animals which have been humanely kept in a natural uncrowded environment free from growth promoters and antibiotics. Meat can be supplied from as little as 1/2lb packs of sausages to a large freezer order, packed and labelled.

● all year Wed, Thur, Sat 8.30-12.30, 1.30-5, Fri 8.30-12.30, 1.30-7

🏠 Map 1 E5
Manor House Folk Museum

West Street, Alford, Lincolnshire
Tel. Alford (05212) 6385

In town centre.

A thatched Elizabethan manor house which is now a folk museum with interesting local history displays. Exhibits include machinery and furnishings from an old sweet factory that made pear drops, a collection of Victorian kitchenware and equipment from an old dairy.

☞ adults 30p, children 15p
● May-Sep Mon-Fri, Bank Hol weekends 10.30-1, 2-4
Facilities: 🚻 ♿

🌾 Map 1 D3
Maud Foster Mill

Willoughby Road, Boston, Lincolnshire
Tel. Boston (0205) 52188

In town centre.

Visitors can look around this working 5-sailed windmill which sells its own stoneground flour in sizes ranging from 3 1/2lb bags to 70lb sacks.

☞ adults 60p, children 30p
● Apr-Dec Wed 10-5, Sun 2-5
Facilities: 🚗

● **Alford Town Centre**

MAP 1

Map 1 E5
Mawthorpe Museum
Woodlands, Mawthorpe,
Alford, Lincolnshire LN13 9LU
Tel. Alford (05212) 2336
*From Alford follow B1196
southwards for 2 miles to
Mawthorpe.*

This privately-owned farm
museum features steam
engines, a fair organ, dairy,
grocer's shop and, in
September, exhibitions of
threshing.

☞ adults 50p, senior citizens &
children 35p
● by appointment
Facilities: ☕ wc ⛟ ♨

Map 1 B5
**Museum of Lincolnshire
Life**
Burton Road, Lincoln,
Lincolnshire LN1 3LY
Tel. Lincoln (0522) 28448
In city centre. Signposted.

The importance of agriculture
in the history of Lincolnshire is
shown in the exhibits at this
museum. Visitors can see a
kitchen display from about
1900, a row of shop interiors
including a Co-op grocery and a
variety of agricultural
implements and machinery.

☞ adults 40p, children 20p
● May-Sep daily 10-5.30;
Oct-Apr Mon-Sat 10-5.30,
Sun 2-5.30
Facilities: ♿ wc ⛟ ♨
★ traditional cooking on
museum's cast iron range —
telephone for details

Map 1 D3
Sibsey Trader Windmill
Sibsey, Boston, Lincolnshire
Tel. Spalford (0522) 27468
*From Boston follow A16
northwards, after 5 miles turn
left onto unclassified road for ½
mile to Sibsey. Signposted.*

This mill is one of England's few
remaining 6-sailed corn mills
and is owned by English

Map 1 B1
THE GEORGE
71 St Martin's, Stamford,
Lincolnshire PE9 2LB
Tel: Stamford (0780) 55171
In town centre.

A traditional English inn
which was once one of the
main coaching inns. Their
recipe for Summer Pudding is
simple, delicious and fresh.
● daily Meals: 12.30-2.30,
7.30-10.30
Price range £3-20
Seats 150
Cards: Access, Amex, Diners,
Visa
Facilities: ♀ ♨ ♿ ⛟

SUMMER PUDDING

*12oz raspberries
1lb blackcurrants
1lb blackberries
4oz sugar
2 tbsp water
1 medium white loaf sliced*
Place all the ingredients
except the bread into a
saucepan. Cook gently to
soften the fruit and dissolve
the sugar. Allow to cool, drain
the fruit and save the juices.
Line a pudding basin with
slices of bread, add some of
the fruit and cover with a
slice of bread. Repeat 4 times
to make 4 layers setting aside
a little fruit for decoration.
Pour the juices over the
pudding, weight it down and
chill for a couple of hours.
Turn out onto a plate and
decorate.

Heritage. Built in 1877 it was
working until 1953. At one time
there were about 800 corn
mills in Lincolnshire, at least 25
of which had 6 sails. Visitors can
follow a self-guided tour
around the mill and also look at
an exhibition on how the mill
works.

☞ adults 50p, senior citizens
35p, children 25p

● Apr-Sep Mon-Sat 9.30-6.30,
Sun 2-6.30
Facilities: wc ⛟ ♨
★ milling & threshing days
during the year — telephone
for details

Map 1 B1
**Stamford Steam Brewery
Museum**
All Saints Street, Stamford,
Lincolnshire PE9 2PA
Tel. Stamford (0780) 52186
In town centre.

At the turn of the century
steam breweries existed in
many towns. Today, only the
Stamford Steam Brewery
Museum remains intact.
Originally a timber-framed
medieval dwelling, it has been
both a malthouse and brewery.
Unusually, the museum still
houses all the original 19thC
equipment such as the mash
tun, cooler, coppers and crown
corkers. An audio-visual display
explains each stage of the
brewing process, bringing alive
the sounds and smells of a
brewery in full production.
Collectors' Beer, made on the
premises, is for sale.

☞ adults £1.20, senior citizens
60p, children (over 5) 60p
● Apr-Sep Wed-Sun, Bank Hols
10-4, closed Wed after Bank
Hols
Facilities: wc

MAP 2 EAST ENGLAND

Map showing East England with locations including:

5 — Hunstanton, Holkham, THE SMITHY, Wells-next-the-Sea, A H ATHILL, CLEY SMOKE HOU, Blakeney, Brancaster, 149

4 — NORFOLK LAVENDER, Docking, LETHERINGSETT WATERMILL, THE HOLT CHEESE SHOP AND DELICATESSEN, Little Walsingham, PARK FARM, Snettisham, SNETTISHAM WATERMILL, GREAT BIRCHAM WINDMILL, Sandringham, 148, Saxth, Fakenham, Guist, SALLE MOOR HALL

3 — Hillington, King's Lynn, Weasenham, ELMHAM WINES, Narborough, LEXHAM HALL, NORFOLK RURAL LIFE MUSEL, CASTLE ACRE PRIORY, DUNHAM MUSEUM, East Dereham, Bawdeswell

2 — Outwell, WELLE MANOR HALL, Market, Fincham, Swaffham, ADLARD'S RESTAURANT, Wymondham, Watton, Attleborough, Southery, Mundford, New Buckenh

1 — Littleport, Brandon, Thetford, Elveden, Kenninghall, Diss, Ely, Botesdale, Stretham, Mildenhall

A   B   C   D

Until the mid-18th century the Herring Fair held in Great Yarmouth lasted for 40 days, such was its popularity. People would come from miles to drink, dance and eat the fresh, salted or smoked herrings. In October, every year, they still hold special thanksgiving services for the 'Harvest of the Sea' in Great Yarmouth. The churches are hung with fishermen's nets and the porches are decorated with fish — traditionally 39 varieties are used in honour of the 39 Articles of the Church of England.

♪ **Map 2 D5**
A H Athill
Scaldbeck Barn, Morston, Holt, Norfolk NR25 7BJ
Tel. Cley (0263) 740306
From Blakeney follow A149 westwards for 2 miles to Morston. Signposted.

Andrew Athill runs a small friendly business offering fresh shellfish and local fish. He sells his own oysters throughout the year by the half-dozen and mussels from September to April by the pint or gallon. He will supply cockles to order,

NORFOLK

plus mullet, dabs and whitebait in season. Visitors can view the oyster beds by appointment.

☞ free
◑ all year daily any reasonable time
Facilities: 🚻 🚌

Map 2 F3
The Broads Museum
Sutton Windmill, Sutton, Nr Stalham, Norfolk NE12 9RZ
Tel. Stalham (0692) 81195

From Stalham follow A149 southwards, after 1½ miles turn left onto unclassified road for ½ mile to Sutton. Signposted.

The Broads Museum is sited at Sutton Mill, Britain's tallest windmill, which was built in 1789 and milled corn up to 1940. The museum has a wide range of historic kitchen equipment, including apple peelers, marmalade cutters and pudding boilers. Also on show are a range of coopers' barrel-making tools and the mill's historic machinery. The museum sells homemade jams.

☞ adults £1.00, children 50p
◑ 15 May-Sep daily 10-6; Apr-14 May Sun-Wed 1.30-5.30
Facilities: 🍴 🚻 🚌 ⛺

🍴 tea room serves 4 kinds of tea & coffee

Map 2 C3
Castle Acre Priory
Stocks Green, Castle Acre, King's Lynn, Norfolk PE32 2AF
Tel. Castle Acre (0760) 5394

From Swaffham follow A1065 northwards, after 4 miles turn left onto unclassified road for ½ mile to priory. Signposted.

Castle Acre was founded around 1090 as a Cluniac priory. The monastic herb garden has been newly created by English

161

MAP 2   EAST ENGLAND

Heritage and grows herbs similar to those grown in the Middle Ages. Herb plants can be bought from the shop.

☞ adults 1.00, senior citizens 75p, children 50p
● Apr-Sep daily 9.30-6.30; Oct-Mar Wed-Sun 9.30-4
Facilities: ♿ 🚻 🚗 ♨

REGIONAL RECIPE

PIG'S FRY

A local farm labourer's dish which is traditionally served with dumplings.

2lb pig's fry
2oz seasoned flour
2oz dripping

Heat the oven to gas 4 (350F, 180C). Cut the prepared fry into small pieces and roll in the seasoned flour. Put in a greased roasting tin and cover with water, leaving the top of the meat sticking out, and dot with dripping. Bake for 1 hour.

Map 2 D5
Cley Smoke House
Cley, Holt, Norfolk
Tel. Cley (0263) 740282

From Blakeney follow A149 eastwards for 1 mile to Cley.

Visitors can see herrings, salmon and cod's roe being smoked at this small-scale traditional fish smokery. They are all on sale as are homemade pâtés and rollmops in cider vinegar.

☞ free
● Apr-mid Oct daily 9-5.30; mid-Oct-Mar daily 10-4.30

Map 2 E5
Cromer Museum
East Cottages, Tucker Street, Cromer, Norfolk NR27 9HB
Tel. Cromer (0263) 513543

In town centre. Signposted.

Cromer has long been famous for its crabs and while the local

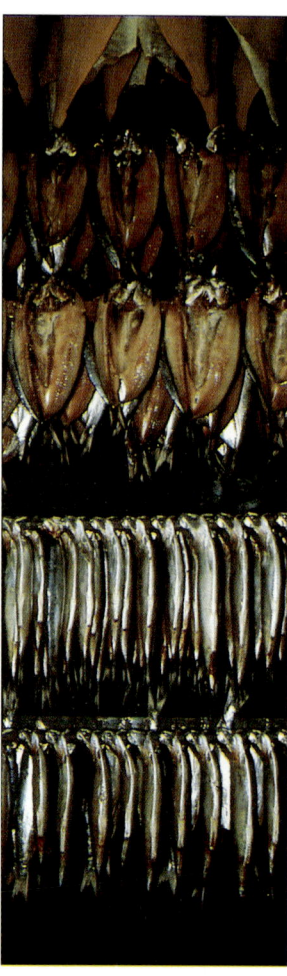

● **Reggie Jonas's smoke house, Cromer**

fishing fleet has been in decline for many years, a handful of boats still bring in crabs, herrings, cod and whelks at different times of the year. A highlight of the museum is a real fisherman's cottage of 90 years ago fitted with the original range and working gaslights.

☞ Spring Bank Hol-Sep 30p, Oct- Spring Bank Hol 20p
● all year Mon 10-1, 2-5, Tue-Sat 10-5, Sun 2-5
Facilities: 🚻

★ Aug cooking on the fisherman's cottage range

Map 2 C3
Dunham Museum
Old Station House, Little Dunham, King's Lynn, Norfolk PE32 2EJ
Tel. Swaffham (0760) 23073

From Swaffham follow A47 eastwards, after 4 miles turn left onto unclassified road for 2 miles to Little Dunham. Signposted.

A museum of everyday life situated in the former Little Dunham railway station, which boasts over 1,000 items. Kitchen and dairy exhibits include a cottage stove, ham press, butter churns, honey spinners and an egg incubator. Guided tours are available.

☞ adults £1.00, children 25p
● Apr-Sep daily 10-5.30; Oct-Mar daily 11-3
Facilities: ♿ 🚻 🚗 ♨ /⚊

Map 2 D3
Elmham Wines
Elmham House, North Elmham, Dereham, Norfolk NR20 5JY
Tel. Dereham (0362) 81571

From East Dereham follow B1110 northwards for 6 miles to North Elmham.

The first experimental vines were planted on the Elmham Estate in 1966. Following encouraging results the first commercial acreage was planted in 1970-71 and the vineyards now cover 6 acres on

MAP 2

3 sites. The wines, which are made and bottled on the estate, are produced mainly from the Madeline-Angevine and Müller-Thurgau vines, although the latter are gradually being replaced. In addition there are several other varieties including Kerner and Huxelrebe. The winery is situated in a pantiled 18thC building and is equipped with a modern wine press and fermentation tanks. Elmham Park dry and medium-dry wines have been exported to Australia and the United States. Elmham House Norfolk Apple Wine is also produced in the winery from freshly pressed English apples.

☞ £1.00
◑ by appointment
Facilities: ▨ 🚗 ♨

❦ Map 2 E4
Felbrigg Hall
Felbrigg, Norwich,
Norfolk NR11 8PR
Tel. West Runton (026375) 444

From Cromer follow A148 south westwards, after 2 miles turn left onto B1436 for 1 mile to house on right. Signposted.

Felbrigg Hall, now owned by the National Trust, is one of the finest 17thC houses in Norfolk. A special feature is its restored walled garden which has a traditional layout of herbaceous borders and includes greenhouses, vegetables, fruit trees and a herb border. Visitors can also see the magnificent restored dovecote. The old kitchen is now the restaurant and one wall is full of gleaming copper pans. The shop sells a selection of National Trust products including teas, preserves, mustards and chocolates.

☞ hall & gardens: adults £2.50, children (under 17) £1.25; gardens: 50p
◑ 2 Apr-Oct Mon, Wed, Thur, Sat, Sun 1.30-5.30

Facilities: ☕ ◖◗ ▨ 🚗 ♨
◖◗ lunches & teas including homemade dishes from traditional local recipes served in licensed restaurant

❦ Map 2 F2
Daphne ffiske Herbs
Rosemary Cottage, The Street,
Bramerton, Norwich,
Norfolk NR14 7DW
Tel. Surlingham (05088) 8187

From Norwich follow A146 south eastwards, after 4 miles turn left onto unclassified road for 1 mile to Bramerton.

A well-established herb nursery with a wide range of plants on display. Visitors can buy labelled herb plants in containers.

☞ free
◑ Mar-Sep Thur-Sun, Bank Hols 10-4
Facilities: 🚗

✻ Map 2 B4
Great Bircham Windmill
Great Bircham, King's Lynn,
Norfolk PE31 6SJ
Tel. Syderstone (048523) 393

From Docking follow B1153 southwards for 3 miles to Great Bircham. Signposted.

There was a windmill on this site in 1769 but the current 5-floor tower mill dates from 1846, with the bakery added slightly later. Milling ceased in the 1930s but the bakery was still in use until 1950. Visitors are welcome to wander around the fully restored mill and see the bakery with its original oven, dough trough and baking implements.

☞ adults £1.00, senior citizens 85p, children 60p
◑ 22 May-Sep Sun-Fri 10-6; 3 Apr-22 May Sun, Wed, Bank Hols 10-6
Facilities: ◖◗ ▨ 🚗
◖◗ tea rooms serve cream teas & homemade cakes

▨ Map 2 D4
The Holt Cheese Shop and Delicatessen
35 Market Place, Holt, Norfolk
Tel. Holt (0263) 713883

In town centre.

A wide variety of home-produced farmhouse cheese is on sale at this delicatessen which also specialises in genuine Italian salamis and Parma ham. It sells fresh pasta, homemade sauces and pastries, and the local herbal drink, Norfolk Punch.

● all year Mon-Sat 9-5

✻ Map 2 D4
Letheringsett Watermill
Riverside Road, Letheringsett,
Nr Holt, Norfolk NR25 7YD
Tel. Holt (0263) 713153

From Holt follow A148 westwards for 1 mile to Letheringsett. Signposted.

On a site listed in the Domesday Book, this working watermill demonstrates the craft of grinding corn into 100% wholewheat flour, which is for sale along with bakers' white flour.

☞ adults 50p, children 25p; demonstrations: adults £1.00, senior citizens 75p, children 25p
● 3 Apr-Sep Tue-Fri 9-1, 2-5, Sat 9-1, Sun, Bank Hols 2-5; Oct-Easter Tue-Fri 9-1, 2-5, Sat 9-1
Facilities: 🚗 ♨

✐ Map 2 C3
Lexham Hall
Nr Litcham, King's Lynn,
Norfolk PE32 2QJ
Tel. Fakenham (0328) 701288

From Litcham follow B1145 westwards, after ½ mile turn left onto unclassified road for ½ mile to vineyard on left.

Part of a large family-owned farming estate, the vineyard consists of 8 acres producing some 16,000 bottles of dry white wine a year. All 4

MAP 2   **EAST ENGLAND**

varieties can be bought at the estate office.

☞ estate office: free
◗ all year Mon-Fri 8.30-4.30 by appointment
Facilities: 🚗

🦌 Map 2 E3
The Mousetrap
2 St Gregory's Alley, Norwich, Norfolk NR2 1ER
Tel. Norwich (0603) 614083
In city centre.

This shop stocks a wide range of top quality cheeses and specialises in farmhouse varieties from Britain, southern Ireland and France. Fresh pasta is made on the premises and also smoked salmon pâté. Other produce includes a small

selection of cold meats, olives, olive oil, biscuits, a range of pasta sauces, houmous, taramasalata and some vegetarian specialities.
◗ all year Tue-Sat 9-5, Mon 10-2, closed Bank Hols

🦌 Map 2 E3
The Mustard Shop
3 Bridewell Alley, Norwich, Norfolk NR2 1AQ
Tel. Norwich (0603) 627889
In city centre.

To mark the 150th anniversary of their founding, Colmans opened the Mustard Shop. Restored and decorated in late 19thC style, the shop houses a mustard museum with displays

on the history and production of Colmans' mustard. A wide range of mustards is on sale, from 3 traditional blends to a selection of powder mustards made specially for the shop including dry mustard with tarragon and thyme, dry crunchy mustard and the genuine double superfine. There are 11 flavours in prepared form, including 3 French speciality mustards and a range of English herbal mustards. Many of the articles offered for sale, which include pottery and linen items, are packaged in designs taken from the Company's archives and are unique to the shop.
◗ all year Mon, Wed, Fri, Sat 9-5.30, Tue 9.30-5.30

🌿 Map 2 B4
Norfolk Lavender
Caley Mill, Heacham, King's Lynn, Norfolk PE31 7JE
Tel. Heacham (0485) 70384
From Hunstanton follow A149 southwards for 3 miles to farm. Signposted.

Norfolk Lavender is the only lavender farm in England. Almost 100 acres of lavender grow on this beautiful riverside site with varieties differing in size, colour and fragrance. There is also a herb garden including culinary, aromatic and decorative plants. Guided tours are available which take in the

● **The Mustard Shop, Norwich**

MAP 2

• **Norfolk Lavender**

drying barn and working distillery during the harvest. Both herb and lavender plants are on sale at the Conservatory Shop along with lavender gifts and toiletries.

☞ free; guided tours 70p
◑ grounds: Whitsun-Sep daily 10-5.30; Oct-Whitsun Mon-Fri 9-4; shops: Easter-Sep daily 10-5.30; gift shop: Oct-Easter Mon-Fri 9-4
Facilities: 🖥 🍴 ♿ 🚾 🚗
🍴 Millers Cottage tea room serves cream teas, homemade cakes & light lunches; open Easter-Spring Bank Hol Sat, Sun 2.30-5.30, Spring Bank Hol-Sep daily 10.30-5.30

🏬 Map 2 D3
Norfolk Rural Life Museum
Beech House, Gressenhall, East Dereham, Norfolk NR20 4DR
Tel. Dereham (0362) 860563
From East Dereham follow B1110 northwards, after 2 miles turn left onto B1146 for ¹/₂ mile to museum. Signposted.

The Norfolk Rural Life Museum's collection of agricultural instruments and dairy equipment is one of the finest in the country. It paints a fascinating picture of farm life in the days of horse and steam power. Many of the implements were made by local foundries and Craftsmen's Row contains authentic reconstructions of

the artisans' shops as well as a village bakery, seed merchant's shop and village general store. Cherry Tree Cottage is a typical farmworker's cottage with a kitchen containing a blackleaded range, stone sink and iron water-pump. The garden is planted with old fashioned flowers, fruit trees and traditional vegetables. Holiday activities are arranged for children.

☞ adults 60p, children (4-16) 10p
◑ 3 Apr-Oct Tue-Sat, Bank Hols 10-5, Sun 2-5.30
Facilities: 🍴 ♿ 🚾 🚗 🛈
★ 28 Aug harvest tea where traditional tea is served

🍴 tea room, open Sun pm, serves homemade cakes & scones

🐓 Map 2 B4
Park Farm
Snettisham, King's Lynn, Norfolk PE31 7NQ
Tel. Dersingham (0485) 41244
In village. Signposted.

Park Farm has all the usual farm animals — cattle, sheep, pigs, chickens and goats — but a farm tour will also introduce visitors to deer and crayfish ranching. There are 3 farm trails to follow and an interpretation centre with audio-visual displays showing what happens on the farm during a typical working year. The farm is known for its free-range eggs, crayfish and venison, which can be bought from the farm shop.

☞ adults £1.50, senior citizens £1.25, children (under 18) 70p
◑ Apr-Sep Sun-Fri 10.30-5.30
Facilities: 🖥 🍴 ♿ 🚾 🚗 🛈
★ Jul & Sep sheep-shearing & sheep dipping

🍾 Map 2 E1
Pulham Vineyards
Mill Lane, Pulham Market, Diss, Norfolk IP21 4XL
Tel. Pulham Market (037976) 672

• **Village shop, Norfolk Rural Life Museum**

MAP 2   **EAST ENGLAND**

From Long Stratton follow A140 southwards, after 3 miles turn left onto B1134 for 1 mile to Pulham Market. Signposted.

Visitors are welcome on self-guided or accompanied tours of this vineyard and winery. The Magdalen wines produced here can be tasted and bought and strawberries and vegetables are also available in season.

☞ tour & tasting: £1.75
◐ sales: all year daily 10.30-5; tour: May-Sep by appointment
Facilities: 🚻 🚗 ♨

● **Pulham Vineyards near Diss, Norfolk**

☺ Map 2 D4
Salle Moor Hall
Salle, Reepham, Norwich, Norfolk NR10 4SB
Tel. Norwich (0603) 870247

From Bawdeswell follow B1145 north eastwards, after 5 miles turn left into Woodallington Road for ½ mile to Salle. Signposted.

A pick your own farm selling strawberries, raspberries, gooseberries, blackcurrants and broad beans which are also available ready-picked.
◐ end Jun-mid Aug Tue-Sat 9-5, Sun 9-1
Facilities: 🚻 🚗 ♨

🎣 Map 2 C5
The Smithy
Brancaster Staithe, King's Lynn, Norfolk
Tel. Brancaster (0485) 210638

From Brancaster follow A149 eastwards for 1 mile to Brancaster Staithe. Signposted.

Harbourmaster Mervyn Nudds farms mussels in Brancaster Harbour — the only EEC-recognised pollution-free

harbour in England and Wales. At low water visitors can walk to the mussel beds ½ mile away but they should remember to bring their boots. Mussels are sold in season, from September to April.

☞ free
◐ by appointment

🏚 Map 2 B4
Snettisham Watermill
The Mill House, Snettisham, King's Lynn, Norfolk PE31 7QJ
Tel. Hencham (0485) 42180

In village. Signposted.

This mill is a working museum with its original 'high technology' 18thC machinery. The miller demonstrates how the mill works and how stoneground flour is produced. An accompanying exhibition traces the history of the mill together with that of the village of Snettisham. Visitors can stroll by the delightful gardens and mill pool and feed the ducks with bread baked with Snettisham flour. Stoneground wholemeal flour is sold from the mill shop in 3½lb bags along with a variety of homemade

jams and preserves including banana chutney and marmalade and Norfolk punch and honey.

☞ adults 80p, senior citizens 70p, children (3-16) 40p
◐ May Sat, Sun, Thur, Bank Hols 10-5.30; 9 Jul-11 Sep Sat, Sun, Wed, Thur, Bank Hols 10-5.30 or by appointment
Facilities: 🚗

🏚 Map 2 F4
Stow Mill
Paston, North Walsham, Norfolk NR28 9TG
Tel. Mundesley (0263) 720298

From Mundesley follow B1159 southwards for ¼ mile to mill.

This corn windmill has recently been restored to working order and visitors are welcome.
☞ adults 20p, children 10p
◐ all year daily 9-5

☺ Map 2 E4
Tylers
The Cedars, Thorpe Market Road, Roughton, Norwich, Norfolk NR11 8TB
Tel. Southrepps (026379) 777

From Cromer follow A140 southwards, after 3½ miles turn

166

MAP 2

left onto B1436 for ½ mile to farm.

A pick your own farm and shop selling a good range of seasonal fruits and vegetables. Some unusual varieties of apples are for sale and all are available ready-picked as are most of the vegetables. Ice cream made from farm grown fruit is also for sale.

● end Jun-Dec Mon-Fri 9-6, Sat 9-5
Facilities: ▧ 🚐 ♨

🦂 Map 2 A2
Welle Manor Hall
Upwell, Norfolk PE14 9AB
Tel. Wisbech (0945) 772121

From Outwell follow unclassified road southwards for 2 miles to Upwell. Signposted.

This fortified manor house and church, occupied by Benedictine monks between 974 and 1539, has some of the earliest brickwork in Norfolk. It is also the home of the medieval herbal drink, Norfolk Punch, which is still made in the traditional manner. Visitors are welcome to tour the herborium and taste the punch. Herbal teas, Norfolk Delight sweetmeat, Christmas puddings, teatowels and of course punch are sold in the shop. There is also a unique silenium mineral spa — the only one in England — and a craft museum with a collection of Lafayette photographs and equipment, horse-drawn vehicles and agricultural implements.

☛ guided tour & punch tasting: adults £1.00
● all year 1st Sun of month tour at 3pm
Facilities: 🚌 🍴 ♿ ▧ 🚐 ♨ ⛟
🍴 restaurant serves lunches, teas & dinners with organic foods, including vegetarian dishes

NORFOLK TURKEYS
The Norfolk black turkey, with its distinctive and subtle flavour, is once again bred and for sale in this area.

☺ Map 2 E3
White House Farm
Sprowston, Norwich, Norfolk
Tel. Norwich (0603) 419357

From Norwich follow A1151 north eastwards, after 3 miles turn right at Blue Boar Inn onto unclassified road for ½ mile to farm on left. Signposted.

This pick your own farm and shop sells strawberries, gooseberries, raspberries, blackberries, blackcurrants, apples and plums. Home-produced asparagus is a speciality and the shop also stocks locally grown onions and potatoes in season.

● mid Jun-Jan daily; Apr-mid Jun Sat-Sun
Facilities: ▧ 🚐 ♨ ⛟

RESTAURANT RECIPE

🍷 Map 2 D2
ADLARD'S RESTAURANT
16 Damgate Street, Wymondham, Norwich, Norfolk NR18 0BQ
Tel: Norwich (0953) 603533
In village.

This old building was once a butcher's shop and there is still plenty of butcher's paraphernalia about the place. Their recipe for Warm Wild Duck En Croute with a port and cinnamon sauce makes a rich and moist dish.

● Tue-Sat Meals: evenings only
Price range £16 - 3 courses, £17.50 - 4 courses
Seats 25
Facilities: 🍷 ♿

WARM WILD DUCK EN CROUTE with a port and cinnamon sauce

4oz breast of wild duck
4oz lean pork
4oz pork back fat
2 tbsp reduced wild duck stock
a little port
a little brandy
quatre épices
seasoning
eggwash
puff pastry
vegetables for sauce: onion, celery, carrot
tomato puree
cinnamon stick
2 shallots chopped
unsalted butter

Heat oven to gas 5 (375F, 190C). Mince the meats and fat finely, add the stock, alcohol, seasonings and chill. Roll out 6 circles of pastry ¹⁄₁₆-inch thick, 4½-inch diameter and make a further 6 of 1½-inch diameter. Put the larger circle - one at a time - in a floured cup or salad bowl, spoon the mixture into the centre, cover with the smaller circle and turn out onto a floured board. Glaze the edges of the pastry with the eggwash, roll it up to enclose the meat, seal, brush lightly with the eggwash, pierce to make 2 air-holes and rest in fridge. To make the sauce: roast the duck carcase for about 20 minutes adding the onion, celery, carrot and tomato puree for the last 10 minutes. Put the bones in a saucepan, cover with water, season and simmer for 4 hours. Pass the stock through a sieve and reduce by half. Break up the cinnamon stick, cook in a little butter with the chopped shallots until soft, deglaze the pan with port, add the stock and reduce for 3 - 5 minutes. Meanwhile cook the meat parcels on a heavy tray lined with greaseproof paper for 15 minutes until golden brown. Beat a little unsalted butter into the sauce and serve with the duck.

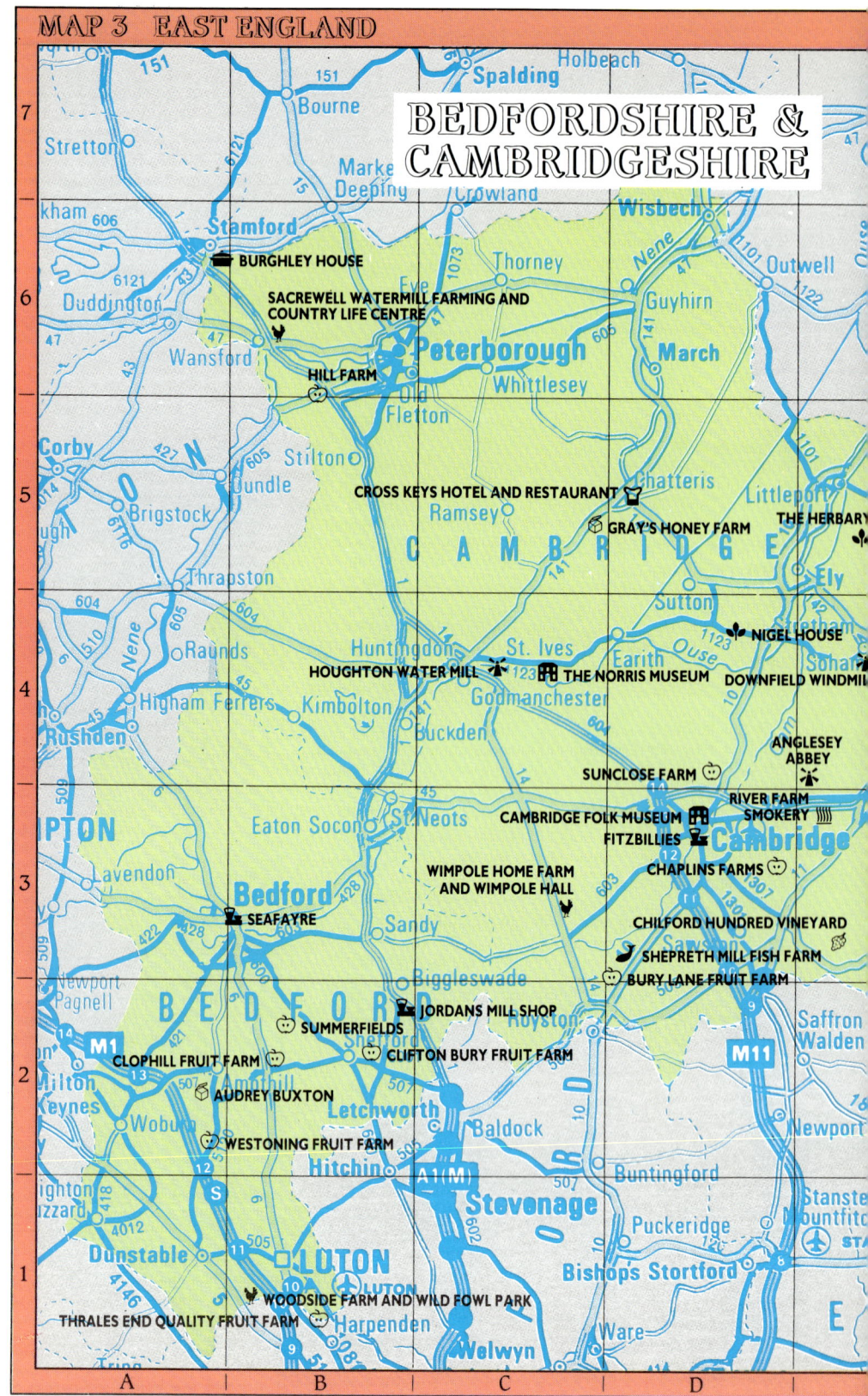

MAP 3   EAST ENGLAND

BEDFORDSHIRE & CAMBRIDGESHIRE

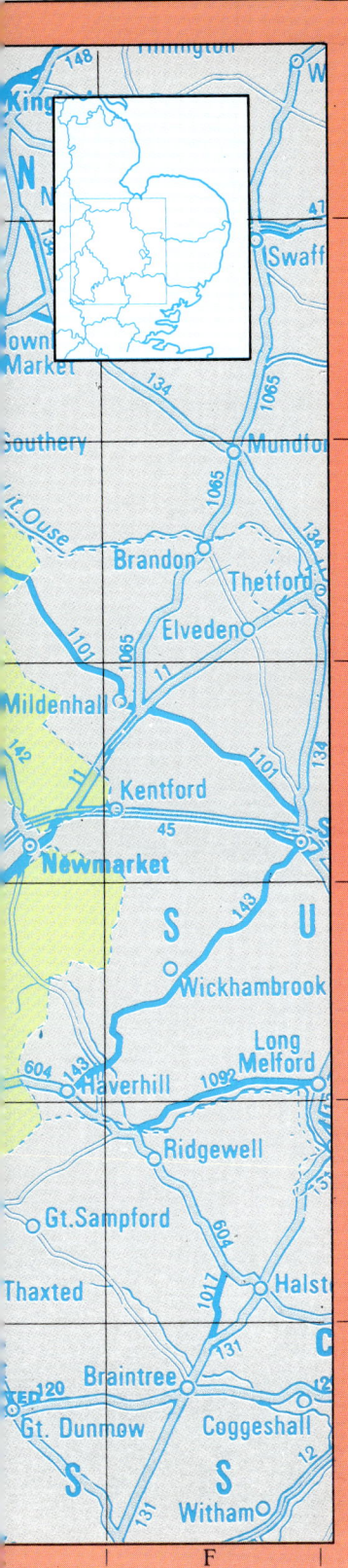

This is a fine part of the country dominated — in all senses of the word — by the University and its surrounding town. Rupert Brooke wrote: "And Cambridgeshire of all England The Shire for Men who Understand". University aside, there is plenty to visit. The area is famous for its market gardens and grows fruit and vegetables for the markets of London. Look out for asparagus and Cambridge greengages which ripen towards the end of summer and, provided there has been plenty of sun, are sweet and juicy. Cambridge Early — that prolific variety of strawberry — was developed in this area, although its popularity is now on the decline.

🏃 Map 3 E4
Anglesey Abbey
Lode, Cambridge,
Cambridgeshire CB5 9EJ
Tel. Cambridge (0223) 811200
From Cambridge follow A1303 eastwards, after 2½ miles turn left onto B1102 for 2 miles to Abbey on left. Signposted.
Built in about 1600, Anglesey Abbey is associated with the Augustinian order and has an ornamental 100-acre garden which was laid out this century by the first Lord Fairhaven. Visitors are invited to tour the working mill in the grounds and stoneground flour is for sale in the shop.

🎟 abbey & grounds: adults £3.50, children £1.75; gardens only: adults £1.50, children 75p
● abbey: 2 Apr-16 Oct Wed-Sun 1.30-5.30; gardens: 2 Apr-3 Jul Wed-Fri 1.30-5.30, Sat, Sun, Bank Hols 12-5.30; 4 Jul-16 Oct Wed-Sun 1.30-5.30
Facilities: ⏍ 🅆🄲 🚗 🚼
★ 1st Sun in month demonstrations of milling
⏍ lunches & teas including rolls & cakes made from own flour

🍲 Map 3 A6
Burghley House
Stamford, Lincolnshire PE9 3JY
Tel. Stamford (0780) 52451
From Stamford follow B1443 south eastwards for 1 mile to house. Signposted.
Burghley House, home of the Cecil family for over 400 years, dates back to Elizabethan times. In the oldest parts of the buildings visitors can see the original 16thC kitchen with its large collection of copper cooking utensils. The Great Hall houses the largest solid silver wine cooler in the world. The 18thC Orangery, designed by 'Capability' Brown in the Gothic Revival style, is now used as a licensed coffee shop.

🎟 adults £3.00, children (under 14) £1.70
● Easter-9 Oct daily 11-5, closed 10 Sep
Facilities: ⏍ ⏍ 🅆🄲 🚗 🚼
⏍ specialities include local pork pies, homemade cakes & biscuits; salad table 12-2

CHELSEA BUNS

Sold at Fitzbillies, Trumpington Street in Cambridge, these are deliciously gooey and sticky. Their recipe is a famous well-kept secret.

😋 Map 3 D3
Bury Lane Fruit Farm
Bury Lane, Melbourn, Royston, Hertfordshire SG8 6DF
Tel. Royston (0763) 60418
From Royston follow A10 north eastwards for 2 miles to farm on left just before Melbourn. Signposted.

A pick your own farm with a shop selling seasonal fruit and vegetables including strawberries, pears, stick beans and sweet corn. Unusual varieties of apples and Cambridge greengages are a speciality. Also on sale are farm produced cider and apple juice.
● all year daily 9-5
Facilities: 🅆🄲 🚗 🚼

MAP 3   EAST ENGLAND

⌾ Map 3 A2
Audrey Buxton
38 Maulden Road, Flitwick,
Bedfordshire
Tel. Flitwick (0525) 712466
*From Ampthill follow B530
westwards, after 1 mile turn left
onto A507 for 1 mile, then turn
right onto unclassified road for ½
mile to bungalow on left.*

This small apiary produces
delicious Bedfordshire honey
made from a mixture of nectar
collected from oil seed rape,
lime, blackberry, willow herb,
sycamore and horse chestnut,
which combine to give it an
unusual and satisfying blend of
flavours. Honey is for sale in jars
and when available — normally
in late July and August — by the
cut comb. Audrey is happy to
talk to visitors and show them
around her apiary.

☞ free
◑ any reasonable time by
appointment

⌂ Map 3 D3
Cambridge Folk Museum
2-3 Castle Street, Cambridge,
Cambridgeshire CB3 OAQ
Tel. Cambridge (0223) 355159
In town centre.

The Cambridge Folk Museum,
housed in the original premises
of the old White Horse Inn,
brings back to life everyday
scenes of the past. The kitchen
features a late 18thC grate,
cooking and laundry equipment
including an early gas cooker
manufactured in 1895 and a
pressure cooker from 1938.
There is a splendid 18thC
dresser which is used to display
all sorts of cooking gadgets
including a flywheel operated
food chopper and a marmalade
cutter. In the farm room there
is an exhibition of dairy
products — milking pails and
stools and even the basket in
which the famous Cambridge
Yard Butter was carried. The

original bar of the White Horse
Inn has been preserved as it
was in 1934 and visitors can see
handmade, mould blown wine
bottles, stoneware, glass casks
and pewter pots and measures.
The kitchen is used by a local
bakery to produce 'Mrs Beeton'
recipe products.

☞ adults 80p, senior citizens &
children 40p
◑ all year Mon-Sat 9.30-5.00,
Sun 2.30-4.30
Facilities: ♿ ♨ ⚱

♟ Map 3 D5
CROSS KEYS HOTEL AND RESTAURANT
16 Market Hill, Chatteris,
Cambridgeshire
Tel: Chatteris (03543) 3036
In town centre.

This pretty 16thC coaching
inn has an interesting
collection of antique clocks
and rifles.
◑ Mon-Sun Meals: until
10pm, closed Sun evenings to
non-residents
Price range £1.50-12
Set L £5.95
Seats 40
Cards: Access, Amex, Diners,
Visa
Facilities: ♟♨♿🚗

LOCAL RAINBOW TROUT

for each person take:
1 8oz trout
2oz prawns
2oz asparagus tips
½ pint white sauce
butter

Clean and gut the trout. Mix
the prawns and asparagus in
the white sauce and spoon
into the trout. Brush the fish
with melted butter and grill
for 8 minutes, then turn over
and grill for a further 8
minutes. Serve with fresh
seasonal vegetables.

☺ Map 3 D3
Chaplins Farms
"Bounds", 9 Doggett Lane,
Fulbourn, Cambridge,
Cambridgeshire CB1 5BT
Tel. Cambridge (0223) 880722
*From Cambridge follow A1307
south eastwards, after 1½ miles
turn left onto A1134 for 1 mile,
then turn right onto unclassified
road for 3 miles to Fulbourn.*

A pick your own farm with a
shop selling an interesting
variety of soft fruits including
autumn perpetual
strawberries. Other produce
for sale includes farm honey,
free-range eggs, delicious ice
cream and homemade jams.
Some vegetables are also
available.
◑ Jun-Oct daily 10-6
Facilities: 🚗 ⚱

✍ Map 3 E3
**Chilford Hundred
Vineyard**
Chilford Hall, Balsham Road,
Linton, Cambridge,
Cambridgeshire CB1 6LE
Tel. Cambridge (0223) 892641
*From Cambridge follow A1307
south eastwards for 7 miles and
continue on A604 for 3 miles,
then turn left onto B1052 for 2
miles to farm on left. Signposted.*

This vineyard was first planted
in 1972 and now produces 2
varieties of white wine. Visitors
can follow a trail around the
vineyard and winery, taste the
wines and receive a souvenir
glass. The vineyard grows
Müller-Thurgau, Ortega,
Huxelrebe, Siegerrebe and
Schönburger vines, all
cultivated without herbicides
or insecticides. Visitors can also
buy vines, wine accessories,
jams, biscuits and gift hampers.
☞ adults £1.95
◑ May-Sep Mon-Sat 10.30-5,
Sun 11-5
Facilities: 🍷🍴♿♿🚗⚱
★ 24-25 Sep English country
weekend — food from local
producers on show

• **Chilford Hundred Vineyard**

Map 3 B2
Clifton Bury Fruit Farm
Stanford Lane, Clifton, Shefford, Bedfordshire
Tel. Hitchin (0462) 814785

From Shefford follow A507 eastwards, after 1½ miles turn left onto unclassified road for ¼ mile to Clifton Bury, then turn left into Stanford Lane for ¼ mile to farm on right.

A pick your own farm specialising in main crop strawberries and raspberries. Gooseberries and red and blackcurrants are also available, as well as Victoria plums and sweet corn in September.
◐ end Jun-early Aug Tue, Wed, Fri-Sun 10-6, Thur 10-8; Sep Sat, Sun 10-5
Facilities: WC

Map 3 B2
Clophill Fruit Farm
Clophill, Ampthill, Bedfordshire
Tel. Silsoe (0525) 61456

From Luton follow A6 northwards, after 11 miles turn right at Flying Horse Inn onto unclassified road for ½ mile to farm on left.

A pick your own farm and shop selling most berries and currants throughout the season including loganberries and tayberries. Twelve different varieties of strawberries are an unusual speciality. All fruits can be picked to order. Also on sale is a selection of local produce including cream, honey and selected vegetables.
◐ end Jun-Aug daily 9-9
Facilities: WC

Map 3 E4
Downfield Windmill
Fordham Road, Soham, Ely, Cambridgeshire
Tel. Ely (0353) 720333

From Soham follow A142 southwards for 1 mile to mill on right at junction with A1123.

The Downfield Mill dates partly from 1726 and was restored from 1975-80 when it started grinding again. One of the few windmills that work all year, it has 2 pairs of millstones, one wind driven, the other engine powered. Visitors can see the whole milling process. Organic and non-organic wholemeal and brown flour, stoneground oatmeal, ryemeal, barley and maize meal, bran and wheat gluten can be bought from the mill's shop.
☞ adults 60p, children 30p
◐ all year Sun, Bank Hols 11-5
Facilities: WC

• **Downfield Windmill**

Map 3 D3
Fitzbillies
52 Trumpington Street, Cambridge, Cambridgeshire CB2 1RG
Tel. Cambridge (0223) 352500

In city centre.

There are 2 branches of this tea room in Cambridge both of which have become almost as much institutions as the university. Renowned for its breads, pastries, sponges,

MAP 3   **EAST ENGLAND**

muffins, lardy cakes and delicious ice-cream sundaes, Fitzbillies is most famous for its sticky Chelsea buns made from a secret recipe. A range of savoury dishes such as vol-au-vents, quiches, pies and sandwiches are popular at lunch times. Handmade chocolates are also on sale and celebration cakes for birthdays and weddings can be ordered. Traditional and exotic teas and coffees are provided by Lays and these can also be bought to take home. Other branch at 50 Regent Street, Cambridge.
⬤ Trumpington Street: all year Mon-Sat 8-5; Regent Street: Easter-end Aug Mon-Sat 9-5, Sun 11-6; Sep-Mar Mon-Sat 9-5 Facilities: 🍽️ ⬤ 🚻

⬧ Map 3 C5
Gray's Honey Farm
Cross Drove,
Warboys, Huntingdon,
Cambridgeshire PE17 2JQ
Tel. Chatteris (03543) 3798

From Chatteris follow A141 south westwards, after 2 miles turn left into Cross Drove Road for ¼ mile to farm on left. Signposted.

Visitors to this honey farm may watch the bees at work in the observation hive and are welcome to wander in the exhibition area with displays on bee-keeping past and present. Visitors are also invited to have a go at making their own beeswax candles. Honey from the farm is sold in jars and by cut comb. The shop also sells Australian and whisky and rum-flavoured honey and a range of honey products including confectionery and biscuits.

☞ adults 50p, children 25p
⬤ exhibition & shop: Apr-Oct Mon-Sat 10.30-6.30; shop only:

Nov-Mar Tue-Sat, Bank Hols 2-5
Facilities: 🍽️ 🚻 🚗 🐾
🍽️ honey teas served

🌿 Map 3 E5
The Herbary
Mile End, Prickwillow, Ely, Cambridgeshire CB7 4SJ
Tel. Prickwillow (035388) 456

From Ely follow B1382 eastwards for 4½ miles to Prickwillow. Signposted.

This 3-acre herb farm is owned by a husband and wife team who supply herbs all year to wholesale markets, hotels and restaurants throughout Britain. On a tour of the farm visitors can see 70 species of culinary herbs growing in fields and poly-tunnels as well as a formal herb garden and a pot plant nursery. They can stroll through the pleasant 19thC orchard and garden and have tea under the trees. Fifteen varieties of culinary herbs are on sale at all times, either fresh-cut or

⬤ **A Fitzbillies speciality**

MAP 3

● Jordans Mill Shop

container-grown, but from April to October a larger selection is available. The proprietors or their qualified staff are always on hand to discuss the growing and use of culinary herbs. Fen-grown exotic vegetables and edible flowers are also sold in season as are herb jellies, vinegars and mustards.

☞ free
◐ all year daily 8-7
Facilities: 🍽 🍴 wc 🚗
★ occasional seminars on herb cookery & herb growing with nationally known speakers & demonstrators
🍴 lunches & teas include herb salads, crudités with herb dips, herb-flavoured cheeses, local goats' cheese, homebaked ham & roast beef

☺ Map 3 B6
Hill Farm
Chesterton, Peterborough, Cambridgeshire PE7 3UH
Tel. Peterborough (0733) 233270

From Peterborough follow A605 south westwards for 4 miles to farm. Signposted.
A pick your own farm selling a good range of seasonal soft fruit and some vegetables including sweet corn and potatoes. All produce is also available ready-picked and some in frozen packs.
◐ end Jun-mid Aug Mon-Fri 9-8, Sat, Sun 9-6
Facilities: 🍽 wc 🚗 🍴

✶ Map 3 C4
Houghton Water Mill
Houghton, Huntingdon, Cambridgeshire PE17 2AZ
Tel. St Ives (0480) 301494
From Huntingdon follow A1123 eastwards, after 2 miles turn right onto unclassified road for ½ mile to mill. Signposted.
Houghton Mill, in a beautiful island setting on the River Great Ouse, is owned by the National Trust. A milling museum with machinery dating back over 200 years, it runs on

the first weekend of every month and makes and sells stoneground wholemeal flour.
☞ adults 80p, children 40p
◐ Easter-18 Sep Sat-Wed 2-5.30
Facilities: wc

⛏ Map 3 B2
Jordans Mill Shop
Holme Mills, Biggleswade, Bedfordshire SG18 9JX
Tel. Biggleswade (0767) 318222

From Biggleswade follow A6001 southwards, after 1 mile turn right onto unclassified road for ¼ mile to mill.

Set on the River Ivel amidst delightful scenery, Jordans Mill Shop offers a full range of products from the country's leading wholefood manufacturer. There are 30 items from cereals and flours to crunchy bars, as well as a variety of local craft products to choose from.
◐ all year Mon-Fri 9.30-1, 2-5, Sat 9.30-12.30
Facilities: wc 🚗

MAP 3　　　　　　　**EAST ENGLAND**

❧ Map 3 D4
Nigel House
High Street, Wilburton, Ely,
Cambridgeshire CB6 3RA
Tel. Ely (0353) 740824

*From Stretham follow A1123
westwards for 1½ miles to
Wilburton.*

Nigel House is a private herb
garden which grows over 220
different culinary, aromatic,
medicinal, Biblical and
Shakespearian herbs. Herbs are
sold fresh cut in bunches, in
pots and dried. Dried flowers
are also available.

☞ free
● May-Sep Thur-Tue 10-6
Facilities: 🚾 ♨

🏛 Map 3 C4
The Norris Museum
The Broadway, St Ives,
Huntingdon,
Cambridgeshire PE17 4BX
Tel. St Ives (0480) 65101

In town centre.

The Norris Museum shows the
history of Huntingdonshire's
rural life through agricultural
and archaeological exhibits.
Amongst the displays are the
remains of a 2,000-year-old
Roman dinner. There is also a
library and riverside garden.

☞ free
● Jan-Apr, Oct-Dec Tue-Fri 10-1,
2-4, Sat 10-12; May-Sep Tue-Fri
10-1, 2-5, Sat 10-12, 2-5, Sun 2-5

〰 Map 3 E3
River Farm Smokery
Great Wilbraham Road,
Bottisham, Nr Newmarket,
Cambridgeshire
Tel. Cambridge (0223) 811382

*From Cambridge follow A1303
eastwards, after 6 miles turn
right into Great Wilbraham Road
for ¼ mile to smokery.
Signposted.*

This smokery cures and
smokes a wide range of meats

and fish in the traditional way
over Fenland peat, fine English
oak and hardwoods. Its range of
smoked fish includes salmon,
trout, eel, pike, cockles, mussels
and tunny and its range of
smoked meats includes hams,
tongue, duck, pheasant and
quail. The smokery also makes
a range of smoked pâtés
including trout, mackerel,
salmon, salmon and shrimp and
other delicacies like potted
brown shrimps, potted cockles
in garlic butter and potted
salmon with dill. Visitors are
welcome to view the smokery
by appointment.

☞ free
● by appointment
Facilities: 🚐

♥ Map 3 B6
**Sacrewell Watermill
Farming and Country Life
Centre**
Sacrewell,
Thornhaugh, Peterborough,
Cambridgeshire PE8 6HJ
Tel. Stamford (0780) 782222

*From Stamford follow A1
southwards, after 5 miles turn
left onto A47 for ¼ mile to mill on
left. Signposted.*

Sacrewell is a farm, museum
and watermill. The 530-acre
working farm has 2 trails, one
guided on the farm trailer and
the other unaccompanied. The
museum houses a collection of
items illustrating almost every
aspect of rural life including
farming, crafts and trades. The
watermill is on a site used since
1086 and is in full working
order. Two farmhouse gardens
and orchards are also open and
there are pick your own fruit
and vegetable sections in
season. Locally produced honey
is sold in the shop.

☞ adults £1.50, senior citizens
& children £1.00
● Apr-Oct Sun, Bank Hols 2-6
Facilities: 🍴 🚾 🚐 ♨ ♿

🦞 Map 3 B3
Seafayre
18 Greyfriars, Bedford,
Bedfordshire
Tel. Bedford (0234) 68738

In town centre.

This popular fishmongers
always has a lovely display of
fresh fish and shellfish. It sells a
wide variety of fish including a
good selection of smoked fish,
much of which is undyed, such
as Loch Fyne kippers, smoked
haddock, buckling, hot-smoked
trout and its own homemade
smoked salmon pâté. The
shop's own boats in Cornwall
supply quality English-caught
fish and it has an extensive
range of more exotic fish
including flying fish, fresh tunny,
sardines, squid, octopus and
cuttlefish, plus frozen swordfish
steaks. It always has a selection
of shellfish including oysters
and mussels in season. The
shop is also licensed to sell
game and has pheasant,
partridge, teal, woodcock,
pigeon, rabbit, hare, and
delicious homemade game pies
in season.

● all year Tue-Sat 6-6

🎣 Map 3 D3
Shepreth Mill Fish Farm
Shepreth Mill, Nr Royston,
Hertfordshire SG8 6QZ
Tel. Royston (0763) 60351

*From Royston follow A10 north
eastwards, after 5 miles turn left
onto unclassified road for ¼ mile
to Shepreth.*

Visitors to this trout farm may
feed the fish as well as hire
tackle to catch their own trout.
The 3.9-acre farm produces
500,000 fish a year, from eggs to
10lb brood stock, and has its
own smokery. Fresh and
smoked trout, smoked trout
pâté, trout pies, ice cream and
soft drinks are for sale.

☞ 40p
● all year Mon-Sat 9-5.30, Sun
11-4.30
Facilities: 🍽 🚾 🚐 ♨

MAP 3

☺ **Map 3 B2**
Summerfields
Rook Tree Farm,
Haynes, Bedford,
Bedfordshire MK45 3PT
Tel. Haynes (023066) 400
*From Bedford follow A600
southwards for 4 miles to farm
on right.*

A pick your own farm with a
shop selling a good range of
seasonal soft fruit and some
vegetables including beans and
peas. Mangetout, marrows,
peppers and courgettes are a
speciality. Also for sale are
locally produced jams, honey
and eggs. Refreshments and
tractor rides are available
during the strawberry season.
● May, Aug-Dec daily 10-6;
Jun-Jul daily 10-8
Facilities: ▨ ▥ ▧ ⚠

☺ **Map 3 D4**
Sunclose Farm
Butt Lane, Milton, Cambridge,
Cambridgeshire CB4 4DQ
Tel. Cambridge (0223) 860522
*From Cambridge follow A10
northwards, after 4 miles turn
left onto unclassified road for ¼
mile to farm.*

A pick your own farm selling
strawberries, raspberries,
tayberries and currants
including whitecurrants. All
produce is available ready-
picked as are potatoes. Local
cream is also sold.
● all year Mon-Fri 9-8, Sat-Sun
9-6
Facilities: ▨ ▥ ▧

☺ **Map 3 B1**
**Thrales End Quality Fruit
Farm**
Thrales End, Harpenden,
Hertfordshire AL5 3NS
Tel. Harpenden (05827) 460919
*From Harpenden follow A1081
north westwards for 2 miles to
farm. Signposted.*

A pick your own farm
specialising in raspberries,

strawberries, gooseberries and
tayberries. All produce in the
shop comes straight from the
field and can be ready-picked to
order.
● Jun-Aug daily 9.30-7
Facilities: ▥

☺ **Map 3 A2**
Westoning Fruit Farm
Toddington Road, Westoning,
Bedfordshire
Tel. Flitwick (0525) 715635
*From Ampthill follow A5120
southwards for 5 miles to farm.
Signposted.*

This pick your own farm offers
gooseberries, strawberries,
raspberries, red and
blackcurrants, loganberries and
Victoria plums. It offers a
weekday discount for senior
citizens.
● mid Jun-Sep Tue-Fri 2-6 Sat,
Sun 10-6
Facilities: ▥ ▧ ⚠

🐦 **Map 3 C3**
**Wimpole Home Farm and
Wimpole Hall**
Arrington, Nr Royston,
Hertfordshire SG8 0BW
Tel. Cambridge (0223) 207257
*From Cambridge follow A603
south westwards, after 8 miles
turn right onto unclassified road
for 1 mile to farm. Signposted.*

Presented to the National Trust
by Kipling's daughter, Mrs
Bambridge, Wimpole Hall is the
largest 18thC house in
Cambridgeshire and stands in
grounds landscaped by Charles
Bridgeman, Humphrey Repton
and 'Capability' Brown. There is
a Victorian dairy, a stable block
which contains a visitors'
reception area and the Great
Barn, designed by Sir John
Soane. This barn houses a
museum with displays of farm
machinery and implements.
Rare breeds of livestock graze
in the surrounding 350 acres of
grassland and videos are shown
in the Film Loft. Heavy horse
cart rides are available and a

shop sells National Trust goods.
☞ adults £2.00, NT members
& children £1.00
● hall: Apr-Oct Tue-Thur, Sat,
Sun, Bank Hols 1-5; farm: Apr-
Oct Tue-Thur, Sat, Sun, Bank
Hols 10.30-5
Facilities: ▨ ▥ ▥ ▥ ▧ ⚠
▥ homecooked buffet lunches
& teas with homemade bread &
cakes served in Great Dining
Room, light refreshments &
confectionery sold in main
farmyard

🐦 **Map 3 B1**
**Woodside Farm and Wild
Fowl Park**
Mancroft Road, Slip End, Luton,
Bedfordshire LU1 4DG
Tel. Luton (0582) 841044
*From Luton follow B4540 south
westwards for 3 miles to farm on
right.*

Begun as a small egg-producing
business in 1974, this farm and
wild fowl park now covers 6
acres and has many pure,
commercial and rare breeds of
livestock including ducks,
chickens, guinea fowl, swans,
goats, sheep, pigs, rabbits,
ponies and fallow deer. Despite
a disastrous fire in 1980 the
farm shop has twice won the
National Farm Shop Award,
selling fresh fruit and
vegetables, milk, yoghurt, goats'
milk products, trout, fresh and
frozen poultry, homemade
biscuits, jams, marmalade,
honey, cooked meats, cold
drinks, tea, coffee and wine.
Visitors may tour the park and
farm premises and collect their
own eggs from the free-range
unit. The Bedfordshire Poultry
Centre was added in 1983 and
supplies poultry-keeping
equipment.
☞ park: adults 90p, senior
citizens & children 60p
● park: Mar-Oct Mon-Sat
9.30-dusk; shop: Mon-Fri 8-
5.30, Sat 8-5
Facilities: ▥ ▥ ▧ ⚠

MAP 4 EAST ENGLAND

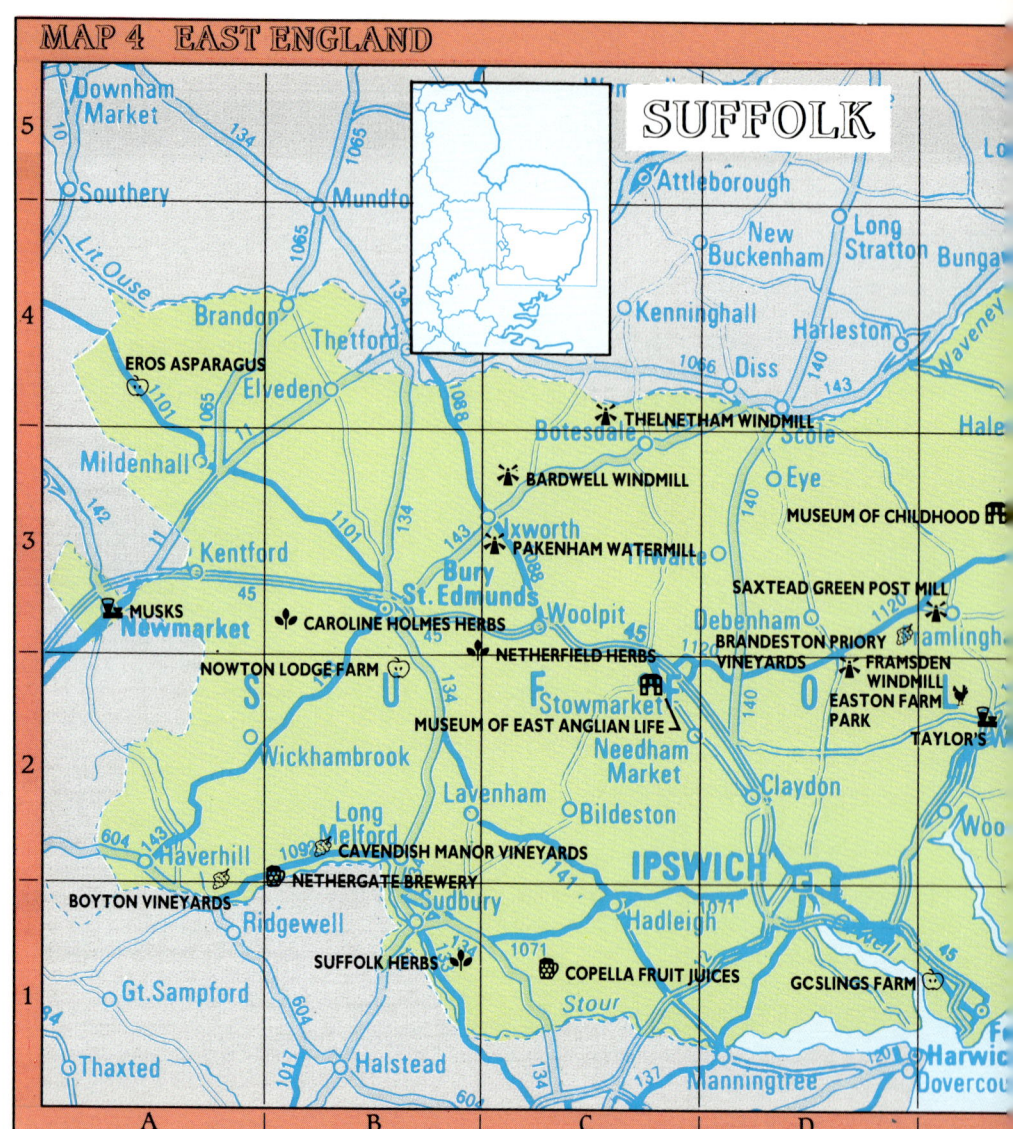

Suffolk is always a joy to visit. Whether you decide to explore the coastland with its inlets and estuaries or to drive around the rolling countryside with its bright yellow mustard fields and gentle slopes strewn with vineyards, it will certainly please you. A popular local dish is 'swimmers' — delicious dumplings made with bread rather than suet dough. They are so light they float in soups or stews and can be eaten in a variety of ways — flavoured with herbs or cheese or served plain coated in treacle.

Map 4 C3

Bardwell Windmill
Bardwell, Bury St Edmunds,
Suffolk IP31 1AD
Tel. Stanton (0359) 51331

From Ixworth follow A143 north eastwards, after ¼ mile turn left onto unclassified road for 2 miles to Bardwell. Signposted.

Bardwell Windmill is a Georgian village tower mill built around 1825 and a typical Suffolk example. It is believed to be one of only two in the country still working full time. The windmill was completely restored in 1986 and now grinds corn as it did 150 years

From Haverhill follow A604 south eastwards, after 3 miles turn left onto A1092 for ¼ mile, then turn left onto unclassified road towards Boyton End for ½ mile to vineyard on left. Signposted.

Boyton Vineyards was planted in 1977 and produces medium dry wine from the Müller-Thurgau and Huxelrebe vines. Tours of the vineyards and cellars include the opportunity to taste different wines. At the wine lodge visitors may purchase wine by the bottle or case and 1 to 2-year-old rooted vine cuttings to grow in the garden.

☞ adults £1.00, accompanied children free

◑ vineyard: May-Nov Sat,Sun or by appointment; wine lodge: all year daily

Facilities: 🚻 🚐 🍽 ♿

⌖ Map 4 D3
Brandeston Priory Vineyards
The Priory, Brandeston, Nr Woodbridge, Suffolk IP13 7AU
Tel. Earl Soham (072882) 462

From Framlingham follow B1119 westwards, after 1½ miles turn left onto A1120 for 1 mile, then turn left in Earl Soham onto unclassified road for 1 mile to vineyard. Signposted.

Brandeston Priory Vineyards produce English wines from their own vineyards, planted with Müller-Thurgau and Schönburger vines. Planted in 1975 the vines are now thought to be in their prime, producing a light, fresh and fruity wine. The gardens feature a yew walk, a scented rose garden, apple, pear and cherry trees and a woodland walk with picnic area. Wines, ciders, local preserves, honey and mustards are on sale in the shop.

☞ adults £1.60, children (under 14) free

◑ May-Sep Mon-Fri, Bank Hols 10.30-5 or by appointment

Facilities: 🚻 🚐 🍽 ♿

⌖ Map 4 E3
Bruisyard Wines
Church Road, Bruisyard, Saxmundham, Suffolk IP17 2EF
Tel. Badingham (072875) 281

● **Bruisyard St Peter Winery**

ago. Tours are available and visitors can buy bags of stoneground flour, muesli and other health foods.

☞ adults 60p, children & senior citizens 30p

◑ all year Mon-Fri 9-5, Sat, Sun 2-5

Facilities: 🍽

★ Suns — steam flour milling demonstration — telephone for details

---

⌖ Map 4 A2
Boyton Vineyards
Boyton End, Stoke-by-Clare, Suffolk CO9 4AN
Tel. Haverhill (0440) 61893

MAP 4　　　　**EAST ENGLAND**

From Framlingham follow B1119 eastwards, after 2 miles turn left onto unclassified road for 2 miles to Bruisyard. Signposted.

The Bruisyard vineyard and winery produce the award-winning Bruisyard St Peter wine. The 10-acre vineyard at Bruisyard was planted in 1974/5 with Müller-Thurgau vines. The grapes are harvested in late October and each stage of the wine-making process may be seen. Tours of the vineyard and winery, as well as demonstrations and tastings, are available. Wine can be bought by the bottle or case and apple wine, apple juice and ice creams are also for sale.

☞ adults £1.80, senior citizens £1.60, children (under 14) free
◗ Easter Sun-Nov daily 10.30-5
Facilities: 🚻 🚗 👶 ⛺

Map 4 F2
The Butley-Orford Oysterage
Market Hill, Orford, Suffolk IP12 2LQ
Tel. Orford (0394) 450277
In town centre.

The Butley Oysterage, run for over 35 years by the Pinney family, is renowned as one of the finest fish smokers in England. Sadly, the oyster farm and smokery are not open to visitors, but the shop sells a wide range of smoked fish including salmon, trout, mackerel, bloaters and kippers. It also sells fresh locally caught fish.

◗ Apr-Sep Mon, Wed-Sat 9-6, Tue 9-1; Oct-Mar Mon, Wed-Sat 9-4, Tue 9-1
Facilities: 🍴
🍴 lunches & dinners served in licensed restaurant specialising in fish & smoked products

Map 4 E2
Calluna Farm
Lodge Road, Hollesley, Woodbridge, Suffolk IP12 3RR
Tel. Shottisham (0394) 411927
From Woodbridge follow A1152 eastwards, after 2 miles turn right onto B1083 for 5 miles, then turn left at Shottisham onto unclassified road for 2 miles to Hollesley. Signposted.

Calluna Farm is one of the few farms in East Anglia which keeps sheep for milk and cheese-making. Visitors can watch sheep milking on Friday, Saturday and Sunday afternoons and see where the cheese and yoghurt are made. The farm sells yoghurt, cheese, home-produced lamb and local beef and pork.

☞ adults 75p, senior citizens & children (over 5) 50p
◗ farm: Apr-Sep daily 10-5, closed 30 May-3 Jun; shop: all year daily 10-5
Facilities: 🍽 🚻 🚗 👶
★ Fri-Sun milking 3pm

Map 4 B2
Cavendish Manor Vineyards
Nether Hall, Cavendish, Sudbury, Suffolk CO10 8BX
Tel. Glemsford (0787) 280221
From Long Melford follow A1092 westwards for 3 miles to Cavendish. Signposted.

The first vines were planted at Cavendish Manor in 1972 and 3 years later they produced a national prize-winning wine. Visitors to Cavendish Manor may tour the vineyard, taste the wine and visit the period manor house with its interesting collection of country bygones. Wine by the bottle, case or gift pack can be bought together with fruit juice and English vineyard mustard.

☞ adults £1.50, senior citizens £1.00, children free
◗ all year daily 11-4
Facilities: 🚻 🚗 👶

Map 4 C1
Copella Fruit Juices
Hill Farm, Boxford, Colchester, Essex CO6 5NY
Tel. Boxford (0787) 210348
From Sudbury follow A134 south eastwards, after 5½ miles turn left onto B1068 for ½ mile, then turn left onto unclassified road for ½ mile to farm on right. Signposted.

This family-run farming and processing business, set in beautiful Suffolk countryside on the edge of Dedham Vale, produces a variety of top quality, freshly pressed English fruit juices under the 'Copella' brand name. The farm grows apples, particularly Cox's Orange Pippins, in a 200-acre orchard, as well as blackcurrants and organic wheat. Seven blends of fruit juices are made — apple, pear, strawberry, blackcurrant, cherry, carrot and guava — and these can be bought from the shop together with apples in season — August to March. Also available is a range of organic products including 'Peake's' Organic Apple Juice which varies in flavour throughout the year depending on the varieties of apples used.

☞ free
◗ all year Mon-Fri 9-5
Facilities: 🚻 🚗

MAP 4

● **The Victorian Dairy at Easton Farm Park**

🐓 Map 4 E2
Easton Farm Park
Easton, Nr Woodbridge,
Suffolk IP13 OEQ
Tel. Wickham Market (0728)
746475
*From Wickham Market follow
B1078 westwards, after ½ mile
turn right onto unclassified road
for 1½ miles to Easton.
Signposted.*

Easton Farm Park provides
visitors with an opportunity to
compare old and modern farm
methods. The Victorian dairy,
with its marble shelves and
fountain, can be seen alongside

a modern dairy centre. From
the overhead viewing gallery
the complete milking operation
can be watched. An exhibition
on farming in East Anglia gives
information about modern
cereal and vegetable
production. Other features of
the farm park include a nature
trail, exhibition of country
bygones, pets' corner and farm
animals including rare breeds.
🎟️ adults £2.00, senior citizens
£1.50, children £1.00, Sat
reduced rates & facilities
● Easter-Oct daily 10.30-6
Facilities: 🚾 🚗 ⛺

🥓 Map 4 E3
Emmetts Stores
High Street, Peasenhall,
Saxmundham, Suffolk IP17 2HJ
Tel. Peasenhall (072879) 250
*From Yoxford follow A1120
westwards for 3 miles to
Peasenhall.*

This village store specialises in
bacon and hams cured in a
variety of ways and smoked
over oak sawdust. As well as
Suffolk cider and York hams,

they make a sweet pickle ham
with a 'secret' recipe of beer
and black treacle. The result is
very similar to a traditional
Suffolk cure — a sweet
succulent ham covered with a
black rind. They also make their
own sausages which are
available fresh or smoked.
● all year Mon-Sat 9-12

🍅 Map 4 A4
Eros Asparagus
Little Paddocks, Kennyhill, Bury
St Edmunds, Suffolk IP28 8DS
Tel. Burnt Fen (035375) 394
*From Mildenhall follow A1101
north westwards for 4 miles to
Kennyhill.*

This asparagus farm is open all
the year round. Visitors are free
to wander round on their own
or go on the guided tour during
the short spring season. The
asparagus is grown without
artificial fertilisers or pesticides
and can be bought from the
shop.
🎟️ tours: £1.00
● all year daily 9.30-4.30; tours:
May, Jun 12.00 by appointment
Facilities: 🚾 🚗 ⛺

🎯 Map 4 D2
Framsden Windmill
Old Mill House, Framsden, Nr
Stowmarket, Suffolk IP14 6HB
Tel. Helmingham (047339) 328
*From Ipswich follow B1077
northwards, after 10 miles turn
right onto unclassified road for ¼
mile to Framsden.*

At Framsden visitors can see
how an 18thC post mill was
modernised in the 19thC to
become a semi-automatic
windmill. One of the additions
was a bolter or wire machine
for separating the flour. The
windmill is still occasionally
used to grind flour. A museum
of country bygones includes a
collection of everyday items
from farm and cottage life.
🎟️ adults 80p, children 40p
● by appointment
Facilities: 🍴 🚗 ⛺

MAP 4　　　　　　　　　　　EAST ENGLAND

☺ Map 4 E1
Goslings Farm
Trimley St Martin, Ipswich,
Suffolk IP1O ORZ
Tel. Ipswich (0394) 273361

*From Ipswich follow A45 south
eastwards, after 6 miles turn
right onto unclassified road for ¼
mile to Trimley St Martin and
farm on right. Signposted.*

A pick your own farm with a
shop selling a good range of
seasonal vegetables, including
broad and runner beans.
Mangetout, squash and
pumpkins are a speciality and
local free-range eggs and Jersey
cream are available.
◑ May-Dec Tue-Sun 10-4.30;
fruit season: daily 10-7.30
Facilities: ᵂᶜ 🚗

☺ Map 4 E4
Grange Farm Orchards
Barsham, Beccles,
Suffolk NR34 8JN
Tel. Beccles (0502) 715008

*From Beccles follow A1062
westwards for 2 miles to
Barsham. Signposted.*

A pick your own farm selling all
fruits in season, including
strawberries, raspberries,
gooseberries and blackcurrants.
Potatoes, apples and pears are
also available ready-picked.
◑ Jun-Oct daily 9-5
Facilities: ᵂᶜ 🚗 ♨

❧ Map 4 B3
Caroline Holmes Herbs
Denham End Farm,
Denham, Bury St Edmunds,
Suffolk IP29 5EE
Tel. Bury St Edmunds (0284)
810653

*From Bury St Edmunds follow
A45 westwards, after 5 miles
turn left at Barrow exit onto
unclassified road for 2 miles to
Denham End. Signposted.*

To encourage the growing and
eating of fresh herbs, this small
specialist nursery invites visitors
to spend a day looking,
touching and tasting, or an
afternoon or evening learning
more about herbs. On sale are
120 varieties of herbs from 50p
upwards, some in specialist
containers. Fresh herbs are
picked to order.
☞ free
◑ all year Sat 10-6 or by
appointment
Facilities: 🚗
★ 18 & 30 Jun, 3 Jul, 22 Sep
herb day courses for cooks

🎣 Map 4 F5
Lowestoft Fishing Industry
Waveney District Council,
Recreation and Amenities
Department, The Esplanade,
Lowestoft, Suffolk NR33 0QF
Tel. Lowestoft (0502) 565989

In town centre. Signposted.

For those who have ever
wondered how fish reach the
table from the sea, Lowestoft
Fishing Industry is well worth a
visit. A 2-hour guided tour
explores the methods used to
catch, prepare and package fish
for the wholesaler. It takes in
the ice factory, fish preparation
area and there is even an
opportunity to board a trawler.
A variety of fish including
shellfish, cod and prime fish can
be bought from the
wholesalers' stock.
☞ adults £1.20, senior citizens
& children 60p
◑ mid Jul-mid Sep Tue-Fri by
appointment
Facilities: 🚗

🏛 Map 4 E3
Museum of Childhood
St Jacobs Farm, St Jacobs Hall,
Laxfield, Woodbridge,
Suffolk IP13 8HY
Tel. Ubbeston (098683) 657

*From Halesworth follow B1117
south westwards for 6 miles to
museum on left. Signposted.*

St Jacobs Hall is a listed moated
hall built in the 16thC with
18thC additions. Home of the
Tina Reynolds Collection of
Antique Toys, it has an
assortment of toys and
playthings dating from 1800-
1960. The Hall is set in a family-
run 12-acre smallholding
stocked with rare breeds of
farm animals such as
Southdown sheep, Dexter
cows and Gloucester Old Spot
pigs as well as horses, goats and
poultry. The family is interested
in self-sufficiency and has a
kitchen garden stocked with a
variety of vegetables, plus a
small amount of crops grown
for the livestock. Visitors can
explore the farm by following
the nature trail which
encounters a wealth of wildlife.
There is also a small dairy and
displays of kitchen equipment
and agricultural implements. A
small craft shop sells interesting
local items.
☞ adults £1.00, children 50p
◑ Easter-Sep Tue-Thur 10-5,
Sun, Bank Hols 12-5; Oct-Mar
Sun, Bank Hols 12-5
Facilities: 🍴 ♿ ᵂᶜ 🚗 ♨ ⚠
🍴 homemade teas served

🏛 Map 4 C2
**Museum of East Anglian
Life**
Stowmarket, Suffolk IP14 1DL
Tel. Stowmarket (0449) 612229

In town centre. Signposted.

East Anglia's open air museum
is attractively set on the River
Rattlesden. Reconstructed
buildings and agricultural
displays on farming featuring
carts, wagons and agricultural
implements, bring local history
to life. One exhibit shows the
farming year, from sowing
through harvesting to
processing. The Alton

MAP 4

Watermill is a working mill dating from the 18thC. Now carefully reconstructed, it grinds grain on special exhibition days. Remus, a working Suffolk Punch horse, is very much a part of the 'life' of the museum and can be seen at work on the site. The story of the region's strong industrial heritage is represented, with 3 steam traction engines built for agricultural use.

☞ adults £1.80, children £1.00
◐ Apr-Oct Mon-Sat 11-5, Sun 12-5
Facilities: ⚫ ᵂᶜ 🚗 ᵜ
★ various events & demonstrations held during year
⚫ cream teas with homemade scones & cakes

🎋 Map 4 A3
Musks
1 The Rookery, Newmarket, Suffolk
Tel. Newmarket (0638) 661824
In town centre.

Suppliers of the renowned Musks' Newmarket sausages to Her Majesty Queen Elizabeth the Queen Mother, which are made on the premises, this high-class delicatessen also stocks a wide range of luxury foods including smoked salmon and Parma ham.
◐ all year Mon, Tue, Thur-Sat 9-1, 2-5, Wed 9-1; closed Bank Hols

🌿 Map 4 B3
Netherfield Herbs
37 Nether Street, Rougham, Nr Bury St Edmunds, Suffolk IP30 9LW
Tel. Beyton (0359) 70452
From Bury St Edmunds follow A45 eastwards, after 3 miles turn right onto unclassified road towards Rougham for ½ mile, then turn right onto unclassified road for 1 mile, then turn left into Nether Street.

Netherfield Herbs is a small herb farm owned by Lesley

Bremness who not only designed the garden here, but also designed the herb garden on BBC TV's Pebble Mill at One. She has presented 7 TV series using herbs. The demonstration garden is small and private and makes a pleasant haven for keen herb enthusiasts. Over 150 varieties of herbs are on sale at the farm and plants can be bought in 3-inch pots. A selection of herb related products can also be bought including herb pillows and pot-pourri, aromatic oils made from natural plant essences and a range of apple-based herb jellies.

☞ free
◐ all year daily 10.30-6
Facilities: 🚗 ✗

🍺 Map 4 B2
Nethergate Brewery
11-13 High Street, Clare, Suffolk CO10 8NY
Tel. Clare (0787) 277244
From Long Melford follow A1092 westwards for 6 miles to Clare.

This is a totally traditional small brewery producing ale in barrels only. The beer is highly acclaimed, winning the prize of Supreme Beer at the 1987 Cambridge Beer Festival. There are conducted tours of the brewery and visitor's can sample the beer. As a souvenir of the day beer in 4½ gallon packs is for sale.

☞ £1.00 including a pint of beer
◐ by appointment
Facilities: ᵂᶜ

RESTAURANT RECIPE

🍴 Map 4 F4
THE CROWN
90 High Street, Southwold, Suffolk IP18 6DP
Tel: Southwold (0502) 722275
In town centre.
People travel for miles to eat at the Crown. One of the reasons is their Fish Pie which makes use of the wonderful supplies of local fish.
◐ Mon-Sun Meals: 12-2, 7-10
Price range Set L £9, £11 Set D £11, £13
Seats 27
Cards: Access, Amex, Visa
Facilities: 🍷 🚗

CROWN FISH PIE
12oz conger eel cut into 1-inch cubes
12oz monkfish cut into 1-inch cubes
1 pint mussels cooked and removed from shells
4oz whole prawns peeled
2oz black olives stoned and halved
4 tomatoes skinned and seeded
3 cloves of garlic peeled and chopped

2 shallots roughly chopped
pinch of saffron
salt
black pepper
parsley chopped
thyme chopped
juice of half a lemon
5fl oz white wine
4fl oz fish stock or water
4 tbsp olive oil
1½lb potatoes pre-cooked and sliced ¼-inch thick
1oz melted butter
rouille:
mayonnaise
anchovies
tomato purée
garlic
pinch of cayenne pepper

Heat oven to gas 5 (375F, 190C). In a deep ovenproof dish put the fish, mussels, prawns, olives, tomatoes, garlic and shallots. Add a pinch of salt, black pepper, parsley, thyme, lemon juice, white wine and stock. Sprinkle with olive oil, arrange sliced potatoes on top and brush with melted butter. Bake for 25-30 minutes until lightly browned. For the rouille mix together the ingredients to taste and serve.

MAP 4   **EAST ENGLAND**

😊 Map 4 B2
Nowton Lodge Farm
The Briars, Nowton, Bury St
Edmunds, Suffolk IP29 5NB
Tel. Bury St Edmunds (0284)
68990

*From Bury St Edmunds follow
A134 southwards, after 2 miles
turn right onto unclassified road
for ½ mile to Nowton.
Signposted.*

A pick your own farm with a
shop selling seasonal soft fruits
including strawberries,
raspberries, gooseberries and
red and blackcurrants.
Vegetables such as potatoes are
sold all year round as are free-
range eggs, dairy produce and
honey. Cold drinks and ice
cream are also available.
◗ all year daily 10-5
Facilities: 🚻 🚌 ☕

🍺 Map 4 F4
Oulton Broad Brewery
Unit 20, Harbour Road, Oulton
Broad, Suffolk NR32 3LZ
Tel. Lowestoft (0502) 87905

*From Lowestoft follow A146
westwards for 1 mile to Oulton
Broad and brewery on
waterfront. Signposted.*

Taking only the best East
Anglian malted barley and
hops, the Oulton Broad

Brewery produces Excelsior
Bitter with methods used
before 1880. Excelsior Bitter is
brewed without sugar, extracts
or chemical additives and is
allowed to mature naturally. A
visit includes a tour of the
brewery and tasting of both
Excelsior Bitter and the
brewery's own label wine.
There is also a museum which
displays pub and fishing
traditions from the turn of the
century to the 1930s. Beer is on
sale in ½ and 1 gallon jugs,
tappits, polypins and firkins.
The wine is available in bottles
and litres.
☞ free
◗ all year Mon-Fri 9-6; Jun-Sep
Sat, Sun 9-12
Facilities: 🚻 🚌
★ 'take home' beer festival of
non-chemical beer & wines,
telephone for details

🏭 Map 4 C3
Pakenham Watermill
Suffolk Preservation Society,
Grimstone End, Pakenham,
Bury St Edmunds,
Suffolk IP31 2LZ
Tel. Beyton (0359) 70570

*From Bury St Edmunds follow
A143 north eastwards, after 6
miles turn right onto unclassified
road for ¼ mile to mill.
Signposted.*

This 18thC working watermill
has been owned by the Suffolk
Preservation Society since 1978.
The Domesday Book records a
mill on the site in 1086, showing
that corn has been ground here
for at least 900 years. The
Society offers visitors a guided
tour of the mill and
demonstrations of corn milling.
Wholemeal stoneground flour
is for sale in 0.5, 1.5 and 5Kg
bags.
☞ adults 90p, children 40p
◗ May-Sep Wed, Sat, Sun, Bank
Hols 2.30-5.30 or by
appointment
Facilities: ☕ ♿ 🚻 🚌 ☕ 🏭

〰 Map 4 F4
Raglan Smoke House
Raglan Street, Lowestoft,
Suffolk
Tel. Lowestoft (0502) 81929
In town centre.

This 200-year-old smoke house
is the only one remaining of the
135 which were in Lowestoft
until the 1950s. It still uses its
old implements and smokes in
the traditional way. Visitors are
taken on a tour of the smoke
rooms and work area where
they will see demonstrations of
how fish was smoked in the
19thC. Kippers are the speciality
here and are all smoked
without dye or added
flavourings. A wide variety of
other fish is smoked including
haddock, cod, trout, sprats and
bloaters. These and numerous
other fish and shellfish are
available from the shop.
☞ free
◗ all year Mon-Fri 8-5, Sat 8-12

🏭 Map 4 E3
Saxtead Green Post Mill
The Mill House, Saxtead Green,
Woodbridge, Suffolk
Tel. Framlingham (0728) 82789
*From Framlinghan follow B1119
westwards for 2 miles to mill at
junction with A1120. Signposted.*

● **Pakenham Watermill**

MAP 4

An elegant white windmill dating from 1796 and one of the finest examples of a traditional Suffolk post mill. It has been restored to working order by English Heritage and visitors can climb up to the 'buck' to view the machinery.

☞ adults 75p, senior citizens 55p, children 35p
◗ Apr-Sep Mon-Sat 9.30-6.30

❧ Map 4 B1
Suffolk Herbs
Sawyers Farm, Little Cornard, Sudbury, Suffolk CO10 0NY
Tel. Bures (0787) 227247

From Sudbury follow B1508 southwards, after 3 miles turn left into Spout Lane for ¼ mile, then turn right to farm. Signposted.

This nursery sells a wide range of organically grown plants and seeds. The range includes culinary, medicinal and fragrant herbs and British, Chinese and Oriental vegetables. Books and ointments are also for sale.

☞ free
◗ all year Sat 9-5.30
Facilities: 🚗

☎ Map 4 E2
Taylor's
66-70 The Hill, High Street, Wickham Market, Suffolk IP13 0QU

Tel. Wickham Market (0728) 747207

In town centre. Signposted.

This grocer's shop, furnished in antique decor and run by the Taylor family since 1914, stocks a wide variety of locally smoked fish, cheeses, meats, pâté, stoneground flour and exotic foods and fruits. The museum has bygone food and drink packaging and utensils.

◗ all year Wed-Sat 10.30-5
Facilities: 🍽 🚻 📶 🚗
★ Nov wine & cheese tasting at Christmas show
🍽 licensed restaurant in 17thC cellar serves light meals featuring homemade quiches, pickles & sweets

🌾 Map 4 C4
Thelnetham Windmill
Mill Road, Thelnetham, Nr Diss, Suffolk IP22 1JZ
Tel. Ipswich (0473) 726996

From Diss follow A1066 westwards, after 5 miles turn left onto B1113 for 2 miles, then turn right onto unclassified road for 2 miles through Thelnetham, then turn right onto unclassified road for ¼ mile to mill on left.

A post mill stood on this site in the 18thC but the present tower mill — the oldest in Suffolk — dates from 1819. The mill fell into disuse in 1924 but was restored between 1980 and 1986 by volunteers of the Suffolk Mill Group. It is now fully operative, grinding flour and other grain products. Visitors can tour the building and see displays of implements and photographs of other local windmills. A number of flours are for sale including stoneground organic wholemeal, white unbleached, refined bran and rough bran in bags from 3½ to 70lb.

☞ free
◗ 3 Apr-Oct Sun, Bank Hols 11-7 or by appointment
Facilities: 📶 🚗

● **Thelnetham Windmill**

SAMPHIRE

Try and sample samphire - a seaweed which is delicious lightly blanched and served tossed in butter or orange juice.

❧ Map 4 F4
Westhall Herbs
Church Lane, Westhall, Nr Halesworth, Suffolk IP19 8NU
Tel. Brampton (050279) 646

From Halesworth follow B1124 north eastwards, after 3 miles turn left onto unclassified road for ½ mile to Westhall.

Westhall grows over 80 varieties of organically grown herbs. Talks and demonstrations are given by appointment. A small gift shop sells herb plants in 3½-inch or 5-inch pots along with herb teas and cakes.

☞ free
◗ Apr-Oct Sat, Sun 10-5, Mon-Fri 2-5 or by appointment
Facilities: 🍽 📶 🚗
🍽 teas served including homemade herb cakes, sesame scones, orange & mint loaf & caraway cake

MAP 5 EAST ENGLAND

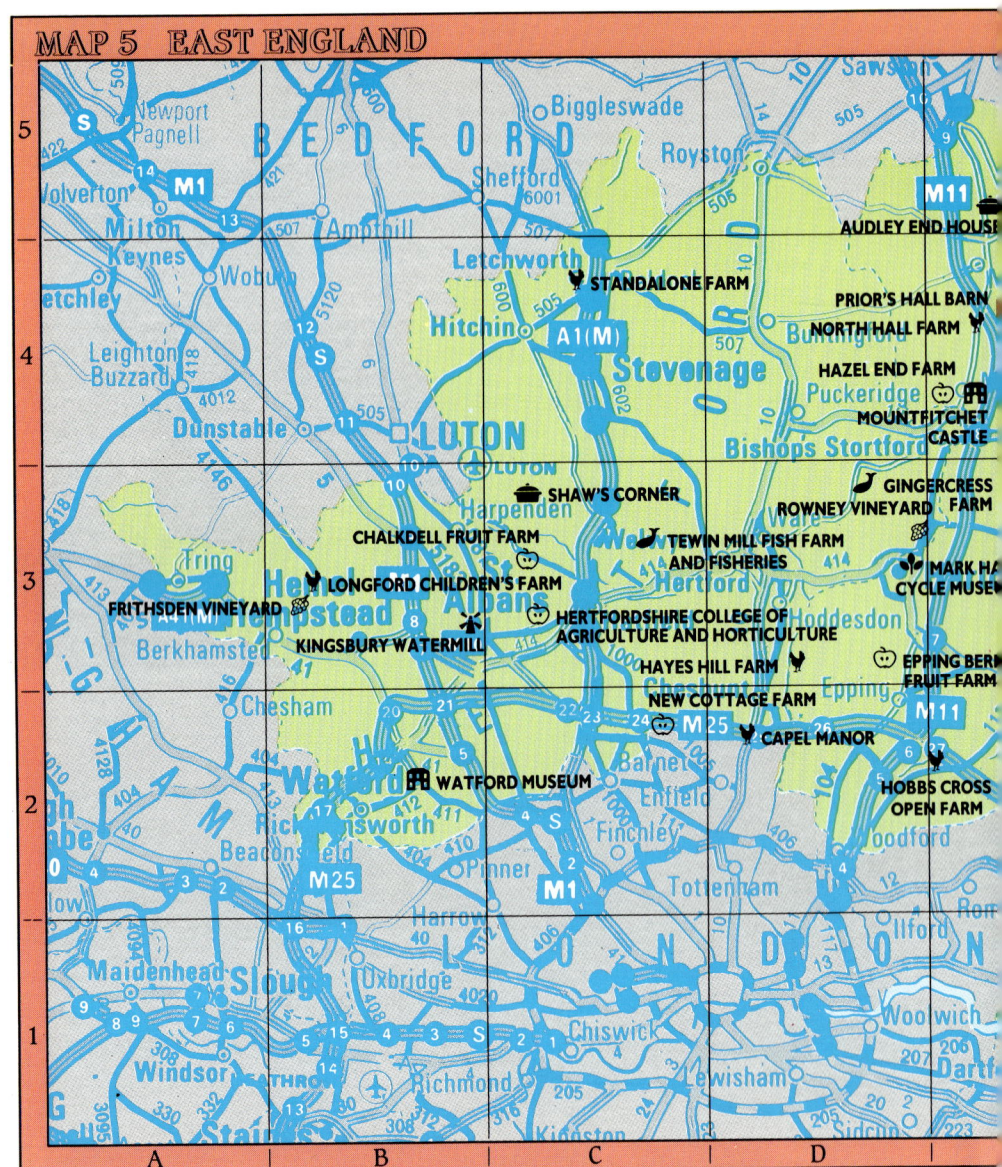

Every Leap year in June the presentation of a flitch — or side — of bacon takes place in Dunmow in Essex. It is given to the married couple who can prove that they have never repented of their union, quarrelled or erred in any way for at least a year and a day. The 'Flitch Trials', where they have to prove their case, are a good natured affair. The winners receive one flitch whilst another is cut up between the other couples brave enough to have entered.

Map 5 E5
Audley End House
Saffron Walden, Essex CB11 4JF
Tel. Saffron Walden (0799) 22399

From Saffron Walden follow B1052 westwards, after ¼ mile turn right onto unclassified road for ¾ mile, then turn right onto B1383 for 100 yards to house on right. Signposted.

A palatial 17thC country house set in a landscaped park, Audley End is now owned by English Heritage. It has many attractions including the

Map labels:

604 143
Haverhill
1092
Long Melford
134
Bildeston
141
IPSWICH
Sudbury
Hadleigh
1071
151
Ridgewell
751
134
1071
12
Neil
45
Gt.Sampford
604
Stour
Manningt
137
Har
Dover
120

GRACES FRUIT FARM
Thaxted
THAXTED WINDMILL
1017
THE BREWERY CHAPEL MUSEUM
Colchester
CRAPES FRUIT FARM
BRADFIELD FRUIT FARM
sted itchet
STANST
120
Braintree
Dunmow
BOCKING WINDMILL
LINDEN LADY CHOCOLATES
Marks
A GREEN AND SONS
OLIVERS ORCHARD
133
Weeley
136
Wivenhoe
Won t
THE STARR RESTAURANT
FELSTED VINEYARDS
Coggeshall
12
BROOK FARM
Brightlingsea
Frinto
CAMMAS HALL FRUIT FARM
KINGS FARM
Witham
HOLE FARM
LODGE FARM
EAST MERSEA FARM
N E ELSWORTH AND SON
Clacton on Se
151
W. Mersea
Chelmsford
1060
130
414
Blackwater
Maldon
414
130
Bradwell on Sea
ipping Ongar
Cold Norton
NEW HALL VINEYARD
Burnham on Crouch
MOUNTNESSING WINDMILL
Billericay
129
132
THE LIMES FARM SHOP
Brentwood
23 128
MARSH FARM COUNTRY PARK
BARLEYLANDS FARM MUSEUM
Rayleigh
Foulnes
25
30
Basildon
M25
128 1014
LORKINS FARM
13
Shoeburyness
Canvey
SOUTHEND on Sea
sett
ays
ilbury
226
228
Grain
Sheerness
Gravesend
Stroo
ham
Isle of 2231
Leysdown
Herne
Birchin

ESSEX & HERTFORDSHIRE

F   G   H   I

butler's pantry, where visitors can see the Braybrooke family silver. The old kitchen — with its kitchen range and equipment — now houses the gift shop. The dining parlour on the ground floor was the first room here designed by the famous architect, Robert Adam, in the 18thC. At this time dinner was served in the afternoon and the green decoration was intended to lead the eye out across the landscaped lawns. The walls were hand-painted rather than covered with fabric so that they

● **Audley End House**

185

● Soyer's miniature kitchen, 1847

did not 'retain the smells of the victuals'. The impressive dining room on the first floor was created in 1825 in Jacobean style and the table is now laid for dinner with a Sèvres dessert service and some of the family silver.

☞ adults £2.50, senior citizens £1.85, children £1.25
● Apr-9 Oct Tue-Sun 1-5
Facilities: 🚤 🍴 ♿ wc 🚗 🛝

🏠 Map 5 F2
Barleylands Farm Museum
Barleylands Farm,
Barleylands Road, Billericay,
Essex CM11 2UD
Tel. Basildon (0268) 282090
From Billericay follow A129 south eastwards for 1½ miles to farm. Signposted.

Barleylands combines a pick your own farm and an agricultural museum. Visitors can pick a wide variety of soft fruits and vegetables or buy from the shop, where freshly shelled peas are a speciality in

July and August. The museum houses an extensive collection of vintage farm machinery and agricultural mementos, including a pair of Fowler steam engines complete with implements.

☞ museum: adults £1.00, senior citizens & children 50p
● Oct-Mar Wed-Sat 11-4.30, Sun 1-5; Apr-Sep Wed-Sat 11-5, Sun 1-5.30
Facilities: 🚤 ♿ wc 🚗
★ late summer steam rally & craft fair

🏕 Map 5 F4
Bocking Windmill
Bocking Church Street, Bocking, Braintree, Essex CM7 6HR
Tel. Braintree (0376) 46806
From Braintree follow A131 northwards, after ½ mile turn left onto B1053 for ½ mile, then turn right into Bocking Church Street for ¼ mile to mill.

A preserved 1830's post mill, last worked just prior to the First World War. It is now a

windmill museum with exhibits on the history of milling.
☞ free
● by appointment

😊 Map 5 I4
Bradfield Fruit Farm
The Street, Bradfield,
Manningtree, Essex CO11 2UU
Tel. Wix (025587) 696
From Manningtree follow B1352 eastwards, after 2 miles turn right onto unclassified road for ½ mile to Bradfield. Signposted.

A shop selling apples, plums and specialities including Morello cherries and Russets. In May visitors can enjoy the blossom walk.
● mid Aug-Dec daily 8.30-6
Facilities: wc 🚗

🏠 Map 5 G4
The Brewery Chapel Museum
Adams Court, Halstead, Essex
In town centre.

This local museum is located in the unlikely setting of a chapel within the Adam and Sons Brewery. It stages a variety of thematic exhibitions all related to local history.
☞ free
● Apr-Oct Sat 10-12.30, 2-4.30, Sun 2-4.30
Facilities: 🚗

😊 Map 5 H4
Brook Farm
Great Bentley, Colchester,
Essex CO7 8QP
Tel. Colchester (0206) 250430
From Brightlingsea follow B1029 northwards, after 3 miles turn right onto unclassified road for 1 mile to farm on right. Signposted.

A pick your own farm with a seasonal farm shop selling an extensive range of farm produce including fruit and

MAP 5

vegetables, meat, eggs and honey. Also on sale are dried flowers and herbs. Farm livestock and poultry are an added attraction.
◑ Jun-Aug daily 9-7
Facilities: 🚾 🚙 ☺

☺ Map 5 E3
Cammas Hall Fruit Farm
Hatfield Broad Oak, Bishop's Stortford, Hertfordshire CM22 7JT
Tel. Hatfield Broad Oak (027970) 777

From Bishop's Stortford follow A120 eastwards, after 5 miles turn right onto B183 for 3 miles to Hatfield Broad Oak, then turn left onto unclassified road for 1/2 mile to farm on left. Signposted.

With 25 years of experience behind it, this fruit farm offers an enjoyable day out and 27 acres of strawberries, raspberries, gooseberries and redcurrants ready for picking. There are also picnic facilities, a marked nature trail, a farm shop and a garden centre.
◑ Jun-Aug Mon-Fri 9-8, Sat, Sun 9-5
Facilities: 🍽 🚾 🚙 ☺

♥ Map 5 D2
Capel Manor
Bullsmoor Lane, Waltham Cross, Hertfordshire EN7 5HR
Tel. Lea Valley (0992) 763849

From Enfield follow A10 north eastwards, after 2 miles turn left into Bullsmoor Lane for 1/4 mile, then turn right to manor. Signposted.

This educational farm and 50-acre wooded estate has a full range of livestock — pigs, sheep, cattle, and poultry — and features both modern and rare breeds. Expert teachers are happy to conduct visitors on guided tours and there are

many special event days. The horticultural and environmental centre has several heated glasshouses with tropical plants and the surrounding estate grows a varied collection of trees, fruit, vegetables and herbs. Many educational courses are available.
☞ adults £1.00, children 80p
◑ 28 Mar-26 Oct Mon-Fri 10-4.30, Sat, Sun 2-5.30; 27 Oct-27 Mar Mon-Fri 10.4.30
Facilities: ♿ 🚾 🚙 ☺ ⚠
★ craft fairs, farm day

REGIONAL RECIPE

COLCHESTER PUDDING

A popular dish in this area and a luxurious version of the old nursery pudding.

1½oz tapioca
1¾ pint milk
salt
rind of 1 lemon grated
vanilla essence
3 egg whites
1lb stewed fruit
8oz caster sugar
6 egg yolks
5fl oz double cream

Heat oven to gas 4 (400F, 200C). Warm 1 pint of milk in a pan, sprinkle in the tapioca with a pinch of salt, stirring continuously, bring to the boil over a gentle heat and simmer for about 10 minutes, or until soft. Add the lemon rind and a few drops of vanilla essence. Put a layer of stewed fruit in an ovenproof serving dish and cover with the tapioca mixture. Make a custard from the egg yolks, 3oz sugar and the rest of the milk and the cream. Pour over the tapioca. Whisk the egg whites stiffly and fold in the last 5oz of sugar to make a meringue. Spread the meringue over the custard and bake the pudding until a delicate brown. Serve cold.

☺ Map 5 C3
Chalkdell Fruit Farm
Coleman Green Lane, Wheathampstead, St Albans, Hertfordshire AL4 8ER
Tel. Wheathampstead (058283) 3752

From Harpenden follow B652 north eastwards, after 1/2 mile turn right onto B653 for 3 miles, then turn right into Coleman Green Lane for 1/2 mile to farm. Signposted.

A pick your own farm selling seasonal soft fruit including autumn-fruiting strawberries. Free maps are provided for country walks.
◑ mid Jun-end Sep daily 9-7
Facilities: 🚾 🚙 ☺

☺ Map 5 G4
Crapes Fruit Farm
Rectory Road, Aldham, Colchester, Essex CO6 3RR
Tel. Colchester (0206) 210406

From Marks Tey follow unclassified road northwards for 1 mile to Aldham. Signposted.

A farm shop selling soft and top fruit including the largest selection of apples in England. John Tam grows over 150 different varieties including Ellisons Orange, Orlean's Reinette, Peasgood Nonesuch and D'Arcy Spice. Visitors can taste before buying, wander around the orchards and chat to the owner and his wife who know just about everything there is to know about apples.
◑ all year Mon-Sat 8-5, closed Bank Hols

☺ Map 5 H3
East Mersea Farm
East Mersea Hall, East Mersea, Colchester, Essex CO5 8TJ
Tel. West Mersea (0206) 383215

From West Mersea follow B1025 northwards, after 1½ miles turn right onto unclassifed road for 2 miles to.farm on left. Signposted.

A pick your own farm with a shop and general store selling

many soft fruits including strawberries, raspberries and tayberries. Also on sale is a wide range of vegetables, cut flowers and farm produced beef, eggs, local hams and bacon. The farm is near the sea and pony rides are available.

● mid Jun-end Oct daily 9-7
Facilities: 🚻 🚗 ♨

😊 Map 5 I3
N E Elsworth and Son
Park Fruit Farm, Pork Lane, Great Holland, Frinton-on-Sea, Essex CO13 0ES
Tel. Frinton (0225) 674621

From Clacton-on-Sea follow B1032 north eastwards for 3 miles to Great Holland. Signposted.

A pick your own farm with a shop selling apples, pears, plums, apple juice, honey and free-range eggs. All produce can be ready-picked and packaged, including special packs for Christmas.

● mid Aug-Mar Mon-Sat 9-5, Sun 10-12, 2-4
Facilities: 🚻 🚗 ♨

🌱 Map 5 D3
Epping Berry Fruit Farm
Upland Road, Epping Upland, Epping, Essex CM1 6PB
Tel. Epping (0378) 78400

From Epping follow B181 northwards, after 2 miles turn right into Upland Road for ¼ mile to farm. Signposted.

This is a unique farm in that all crops are grown organically. Neither crops nor soil are treated with any chemicals, artificial fertilizers or pesticides, instead the animals are kept to provide manure. Visitors can follow the Herbal Fruit Trail to discover how the farm encourages conservation with re-planting schemes. The visitor centre explains how fruit is grown organically and also houses a photographic exhibition which shows what it is like to work on a farm in Britain. Visitors can pick fruit by prior arrangement, including many varieties of English soft fruit and vegetables. These, along with a range of wholefoods, are on sale at the farm shop.

🚂 before 11.30 free; adults £1.00, children (under 5) free, family ticket £2.50, adult season ticket £1.50, family season £4.00
● Jun-Sep daily 9.30-6
Facilities: 🍴 🚻 🚗 ♨ ⚖
🍴 teas served with homemade wholefood cooking

🍇 Map 5 F4
Felsted Vineyards
The Vineyards, Crix Green, Felsted, Essex CM6 3JT
Tel. Chelmsford (0245) 361504

From Chelmsford follow A130 northwards, after 6 miles turn right onto B1417 for 3 miles through Felsted to Bannister Green, then turn right onto unclassified road for 2 miles to vineyard.

This was the first commercial vineyard to be planted in Essex this century. Visitors are welcome to tour the vineyard

● Oyster Day

MAP 5

and use the picnic area. Felsted wines are on sale at the shop, as well as vines and fruit juices.
☞ 50p
● all year Tue-Sun 10-7
Facilities: 🚻 🚗 ⛲ /🏔

🍷 Map 5 B3
Frithsden Vineyard
38 Crouchfield,
Hemel Hempstead,
Hertfordshire HP1 1PA
Tel. Hemel Hempstead (0442) 57902

From Hemel Hempstead follow A4146 northwards, after 2 miles turn left onto unclassified road for 1 mile, then turn left onto unclassified road for 1/4 mile, then turn right onto unclassified road for 1/4 mile, then turn right to vineyard.

This vineyard was established 16 years ago and produces wines from Müller-Thurgau, Kerner, Sieger and Reichensteiner grape varieties. Visitors can follow tours around the estate and winery and buy wine by the bottle or case.
☞ free
● Jun-Sep Sun 11.00 or by appointment
Facilities: 🚻 🚗

🐟 Map 5 D3
Gingercress Farm
Widford Road, Much Hadham,
Hertfordshire SG10 6AT
Tel. Much Hadham (027984) 2225

From Bishop's Stortford follow B1004 south westwards for 5 miles to farm on left.

This was originally a watercress farm, but is now a fish farm breeding trout, pond fish and aquatic plants. Visitors can follow the self-guided farm trail, join a conducted tour and catch their own trout. There is also a smokery and various smoked fish products, including pâté, are for sale in the shop as well as other smoked foods, a wide range of fresh and frozen fish and eggs. Visitors are welcome to taste the produce.
☞ farm: adults 50p, children (under 12) free; rod £1.00
● all year Tue-Sun 10-6
Facilities: 🚤 🍴 🚻 🚗 ⛲ /🏔
🍴 cream teas served with homemade scones, cakes & ice cream

🍎 Map 5 E4
Graces Fruit Farm
Wimbish, Nr Saffron Walden,
Essex CB10 2XP
Tel. Thaxted (0371) 830387
From Saffron Walden follow B184 south eastwards for 4 miles to farm. Signposted.

A pick your own farm with a shop selling seasonal fruits, potatoes, local free-range eggs, honeycombs and apple juice. There is also a farm trail.
● all year daily 9-5
Facilities: 🚻 🚗 ⛲ /🏔

🐟 Map 5 H4
A Green and Sons
17 Eld Lane, Colchester,
Essex CO1 1LS
Tel. Colchester (0206) 576731
In town centre.

This family-run business has been smoking fish for the shop for over 100 years. They are particularly famous for their home-smoked haddock which is smoked naturally without dyes or additives. They also stock a wide selection of both fresh and smoked fish — about 40 different varieties at any one time — and also make their own fish pâtés. Crabs and whelks, cooked on the premises, can be bought in season.
● all year Tue-Sat 7.30-5.15

🐷 Map 5 D3
Hayes Hill Farm
Stubbins Hall Lane, Crooked Mile, Waltham Abbey, Essex
Tel. Nazeing (099289) 2291
From Waltham Abbey follow B194 northwards for 1 1/2 miles to farm on left. Signposted.

Part of the huge Lee Valley leisure park, Hayes Hill Farm and the adjoining Holyfieldhall Farm offer visitors the chance to see farm animals and crops at close quarters. At 2.45 every day on Holyfieldhall Farm the herd of Friesian cows is milked and a special gallery allows a good view. In autumn wheat is harvested and in spring there are many new-born animals to see, including kids, piglets, rabbits and chicks.
☞ adults £1.20, children 75p
● all year Mon-Fri 10-4.30, Sat, Sun, Bank Hols 10-4.45
Facilities: 🚤 ♿ 🚻 🚗 ⛲ /🏔

🍎 Map 5 E4
Hazel End Farm
Hazel End, Bishop's Stortford,
Hertfordshire CM23 1HG
Tel. Bishop's Stortford (0279) 813241
From Bishop's Stortford follow B1383 northwards, after 2 miles turn left onto unclassified road for 1/4 mile, then turn left onto unclassified road for 1/2 mile to Hazel End. Signposted.

A pick your own farm selling seasonal fruit including rhubarb, strawberries, raspberries and blackcurrants. Broad and runner beans, potatoes, onions and sweet corn are also available. The farm is attractively situated by a river and a vineyard.
● Apr-Oct Mon-Fri 9-5, Sat, Sun 9-6
Facilities: 🚻 🚗 ⛲

MAP 5　　EAST ENGLAND

RESTAURANT RECIPE

♈ Map 5 E4

THE STARR RESTAURANT

Market Place, Great Dunmow, Essex CM6 1AX
Tel: Great Dunmow (0371) 4321

In town centre. Signposted.

A friendly restaurant situated in a building part of which dates from the 15thC.

◖Mon-Sun Meals: 12-1.30, 7-9.30; closed Sat L, Sun D, 2 weeks at Christmas, 3 weeks in Aug
Price range Set L £12.95 Set D £22 Sun L £15 Sat D £25
Seats 60
Cards: Access, Diners, Visa
Facilities: ♿ 🚗 ♈ 🎪

SAUTÉED FRESH SCALLOPS

18 fresh scallops
1 large carrot thinly sliced
1 small leek thinly sliced
4oz baby mangetout
small cube of clarified butter
seasoned flour
chervil
Beurre Blanc:
1 tbsp white wine
ground black pepper
4oz butter

Slice the scallops crossways into 3 and toss in seasoned flour. Heat the clarified butter in a small frying pan and sauté the scallops for 5-7 minutes until just firm, remove and keep warm. Add the leek,.carrot and mangetout and cook quickly until crisp. To make Beurre Blanc: reduce the wine and pepper by a third, cut butter into 1-centimetre cubes and very gradually beat into the wine over a low heat taking care not to let it separate. Arrange the scallops and vegetables on a plate, pour over the sauce and decorate with chervil.

🍎 Map 5 C3

Hertfordshire College of Agriculture and Horticulture

Oaklands, St Albans, Hertfordshire AL4 0JA
Tel. St Albans (0727) 50651

From St Albans follow A414 eastwards, after 1½ miles turn left onto unclassified road for ¼ mile to college.

A pick your own farm selling an interesting range of top and soft fruit including strawberries, raspberries, loganberries, apples and pears. Also on sale are selected vegetables and salads. All produce comes straight from the field.

◖telephone (0727) 53641 for opening times
Facilities: 🚾 🚗 🎪

♥ Map 5 E2

Hobbs Cross Open Farm

Theydon Garnon, Nr Epping, Essex CM16 7NY
Tel. Theydon Bois (037881) 2882

From Chipping Ongar follow A113 southwards, after 4½ miles turn right just after passing under M25 onto unclassified road for 2 miles, then turn right onto unclassified road for ½ mile to farm on right. Signposted.

Hobbs Cross comprises 6 farms covering about 1,000 acres. It supports a dairy herd of 400 cows and calves, a herd of breeding sows and sheep, goats, hens, chicks, donkeys, bees, deer, ducks, geese and rabbits. Visitors can see the whole story of milk production from cows being fed, through milking — 1.30-4 every day — to the pasteurisation and bottling process. The shop sells milk, ice cream, single and double cream and jars of honey along with vegetables, fruit, homemade jams and preserves.

☛ adults £1.50, senior citizens & children £1.00

◖farm: all year daily 10-5; shop: all year daily 7-6
Facilities: 🍽 🍴 ♿ 🚾 🚗 🎪 ⚲
🍴 cafe serves lunches & cream teas

🍎 Map 5 G3

Hole Farm

Rivenhall, Witham, Essex CM8 3HB
Tel. Kelvedon (0376) 70434

From Witham follow A12 north eastwards for 3 miles to farm on right. Signposted.

A pick your own farm with a shop selling strawberries, raspberries and red and blackcurrants in season as well as an interesting range of vegetables. Sweet corn and dried flowers are a speciality. Free-range eggs, cream and potatoes are also on sale. From August the barns are hung with dried flowers and refreshments are available.

◖end Jun-mid Oct daily 9-6
Facilities: 🚾 🚗 🎪

🍎 Map 5 F3

Kings Farm

Ford End, Chelmsford, Essex CM3 1LN
Tel. Pleshey (024537) 235

From Chelmsford follow A130 north westwards for 7 miles to farm, ½ mile beyond Ford End. Signposted.

A pick your own farm with a shop selling an extensive range of soft fruits, apples and pears. Autumn raspberries are a speciality and free-range eggs are also sold.

◖Jun-Dec daily 9-6; Jan-Mar Mon-Sat 9-6
Facilities: 🚾 🚗

✹ Map 5 B3

Kingsbury Watermill

St Michaels Village, St Albans, Hertfordshire AL3 4SJ
Tel. St Albans (0727) 53502

In town centre. Follow signs to 'Roman Verulamium'.

MAP 5

This Elizabethan watermill was used for the milling of flour until 1936 and was restored as a museum in 1973. The mill is now in working condition once more and contains a display of old dairying and farming implements.

adults 60p, senior citizens 40p, children 30p

Apr-Oct Wed-Sat 11-6, Sun 12-6; Nov-Mar Wed-Sat 11-5, Sun, Bank Hols 12-5
Facilities:

light lunches & teas served in the Waffle House; freshly-baked waffles with organic & wholefood ingredients a speciality

Map 5 G2
The Limes Farm Shop
Southminster Road, Burnham-on-Crouch, Essex CM0 8QE
Tel. Maldon (0260) 782051

From Burnham-on-Crouch follow B1021 northwards for ¼ mile to farm on left. Signposted.

A pick your own farm with a shop selling a full range of English soft and cane fruits. Most vegetables are available in season, as are eggs. Specialities include mangetout, squashes and kohlrabi. All produce is available ready-picked.

shop: all year Mon, Wed-Sat 8.30-6, Sun 8.30-1; PYO: late Jun- early Aug daily 8.30-6
Facilities:

Map 5 G4
Linden Lady Chocolates
Walnut Tree Farm, Birch Road, Copford, Nr Colchester, Essex CO6 1DR
Tel. Colchester (0206) 330240

From Colchester follow B1022 south westwards, after 3 miles turn right onto unclassified road for 1 mile to Copford Green.

All products at this factory are made by hand using exclusive recipes. Young staff are trained here in the traditional skills of chocolate-making. Tours of the

● **Making chocolates by hand, Linden Lady Chocolates**

factory are available, mornings being the best time to see the chocolates being made. It may be possible to see mint creams being hand-dropped, something unique to this factory. Chocolates made on the premises are available for sale.

free

shop: all year Mon-Fri 9-4.30; factory: all year Mon-Fri 9-1
Facilities:
★ Easter egg-making

Map 5 F3
Lodge Farm
Hatfield Road, Witham, Essex CM8 1EJ
Tel. Witham (0376) 512009

From Witham follow B1389 south westwards for ½ mile to farm on right. Signposted.

A pick your own farm selling strawberries, raspberries, red and blackcurrants, gooseberries and cut flowers. Potatoes and broad beans are available in season. All produce is available ready-picked or sold straight from the field.

Jun-Aug Mon-Fri 10-8, Sat, Sun 9-6
Facilities:

Map 5 B3
Longford Children's Farm
St Margaret's, Great Gaddesden, Hemel Hempstead, Hertfordshire HP1 3BZ
Tel. Little Gaddesden (044284) 3471

From Hemel Hempstead follow A4146 north westwards, after 2½ miles turn left onto unclassified

MAP 5   EAST ENGLAND

● **The kitchen at the re-constructed Norman castle of Mountfitchet**

road for ¼ mile to Great Gaddesden. Signposted.

This small family farm is ideal for children. They are welcome to wander around and meet the farmyard pets which include sheep, goats, pigs, bantam chickens, hens and ducks. The farm shop sells a variety of free-range eggs in season — chicken, duck, goose, quail and guinea fowl, as well as goats' milk and yoghurt, biscuits and preserves.

☞ 50p
● all year daily 9-5
Facilities: 🚻 🚌

☼ Map 5 E1
Lorkins Farm
Conways Road, Orsett,
Essex RM16 3EL
Tel. Grays Thurrock (0375)
891439

From Orsett follow B188 northwards for 1 mile to farm. Signposted.

A farm shop selling a wide range of vegetables, salads and fruit with the emphasis on locally grown produce. Specialities include homemade jams and preserves, pickles, fudge, free-range eggs, cakes, and Burnham mustard. Also on sale are a range of local crafts and dried flower arrangements. Visitors are welcome to look at the traditional farm buildings and children can feed the chickens and rabbits.
● all year Tue-Sun, Bank Hols 9-6
Facilities: 🚻 🚌

❦ Map 5 D3
Mark Hall Cycle Museum
Muskham Road, off First Avenue, Harlow, Essex
Tel. Harlow (0279) 39680

From Harlow follow A414 northwards, after 1 mile turn left at junction with B183, then immediately right to museum on right. Signposted.

Begun in 1948 by John Collins, this is one of the largest collections of bicycles in the country. The collection is housed in 5 galleries of the converted stable block of Mark Hall, the Collins' family home. The exhibits cover the evolution of the bicycle from the 'hobby horse' of 1818 through the pennyfarthing and safety bicycles to the modern machine. There is also a wide range of specialist and tradesmens' bicycles once commonly used by butchers' and bakers' boys. Behind the museum are 3 walled gardens: the 2 small ones are laid out as a 17thC herb garden and an ornamental fruit garden, while the large one is divided into sections showing a rose garden, herbaceous garden, vegetable garden and a typical cottage garden.

☞ free
● all year daily 10-5
Facilities: ♿ 🚻 🚌

⚑ Map 5 F2
Marsh Farm Country Park
Marsh Farm Road,
South Woodham Ferrers,
Essex CM3 5LD
Tel. Chelmsford (0245) 321552

MAP 5

From Chelmsford follow A130 south eastwards, after 9 miles turn left onto A132 for 3 miles to South Woodham Ferrers. Signposted.

Marsh Farm is a working farm which gives visitors an insight into the agricultural industry, particularly meat production. Beef cattle, sheep and pigs are kept commercially here. The route round the farm is self-guided and the buildings have been specially designed with walkways so that visitors can see some of the animals which are kept in the farm buildings all year. Stockmen can be seen at work shearing and lambing in season. The visitor centre, housed in an attractive 19thC barn, has displays and video units providing information about farming and the countryside. There is also a nature reserve at the eastern end of the park.

☞ adults 80p, senior citizens & children (3-16) 40p, family season ticket £7.50
◐ all year Mon-Fri 10-4.30, Sat, Sun, Bank Hols 10-5.30; Oct-Feb closed for lunch 12.30-1.30; winter farm closes at dusk
Facilities: 🚌 🍴 ♿ 🚾 🚗 👶
🍴 farmhouse teas with homemade cakes, biscuits & scones, light lunches with baked potatoes, pasties & pies

---

🏰 **Map 5 E4**
Mountfitchet Castle
Bayley Walls, Stansted,
Essex CM24 8SP
Tel. Bishop's Stortford (0279) 813237/815035

From Bishop's Stortford follow B1383 northwards, after 2 miles turn right to castle.

When William the Conqueror came to Britain in 1066 his cousin, the Duke of Boulogne, built a fine motte-and-bailey castle. In 1215 this stronghold was razed to the ground in revenge against Richard de Mountfitchet, one of the 25

barons who forced King John to sign the Magna Carta. On the mound that remained, Mountfitchet castle and village were rebuilt, thus creating the only reconstructed Norman Motte-and-Bailey castle in the world. It shows how the Normans lived, what they ate, the crops they grew and the animals they kept. On display are agricultural implements, a vineyard and a herb garden. A reconstructed medieval kitchen displays food eaten during the Norman period. Eggs from the village farm can be bought from the farm shop.

☞ adults £2.75, senior citizens £2.00, children £1.75
◐ 13 Mar-13 Nov daily 10-5
Facilities: 🚌 🍴 🚗 👶
★ Spring Bank Hol week wild flower & herb festival
🍴 teas served with homemade cakes, pies & scones baked to medieval recipes using natural ingredients

---

🪁 **Map 5 E2**
Mountnessing Windmill
Roman Road, Mountnessing,
Brentwood, Essex
Tel. Chelmsford (0245) 352232
From Brentwood follow A1023 north eastwards, after 1½ miles turn left onto B1002 for ½ mile to mill.

This working windmill, built in 1807, is the only one in Essex which regularly grinds flour, which is for sale in 3lb bags. Visitors can also see a display of rural implements in the mill.

☞ free
◐ 1 & 30 May, 26 Jun, 31 Jul, 29 Aug, 25 Sep, 23 Oct 2-5
Facilities: 🍴 🚗 👶 🅿

🕓 **Map 5 C2**
New Cottage Farm
Ridgeway, Potters Bar,
Hertfordshire EN6 5QT
Tel. Potters Bar (0707) 43033
From Enfield follow A110 westwards, after 1 mile turn right onto A1005 for 3 miles to farm on right. Signposted.

A pick your own farm selling strawberries, raspberries, tayberries, gooseberries and redcurrants. Vegetables for sale include peas, dwarf and broad beans, courgettes, cabbage and broccoli.

◐ end Jun-end Aug daily 9-6.30
Facilities: 🚾 🚗 👶

🍷 **Map 5 G2**
New Hall Vineyard
Chelmsford Road, Purleigh,
Nr Maldon, Essex CM3 6PN
Tel. Maldon (0621) 828343
From Maldon follow B1018 southwards, after 4 miles turn right onto unclassified road for 1 mile, then join B1010 for 1 mile to Purleigh. Signposted.

The Greenwood family own and run 22 acres of vines at New Hall and have won various awards for their wines over the years. The wines are identified by the grape variety and include Huxelrebe, Müller-Thurgau, Pinot Gris, Pinot Noir, Zweigeltrebe and Bacchus. The wines should be drunk cool or slightly chilled, including the light red which can be enjoyed young but improves with age. The vineyard is open for visits and sales are made from the cellars. There is also a mixed farm, a nature trail and fishing.

☞ free
◐ cellar & shop: all year Mon-Fri 10-6, Sat, Sun 10-1.30; tours: end May-Sep by appointment
Facilities: 🚾 🚗 👶 🅿
★ 24-25 Sep English wine festival with wine tastings, tours, Colchester oysters & many other events

---

🍷 **Map 5 E4**
North Hall Farm
Quendon, Saffron Walden,
Essex CB11 3XP
Tel. Saffron Walden (0799) 88429
From Newport follow B1383 southwards for 2 miles to Quendon.

MAP 5   EAST ENGLAND

All the stock on this farm is reared organically without the use of additives or growth promoters. Visitors may tour the farm and buy from a selection of pork, bacon and beef, as well as free-range eggs.

☞ free
● all year by appointment
Facilities: ▥ 🚗

😊 Map 5 H4
Olivers Orchard
Olivers Lane, Gosbecks Road, Colchester, Essex CO2 OHH
Tel. Colchester (0206) 330208

From Colchester follow B1022 south westwards, after 1 mile turn left at Leather Bottle Inn into Gosbecks Road for ¼ mile, then turn right into Olivers Lane for 1 mile to orchard. Signposted.

A pick your own farm with a shop selling an extensive range of seasonal fruit and vegetables as well as homemade jams, honey, cider and apple juice. Also on sale are unusual varieties of apples and autumn strawberries. The farm also has a cider bar, a farm nature trail and a conservation centre.

● end Jun-end Oct Mon-Thur 9-dusk, Fri-Sun 9-6; Nov-Dec Sat, Sun 9-6
Facilities: ▥ 🚗 ☕ ⛺

🏠 Map 5 E4
Prior's Hall Barn
Widdington, Nr Saffron Walden, Essex
Tel. Saffron Walden (0799) 41047

From Saffron Walden follow B1052 south westwards, after 2 miles turn left onto B1383 for 2½ miles, then turn left onto unclassified road for 1 mile to Widdington. Signposted.

One of the finest medieval barns in South East England, measuring 124 by 38 feet and 33 feet high, it has a number of peculiar features. It was used to store the year's harvest, mostly corn, which was not threshed at harvest time as today, but stored in sheaves and threshed in the barn during the winter.

☞ adults 50p, senior citizens 35p, children 25p
● Apr-Sep Sat-Sun 9.30-6.30
Facilities: ♿ 🚗

🍇 Map 5 D3
Rowney Vineyard
Rowney Farm, Chaseways, Sawbridgeworth, Hertfordshire CM21 OAS
Tel. Harlow (0279) 725390/ 723535

From Harlow follow A1184 northwards, after 1 mile turn left into Chaseways Road for ¼ mile to vineyard.

● **An exotic range of pumpkins for Hallowe'en at Olivers Orchard**

• **Pick your own at Olivers Orchard**

Vines were first planted here in 1976 and since then Rowney Farm has expanded to $2\frac{1}{2}$ acres. Four wines are produced: 2 whites, one of the familiar Müller-Thurgau variety; a rosé and a red made from the promising Austrian black grape Zweigeltrebe. All are priced below £3.80 a bottle. Rowney also offers 2 'county wines', blended from grapes and apples.

free

all year Sat, Sun 10-5, Mon-Fri by appointment

Facilities:

Map 5 C3

Shaw's Corner

Ayot St Lawrence, Nr Welwyn, Hertfordshire AL6 9BX
Tel. Stevenage (0438) 820307

From Harpenden follow B653 eastwards for 2 miles to Wheathamstead, then turn left onto B651 for 2 miles, then turn right onto unclassified road for 1 mile to house. Signposted.

This Edwardian villa was the home of George Bernard Shaw from 1906 until his death in 1950. Many of the rooms remain unaltered and contain Shaw's personal belongings. His kitchen and scullery, however, have recently been restored and are open to visitors. They are now as they would have been in the 1920's, with a splendid range and artefacts of the period including a dresser with its shelves full of china, some of which belonged to Shaw. He was a vegetarian and this is where all his food would have been prepared. The scullery is fully equipped and contains cookery books of the period and kitchen implements.

adults £1.60, children 80p

Apr-Oct Wed-Sat 2-5.30, Sun, Bank Hols 12-5.30

Facilities: WC

Map 5 C4

Standalone Farm

Wilbury Road, Letchworth Garden City, Hertfordshire SG6 4JN
Tel. Letchworth (0462) 686775

On northern edge of town.

This 170-acre working farm raises cattle, sheep, pigs and poultry. Visitors can follow the farm nature trail, watch milking demonstrations and see the Shire horses, goats and turkeys as well as the collection of old farm machinery. Fresh eggs are for sale.

adults £1.00, senior citizens & children (over 3) 40p

30 Mar-Oct daily 11-5

Facilities: WC

Map 5 C3

Tewin Mill Fish Farm and Fisheries

Kingsbridge, Tewin, Nr Welwyn, Hertfordshire AL6 0LJ
Tel. Tewin (043871) 6019

From Welwyn follow B1000 eastwards for 1 mile to farm.

Visitors to this fish farm and water-garden centre are welcome to walk around the premises, feed the fish and catch their own trout from the ponds. Fresh trout are sold in sizes varying from 10oz to 10lb and smoked trout and salmon are also available.

rod £3.00

all year daily 9-5.30

Facilities: WC

Map 5 E4

Thaxted Windmill

Thaxted, Essex CM6 2PY
Tel. Thaxted (0371) 830366

In village.

Visitors to this windmill are welcome to view the machinery and the exhibits in the rural museum on the ground and first floors.

adults 40p, children 20p

May-Sep Sat, Sun, Bank Hols 2-6

Facilities:

Map 5 B2

Watford Museum

194 High Street, Watford, Hertfordshire WD1 2HG
Tel. Watford (0923) 32297

In town centre.

Formerly the offices of Benskins Brewery, this building now houses a museum of local history and art and features a large display on the history of brewing.

free

all year Mon-Sat 10-5

Facilities: WC

· CALENDAR OF EVENTS ·

MAY

Stilton Cheese Rolling Festival
2 May
An old custom which takes place at Stilton, near Peterborough in Cambridgeshire.

English Civil War Battle
29-30 May
A re-enactment by the English Civil War Society which includes period cooking, at Audley End House, near Saffron Walden, Essex.

JUNE

Dunmow Flitch Ceremony
11 June
This ceremony, dating from the 13thC, only takes place on leap years, when married couples compete for a flitch side of bacon, at Great Dunmow, Essex.

AUGUST

Colchester Oyster Feast and Ceremonies
28 Aug-2 Sep
Traditional annual ceremonies include the Oyster Feast in Colchester, Essex - guests are invited by the Mayor, although some tickets are available by ballot.

SEPTEMBER

Whitebait Festival
September
An annual ceremony following which the 'catch' is eaten at Thorpe Bay Yacht Club, Thorpe Bay, Essex.

AGRICULTURAL SHOWS

A number of annual agricultural shows are held in East Anglia — they are normally a good source of local produce. The following are a selection:

MAY

South Suffolk Agricultural Show
14 May at Ampton, Bury St Edmunds, Suffolk.

Hadleigh Agricultural Show
21 May at Hadleigh, Suffolk.

Hertfordshire Show
27-29 May at Redbourn, near St Albans, Hertfordshire.

JUNE

The Suffolk Show
1-2 June at Ipswich, Suffolk.

Essex County Show
7-9 June at Great Leighs, Chelmsford, Essex.

Lincolnshire County Show
22-23 June at Grange-de-Lings, Lincoln, Lincolnshire.

Royal Norfolk Show
29-30 June at New Costessey, Norwich, Norfolk.

JULY

Tendring Hundred Show
9 July at Manningtree, Essex.

South Bedfordshire Show
9-10 July at Toddington, Bedfordshire.

East of England Show
19-21 July at the East of England Showground, Peterborough, Cambridgeshire.

SOUTH WEST ENGLAND

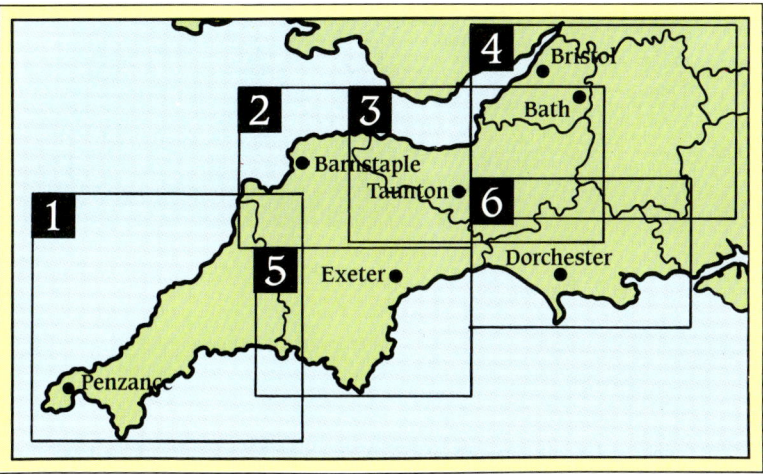

=SOUTH WEST= ENGLAND

by Geraldene Holt
COOKERY WRITER

Sometimes, in the evening when I go out to shut in the geese, I stroll to the top of the orchard and pause to take in the sunset. Looking west into the fading day I can see the ancient granite stones of Haytor on Dartmoor, while to the south there is the break in the hills that lie between our village and the coast. This is Sidmouth Gap and through it funnels the warm, balmy air of the Gulf Stream. Away to my left the giant counterpane of rolling green fields stretches to Somerset and beyond — a region that here in Devon is known as 'up country'.

About a dozen years ago, during the worst drought of the century, we moved down here to the West Country. In the years since I have come to know well the beautiful and varied countryside of Devon and the five surrounding counties that make up the South West of England.

At first we grew and farmed almost all our own food. We kept pigs and sheep, geese and chickens.

But gradually they and their descendants were eaten and our lives turned more to writing than to farming. We began to look elsewhere for food that was as good, as pure and delicious as the food we ourselves had grown. Shopping became a series of expeditions, each one in search of fine food.

I remember visiting a farmer's wife in a steep wooded valley on the far side of Honiton; she made her own clotted cream and farmhouse cheeses and they tasted superb. Someone told me about the magnificent bacon and ham to be had if I made the journey to Heal Farm in North Devon. On the way home I spotted a sign saying Heather Hohey for sale, we bought some and it was a rare treat, even in Devon. There were trips to Dorset for blueberries and to Cornwall for Fowey River crabs.

We discovered a renaissance of interest in producing fine food in a region already famous for its quality of ice cream and butter, its apples, cider and pork. Not only are good traditional cheeses finding an expanding market but some enthusiasts — often newcomers to farming — are starting to make new cheeses, like Cornish Yarg, Devon Garland and Beenleigh Blue. Fine cheeses are being made not only with cows' milk but also from goats' and sheep's. Now, high quality cheese-mongers and top restaurants in London are keen to stock them.

West Country game and fish, stoneground flours and unusual herbs, even local wines and liqueurs from Dittisham, are all gaining a national reputation. Although there are, I believe, more miles of road in Devon than in the whole of Belgium, finding these food producers, often hidden away down never-ending lanes, is an enjoyable and rewarding mission.

The sea-borne trade from Bristol and Falmouth, Plymouth and Swanage has played an important part in the history of English food. Sailing ships which exported tin ore or china clay returned laden with exotic spices, cane sugar and fruit. Even today the world's costliest spice, saffron, is used in Cornish saffron bread, glowing yellow and studded with currants.

The South West is still largely rural. Thankfully, much of it remains unspoilt; huge tracts of Bodmin Moor, Dartmoor and Exmoor and parts of the Mendips and Quantocks are little changed from 1,000 years ago. Sheep have roamed these lands and brought riches to the region for generations and still graze freely. The fertile soil of Devon's red land yields wheat, barley and cider apples. Dairy cattle feed on the lush grass to give a rich milk and cream which is world famous.

The food here is worth waiting for and you'll enjoy discovering fine food far more when you take your time.

Geraldine Holt

MAP 1   SOUTH WEST ENGLAND

CORNWALL

7

6

5

4

Padsto

St. Columb
Major

Newquay

TRERICE   DAIRYLAND

Mitchell

Freddon

C O

St.
Aust

3058

3

St. Agnes

THE ORIGINAL CORNISH SCRUMPY
COMPANY

CHACEWATER VINEYARD

Truro

Grampou

Tregon

St. Ives

WAYSIDE MUSEUM

Redruth

SHIRE HORSE FARM AND CARRIAGE MUSEUM

Camborne   PARKINSON HERBS

Hayle

PELOE DAIRY FARM

St. Mawes

Penryn

2

St. Just   Penzance

Marazion

Breage

Falmouth

Falmouth Bay

TRENGWAINTON GARDEN

THE SAIL LOFT

W HARVEY AND SONS

Land's
End   Sennen

Mount's
Bay

Helston

CORNISH HERBS

St.
Keverne

DUCHY OF CORNWALL OYSTER FARM

ROSKILLY CREAM AND ICE CREA

1

Coverack

Lizard

Lizard Pt

A   B   C   D

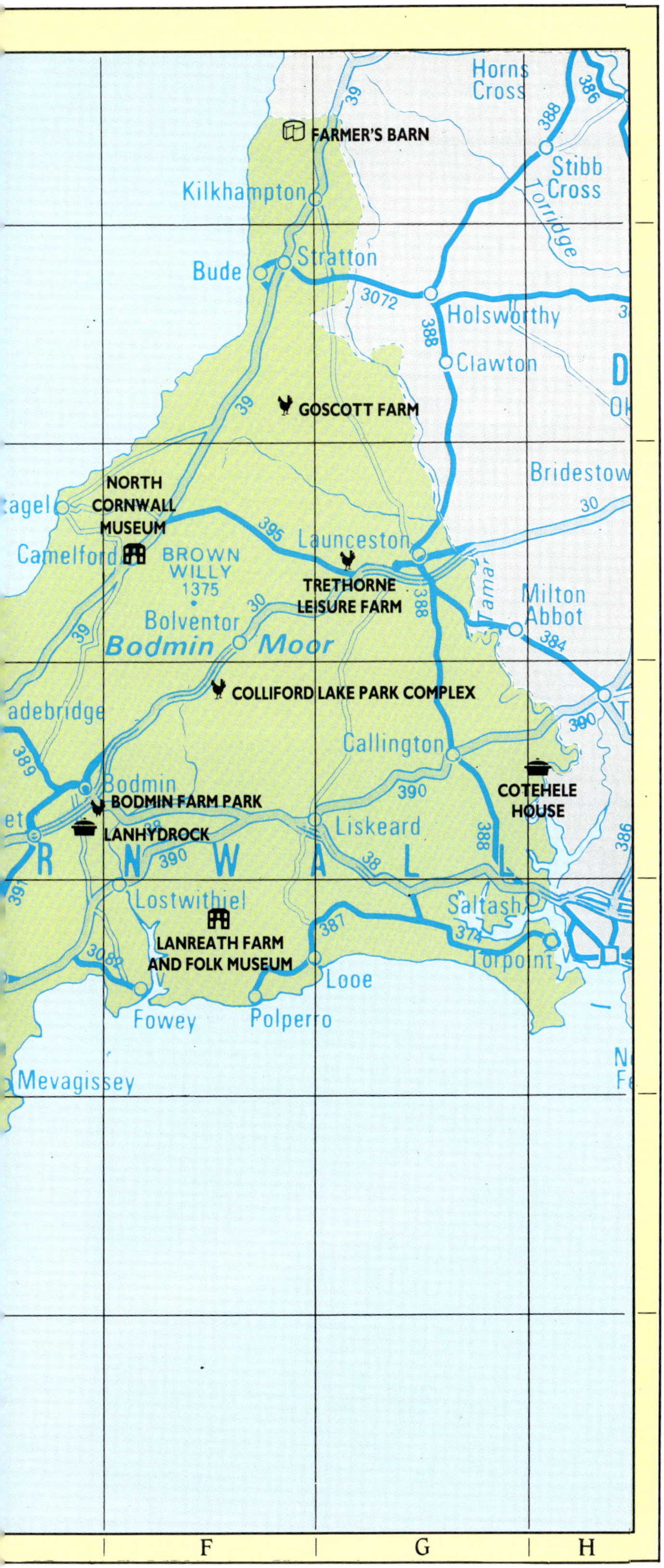

Cornwall, the most southern county in Britain, has one great advantage — an early spring. Here daffodils bloom in February, new potatoes crop in May and cows are put out to pasture long before the rest of the country. The best Cornish clotted cream comes from the milk of the Guernsey or Jersey cows which is rich and creamy with a high butterfat content. Try it for tea with Cornish Splits, soft buns served with either jam or 'thunder and lightning' — clotted cream and treacle or golden syrup.

🍴 Map 1 E4
Bodmin Farm Park
Bodmin, Cornwall PL30 4AT
Tel. Bodmin (0208) 2074
From Bodmin follow A38 southwards, after 2 miles turn right to museum. Signposted.

Children will love this opportunity to see a full range of animals on a traditional mixed farm. They can ride a pony or donkey and follow a fascinating nature trail. There is also an exhibition of horse-drawn implements and old farm tools which highlight the contrast between farming past and present. Farm produce including cream and eggs is for sale from the shop.

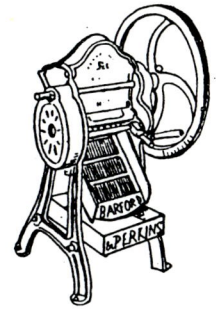

🎟 adults £1.80, children 90p
● May-Sep Sun-Fri 10-5
Facilities: 🍴 🚻 🚗 ♿ ⚠
🍴 teas served with cream & milk from farm

Map labels:

Horns Cross
FARMER'S BARN
Kilkhampton
Stibb Cross
Bude
Stratton
3072
Holsworthy
Clawton
GOSCOTT FARM
Bridestow
NORTH CORNWALL MUSEUM
Camelford
BROWN WILLY 1375
Launceston
TRETHORNE LEISURE FARM
Milton Abbot
Bolventor
Bodmin Moor
COLLIFORD LAKE PARK COMPLEX
Callington
BODMIN FARM PARK
COTEHELE HOUSE
LANHYDROCK
Liskeard
Lostwithiel
Saltash
LANREATH FARM AND FOLK MUSEUM
Torpoint
Looe
Fowey
Polperro
Mevagissey

F G H

201

Map 1 C3
Chacewater Vineyard
Twelveheads Road,
Chacewater, Truro,
Cornwall TR4 8SN
Tel. Truro (0872) 560868

*From Truro follow A390
westwards, after 2 miles turn left
onto unclassified road for 2 miles
to Chacewater, then turn left into
Twelveheads Road to vineyard.*

Wine and cider are produced at
this West Country vineyard and
potted herbs from the herb
nursery are also for sale.
Visitors are welcome to stroll
along the river walk and see the
breeding grounds of geese and
rare dragonflies.

free

all year daily 9-6
Facilities:

Map 1 F4
**Colliford Lake Park
Complex**
Colliford Lake Park, Liskeard,
Cornwall PL14 6PZ
Tel. Cardinham (020882) 335

*From Launceston follow A30
south westwards, after 15 miles
turn left to farm. Signposted.*

Set on Bodmin Moor at the north
edge of Colliford Reservoir,
this 60-acre park has many rare
breeds of domestic and wild
animals and birds and a pets'
corner where children can play.

park: adults £2, senior
citizens £1.60, children £1.00;
rest of complex all year: free

park: Apr-Oct daily 10-dusk;
rest of complex: all year daily
10-dusk
Facilities:

12thC Cornish long house
serves real ale & bar snacks;
candle-lit restaurant serves teas
& dinners with English country-
style food

Map 1 C1
Cornish Herbs
Trelowarren, Mawgan-in-
Meneage, Nr Helston,
Cornwall TR12 6AD
Tel. Mawgan (032622) 374

*From Helston follow A3083
southwards, after 2 miles turn
left onto B3293 for 1 mile, then
turn left onto unclassified road
for 1 mile to estate. Signposted.*

Trelowarren, a 1,000-acre
estate, has been the home of
the Vyvyan family since 1427. It
is now the home of Cornish
Herbs, a small specialist grower

● **The milking parlour, Dairyland**

MAP 1

offering a selection of culinary, medicinal and aromatic plants along with some more distinctive Alpine and house varieties. All plants are for sale individually or in 3 special packages of 10 perennials which are ideal for the beginner.

☞ free
● 15 Mar-14 Jul, Sep Tue-Sun 12-5; 15 Jul-Aug Mon-Sun 12-5
Facilities: ⦿ & wc

⛵ Map 1 H4
Cotehele House
St Dominick, Nr Saltash, Cornwall PL12 6TA
Tel. Liskeard (0579) 50434

From Callington follow A388 southwards, after 3 miles turn left onto unclassified road for 2 miles to St Dominick, then continue through village for ½ mile to house. Signposted.

This 1,300-acre estate, including a fortified manor house, quay and watermill, belonged to the Edgcumbe family from 1353 until it passed to the National Trust in 1947. The house itself was allegedly slept in by Charles I and has scarcely been altered since 1627. The medieval kitchen has a cloam oven and a salamander for browning cakes while other rooms contain 18thC pewter, Delftware and Victorian copper ale warmers. The nearby quay has a maritime museum, a watermill with a working cider press and audio- visual displays. Herbs, plants and confectionery are for sale in the shop.

☞ house, gardens & mill: adults £3.20, children (5-17) £1.60; gardens & mill: adults £1.50, children (5-17) 75p
● Apr-Oct Sat-Thur 11-6.00
Facilities: ⛲ ⦿ ⚗ ⛟
⦿ restaurant in barn serves homecooked local dishes & tea room on quay serves snacks & Cornish cream teas

---

📷 Map 1 D3
Dairyland
Tresillian Barton, Summercourt, Newquay, Cornwall TR8 5AA
Tel. Mitchell (087250) 246

From Newquay follow A392 south eastwards, after 2 miles join A3058 for 2 miles to farm on left. Signposted.

Regular talks on farming are given here and, for those who do not wish to actually hand-milk a cow themselves, an elevated platform offers a fine view of the genuine rotary milking parlour. This farm park also has a nature trail, breeds sheep and cattle and grows fodder crops. The shop sells milk, cream, cheese and fresh vegetables.

☞ adults £2.80, senior citizens £2.30, children £1.40
● Easter, May-Sep daily 10-6; Apr, Oct daily 1.30-5.30
Facilities: ⦿ & wc ⚗ ⛟ ⚗
⦿ cream teas with homemade pastries & scones

🦪 Map 1 C2
Duchy of Cornwall Oyster Farm
Port Navas, Falmouth, Cornwall TR11 5RJ
Tel. Falmouth (0326) 40210/713

From Penryn follow B3291 south westwards, after 6 miles turn left onto unclassified road for 3 miles to Port Navas.

With beds in the Helford and Racuil rivers, this is the only oyster farm in Cornwall. Visitors are welcome to tour the purification plant at Port Navas where they can watch the unloading, pumping, cleaning and packing of the shellfish. Native and Pacific oysters, mussels and clams may be purchased at the shop or ordered to be sent by rail.

☞ free
● all year Mon-Fri 8-4, Sat, Sun 8-11
Facilities: wc ⚗

🍴 Map 1 B2
THE SAIL LOFT
The Harbour, Nr Marazion, St Michael's Mount, Cornwall
Tel: Penzance (0736) 710748

From Marazion cross to St Michael's Mount by foot across causeway when open, or take a boat.

This converted net loft looks over Mount's Bay and across to Marazion and Penzance. The food, all cooked on the premises, is fresh and homely. The thick, substantial Artichoke and Split Pea Soup is typical of the restaurant's style.

● Apr-end Oct, closed Thur
Apr-May Meals: 10.30-12.15, 12.15-2.30, 2.30-5.30
Price range £1.00-5.00
Seats 100
Cards: Access, Amex, Visa
Facilities: & ⚗ ⛵ ⚗

ARTICHOKE AND SPLIT PEA SOUP

2oz butter
1 small onion chopped
2lb Jerusalem artichokes peeled
½lb split peas soaked overnight and washed
2 pints chicken stock
mace
cream
fresh parsley

Melt the butter and add the onion and artichokes. After 5 minutes add the split peas and enough stock to make as thick or thin as liked. Bring to the boil, then simmer for 30 minutes. Add a touch of mace. Finish with cream and parsley.

📷 Map 1 F7
Farmer's Barn
Gooseham, Morwenstow, Nr Bude, Cornwall EX23 9PG
Tel. Morwenstow (028883) 251 day, 481/379 evening

MAP 1   SOUTH WEST ENGLAND

From Kilkhampton follow A39 northwards, after 2 miles turn left onto unclassified road for 2 miles, then turn right at Shop village onto unclassified road for ½ mile to Gooseham and farm on right just beyond village. Signposted.

The 85-strong flock of pure and crossbred Friesland ewes established by Joy Savage at Farmer's Barn in 1983 produces milk, yoghurt and a mild soft cheese flavoured with local herbs. Visitors may watch the milking and buy ewes' milk, plain and herb cheese, herbs and wild flowers from Rectory Tea rooms in Morwenstow village.

☞ free
● farm: by appointment
Facilities: 🍴 🚻 ♿ 🐄

🍴 Cornish cream teas & wholefoods served at Rectory Tea rooms in Morwenstow — open 27 Mar-2 Oct daily 10.30-6; specialities include naturally flavoured ewes' milk desserts, ice cream, pies, Cornish pasties & cakes; vegetarians catered for

🌱 **Map 1 F6**
Goscott Farm
Week St Mary, Nr Bude,
Cornwall EX22 6UU
Tel. Week St Mary (028884) 434

From Bude follow A39 southwards, after 5 miles turn left onto unclassified road for 2 miles to Week St Mary, then turn right onto unclassified road for ½ mile to farm. Signposted.

This stock-rearing farm is dedicated to conservation and visitors are able to explore, study or simply enjoy the valley by taking the Farm Trail — 3½ miles through many differing habitats. The trail begins with a restored Victorian pond; this was the main reservoir for the water that drove a water wheel to power farm machinery. An example, the Bates Threshing Machine, can be seen in the old Victorian barn. The trail also passes through ancient woodlands and Iron Age and medieval settlements.

☞ adults £1.25, children 50p
● Apr-Oct daily dawn-dusk
Facilities: 🍴 🚻 ♿

🦐 **Map 1 B2**
W Harvey and Sons
Newlyn, Penzance,
Cornwall TR18 5HF
Tel. Penzance (0736) 62734

From Penzance follow A3077 coast road south westwards, after 1 mile turn right at Newlyn Bridge onto unclassified road for 200 yards to shop on left.

This shellfish merchant specialises in Cornish crabs either in packs of hand-picked meat or as whole cooked crabs freshly boiled on the premises. Also for sale are smoked mackerel fillets, frozen haddock fillets and frozen whole and peeled prawns.

● May-Oct Tue-Fri 9-12.45, 2-4.45, Sat 9-11.45; closed Bank Hols

CORNISH PASTIES
This is the county to find the real Cornish Pasty. Traditionally it should be filled with beef, liver, potatoes, turnip, carrots and onion.

● **Goscott Farm, near Bude**

MAP 1

M STEWART

• **Lanreath Farm and Folk Museum**

🏠 Map 1 E4
Lanhydrock
Nr Bodmin,
Cornwall PL30 5AD
Tel. Bodmin (0208) 3320

*From Bodmin follow B3268
southwards, after 3 miles turn
left onto unclassified road for 1
mile to house. Signposted.*

Thirty-six rooms are open to
view in this 17th and 19thC
mansion now owned by the
National Trust. The fascinating
Victorian kitchen and food
preparation rooms feature a
roasting spit and an impressive
'batterie de cuisine'. Visitors
may also see the dairy and
bakery and tour the gardens.
Confectionery and gifts are for
sale at the National Trust shop.

🐝 house, garden & grounds:
adults £3.20, children £1.60;
gardens & grounds: adults
£1.60, children 80p
◐ Apr-Oct daily 11-6
Facilities: 🍴 ♿ 🚻 🚗 🖤
🍴 lunches & teas served in
licensed restaurant include
wide range of regional dishes

REGIONAL RECIPE

PILCHARD HOT-POT

*3lb pilchards
4oz butter
2oz flour
1 tsp tomato puree
2 pints milk
salt & pepper
1lb potatoes par-boiled and
sliced
2oz Cheddar grated*

Heat oven to gas 4 (350 F,
180C). Clean and scale the
fish, split open and remove
the bones. Lay the fish in a
greased fireproof dish. Melt
2oz of the butter, stir in the
flour and tomato puree, then
add the milk, salt and pepper.
Stir until the sauce boils and
thickens. Pour the sauce over
the fish and arrange the
sliced potatoes on top; dot
with the remaining butter and
sprinkle with cheese. Bake
for 15 minutes and place
under a hot grill to brown
before serving.

🏠 Map 1 F3
**Lanreath Farm and Folk
Museum**
Churchtown, Lanreath, Looe,
Cornwall PL13 2NX
Tel. Lanreath (0503) 20321/
20349

*From Looe follow A387
westwards, after 2½ miles turn
right onto B3359 for 4 miles,
then turn left onto unclassified
road for ½ mile to Lanreath.
Signposted.*

A small mixed farm and folk
museum where visitors can see
goats, rabbits and guinea-pigs
and visit the museum in the
tithe barn. This features an old
world kitchen with butter
churn, cloam oven and cream
separator. The upper floor
houses mill workings and a
tractor section contains
threshing machines, potato
riddles and a cider mill and
press. Cornish ice cream is sold
and fishing permits are
available.

🐝 adults £1.25, children 75p
◐ Easter-May, Oct daily 11-1, 2-5;
Jun-Sep daily 10-6
Facilities: 🐷 🍴 ♿ 🚻 🚗 🖤 ⛽
★ Easter-Sep craft
demonstrations
🍴 café & tea garden serve
homemade Cornish pasties,
cream teas & cakes

MAP 1　　　　　**SOUTH WEST ENGLAND**

Map 1 F5
North Cornwall Museum
The Clease, Camelford,
Cornwall PL32 9PL
Tel. Camelford (0840) 212954
In town centre. Signposted.
This privately-owned museum
is housed in a building that was
originally used for making
coaches and wagons. Whilst it
sets out to recall general rural
life in the North Cornwall of 50
to 100 years ago, there is an
emphasis on farming, with
numerous dairy and cider-
making exhibits. The kitchen
has a particularly interesting
collection of cloam ovens,
domestic earthenware pottery
and original kitchen gadgets,
such as a cherry stoner, apple
peeler and butter churn. A
special reconstruction of a
moorland cottage vividly
portrays rural domestic living at
the turn of the century.
adults £1.00, senior citizens
50p, children 25p
● Apr-Sep Mon-Sat 10.30-5
Facilities:

Map 1 D3
**The Original Cornish
Scrumpy Company**
Callestock Cider Farm,
Penhallow, Truro,
Cornwall TR4 9LW
Tel. Truro (0872) 573356
*From Truro follow A390 north
westwards, after 4 miles turn
right onto A30 northwards for 2
miles, then turn left onto
unclassified road to Callestick.
Signposted.*
Visitors are invited to see how
cider-making has been
practised and developed over
the years. Farmhouse scrumpy
was originally made to pay
casual farm labourers for their
work at harvest time. This farm
carries out the complete cider-
making process, from growing
the apples to labelling the

bottles. Five acres of orchards
have been planted and apple
pressing, fermenting and
bottling all take place on site —
and are on show to visitors.
Cider in various quantities and
containers, including
stoneware, is for sale and other
country wines are also
available.
free
● Mar-Dec Mon-Sat 9-6
Facilities:

Map 1 D2
Parkinson Herbs
Barras Moor Farm,
Perran-ar-Worthall, Truro,
Cornwall TR3 7PE
Tel. Truro (0872) 864380
*From Truro follow A39
southwards for 5 miles to Perran-
ar-Worthall. Signposted.*

Here visitors can find all
manner of herbs grown in pots
for planting out or freshly cut
and pre-packed for cooking and
freezing. They also sell a variety
of bouquet garnis including
some specially blended for fish
and egg dishes, and sachets for
mulled wine. Look out for their
herbal teas — mint, lemon
balm and peppermint — tea
infusers and a selection of
homemade jams, marmalades,
chutneys, relishes, vinegars,
jellies and wholegrain
mustards.

free
● all year daily 9-5
Facilities:

Map 1 C2
Peloe Dairy Farm
Praze-an-Beeble, Nr
Camborne, Cornwall TR14 9PG
Tel. Camborne (0209) 831284
*From Camborne follow B3303
southwards, after 3 miles turn
left onto B3280 for 1 mile, then
turn left at school onto
unclassified road for ¾ mile to
farm. Signposted.*
This dairy farm also keeps
sheep and pigs. Visitors can
meet the friendly farmyard
animals, watch the cows being
milked, take a tractor ride,
follow the nature trail or try the
farm's own assault course. Milk
and fresh eggs are for sale.
adults £1.20, senior citizens
90p, children 60p
● May-Sep Mon-Sat 11-6
Facilities:
Cornish cream teas served

Map 1 D1
**Roskilly Cream and Ice
Cream**
Tregellast Barton, St Keverne,
Helston, Cornwall TR12 6NX
Tel. St Keverne (0326) 280479
*From St Keverne follow
unclassified road southwards to
Tregellast Barton, after ¼ mile
turn right onto unclassified road
to farm immediately on left.*
The milk from this dairy farm's
85 head of Channel Island cows
is used to make the famous
Cornish clotted, double and
whipped cream. Although
cream has been made here for
27 years, a relatively new
venture is the production of ice
cream. The farm is run as
organically as possible, without
fertilisers or sprays and they use
no artificial colours, flavours or
additives in their products. All
produce is available in the shop.
● all year daily 9-5

MAP 1

Map 1 C2
Shire Horse Farm and Carriage Museum
Lower Gryllis Farm, Treskillard, Redruth, Cornwall TR16 6LA
Tel. Camborne (0209) 713606

From Redruth follow A393 southwards, after 1/2 mile turn right onto B3297 for 1 1/2 miles, then turn right onto unclassified road for 1 1/2 miles, then turn left just after Piece village onto unclassified road for 1/4 mile to museum on left in Treskillard. Signposted.

Here is an opportunity to take a guided tour of a working farm and learn more about rural life in the farm's museum.

☞ adults £1.75, children £1.00
◑ April-Oct daily 10-6
Facilities: 🍽 ♿ 🚻 🚌 ⛺
🍽 farmhouse cream teas served

Map 1 B2
Trengwainton Garden
Nr Penzance,
Cornwall TR20 8RZ
Tel. Penzance (0736) 63021

From Penzance follow B3312 north westwards for 2 miles to garden on left. Signposted.

This large garden, owned by the National Trust, has splendid views across Mounts Bay and is particularly colourful in spring and autumn. The Victorian walled kitchen garden has raised sloping beds and because of its sheltered position and the temperate climate grows many vegetables which cannot be grown in the open elsewhere in England.

☞ adults £1.40, children 70p
◑ Mar-Oct Wed-Sat, Bank Hols 11-6
Facilities: 🍽 ♿ 🚻 🚌
🍽 teas available at Trengwainton Farm House

Map 1 D3
Trerice
St Newlyn East, Nr Newquay, Cornwall TR8 5JJ
Tel. Newquay (0637) 875404

From Newquay follow A392 eastwards, after 2 1/2 miles turn right onto A3058 for 1 mile, then turn right at Kestle Mill onto unclassified road for 3/4 mile to house. Signposted.

Trerice is a small Elizabethan manor house owned by the National Trust. A variety of plants are grown in its summer garden and of particular interest is an orchard of Cornish apple trees.

☞ adults £2.40, children £1.20
◑ Apr-Oct daily 11-6
Facilities: 🍽 ♿ 🚻 🚌 ⛺
🍽 lunches & teas served in Barn

Map 1 G5
Trethorne Leisure Farm
Kennards House, Launceston, Cornwall PL15 8QE
Tel. Launceston (0566) 86324

From Launceston follow A30 westwards, after 3 miles turn right onto A395 for 1/4 mile to farm on right. Signposted.

Visitors to this 140-acre dairy farm are invited to milk cows, ride donkeys and ponies, see cream being made, watch chicks and ducklings hatch, feed lambs and goats and play with rabbits. Free-range eggs and cheese and cream made from the farm's own milk are for sale. For children there is crazy golf, skittles, garden chess and an adventure playground.

☞ adults £2.00, senior citizens & children £1.00
◑ Mar-Nov Mon-Sat 10-6
Facilities: 🍽 ♿ 🚻 🚌 ⛺ 🎡
🍽 cream teas with lots of homemade cream, homemade pasties, cakes, sausage rolls, & ploughman's lunches

Map 1 B2
Wayside Museum
Zennor, Nr St Ives, Cornwall TR26 3DA
Tel. Penzance (0736) 796945

From St Ives follow B3306 westwards, after 4 1/2 miles turn right to museum. Signposted.

Wayside is one of the oldest private museums in Britain, with a collection drawn from the local parish. It features cooking equipment from 3,000 BC to the 1930's. On show are 16th and 19thC kitchens, a dairy, a watermill and a small herb garden. The museum contains a number of Iron and Bronze Age stone handmills for grinding corn. Local honey is for sale.

☞ adults 95p, children 50p
◑ 28 Mar-Oct daily 10-dusk
Facilities: 🍽 🚻 🚌

● **Trerice**

MAP 2 SOUTH WEST ENGLAND

This is one of the most interesting areas of rural food production. Here, surrounded by dramatic countryside, you will find all sorts of exciting produce from rare breed pigs to trout. Salmon and trout from the river Tamar are sometimes available in local restaurants and it would be a shame not to try Hog's Pudding, a local white pudding which is only for sale in Barnstaple.

♥ Map 2 E1
Bickleigh Mill
Bickleigh, Nr Tiverton,
Devon EX16 8RG
Tel. Bickleigh (08845) 419
In town centre. Signposted.
A 19thC farm, agricultural museum, fishing centre,

watermill and bakery are just some of the attractions to be found at Bickleigh, so allow plenty of time to wander around. Bickleigh has reconstructed a live working farm at the turn of the century. Visitors may watch or join in the hay-making, sheep-shearing

and hand-milking. There are also rare breeds of cattle, pedigree goats, Jacob sheep, pigs, donkeys and an extensive range of poultry. The farmhouse kitchen has been rebuilt to show the many household duties the farmer's wife used to perform such as clotted cream and cider-making. There is also a fishing centre where visitors can feed rainbow trout, hire a rod, receive tuition and buy fresh or smoked trout. Homemade natural and specialist foods made in the bakery, cows' and goats' milk, locally made cheese and pâtés and an interesting

From Ilfracombe follow B3230 southwards, after 3½ miles turn left onto B3343 for 2½ miles, then turn left onto unclassified road for 200 yards, then turn left onto unclassified road for ¼ mile to farm. Signposted.

Set in an area of outstanding natural beauty, visitors to this dairy farm may watch the milking from a viewing gallery or have a go at hand-milking the cows and goats themselves. The many farm animals also include a large herd of Shetland ponies, and feeding by bottle of the baby animals is welcome. There are tractor and trailer and horse and cart rides and a nature trail. Free-range eggs, organic pork and goats' milk are for sale in the shop.

☞ adults £2.00, senior citizens & children (3-16) £1.00
◑ Mar Sun 10.30-6; Apr, Oct Wed, Thur, Sun, Easter Mon 10.30-6; May-Sep Sun-Fri 10.30-6
Facilities: 🍽 🚻 🚗 ♨ ⚠
🍽 food bar serves ploughman's, jacket potatoes, homemade biscuits, sandwiches & pasties

---

🎣 Map 2 E1
Burn Valley Trout Ponds
Burnhayes, Silverton, Exeter, Devon EX5 4BU
Tel. Bickleigh (08845) 282

From Bickleigh follow unclassified road eastwards towards Butterleigh, after ½ mile turn right onto unclassified road for ¼ mile to farm on right. Signposted.

Burn Valley has created an environment as close to nature as possible for its rainbow trout. The 1½ acres of ponds are large, irregularly shaped and lightly stocked. Feed water comes from springs in the valley and the River Burn, providing fauna with which the trout are fed. The result is a free-range fish, pink and firm-fleshed. Visitors are welcome to look around the farm and smokery and to feed the fish. The farm also has a flock of pedigree Jacob sheep and an abundance of wild mallard ducks. The shop sells hot and

cold-smoked trout, trout pâté and fresh fish. The pâté comes in 5oz tubs, the hot-smoked trout in vacuum packs and the cold-smoked trout in 4-5oz sizes.

☞ free
◑ all year daily 2-6
Facilities: 🚗

〰 Map 2 E1
Devon Quail
Poole Farmhouse, Thorverton, Exeter, Devon EX5 5PN
Tel. Exeter (0392) 860946

From Bickleigh follow A396 southwards, after 3 miles turn right onto unclassified road for 2 miles through Thorverton to farm on left.

Devon Quail is one of the few commercial quail farms in Britain. It offers a selection of quality produce from its flocks of quail and guinea fowl with all the birds reared under non-intensive systems. Visitors are welcome to watch demonstrations in the poultry farm and in the smokery where local English oak and apple wood are used and may taste the produce. Fresh, frozen and smoked poultry and game such as rabbit, partridge, pheasant and pigeon as well as quail and guinea fowl are available from the shop. Quails' eggs — fresh, smoked, bottled and Scotch, with a choice of sausage meat from Heal Farm — are for sale as well as pâtés made from either quails' eggs and sherry or smoked rabbit and cider.

☞ free
◑ all year Mon-Sat 9-6, closed Bank Hols
Facilities: 🚗

🎣 Map 2 D2
Exmoor Trout
North Molton, Devon EX36 3JJ
Tel. North Molton (05984) 321

selection of West Country food are all for sale in the shop.
☞ adults £3.00, children £2.00, rod £1.00
◑ Apr-Oct daily 10-6; Nov, Dec daily 10-5; Jan-Mar Sat, Sun 10-5
Facilities: 🍽 🍴 ♿ 🚻 🚗 ♨ ⚠
🍴 famous for its homemade food & Devonshire cream teas

🐾 Map 2 C3
Bodstone Barton Working Farm and Country Park
Bodstone Barton, Combe Martin, Devon EX34 0NT
Tel. Combe Martin (027188) 3654

MAP 2　　　　**SOUTH WEST ENGLAND**

From South Molton follow unclassified road northwards for 3 miles through North Molton, then turn left to farm just before bridge. Signposted.

Here rainbow trout are farmed in the unpolluted waters of the River Mole. Over 1 million eggs are incubated every year, mostly from the farm's own breeding stock, although some eggs are imported from California and Tasmania. Visitors can stroll around the hatchery, rearing tanks and stew ponds and even choose their own fish. Some of the trout are grown to as large as 10lb whilst the smallest weigh around 12oz. The farm also sells whole hot-smoked trout, cold-smoked sides, pre-sliced 4oz packs and smoked trout pâté.

☞ free
◗ all year daily 8.30-5.30
Facilities: ▥ ⇋

HEAL FARM

QUALITY TRADITIONAL MEATS
Produced naturally at a
Rare Breeds Survival Trust Approved Centre

We are a Rare Breeds Survival trust Approved Centre specialising in traditional breeds of pigs—Middle Whites, Gloucestershire Old Spots, Tamworths and Berkshires. As our pigs are reared in a non-intensive system, without the aid of growth-promoters, etc., they take longer to mature, thus producing a carcase which is infinitely superior in quality, texture and flavour. The beef cattle and lambs are reared to the same exacting standards. Our methods of meat production are as old-fashioned as our livestock, and you can taste the virtues of both.

HEAL FARM
—Quality Traditional Meats—
(ANNE PETCH)
Kings Nympton, Umberleigh, Devon EX37 9TB
Tel. South Molton (STD 076 95) 2077

🍎 Map 2 C2
Hancock's Cider and Mineral Waters
Clapworthy Mill, South Molton, Devon EX36 4HU
Tel. South Molton (07695) 2678
From South Molton follow B3226 south westwards for 3 miles to mill on left in Clapworthy. Signposted.

At Hancock's the art of cider-making has been handed down from father to son for 5 generations. The mill is worth visiting both to see the traditional cider-making equipment and to taste the ciders and mineral waters. Tours around the mill include a film of the autumn cider pressing. Scrumpy, dry, medium and sweet ciders are sold in stone jars, bottles and on draught in the off-licence.

☞ adults £1.00, children 50p
◗ 31 Mar-Oct Mon-Sat 9-1, 2-5.30, Sun 10.30-1
Facilities: ▱ ▥ ⇋ ☖

🐟 Map 2 C2
Head Mill Trout Farm
Umberleigh, Devon EX37 9HA
Tel. Chulmleigh (0769) 80862
From South Molton follow B3226 south westwards for 8 miles to farm on right. Signposted.

Located in the Wildfowl Trust's North Devon conservation area of King's Nympton Park, this is the largest working trout farm in the West Country. To obtain the best flavour all tanks and ponds are solid-based which avoids the earthy taste often found in fish in contact with mud. Visitors may stroll around the farm, see trout at all stages of their development and watch oak smoking and brining in the smokery. The shop sells fresh and smoked

trout, whole smoked trout fillets in vacuum packs and smoked trout pâté. Speciality products include potted trout with herbs in 3oz tubs, available from Easter to Christmas, presentation packs of 12 smoked-trout fillets and 4¼lb tubs of pâté.

☞ free
◗ all year daily 9.30-6
Facilities: ▥ ⇋

🎥 Map 2 C2
Heal Farm Quality Traditional Meats
King's Nympton, Umberleigh, Devon EX37 9TB
Tel. South Molton (07695) 2077
From South Molton follow B3226 south westwards, after 5 miles turn left to farm.

MAP 2

● **Some of the 'real' meat products, Heal Farm**

This Rare Breeds farm was founded in 1981 and specialises in non-intensively reared animals fed with natural feed only. Over 100 'real meat' products are processed in the butchery and all the brining and smoking is done on the

premises. The farm itself is not open to visitors but produce can be bought in the shop, including cider-cooked hams, 9 varieties of sausage, all cuts of pork, beef, lamb and venison, dried and salt beef, pâté, burgers and salami, and hampers. Animals can be seen grazing in the paddocks in the summer.
◑ all year Mon-Fri 9-5, Sat 10-4, Sun, Bank Hols by appointment
Facilities: ▨ ⛟

🍷 Map 2 E1
Highfield Vineyards
Long Drag Hill, Tiverton,
Devon EX16 5NF
Tel. Tiverton (0884) 256362

From Tiverton follow A373 westwards for 1 mile to vineyard on right. Signposted.

The 3 acres of this vineyard are sited 400 feet above sea level for maximum warmth and shelter during the growing season. Two early ripening grape varieties have been planted — the Madeleine Angevine from the Loire and Siegerrebe from Germany. The other vines grown are the Scheurebe and the spicy Gewürztraminer and they are all planted on the double Guyot system. The shop, open for tasting and purchasing wines, also sells cider, liqueurs, honey, mustard and chutney. Tours of the vineyard are available all year except harvest time, which usually falls in September.
☞ free
◑ all year Mon-Sat 10-6
Facilities: ▨ ⛟

🐚 Map 2 C2
Hurstone Farm Dairy Products
Hurstone Farm,
Chittlehamholt, Umberleigh,
Devon EX37 9PG
Tel. Chittlehamholt (07694) 514
From Barnstaple follow A377 southwards, after 8 miles turn left onto B3227 for 2 miles then turn right onto unclassified road for 1½ miles, then turn right onto

unclassified road for ¼ mile to farm.

This small dairy farm separates and cooks the milk from its herd of Jersey and Guernsey cows to make fresh Devon clotted cream. Visitors may watch the whole production process, tour the dairy and buy both the clotted and double cream as well as farm eggs.
☞ free
◑ all year daily 9-7
Facilities: ▨ ⛟

🍴 Map 2 A2
The Milky Way
Downland Farm,
Higher Clovelly, Nr Bideford,
Devon EX39 5RY
Tel. Clovelly (02373) 255
From Clovelly follow B3237 southwards, after 1 mile turn left at Clovelly Cross onto A39 for 1 mile, then turn right to farm. Signposted.

A traditional farmhouse welcome is extended to visitors to this West Country dairy farm. They can watch 160 cows being milked in an ultra-modern parlour, try handmilking and even bottle-feeding baby animals. An 11,000 square foot display depicts rural life and shows scenes from the kitchen, dairy and salting room. A wide range of locally made farmhouse products are for sale including cheese, yoghurt, butter, cream, milk, cakes, lemon curd, honey and ice cream.
☞ adults £2.00, senior citizens & children (over 3) £1.00
◑ Easter-Sep daily 12-6
Facilities: 🍴 ♿ ▨ ⛟ 🍴
🍴 cream teas served

🍴 Map 2 C3
North Devon Farm Park
Marsh Farm, Landkey,
Barnstaple, Devon EX32 0NN
Tel. Barnstaple (0271) 830255
From Barnstaple follow A361 south eastwards for 3 miles to farm. Signposted.

MAP 2　　SOUTH WEST ENGLAND

Set in 25 acres of unspoilt countryside, this Rare Breeds centre claims to feature, amongst its animals and poultry, the world's only collection of 49 breeds of British sheep. There is also a fish farm where visitors can catch their own trout and several fields where they can pick their own fruit and vegetables, including strawberries, raspberries, gooseberries, red and blackcurrants, broad beans, runner beans and peas.

☞ adults £1.50, children 70p, rod & bait £1.25, fish caught £1.30 per lb
◑ May-Sep daily 10-5
Facilities: 🍴 🚻 🚗 🛝 ⛺

🏹 Map 2 C4
The Old Corn Mill
Hele Bay, Ilfracombe, Devon
Tel. Barnstaple (0271) 63162
From Ilfracombe, follow A399 eastwards, after ½ mile turn right onto unclassified road for ¼ mile, then turn left to mill. Signposted.

Derelict for 30 years, this 16thC watermill has been painstakingly restored to its original condition. Now once again its 18 foot overshot wheel is at work producing wholemeal flour. Visitors can

tour the mill and learn all about the process from equipment and information boards on display. Wheatflakes and 4 grades of wholemeal flour can be bought in small or large packs.

☞ adults £1.00, children 50p
◑ Easter-Oct Mon-Fri 10-5, Sun 2-5
Facilities: 🚻 🚗

🐚 Map 2 D2
Quince Honey Farm
North Road, South Molton, Devon EX36 3AZ
Tel. South Molton (07695) 2401
From South Molton follow A361 northwards for ¼ mile to farm on left. Signposted.

● **The bees, Quince Honey Farm**

This unique indoor apiary has 20 colonies of bees with up to 1 million workers. There are specially designed viewing galleries and glass booths so that visitors can watch the bees from all sides in complete safety. The hives open to reveal young bees and larvae sealed in their cells, drones and workers busy feeding them and the new honey and pollen being stored in the honeycomb. Honey and beeswax products are for sale in the shop.

☞ adults £2.00, children (5-16) 75p
◑ Easter-Sep daily 9-6; Oct-Easter daily 9-5
Facilities: 🍴 🍽 🚻 🚗 ⛺
🍽 honey cream teas served

🦞 Map 2 B3
Sylvester's Seafoods
2 Holt Cottages, Richmond Road, Appledore, Nr Bideford, Devon EX39 1QN
Tel. Bideford (02372) 79101
From Westward Ho! follow B3236 eastwards for 2 miles to Appledore.

People have fished for salmon in this estuary since the 9thC and the practice still goes on — between April and August fishermen can be seen casting their Seine nets from the river bank. Sylvester's also fishes throughout the year, landing many different varieties including plaice, cod, bass, sole, live lobsters and other local shellfish. They also sell fresh and smoked Devon salmon, local smoked mackerel and crab meat. Although visitors can watch the fishing and landing from Appledore Quay — about ½ mile away — products are sold at quayside prices only if ordered in advance — 3-5 days notice. Charter facilities for sea fishing can also be arranged.
◑ by appointment
Facilities: ♿ 🚗

● **The Old Corn Mill, Ilfracombe**

MAP 2

ⓢ Map 2 A1
Thorne Farm
Pancrasweek, Holsworthy,
Devon EX22 7JD
Tel. Holsworthy (0409) 253342

*From Holsworthy follow A3072
westwards, after 2 miles turn
right onto unclassified road for ¼
mile to farm. Signposted.*

This working dairy farm has set
aside 50 acres as a Nature
Reserve and visitors can follow
the trails. They can also watch
the cows being milked from a
viewing gallery. The farm's
speciality is ice cream made
with natural ingredients with
no artificial colours or additives
and it is on sale in packs ranging
from 100ml to 4 litres.

☞ adults 50p, senior citizens &
children 25p
◗ Apr-Sep daily 9-5 or by
appointment
Facilities: ⏹ ⚏ 🚗 ♨ ⚠
⏹ Devon cream teas served

JUNKET
With all their milk, junket is a
local favourite. Made with
milk, sugar and rennet,
junket should always be
eaten very fresh.

⊞ Map 2 E1
Tiverton Museum
St Andrew Street, Tiverton,
Devon EX16 6PH
Tel. Tiverton (0884) 256295

In town centre.

Tiverton Museum claims to be
one of the largest privately-
managed museums in the
South West. Housed in an old
Tiverton school it has a
wonderful collection of
agricultural implements
including a cider press from
1670 and a pair of wooden
scales first used in 1693. The
display of domestic equipment
and utensils features a
reconstruction of a typical
laundry room, while the
crueller side of rural life is

reflected in the collection of
animal — and man — traps.

☞ free
◗ Feb-Dec Mon-Sat, Bank Hols
10-30-4.30
Facilities: ⚏

ⓢ Map 2 F2
Waterloo Farm
Clayhidon, Cullompton,
Devon EX15 3TN
Tel. Hemyock (0823) 680273

*From Cullompton follow B3181
northwards for 3 miles, continue
onto B3391 for 4 miles, then turn
right at Culmstock onto
unclassified road for 5 miles
through Hemyock and Rosemary
Lane, then continue for ½ mile
and turn left at Clayhidon to
farm. Signposted.*

Set 800 feet above sea level in
an area of outstanding natural
beauty, this 30-acre sheep farm
produces award-winning
yoghurt and fudge from
Friesland ewes' milk. There are
daily demonstrations of sheep
milking and visitors are
welcome to mix with the
friendly animals. Milk, yoghurt,
fudge and fudge yoghurt are for
sale.

☞ adults 60p, children 30p
◗ all year daily 3-6
Facilities: 🚗 ♨

⊟ Map 2 C1
Wheatland Farm
Winkleigh, Devon EX19 8DJ
Tel. Winkleigh (083783) 361

*From Winkleigh follow B3220
northwards, after ½ mile turn
right onto unclassified road for 1
mile to farm on right. Signposted.*

This dairy farm uses all its own
products in its cheese and
butter. Only untreated milk, salt
and vegetarian rennet go into
the handmade cheeses with
fresh grown herbs added for
taste. Visitors may watch the
dairy at work, learn farming
techniques in the Interpretation
Centre and sample several
varieties of herb and mould-

ripened cheeses. Individual
hard cheeses are sold cut or in
2lb and 4 to 5lb weights while
the mould-ripened varieties
come in 8oz sizes. Herb butter
is also sold.

☞ free
◗ farm: Apr-Sep Mon-Sat 9-5;
cheese sales: all year
Facilities: 🚗 ♨

ⓥ Map 2 F1
Whitmoor House Vineyard
Whitmoor House, Ashill
Cullompton, Devon EX15 3NP
Tel. Craddock (0884) 40145

*From Cullompton follow B3181
northwards for 3 miles, continue
onto B3391 for 3 miles, then turn
right at Craddock onto
unclassified road for 1 mile to
Ashill, then follow unclassified
road southwards for ½ mile to
farm on right. Signposted.*

The grounds of Whitmoor
House were formerly part of
the Dunkeswell Abbey estate
where monks grew vines
before they were dispersed in
the 16thC. The present 2½-acre
vineyard, begun in 1981,
produces a medium dry white
wine from Madeleine Angevine
grapes. Recent plantings
include Seyval Blanc, Leon
Millot and Triomphe d'Alsace.
Visitors may tour the vineyard
and winery and sample the
wines and cider — including
naturally fermented Devon
scrumpy. Wine is available by
the bottle or case in 70cl, litre,
2½-litre and 5-litre quantities.

☞ free
◗ Apr-Oct Mon, Wed-Sat 10-5,
Sun 12-4; Nov-Mar by
appointment
Facilities: ⚏ 🚗

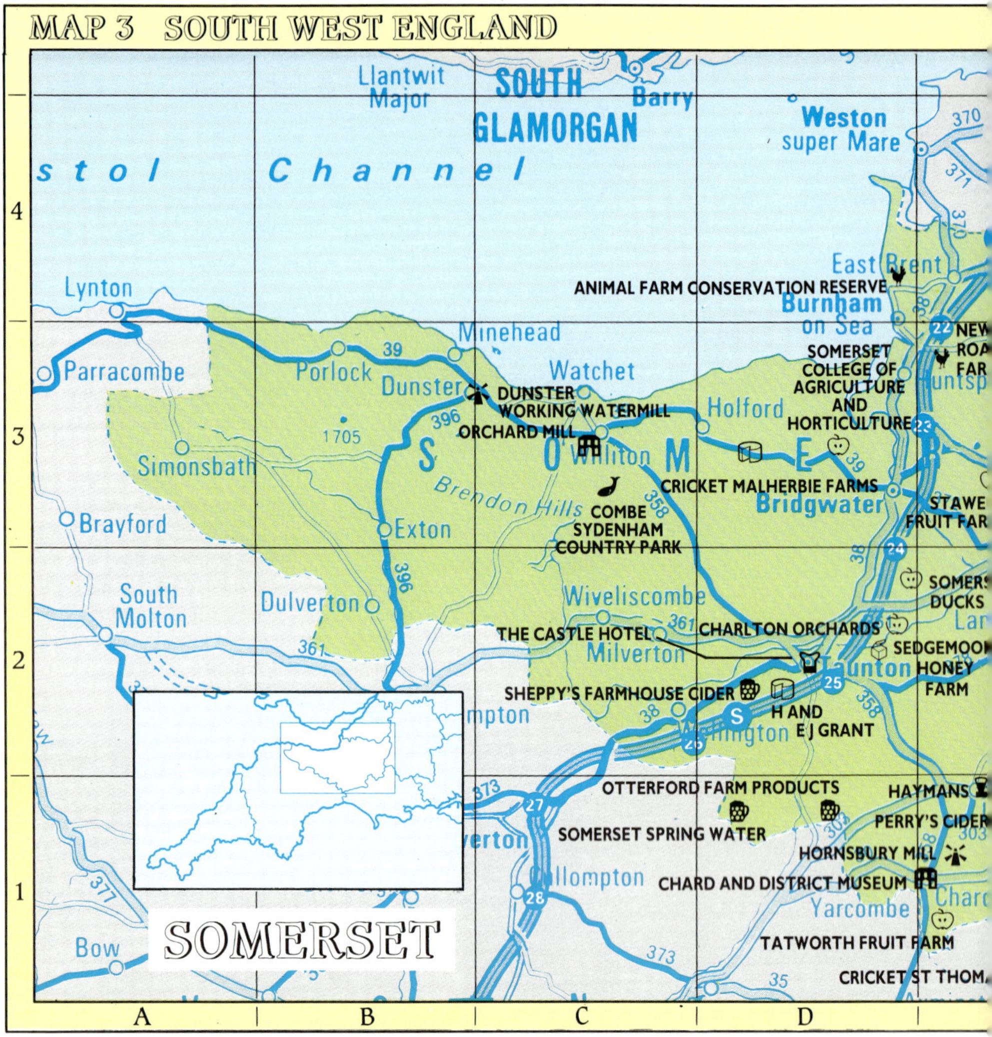

MAP 3 SOUTH WEST ENGLAND

Llantwit Major

SOUTH GLAMORGAN

Barry

Weston super Mare

370

311

370

s t o l   C h a n n e l

4

Lynton

ANIMAL FARM CONSERVATION RESERVE

East Brent

Burnham on Sea

22 NEW

Parracombe

Minehead

39

Porlock

Dunster

DUNSTER WORKING WATERMILL

Watchet

Holford

SOMERSET COLLEGE OF AGRICULTURE AND HORTICULTURE

ROA FAR

huntsp

3

1705

396

ORCHARD MILL

Whiton

S   O   M

E

23

38

Simonsbath

Brendon Hills

COMBE SYDENHAM COUNTRY PARK

CRICKET MALHERBIE FARMS

Bridgwater

STAWE FRUIT FAR

Brayford

Exton

538

24

South Molton

Dulverton

361

396

Wiveliscombe

SOMERS DUCKS

Lar

361

THE CASTLE HOTEL

Milverton

CHARLTON ORCHARDS

SEDGEMOOR HONEY FARM

2

SHEPPY'S FARMHOUSE CIDER

mpton

25

38

aunton

38

358

25

H AND E J GRANT

ington

S

373

27

OTTERFORD FARM PRODUCTS

HAYMANS

SOMERSET SPRING WATER

PERRY'S CIDER

303

verton

llompton

HORNSBURY MILL

Chard

28

CHARD AND DISTRICT MUSEUM

Yarcombe

1

377

Bow

SOMERSET

373

TATWORTH FRUIT FARM

35

CRICKET ST THOM.

A   B   C   D

Wine has been produced here for centuries, as can be seen from the stone carvings at Wells. During the 13thC when the cathedral was built the stonemasons working on the columns had a free hand to decorate the capitals with scenes from country life. One column carries a delightful sequence of 4 carvings showing a local farmer hearing the news that his grapes had been stolen and how he took the thieves to task. One of the carvings was chosen by Wootton Vineyard as their label and now graces their bottles.

♥ Map 3 D4
Animal Farm Conservation Reserve
Red Road, Berrow,
Nr Burnham-on-Sea, Somerset
Tel. Brean Down (027875) 628

From Burnham-on-Sea follow B3139 northwards for 1 mile to Berrow, then continue onto unclassified road for 1½ miles to farm on right. Signposted.

This conservation reserve offers a great deal to the visitor. With extensive nature trails and a pets' corner there are many opportunities to feed and make friends with a variety of farm animals, including several rare breeds. There is also an interesting display of vintage farming machinery.

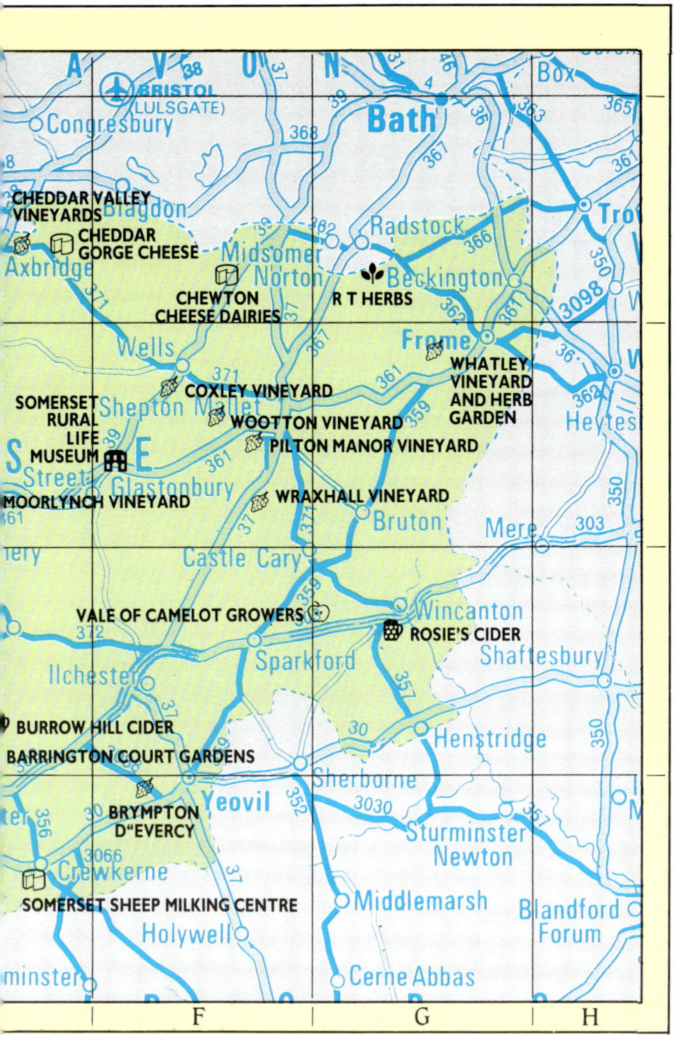
BRISTOL
(LULSGATE)
Congresbury
Bath
Box
Radstock
Trow
CHEDDAR VALLEY VINEYARDS
Blagdon
CHEDDAR GORGE CHEESE
Axbridge
Midsomer Norton
Beckington
CHEWTON CHEESE DAIRIES
R T HERBS
Wells
Frome
WHATLEY VINEYARD AND HERB GARDEN
COXLEY VINEYARD
SOMERSET RURAL LIFE MUSEUM
Shepton Mallet
WOOTTON VINEYARD
PILTON MANOR VINEYARD
Heytes
Street
Glastonbury
MOORLYNCH VINEYARD
WRAXHALL VINEYARD
Bruton
Mere
Castle Cary
VALE OF CAMELOT GROWERS
Wincanton
ROSIE'S CIDER
Shaftesbury
Sparkford
Ilchester
BURROW HILL CIDER
BARRINGTON COURT GARDENS
Henstridge
Sherborne
Yeovil
BRYMPTON D"EVERCY
Sturminster Newton
Crewkerne
SOMERSET SHEEP MILKING CENTRE
Middlemarsh
Blandford Forum
Holywell
Cerne Abbas
F
G
H

☞ adults £1.25, children (under 16) 75p
◐ May-Sep 10-5 daily
Facilities: ☕ 🍽 WC 🚗 🧺 ⛺
★ food & wine fair — telephone for details

✿ Map 3 E2
Barrington Court Gardens
Barrington Court, Ilminster, Somerset TA19 0NQ
Tel. South Petherton (0460) 41480

From Ilminster follow B3168 northwards, after 3 miles turn right onto unclassified road for 1 mile through Barrington to house. Signposted.

Barrington Court consists of a farm, extensive grounds and the largest kitchen garden in Somerset. The farm has a trail which wanders through both arable and dairy farmland, giving a good impression of modern farm life. The walled kitchen garden, laid out to plans approved by Gertrude Jekyll, is pleasant simply to stroll through, but also offers pick your own soft fruit. A shop sells vegetables, soft fruit, honey, plants, country wines and cider.

☞ adults £2.50, senior citizens £2.00, children (over 12) £1.50
◐ Easter Sun-28 Sep Sun-Wed 2-5.30
Facilities: ☕ 🍽 ♿ WC 🚗 🧺 ⛺
🍽 homemade cream teas served

🍇 Map 3 F1
Brympton d'Evercy
Brympton, Yeovil, Somerset BA22 8TD
Tel. Yeovil (0935) 862528

From Yeovil follow A30 south westwards, after 2 miles turn right onto unclassified road for ¾ mile to house on right.

BRYMPTON
English White Table Wine
70cl

The owners of Brympton d'Evercy, Charles and Judy Clive-Ponsonby-Fane, have created the first apple brandy distillery in the West Country for 200 years. Visitors are free to wander around the vineyard

● **Brympton d'Evercy**

MAP 3   SOUTH WEST ENGLAND

and the grounds and to enjoy its fruits — the wine, along with the cider, is on sale now, but they will have to wait until 1990 for the apple brandy. Apart from the winery there is a 14thC priest's house with an exhibition of cider-making and coopering through the ages, and part of the grounds have been given over to a pick your own area, offering a variety of soft fruits. A souvenir shop sells local honey and sweets, as well as the liquor made on the premises.

☞ adults £2.30, senior citizens (Mon-Wed) £2.00, children £1.00
● Easter weekend, May-28 Sep Sat-Wed 2-6
Facilities: 🍲 🍴 📶 🚗 ⛺
🍴 cream teas served

CHEDDAR CHEESE

This is the land of the traditional farmhouse Cheddar. Look out for the mini cloth-bound, cylindrical cheeses; they make excellent presents.

🐝 Map 3 E2
Burrow Hill Cider

Burrow Hill, Kingsbury Episcopi, Martock, Somerset TA12 5BU
Tel. South Petherton (0460) 40782

From Ilminster follow B3168 northwards, after 5 miles turn right at Hambridge onto unclassified road for 2 miles to farm on left.

Burrow Hill is an award-winning cider farm, with over 4,000 apple trees in its orchard. Visitors can see its 100-year-old cider house, huge cider vats and other old cider-making equipment. It also has a mobile French Calvados still, a rare sight in England. Visitors are encouraged to taste all the farm's ciders which are on sale, draught and bottled. The farm also sells apple juice, cider

vinegar, milling spices, apples and raspberries.

☞ free
● all year Mon-Sat 9-6
Facilities: 📶 🚗 ⛺

🏛 Map 3 E1
Chard and District Museum

Godworthy House, High Street, Chard, Somerset
Tel. Chard (0460) 20250

In town centre.

Founded in 1235 by Jocelyn, Bishop of Bath, Chard was originally a wool town. Today the museum celebrates 750 years of history through a number of interesting exhibits. There is a reconstructed row of shops and factories, a cider mill — complete with horse-drawn press, a selection of dairy and kitchen equipment and a barn full of vintage waggons, ploughs and farm machinery.

☞ adults 60p, senior citizens 30p, children 10p
● 17 May-1 Oct Mon-Sat 10.30-4.30; Aug daily 10.30-4.30
Facilities: 📶 ⛺

😊 Map 3 D2
Charlton Orchards

Charlton Road, Creech St Michael, Taunton, Somerset TA3 5PF
Tel. West Monkton (0823) 412959

From Taunton follow A361 north eastwards, after 3 miles turn right at junction with A38 onto unclassified road for 1 mile to orchards on left. Signposted.

This farm shop sells over 20 different sorts of apple, including several old and less common varieties, all graded by size and quality. Pears, plums, damsons, raspberries and gooseberries are also for sale.
● mid Aug-Oct Mon-Fri 3.30-6, Sat-Sun 10-5
Facilities: 📶 🚗

🏠 Map 3 E4
Cheddar Gorge Cheese

The Cliffs, Cheddar, Somerset BS27 3QA
Tel. Cheddar (0934) 742810.

From Wells follow A371 north westwards, after 8 miles turn right onto B735 for ½ mile to cheese-makers, 200 yards from Cox's Cave. Signposted.

● **Filling the cheese moulds**

● **Cheeses ripening in the cheese store**

The only cheese-maker in Cheddar, this company still makes cheese the traditional way, using equipment which is over 100 years old. Visitors may watch the process, see an explanatory film and finally taste the product. There is also a small exhibition of old cider-making equipment, including an apple masher, press and sawdust filter. There are 2 shops on the premises: the Old Country Store selling cheeses

MAP 3

from wedges and truckles to 80lb pieces; and Mangel Wurzel's Scrumpy Cider Shop, selling cider and country wines.

☞ adults 50p, senior citizens & children 25p
◑ all year daily 11-5
Facilities: 🍽 ⬛ 🚗
🍽 licensed restaurant serves cheese & local ciders

🍃 Map 3 E4
Cheddar Valley Vineyards
Stoneleys, Hillside, Axbridge, Somerset BS26 2AN
Tel. Axbridge (0934) 732280
In village. Signposted.

There was a vineyard close by this site in Roman times but the present one was planted in 1983 with 800 Müller-Thurgau vines. Since then 1,400 new vines have been added, including Reichensteiner, Auxerrois, Schönburger and Pinot Gris. Axbridge wines, whether dry, medium or medium dry, are characterised by their flowery bouquet and fresh, fruity taste. Tastings are free and visitors are welcome to wander around the vineyard. Wine is sold by the bottle, case or gift pack and the shop also sells herbs, perennial plants and home-grown vegetables and fruit.

☞ free
◑ Apr-Oct Wed-Sun 10-7
Facilities: ⬛ 🚗 ⛺

🏠 Map 3 F4
Chewton Cheese Dairies
Priory Farm, Chewton Mendip, Somerset BA3 4NT
Tel. Chewton Mendip (076121) 666
From Wells follow A39 northwards, after 6 miles turn left onto unclassified road for ¼ mile to farm on left.

This traditional cheese dairy uses the milk from its own herds to make Cheddar, butter and cream. Visitors may see the animals, watch the cheese-

● **A day-old Cheddar cheese, Chewton Cheese Dairies**

making and visit the store where the cheeses are matured for up to 12 months. A shop sells all the produce as well as other local cheeses, sausages, homemade breads, cakes, Somerset cider and wine. Guided tours are available.

☞ adults 50p
◑ all year daily 12-2; guided tours: May-Sep, or by appointment
Facilities: 🍽 ⬛ 🚗 ⛺ 🏛
🍽 speciality ploughman's lunches & fresh salads, homemade cakes

---

🎵 Map 3 C3
Combe Sydenham Country Park
Monksilver, Taunton, Somerset TA4 4JG
Tel. Wiveliscombe (0984) 56284
From Watchet follow B3190 southwards, after 2½ miles turn left onto B3188 for 2½ miles to farm on left. Signposted.

Not many trout farms can claim a location in the grounds of an Elizabethan hall in Drake country. The valley ponds and leat system originally laid out in Sir Francis Drake's time are now freshwater lakes breeding pink-fleshed rainbow trout. Visitors are encouraged to feed the fish or catch them — fishing lessons are available. The trout

is smoked traditionally in the smokery, over oak wood chips. Other features at Combe Sydenham include a country park with fallow deer, a herb garden and a working corn mill. Fresh and smoked trout, as well as pâté, are for sale in sizes ranging from 8oz to 14lb freezer and catering packs.

☞ country park: £1.60
◑ country park: 28-30 Mar, Jun-Sep Mon-Fri 10.30-6; Apr, May, Oct Mon-Fri 10.30-5
Facilities: 🍽 ⬛ 🚗 ⛺
🍽 lunches & teas include trout salad & homemade pastries

🍃 Map 3 F3
Coxley Vineyard
Coxley, Nr Wells, Somerset BA5 1RQ
Tel. Wells (0749) 73854
From Wells follow A39 southwards for 2 miles to Coxley. Signposted.

Situated in the heart of cider country a vineyard may well make a refreshing change. This vineyard offers trails around the terraces, wines made on the premises are on sale in the house and all visitors are encouraged to taste them.

☞ free
◑ all year daily any reasonable time
Facilities: 🍽 ⬛ 🚗 ⛺

217

MAP 3 — SOUTH WEST ENGLAND

REGIONAL RECIPE

SOMERSET CASSEROLE

This delicious recipe makes good use of the strong local alcohol - cider.

2lb cod filleted
2½oz butter
salt & pepper
4oz mushrooms sliced
4oz tomatoes skinned and sliced
½ pint cider
1½oz flour
1lb creamed potatoes
grated cheese

Heat the oven to gas 5 (375F, 190C). Cut the fish into small cubes and place in a shallow buttered fireproof dish. Season. Add mushrooms, tomatoes and cider and dot with butter. Cover and bake for 25 minutes. Strain off the liquid and set aside. Melt 1½oz of the butter, stir in the flour and gradually add the liquid. Bring this sauce to the boil and cook for a few minutes. Pour the sauce over the fish. Place a border of potatoes around the inside of the dish and sprinkle with cheese. Brown in a hot oven until the cheese is bubbling.

🏠 Map 3 D3
Cricket Malherbie Farms
Stowey Court Farm,
Nether Stowey, Bridgwater,
Somerset TA5 1LL
Tel. Bridgwater (0278) 732989
From Bridgwater follow A39 westwards for 8 miles to farm. Signposted.

This farm's dairy produces farmhouse Cheddar, salted and unsalted butter and clotted, double and whipping cream. The farm shop sells all these and also a wide range of other country produce including a selection of fruit and vegetables, dairy ice cream and cider. Visitors are welcome to watch the cheese-making.

218

☞ free
● May-Sep Mon-Sat 8-5, Sun 10-3; Oct-Apr Mon-Sat 8-5
Facilities: 🚻 🚗

🌷 Map 3 E1
Cricket St Thomas
Chard, Somerset TA20 4DB
Tel. Winsham (046030) 755
From Chard, follow A30 eastwards, after 3 miles turn right to house. Signposted.

If Cricket St Thomas looks familiar it's because the house was used for the filming of the BBC TV series 'To the Manor Born'. The 16 acres of gardens include a wildlife park, railway, dairy farm, children's farm and agricultural museum. The dairy, which is open to the public, has viewing galleries and processes home-produced milk. The children's farm has a fine display of Shire horses and the country life museum illustrates farming through the ages. The estate also contains several shops including a Taste of Somerset speciality food shop. Farm and dairy produce is sold, including many different flavours of sorbet and ice cream.

☞ adults £3.50, children £2.50
● Apr-Oct daily 10-6; Nov-Mar daily 10-5 or dusk
Facilities: 🍴 🚻 🚗 🛝 ⚒
★ calendar of events planned
🍴 homemade lunches & teas served in large café

✴ Map 3 C3
Dunster Working Watermill
Mill Lane, Dunster,
Nr Minehead,
Somerset TA24 6SW
Tel. Dunster (0643) 821759
In village.

Dunster Mill was mentioned in the Domesday Book in 1086 and today is once more a working mill producing stoneground wholewheat flour. The mill extends over 3 floors and now contains a museum, with an interesting collection of farm implements and a shop selling Dunster flour, bread, cakes, gifts, locally made jams, sweets and honey.

☞ adults £1.00, children 50p
● Apr-Jun, Sep Sat-Wed 11-5; Jul-Aug daily 11-5; Oct Sat-Wed 12-4

🏠 Map 3 D2
H and E J Grant
Hamwood Farm, Trull,
Somerset TA3 7NX
Tel. Blagdon Hill (082342) 248
From Taunton follow B3170 southwards, after 2½ miles turn right onto unclassified road for 2½ miles to Trull.

This dairy farm keeps 180 Friesian cows and makes traditional farmhouse Cheddar cheese and hand-rolled butter from the unpasteurised milk. Visitors are welcome to view the dairy, watch the cheese-making and taste the cheese. Butter and cheese, cut to size, are for sale.

☞ free
● all year Mon-Fri 9-5, Sat 9-1
Facilities: 🚻 🚗

🍞 Map 3 E1
Haymans
11 Silver Street, Ilminster,
Somerset TA19 0DH
Tel. Ilminster (04605) 3931
In town centre.

Established in 1891, this shop sells a wide range of homebaked breads and cakes from its bakery 3 miles away in Ilton. They include local specialities including a particularly delicious lardy cake. There is also a branch in Chard.
● all year Mon-Wed, Fri, Sat 9-5.30, Thur 9-2; closed Bank Hols
Facilities: 🍴 🚻
★ spring sugarcraft demonstration by appointment
🍴 lunches & teas served in restaurant including homemade dishes like cottage pies, steak & kidney pies

MAP 3

✻ Map 3 E1
Hornsbury Mill
Nr Chard, Somerset TA20 3AQ
Tel. Chard (04606) 3317

From Chard follow A358 northwards for 2 miles to mill on left. Signposted.

Visitors to this mill can watch the great water wheel rotating behind glass as they feast on local produce in the restaurant. Although the present building dates from 1800 there has been a mill on the site since 1327.

Visitors can also stroll round the 5 acres of garden, feed fish in the trout lake and visit the museum with its exhibits of kitchen and agricultural equipment. Homemade fudge and jams are for sale.

☞ free
◕ Apr-Sep daily 10.30-6; Oct-Dec, Mar Wed-Sun 10.30-6
Facilities: ☕ ⑩ ♿ ⓦⓒ 🚗
⑩ speciality cream teas with homemade scones, jams & award-winning clotted cream

---

🍷 Map 3 E3
Moorlynch Vineyard
Moorlynch, Bridgwater, Somerset TA7 9BU
Tel. Ashcott (0458) 210393

From Street follow A39 westwards, after 5 miles turn left onto unclassified road for ½ mile to Moorlynch. Signposted.

Set in the Polden Hills, this vineyard is believed to have been part of the medieval Glastonbury Abbey estate. The 12 acres of vines produce a blended white, from Müller-Thurgau, Madeleine Angevine and Seyval Blanc grapes, and 2

● **English vines, Moorlynch Vineyard**

single-grape wines: Würzer and Schönburger. The first vintage, in 1983, won an English Vineyards Association award and the proprietor went on to gain the title of South West England's Best Winemaker in 1986. The surrounding farm has free-range pigs, cattle and chickens bred without the use of hormones or antibiotics. Visitors may tour the vineyard, winery, wine bar and farm and buy wine — by the bottle or case — jam, chutney, pies, homemade bread, mustard and large freezer packs of pork.

☞ free
◕ farm & vineyard: May-Sep daily 10-6; shop: all year daily 10-6
Facilities: ⑩ ♿ ⓦⓒ 🚗

🍴 Map 3 E3
New Road Farm
New Road, East Huntspill, Nr Highbridge, Somerset TA9 3PZ
Tel. Burnham-on-Sea (0278) 783250

From Huntspill follow A38 northwards, after ½ mile turn right onto unclassified road for 1½ miles to farm on right just after motorway bridge. Signposted.

● **A Somerset cream tea at Hornsbury Mill**

MAP 3

SOUTH WEST ENGLAND

There has been a farm at New Road since the late 17thC and the 300-year-old farmhouse is a listed building. In former times cider and both Cheddar and Caerphilly cheese were produced but today it is a mixed farm, with 200 sheep, 150 free-range hens, cattle, goats, pigs and rare breeds raised on the 70-acre site. Visitors may watch regular demonstrations of milking, sheep-shearing, haymaking, farrowing and incubation and can buy milk, clotted cream, free-range eggs and vegetables in the shop.

☞ adults £1.50, senior citizens & children £1.00
● Easter-mid Oct Tue-Sun, Bank Hols 10-6
Facilities: |●| & ⚐ ❤ /Å\
|●| homemade lunches & teas served in farmhouse

🏠 Map 3 C3
Orchard Mill
Off Bridge Street, Williton, Taunton, Somerset TA4 4NS
Tel. Williton (0984) 32133
From Williton follow A39 westwards, after ½ mile turn left onto unclassified road to mill. Signposted.

An early 17thC watermill is home to this unusual rural life museum. The large overshot water wheel still works and visitors can see how wheat was ground by nothing more than the power of water. Agricultural implements and domestic exhibits fill out the picture of everyday Victorian and Edwardian life.

☞ adults 75p, children (under 14) 35p
● Mar-Apr, Oct-Dec Wed-Sun; May-Aug Tue-Sun 10-6
Facilities: ▬ |●| & ⚐ ⚐ /Å\
|●| Taste of Somerset buffets with home-prepared local produce & vegetarian dishes served in Mill House, cream teas served in Orchard Garden

🌸 Map 3 D1
Otterford Farm Products
Higher Whatley Farm, Higher Whatley, Otterford, Chard, Somerset TA20 3QL
Tel. Chard (046034) 477
From Taunton follow B3170 southwards, after 10 miles turn left onto unclassified road towards Bishopswood for ¼ mile, then turn left to farm.

Lovers of mineral water can taste the farm's spring water and inspect its bottling factory. For centuries this natural spring water has been noted for its freshness and purity and, more recently, for its very low sodium content. The farm shop sells the water by the bottle or in cases of 12 and also has cheese, wine, cider, pâté, butter, cream and ice cream for sale.

☞ free
● by appointment
Facilities: |●| ⚐ ⚐ ❤
|●| teas served with cakes, scones, local cream & jam

▽ Map 3 D2
THE CASTLE HOTEL
Castle Green, Taunton, Somerset TA1 1NF
Tel: Taunton (0823) 272671
In town centre.

The Castle Hotel has built up a fine reputation for its restaurant. What is particularly encouraging is how they make a point of using local produce - to excellent effect.
● daily Meals: 12.30-2, 7.30-9
Price range £10-30
Seats 65
Cards: Access, Amex, Diners, Visa
Facilities: & ⚐ ⚐

DUCK TERRINE
To make one terrine use a 1lb bread loaf tin.
12 rashers bacon
8oz veal kidneys minced and marinaded in madeira
2 duck breasts marinaded in brandy
1 pork fillet marinaded in port
¾lb chicken livers trimmed
1oz pistachio nuts
¼ pint duck stock reduced
seasoning to taste
10 leaves gelatine
3 tbsp redcurrant jelly
¾ pint port
Pastry to line the mould:
1lb flour
6oz butter
3 eggs
1 egg yolk

2oz orange juice
orange zest
water
salt

Heat oven to gas 6 (400F, 200C). Pastry: melt the butter and add all·the wet ingredients. Mix with the flour and knead to a workable paste adding water if necessary. Allow to rest. Duck terrine: line the mould with the pastry and lay the rashers of bacon on the pastry, covering the whole of the inside. Place the minced veal kidney into the base of the mould, lay a duck breast across the top with a sprinkling of pistachio nuts. Place a pork fillet through the centre of the mould and the chicken livers either side. Lay the other duck breast on top and continue to fill with the minced veal kidneys and pistachios. When at the top of the mould, fold in the rashers of bacon to cover and place a lid of pastry on top. Make a hole in the centre of the pastry and leave to rest for about one hour and then cook for 55-60 minutes. Meanwhile make the port jelly by dissolving the gelatine and redcurrant jelly in the port and duck stock, remove from the heat and slowly add to the terrine through the hole in the lid until filled. When cool refrigerate and leave to rest for one day before serving.

MAP 3

Map 3 E1
Perry's Cider
Dowlish Wake, Ilminster,
Somerset TA19 0NY
Tel. Ilminster (04605) 2681

From Ilminster follow A303 eastwards, after 1/4 mile turn right onto unclassified road for 1 1/2 miles to Dowlish Wake.

Autumn is the best time to visit this traditional cider-maker when the local crop of apples is pressed and prepared for fermentation. The draught farmhouse cider is free from all colouring, artificial sweeteners or flavourings and is offered for tastings. Vintage sweet, medium and dry cider, and ordinary sweet, medium and dry cider is produced and can be bought from 4 pints upwards or in stone jars from 1/2 pint to 2 gallons. The attached museum tells the history of cider-making through original equipment and photographs.

free
all year Mon-Fri 9-1, 2-5.30, Sat, Spring & Summer Bank Hols 9.30-1, 2-4.30, Sun 9.30-1, closed winter Bank Hols
Facilities: 🚻 ♿ 🚗

Map 3 F3
Pilton Manor Vineyard
The Manor House,
Pilton, Shepton Mallet,
Somerset BA4 4BE
Tel. Pilton (074989) 325

From Shepton Mallet follow B3136 south westwards, after 2 miles join A361 for 1 mile to Pilton, then turn left onto unclassified road for 1/4 mile to house on right. Signposted.

Vines were first planted on this estate by the monks of Glastonbury Abbey in the mid-12thC and the tradition has continued up to this day. Visitors are welcome to watch wine-making videos in the 13thC dovecote, see grape-processing equipment in the winery, visit the 14thC cellars and, of course, taste the wines produced. Wine is for sale by the glass, bottle or case and vines can also be bought. A trout stream offers further distraction if needed.

free
Jun-mid Sep Wed-Fri 12-2.30; Jul-Aug Wed-Sat 12-2.30; mid Aug-mid Sep Sun, Bank Hol 12-6
Facilities: 🍽 🚻 🚗

🍽 wine bar serves light lunches — specialities include homemade stuffed vine leaves & local farmhouse Cheddar cheese

Map 3 G2
Rosie's Cider
Rose Farm, Lattiford,
Holton, Nr Wincanton,
Somerset BA9 8AF
Tel. Wincanton (0963) 33680

From Wincanton follow A371 westwards, after 1/2 mile turn left onto A357 for 1 mile to farm on left in Lattiford. Signposted.

In 1982, the 400-year-old tradition of farmhouse cider-making was revived at Rose Farm. This regeneration of a traditional industry encouraged local orchard owners to harvest crops rather than let them rot on the ground. In fact, cider apple trees are actually being planted again, helping to stem a long decline in Somerset cider orchards. Rosie's Cider took the Royal Bath and West Farmhouse Cider Championship in 1987 and they are keen to explain the cider-making process to any interested visitors. They offer free tastings highlighting the regional variations in flavour

● **Rose Farm, a 15th century Somerset cider farmstead**

221

MAP 3

SOUTH WEST ENGLAND

and sell dry, medium and sweet ciders in plastic, glass or stone containers. Apple juice and gifts are also on sale.

☞ free
● all year daily 8.30-7.30
Facilities: 🚗 ☕

❧ Map 3 G4
R T Herbs
Orange Farm, Kilmersdon,
Nr Radstock, Bath,
Avon BA3 5TD
Tel. Midsomer Norton (0761) 35470

From Radstock follow B367 southwards, after 2 miles turn left onto B3139 for 2 miles to Kilmersdon.

Situated in a conservation area, this well-stocked herb farm is owned by Richard and Alice Taylor who encourage visitors to learn more about the use of herbs before choosing which plants to buy. Their farm contains a number of unusual herbs, such as alecost, a tonic herb once used to flavour beer, and borage whose flowers are used for fruit cups and whose chopped leaves taste of cucumber.

☞ adults 60p, senior citizens & children free
● all year daily 10-5
Facilities: 🚾 🚗 ☕ ⚠

☙ Map 3 D2
Sedgemoor Honey Farm
53 West View,
Creech St Michael,
Somerset TA3 5DU
Tel. Henlade (0823) 442734

From Taunton follow A361 north eastwards, after 2½ miles turn right onto unclassified road for 1 mile to Creech St Michael.

Visitors can buy 2 varieties of home-produced honey from this small producer — Somerset honey or Exmoor heather honey, either set or runny. Honeycombs are normally available in late May and at the end of August.

☞ free
● any reasonable time or by appointment

222

🍎 Map 3 D2
Sheppy's Farmhouse Cider
Three Bridges,
Bradford-on-Tone, Taunton,
Somerset TA4 1ER
Tel. Bradford-on-Tone (082346) 233

From Taunton follow A38 westwards for 3 miles to farm on left. Signposted.

● **Sheppy's cellars and the modern cider press room**

The Sheppy family have been making cider here since the early 1800s, winning over 200 awards and 2 gold medals for their efforts. There are 42 acres of cider orchards growing a variety of apples including Kingston Black, Yarlington Mill, Dabinett, Stoke Red and Tremlett's Bitter. In the cellar and modern press room visitors can see how the apple crop is processed each autumn while the museum shows how the same things were done in times past. Ciders, cream and cheeses are all on sale.

☞ free
● Apr-Sep Mon-Sat 8.30-7, Sun 12-2; Oct-Dec Mon-Sat 8.30-6, Sun 12-2; Jan-Mar Mon-Sat 8.30-6
Facilities: 🚾 🚗 ☕

☺ Map 3 D3
Somerset College of Agriculture and Horticulture
Cannington, Bridgwater,
Somerset TA5 2LS
Tel. Combwich (0278) 652226

From Bridgwater follow A39 westwards, after 4 miles turn right in Cannington into East Street for ¼ mile to college.

The college is open for pick your own soft fruit, broad beans, runner beans, sweet corn, apples and pears. The shop sells the produce ready-picked.

● PYO: 12 Sep-24 Oct Wed-Sun 2-5; shop: all year Mon-Fri 10-12, 2-4
Facilities: 🚾 🚗

☺ Map 3 D2
Somerset Ducks
Greenway Farm,
North Newton, Bridgwater,
Somerset TA7 0DS
Tel. North Petherton (0278) 662656/663800

From Bridgwater follow A38 southwards, after 3 miles turn left at North Petherton onto unclassified road for 1½ miles to North Newton.

The shop on this duck farm sells oven-ready ducks, portions and halves; boned, cooked ducks stuffed in various ways; duck and orange pie and duck pâté and sausages. All the produce is fresh and contains no added preservatives.

● by appointment
Facilities: 🚾

🏠 Map 3 F3
Somerset Rural Life Museum
Abbey Farm,
Chilkwell Street, Glastonbury,
Somerset BA6 8DB
Tel. Glastonbury (0458) 32903

MAP 3

● A display at Sheppy's Farm Museum

MAP 3　　　　　**SOUTH WEST ENGLAND**

In town centre. Signposted.

Old farm buildings and a magnificent barn provide an appropriate setting for this rural life museum. A farmhouse kitchen recaptures the atmosphere of the 1890s, with its cast iron range, cooking equipment and gadgets. In the cellar a cheese room tells the story of Cheddar cheese-making in Somerset. One exhibit of particular interest is a cheese mould carved with the Royal Coat of Arms — it was used to press a truckle of Cheddar cheese made for Queen Victoria's wedding. Demonstrations in the dairy are held throughout the summer using hand butter-making equipment, such as the end-over-end churn butter worker. There are also several vintage cider presses and mills which are still used for cider-making.

☞ adults 60p, senior citizens & children 20p

● Easter-Oct Mon-Fri 10-5, Sat, Sun 2-6; Nov-Mar Mon-Fri 10-5, Sat, Sun 2.30-5

Facilities: ▆ ▌& ⚏ ▆ ❦

★ mid Oct cider-making weekend

▌teas served including cider cake

▢ Map 3 E1
Somerset Sheep Milking Centre
Higher Folly Farm, Crewkerne, Somerset TA18 8PN
Tel. Crewkerne (0460) 76966

From Crewkerne follow B3165 south westwards, after 1 mile turn left onto unclassified road for ¼ mile to farm on left. Signposted.

This dairy sheep farm has 200 pedigree Friesland ewes producing milk for yoghurt, cheese and related foods. Visitors may see the sheep and lambs with their traditional

collars and bells, watch milking, either live or on video, and learn the history of sheep dairying in the Information Centre. There is also a video on cheese-making and tastings of milk, cheese and the farm's unique sheep's milk fudge. A shop sells sheep's milk, sheep's milk cheese, prize-winning yoghurts, fudge, ice cream and frozen sheep's milk lollies. All products are free from artificial preservatives and additives. Culinary and aromatic herbs and craft products are also sold.

☞ adults £1.20, senior citizens & children (4-15) 60p

● shop: all year daily 9.30-5.30; farm: Apr-Sep Tue-Sun, Bank Hols 10-5.30; Jul-Aug daily 10-5.30; or by appointment

Facilities: ▆ ▆

▩ Map 3 D1
Somerset Spring Water
The Firs, Biscombe, Churchstanton, Taunton, Somerset TA3 7PZ
Tel. Churchstanton (082360) 385

From Taunton follow unclassified road southwards for 1 mile to Trull, continue for 3 miles through Blagdon Hill to Churchstanton, continue for ½ mile, then turn right to Stapley and Biscombe. Signposted.

Dating from 1799 'The Wells' is a spring originating deep down in the Neroche Forest and emerging at Rainbow Hill, 900 feet above sea level. The natural, pure spring water rises out of the ground through flint and Jurassic rock and from there is gravity fed direct to the bottling plant. A walk to the spring is a nature trail in itself. Somerset Spring Water, ideal for lemon and herbal teas, fruit and soft drinks and as a mixer with alcohol, has won many accolades since its launch in 1986.

☞ free
● Mar-Oct daily 10-6, Nov-Feb daily 10-dusk

☺ Map 3 E3
Stawell Fruit Farm
Stawell, Bridgwater, Somerset TA7 9AE
Tel. Bridgwater (0278) 722732

From Bridgwater follow A39 north eastwards, after 5 miles turn right onto unclassified road for ½ mile to Stawell.

Pick your own apples — 21 varieties — blackberries and damsons at this fruit farm. Free-range eggs are also available.

● PYO: mid Aug-Oct Wed-Sun 11-5; shop: Oct-May telephone for opening hours

---

☺ Map 3 E1
Tatworth Fruit Farm
Tatworth, Chard, Somerset TA20 2SG
Tel. Chard (0460) 20272

From Chard follow A358 southwards, after 2 miles turn left onto unclassified road to farm.

This pick your own farm offers soft fruits, vegetables and 17 varieties of apples. The farm shop also stocks local cream, Somerset honey, farmhouse cider and wine from Pilton Manor and Wootton vineyards.

● all year Mon-Sat 9-5, Sun, Bank Hols 10.30-5

Facilities: ▆ ▆

☺ Map 3 G2
Vale of Camelot Growers
Woolston, North Cadbury, Yeovil, Somerset BA22 7BJ
Tel. North Cadbury (0963) 40280

From Sparkford follow A303 eastwards, after 2 miles turn left onto unclassified road for ½ mile to North Cadbury, then turn right onto unclassified road for ¾ mile to farm on right. Signposted.

MAP 3

This pick your own farm offers the usual soft fruits, including worcesterberries, grown on naturally fertile soils, while the farm shop supplements the range with organically grown vegetables and local Jersey cream.
◐ mid Jun-Jul daily 9-7
Facilities: 🚾 🚗 ⛺

🍇 Map 3 G3
Whatley Vineyard and Herb Garden
Whatley, Frome, Somerset BA11 3LA
Tel. Nunney (037384) 467
From Frome follow unclassified road westwards for 2 miles to Whatley and vineyard on right just before church. Signposted.
This 4-acre vineyard was planted in 1979 and includes a winery and walled herb garden. Five types of vine have been planted to produce some interesting white wines. The herb garden, arranged in the shape of a cross, includes culinary, medicinal, aromatic

and cosmetic varieties which may be bought dried or as pot plants. Homemade food using herbs and flowers is for sale along with the wines and flavoured mustards.
☞ free
◐ Apr-Oct Wed-Fri, Bank Hols 10-6
Facilities: 🚾 🚗
★ 3-day courses on growing & cooking herbs & growing & tasting wines

🍇 Map 3 F3
Wootton Vineyard
North Wootton, Shepton Mallet, Somerset BA4 4AG
Tel. Pilton (074989) 359
From Wells follow A39 south westwards, after 1 mile turn left onto unclassified road for 2½ miles to North Wootton, then turn left onto unclassified road for ½ mile to vineyard.
This 6-acre vineyard planted in 1971 in the foothills of the Mendips now produces dry white wines from 4 varieties of grape: Müller-Thurgau, Seyval, Auxerrois and Schönburger.

The winery produces 100,000 bottles a year and visitors may watch the processing and tour the vineyard. Wine may be bought by the bottle or case and wine mustard is also for sale.
☞ free
◐ all year Mon-Sat 10-1, 2-5
Facilities: 🚗

🍇 Map 3 F3
Wraxhall Vineyard
Wraxhall, Shepton Mallet, Somerset BA4 6RQ
Tel. Ditcheat (074986) 486
From Shepton Mallet follow A37 southwards, after 5 miles turn left onto unclassified road for ¼ mile to vineyard. Signposted.
The southern slopes of the Mendip Hills are home to these vines, grown on a high-wire system known as the Geneva Double Curtain. Pioneered on America's east coast and designed for rich northern soils, the vines hang down to create leafy avenues — in complete contrast to continental vineyards. The principal blend, Müller-Thurgau and Seyval grapes, yields a fruity, fragrant medium-dry white wine. A refreshing, unusual wine is produced by the Madeleine Angevine grape. Some red varieties have also been planted. Visitors are welcome to look around unaccompanied, taste the wines before buying or enjoy them on the premises with lunch. For those who want to make their own, vines can be bought.
☞ free
◐ shop: all year daily 9-5
Facilities: 🍴 🚾 🚗 ⛺
🍴 light lunches served in wine bar Jul-mid Sep during licensing hours include local cheese, homemade mackerel pâté & other dishes

● **Rows of vines at Whatley Vineyard**

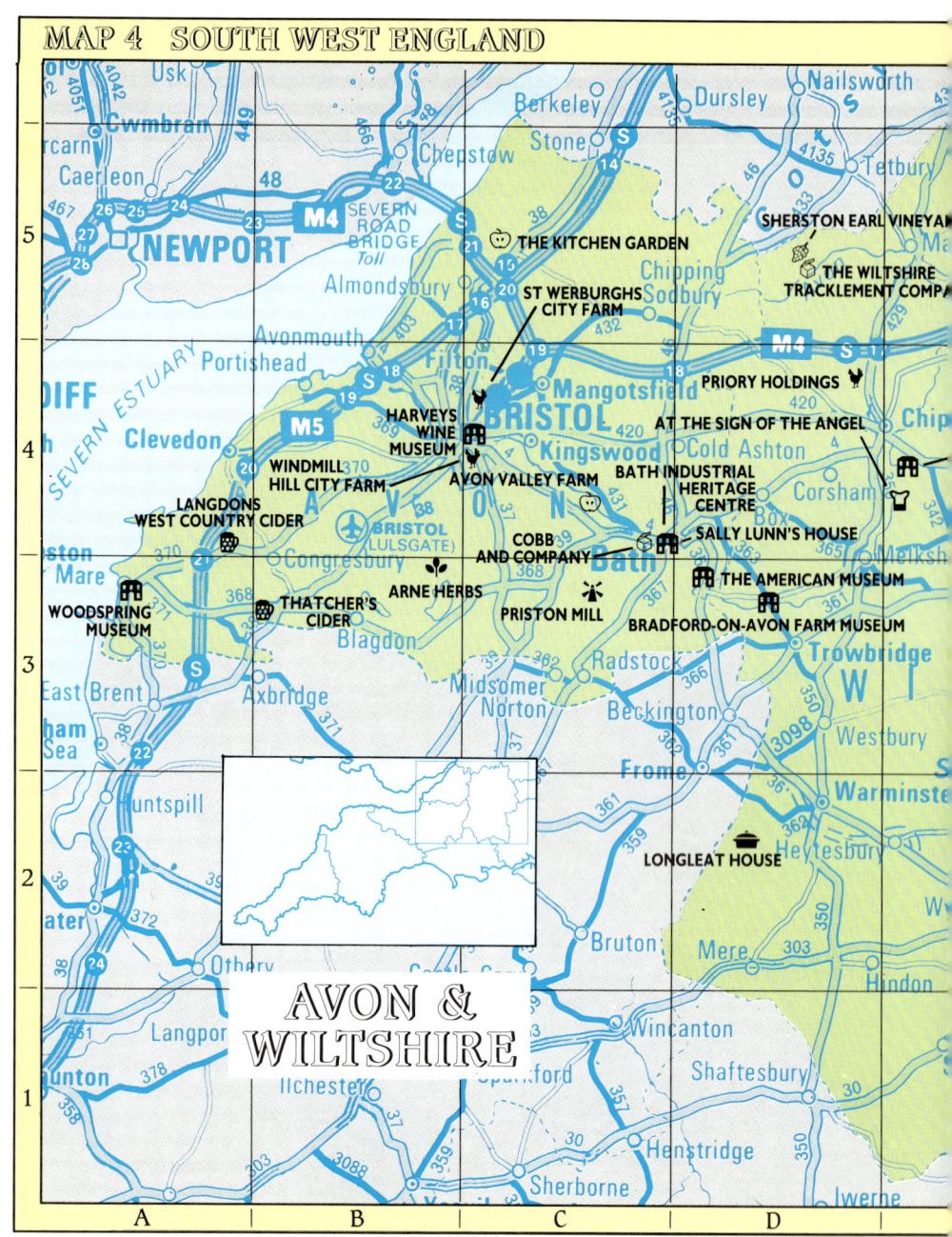

MAP 4   SOUTH WEST ENGLAND

AVON &
WILTSHIRE

Bath, elegant and imposing, features high on tourists' lists. It has also lent its name to many specialities: Bath Chaps — made from salted and cured pig's cheek; Bath Polony — a savoury sausage of minced pork and spices in a bright red skin; Bath Olivers — a water biscuit invented by Dr Oliver, the town's first physician; and Bath Buns — best eaten in the Pump Room, a building of great Georgian elegance where you can also take the waters.

Map 4 D3

The American Museum
Claverton Manor, Bath,
Avon BA2 7BD
Tel. Bath (0225) 60503

From Bath follow A36 southwards, after 2 miles turn right onto unclassified road for ¼ mile to museum on right. Signposted.

The American Museum is the

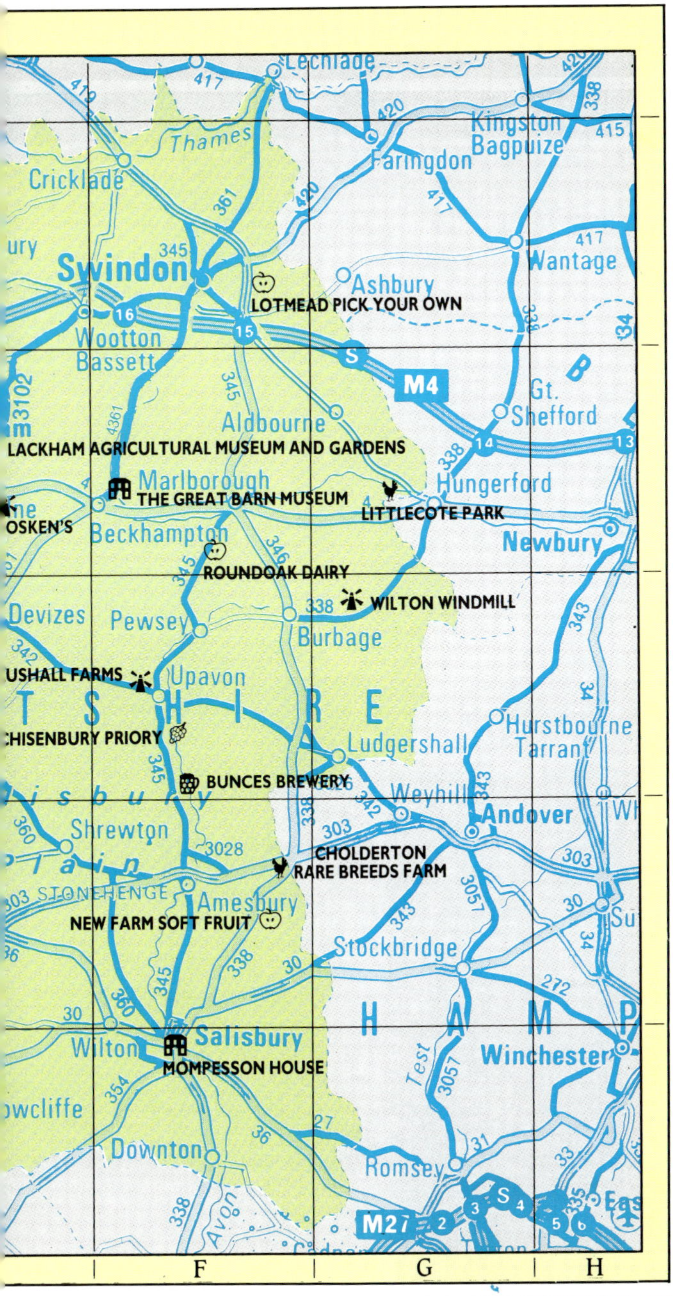

The map area contains the following labels:

Lechlade · Kingston Bagpuize · Faringdon · Thames · 417 · 420 · 338 · 415 · Cricklade · 361 · Wantage · Swindon 345 · Ashbury · LOTMEAD PICK YOUR OWN · Wootton Bassett · 16 · 15 · 34 · 345 · M4 · Gt. Shefford · 14 · 13 · Aldbourne · 338 · LACKHAM AGRICULTURAL MUSEUM AND GARDENS · Marlborough · Hungerford · THE GREAT BARN MUSEUM · LITTLECOTE PARK · OSKEN'S · Beckhampton · Newbury · ROUNDOAK DAIRY · 346 · 343 · Devizes · Pewsey · 338 · WILTON WINDMILL · Burbage · USHALL FARMS · Upavon · Hurstbourne Tarrant · 34 · CHISENBURY PRIORY · Ludgershall · 345 · BUNCES BREWERY · Weyhill · 343 · Shrewton · 303 · Andover · 360 · 3028 · 303 · CHOLDERTON RARE BREEDS FARM · 303 · STONEHENGE · Amesbury · 3057 · 30 · NEW FARM SOFT FRUIT · 343 · Stockbridge · 272 · 30 · 360 · H A M P · Wilton · Salisbury · Winchester · MOMPESSON HOUSE · Test · 3057 · owcliffe · 354 · 27 · Downton · 36 · Romsey · 31 · 33 · 338 · M27 · 2 · 3 · 4 · 5 · 6 · Eas

F   G   H

---

and herbs from the garden. A particularly interesting speciality is gingerbread made according to George Washington's mother's recipe and prepared in a beehive oven.

🏛 museum & grounds: adults £2.75, senior citizens & children £2.25; grounds only: £1.00
◑ Apr-Oct Tue-Sun 2-5, Bank Hols 11-5
Facilities: ⛴ ⼁ WC 🚗 🚐

❧ Map 4 B3
Arne Herbs
Limeburn Nurseries, Chew Magna, Bristol, Avon BS18 8QW
Tel. Chew Magna (0272) 333399

From Bristol follow A38 south westwards, after 5 miles turn left onto B3130 for 3 miles, then turn left into Limeburn Hill Road for ¼ mile to nurseries on left. Signposted.

Anthony Lyman-Dixon and Helen Lee, the owners of these nurseries, are delighted to help both professional and amateur chefs to improve their knowledge of herbs. Over 350 varieties are grown and are for sale, including nasturtium and eau de cologne mint. Chinese vegetables are offered for sale, also eggs from the nurseries' own Belgian bantams. Visitors are advised to telephone in advance if they have any particular requests. There is an informal trail and the rare sight of a field that has never been ploughed.

🏛 free
◑ by appointment
Facilities: 🚗 ⼁
⼁ elaborate picnics by arrangement

---

only museum of its kind outside the United States. It aims to bring to life the history of America between the 17th and 19thC. Housed in Claverton Manor, the museum has extensive grounds which include a herb garden, an American arboretum and a replica of George Washington's own garden. American cookies are for sale, along with homemade jams, marmalade

● **Claverton Manor, home of the American Museum**

MAP 4   **SOUTH WEST ENGLAND**

☺ Map 4 C4
Avon Valley Farm
Pixash Lane, Bath Road,
Keynsham, Bristol,
Avon BS18 ITS
Tel. Bristol (0272) 862173/
865742

*From Bristol follow A4 south
eastwards, after 4 miles turn left
at Saltford into Pixash Lane for ½
mile to farm. Signposted.*

This 60-acre pick your own
farm, one of the largest in the
South West, offers most of the
usual soft and top fruit,
vegetables and potatoes. They
will sell their own produce
ready-picked to order. There is
also a country park and farm
animals to see and fishing is
available.
◑ telephone for times
Facilities: 🍴 wc ♿ 👶 🛖

WILTSHIRE SAUSAGES

Look out for Wiltshire
sausages which are full of
pork and interestingly
flavoured with sage.

🏠 Map 4 C4
**Bath Industrial Heritage
Centre**
Camden Works, Julian Road,
Bath, Avon BA1 2RH
Tel. Bath (0225) 318348

In city centre. Signposted.

Connoisseurs of drinking water
will enjoy this unique
opportunity to visit a Victorian
mineral water manufacturer.
Although no water is for sale,
the 19thC machinery, still in
working order, is fascinating to
watch. There is also a large
collection of original 'water'

bottles — some 10,000 in all —
embracing all varieties of what
the Victorians called water,
including orange champagne,
lithia water and ginger beer.
☞ adults £1.00, senior citizens
& children 50p, family ticket (2
adults & children) £2.00
◑ Feb-Nov daily 2-5; Dec-Jan
Sat, Sun 2-5
Facilities: 🍴 wc

🏠 Map 4 D3
**Bradford-on-Avon Farm
Museum**
The Tithe Barn,
Bradford-on-Avon, Wiltshire
Tel. Bradford-on-Avon (02216)
4783

*From Trowbridge follow A363
north westwards for 3 miles to
Bradford-on-Avon. Signposted.*

This 14thC barn, owned by
English Heritage, contains an
interesting exhibition on
farming and country life in
Wiltshire from the Victorian
and Edwardian eras. It includes
a restored collection of farming
tools and equipment displayed
with contemporary
photographs.
☞ adults £1.00, senior citizens
75p, children 50p
◑ Apr-Oct daily 10-6
Facilities: ♿

🍺 Map 4 F3
Bunces Brewery
The Old Mill, Mill Road,
Netheravon, Salisbury,
Wiltshire SP4 9QB
Tel. Stonehenge (0980) 70631

*From Amesbury follow A345
northwards, after 4 miles turn
right in Netheravon to mill.
Signposted.*

Bunces specialises in brewing a
well-hopped beer with a
distinctive flavour and
supplying free houses from
Surrey to Somerset with its
products. The brewery, a Grade
II listed building, uses traditional
methods to produce a
memorable cask-conditioned

● **The Essence Room, Bath Industrial Heritage Centre**

MAP 4

bitter. Visitors can admire the complex brewing procedures in pumps and fermenting vessels and watch as the finished ale is racked by gravity into steel or wooden casks. Two types of beer are for sale: Best Bitter, in 18 and 9 gallon barrels for the wholesale market, and Benchmark in 4 and 2 gallon, 8 and 4 pint units for the home consumer.

☞ adults £1.00
◑ all year evenings by appointment
Facilities: 🚾 🚗 ☕

Map 4 F3
Chisenbury Priory
Nr Pewsey, Wiltshire SN9 6AQ
Tel. Stonehenge (0980) 70406

From Upavon follow A342 southwards, after ¼ mile keep right onto unclassified road for 1 mile. Signposted.

This medieval house with an 18thC facade offers visitors a tour of its 5 acres of gardens, vineyard and winery. Its English table wine is made from a single variety of grape — Bacchus — and visitors are welcome to taste it. This and wine from other local vineyards are for sale by the case and bottle. Plants from the garden may also be bought.

☞ gardens: adults £1.20, children (over 6) 50p
◑ May, Sep Wed 2-6; Jun-Aug first Sun in month, Wed 2-6, or by appointment
Facilities: 🍴 🚾 🚗
🍴 teas served with homemade scones, cream & strawberry jam

Map 4 F2
Cholderton Rare Breeds Farm
Amesbury Road, Cholderton, Salisbury, Wiltshire SP4 0EW
Tel. Cholderton (098064) 438

From Amesbury follow A303 eastwards for 5 miles to farm on right at junction with A338. Signposted.

●**Butter churn and cheese presses, The Great Barn Museum**

This unusual farm boasts a variety of rare farmyard breeds, with almost all the animals being endangered species. For children there is a pet animal yard, play area and an educational history of the chicken. There are also formal gardens, a woodland walk and a picnic area by a wild fowl pond. Free-range eggs and honey are sold when available.

☞ adults £1.60, senior citizens £1.00, children 80p
◑ Apr-Oct daily 10-6
Facilities: 🛍 🍴 🚾 🚗 ☕ 🅿
🍴 restaurant in flintstone farmhouse serves 3-course homemade cooked meals; cafeteria next door serves hot snacks, homemade cakes & clotted cream teas

Map 4 C4
Cobb and Company
The Bakery, Lansdown View, Twerton, Bath, Avon
Tel. Bath (0225) 23120

From Bath follow A36 westwards, after 1 mile turn left into Jews Lane to bakery. Signposted.

Founded in 1866, Cobb and Company is the oldest established bakery in Bath and is still managed by the same family. There is a showroom and a guide to the bakery, where the company bakes the original Bath bun as well as traditional breads and sugar craft work. All produce can be bought at their 2 shops at 11 Westgate Street and 1 Lower Borough Walls in the centre of Bath.

☞ free
◑ all year Mon-Sat 8-1 by appointment, closed Bank Hols
Facilities: 🚾 🚗

Map 4 F4
The Great Barn Museum
Avebury, Wiltshire SN8 1RF
Tel. Avebury (06723) 555

229

MAP 4　　　　　**SOUTH WEST ENGLAND**

From Marlborough follow A4 westwards, after 5 miles turn right onto B4003 for 1 mile to Avebury.

The Great Barn houses a collection of exhibits illustrating Wiltshire life, its culture and history from the 17thC to the present day. These include a good selection of agricultural implements and dairy equipment. The Wiltshire Folk Life Society publishes several Wiltshire recipes and a book on Christmas customs and traditions. The museum also sells fudge, sweets and books on Wiltshire recipes.

☞ adults 80p, senior citizens & children (over 5) 40p, family ticket (2 adults & 2 children) £1.90

◑ mid Mar-end Oct daily 10-6; Nov-mid Mar Sat 1-5, Sun 11-5
Facilities: 🍽 ♿ 🚗 ⛰

★ weekends devoted to locally produced food, telephone for details

🍽 licensed wholefood restaurant adjoining; all food, including bread, made on premises

---

🏛 Map 4 C4
Harveys Wine Museum
12 Denmark Street, Bristol, Avon BS1 5DQ
Tel. Bristol (0272) 277661

In city centre.

Birthplace of Harveys famous Bristol Cream Sherry, this museum is the only one of its kind in Britain. It tells the story of wine-making through articles used in wine production, service and consumption. The museum is housed in a set of 13thC cellars which originally served as store rooms for a medieval hospital. Later, in the closing years of the 18thC, a merchant named William Perry came to Denmark Street and began to use the cellars beneath for his trade in the wines of Spain and Portugal. The company he founded later

became Harveys of Bristol. The exhibits include antique corkscrews, bottles, decanters, silver and a fine collection of 18thC English drinking glasses. The museum shop sells a good range of wines and spirits, together with wine paraphernalia.

☞ adults £1.00
◑ all year Fri 10-12; Mon-Thur by appointment
Facilities: ♿

🌾 Map 4 E4
Hosken's
Mill Farm, Blackland, Nr Calne, Wiltshire SN11 8PR
Tel. Calne (0249) 814507

From Calne follow A4 eastwards, after 2 miles turn right onto unclassified road for ½ mile to mill.

This is a water-driven flour mill which visitors are welcome to walk around. It produces a high quality stoneground wholemeal flour which is sold in 1.5 and 15Kg packs.

☞ free
◑ all year daily 8-5

☺ Map 4 C5
The Kitchen Garden
Old Down House, Tockington, Bristol, Avon BS12 4PG
Tel. Thornbury (0454) 413605

From Almondesbury follow A38 north eastwards, after 1 mile turn left onto B4461 for 1½ miles to Tockington, then turn right and immediately left onto unclassified road for 1 mile to house on left. Signposted.

Visitors can pick their own fruit and vegetables here and also visit the farm shop which specialises in home-grown, additive-free produce. Their impressive list includes ice cream, sherbets, sorbets, yoghurt, cheeses, smoked meats, sausages, organic flour, biscuits, sweets and jams.
◑ Apr-Oct Tue-Sun 9-7; Nov-Mar telephone for details
Facilities: ♿ 🚗 🍴

🍷 Map 4 E4
AT THE SIGN OF THE ANGEL
Church Street, Lacock, Wiltshire SN15 2LA
Tel: Lacock (024973) 230

From Chippenham follow A350 southwards, after 3 miles turn left onto unclassified road for ¼ mile to Lacock.

Most of the food served in this restaurant is home produced – the vegetable plot, chickens and ducks are at the foot of the garden. Guests will eat at varnished wooden tables in the candle-lit dining room.

◑ Mon-Sat D, Mon-Fri, Sun L
Meals: 1-1.30, 7.30-8
Price range Set L £15.00, Set D £19.50
Seats 40
Cards: Access, Visa
Facilities: 🍷

BROWN BREAD ICE CREAM
to make one gallon:
6 egg yolks
8oz light brown sugar
2 pints milk
1 tsp vanilla essence
1 large brown loaf
1 tbsp caster sugar
½ pint double cream

Heat oven to gas 3 (320F, 160C). Whisk the brown sugar and egg yolks in a bowl. Heat the milk to just below boiling point and pour it over the mix, whisking continuously until the mixture thickens. Stir in the vanilla essence and leave to cool. Meanwhile reduce the brown loaf to breadcrumbs and spread on a baking sheet, sprinkle with caster sugar and bake for 30 mins until crisp and brown. Cool, add to the ice cream mixture, stir in the double cream and freeze.

MAP 4

⛊ Map 4 E4
Lackham Agricultural Museum and Gardens
Lacock, Chippenham,
Wiltshire SN15 2NY
Tel. Chippenham (0249) 656111

*From Chippenham follow A350
southwards, after 2½ miles turn
left to Lackham House.
Signposted.*

This is a farm and rural life
museum which has special
sections on dairying, cider-
making, bee-keeping and
agricultural equipment and
buildings. The 1-acre walled
garden has a magnificent
display of flowers, some of
which may be bought from the
greenhouse.

☞ adults £1.50, children 75p
● Easter-Oct daily 11-4 by
appointment
Facilities: 🚾 🚐 ♨

✿ Map 4 A4
Langdons West Country Cider
The Cider Mill, Hewish,
Weston-super-Mare,
Avon BS24 6RR
Tel. Weston-super-Mare (0934)
833433

*From Weston-super-Mare follow
A370 north eastwards, after 5
miles turn left onto unclassified
road towards Wick St Lawrence
for ¼ mile to mill. Signposted.*

Visitors to this cider mill during
September to November —
the harvest season — can
watch the cider-maker
producing farmhouse cider,
perry and apple juice. Visitors
are welcome at any time of the
year to tour the premises and
sample the produce. Perry,
apple juice and cider drawn
straight from the wood are for
sale in 70cl, 1 and 2 litre, ½ and
1 gallon bottles. Local Cheddar
cheese, Stilton, free-range eggs,
presentation stoneware, cider
mugs and gifts are also sold.

☞ free
● May-Sep Mon-Sat 9-8, Sun
12-2, Oct-Apr Mon-Sat 9-6,
Sun 12-2
Facilities: ♿ 🚾 🚐

♥ Map 4 G4
Littlecote Park
Hungerford,
Berkshire RG17 0SS
Tel. Hungerford (0488) 84000

*From Hungerford follow A4
westwards, after 2½ miles turn
right onto unclassified road for 1
mile, then turn left to house.
Signposted.*

Littlecote Park offers a wide
range of attractions for all ages.
The farm covers 2,000 years of
history from the Romans to the
present day and includes a Rare
Breeds farm, Roman villa, herb
garden and 'potager'. All
Littlecote's workers wear 17thC
period costume and visitors can
watch them shear sheep during
the season. The Roman villa
discovered at Littlecote has
been extensively excavated and
the finds are on show in the
museum. The herb gardens
grow over 150 varieties of herb
for culinary, decorative and
medicinal use. The 'potager' is a
combination of an ornamental
vegetable and a functional
kitchen garden. Vegetables,
fruit and herbs are on sale in
the garden centre shop, along
with free-range eggs, honey
and goats' milk.

☞ adults £3.50, senior citizens
£3.00, children £2.50
● 27 Mar-Oct daily 10-6
Facilities: 🍴 ⛴ ♿ 🚾 🚐 ♨ /🅿

🍽 Map 4 D2
Longleat House
Warminster,
Wiltshire BA12 7NN
Tel. Maiden Bradley (09853) 551

*From Warminster follow A362
westwards, after 2 miles turn left
onto unclassified road for 2 miles
to house. Signposted.*

This Elizabethan manor house,
with gardens landscaped by
'Capability' Brown in 1757, was
the first stately home to be
opened to the public. The
magnificent restored Victorian
kitchen has models of food in
preparation on display on its
tables, its original ranges, a
copper 'batterie de cuisine' and
dressers displaying a collection
of china. In the state dining
room the table is laid for dinner.
Other attractions include the
Safari Park, the Doctor Who
exhibit, a railway, boat rides, a
pets' corner, the world's largest
maze, lakes for fishing, a
butterfly garden and an
orangery.

☞ house: adults £2.80, senior
citizens £2.30, children £1.00;
gardens: 50p
● house & gardens: all year daily
10-4; kitchens: Easter-Oct daily
10-6
Facilities: ⛴ 🍴 ♿ 🚾 🚐 ♨ /🅿
🍴 cream teas & light lunches
served in Old Cellar Café; also a
restaurant & pub

☺ Map 4 F5
Lotmead Pick Your Own
Lotmead Farm, Wanborough,
Nr Swindon, Wiltshire
Tel. Swindon (0793) 790137

*From Swindon follow A420
eastwards, after 1½ miles turn
right onto Ermin Way for 1 mile
to farm. Signposted.*

This pick your own farm offers
6 varieties of strawberries and
3 of raspberries including late
varieties of both, as well as
blackcurrants, gooseberries and
a range of vegetables such as
broad and runner beans and
sweet corn. The shop sells
these ready-picked and also
cream and eggs.

● mid Jun-Oct daily 9.30-8.30 or
dusk
Facilities: ⛴ 🚾 🚐 ♨ /🅿

MAP·4   **SOUTH WEST ENGLAND**

🏠 Map 4 F1
Mompesson House
The Close, Salisbury,
Wiltshire SP1 2EL
Tel. Salisbury (0722) 335659
In town centre.

Originally built for Charles
Mompesson in 1701 and now
the home of the Townsend
family, this is one of the finest
18thC houses in the Cathedral
Close of Salisbury. As well as
notable plasterwork and period
furniture it also has a fine and
important collection of 18thC
English drinking glasses.
☞ adults £1.50, children 70p
● 2 Apr-30 Oct Sat-Wed
12.30-6 or dusk
Facilities: &

☺ Map 4 F2
New Farm Soft Fruit
35 Beech Field, Newton Toney,
Salisbury, Wiltshire SP4 0HQ
Tel. Cholderton (09864) 359
*From Salisbury follow A338 north
eastwards, after 7 miles turn
right onto unclassified road for ¹/₂
mile to farm. Signposted.*

A pick your own farm with
strawberries, raspberries,
blackcurrants, gooseberries and
broad beans, which also sells
the produce ready-picked.
● mid Jun-Jul daily 10-8
Facilities: 🚗 🛝

❦ Map 4 D4
Priory Holdings
Kington St Michael,
Chippenham,
Wiltshire SN14 6JR
Tel. Chippenham (0249) 75222
*From Chippenham follow A429
northwards, after 2 miles turn
left onto unclassified road for 1¹/₂
miles through Kington St
Michael, then turn left onto
unclassified road for ¹/₄ mile, then
turn right to farm on left.*

A 26-acre almost self-sufficient
mixed farm producing beef,
lamb, chickens, vegetables, fruit
and honey. Visitors are

● **Priston Mill, in continuous use since the 10th century**

welcome to tour the farm and
may see sheep being milked
from April to September and
lambing and calving in season.
Fresh and frozen sheep's milk
and yoghurt are for sale.
☞ free
● by appointment
Facilities: 🚻 🚗 🛝

✈ Map 4 C3
Priston Mill
Priston, Nr Bath,
Avon BA2 9EQ
Tel. Bath (0225) 23894/29894
*From Bath, follow A367 south
westwards, after 3 miles turn
right onto B3115 for 1 mile to
Priston. Signposted.*

This working watermill is in the
1987 'Guinness Book of
Records', as holding the record
for the longest continuous use.
The mill goes back to 931.

Today, the mill is part of a 300-
acre mixed farm, complete with
nature trails and animals. It still
produces wholewheat
stoneground flour, which is on
sale in 1.5 and 25Kg packs.
☞ adults 85p, senior citizens
60p, children (under 13) 50p
● Easter-Sep Mon-Sat 2.15-5,
Sun, Bank Hols 11 - 12.45, 2.15-5
Facilities: 🍽 🍴 🚻 🚗 🛝 ⛰

☺ Map 4 F4
Roundoak Dairy
Levetts Farm, Clench
Common, Marlborough,
Wiltshire SN8 4DS
Tel. Marlborough (0672) 52035
*From Marlborough follow A345
southwards for 2 miles to farm.*

Martin Pitt keeps over 20,000
free-range hens, 50 milking
sheep and 20 goats for cheese

MAP 4

production and about 60 geese on his 420-acre mixed downland farm. The farm sells free-range hen and goose eggs and also makes 5 different types of soft cheese from both the sheep's and goats' milk and Levett's Larder mayonnaise which is made by hand. All the produce is free from additives, colourings and antibiotics; the poultry are fed on grain grown on Levetts Farm with a small addition of ground oyster shell to ensure maximum shell strength with minimum porosity to improve the keeping quality. Visitors are welcome to tour the dairy, watch a demonstration of sheep milking and taste the produce.

☞ £1.00

◑ all year by appointment

Facilities: 🚻 🚗 ⛺

✾ Map 4 F3

Rushall Farms

Rushall, Nr Pewsey, Wiltshire
Tel. Stonehenge (0980) 630335/630264

From Pewsey follow A345 south westwards, after 4 miles turn right onto unclassified road for ¼ mile to Rushall.

In 1970 Rushall Farm set out to produce organically grown wholemeal flour. Gradually each field was scheduled 'chemical free', a lengthy process since it can take 3 years for the chemicals to disappear. Today, this is the largest organic farm in Britain, growing wheat for wholemeal flour which is stoneground in the farm's own mill. Visitors are welcome to look around the Simon Barron Stone Mill where the wheat is dried, stored and milled. Bread, rolls and croutons are baked to order every Tuesday and Friday, when visitors can also see baking demonstrations and buy bags of flour and pearl barley to try for themselves.

● **The café, St Werburghs City Farm**

☞ telephone for details

◑ all year Mon-Fri 7.10-12.30, 1.30-4.30, Sat 7.10-10.00

Facilities: 🚻 🚗

🐓 Map 4 C4

St Werburghs City Farm

Watercress Road,
St Werburghs, Bristol,
Avon BS2 9YJ
Tel. Bristol (0272) 428241

From Bristol city centre follow signs to M32, leave road just before motorway and join roundabout, take second exit, turn right into Summers Road, then right into Roseberry Avenue, and left into Mina Road, follow signs to St Werburghs City Farm.

The outskirts of a large city is an unexpected setting for this combination of small farm, shop, 'gnome-built' wholefood café and playground. The emphasis is on vegetarian, wholefood and organic produce served in the café. Farm produce is also for sale, including goats' milk, free-range eggs, organic vegetables and meats, soft cheese, wholefoods, preserves and herbs.

☞ free

● Apr-Oct daily 8-6; Nov-Mar daily 9-5; tours by appointment

Facilities: 🍴 & 🚻 ⛺ 🅿

★ Jun summer farm fair

MAP 4   **SOUTH WEST ENGLAND**

🏠 Map 4 C4
Sally Lunn's House
4 North Parade Passage, Bath,
Avon BA1 1NX
Tel. Bath (0225) 61634
In city centre.
Reputed to be the oldest house
in Bath, visitors to the museum
can still see the original kitchen
bakery, complete with faggot
oven, Georgian cooking range
and baking utensils, where Sally
Lunn, a French Huguenot
refugee, created the famous
bun named after her. Whilst
the recipe for this rich festival
bread, based on the French
brioche, remains a closely
guarded secret, the Sally Lunn is
still baked on the premises

today and can be bought and
eaten as a savoury or sweet
snack.
🎫 museum: adults 30p, senior
citizens & children free
● museum: all year Mon-Sat
10-1
Facilities: 🍺 🍴 📶
🍴 licensed refreshment house
serves Sally Lunn's in a variety
of ways

🍷 Map 4 D5
Sherston Earl Vineyards
Sherston, Malmesbury,
Wiltshire SN16 OPY
Tel. Malmesbury (0666) 840716
*From Malmesbury follow B4040
westwards for 5 miles to
Sherston. Signposted.*
This 3-acre vineyard and
orchard makes its own English
wine and country wines. It is
one of the few remaining places
to have a cider apple orchard
for producing 100% ciders
matured in oak. Visitors are
welcome to walk around both
the vineyard and orchard
where trees are labelled and
amusements for children are
provided. A shop sells
strawberries and some
interesting local foods such as
free-range eggs pickled in cider
vinegar, pickled shallots and
cabbage, mulled spices and
hedgerow jellies. Apart from
still and sparkling cider, the
vineyard sells some unusual
wines, including elderflower
and grape, strawberry and a
sparkling gooseberry wine
made by the champagne
method.
🎫 free
● all year Mon-Sat 10-5.30,
Sun 12-2
Facilities: 📶 🚍 ♿

● Sally Lunn's House, built around 1482

🍺 Map 4 B3
Thatcher's Cider
Myrtle Farm, Sandford, Bristol,
Avon BS19 5RA
Tel. Banwell (0934) 822862

MAP 4

From Blagdon follow A368 westwards for 7 miles to Sandford. Signposted.

This family business was established in 1904 and welcomes visitors all year, though perhaps the most interesting time to visit is during the cider-making season, from October to Christmas, when the farm is at its busiest. Cider is sold in various sizes, from 2 litre bottles to 5 gallon barrels.

☞ telephone for details
◐ all year Mon-Sat 8-6, Bank Hols 8-1
Facilities: ♿ ⚾ 🚗

✈ Map 4 G3
Wilton Windmill
Wilton, Marlborough, Wiltshire
Tel. Marlborough (0672) 870212
From Hungerford follow A338 southwards, after 7 miles turn right onto unclassified road for 1 mile to Wilton. Signposted.

This is one of Wiltshire's working windmills. It was restored in 1976 and is now run by the Wilton Windmill Society, a voluntary organisation. The 167-year-old mill is open to visitors who, wind permitting, may watch flour being stoneground in the traditional way. Guided tours are available at selected times and flour can be bought in 1.5Kg bags.

☞ adults 60p, children 30p
◐ Easter-Sep Sun, Bank Hols 2-5 or by appointment
Facilities: 🚗 ⚾

🐚 Map 4 D5
The Wiltshire Tracklement Company
38 High Street, Sherston, Malmesbury, Wiltshire SN16 0LQ
Tel. Malmesbury (0666) 840851
From Malmesbury follow B4040 westwards for 5 miles to Sherston. Signposted.

This company manufactures a wide range of meat and cheese tracklements such as herb jellies, mustards and horseradish sauces. Over 20 different varieties of English coarse-ground mustard are made and visitors may view the raw materials, watch the processing and sample the end product.
◐ Mon-Fri 9.30-5, Sat 9.30-1
Facilities: ⚾ 🚗

🐔 Map 4 C4
Windmill Hill City Farm
Philip Street, Bedminster, Bristol, Avon BS3 4DU
Tel. Bristol (0272) 633252
From Bristol city centre follow A38 south westwards, after ½ mile turn left onto unclassified road for ¼ mile to Windmill Hill. Signposted.

This mixed, small-scale organic farm in an urban setting is a registered charity run by volunteers. It has a dairy producing yoghurt, goats' milk and cheese and a butchery where the plucking, jointing and freezing of poultry may be seen. Visitors are invited to see the farm animals, watch craft demonstrations and enjoy a barbeque. A shop sells fruit, vegetables, eggs, goats' milk, cheese and meat.

☞ free
◐ all year daily 8-dusk; Wed usually allocated for the disabled
Facilities: 🍴 ♿ ⚾ ⚾ ⛲
🍴 lunches & teas served in café including homemade cakes, soups, vegetarian & non-vegetarian food; open Tue-Sat 9.30-5, Mon 10-3.30, Sun 12-5

🏛 Map 4 A3
Woodspring Museum
Burlington Street, Weston-super-Mare, Avon BS23 1PR
Tel. Weston-super-Mare (0934) 21028
In town centre. Signposted.

Situated off the seafront, the museum takes visitors back to the Victorian and Edwardian period. Included are reconstructions of a late-Victorian kitchen, a dairy, a cider-making display, various shop signs, an old gas cooker and a Victorian beach picnic scene. There are also displays of fish and fishing in the Severn estuary. Visitors can buy wood and terracotta butter moulds, shortbread moulds, recipe books and reproduction pie funnels.

☞ free
◐ all year Mon-Sat, Bank Hols 10-5; Nov-Feb closed 1-2
Facilities: 🍽 ♿ ⚾

● **The Dairy, Woodspring Museum**

MAP 5 SOUTH WEST ENGLAND

Map labels (geographic):

Okehampton — South Zeal — J G QUICKE AND PARTNERS — BOTTLESCREEN BILL'S — MUSEUM OF DARTMOOR LIFE — E AND P BROMELL — Exeter — DEVON FOODS — Bridestowe — YES TOR 2027 — CASTLE DROGO — WEST TOWN DAIRY — 3F'S PICK YOUR OWN — Topsha — Moretonhampstead — WHITSTONE VINEYARDS — Milton Abbot — DEVON HERBS — Chudleigh — Exm — COUNTRYMAN CIDER — PARKE RARE BREEDS FARM — Dawlish — Teignmout — Tavistock — Two Bridges — Ashburton — Newton Abbot — TORQUAY WINERY AND VINEYARD — MORWELLHAM QUAY — Buckfastleigh — COMPTON CASTLE — orquay — BUCKLAND ABBEY — Yelverton — Dart — South Brent — TICKLEMORE CHEESE SHOP — Totnes — TORBAY — PLYMOUTH — LANGAGE FARM DAIRY PRODUCTS — Paignton — BEENLEIGH MANOR FARM FOODS — CHURCHWARD CIDER — BRITISH FISHERIES MUSEUM — SALTRAM — CROWDY MILL — Torpoint — PLYMOUTH — Ivybridge — CAPTON VINEYARD — Dartmouth — SMITHALEIGH CHILDREN'S FARM AND TEA HOUSE — Modbury — LODDISWELL VINEYARD — MILL LEAT TROUT FARM — LUDBROOK TROUT FARM — Newton Ferrers — Kingsbridge — VALLEY SPRINGS TROUT FARM — Torcross — SALCOMBE DAIRY — Salcombe — SALCOMBE SMOKERS — Start Pt. — Prawle Pt.

One of the attractions of South Devon is that the wild moors and seaside towns are within easy access — so visitors get the best of both worlds. The fertile orchards produce scrumpy, a farmhouse cider originally produced to pay casual farm labourers for their harvest work. Cloudy or clear at its best it is a tart, full, refreshing drink, guaranteed to bring a glow to any cheek.

Map 5 D4
3F's Pick Your Own
New Barn Farm,
Shillingford St George, Exeter,
Devon EX2 9QR
Tel. Exeter (0392) 832218

From Exeter follow A3085 southwards, after 1 mile turn left at roundabout onto unclassified road for 1/2 mile through Alphington, then turn right onto unclassified road for 1 1/2 miles to Shillingford St George, then turn right onto unclassified road for 1/2 mile to farm on right. Signposted.

This farm has both a pick your own section and a vineyard. Visitors are welcome to pick a wide variety of soft and cane fruit, plums and damsons as well as sweet corn, courgettes and broccoli. The vineyard

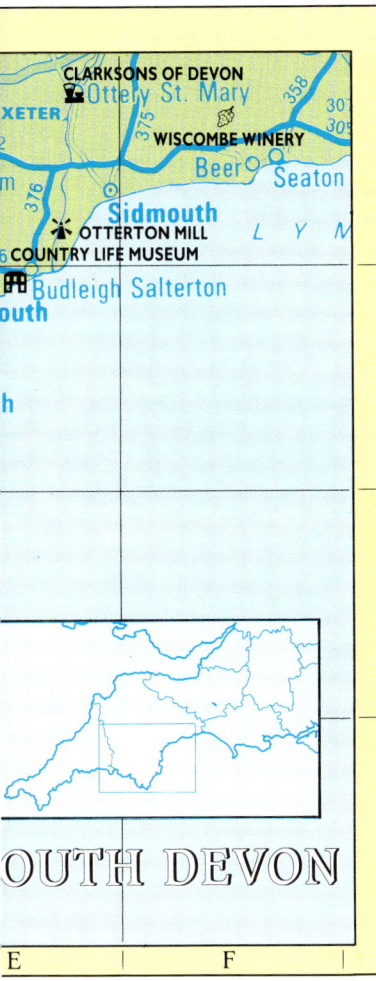

grows white grapes producing Manstree English wine. This can be tasted and bought by the case.

◐ mid Jun-Jul daily 9-6; Aug-Sep Mon-Fri 9-5, Sat 9-1
Facilities: 🚾 🚗 🍼 ⛺

💷 Map 5 D2
Beenleigh Manor Farm Foods
Beenleigh Manor, Harbertonford, Totnes, Devon
Tel. Harbertonford (080423) 234/738

From Totnes follow A381 southwards, after 3 miles turn left onto unclassified road for 1 mile to farm on right. Signposted.

This medieval estate is complete with historic buildings and a hamlet of attached houses. It continues to produce Devon cider in the traditional way — by taking locally grown cider fruits, such as Foxwelp, Sheep's Nose, Sercombe's Natural and Slack-ma-Girdle, crushing them and allowing the juice to ferment and mature slowly. Finally, the cider is poured into hand-coopered casks. The estate also sells pure apple juice, taken from classic English dessert and culinary fruit and a wide selection of local apples.

☞ free
◐ by appointment — telephone for details

🏠 Map 5 D2
British Fisheries Museum
Old Market House, The Quay, Brixham, Devon TQ5 8TB
Tel. Brixham (08045) 2861

In town centre.

Housed in the Old Market House on Brixham Quay, this museum is part of the National Maritime Museum at Greenwich. There are a number of interesting displays on the history of fishing and in particular the development of the fishing boat from the herring buss of the 16thC to the modern motor vessel. A fish shop next door sells locally caught produce.

☞ adults 30p, senior citizens & accompanied children free
◐ Jan-Apr, mid Oct-Dec Tue-Sat 9-1, 2-5.15; May-mid Oct Mon-Sat 9-6, Sun, Bank Hols 10-1, 2-5
Facilities: ♿

💷 Map 5 D4
E and P Bromell
Lower Uppacott, Tedburn St Mary, Nr Exeter, Devon EX6 6AZ
Tel. Tedburn St Mary (06476) 294

From Exeter follow B3212 westwards, after 1½ miles bear right onto unclassified road, the old A30, for 6 miles to Tedburn St Mary. Signposted.

This dairy and cider farm uses locally grown apples to produce dry, medium and sweet cider. Visitors can watch cider-making demonstrations during the season — October-December — and buy the produce in a variety of containers, from 2 pints upwards.

☞ free
◐ all year daily 7-8
Facilities: 🚾 🚗

🏠 Map 5 B3
Buckland Abbey
Yelverton, Devon PL20 6EY
Tel. Yelverton (0822) 853607

From Yelverton follow A386 southwards, after ½ mile turn right onto unclassified road for 2 miles to Abbey. Signposted.

This 13thC monastery was converted into a house by the English naval commander Sir Richard Grenville in 1576. Sir Francis Drake bought it in 1581 and it is now a naval and Devon folk museum. Displays depict 700 years of history from the

● **Buckland Abbey**

MAP 5   SOUTH WEST ENGLAND

days of the great Cistercian monastery, through the Armada period — including Drake's drum — to modern times. A tea room in the historic Tudor kitchen serves homemade food and ice cream. There is a medieval tithe barn to visit as well as a knot garden planted with herbs.

☞ adults £2.80, children £1.40
◑ 20 Jul-Oct daily 11-6, Nov-Mar Wed, Sat, Sun 2-5
Facilities: ♨ ⑩ ᷇ ⑫ ⇔ ᵕ

⚲ Map 5 D2
Capton Vineyard
Capton, Nr Dartmouth, Devon TQ6 0JE
Tel. Blackawton (080421) 452

From Dartmouth follow B3207 westwards, after 3 miles turn right onto unclassified road for 1 mile, then turn left onto unclassified road for ¹/₂ mile to Capton. Signposted.

The Fruit Farm offers pick your own facilities for strawberries, raspberries, gooseberries, blackcurrants, tayberries, loganberries and many vegetables and herbs. There is a pre-historic rural life museum with agricultural implements on display and also a herb garden. The adjoining Capton Vineyard makes pure fruit liqueurs using no artificial colourings or preservatives. The hand-harvested fruit is cold pressed to produce a liqueur matured in oak casks with pure grain spirit. Current varieties are Cassis, Framboise and Frasia. Visitors are welcome to taste the finished product and watch frequent demonstrations on the process. A farm shop sells cider, beer, clotted and double cream, ice cream, English wine and free-range eggs.

☞ vineyard: free; museum: adults 30p, children 15p
◑ Apr-Oct daily
Facilities: ⑩ ⑫ ⇔ ᵕ

● **The kitchen at Castle Drogo**

🍲 Map 5 C4
Castle Drogo
Drewsteignton, Devon EX6 6PB
Tel. Chagford (06473) 3306

From Mortonhampstead follow A382 north westwards, after 4 miles turn right at Sandy Park onto unclassified road for ¹/₂ mile to castle. Signposted.

Built between 1910 and 1930 for Julian Drewe, the founder of a grocery chain, this eccentric granite castle is one of the most remarkable works of Sir Edwin Lutyens. Towering over Dartmoor and the wooded gorge of the River Teign, it has a fascinating Lutyens kitchen which features interesting period equipment.

☞ adults £2.60, children £1.30
◑ Apr-Oct daily 11-6
Facilities: ♨ ⑩ ᷇ ⑫ ⇔ ᵕ
⑩ restaurant serves homemade dishes from local produce

🍵 Map 5 D2
Churchward Cider
Yalberton Farm, Yalberton Road, Paignton, Devon TQ4 7PE
Tel. Paignton (0803) 558157

From Paignton follow A385 westwards, after ¹/₂ mile turn left onto A3022 for ¹/₄ mile, then turn right into Yalberton Road for ¹/₄ mile to farm on left.

Yalberton specialises in both cider and pigs, which means in summer its orchards are full of pigs and new-born piglets. The cider, stored in wooden barrels in a cellar, is on sale all year and visitors are welcome to taste it before purchase. The farm also sells clotted cream, lemonade and a special cider ice cream.

☞ free
◑ Jun-Aug Mon-Sat 9-9, Sun 12-2, 7-9; Sep-May Mon-Sat 10-6, Sun 12-2, 7-8
Facilities: ⇔
★ Sep-Dec cider-making by appointment

🦐 Map 5 E4
Clarksons of Devon
1-7 Alansway, Ottery St Mary, Devon EX11 1NR
Tel. Ottery St Mary (040481) 3581

In town centre. Signposted.

Set in Ottery St Mary on the banks of the River Otter, Clarksons specialise in supplying vacuum-packed high

MAP 5

quality fresh meats, fish and dairy products sold either direct to the customer or by mail order. Food packs available include 10lb assorted cheeses, 20lb gammon and back rashers, 16lb barbecue meats, a gourmet fish pack including smoked salmon, trout, crab, pâté and a 14lb prime beef steak pack. At Christmas they also sell a variety of hampers and a range of hams.

◑ all year Mon-Fri 8-5, closed Bank Hols
Facilities: 🚾 🚗

🛥 Map 5 D2
Compton Castle
Marldon, Paignton, Devon TQ3 1TA
Tel. Kingskerswell (08047) 2112

From Newton Abbot follow A381 southwards, after 2½ miles turn left onto unclassified road for 2 miles to castle. Signposted.

This fortified manor house was built between 1340 and 1530 by the Gilbert family. Sir Humphrey Gilbert, half-brother to Sir Walter Raleigh, and a renowned navigator and founder of the first colony in Newfoundland in 1583, lived here. There is a medieval kitchen which was probably built around 1520 and has an open fireplace which extends for its full width.

☞ adults £1.30, children 65p
◑ Apr-Oct Mon-Thur 10-12.15, 2-5
Facilities: 🚗

🏠 Map 5 E3
Country Life Museum
Sandy Bay, Exmouth, Devon EX8 5BU
Tel. Topsham (039287) 3230

From Exmouth follow A376 eastwards, after 3 miles turn right at Littleham Cross onto unclassified road for ¼ mile to museum on left. Signposted.

This fascinating museum re-creates rural life at the turn of

the century both on and off the farm. The large collection of agricultural implements, machines and tools actually move in slow motion to give a clear idea of how each one worked. There is a typical selection of farmyard animals and an observation beehive fitted with glass so visitors can watch as bees bring back the pollen and make it into honey. A re-created thatcher's cottage features a period kitchen, complete with an authentic range and pots and pans. The role of the local mill is shown through a display which includes an original water wheel and grinding machinery.

☞ adults £1.70, senior citizens £1.00, children (5-16) 60p, family ticket (2 adults & children) £4.00, wheelchair visitors free
◑ Easter-May, Sep daily 10-5; Jun-Aug daily 10-6
Facilities: 🛥 🍴 ♿ 🚾 🚗 🍵 ⛲

REGIONAL RECIPE

DEVONSHIRE SYLLABUB

10oz caster sugar
3 lemons juice and rind
½ pint sherry
5 fl oz brandy
1½ pints double cream

Mix the sugar with the lemon juice, add the rind, sherry and brandy. Warm slightly to dissolve the sugar and infuse the flavour, or leave to stand for three hours. Whip the cream and fold into the liquid. Chill.

🍺 Map 5 A3
Countryman Cider
Felldownhead, Milton Abbot, Tavistock, Devon PL19 0QR
Tel. Milton Abbot (082287) 226

From Milton Abbot follow A384 westwards, after 2 miles turn right onto unclassified road for ½ mile to Felldownhead. Signposted.

Countryman's medium-sweet scrumpy is just one of the ciders from this traditional manufacturer. Visitors are welcome to tour the farm and learn something of the methods used. They can then taste the product and buy a variety of ciders and local mead from the on-site off licence.

☞ free
◑ all year Mon-Fri 8.30-5.30
Facilities: 🚾 🚗

🏭 Map 5 C2
Crowdy Mill
Harbertonford, Totnes, Devon TQ9 7HU
Tel. Harbertonford (080423) 340

From Totnes follow A381 southwards, after 3 miles turn left at Harbertonford onto unclassified road for ½ mile to mill on right.

There has been a watermill on the site of Crowdy Mill for at least 700 years. Now restored, the mill is once again a commercial enterprise, specialising in flours and wholemeals milled from locally grown, organically cultivated grains. Several different wholemeals are ground, including a strong mixture of English and Canadian wheats, and both a standard and organic wholemeal. Produce is for sale in bags from 1.5 to 32Kg.

☞ free
◑ all year Mon-Fri 9-4 or by appointment

🍴 Map 5 D4
Devon Foods
15 Gandy Street, Exeter, Devon
Tel. Exeter (0392) 221525

In town centre.

Devon Foods gathers together the best food and drink from specialist small producers throughout the county. All their suppliers have returned to traditional methods and provide some excellent local

MAP 5　　　　　**SOUTH WEST ENGLAND**

specialities. Cooked meats include traditionally made hams, both on the bone and off, smoked lamb, pâtés and terrines. Fresh trout is available every morning and is also stocked smoked and as pâté. They sell imaginative salads and their cheese selection is among the best outside London. A good range of wines, liqueurs and pastries is also for sale.

◗ all year Mon-Sat 9-5.30, closed Bank Hols

★ frequent tastings & chance to meet producers

CHUDLEIGHS

Chudleighs are the Devon version of Cornish Splits and are often served instead of scones at tea.

❧ Map 5 B3
Devon Herbs
Burn Lane, Brentor, Tavistock, Devon PL19 OND
Tel. Mary Tavy (082281) 285
From Tavistock follow A386 northwards, after 4 miles turn left at Downs Garage in Mary Tavy, then turn right, then turn left to farm on left. Signposted.

Dartmoor National Park makes an attractive setting for this small nursery specialising in culinary, fragrant and medicinal herbs. As well as a traditional herb garden there is a good selection of plants in pots. Staff are happy to take visitors on a tour and give explanations of the produce. Pot grown plants can be bought.

☞ free

◗ Apr-Sep Wed-Sun, Bank Hols 12-6

▢ Map 5 B2
Langage Farm Dairy Products
Higher Langage Farm, Plympton, Plymouth, Devon PL7 5AW
Tel. Plymouth (0752) 337723

From Plymouth follow A38 eastwards, after 5 miles turn left onto B3416 towards Plympton for ¼ mile, then turn right at second roundabout onto unclassified road for ¼ mile, then turn right again onto unclassified road for 200 yards to farm on right. Signposted.

This farm's herd of 250 Jersey cows has been carefully selected and built up over the years to produce a high butterfat-content milk. This is used to full advantage in the thick clotted cream. Visitors can tour the farm, watch the cows being milked and taste the range of dairy ice creams. The shop sells cream, yoghurt, ice cream, cottage cheese, low and full fat cheese and milk.

☞ free

◗ all year daily 10-5; tours by arrangement
Facilities: 🍽🚻🚗
🍽 milk shakes, homemade pies & sausages

✺ Map 5 C2
Loddiswell Vineyard
Lilwell, Loddiswell, Kingsbridge, Devon TQ7 4EF
Tel. Kingsbridge (0548) 550221
From Kingsbridge follow B3196 northwards for 3 miles to vineyard on left, 1 mile beyond Loddiswell. Signposted.

This 6-acre vineyard was planted in 1977 and produces dry and medium-sweet white wines that won the coveted English Vineyards Association Gold Seal award in 1984. Twelve tonnes of grapes are processed into 12,000 bottles of wine every year. The main varieties of grape are Müller-Thurgau, Reichensteiner, Huxelrebe, Siegerrebe and Bacchus, though the red Pinot Noir and Blauburger types have recently been introduced. Visitors may either walk about the vineyard and sampling room or take a guided tour which includes the winery and videos of wine production and rural life. Wines are available by the bottle or case and homemade fudge is also for sale.

☞ adults £2.25 including tasting, children (6-18) 75p
◗ Apr-Oct Mon-Thur 1-6; Jul-Aug Sun-Thur 1-6
Facilities: 🍽🍽♿🚻🚗🧸🏧
🍽 cream teas served

♪ Map 5 C2
Ludbrook Trout Farm
Meadfoot Meadow, Ermington, Ivybridge, Devon PL21 OLQ
Tel. Modbury (0548) 830168

LODDISWELL
ENGLISH TABLE WINE
PRODUCED and BOTTLED by the SAMPSON FAMILY, LILWELL, LODDISWELL, South DEVON, ENGLAND.
70cl

MAP 5

From Ivybridge follow B3211 southwards, after 1½ miles turn left in Ermington onto B3210 for ¼ mile, then turn left onto unclassified road for 200 yards to farm on right. Signposted.

Only the best quality fish are bred in this small restocking trout farm on the Lud Brook. Visitors may view and feed the fish, catch their own — tackle is provided — or buy them fresh from the shop. Whole smoked trout and gourmet speciality cold-cured trout fillets are also available.

🎣 rod £1.25, fish caught £1.20 per lb

◗ all year daily 10-6; fishing: Apr-Oct daily 10-6

Facilities: 👶 🚗 ♨

🎵 Map 5 C2
Mill Leat Trout Farm
The Mills, Ermington, Ivybridge, Devon PL21 9NT
Tel. Modbury (0548) 830172

From Ivybridge follow B3211 southwards for 1½ miles to Ermington.

This working trout farm offers visitors the chance to catch their own fish or buy them fresh or smoked from the shop. There are also farm trails to follow and a craft centre selling locally made items.

🎣 rod £1.15, fish caught £1.15 per lb

◗ all year daily 9-5.30

Facilities: 🥤 🍴 🚾 🚗 ♨

🍴 tea shop specialises in Devon cream teas

🏠 Map 5 A3
Morwellham Quay
Morwellham, Tavistock, Devon PL19 8JL
Tel. Tavistock (0822) 832766

From Tavistock follow A390 westwards, after 2 miles turn left onto unclassified road for 2½ miles to Morwellham. Signposted.

Hidden deep in the Tamar Valley, this great Victorian copper port has been restored to its authentic 1860's condition complete with mines, lime kilns, giant water wheels and

railway. The staff wear period clothes and can be addressed as if they were part of living history. Even the shops sell 19thC produce, with homemade scrumpy bread in Quay Cottage and fresh Devon pasties at the bakery. The Victorian Sweet Shop has traditional sweets. Visitors can

● **Morwellham Quay**

MAP 5   **SOUTH WEST ENGLAND**

● **Take a carriage ride at Morwellham Quay**

try on a Victorian costume, take a carriage ride, watch a slide show and see a Victorian farmyard.

☞ adults £3.95, senior citizens £2.95, children (5-18) £2.45
● 1 Apr-Nov daily 10-5.30 (last admission 4); Nov-Mar daily 10-5
Facilities: ⦿ ⓌⒸ 🚗 ⛺ ⛰
⦿ Ship Inn licensed restaurant serves country fare including Devon pasties & West Country pies; tea rooms serve traditional teas & homemade cakes baked in cottage range (last admission 2.30)

🏛 Map 5 B4
Museum of Dartmoor Life
The Dartmoor Centre,
West Street, Okehampton,
Devon EX20 1HQ
Tel. Okehampton (0837) 3020
In town centre. Signposted.

Housed in an authentic agricultural mill built in 1811, the Museum of Dartmoor Life contains many exhibits including cider-making and dairy equipment, farm

implements, tools and kitchen utensils. A shop sells homemade sweets, cakes, cream and other produce.

☞ adults 50p, senior citizens 40p, children (5-16) 30p
● Apr-23 Jul, 29 Aug-Oct Mon-Sat 10-5; 24 Jul-28 Aug Mon-Sun 10-5; Nov-Mar Mon-Fri 10-4.30
Facilities: ⦿ ⓌⒸ 🚗
⦿ Victorian Pantry tea room serves traditional lunches & cream teas with many local & regional specialities

---

🎋 Map 5 E4
Otterton Mill
Nr Budleigh Salterton,
Devon EX9 7HG
Tel. Colaton Raleigh (0395) 68521/68031
From Budleigh Salterton follow A376 northwards, after 2 miles turn right onto unclassified road for ½ mile to mill on right. Signposted.

This watermill has been grinding grain from the local valley for at least 1,000 years. Visitors may watch the grain as it cascades down from the top of the building, through the

millstones and finally comes out as ground flour. Although actual milling takes place no more than 3 days a week, the machinery is always running. A guided tour, slide show and museum place the mill in context and explain how the machinery works. The flour produced is all stoneground wholemeal and can be bought in the neighbouring bakery, both in 1.5Kg packs and in bulk. The shop also sells homemade gingerbread, honey oat cake, walnut and raisin cake, chocolate coconut biscuits, local jams, wholefoods, wines and ciders.

☞ Apr-Dec adults £1.00, children 50p, Jan-Mar adults 50p, children 25p
● Apr-Sep daily 10.30-5.30; Oct-Mar Mon-Fri 10.30-5.30; Sat-Sun 2-5; telephone for times of running of mill
Facilities: ☕ ⦿ ⓌⒸ ♿ ⛺
★ Easter-Christmas daytime & evening events
⦿ licensed Duckery Restaurant serves wholefood & vegetarian dishes, cream teas, wholemeal scones & free-range eggs

MAP 5

❦ Map 5 D3
Parke Rare Breeds Farm
Parke Estate, Bovey Tracey,
Devon TQ13 9JQ
Tel. Bovey Tracey (0626) 833909

From Chudleigh follow B3344
south westwards for 3 miles to
Bovey Tracey, continue for
¼ mile, then turn right to farm.
Signposted.

Approved by the Rare Breeds
Survival Trust, this farm
features a collection of rare and
indigenous breeds of dairy and
beef cattle, horses, pigs, sheep
and poultry. Some of the
breeds were known to have
been farmed in the Middle
Ages and a few can even be
traced back to prehistoric
times. Set in National Trust
parkland near Dartmoor, the
farm is well equipped for all the
family. A ¾ mile long farm trail
meanders through attractive
countryside and display
paddocks while a pets' corner
and play area has been set up
for young children. The
Interpretation Centre has a
fascinating honey bee museum
with an inspection hive. Home
produced pork and lamb can be
purchased to order.

☞ adults £1.80, senior citizens
£1.40, children (3-14) £1.00
◐ Apr-Oct daily 10-6
Facilities: 🍽️🅿️♿🚗♨️🏧

☘ Map 5 D4
J G Quicke and Partners
Woodley, Newton St Cyres,
Exeter, Devon EX5 5BT
Tel. Exeter (0392) 851222

From Exeter follow A377
northwards, after 4 miles turn
left in Newton St Cyres onto
unclassified road for ½ mile to
farm. Signposted.

Although Quicke's is a mixed
farm containing pigs and arable
and sheep farmland, its
speciality is cheese. There are
many varieties including herb
and smoked Cheddars, as well
as the traditional and double
Gloucester. Milk from the herd
of 300 dairy cows is also used to
produce dairy ice cream, cream
and butter. The traditional
Cheddar is sold as vegetarian
mild, mellow or mature —
depending on storage time —
in 56lb wholes, quarters,
eighths, 3lb packs and wedges.
Herb and smoked Cheddars
come in 7lb and 3lb sizes.
Locally made yoghurt, sheeps'
milk, Stilton and Cheshire are
also for sale.
◐ Mon-Fri 9-5.30, Sat 9-1, closed
Bank Hols
Facilities: 🚗♨️

♟ Map 5 D4
BOTTLESCREEN BILL'S
White Hart Hotel,
South Street, Exeter,
Devon EX1 1EE
Tel: Exeter (0392) 37511

In town centre.

A 16thC building housing an
atmospheric wine bar with
sawdust on the floor and
filled with antiques and
farming machinery. The food
is traditionally English and
the Fisherman's Pie is
particularly homely and
filling.
◐ Mon-Sat Meals: 12-2, 7-10,
Fri-Sat 7-10.30
Price range £6.00
Seats 50
Cards: Access, Amex, Diners,
Visa
Facilities: ♿🚗

FISHERMAN'S PIE

6 fillets of coley skinned
2 pints milk
1lb cheese grated
4oz butter
½ glass white wine
2lb potatoes cooked and
sliced
parsley chopped
black pepper
salt
3oz plain flour

Heat oven to gas ¼ (225F,
110C). Bake the fish in a pint
of milk with plenty of black
pepper and a little salt for 20-
30 minutes. Meanwhile melt
the butter in a pan, add the
flour to make a smooth paste
and remove from heat. Slowly
add the milk stirring
continuously, when a pint
has been added return to
heat, still stirring. As the
sauce comes to the boil add
the cheese, wine, parsley and
plenty of black pepper. Flake
and bone the cooked coley,
put into a dish, add the sauce
and cover with sliced potato.
Coat with grated cheese and
bake until golden brown.

● **A Longhorn bull at Parke Rare Breeds Farm**

MAP 5   SOUTH WEST ENGLAND

Map 5 C1
Salcombe Dairy
Shadycombe Road, Salcombe,
Devon TQ8 8DX
Tel. Salcombe (054884) 3228
In town centre.

Salcombe Dairy is a large
producer of dairy ice cream and
sorbets and makes everything
with traditional ingredients in
the time-honoured manner.
Visitors may sit and watch the
whole manufacturing process
through large windows and
taste the ice cream in the
adjoining shop. A variety of ice
creams and sorbets is available
in sizes from individual portions
to 10-litre packs. Wafers and
cones are also sold.
☞ free
◑ Mar-May, Oct-Jan Mon-Fri
9-5; Jun-Sep daily 9-5
Facilities: 🚗 ⛺

Map 5 C1
Salcombe Smokers
Fore Street, Kingsbridge, Devon
Tel. Kingsbridge (0548) 2006
In town centre.

Salcombe Smokers, right in the
centre of the attractive little
town of Kingsbridge, smokes a
selection of local fish including
salmon, pollock, haddock and

— their speciality — mackerel.
They claim that south Devon
mackerel are better for
smoking as they are less oily
than those caught off Scotland
or Ireland. They also sell locally
caught wet fish.
◑ all year Mon-Wed, Fri 8-5,
Thur, Sat 8-1

Map 5 B2
Saltram
Plympton, Plymouth,
Devon PL7 3UH
Tel. Plymouth (0752) 336546
*From Plymouth follow A379
eastwards, after 2 miles turn left
at Marsh Mills roundabout onto
unclassified road for 1 mile, then
turn left to house. Signposted.*

One of the finest 18thC houses
in the south west, this George II
mansion incorporates Tudor
sections and has a superb
dining room designed by
Robert Adam and completed in
1768. As well as historic
furniture, a porcelain collection
and paintings by Reynolds,
there is also a Tudor Great
Kitchen which was in use until
1962. It contains a huge
Victorian range and a display of
pewter and copper utensils

which give an indication of the
equipment needed for catering
on the 'grand' scale.
☞ adults £3, children £1.50
◑ house: Apr-Oct Sun-Thur
12.30- 6
Facilities: 🚌 🍴 ♿ 🚻 🚗 ⛺
🍴 restaurant serves homemade
food including soups, hot pots,
puddings, scones & breads

Map 5 B2
**Smithaleigh Children's
Farm and Tea House**
Smithaleigh, Plympton,
Devon PL7 5AX
Tel. Plymouth (0752) 893772
*From Ivybridge follow A38
westwards, after 2½ miles turn
left onto unclassified road for ¼
mile to farm on right.*

This farm has been specially
designed with young children in
mind. It has a large collection of
friendly farm animals used to
children, a traditional farmyard
and extensive vegetable and
fruit gardens.
☞ 70p, children (under 2) free
◑ May-Sep Wed-Mon 1-6
Facilities: 🍴 ♿ 🚻 🚗 ⛺
🍴 traditional Devon cream teas
with Devon splits, homemade
jam & cakes; farmhouse teas
including homebaked bread

● **The Great Kitchen, Saltram**

Map 5 D2
Ticklemore Cheese Shop
1 Ticklemore Street, Totnes,
Devon TQ9 5EJ
Tel. Totnes (0803) 865926
In town centre.

A specialist shop that makes its own cheeses and yoghurts. Visitors are welcome to watch the cheese-making and to taste the results. The shop sells a vast selection of other farm produced cheeses, particularly local and West Country varieties. These include Beenleigh Blue and Harbourne Blue as well as the Ticklemore goat and sheep's cheeses. It also sells other dairy produce like its own goat and sheep's milk and yoghurts, cream, butter, free-range eggs and a range of homemade produce including cheesecakes and quiches. The shop will arrange visits to local cheese-makers by appointment.
● all year Mon-Wed, Fri 9.30-5, Thur 9.30-1, Sat 9.30-2

Map 5 D3
Torquay Winery and Vineyard
Scott's Bridge, Kingskerswell Road, Torquay, Devon TQ2 8JT
Tel. Torquay (0803) 62166
From Torquay follow A380 northwards for 1½ miles to vineyard on right.

Pepe, the owner of the vineyard, comes from a wine producing family in Sicily. He has been making wine in England for 20 years, 5 of which have been in Torquay. His vineyard grows white and red grapes and produces both white and red wines. The wine is pressed and bottled on the premises and Pepe will personally show visitors around the vineyard and the winery and they are invited to sample and to buy his wines.
☞ free
● Easter-Oct daily 10-6
Facilities: 🚻 🚗

Map 5 C1
Valley Springs Trout Farm
Sherford, Kingsbridge,
Devon TQ7 2BG
Tel. Frogmore (054853) 574
From Kingsbridge follow A379 eastwards, after 3 miles turn left onto unclassified road for 2 miles to farm. Signposted.

Set in a secluded valley in the South Hams, this is the oldest trout farm in Devon. Visitors may catch their own trout in 1 of the 4 pools or try for big fish, up to 6lb, in the challenge pool. There are regular hour-long guided tours which include videos on farming, breeding, catching and cooking fish. The farm also arranges trout barbecues and has an attractive woodland nature trail. A shop sells fresh, frozen and smoked trout as well as smoked trout pâté, troutburgers and other farm produce.
☞ adults 50p, children 25p, rod £1.50; guided tours adults: £2.00, children £1.25
● Good Friday-Oct daily 10.30- 5.30; guided tours: Wed
Facilities: 🍴 ♿ 🚻 🚗 🍳
🍴 barbecue for visitors to cook their own trout

Map 5 D4
West Town Dairy
West Town, Ide, Nr Exeter,
Devon EX2 9TG
Tel. Longdown (039281) 257
From Exeter follow B3212 westwards, after 2 miles turn left onto the right hand unclassified road turn down the hill for ½ mile to farm. Signposted.

This dairy farm, set in a quiet unspoilt wooded valley, has the perfect location for 2 attractive nature trails. Visitors can ramble through the farm landscape inspecting cattle, pigs and sheep at close quarters. The farm grows wheat and apples organically and these, as well as milk, yoghurt, cheese and eggs can be bought from the farm shop.
☞ free
● Jul-Sep daily 9-4
Facilities: 🍴 🚻 🚗
🍴 homemade cream teas served

Map 5 D3
Whitstone Vineyards
Bovey Tracey,
Devon TQ13 9NA
Tel. Bovey Tracey (0626) 832280
From Newton Abbot follow A382 north westwards for 6 miles to vineyard just after Bovey Tracey.

This Dartmoor vineyard organises special tours and tastings for interested visitors. The wine is sold by the bottle, 3-pack and case.
☞ adults £1.50, children (under 18) free
● sales: Jun-Oct Mon-Sat 10-12; tours: by appointment
Facilities: 🚻 🚗

Map 5 F4
Wiscombe Winery
Southleigh, Colyton,
Devon EX13 6JF
Tel. Farway (040487) 360
From Ottery St Mary follow B3174 eastwards, after 6 miles turn left then immediately right onto unclassified road for 2½ miles to Southleigh. Signposted.

Wiscombe Winery began producing commercial country wines in 1970. The most popular, Devonshire apple white wine, is made from organically grown apples and is matured in oak barrels. Other wines include a rosé made from apples and blackberries and a red from apples and blackcurrants. Visitors are welcome to look round the winery, take a guided tour and sample the wines. These are sold either by the case or in gift packs.
☞ adults £1.50, accompanied children free
● all year Mon-Fri 9-6, Sat 9-1
Facilities: 🚻 🚗

MAP 6   SOUTH WEST ENGLAND

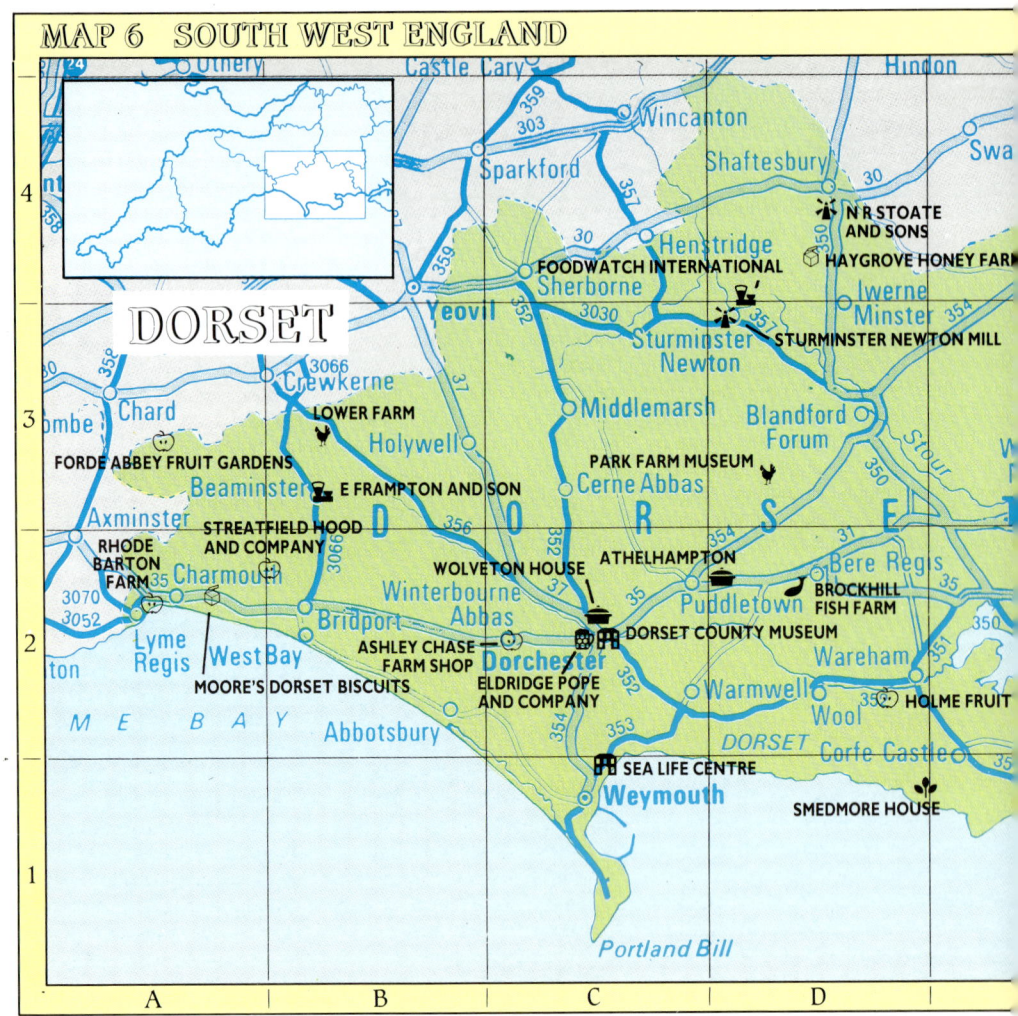

DORSET

The mystery of Blue Vinney cheese from Dorset continues according to Patrick Rance, the great British cheese expert. A hard, almost fat-free cheese, it was made from buttermilk with a blue mould which was acquired naturally or, as it is sometimes claimed, from dirty harnesses or old boots. As cheese-making died out during World War II, so did Blue Vinney. It became increasingly difficult to find and as Patrick Rance suggests, second-rate Stilton was often sold under its name. Whether Blue Vinney is made now or not, no-one seems certain, even though several attempts to track it down have been made. If you see some for sale, try it first to make sure it is the real thing. Otherwise buy Dorset Blue, a full-fat farmhouse cheese.

✴ Map 6 F4
Alderholt Mill
Sandleheath Road,
Alderholt, Fordingbridge,
Hampshire SP6 1PU
Tel. Fordingbridge (0425) 53130

From Fordingbridge follow B3078 westwards for 2½ miles to Sandleheath, then turn left onto unclassified road for ½ mile to mill on right. Signposted.

This 14thC watermill has been restored over the last 6 years and has at last begun to mill flour on a small scale. Part of the mill is now an art gallery and craft shop, where homemade fudge, jam, biscuits and, of course, wholemeal flour can be bought.

☞ free

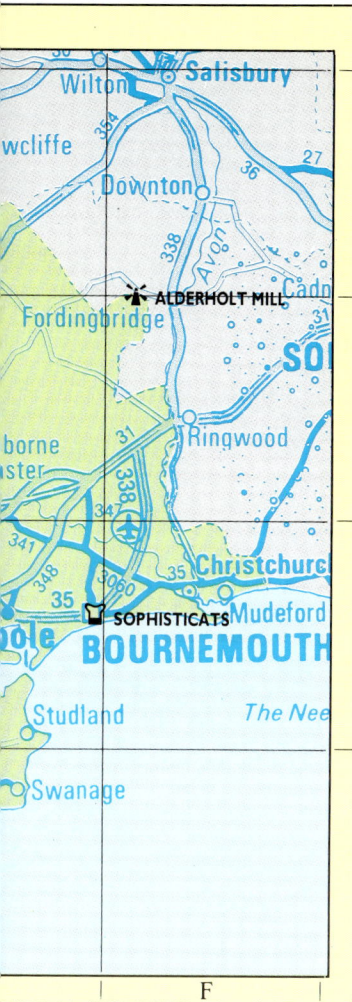

🍲 Map 6 D2
Athelhampton
Dorchester, Dorset DT2 7LG
Tel. Puddletown (030584) 363

From Puddletown follow A35 eastwards for 1 mile to house on left. Signposted.

Athelhampton has been in the same family for the last 5 centuries and also claims to be the legendary site of King Athelstan's palace. The house has a number of impressive state rooms and a large wine cellar with an extensive collection of fine wines. The enormous dovecote, with 1,500 nesting holes, dates from the Middle Ages when doves were a major part of the diet. The house is near the River Piddle and sells its bottled water.

☞ garden: adults £1.25, children free; house & garden: adults £2.25, children £1.00

◑ Easter-Oct Wed, Thur, Sun 2-6; Aug Mon-Thur, Sun 2-6
Facilities: ⏻ & ᵂᶜ ⛟
⏻ Dorset cream teas & homemade cakes served

🎣 Map 6 D2
Brockhill Fish Farm
Brockhill, Bere Regis, Wareham, Dorset BH20 7NH

From Bere Regis follow the Wool Road southwards, after 1 mile turn right onto unclassified road for 1 mile to farm.

The River Piddle is the water source for this quality trout farm at Brockhill. Visitors are welcome to look round the premises and learn how a modern fish farm operates.

☞ free
◑ all year Mon-Fri 9-5, Sat 9-1
Facilities: ᵂᶜ ⛟

🏛 Map 6 C2
Dorset County Museum
High West Street, Dorchester, Dorset DT1 1XA
Tel. Dorchester (0305) 62735

In town centre.

Set in the heart of Wessex this museum illustrates 5,000 years of Dorset county history, from ancient cooking and eating implements to local celebrities such as Thomas Hardy and William Barnes.

☞ adults £1.00, senior citizens & children (over 5) 50p
◑ all year Mon-Sat 10-5

🍺 Map 6 C2
Eldridge Pope and Company
Dorchester Brewery, Weymouth Avenue, Dorchester, Dorset DT1 1QT
Tel. Dorchester (0305) 251251

In town centre.

This traditional brewery takes groups of visitors on guided tours of its premises where they see all the production processes of Eldridge Pope's prize-winning Huntsman Ales. Individuals are welcome to join a tour and to sample the beer.

☞ free
◑ all year Tue-Thur tours at 2.30 by appointment
Facilities: ᵂᶜ

◑ Apr-2 Oct, 15 Nov-24 Dec Tue-Fri, Sun 2-6, Sat, Bank Hols 10-6
Facilities: & ⛟

☺ Map 6 C2
Ashley Chase Farm Shop
Winterborne Abbas, Dorchester, Dorset
Tel. Martinstown (030588) 430

In village centre.

Ashley Chase is the largest producer of farmhouse Cheddar in Dorset, with 1,500 cows producing 1½ tonnes a day. Visitors may taste and buy the cheese in the shop which also sells butter and general provisions.

◑ all year Mon-Sat 9.15-5.30, Sun 10-2
Facilities: ⏻ ᵂᶜ ⛟ ♨

MAP 6 **SOUTH WEST ENGLAND**

Map 6 D4
Foodwatch International
Butts Pond Industrial Estate,
Sturminster Newton,
Dorset DT10 1AZ
Tel. Sturminster Newton
(0258) 73356

From Sturminster Newton follow B3091 eastwards for ¼ mile to Butts Pond Estate. Signposted.

This is the only organisation in the UK, and possibly the world, catering for those with food and environmental allergies. It stocks a vast range of foods for special diets; some made on the premises, others imported from outside companies. Many items are unavailable elsewhere in the UK and include alternative milk products, wheat flour, natural food colourings, fruit juice concentrates and chocolate beans. Although primarily a mail order business, customers are welcome to call personally and look around the warehouse where they can see the products and obtain detailed literature on a number of associated topics.
● all year Mon-Fri 8.30-5
Facilities: WC 🚗

Map 6 A3
Forde Abbey Fruit Gardens
Forde Abbey, Chard, Somerset
Tel. South Chard (0460) 20206/20384

From Chard follow B3162 south eastwards, after 2½ miles turn right at Whatley onto unclassified road for 1 mile to Forde Abbey, then continue for ¼ mile to farm on right. Signposted.

Gooseberries, strawberries, red and blackcurrants, raspberries and tayberries are available here on a pick your own basis. The shop also sells local cream, ice cream and a useful booklet giving freezing and recipe advice.
● Jun-Aug daily 9-7
Facilities: WC 🚗 ☕ ⚠

248

Map 6 B3
E Frampton and Son
18 The Square, Beaminster,
Dorset DT8 3AU
Tel. Beaminster (0308) 862253
In town centre.

This shop was established over 150 years ago by the Frampton family as a butcher and game dealer. He is still a first class butcher, selling his own range of sausages, poultry and game, including venison, but now he also sells a wide range of cheeses. They specialise in regional varieties like Dorset Blue Vinney, Denhay Cheddar, Somerset Brie and goats' cheese as well as a selection from the continent. They also sell locally smoked fish products and yoghurt.
● all year Mon, Tue, Thur-Sat 8-1, 2-5, Wed 8-1, closed Bank Hols
Facilities: 🚗

Map 6 D4
Haygrove Honey Farm
Twyford, Shaftesbury,
Dorset SP7 0JF
Tel. Fontmell Magna (0747) 811855

From Shaftesbury follow A350 southwards, after 2½ miles turn right onto unclassified road for 1½ miles to farm on right in Twyford.

This bee and organic vegetable farm rears queen bees to produce royal jelly as well as ordinary bees for other honey products. Visitors can tour the breeding yard and also buy fresh vegetables, herbs, soft fruit, honey and bees wax. Queen bees, royal jelly and pollen are sold by arrangement.
🚗 free
● all year daily 9.30-6
Facilities: 🚗

Map 6 D2
Holme Fruit
West Holme Farm, Wareham,
Dorset BH20 6AG
Tel. Wareham (09295) 2972

From Wareham follow A352 westwards, after 2 miles turn left onto B3070 for ½ mile to farm on left. Signposted.

This pick your own farm offers most of the usual soft fruits and vegetables as well as apples, plums and sweet corn. The shop also sells more unusual produce such as mangetout, calabrese and globe artichokes as well as local cream, eggs, potatoes and a range of homemade jellies, jams and other preserves.
● mid Jun-Jul 10-7, Aug-Oct 2-5.30
Facilities: WC 🚗 ☕

Map 6 B3
Lower Farm
Chedington, Beaminster,
Dorset DT8 3JA
Tel. Corscombe (093589) 371

From Crewkerne follow A356 south eastwards, after 5 miles turn right at Winyards Gap Inn onto unclassified road for ½ mile to farm. Signposted.

Lower Farm is a 120-acre stock farm with permanent pasture which has remained unploughed for 50 years. Specialising in rare breeds, the farm keeps Tamworth Ginger and Gloucester Old Spot pigs, Jacob and Welsh Mountain sheep, White Park cattle and Suffolk Punch heavy horses. The lakes are stocked with rainbow trout and signal crayfish for fish your own with wheelchair fishing stations for the disabled. Farm-grown lamb

MAP 6

and pork may be ordered and other items, including woollen products from the Jacob sheep, are for sale in the shop.

🐾 free
◑ Apr-Sep daily 10-6; Oct-Mar daily 10-4
Facilities: ♿ 🚻 🚗 ☺

🛍 Map 6 A2
Moore's Dorset Biscuits
The Biscuit Bakery,
Morcombelake, Bridport,
Dorset DT6 6ES
Tel. Chideock (0297) 89253

From Bridport follow A35 westwards for 4 miles to factory on left.

Probably the only biscuit factory open to the public in Britain, visitors are welcome to walk around and see the range of biscuits being made, baked and packed and to sample the end product. Dorset knobs, twice baked with the texture of a rusk, are a local speciality and are delicious with cheese. They are available in the shop as well as other biscuits in a variety of packs and tins.

🐾 free
◑ all year Mon-Fri 9-5, closed Bank Hols
Facilities: 🚻

🐔 Map 6 D3
Park Farm Museum
Park Farm, Milton Abbas,
Blandford, Dorset
Tel. Milton Abbas (0258) 880216

From Blandford Forum follow A354 south westwards, after 5 miles turn right at Winterborne Whitechurch onto unclassified road for 3½ miles past Milton Abbas to farm on right. Signposted.

This is both a working farm and a museum. Traditional farm animals are kept on the 30 acres while the museum focuses on rural life in the past. It has particularly good collections of brewing and kitchen equipment. Visitors are welcome to picnic on the farm and enjoy the countryside views stretching some 30 miles. In poor weather visitors can use the barn. A farm shop sells home-produced eggs, butter, honey and cakes.

🐾 adults £1.00, children 25p
◑ Easter Sat-Oct daily 10-6
Facilities: 🍽 🍴 🚻 🚗 ☺ 🏧

☺ Map 6 A2
Rhode Barton Farm
Lyme Regis, Dorset DT7 3JE
Tel. Lyme Regis (02974) 2611

From Lyme Regis follow A3052 northwards for 1 mile to farm on right. Signposted.

A pick your own farm and a shop selling various soft fruits, vegetables, including asparagus, eggs, quiches, bread, jam, yoghurts, apples and potatoes. Visitors are welcome to walk around the farm.

◑ mid Jun-mid Aug daily 9.30-6
Facilities: 🚗 ☺

🏨 Map 6 C1
Sea Life Centre
Lodmoor Country Park,
Weymouth, Dorset DT4 7SX
Tel. Weymouth (0305) 788255

From Weymouth follow A353 northwards for 1 mile to park. Signposted.

The Sea Life Centre invites visitors to discover the secrets of marine life. Enormous, specially designed tanks bring them face to face with hundreds of exciting sea creatures including octopus and sharks. Masses of more familiar fish, found around the British coast, can be seen in the ocean tunnel, Europe's largest tank, and in the island sands tank where visitors can look down on the fish. 'Touch' pools

● **Lower Farm, Chedington**

249

MAP 6   **SOUTH WEST ENGLAND**

provide an opportunity to handle a variety of small sea creatures.

☞ adults £2.25, senior citizens £1.60, children (3-14) £1.35
● Mar-Nov daily 10-5, mid-summer closes later — telephone for details
Facilities: 🚌 🍴 ♿ 📶 🚗 🐕 /⚠\
🍴 lunches, teas & dinners served in restaurant including fish & chips & cream teas

REGIONAL RECIPE

LETTUCE SOUP

Lettuce soup has always been made in this part of the country during the summer as it's an ideal way of dealing with bolted lettuces.
1 onion chopped
1oz butter
2 lettuces chopped
1 tsp cornflour
2 pints stock
salt & pepper
2 tbsp cream
chervil

Soften the onion in the butter and add the lettuce. Cover and simmer for 2 minutes. Add the cornflour, stir in until smooth, add the stock and simmer for a further 10 minutes. Puree the onion and lettuce and return to the pan. Season to taste, stir in the cream and sprinkle over the chervil.

🌿 Map 6 D1
Smedmore House
Kimmeridge, Wareham, Dorset BH20 5PG
Tel. Corfe Castle (0929) 480717
From Wareham follow A351 southwards, after 1½ miles turn right at Stoborough Green onto unclassified road for 5 miles to Kimmeridge, then turn left onto unclassified road for 1 mile to house on left. Signposted.

The original layout of Smedmore's walled gardens has changed little since Sir William Clavile 'built a little newe house and beautified

it with pleasant gardens' in the early 17thC. Today the traditional kitchen garden, which grows fruit, vegetables and herbs, is run as a commercial concern. A gardener is always on hand to answer questions and visitors are welcome to wander round on their own. Produce from the gardens is for sale from the shop.

☞ house & garden: adults £1.30, children 65p; garden: adults 65p, children free
● Jun-mid Sep Wed, Aug Bank Hol Sun 2.15-5.30
Facilities: 🚌 📶 🚗 🐕

🐟 Map 6 D4
N R Stoate and Sons
Cann Mills, Shaftesbury, Dorset SP7 OBL
Tel. Shaftesbury (0747) 2475
From Shaftesbury follow A350 southwards, after 1½ miles turn right to mill. Signposted.

On a site dating back to the Domesday Book this working Portuguese windmill has been

built on top of a working watermill. Locally grown organic wheat is ground between horizontal millstones powered by the water wheel. Visitors can tour the mill and buy a variety of flours in bags from 8Kg upwards.

☞ free
● all year Mon-Fri 8.30-1, 2-5, closed Bank Hols, telephone before visiting
Facilities: 🚗

🍎 Map 6 B2
Streatfield Hood and Company
Denhay Farm, Broadoak, Bridport, Dorset DT6 5NP
Tel. Bridport (0308) 22770/ 22717

From Bridport follow B3162 northwards, after 1 mile turn left onto unclassified road for 2 miles to Broadoak. Signposted.

This farm shop sells a variety of farm produce including its own traditional farmhouse 'Denhay' Cheddar cheese and butter, also stoneground flour, real ale

● **Swans on the lake at Cann Mills**

MAP 6

chutney, cream, ice cream and bacon.

◐ all year Mon, Thur 9.30-5, closed Bank Hols
Facilities: 🚗

🌾 Map 6 D3
Sturminster Newton Mill
Sturminster Newton,
Dorset DT10 1AG
Tel. Sturminster Newton
(0258) 73151/72275

In town centre. Signposted.

Although the present mill dates from the 16thC there has been a mill here as far back as the 11thC. A new, more efficient water turbine replaced the old water wheel in 1904 and can still be seen in action. Visitors can tour the mill and also buy homemade breads, cakes and of course stoneground wholemeal flours — wheat, rye and malt — in packs from 4lb to 32Kg.

☞ adults 80p, children 40p
◐ May-Sep Tue, Thur, Sat, Bank Hols 11-5, Sun 2.30-5
Facilities: 🍵 🚗 ♨

🛳 Map 6 C2
Wolveton House
Dorchester, Dorset
Tel. Dorchester (0305) 68748

From Dorchester follow A37 northwards, after 1½ miles turn right onto A352 for ¼ mile, then turn right onto unclassified road for ¼ mile to house on right. Signposted.

It seems probable that a house existed on this site in Saxon times but the current building dates largely from when it was inherited by the Trenchard family in 1480. Sir Thomas Trenchard was twice sheriff of Dorset and his great grandson Sir George was an important figure in the court of Elizabeth I. The building has a number of famous ghosts and is featured in a short story by Thomas Hardy. Visitors may tour the house and grounds, including the dining room, parlour, ice house and 16thC garden. An original cider mill and press is still used and visitors are welcome to view the machinery and taste the product. Cider and locally made pottery cider mugs are for sale.

☞ adults £2.00, children £1.00
◐ May-Sep Tue, Fri 2-6
Facilities: ♿ ♨

🍴 Map 6 E2
SOPHISTICATS
43 Charminster Road,
Bournemouth,
Dorset BH8 8UE
Tel: Bournemouth (0202) 291019

In town centre.

A small friendly restaurant with a varied menu serving plenty of local sea food.
◐ Tue-Sat Meals: 7-10
Price range £12-18
Seats 32
Facilities: ♿ 🚻

GOLDEN CRAB

*1lb crabmeat
1 onion finely diced
2 tbsp homemade mayonnaise
1oz mature Cheddar grated
4 slices of bread*

Mix together the crabmeat, the onion and most of the mayonnaise. Toast the bread under a grill on one side only and then spread a little of the mayonnaise on the untoasted side. Pile on the mixture, sprinkle with cheese and grill until golden brown.

● **Wolveton, Dorset**

· CALENDAR OF EVENTS ·

MAY

Country Food and Cider Fayre
1-2 May
Fayre held at the National Shire Horse Centre, Yealmpton, Plymouth, Devon.

The Blessing of the Water
8 May
An annual custom when the waters are blessed for a good fish harvest at Mudeford Quay, Christchurch, Dorset.

Devon County Show
19-21 May
An annual agricultural show held at Whipton, Exeter, Devon.

Kingsteignton Ram Roasting Festival
30 May
An old custom - a ram is spit roasted over an open fire and slices are then distributed in Kingsteignton, near Newton Abbot, Devon. Prior to 1885, a live lamb was drawn around the parish in a flower-garlanded cart.

JUNE

Royal Bath and West Show
1-4 June
An annual agricultural show for top cattle, sheep and pigs, as well as a cheese show, at Shepton Mallet, Somerset.

Royal Cornwall Show
9-11 June
An annual agricultural and horticultural show at Wadebridge, Cornwall.

Ale Tasting and Bread Weighing
30 June
An ancient ceremony dating back to Saxon times - ale tasters and bread weighers parade round all the pubs and bakeries during carnival week, tasting the beer and bread in the streets of Ashburton, Devon.

JULY

10th World Wine Fair
8-16 July
An annual wine fair at Bristol Exhibition Centre, Bristol, Avon.

Marldon Apple Pie Fayre
30 July
A village fair where apple pies are sold according to an old tradition at Marldon, near Paignton, Devon.

AUGUST

Priddy Sheep Fair
18 August
A sheep fair has been held each year for about 700 years at Priddy, near Wells, Somerset.

SEPTEMBER

Cheese and Onion Fayre
14 September
Regional and seasonal produce used to be sold at this fayre - now it is a funfair at Newton Abbot, Devon.

Frome Cheese Show
21 September
An annual show at Frome, Somerset.

OCTOBER

Tavistock Goose Fair
12 October
Traditionally a Michaelmas 'goosey' fair famous for its sales of geese and other livestock, and now a funfair at Tavistock, Devon.

Taunton Cider Barrel Rolling Race
15 October
This takes place at the same time as the annual carnival and cider barrels are rolled down the main streets of Taunton, Somerset.

NOVEMBER

The Great Western Beer Festival
5-8 November
An annual beer festival at Bristol Exhibition Centre, Bristol, Avon.

SOUTH EAST ENGLAND

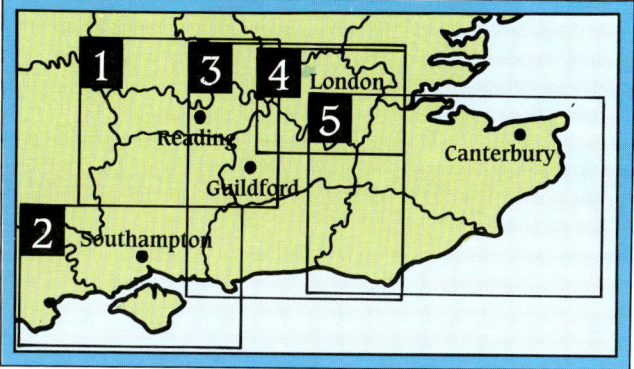

SOUTH EAST ENGLAND

● **Unpacking game, Leadenhall Market**

by Lindsey Bareham

RESTAURANT CRITIC

The most enduring memory of my Kent childhood is apples. Apples were everywhere — they were stored on attic rafters, in cupboards under the stairs and neatly piled between paper in the recesses of the dining room dresser. Windfalls had to be collected from orchards and each summer we made trips further into Kent to follow the now fashionable activity of picking your own. We had more apple pies than I care to remember; apple charlottes, apple compôtes, blackberries with apples, baked apples, apple chutney and always a constant supply of crisp Cox's Orange Pippins to munch on.

As children we went scrumping for apples and plums in the vicarage garden that is now a town house development. We helped pick apples and cut rhubarb on the farm down the lane and during school holidays joined parties to pick Kent cob nuts and watch the gypsies arriving to pick hops. Kent is still famous for its soft fruits and apples. There are farm shops everywhere

and fruit still plays an important part in the local cooking.

When I left home and moved to London in the early sixties I left behind my mother's steak and kidney pie and cherry tarts for the tins of Fray Bentos and at last began to appreciate family Sunday lunches and those inevitable apple pies. We weren't into quality food in those days and most of our eating took place in basement restaurants off the Earls Court Road where you could fill up for around £1.00. But gradually people became more aware of what they ate. Craig Sams, now head of the Whole Earth healthfood empire, opened Ceres, the first wholewheat bakery and Cranks in Marshall Street was just beginning: vegetarianism, brown rice and vegetables were the thing.

I made tentative buying sprees to Soho delicatessens, walked nervously round the supermarkets of Chinatown, tried my first bagel in Brick Lane and began brewing proper coffee. Portobello and its cosmopolitan food market became a Saturday haunt and it was there that I had my first encounter with curried goat.

In 1977 I was asked to write the restaurant column for 'Time Out' and my interest in food, food shops and eventually wine, grew. These days I am, I suppose, what is referred to as 'a foodie'. I earn my living exclusively writing about food, know about virtually every cuisine of the world and am able to take full advantage of the enormous variety of food stuffs available in and around London.

London has it all and is undisputedly the food capital of Britain: the wholesale food markets of Billingsgate, Smithfield and Covent Garden; survivors of a bygone era like the pie and mash shops and jellied eel stalls; food halls in Harrods and Fortnum and Mason; authentic ethnic zones such as Brixton, Chinatown or Southall. Specialists like the 190-year-old cheese shop Paxton and Whitfield, Thai food stores, Japanese fishmongers, bagel bakers and comprehensive fishmongers like Steve Hatt in Islington. We also have some fine cooks' equipment shops and even a book shop dedicated exclusively to the art of food — Books for Cooks.

But there is much more to this region than London or Kent. South East England is the 'region of plenty' in all senses of the word — and has a fine tradition of eating and drinking. It is crammed with vineyards, cider makers, small brewers and even a hop museum. There is a flourishing fishing industry all along the South East's long coastline, with locally caught fish such as dabs, flounders, plaice, mackerel, haddock and mullet, often available straight from the boat. In Hampshire, you can buy venison from the New Forest, trout from the river Test and watercress grown in the pure waters of the chalk streams. The Isle of Wight offers excellent shellfish, fruit and vegetables and, surprisingly, garlic which is even exported to France. In Surrey you'll find small specialist shops and pick your own farms, and in Sussex, Southdown lamb, local goats' cheeses and much, much more.

Lindsey
Bareham

MAP 1 SOUTH EAST ENGLAND

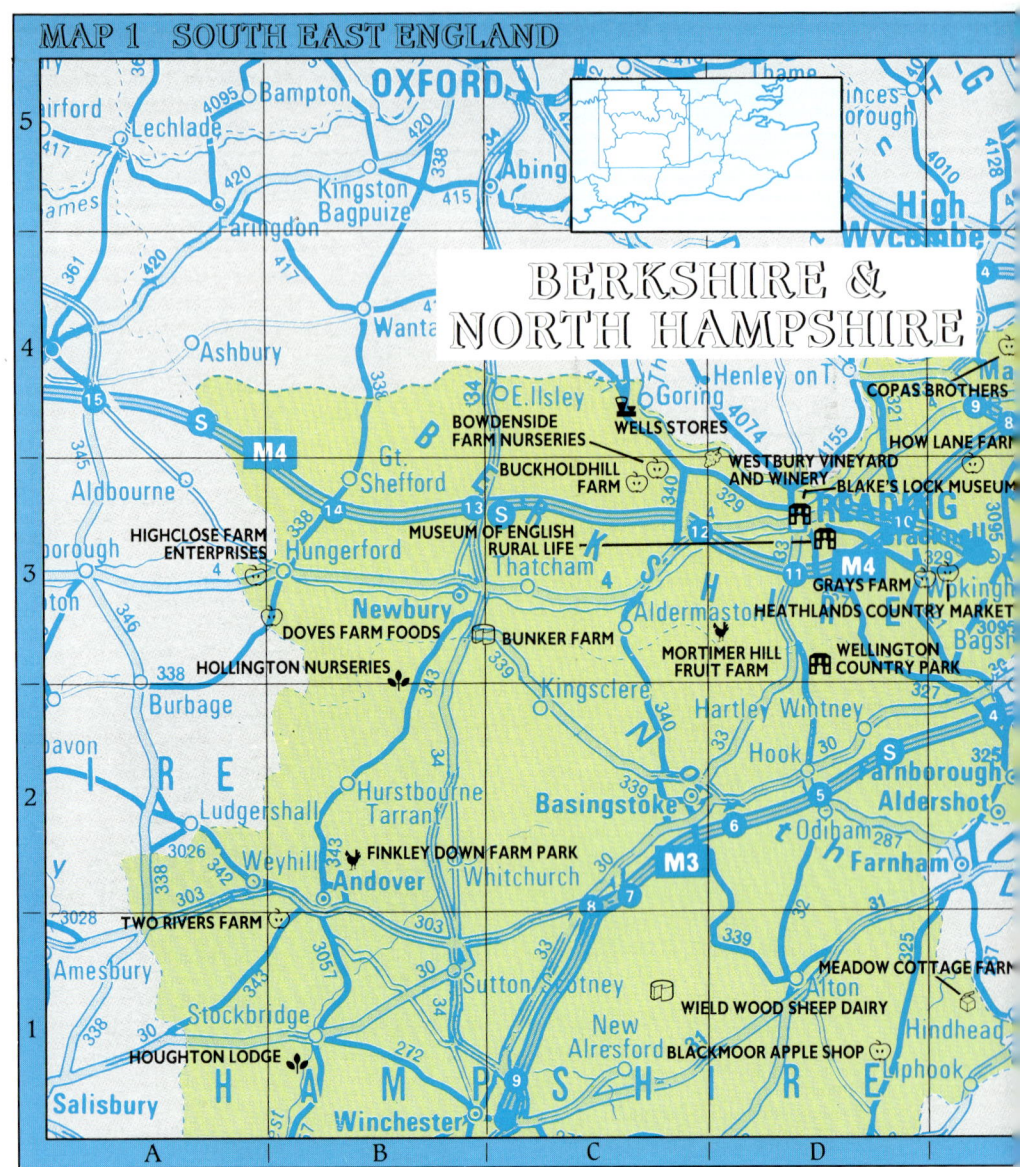

BERKSHIRE & NORTH HAMPSHIRE

As well as wines from grape varieties, this area produces an interesting range of country and fruit wines. In Berkshire you will find elderflower wine and a sparkling gooseberry champagne on sale in several local shops. In Hampshire, Gales, a local traditional brewery, offer in their pubs a range of their own fruit wines.

✉ Map 1 E3
Ascot Vineyard
Ascot Farm, Winkfield Road,
Ascot, Berkshire SL5 7LJ
Tel. Ascot (0990) 23563
From Ascot follow A329

eastwards, after ¼ mile turn left onto A330 for ¼ mile, then turn right to vineyard. Signposted.

This award-winning vineyard was established in 1979 in part of the Crown property of Sunningdale. It was the first

vineyard to be planted here since Henry II forbade English vine-growing to appease his French wife Eleanor of Aquitaine. The estate now boasts 4,000 vines of 7 Anglophile varieties trained on the Guyot system. Visitors may walk in the vineyard, attend talks on viticulture and taste the wines free of charge. Both red and white wine may be bought by the bottle or case.

☞ free
◐ all year daily 12-dusk
Facilities: 🚾 🚐

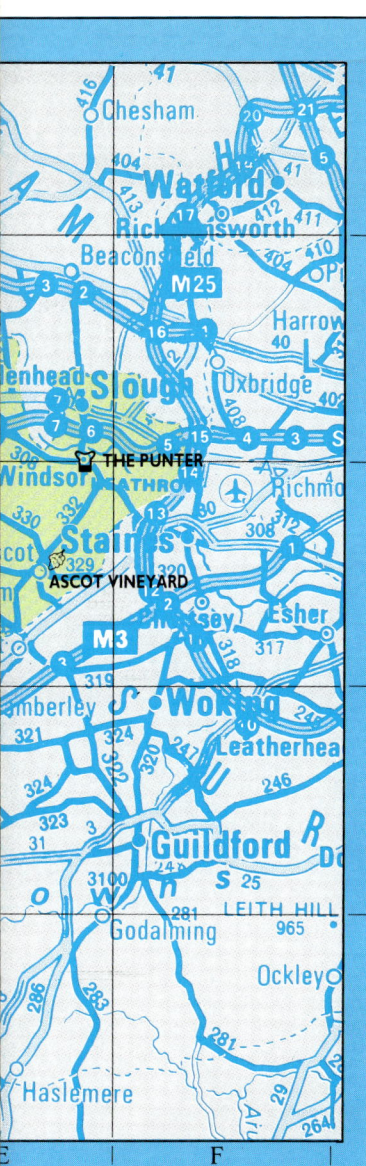

few commercial quince growers in the country. As well as apples and quinces the shop sells fruit wines, ice cream, homebaked products, preserves, English cheeses, eggs, pears and meat with no added hormones.

◗ Easter-mid Oct Tue-Thur 9-4, Fri, Sat 9-5; mid Oct-Easter Tue-Thur 9-4, Fri, Sat 9-5, Sun 11-4
Facilities: 🚗

🏠 Map 1 D3
Blake's Lock Museum
Gas Works Road, Reading, Berkshire RG1 3DH
Tel. Reading (0734) 55911 ext 2242

In town centre. Signposted.

Situated on the banks of the River Kennet, in part of an old pumping station, the museum is a superb example of Victorian industrial architecture and Reading's decorative brickwork, built during a period when the town's growth and wealth were based on two factors — the railway and the biscuit factories, particularly Huntley and Palmers. The displays show 19th and 20thC material and feature a reconstruction of the bakery, Huggin's of Crown Street, exhibits on the history of Cocks' famous Reading Sauce, local confectionery and a local mineral water.

☞ free
◗ all year Mon-Fri 10-5, Sat, Sun 2-5
Facilities: 🚺 🍴

Peasgood Nonesuch, Lord Lambourne, St Edmond and Egremont Russets which are available from August to April. The farm also sells pears, plums, quinces, home-produced honey and free-range eggs.

◗ all year Tue-Sun, Bank Hols 9-5
Facilities: 🚗

😊 Map 1 C3
Buckholdhill Farm
Yattendon Road, Pangbourne, Berkshire RG8 8QE
Tel. Bradfield (0734) 744388

From Goring follow A329 south eastwards, after 4 miles turn right at Pangbourne into Yattendon Road for 3 miles to farm. Signposted.

A pick your own farm with gooseberries, blackberries, red and blackcurrants, peas and broad beans. The shop also sells other locally grown vegetables, honey and free-range eggs.

◗ end Jun-Aug daily 8-7
Facilities: 🚗 🍴

● **Rock's Country Wines, Twyford**

😊 Map 1 D1
Blackmoor Apple Shop
Blackmoor Estate, Blackmoor, Liss, Hampshire GU33 6BS
Tel. Bordon (04203) 3576

From Liphook follow B2131 westwards, after 4 miles turn right onto A325 for 1 mile, then turn left onto unclassified road for 1 mile to Blackmoor. Signposted.

This large farm specialises in many different varieties of apples — available from August to April — and is one of the

😊 Map 1 C3
Bowdenside Farm Nurseries
Bowdenside Farm, Yattendon Road, Pangbourne, Berkshire RG8 8PT
Tel. Pangbourne (07357) 4152

From Goring follow A329 south eastwards, after 4 miles turn right at Pangbourne into Yattendon Road for 1½ miles to farm. Signposted.

This farm shop sells over 20 varieties of apples including traditional fruits such as

🏠 Map 1 B3
Bunker Farm
Basingstoke Road, Greenham Common South, Newbury, Berkshire RG15 8HH
Tel. Newbury (0635) 45535

From Newbury follow A34 southwards, after 1½ miles turn left onto A339 for 200 yards to farm.

This farm specialises in goats but they also keep a few pigs and hens. They aim to produce traditional food without the use of chemicals, growth

257

MAP 1   SOUTH EAST ENGLAND

promoters or preservatives. Visitors can watch cheese being made through an observation window which looks onto the dairy and buy the cheese in the shop. Also on sale are goat and kid meat, pork, ham, bacon and goat and pork sausages.

☞ free

◗ all year Mon-Sat 9-5.30, Sun 10-4

Facilities: 🚻 🚗

⌣ Map 1 E4

Copas Brothers

Lower Mount Farm, Long Lane, Cookham, Berkshire SL6 9EE
Tel. Bourne End (06285) 29596

From Maidenhead follow B4447 northwards for 2 miles to farm.

A pick your own farm offering gooseberries, strawberries, cherries, red and blackcurrants, tayberries, loganberries, plums, broad beans and potatoes. The shop also sells eggs, apples and Christmas poultry.

◗ PYO: end Jun-Oct Wed-Sat 2-7, Sun 10-5; shop: all year Sun 10-1

Facilities: 🚗

⌣ Map 1 B3

Doves Farm Foods

Salisbury Road, Hungerford, Berkshire RG17 0RF
Tel. Hungerford (0488) 84880

From Hungerford follow A338 southwards for 3 miles to farm.

This organic farm produces quality foods with the Soil Association's symbol of organic quality. It has a mill producing stoneground flours and a cheese-making dairy where goats' cheeses are made from the farm's own herd. The shop sells a wide range of products including bread, stoneground flours, grains such as wheat germ, bran and maize meal, wholemeal digestive biscuits, goats' cheeses and a delicious

258

🍴 Map 1 E4

THE PUNTER

50 Thames Street, Windsor, Berkshire
Tel: Windsor (0753) 865565

In town centre. Signposted.

A small, friendly restaurant serving a mixture of English and French food.

◗ Mon-Sun Meals: 12-3, 6.30-11
Price range: £6-16.50
Seats 48
Cards: Access, Amex, Diners, Visa
Facilities: ♿ 🍷 🚗

LAMB AND APRICOT CASSEROLE

olive oil
8oz leg of lamb cubed
1½ onions chopped

1oz celery chopped
4oz carrots chopped
1fl oz red wine
2oz flour sifted
1½oz tomato purée
4oz apricots stoned and halved
2fl oz apricot juice
bayleaf
parsley stalk
1 pint lamb stock

Melt a little oil and gently brown the lamb. Remove from the pan, add the onions, carrots and celery and sweat until soft. Remove and deglaze the pan with red wine. Put all the ingredients back into the pan, add the flour, tomato purée, apricots, apricot juice, bay leaf, parsley stalk and finally the lamb stock. Cover and simmer for 1 hour.

strawberry goats' cheese fromage frais.

◗ all year Mon-Fri 9-5.30, weekends, Bank Hols by appointment

Facilities: 🚗

🐐 Map 1 B2

Finkley Down Farm Park

Finkley Down Farm, Andover, Hampshire SP11 6NF
Tel. Andover (0264) 52195

● **The Royal Kitchen, Windsor Castle**

MAP 1

From Andover follow A3057 northwards, after $\frac{1}{2}$ mile turn right onto A3093 for $\frac{1}{2}$ mile, then turn left at roundabout onto unclassified road for $\frac{1}{2}$ mile, then turn left onto unclassified road for $\frac{1}{4}$ mile to farm on right. Signposted.

Finkley Down specialises in rare breeds of farm animals including poultry, geese, ducks, peacocks, pigs, goats, sheep, rabbits, Shire horses, ponies and donkeys. Visitors can see all the animals and there is a pets' corner for children where they can handle tame, hand-reared baby animals. There is also a countryside museum, housed in an old barn, which includes a collection of bygones and an exhibition called 'Old MacDonald's Farm'.

☞ adults £2.00, senior citizens & children £1.00
● Apr-2 Oct daily 10.30-6
Facilities: 🚌 🍴 ♿ 🚻 🚗 🍵 ⚠
🍴 ploughman's lunches & teas with homemade cakes & scones served

---

REGIONAL RECIPE

WATERCRESS STUFFING

Watercress is widely grown in Hampshire. This is an unusual stuffing for either lamb or chicken.

1 medium onion
2-3 sticks celery chopped
2oz butter melted
1 tsp salt
pepper
3oz watercress finely cut
5oz fresh breadcrumbs
1 egg beaten
a little milk

Mix all the ingredients together using the egg and milk to bind the mixture. Take care the stuffing is not too wet.

☺ Map 1 D3
Grays Farm
Heathlands Road, Wokingham, Berkshire RG11 3AN
Tel. Wokingham (0734) 785386

From Wokingham follow A329 Peach Street eastwards, after $\frac{1}{4}$ mile turn right into Easthampstead Road, then turn right by White Horse Inn into Heathlands Road to farm on right. Signposted.

A pick your own farm and a shop offering strawberries, raspberries, various vegetables, honey and cream.
● 28 May-1 Oct Mon-Sat, Bank Hols 9-6
Facilities: 🚻 🚗 🍵 ⚠

☺ Map 1 E3
Heathlands Country Market
Heathlands Road, Wokingham, Berkshire RG11 3BG
Tel. Wokingham (0734) 787976

From Wokingham follow A329 Peach Street eastwards, after $\frac{1}{4}$ mile turn right into Easthampstead Road, then turn right by White Horse Inn into Heathlands Road to farm on left.

A large range of fruit and vegetables is available on this pick your own farm. The shop also specialises in fresh fish and salmon, oak-smoked on the premises.

● all year Tue-Sun, Bank Hols 9-5.30
Facilities: 🚻 🚗 🍵 ⚠

☺ Map 1 A3
Highclose Farm Enterprises
Bath Road, Hungerford, Berkshire RG17 0SP
Tel. Hungerford (0488) 84341

From Hungerford follow A4 westwards for $1\frac{1}{2}$ miles to farm. Signposted.

A pick your own farm offering strawberries, gooseberries, red and blackcurrants, raspberries, peas, broad beans and mangetout.
● 23 Jun-Jul daily 10-6
Facilities: 🚗

❧ Map 1 B3
Hollington Nurseries
Woolton Hill, Newbury, Berkshire RG15 9XT
Tel. Highclere (0635) 253908

From Newbury follow A343 southwards, after 4 miles turn right onto unclassified road for $\frac{1}{4}$ mile, then turn left onto unclassified road for $\frac{1}{2}$ mile, then turn left onto unclassified road for $\frac{3}{4}$ mile to house on left. Signposted.

Located in a 2-acre walled garden, Hollington Nurseries specialise in culinary, medicinal

● **Tylney Hall, Berkshire**

MAP 1 SOUTH EAST ENGLAND

and aromatic herbs. The nurseries have a number of formal beds plus a water and knot garden and a re-creation of their award-winning display at the Chelsea Flower Show. The extremely wide range of herbs grown includes many unusual varieties for cooking. The shop sells plants, herb products and a number of publications on the subject.

☞ free
● 15 Mar-Sep Mon-Sat 10-5.30, Sun, Bank Hols 11-5; Oct-14 Mar Mon-Fri 10-5
Facilities: ⬛ ⑩ ⬛ 🚗

❧ Map 1 B1
Houghton Lodge
Stockbridge,
Hampshire SO20 6LQ
Tel. Andover (0264) 810502

From Stockbridge follow A30 westwards, after ¾ mile turn left onto unclassified road for 1½ miles to Lodge.

Houghton Lodge, a beautiful 18thC 'Cottage Orne', is set in lovely gardens with fine views over the Test Valley. The old-fashioned greenhouses are of special interest with their 100-year-old vines. Visitors are welcome to pick the grapes themselves as well as the many varieties of espalier apples in the orchards.

☞ gardens: £1.00
● gardens: Mar-Aug Wed, Thur, Bank Hols 2-5 or by appointment
Facilities: ♿ ⬛ 🚗

☺ Map 1 E3
How Lane Farm
White Waltham, Maidenhead,
Berkshire SL6 3JP
Tel. Twyford (0734) 343291

From Windsor follow B3024 westwards, after 5 miles turn left onto A330 for ½ mile, then turn right to rejoin B3024 for 1 mile, then turn left onto unclassified road to farm immediately on left. Signposted.

A good range of pick your own soft fruit and vegetables is available here as well as free-range eggs and honey. Produce is also available ready-picked.
● Jun-Jul daily 10-7; Aug Tue, Thur, Sat 10-6; Sep-early Oct Tue, Sat 10-6
Facilities: ⬛ ⬛ 🚗 ➰

⬙ Map 1 E1
Meadow Cottage Farm
Churt Road, Headley, Bordon,
Hampshire GU35 8SS
Tel. Headley Down (0428) 712155

From Hindhead follow A287 north westwards, after 3 miles turn left at Churt onto unclassified road for 1½ miles to farm on right. Signposted.

This working dairy farm has 90 pedigree Weydown Jersey cows and produces delicious ice cream in a range of flavours. Specialities include fruit sorbets and Slimline Milk Ice — a low fat dessert with the texture of dairy ice cream but containing only one fifth of the fat content.
● all year daily 7-7
Facilities: 🚗
★ regular tastings

♥ Map 1 D3
Mortimer Hill Fruit Farm
Mortimer Hill, Mortimer,
Berkshire RG7 3PG
Tel. Mortimer (0734) 333157

From Reading follow A4 westwards, after 6 miles turn left onto unclassified road for 4 miles to Mortimer. Signposted.

This small family-worked fruit farm specialises in high quality soft fruit. There are over 30 varieties of plums as well as strawberries, gooseberries, tayberries, loganberries and red and blackcurrants. Visitors can follow the farm trail which includes an area of natural woodland and see some interesting farmyard animals including Cochin hens and Vietnamese pot-bellied pigs. The shop also sells ready-picked fruit and a range of homemade produce such as jams, jellies, pickles, fruit vinegars and syrups.

☞ free
● 29 Apr-25 Jun, 9 Sep-2 Oct Fri-Sun 10-4; 26 Jun-31 Jul daily 9-7; 1 Aug-4 Sep daily 10-5.30
Facilities: ⬛ ⬛ 🚗 ➰ /⛰
★ 6 Feb, 5 Nov pruning demonstrations 10-12'
⬛ homemade cookies & ice cream

⊞ Map 1 D3
Museum of English Rural Life
University of Reading,
White Knights, Reading,
Berkshire RG6 2AG
Tel. Reading (0734) 875123 ext 475

● **Soft fruits, Mortimer Hill Fruit Farm**

MAP 1

From Reading follow A327 southwards for 2 miles to university on left. Signposted.

Based in the largest agricultural and food educational establishment in the country, this rural life museum has exhibits on all aspects of agricultural life. There is an extensive collection of kitchen equipment and displays on butter and cheese-making. The museum also has large archive and photographic collections.

☞ adults 50p, children free
◗ all year Tue-Sat 10-1, 2-4.30
Facilities: 🚻 ♿ 🚗 🍽

☺ Map 1 B1
Two Rivers Farm
Cattle Lane, Abbots Ann, Andover, Hampshire SP11 7DS
Tel. Andover (0264) 710365

From Andover follow A343 south westwards, after 1 mile turn right onto unclassified road for ¼ mile to Abbots Ann. Signposted.

This pick your own farm offers strawberries, raspberries, red and blackcurrants and broad beans. Visitors can also see the farmyard animals and chickens.
◗ Jun-Jul daily 9-8
Facilities: 🚻 🚗 🍽

🏫 Map 1 D3
Wellington Country Park
Riseley, Reading, Berkshire RG7 1ST
Tel. Reading (0734) 326444

From Reading follow A33 southwards, after 7 miles turn left onto B3349 for 1 mile to park. Signposted.

Wellington Country Park, on the borders of Hampshire and Berkshire, is the home of the National Dairy Museum. Funded by the National Dairy Council, it has exhibitions of equipment and memorabilia relating to the development of the dairy industry. The museum makes Wellington cheese and

dairy ice cream on the premises and they can be bought in the shop.

☞ adults £1.70, children (5-15) 80p
◗ Mar-Oct daily 10-5; Nov-Feb Sat-Sun 10-5
Facilities: 🚻 ♿ 🚻 🚗 🍽 ⛺

🧀 Map 1 C4
Wells Stores
Streatley, Nr Reading, Berkshire RG8 9HY
Tel. Goring (0491) 872367

From Goring follow B4009 westwards for ½ mile to Streatley.

This specialist cheese shop is known world-wide for its stocks of the best British and French farmhouse cheeses. Run by Patrick Rance and his son Hugh, the shop produces an informative guide to help customers choose, serve and keep cheese and offers free tastings. As well as providing one of the widest selections of unpasteurised British cheeses from sheep's, goats' and cows' milk the shop also sells wine, including a selection of Thames Valley wines and a range of biscuits to go with cheese.
◗ all year Mon-Tue, Thur-Sat 9-1, 2.30-5, Wed 9-1, closed Bank Hols
Facilities: 🚻 🍽

🍇 Map 1 D3
Westbury Vineyard and Winery
Westbury Farm, Purley on Thames, Nr Reading, Berkshire RG8 8DL
Tel. Pangbourne (07357) 3123

From Reading follow A329 north westwards, after 4 miles turn right at Purley into Westbury Lane for ½ mile to farm. Signposted.

Westbury Vineyard and Winery was planted in 1970 and is now one of Britain's bigger vineyards, covering over 15 acres. Many varieties of grapes

are grown producing white, red and rosé wines. The red, from Pinot Noir grapes — used to produce Burgundy — was the first to be made commercially in England since 1914. Visitors are welcome to walk around the vineyard and buy the wines from the shop. A trout lake is available for fishing.

☞ free
◗ all year by appointment
Facilities: ♿ 🚻 🚗 🍽

🧀 Map 1 C1
Wield Wood Sheep Dairy
Wield Wood Estate, Nr New Alresford, Hampshire SO24 9RU
Tel. Alton (0420) 63151

From New Alresford follow B3046 northwards, after 8 miles turn right at Preston Candover onto unclassified road for 1½ miles, then turn right onto unclassified road for ¾ mile to farm on right just before Upper Wield village. Signposted.

Sheep were milked on this historic farm as early as 1250 and today the same work continues. Visitors are welcome to sample the many natural ewes' milk products and buy milk, yoghurt and 'Walda', a Hampshire ewes' milk cheese.

☞ adults 50p, children (under 14) free
◗ Easter-Oct daily 2-5 or by appointment
Facilities: 🚻 🚗

MAP 2   SOUTH EAST ENGLAND

Map (South Hampshire & Isle of Wight)

5 | Wilton Salisbury Winchester West Meon
KIMBRIDGE FARM SHOP
Swallowcliffe
Downton
Romsey
BREAMORE HOUSE
HILL FARM ORCHAR
Eastleigh
M27
MEON
VALLEY
VINEYA
Fordingbridge Cadnam Botley
LONGDOWN ELING TIDE MILL
DAIRY FARM HAMPSHIRE
4 | 354 SOUTHAMPTON M27 FARM MUSEUM
HOCKEYS
Lyndhurst
RINGWOOD BREWERY JOHN STRANGE
Wimborne Ringwood BEAULIEU CHOCOLATE Fareham
Minster PARLOUR
MONTAGU VENTURES Fawley
Brockenburst
Gosport PO
SEA LIFE CENTRE
3 | LYMINGTON VINEYARD Solent The Cowes
Christchurch OSBORNE Spithead Ryde
LYMORE VALLEY HERBS Lymington HOUSE
Mudeford Yarmouth BARTON MANOR
Poole BOURNEMOUTH VINEYARD AND GARDE
PUFFIN FISHERIES Newpor
MILLERS DAMSEL REAL BREAD SHOP ISLE OF WIGH
Studland The Needles Totland THE HOLLANDS Sand
STRAWBERRY
2 | le FARM Shank
Swanage Chale KINGCOB GARLIC
AND SWEET COR
Ventnor
St. Catherine's Pt.

1 | # SOUTH HAMPSHIRE &
ISLE OF WIGHT

A | B | C | D

The inhabitants of Hampshire are unflatteringly nick-named 'Hampshire Hogs'. Not because of any supposed resemblance to these glorious animals but rather because of a fondness for pork products. Pigs once roamed the New Forest and in Edwardian times were supposedly trained to find the only edible truffle in Britain — the tuber aestivium or summer truffle. The New Forest was the hunting ground of the Norman kings and today deer, pigeon, rabbits and hare still roam wild.

Map 2 D2
Adgestone Vineyard
Upper Road,
Adgestone, Sandown,
Isle of Wight PO36 OES
Tel. Isle of Wight (0983) 402503

From Sandown follow A3055 northwards, after 2 miles turn left at Brading into Lower Adgestone Road for ¹/₂ mile, then turn left into Sheep Lane then left to vineyard on right. Signposted.

Founded in 1968, this vineyard is sited on 28 acres of chalky, south-facing slopes. The conditions are well suited to the 3 white grapes grown — Seyval Blanc, Müller-Thurgau and Reichensteiner. All 3 are

⚘ Map 2 D3

Barton Manor Vineyard and Gardens

Whippingham, East Cowes,
Isle of Wight PO32 6LB
Tel. Isle of Wight (0983) 292835

From Cowes follow A3021 south eastwards, after 2 miles turn left onto unclassified road for ¼ mile to Manor. Signposted.

Barton Manor has had a varied history. It began in the 13thC as an Augustinian oratory, was later bought by Queen Victoria and at the turn of the century became Edward VII's island home. Sold by the Crown in 1922, the 6-acre vineyard was planted in 1977 with a variety of vines including Müller-Thurgau, Gewürztraminer and Seyval Blanc. The vineyard now produces 20,000 bottles of white and rosé wine a year and also a dry apple wine. Visitors may tour the vineyard and winery, watch a video on wine-making and taste a selection of the wines. The shop sells wine by the bottle or case.

☞ adults £1.75, senior citizens £1.50, children (under 15) free
◑ Easter, Apr Sat, Sun 10.30-5.30; May-9 Oct daily 10.30-5.30
Facilities: 🍽♿🚻🚗
🍽 homemade salads & teas served

🍫 Map 2 C3

Beaulieu Chocolate Parlour

High Street, Beaulieu,
Hampshire SO4 7YA
Tel. Beaulieu (0590) 612279

From Lymington follow B3054 north eastwards for 6 miles to Beaulieu.

This shop started making its own chocolates 5 years ago using pure couverture from Belgium and natural ingredients for centres. Its range includes a selection of fresh cream truffles, seasonal novelties and personalised products. The Parlour also sells Beaulieu Fruit Cake which is made to its own recipe and a range of jams and marmalades from local fruit.
◑ Apr-Oct daily 9-6; Nov-Mar daily 10-5

🍏 Map 2 E4

Bedhampton Fruit Farm

Lower Road, Old Bedhampton,
Havant, Hampshire
Tel. Havant (0705) 472854

From Havant follow B2150, then B2177 westwards, after 1 mile turn left into Brookside Road, then right into Lower Road to farm. Signposted.

A pick your own farm offering strawberries, raspberries, broad beans, courgettes and potatoes.
◑ Jun-Sep daily 10-7
Facilities: 🍴🚻🚗🏕

🍏 Map 2 E4

Bedhampton Vegetable Farm

40 Acres, Havant Road,
Bedhampton, Havant,
Hampshire
Tel. Havant (0705) 472854

From Havant follow B2150, then B2177 westwards, after 2 miles join A2030 and turn left immediately to farm. Signposted.

A pick your own farm offering a full range of vegetables including mangetout and asparagus. Produce is also available ready-picked.
◑ all year Tue-Sat 10-5
Facilities: 🚻🚗

🏛 Map 2 B4

Breamore House

Breamore, Nr Fordingbridge,
Hampshire SP6 2DF
Tel. Downton (0725) 22233

From Fordingbridge follow A338 northwards, after 3 miles turn left onto unclassified road for ½ mile to house. Signposted.

This Elizabethan manor house was completed in 1583 and has been in the Hulse family since 1748. It is now a countryside museum with an historic kitchen which has a superb collection of copper pans and moulds on display, an 18thC self-service beer wagon and replicas of a dairy, cider house and brewery. A farm cottage has been furnished as it would have been in the 19thC

blended to produce a light, fragrant dry white wine which has won many trophies including the 1974 Sunday Times Gold Medal. Over 70,000 bottles are now produced each year. Visitors may tour the vineyards and winery, taste the wines and buy them by the bottle or case.

☞ free
◑ all year Mon-Fri 9-4.30, Sat 10-12.30
Facilities: 🚻🚗

MAP 2   SOUTH EAST ENGLAND

complete with a table set for tea. The estate also has a carriage museum which houses agricultural machines and horse-drawn carriages. The gardens offer pick your own asparagus.

☞ adults £2.80, senior citizens £1.20, children £1.40
◉ Easter, Apr Tue, Wed, Sun 2-5.30; May-Jul, Sep Tue-Thur, Sat, Sun, Bank Hols 2-5.30; Aug daily 2-5.30
Facilities: ⑩ ⑬ 🚗 ♨
★ poultry & rare breeds show
⑩ teas served including toasted sandwiches, homemade cakes & scones

Eling Tide Mill
🏯 Map 2 C4

The Toll Bridge, Eling Totton, Nr Southampton, Hampshire SO4 4HF
Tel. Southampton (0703) 869575

From Totton follow unclassified road southwards for ³/₄ mile towards Eling to mill on left. Signposted.

Eling Mill is an unusual 18thC mill that is powered by the tide. Situated on Eling causeway, an inlet off the tidal estuary, the mill has sluice gates to hold back the water as the tide rises. When they are opened they drive the mill for up to 5 hours. In the 19thC this type of mill was quite common but now Eling is one of only 3 left in working order. Visitors can follow the progress of the home-grown wheat as it passes through the mill and is ground to flour. There is a video to explain the miller's life and displays on local history. The shop sells stoneground flour and biscuits.

☞ adults 85p, senior citizens 60p, children 50p
◉ all year Wed-Sun, Bank Hols 10-4 or by appointment
Facilities: 🍴 🚗 ♨

Hampshire Farm Museum
🐓 Map 2 D4

Manor Farm, Brook Lane, Botley, Hampshire SO3 2ER
Tel. Botley (04892) 87055

From Botley follow unclassified road southwards for 1 mile to farm. Signposted.

The exhibits on this working farm museum cover the history of farming in Hampshire from 1850 to 1950. Visitors can explore the farm, the farmhouse, barns, outbuildings and workshops and imagine farm life as it used to be. Some of the older buildings house a collection of agricultural implements including steam engines. There are also a number of old breeds of farm animals to be seen including Hampshire Downs sheep, Wessex Saddleback pigs, Guernsey cattle, Golden Guernsey goats and a Shire horse. Free-range eggs are sold from the farm shop.

☞ adults 60p, senior citizens & children 30p
◉ Jan-Mar, Oct-Dec daily 10-5; Apr-Sep daily 10-6
Facilities: 🍴 ⑩ ♿ ⑬ 🚗 ♨

• **The gateway of Beaulieu Abbey**

MAP 2

● **Palace House, Beaulieu Abbey**

the 16th and 17thC are used to make a range of chutneys and jellies. The shop also sells a range of health foods and drinks. The farm's conservation picnic area has trout ponds and barbecue facilities — barbecue packs are also sold in the farm shop. There is also a pets' corner for children.

☞ free
◖ all year Mon-Thur, Sat 9-6, Fri 9-7
Facilities: 🚻 🚗 ⛺ ⛰
★ spring & summer Sats open days with demonstrations & barbecues, telephone for details

---

☺ Map 2 D4
Hill Farm Orchards
Droxford Road,
Swanmore, Southampton,
Hampshire SO3 2PY
Tel. Droxford (0489) 877225

From Fareham follow A32 northwards, after 6 miles turn left onto unclassified road for 1½ miles, then turn right at Swanmore into Droxford Road for ¼ mile to farm on right.

As well as having the largest cherry orchard in Hampshire, Hill Farm specialises in apples and pears including unusual varieties such as Lord Lamborne, Ashmeads Kernel and Red James Grieve. Apple juice is pressed and bottled on the farm and can be bought in the shop, along with ready-picked fruit, vegetables, cheese, cream, country wines and ciders. It is also a pick your own farm and offers a range of soft fruits including white currants and plums together with apples, pears and cherries.
◖ farm shop: all year Mon-Sat 9-5, Sun 10-5; PYO: mid Jun-Oct Mon-Sat 9-5, Sun 10-5
Facilities: 🚻 🚗 ⛺
★ blossom walks & open days

🐦 Map 2 B4
Hockeys
South Gorley, Fordingbridge,
Hampshire SP6 2PW
Tel. Fordingbridge (0425) 52542

From Ringwood follow A338 northwards, after 2 miles turn right onto unclassified road for ½ mile, then turn left onto unclassified road for ¼ mile to farm on right. Signposted.

This traditional beef and lamb farm, dating from the 17thC, is situated in the New Forest where the cattle graze on the rich land. The farming methods have changed very little over the years and no chemicals or growth promoters have ever been used here. All the beef, lamb and pork is produced naturally and is expertly hung, butchered, packed and labelled. Visitors are welcome to tour the farm on the Farm Walk and, on Saturdays, watch demonstrations including sausage-making. The farm shop sells beef, pork, lamb, poultry, venison from the New Forest, homemade sausages, pâtés, faggots, burgers, homecured gammons, bacon and cooked meats. Recipes dating from

---

☺ Map 2 D2
The Hollands Strawberry Farm
Hale Common,
Arreton, Newport,
Isle of Wight PO30 3AR
Tel. Isle of Wight (0983) 865308
From Sandown follow A3056 westwards for 3 miles to farm opposite petrol station.

A pick your own farm and shop offering strawberries, raspberries, cream and tomatoes.
◖ PYO: Jun-Sep daily 9.30-5.30; shop: May-Nov daily 9-7

☺ Map 2 D3
Island Country Foods
Asheybrook, East Ashey Lane,
Ashey, Isle of Wight PO33 4AT
Tel. Isle of Wight (0983) 65686
From Ryde follow A3055 southwards, after 2 miles turn right onto unclassified road for 1 mile, then turn right onto unclassified road for ½ mile to farm on right.

This farm grows a variety of organic vegetables and strawberries which are sold on a pick your own basis or ready-picked from the shop. It also has a free-range herd of rare

MAP 2   SOUTH EAST ENGLAND

breed pigs which provide meat for the shop. Lamb, corn-fed chicken and cream are also for sale.

◖ all year Tue-Sun 9.30-6
Facilities: ᴵᴼᴵ �ʷᶜ �． ᵙ
ᴵᴼᴵ teas with homemade cakes served in farmhouse kitchen

😊 Map 2 C5
Kimbridge Farm Shop
Kimbridge, Romsey, Hampshire SO51 0LE
Tel. Lockerley (0794) 40777

From Romsey follow A3057 northwards, after 3 miles turn left opposite Bear and Ragged Staff Inn to farm. Signposted.

This farm shop sells a large range of locally grown produce. It has fresh trout, asparagus, sweet corn, a wide selection of English cheeses, local cream, free-range eggs, fruit, vegetables, smoked trout and pâtés, jams, local honey, herbs and spices. Visitors can see the farm's bantams, ducks and trout pond.
◖ all year daily 10-1, 2-5
Facilities: 🚐

😊 Map 2 D2
Kingcob Garlic and Sweet Corn
Langbridge Farm, Newchurch, Sandown, Isle of Wight PO36 0NT
Tel. Isle of Wight (0983) 865378/229

From Sandown follow A3056 westwards, after 3 miles turn right onto unclassified road for 1 1/2 miles to Newchurch.

This is the largest commercial garlic and sweet corn farm in Britain. The garlic from this farm is sold all over the country and some is even exported to France. Their latest development is fresh, peeled garlic sold vacuum-packed and visitors can buy this or garlic by the bulb or string. Sweet corn,

early potatoes, early carrots and asparagus are also available in season.
◖ 20 Apr-23 Oct Mon-Fri 9-5, Sat 10-4, Sun 10-1
Facilities: 🚐
★ 14 August 1988 Newchurch garlic festival

● **Tying strings of garlic, Langbridge Farm**

🌱 Map 2 C4
Longdown Dairy Farm
Longdown, Ashurst, Nr Southampton, Hampshire SO4 4UH
Tel. Ashurst (042129) 3326

From Totton follow A35 southwards, after 2 miles turn left onto unclassified road for 1/4 mile to farm on left.

Longdown Dairy Farm, a modern and highly productive dairy farm, was one of the first to open to the public. It has been specially designed so visitors can walk around the whole farm complex without interrupting the routine of the farm workers. A highlight is the daily milking of the 150 Friesian cows in the computerised herringbone parlour, which takes place from 2.30-5. Visitors may also see and feed sheep, goats, pigs, chickens, ducks, rabbits and a rare breed of Iron Age pigs. Information about how the farm runs is available from the farm office which has a display on dairy farming.
☞ adults £1.50, senior citizens £1.25, children (3-13) £1.00
◖ 26 Mar-Oct school hols & half terms 11-5, telephone for details
Facilities: ʷᶜ 🚐

🐚 Map 2 C3
Lymington Vineyard
Wainsford Road, Pennington, Lymington, Hampshire SO41 8LB
Tel. Lymington (0590) 72112

From Lymington follow A337 south westwards, after 1/4 mile turn right onto unclassified road for 1/2 mile to Pennington. Signposted.

Visitors are welcome to walk around this award-winning vineyard and winery. The wines are for sale by the bottle or case.
☞ telephone for details
◖ May-Sep Sun-Fri 10.30-4.30
Facilities: ʷᶜ 🚐

REGIONAL RECIPE

HAMPSHIRE DROPS

4oz butter
4oz caster sugar
2 eggs
4oz cornflour
4oz plain flour
1/2 tsp baking powder
jam

Heat oven to gas 3 (325F, 160C). Cream the butter with the sugar until fluffy, beat in the eggs and mix in the cornflour and flour sifted with the baking powder. Beat to a fairly stiff consistency. Drop teaspoons of the mixture onto greased baking trays and bake for 30 minutes. Leave to cool, then sandwich together with jam.

🌿 Map 2 C3
Lymore Valley Herbs
Lymore Lane, Milford-on-Sea, Hampshire SO41 0TX
Tel. Lymington (0590) 42030

From Lymington follow A337 south westwards, after 2 miles turn left onto B3058 for 1/4 mile, then turn left onto unclassified road for 1/2 mile to farm on left. Signposted.

Lymore Valley Herbs, close to the New Forest, is a herb farm

MAP 2

● Kingcob garlic, Langbridge Farm

MAP 2

SOUTH EAST ENGLAND

with demonstration herb gardens and orchards which visitors are welcome to explore. Pot-grown herbs and an extensive selection of terracotta containers are for sale in the shop.

☞ free

◑ Apr-Sep Tue-Sun 9-5 or by appointment

🍃 Map 2 D4

Meon Valley Vineyard

Hill Grove,
Swanmore, Southampton,
Hampshire SO3 2PZ
Tel. Droxford (0489) 877435

From Fareham follow A32 northwards, after 6 miles turn left onto unclassified road for 1 mile to vineyard on right.

This vineyard was established in 1977 on a site previously used for growing strawberries. It produces and bottles its own red, white and rosé wines from a variety of grapes. It also produces a range of country wines from pure fruit juices, mead and cider. Visitors are welcome to tour the vineyard, where they will see the vines growing on the Geneva double curtain system, after which they can taste the wines. The busiest and perhaps most interesting time of year to visit is between mid- September and mid- November when harvesting and wine-making takes place. The shop sells the full range of wines produced including Hill Grove Wines, cider and mead by the bottle or case as well as speciality fudge made from natural ingredients.

☞ £1.50 including wine tasting

◑ Easter-1 Oct by appointment
Facilities: 🚾 🚗

268

🦞 Map 2 C2

Millers Damsel Real Bread Shop

Avenue Road, Freshwater,
Isle of Wight PO40 9UT
Tel. Isle of Wight (0983)) 752516

From Totland follow A3055 eastwards for 1½ miles to Freshwater.

This shop not only has its own bakery but also its own watermill where wholemeal flour is still milled. Specialities include wheat wafers, shortbread and other sweet biscuits such as Calbourne crunchies and ginger shorties. The shop also stocks a comprehensive range of fine foods including wholefoods, herbs, spices, teas and coffees.

◑ all year Tue, Wed, Fri, Sat 9-1, 2.15-4.30, Mon, Thur 9-1

VENISON

In the New Forest take advantage of the game. You can buy excellent venison, trout and pheasant and a number of butchers do a brisk trade in venison sausages. Markets often hold meat auctions where, if you are lucky, you can find some excellent bargains.

🍃 Map 2 C3

Montagu Ventures

John Montagu Building,
Beaulieu, Brockenhurst,
Hampshire SO42 7ZN
Tel. Beaulieu (0590) 612345

From Lymington follow B3054 north eastwards for 6 miles to Beaulieu. Signposted.

The herb garden here is in the delightful setting of Beaulieu Abbey cloisters. The shop in the palace house sells the estate's own white wine as well as homemade preserves and biscuits.

☞ adults £4.40, senior citizens £3.60, children (4-16) £3.00

◑ May-Sep daily 10-6; Oct-Apr daily 10-5; vineyard tours by appointment
Facilities: 🚾 🍴 ♿ 🚾 🚗 🍳

🍴 full range of food & drink served in licensed Brabazon Food Court

🍃 Map 2 E2

Morton Manor Vineyard

Morton Manor, Brading,
Isle of Wight PO36 0EP
Tel. Isle of Wight (0983) 406168

From Sandown follow A3055 northwards for 1½ miles to Morton. Signposted.

Visitors are welcome to look round this 2-acre vineyard, see the winery display and visit the museum of antique wine-making equipment. They can sample the fine wines and buy them by the glass or bottle. Vines are also on sale.

☞ adults £1.50, senior citizens £1.25, children 60p

◑ 3 Apr-Oct Sun-Fri 10-5.30
Facilities: 🚾 🍴 🚾 🚗 ♿

🍴 lunches & teas served in licensed Thatched Cottage tea rooms & wine bar; food includes homemade cakes, scones, & local gâteaux

🍲 Map 2 D3

Osborne House

East Cowes,
Isle of Wight PO32 6JY
Tel. Isle of Wight (0983) 200022

From Cowes follow A3021 south eastwards for 1½ miles to house on left. Signposted.

Osborne House was Queen Victoria's seaside home and has been described as the 'high noon' of the Victorian age. The dining room includes 8 miniature chairs and a table made for the royal children. The Swiss Cottage museum in the gardens houses curiosities that the various royals collected as children including a miniature grocery shop.

MAP 2

☞ adults £2.50, senior citizens £1.85, children £1.25
◑ Apr-Oct daily 10-5
Facilities: ▇ ⦿ ⅋ ⅏ 🚗 ⛺

🦞 Map 2 C3
Puffin Fisheries
Saltern Wood Quay, Yarmouth, Isle of Wight PO41 0SE
Tel. Isle of Wight (0983) 760090

From Yarmouth follow A3054 westwards, after ¼ mile turn right to quay. Signposted.

Puffin Fisheries ensures the freshness of its produce by keeping up to 100lb of live lobsters and 800lb of live crabs in holding tanks. Visitors can choose their specimen and then have it cooked on the premises ready to take away. A complete range of locally caught, fresh fish is also available including Dover sole, plaice, skate, mullet and bass.
◑ Mar-Apr, Oct Tue-Sun 9-5; May- Sep daily 9-5; Nov-Mar Tue-Sat 9-5
Facilities: ⅏ 🚗 ⛺

🍺 Map 2 B4
Ringwood Brewery
138 Christchurch Road, Ringwood, Hampshire BH24 3AP
Tel. Ringwood (0425) 471177

In town centre.

This small independent brewery, established 10 years ago, produces a range of real ales including a prize-winning strong ale, Old Thumper. Visitors are welcome to visit the brewery by appointment and to taste the beer before buying it in the shop. Four beers are produced — Best Bitter, Fortyniner, XXXX Porter and Old Thumper — and are sold in containers ranging from 4 to 72 pints. Mustard and chutney, made with Old Thumper, are also on sale.
☞ free
◑ shop: all year Mon-Fri 10-5, Sat 10-12, closed Bank Hols; tours Sep-Nov, Jan-Mar 6.30 by appointment
Facilities: ⅏ 🚗

🐠 Map 2 E3
Sea Life Centre
Clarence Esplanade, Southsea, Portsmouth, Hampshire PO5 3PB
Tel. Portsmouth (0705) 734461

From Portsmouth follow A288 south eastwards for 1½ miles to Southsea.

The Sea Life Centre invites visitors to explore its breathtaking wealth of fascinating marine life. Surrounded by thousands of gallons of water they will come face to face with hundreds of exciting sea creatures, from octopus to conger eels. The Ocean Reef is Europe's deepest tank and includes fish that live in the depths of the ocean and which would not normally be seen. 'Touch' pools provide the opportunity to handle a number of interesting sea creatures.
☞ adults £2.40, senior citizens £1.75, children £1.55
◑ all year daily 10-7
Facilities: ▇ ⦿ ⅋ ⅏ 🚗 ⛰

🦞 Map 2 C4
John Strange
16 High Street, Lyndhurst, Hampshire
Tel. Lyndhurst (042128) 3300

In town centre.

John Strange is one of the best known game butchers in England. The shop's speciality is New Forest venison to which it has exclusive rights. The venison is sold either fresh, butchered into various cuts, or as pies, pâtés and sausages all made on the premises.
◑ all year Mon-Sat 9-5, Sun telephone for details
Facilities: 🚗 ⛺

● **Freshly caught lobster**

MAP 3   SOUTH EAST ENGLAND

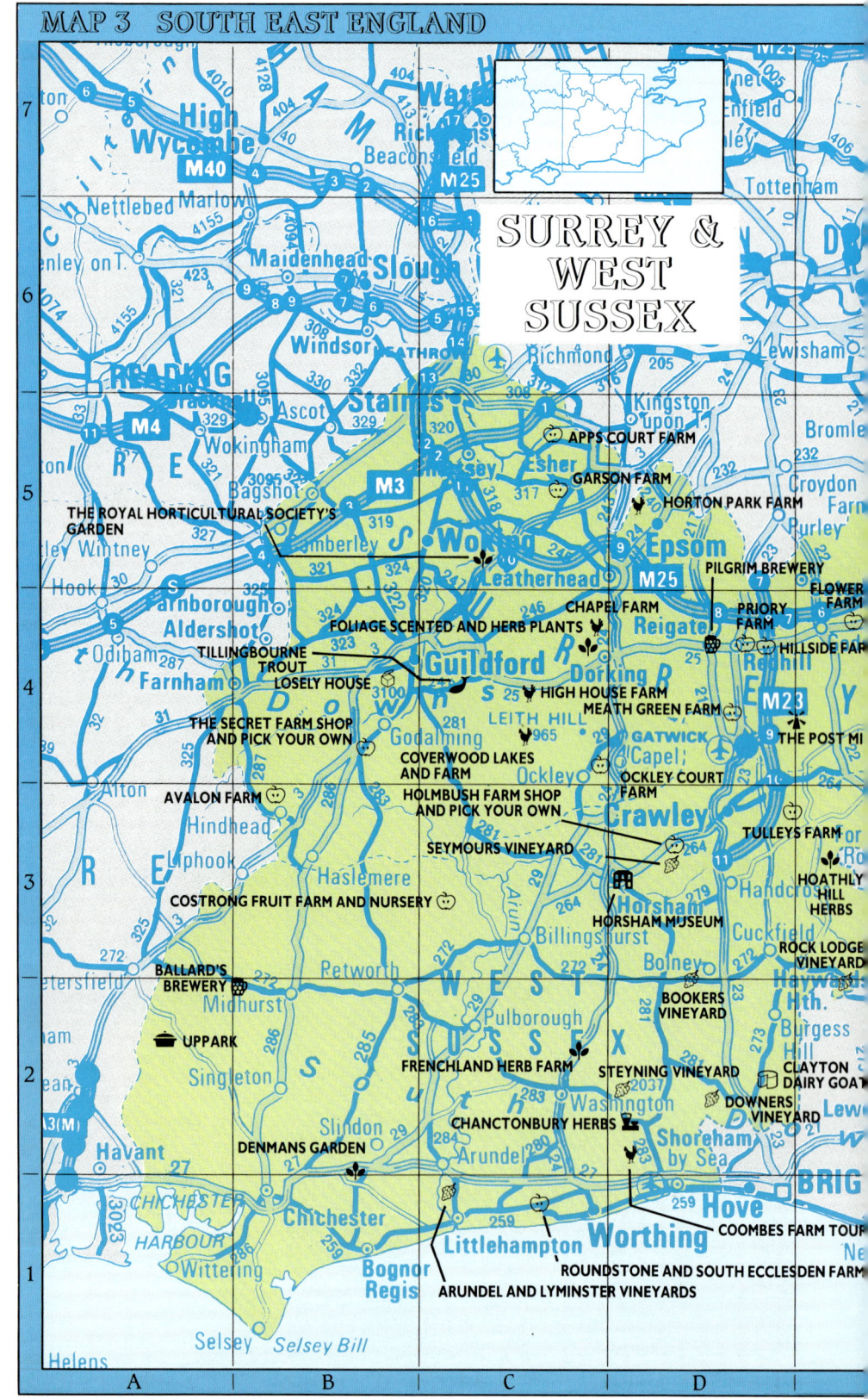

SURREY &
WEST
SUSSEX

The whole of South East England is packed with vineyards. It is a developing industry and, as our winemakers gain confidence and experience, so the quality of the wine improves. There are over 40 varieties of grapes suitable for growing in this country, the main ones being Müller-Thurgau, Reichensteiner, Huxelrebe and Seyval Blanc and these produce a wine with a pleasant bouquet and a freshness and crispness which is not dissimilar in character to German wine.

☺ Map 3 C5
Apps Court Farm
Hurst Road, Walton-on-Thames, Surrey KT12 2EG
Tel. Walton-on-Thames (0932) 244822

From Esher follow A307 north eastwards, after 1 mile turn left onto A309 for 2 miles, then turn left onto A3050 for 2½ miles to farm. Signposted.

This pick your own farm offers soft fruit and vegetables from June to October. Visitors may pick pumpkins, mangetout and celeriac while the farm shop stocks eggs, preserves, honey, dairy products, ice cream, goats' milk and dried fruits.
◗ shop: all year daily Mon-Sat 9-5, Sun 9-2; PYO: Jun-Oct daily 9-7
Facilities: ⓦ 🚗 ♨ ⚑

🍇 Map 3 C1
Arundel and Lyminster Vineyards
The Vineyard,
Church Lane, Lyminster,
West Sussex BN17 7QF
Tel. Arundel (0903) 883393

From Arundel follow A284 southwards for 1 mile to Lyminster.

In 1763 the Duke of Norfolk's vineyard at Arundel Castle produced '60 pipes of palatable Burgundy type wine'. Today, a mile south of the castle, the tradition continues with the Arundel and Lyminster Vineyards which produce the Arun Valley table wines. Visitors may walk about the estate and taste the wines in the 400-year-old barn. Arun Valley wines and honey are on sale.

☞ free
◗ May-Oct daily 2-dusk
Facilities: ⓦ 🚗 ♨
🍴 spit roasts for parties of 10 or more

☺ Map 3 B3
Avalon Farm
The Packhouse, Tilford Road, Churt, Farnham,
Surrey GU10 2NA
Tel. Hindhead (042873) 5161

From Hindhead follow A287 northwards, after ¼ mile turn right onto unclassified road for 1 mile to farm on left.

This 80-acre farm offers a huge range of pick your own fruit and vegetables including blueberries, squash, mangetout, cherries and late crop strawberries. The shop also sells apples and pears as well as local cream and ice cream.
◗ Jun-Jul daily 9-8, Aug-Dec daily 9-5
Facilities: ⓦ 🚗 ♨

🍺 Map 3 B2
Ballard's Brewery
Elsted Marsh, Elsted, Midhurst, West Sussex GU29 0JT
Tel. Midhurst (073081) 4936/3662

From Midhurst follow A272 westwards, after 2 miles turn left onto unclassified road for 1½ miles to Elsted Marsh.

A small, real ale country brewery that is one of only half a dozen in the UK to comply with the German Reinheitsgebot brewing purity standards. Visitors are welcome to tour the premises and taste the beer which can be bought in 4½ and 9 gallon containers or in pints in the adjoining pub.

MAP 3   SOUTH EAST ENGLAND

☞ free; evening tours: telephone for details

◑ all year Mon-Fri 9-5, evening tours by appointment

Facilities: 🍽 🚻 ♿

🍴 homecooked meals served in pub

🌿 Map 3 D2

Bookers Vineyard

Foxhole Lane, Bolney, West Sussex RH17 5NB

Tel. Bolney (044482) 575

From Bolney follow A272 westwards after ½ mile turn right into Foxhole Lane for ½ mile to vineyard on left.

In the heart of rural Sussex, this vineyard is carrying on a tradition brought to Britain by the Romans nearly 2,000 years ago. It produces a classic Müller-Thurgau white wine, Bolne, which has been awarded the English Vineyards Association's Seal of Merit. Visitors can enjoy a pleasant walk around the vineyard and its stream and waterfalls and then taste the wine produced. They may also see the herd of dairy goats whose milk is used to make cheese and yoghurt and, occasionally, watch cheese-making. The vineyard shop sells wine, a wide selection of goats' cheeses, yoghurt and milk, as well as herb plants and vines.

☞ free

◑ vineyard: Easter-Oct Wed, Sat, Sun, Bank Hols 12-dusk or by appointment; shop: all year daily 9-5

Facilities: 🍴 🚻 ♿

🌿 Map 3 D2

Chanctonbury Herbs

104 High Street, Steyning, West Sussex BN4 3RD

Tel. Steyning (0903) 815000

From Shoreham-by-Sea follow A283 northwards for 5 miles to Steyning.

This specialist herb shop sells a range of herbal foods including

chutneys, marmalades, mustards, vinegars, teas and herb plants.

◑ all year Mon-Sat 9.30-5.30, closed Bank Hols

🐔 Map 3 C4

Chapel Farm

Westhumble, Dorking, Surrey RH5 6AY

Tel. Dorking (0306) 882865

From Dorking follow A24 northwards, after 2 miles turn left onto unclassified road for ¼ mile to Westhumble.

This 220-acre working family farm is set in an area of outstanding natural beauty close to Boxhill. A guided tour allows visitors to see the extensive farm buildings, some over 400 years old, and watch and handle a variety of farm and domestic animals. There is also a farm animal trail which visitors can follow unaccompanied. A shop sells garden plants, dried flowers, and apple juice.

☞ animal trail: £1.00; guided tour: £1.50

◑ Mar-Oct daily 10.30-2.30, guided tours by appointment

Facilities: 🚻 ♿ 🧺 ⛺

★ 8 May cowpie rally

📖 Map 3 D2

Clayton Dairy Goats

Holt Valley Farm, Underhill Lane, Clayton, Nr Hassocks, West Sussex BN6 9PL

Tel. Hassocks (07918) 5158

From Brighton follow A23 northwards, after 6 miles turn right onto A273 for 1 mile to Clayton. Signposted.

This goat and sheep farm has a small dairy where the owner makes and presses goats' cheese. His specialities are fresh herb-flavoured and well-ripened mature cheeses.

Visitors can see the goats and also the rare breed of South Down sheep. The farm's own cheese, milk and yoghurt is for sale all year round.

☞ free

◑ by appointment

Facilities: 🚻 ♿

🐔 Map 3 D2

Coombes Farm Tours

Church Farm, Coombes, Lancing, West Sussex BN15 0RS

Tel. Brighton (0273) 452028

From Worthing follow A27 eastwards, after 3 miles turn left past Lancing College onto unclassified road for 2 miles to farm. Signposted.

This 1,000-acre working mixed farm offers a 1½ hour tractor and trailer tour led by the farmer's daughter, Jenny. She shows visitors the farm's 700 acres of downland grazed by 500 ewes producing about 800 lambs a year. She then moves on to the 300 acres of alluvial brookland where wheat is grown and 80 beef cows are kept in pastures.

☞ adults £1.75, senior citizens £1.50, children £1.00

◑ Mar-Oct daily during daylight hours by appointment

Facilities: 🍴 🚻 ♿ 🧺 ⛺

MAP 3

☺ Map 3 C3
Costrong Fruit Farm and Nursery
Plaistow Road, Kirdford,
West Sussex RH14 0LA
Tel. Kirdford (040377) 391

From Billingshurst follow A272 westwards, after 2 miles turn right at Wisborough Green onto unclassified road for 2 miles to Kirdford, then turn right onto unclassified road for 1 mile to farm.

This 80-acre farm offers the usual pick your own fruit and vegetables including 15 varieties of apples, early glass-grown strawberries, melons and seedless grapes. The shop sells the produce ready-picked and also local cream, honey and eggs.
● all year daily 10-5
Facilities: 🚻 🚗

❦ Map 3 C4
Coverwood Lakes and Farm
Peaslake Road, Ewhurst,
Cranleigh, Surrey GU6 7NT
Tel. Dorking (0306) 731101

From Dorking follow A25 westwards, after 7 miles turn left onto unclassified road for 3 miles to Peaslake, then continue on unclassified road towards Ewhurst for 2 miles to farm.

Coverwood Farm, in the Surrey Hills, has one of the leading herds of pedigree Poll Hereford cattle in south east England. Visitors are welcome to walk around the farm on a trail which allows them to see cattle and sheep of all ages, from calves and lambs to stock bulls and rams. The gardens are also open.
☞ adults £1.50, children (5-16) 50p
● 5 Jun, 8 Jun, 12 Jun 2-6.30
Facilities: 🍴 🚻 🚗
🍴 teas served with homemade cakes

🌿 Map 3 B2
Denmans Garden
Clock House, Denmans,
Fontwell, Nr Arundel,
West Sussex BN18 0SU
Tel. Eastergate (024368) 2808

From Chichester follow A27 eastwards, after 5 miles turn right onto unclassified road for ¼ mile to garden. Signposted.

This 3½-acre garden was created by the Robinson family in the 1940s and is now owned by the well-known garden writer John Brookes. It has a remarkable collection of plants and includes a walled herb garden. The Clock House runs courses in garden design while the plant centre and shop sells rare plants, herbs, teas, bouquets garnis and a range of preserves.
☞ adults £1.50, senior citizens £1.40, children 80p
● 29 Mar-Oct Tue-Sun, Bank Hols 10-6
Facilities: 🍴 ♿ 🚻 🚗 🍵
★ 4 Jun, 9 Jul day seminars on the history & uses of herbs
🍴 teashop serves vegetarian lunches by prior arrangement & teas with homemade cakes

---

SUSSEX CRABS
Along the coast you can find fresh crabs and winkles on sale at seaside stalls.

⌘ Map 3 D2
Downers Vineyard
Clappers Lane,
Fulking, Henfield,
West Sussex BN5 9NH
Tel. Poynings (079156) 484

From Shoreham-by-Sea follow A283 northwards, after 3 miles turn right onto A2037 for ½ mile, then turn right onto unclassified road for 2½ miles to Fulking, then turn left into Clappers Lane for ½ mile to vineyard. Signposted.

Visitors to this 7-acre vineyard may follow a trail to see the Müller-Thurgau vines and enjoy magnificent views of the South Downs. The wine can be bought in the shop by the bottle or case.
☞ adults £1.00, accompanied children free
● vineyard: Jun-mid Oct daily 11- dusk; shop: all year daily 11- dusk
Facilities: 🚗

☺ Map 3 E4
Dry Hill Farm
Dormansland, Lingfield,
Surrey RH7 6PD
Tel. Dormans Park (034287) 472

From East Grinstead follow A264 eastwards, after 2½ miles turn left onto unclassified road for 1 mile to farm on right. Signposted.

A pick your own farm offering a wide range of soft fruit, apples — including some early varieties — and mangetout. The shop also sells local honey, Jersey cream, apple juice and ice cream.
● Jun, Jul daily 9-7, Aug-Oct daily 10-5
Facilities: 🚻 🚗 🍵 ⛺

☺ Map 3 E4
Flower Farm
Flower Lane, Godstone,
Surrey RH9 8DE
Tel. Godstone (0883) 843636

From Godstone follow A25 eastwards for 1 mile to farm. Signposted.

A pick your own farm offering the usual soft fruits and vegetables including autumn strawberries, raspberries, mangetout and pumpkins. The shop also sells eggs, cream and ready-picked potatoes and calabrese.
● Jun-Oct daily 9-6
Facilities: 🚗 🍵

MAP 3 **SOUTH EAST ENGLAND**

❧ Map 3 C4
Foliage Scented and Herb Plants
Ranmore Common, Dorking, Surrey RH5 6SX
Tel. East Horsley (04865) 2273/4731

From Dorking follow unclassified road westwards towards East Horsley, after 1 mile turn right by Ranmore Arms Pub into Crocknorth Road to garden.

This herb farm has over 200 varieties of culinary and aromatic herbs all of which can be bought as plants. Visitors may take a guided tour of the garden and learn how the plants are cultivated.

☞ adults £1.00
◑ Apr-Sep daily 10-6, open Bank Hols
Facilities: 🚗

❧ Map 3 C2
Frenchland Herb Farm
Frenchland House, Ashington, West Sussex RH20 3DF
Tel. Ashington (0903) 892476

FRENCHLAND HERB FARM

FRENCHLAND HOUSE
ASHINGTON
PULBOROUGH
SUSSEX RH20 3DF

ASHINGTON (0903) 892476

From Horsham follow A24 southwards for 12 miles to Ashington. Farm difficult to find — please telephone for directions.

This herb farm grows a huge variety of plants and supplies retailers with fresh cut herbs for cooking. Over 50 varieties of herbs are grown, including 9 different types of thyme and 3 of basil. Visitors are welcome to look round the farm.

☞ free
◑ by appointment

😃 Map 3 C5
Garson Farm
Winterdown Road, Esher, Surrey KT10 8LS
Tel. Esher (0372) 64389

From Esher follow A307 south westwards, after ½ mile turn right into Hawkshill Way for ¼ mile, then turn left at Prince of Wales Inn into Winterdown Road for ¼ mile to farm.

Garson Farm has 180 acres of pick your own soft fruits, apples and vegetables. It also grows some more unusual crops including elderflowers, elderberries, whitecurrants and pumpkins. There is a garden centre and a shop sells ice cream, Somerset cheese, apple juice, health foods, jams and biscuits.

◑ mid Jun-mid Aug daily 9-7; mid Aug-mid Jun Mon-Sat 9-5, Sun 10-5
Facilities: 🚾 🚗 ⛱ /🔥

🏠 Map 3 E4
Haxted Watermill and Museum
Haxted Road, Nr Edenbridge, Kent
Tel. Oxted (0883) 722388

From Edenbridge follow unclassified road westwards towards Lingfield for 2 miles to mill. Signposted.

This Elizabethan watermill has 14thC foundations and 16thC

machinery still in everyday use. The mill is now a museum where visitors may listen to a taped historical commentary and view milling and agricultural exhibits including a number of working models.

☞ adults £1.50, senior citizens £1.00, children 75p
◑ Apr-May Sat, Sun, Bank Hols 12-5; Jun-Sep daily 12-5
Facilities: 🍽 🚾 🚗 ⛱ /🔥
🍽 restaurant specialising in fish & seafood serves lunches, teas & dinners

🌷 Map 3 C4
High House Farm
Shere, Nr Guildford, Surrey GU5 9JE
Tel. Shere (048641) 2976

From Guildford follow A25 south eastwards, after 4 miles turn right onto unclassified road for ¼ mile to Shere. Signposted.

High House Farm, as well as being an organic sheep farm, grows organic grain and potatoes. Visitors can see demonstrations of sheep-shearing, spinning and weaving, as well as corn flailing, dressing and milling. Agricultural implements are on display. Guided tours are available around the farm and farm buildings.

☞ adults £2.00, senior citizens & children £1.50
◑ Easter-Oct Sat, Sun, Bank Hols tours at 10, 2 & 4; Wed-Fri by appointment

😃 Map 3 D4
Hillside Farm
Coopers Hill Road, Nutfield, Redhill, Surrey RH1 4HX
Tel. Nutfield Ridge (0737) 822645

From Redhill follow A25 eastwards, after 2 miles turn right at Crown Inn into Coopers Hill Road for ¾ mile to farm on left. Signposted.

MAP 3

A pick your own farm where organic based fertilisers produce a good range of soft fruit and vegetables. The shop also sells marrows, apple juice, cream and ice cream.
◐ Jun-Jul daily 9-8; Aug-Sep daily 9-6
Facilities: 🚗 ♨ ⚠

CHICHESTER PUDDING

1 pint milk
6 eggs separated
3oz sugar
6oz fresh white breadcrumbs
cinnamon

Heat oven to gas 4 (350F, 180C). Heat the milk until warm and pour into the 6 egg yolks beaten with the sugar. Mix well then strain. Blend the breadcrumbs and cinnamon into the custard, beat the egg whites until stiff and then fold into the mixture to give a marbled effect. Pour into a buttered 2 pint dish and stand the dish in a baking tray of hot water. Bake for 30-40 minutes, or until custard is set.

🌿 Map 3 E3
Hoathly Hill Herbs
Hoathly Hill, West Hoathly, West Sussex RH19 4SJ
Tel. Sharpthorne (0342) 810399

From Haywards Heath follow B2028 northwards, after 5 miles turn right onto unclassified road for 2 miles to West Hoathly. Signposted.

This display herb garden is part of a neighbourhood community project which uses organic methods and principles. The garden has over 200 varieties of herbs, all of which are labelled for visitors. Herb plants are sold in 3½-inch and 1 litre pots.
☞ free
◐ 30 Apr-30 Sep Wed, Fri 2-5.30 or by appointment
Facilities: ♿ 🚗

😋 Map 3 D3
Holmbush Farm Shop and Pick Your Own
Crawley Road, Faygate, Horsham, West Sussex RH12 4SE
Tel. Faygate (029383) 674/566

From Crawley follow A264 westwards for 3 miles to farm. Signposted.

A pick your own farm offering soft fruit and vegetables. The shop sells the produce ready-picked and also the farm's own lamb, locally produced meat, game, pies, sausages, frozen fish and cream.
◐ PYO: telephone for details; shop: all year Mon-Sat 9-5
Facilities: 🚗 ♨

🏛 Map 3 D3
Horsham Museum
9 The Causeway, Horsham, West Sussex RH12 1HE
Tel. Horsham (0403) 54959

In town centre.

Horsham Museum, housed in a timber-framed building, is a general museum with exhibits on the domestic and agricultural life of the area. A Victorian kitchen display shows equipment used to prepare food while old farming tools and machinery can be seen in the Sussex Barn. Outside, the museum has a walled garden with herbs and unusual plants.
☞ free
◐ Apr-Sep Tue-Sat 10-5; Oct-Mar Tue-Fri 1-4, Sat 10-5

🐓 Map 3 D5
Horton Park Farm
Horton Lane, Epsom, Surrey
Tel. Epsom (03727) 43984

From Epsom follow B284 northwards, after 1 mile turn left onto unclassified road for ½ mile to farm. Signposted.

Horton Park Farm is open for visitors to look round and see a variety of farm animals including cows, goats, sheep, rabbits, ponies and poultry. A shop sells fresh eggs.
☞ adults £1.10
◐ all year daily 10-6
Facilities: 🍴 ♿ 🚻 🚗 ♨ ⚠

MAP 3 SOUTH EAST ENGLAND

⑤ Map 3 B4
Loseley House
Guildford, Surrey GU3 1HS
Tel. Guildford (0483) 571881

From Guildford follow A3 south westwards, after 1 mile turn left onto B3000 for ½ mile to house on right. Signposted.

Loseley Park Estate covers some 1,400 acres of farms and woodlands. Over 700 Jersey cattle are kept here providing milk and cream for the famous Loseley dairy products. A variety of organic crops are grown for milling and cereal products. Visitors are welcome to follow a farm trail and see the famous Jersey herd as well as many breeds of sheep, pigs, peacocks and poultry. The shop sells the full range of Loseley dairy products including cream, milk, yoghurts, ice creams and gateaux. It also stocks Loseley cereal products such as stoneground wholemeal flour, quiches, bread and biscuits.

☞ farm tour: adults £2.20, children £1.40; farm walk: £1.20
● shop: 30 May-Sep Wed-Sat, Bank Hols 11.30-5; farm tour: Apr- Oct Mon, Sat by appointment
Facilities: ⬛ ⦿ & ⬛ ⊕ ⛨ ⋔
⦿ wholefood lunches & teas served in magnificent 17thC tithe barn include cakes, scones & biscuits made from Loseley products

─────────

☺ Map 3 D4
Meath Green Farm
Horley, Surrey RH6 8H2
Tel. Horley (0293) 773000

From Reigate follow A217 southwards, after 4 miles turn left onto unclassified road for 1 mile to Meath Green.

This pick your own farm offers strawberries, raspberries, broad beans, courgettes, runner beans, sweet corn, mangetout, cherry tomatoes and peppers. The shop sells the produce ready-picked and also a variety of other farm produce including cream and unpasteurised milk.
● all year daily 9-6
Facilities: ⊕ ⛨

─────────

☺ Map 3 C4
Ockley Court Farm
Ockley, Dorking,
Surrey RH5 5LS
Tel. Dorking (0306) 711365/ 711321

From Ockley follow A29 northwards, after ½ mile turn right onto B2126 for ¼ mile to farm on right. Signposted.

There are 50 acres of pick your own crops at Ockley Court with a wide range of fruit and vegetables. The shop also sells local goats' cheese, eggs, cream and apple juice.
● Shop: May, Nov-Feb daily 9-5; Jun-Oct daily 9-8 or dusk; PYO: Jun-Oct daily 9-8 or dusk
Facilities: ⬛ ⊕ ⛨

─────────

🍺 Map 3 D4
Pilgrim Brewery
West Street, Reigate,
Surrey RH2 9BL
Tel. Reigate (0737) 222651

In town centre. Signposted.

The only brewery in Surrey, Pilgrim offers tours and tastings and the chance to relax in their beer room. Beer is for sale in containers from 1 pint up to 3 gallons.
☞ free
● all year by appointment
Facilities: & ⬛ ⊕ ⛨

─────────

🌾 Map 3 E4
The Post Mill
Outwood Common, Nr Bletchingley, Surrey RH1 5PW
Tel. Smallfield (034284) 3458

From Redhill follow A23 southwards, after 3 miles turn left at Salfords onto unclassified road for 3 miles to Outwood. Signposted.

Built in 1665, this is probably one of England's oldest working windmills. Visitors can look round the mill and visit the small museum with its collection of old farm tools. Wholemeal flour is for sale.
☞ adults 60p, children 40p
● Easter-Oct Sun, Bank Hols 2-6
Facilities: & ⬛ ⊕ ⛨

─────────

☺ Map 3 D4
Priory Farm
Nutfield, Redhill,
Surrey RH1 4EJ
Tel. Nutfield Ridge (0737) 822484

From Redhill follow A25 eastwards, after 1½ miles turn right at Nutfield into Mid Street, then right fork into Sandy Lane to farm on right. Signposted.

Beginning with asparagus and rhubarb in May and ending with squashes, pumpkins and apples in October, Priory Farm offers a large selection of fruit and vegetables on a pick your own basis. These include a wide variety of English cherries and blueberries. Produce is also available ready-picked and there are facilities for fishing.
● May, Aug-Oct daily 9-6; Jun-Jul daily 9-8
Facilities: ⬛ ⬛ ⊕ ⛨ ⋔

─────────

🍇 Map 3 E2
Rock Lodge Vineyard
Scaynes Hill,
West Sussex RH17 7NG
Tel. Scaynes Hill (044486) 224

From Haywards Heath follow A272 eastwards for 3 miles to vineyard just beyond Scaynes Hill. Signposted.

Established in 1961 Rock Lodge Vineyard is one of the oldest vineyards in England. Visitors are welcome to follow a trail through 4 acres of Müller-Thurgau vines which produce about 40,000 bottles of wine a year. Wine and cider can be bought from the shop by the bottle or case.

MAP 3

• **Picking apples in the orchard, Wisley**

free — groups only
all year Mon-Sat 9-1, 2-6
Facilities: 🚻 🚗

☺ Map 3 C1
Roundstone and South Ecclesden Farms
Littlehampton Road, Ferring, Worthing, West Sussex BN12 6PW
Tel. Rustington (0903) 770670
From Worthing follow A259 westwards for 4 miles to Ferring.
A very large range of fruit and vegetables is on offer at these pick your own farms. Produce includes apples, rhubarb,

tayberries, broad beans, calabrese, Chinese leaves, mangetout, marrows, onions, pumpkins and spinach.
mid Jun-Sep daily 9-5
Facilities: 🚻 🚗 ⛄

🌿 Map 3 C5
The Royal Horticultural Society's Garden
Wisley, Woking, Surrey GU23 6QB
Tel. Guildford (0483) 224234
From Guildford follow A3 north eastwards, after 6 miles turn left onto unclassified road for ¼ mile to garden on left. Signposted.

These world-famous gardens show every aspect of gardening at its best. They have an extensive fruit collection with over 700 varieties which include many old ones, 100 different varieties of pears, as well as plums, kiwi fruit, peaches and nectarines. The gardens are important for conservation as many of the species are in danger of disappearing and are only found at Wisley. Fruit, and vegetables, are grown on a small scale basis in the model gardens and a range of more unusual examples like Cape

277

• **Part of the model orchard, Wisley**

gooseberries, can be seen here throughout the year. Salad crops, protected by glass, are cultivated during the winter. Visitors can also see the allotment-sized plot and pick up some ideas for their own allotments. The herb garden contains a selection of culinary and medicinal herbs. Fruit and vegetables are on sale from the shop in season.

☞ adults £2.50, children (6-14) & disabled £1.00
◐ all year Mon-Sat 10-sunset
Facilities: ☕ 🍴 ♿ WC 🚗 🧺

Map 3 B4
The Secret Farm Shop and Pick Your Own
Chapel Lane, Milford, Godalming, Surrey GU8 5HU
Tel. Guildford (0483) 426789/426543

From Godalming follow A3100 south westwards for 2 miles to Milford: farm shop on right just before joining A3; for the PYO turn left into Church Road and left again into Station Lane to farm on right.

A wide range of soft fruits and vegetables are available on a pick your own basis including speciality salad crops like oakleaf lettuce, corn salad, little gem and all-year-round spinach. The shop sells these ready-picked and other local produce as well as over 100 different cheeses and the farm's free-range eggs, meat, pâtés, bread and cakes.

◐ PYO: Jun-Sep daily 9-7; shop: all year Mon-Thur 9-5.30, Fri 9-6, Sat 9-4.30
Facilities: WC 🚗 🧺 ⛺

Map 3 D3
Seymours Vineyard
Forest Road, Horsham, West Sussex RH12 4HL
Tel. Horsham (0403) 52397

From Horsham follow A264 north eastwards, after 1 mile turn right onto unclassified road for 2 miles to vineyard on left.

This small 5-acre vineyard and winery is situated on the edge of St Leonard's Forest. It grows Seyval Blanc, Kerner and Schönburger vines trained on the double Guyot system. Visitors may follow the vineyard walk, see the vines and look at experimental varieties being grown under cover in tunnels. A shop sells the wine and also English mustards, chutneys and herbal wine mixes.

☞ adults £1.25, children free
◐ vineyard: Jul-Oct Thur-Sat 10-6; shop: Jul-Oct Thur-Sat 10-6; 1-24 Dec Tue-Sat 10-6
Facilities: WC 🚗

Map 3 D2
Steyning Vineyard
Nash Hotel, Horsham Road, Steyning, West Sussex BN4 3AA
Tel. Steyning (0903) 814988

From Washington follow A283 eastwards, after 3 miles turn left onto B2135 for ½ mile, then turn right onto unclassified road for ¼ mile to farm. Signposted.

Steyning Vineyard has an idyllic setting on the edge of the South Downs. Visitors are welcome to walk among the vines and learn about growing grapes and making wine. The Nash English wine produced here can be tasted at the Nash Hotel. Wine is for sale in the shop by the bottle or case.

☞ free
◐ all year daily 10.30-dusk
Facilities: ♿ WC 🚗 🧺
★ tutored wine tastings — telephone for details

Map 3 C4
Tillingbourne Trout
Albury Mill, Albury, Guildford, Surrey GU5 9AA
Tel. Shere (048641) 2567

MAP 3

From Guildford follow A281 southwards, after 2 miles turn left onto A248 for 2½ miles farm. Signposted.

At this trout farm set in the Surrey hills visitors can watch, feed, catch and buy the fish. The farm has its own smokery and sells a variety of smoked products including salmon, trout — both vacuum packed in slices and as fillets — and smoked trout pâté.

☞ rod £1.50
◑ all year daily 9.15-5.15
Facilities: ⬛ ⬜ 🚗 🍽 🏠

☺ Map 3 D3
Tulleys Farm
Turners Hill, Nr Crawley, West Sussex RH10 4PD
Tel. Copthorne (0342) 715365/ 715856

From East Grinstead follow B2110 south westwards, after 4 miles turn right just after Turner's Hill onto unclassified road for 1½ miles to farm on left. Signposted.

All produce on this farm is grown using only natural organic fertilisers. Visitors can pick most soft fruits and vegetables here including red and blackcurrants, spinach, calabrese, sweet corn and red cabbage.

◑ mid Jun-Aug daily 9.30-8; Sep daily 9.30-6; Oct, Nov Sat, Sun 9.30-6
Facilities: ⬜ 🚗 🍽 🏠

⬛ Map 3 A2
Uppark
South Harting, Petersfield, Hampshire GU31 5QR
Tel. Harting (073085) 317/458

From Petersfield follow B2146 south eastwards, after 5 miles turn left onto unclassified road for ¼ mile to house. Signposted.

Situated high on the South Downs with extensive views to the south coast, Uppark was built in about 1690 and is now owned by the National Trust. Visitors can see Uppark's magnificent Victorian kitchen which was used until 1968. It contains a dresser from the original 17thC kitchen which displays the copper 'batterie de cuisine', an open range, brick-built charcoal-fired warmers and a white marble mortar. The butler's pantry illustrates aspects of his duties like washing, cleaning and polishing the glass and silver and uncorking, decanting and serving the wine. The housekeeper's room is lined with cupboards for the storage of china and linen while the still-room is packed with shelves for storing preserves, pickles, tea, coffee, cakes and biscuits; the large vaulted beer cellar can also be seen.

☞ adults Mon-Sat £2.00, Sun & Bank Hols £2.50
◑ Apr-Sep Wed, Thur, Sun, Bank Hols 2-5.30
Facilities: 🍴 ♿ ⬜ 🚗

● **The kitchen at Uppark**

MAP 4   SOUTH EAST ENGLAND

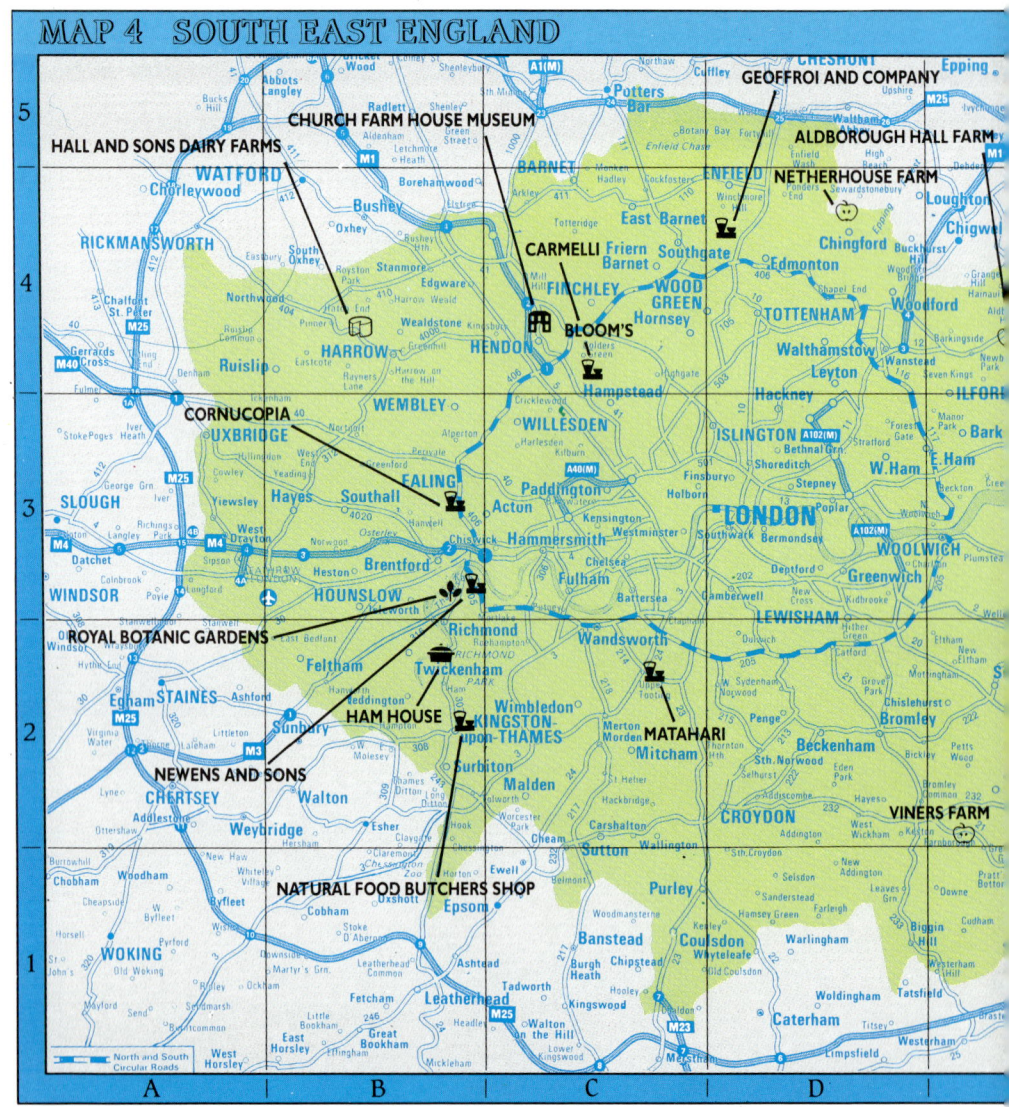

London is a shopper's paradise — there is virtually nothing that you cannot buy. Its inhabitants have settled here from all over the world and the resulting ethnic shops are a joy to visit. Everybody goes to the Food Hall at Harrods at least once in their lives, but how many people have scoured Gerrard and Lisle Streets in the heart of Chinatown, where carp swim in freshwater tanks and won-ton skins nestle next to dim-sum dumplings?

scallops, oysters and a wide selection of fresh fish are available as well as some of the best Scotch smoked salmon in London. The market also sells wines specially chosen to complement the fish.
◗ all year Mon, Sat 9-5, Tue-Fri 9-7
Facilities: 🍽

Albert Wharf Market
Map 4 C3
35 Parkgate Road,
London SW11 4NP
Tel. London (01) 228 8810
For details consult a London street guide.

This fishmarket has 2 boats of its own and contracts a further 14 in Scotland and Cornwall. Specialising in live shellfish, it brings them straight from the coast and keeps them live in seawater tanks until sold. Lobsters, crabs, langoustines,

Aldborough Hall Farm
Map 4 E4
Aldborough Hatch, Ilford,
Essex TG2 7TD
Tel. London (01) 597 6540
For details consult a London street guide.

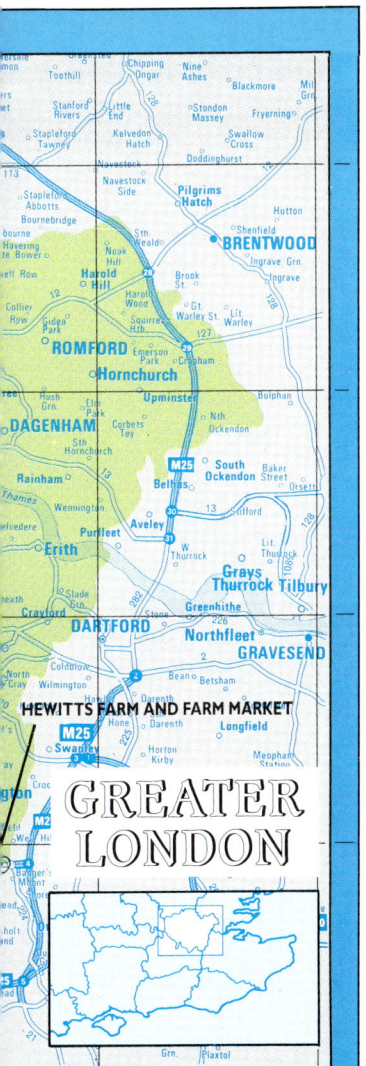

GREATER
LONDON

HEWITTS FARM AND FARM MARKET

F

CENTRAL LONDON LISTINGS

Due to their number, Central London listings are shown below. To locate a listing, please consult a London street guide.

MAP C3

- ALBERT WHARF MARKET
- R ALLEN AND COMPANY
- O BARTHOLDI AND SONS
- BOOKS FOR COOKS
- I CAMISA AND SON
- CHARBONNEL ET WALKER
- THE CHELSEA PHYSIC GARDEN
- KEN CONDON
- THE CURRY SHOP
- ELM FARM
- FORTNUM AND MASON
- FRATELLI CAMISA
- FREIGHTLINERS CITY FARM
- GOLDEN GATE CHINESE SUPERMARKET
- GOLDEN GATE GROCERS
- THE GREEK FOOD CENTRE
- HARRODS FOOD HALLS
- HOBBS AND COMPANY
- JEROBOAMS
- C LIDGATE
- KEN LO'S KITCHEN SHOP
- NEAL'S YARD DAIRY
- NEW COVENT GARDEN MARKET
- PAXTON AND WHITFIELD
- RICHARDS
- THE RITZ
- ROCOCO CHOCOLATES
- THE SCIENCE MUSEUM
- SEE WOO HONG
- SLATER AND COOKE

MAP D3

- BILLINGSGATE MARKET
- F COOKE AND SONS
- THE GEFFRYE MUSEUM
- STEVE HATT
- SMITHFIELD MARKET
- SPITALFIELDS MARKET

---

find it little changed since it opened 130 years ago. There is still sawdust on the floor and traditional wooden chopping blocks behind the counter. Allen's specialise in the finest quality Scotch beef, milk-fed Dutch veal, English lamb, salt beef, sausages and game. They hang all their own meat and cut orders to customers' requirements.

◑ all year Mon-Fri 5-4, Sat 5-1

Map 4 C3
O Bartholdi and Sons
4 Charlotte Street, London W1
Tel. London (01) 636 3762
For details consult a London street guide.

This family business specialising in Swiss food was established in 1928. It now makes over 250 meat products including most types of Swiss sausage. Swiss cheeses, from both the family's own cheese factory and other producers, are imported from Switzerland. The shop also sells biscuits, jams, Swiss chocolates and other delicatessen items.

◑ all year Mon-Fri 9-6

Map 4 D3
Billingsgate Market
West India Dock Road, London E14
Tel. London (01) 515 2655
For details consult a London street guide.

A 152-acre pick your own farm selling a wide range of vegetables and fruits including strawberries and raspberries throughout the season. The shop also sells free-range eggs.

● Sep-May Tue-Sat 9-5, Sun 10-1; Jun-Aug Tue-Sat 9-6, Sun 10-4
Facilities: ▦ 🚗 ⛱

Map 4 C3
R Allen and Company
117 Mount Street, London W1
Tel. London (01) 493 0258
For details consult a London street guide.

This is the oldest retail butcher in London and customers will

Tom, Jerry and Logic tasting Wine in the Wood, at the London Docks.

● **Tasting wine, London Docks**

281

MAP 4 **SOUTH EAST ENGLAND**

About 60 firms trade in Billingsgate, London's wholesale fish market. They sell a good selection of British-caught fish as well as imported fish from as far away as the Seychelles, New Zealand, the Caribbean and the southern USA. Exotic species include fresh tunny, swordfish, bourgeois and vara-vara. Many firms have their own smokeries and sell a variety of smoked fish.

◗ all year Tue-Sat 5.15-8.30

✿ Map 4 C4
Bloom's
130 Golders Green Road,
London NW11
Tel. London (01) 455 1338
For details consult a London street guide.

Opened in 1921 by Morris Bloom, Bloom's is now run by the fourth generation of the family. The licensed restaurant has a take-away bar which specialises in Jewish food such as salt beef sandwiches, potato lutkes and gefilte fish. The original Bloom's is at 90 Whitechapel High Street, London E1.

◗ all year Sun-Thur 9-9.30, Fri 9-3
Facilities: 🍽️ 🍴
🍴 licensed restaurant open all year Mon-Thur 11.30-9.30, Sun 10.30-9.30

✿ Map 4 C3
Books for Cooks
4 Blenheim Crescent,
London W11 1NN
Tel. London (01) 221 1992
For details consult a London street guide.

Books for Cooks is unique. It is the only bookshop in Britain to stock just about every cookery book still in print which has been published within the last 5 years. If they have not got what you want, provided you can

supply the name of the book and the publisher, they can find it for you. With over 4,000 titles published in Britain and overseas and a wide range of food magazines to browse through, visitors cannot fail to find out the latest food news and trends. The shop is well-known as a meeting place for chefs and writers and Heidi Lascelles, the owner, runs demonstrations, informal discussions and offers plenty of advice. There is also a small café run from the demonstration kitchen which often tests and serves recipes from new books in stock.

◗ all year Mon-Sat 9.30-6, closed Bank Hols
Facilities: 🍴 🚻
★ cookery demonstrations by authors, ring for details

✿ Map 4 C3
I Camisa and Son
61 Old Compton Street,
London W1V 5PN
Tel. London (01) 437 7610
For details consult a London street guide.

This family-run Italian grocers has been established for about 8 years. It specialises in freshly-cut cured and cooked meats such as salamis and Parma hams. A wide range of fresh pasta is made daily, including vegetarian tortelloni with spinach, ricotta and parmesan cheese. The shop imports its own brand of olive oil, olives, parmesan and other Italian cheeses. Fresh Piedmontese truffles and dried mushrooms are for sale in season.

◗ all year Mon-Sat 8.30-6

✿ Map 4 C4
Carmelli
128 Golders Green Road,
London NW11
Tel. London (01) 455 2074
For details consult a London street guide.

This Jewish bakery specialises in kosher food. Bagels, croissants, cheesecakes, Danish pastries, strudels, Bourekas and biscuits are baked fresh every day. Bagels filled with smoked salmon are available to take away.

◗ all year Sun-Fri 7-11

✿ Map 4 C3
Charbonnel et Walker
1 Royal Arcade,
28 Old Bond Street,
London W1X 4BT
Tel. London (01) 491 0939
For details consult a London street guide.

This shop was set up in 1875 under the patronage of Edward VII and has been supplying delicious chocolates ever since. The superior handmade chocolates are made in Tunbridge Wells and are supplied to Royal households. Specialities include dark chocolates, strawberry truffles in white chocolate, all kinds of liqueur truffles, Charbonnels, mocha batons, cartridge shaped Cartouches with boiled lemon or mint centres, cracknel, soft fondants, maple brazils and sugared almonds.

◗ all year Mon-Fri 9-5.30, Sat 10-4

❀ Map 4 C3
The Chelsea Physic Garden
66 Royal Hospital Road,
London SW3
Tel. London (01) 352 5646
For details consult a London street guide.

Founded in 1673, the Chelsea Physic Garden is an important centre for the study of horticulture. It includes a herb garden with well labelled culinary and medicinal plants. There are also explanatory leaflets on using the plants. The garden has a number of more unusual fruit trees including

MAP 4

mulberry, quince, medlar and the largest olive tree in England. Herb plants are for sale in the shop.

☞ £1.50, children £1.00
◐ 10 Apr-23 Oct Wed, Sun 2-5, 24-27 May daily 12-5
Facilities: 🍽 ♿ ⚿

🏠 Map 4 C4
Church Farm House Museum
Greyhound Hill, Hendon, London NW4 4JR
Tel. London (01) 203 0130

For details consult a London street guide.

This museum is housed in a mid-17thC Grade II listed building, the oldest of its type in the area. It features a splendid reconstruction of an early 19thC farmhouse kitchen,

● Church Farm House Museum

complete with a huge fireplace, bake oven, spit and chimney crane. The dining room has been furnished in 18thC country style.

☞ free
◐ all year Mon, Wed-Sat 10-1, 2-5.30, Tue 10-1; Sun 1-5.30
Facilities: ⚿ 🚗 ☕

🦞 Map 4 C3
Ken Condon
363 Wandsworth Road, London SW8 2JJ
Tel. London (01) 622 2934

For details consult a London street guide.

This family-run fishmongers and smokery has been established for over 100 years. A wide range of fish is smoked including salmon, haddock, buckling, bloaters, mackerel, sprats and trout. There is also a good selection of shellfish which can be bought boiled or alive. The shop stocks some exotic fish with produce from Asia, the West Indies and the Caribbean. A number of fish kettles are available for customers to borrow free of charge.
◐ all year Mon 9-12, Tue, Wed, Fri 9-5.30, Thur 9-1, Sat 9-4.30

● **An East London eel and pie shop**

🦞 Map 4 D3
F Cooke and Sons
41 Kingsland High Street, London E8 2JS
Tel. London (01) 254 2878

For details consult a London street guide.

This eel pie shop was the first of the Victorian fast food shops and has been run by the same family for 4 generations. The shop sells live and jellied eels, hot eels with mashed potatoes and parsley sauce and freshly baked steak and kidney pies. Customers are welcome to take a short tour of the premises and see where up to 8 tons of live eels are kept in specially adapted tanks.
◐ all year Mon, Thur 10-8, Tue-Wed 10-6, Fri-Sat 10-10, closed Bank Hols, tours by appointment

● **A kitchen of the 1820's at Church Farm House Museum**

MAP 4   **SOUTH EAST ENGLAND**

☕ Map 4 B3
Cornucopia
64 St Mary's Road, Ealing,
London W5 5EX
Tel. London (0I) 579 943I

*For details consult a London
street guide.*

A delicatessen selling a large
selection of wholefoods
including flour, nuts, raisins,
cereals, organic wine and cider
and baby foods. They offer
over I00 continental and British
cheeses such as Devon Garland
and Wedmore — a hard cheese
with a layer of fresh herbs
through the centre. Also
available is their homemade
fresh pasta and ravioli and fresh
yeast for keen bread-makers.
◐ all year Mon-Sat 9-5.30,
closed Bank Hols
Facilities: ♿

☕ Map 4 C3
The Curry Shop
37 The Market,
Covent Garden,
London WC2
Tel. London (0I) 240 5760

*For details consult a London
street guide.*

This shop opened in March
1985 and specialises in Indian,
Thai, Chinese, Middle Eastern
and Malaysian ingredients. It
now stocks over I,000 different
lines of spices, dried
ingredients, cookbooks,
equipment, tableware and
oriental deep-frozen foods.
◐ all year Mon-Sat II-8, Sun I2-
6
Facilities: 🍽
🍽 take-away samosas & other
hot snacks

🌾 Map 4 C3
Elm Farm
Gladstone Terrace, Battersea,
London SW8 3BA
Tel. London (0I) 627 II30

*For details consult a London
street guide.*

Elm Farm is a small working
farm right in the middle of

● **Berwick Street Market, London**

London. It keeps a number of
goats, calves, sheep, chickens,
ducks, rabbits, bees and also
runs a market garden. Visitors
are encouraged to become
involved with the practical side
of food production and allowed
to have a go at milking goats or
making yoghurt. The shop sells
free-range duck and hens' eggs,
yoghurt, goats' and sheep's
milk, vegetables and herbs.
🚗 free
◐ all year Tue-Thur, Sat-Sun
8.30-5
Facilities: 🍽 🍴 ♿ 🚾 🚗
🍴 teas & snacks served Tue-
Thur using fresh produce &
include salads, baked potatoes
& pizzas

☕ Map 4 C3
Fortnum and Mason
I8I Piccadilly, London WI
Tel. London (0I) 734 8040

*For details consult a London
street guide.*

Established in I707 as a small
grocery business, Fortnum and
Mason is now famous all over
the world. Many products are
produced and packaged
exclusively for them. The
provisions department
specialises in cooked meats,
cheeses and smoked fish, while
the bakery sells produce baked
on the premises. The dried
goods section includes exotic
mustards, sauces and relishes

MAP 4

and the famous tea department sells over 30 different teas blended specially for them. They have supplied food hampers since 1851.

◗ all year Mon-Sat 9-5.30
Facilities: 🚍 ⭐

⭐ 3 restaurants: St James on 4th floor serves salads, lunches & afternoon tea at 3pm accompanied by a piano player; The Patio & The Fountain, open 9-midnight, serve light refreshments

---

🏛 Map 4 C3
Fratelli Camisa
1A Berwick Street,
London W1V 3RG
Tel. London (01) 437 7120
For details consult a London street guide.

Established in 1929, this family-run Italian grocers has become a Soho institution. It specialises in Italian and English cheese with over 100 different varieties in stock. Italian specialities include buffalo Mozzarella, fresh goats' cheeses and 3 types of Pecorino — sardo, romano and tuscan. The English selection is no less varied with an unusual smoked Caerphilly, single Gloucester and 14-month-old farmhouse Cheddar from Chewton Mendip in Somerset. Fresh pasta is made daily on the premises and there is a choice of over a dozen different olive oils. Vegetables are imported regularly from southern Italy including sun-dried tomatoes, artichoke hearts, aubergines and wild onions. A speciality is 4-year-old Balsami vinegar which is made from regional wines around Modena in northern Italy and matured in wooden casks. Also branch at 53 Charlotte Street, London W1.

◗ all year Mon-Wed, Fri-Sat 9-6, Thur 9-2

🌱 Map 4 C3
Freightliners City Farm
Sheringham Road, London N7
Tel. London (01) 609 0467
For details consult a London street guide.

This is a working city farm with a wide variety of farm animals kept in 2½ acres of yards, paddocks and a small field. Animals include goats, cows, sheep, a pig, a pony, ducks, geese and chickens. Visitors are welcome to look around and join in farm activities such as milking, feeding, mucking out and gardening. The shop sells goats' milk and yoghurt, free-range chicken and duck eggs and sometimes also stocks herb plants and meat.

🅿 free
◗ all year Tue-Sun 11-1, 2-5
Facilities: 🚾 ♿ 🅿

🏨 Map 4 D3
The Geffrye Museum
Kingsland Road,
London E2 8EA
Tel. London (01) 739 8368
For details consult a London street guide.

This museum is housed in an interesting building originally constructed as almshouses by the Worshipful Company of Ironmongers in the 17thC. Its collections specialise in urban domestic life and interior design from 1600 to 1940. Exhibits are arranged in a series

● **An open-hearth kitchen of the type used in the 18th and 19th centuries**

MAP 4   SOUTH EAST ENGLAND

of room settings and include a kitchen interior.

☞ free

◗ all year Tue-Sat 10-5, Sun 2-5
Facilities: 🍽️ 🆆🅲 🚻 🍵 /🚹\

🏪 Map 4 D4
Geoffroi and Company
65 Station Road,
Winchmore Hill,
London N21 3NB
Tel. London (01) 360 8289
For details consult a London street guide.

Geoffroi's husband and wife team makes delicious handmade quality chocolates. Fresh cream truffles are their speciality. These are made from natural ingredients and flavoured with real liqueurs like Amaretto, Benedictine, Brandy, Cointreau, Kirsch and Grand Marnier. The shop also sells a range of gourmet preserves, jellies, chutneys, sauces, nuts, and a selection of quality teas and fresh ground coffees. Truffle cake is made to order.
◗ all year Tue-Fri 10.30-7, Sat 10-5
Facilities: 🆆🅲

🏪 Map 4 C3
Golden Gate Chinese Supermarket
14 Lisle Street, London WC2
Tel. London (01) 437 0014
For details consult a London street guide.

This Chinese supermarket in the centre of Chinatown serves virtually every imaginable exotic food. Its stock includes not just general Chinese foodstuffs but Malaysian, Thai, and Singaporean produce as well. It keeps live lobsters and crabs and stocks fresh bean curd, Chinese pork sausages and bean sprouts. It also sells fresh herbs such as lemon grass, pandang and lime leaves, galanga and chillis, as well as a number of Chinese health products such as Royal Jelly and
286

Ginseng. The shop has a selection of frozen dim-sum and fresh dumplings and won-tons are made each day.
◗ all year daily 9-9

🏪 Map 4 C3
Golden Gate Grocers
16 Newport Place,
London WC2
Tel. London (01) 437 6266
For details consult a London street guide.
A sister shop to the Golden Gate Supermarket this branch sells exotic vegetables and fruit from the Far East. Produce includes lychees, mangosteens, Japanese pears, rambutans and persimmons.
◗ all year daily 10-8

🏪 Map 4 C3
The Greek Food Centre
12 Inverness Street,
London NW1
Tel. London (01) 485 6544
For details consult a London street guide.
Family-owned and run for 36 years, this shop sells all kinds of Mediterranean food including Egyptian, Cypriot and Lebanese, as well as Greek. It has an excellent range of olives and olive oil and a wide variety of dried pulses, burghul, couscous, pastas, herbs and spices. It also sells fresh salads, taramasalata and spices.
◗ all year Mon-Sat 9.30-5.30

🏠 Map 4 B4
Hall and Sons Dairy Farms
Pinner Park Farm,
George V Avenue, Pinner,
Middlesex HA5 4SU
Tel. London (01) 863 1075
For details consult a London street guide.
Established in 1857, this is the largest farm in London with 200 acres supporting 400 head of dairy cattle. It has its own circular milking parlour, a dairy

and a creamery. The farm specialises in making ethnic Indian products such as 'mawa' which is used in Indian sweets, shrikand, channa and paneer. Visitors may buy these products as well as goats' milk yoghurt.
☞ free
◗ all year Mon-Sat 9-1
Facilities: 🆆🅲 🚚

● **Lemonade, half-penny a glass, Ludgate Hill**

🍲 Map 4 B2
Ham House
Ham, Richmond,
Surrey TW10 7RS
Tel. London (01) 940 1950
For details consult a London street guide.
Administered by the Victoria and Albert Museum, Ham House has been totally restored to its 17thC splendour. Visitors may take a tour of the kitchens which include a working spit jack and a larder with reproduction period food. The grounds feature an 18thC dairy with original fittings and a restored 19thC icehouse. The orchard has been planted with 17thC varieties of pears, apples, figs and plums while the restored 17thC formal garden includes herbs and grape vines. The National Trust shop sells jams, chutneys, chocolates and English teas.

MAP 4

☞ adults £1.80, senior citizens & children (under 16) 90p
◐ all year Tue-Sun, Bank Hols 11-5
Facilities: ⬛ ⦿ ⚬ 🚻 🚗 ☺
⦿ homemade snacks, light lunches & cream teas served in the Orangery

---

🔋 Map 4 C3
Harrods Food Halls
Knightsbridge, London SW1
Tel. London (01) 730 1234
For details consult a London street guide.

The small grocers shop which started in 1849 is now one of the major attractions in Harrods. Six food halls sell an enormous range of produce — the Charcuterie Hall alone has over 500 varieties of cheeses. Much of the produce is from small British producers and all is carefully chosen for the highest quality. There is also a wide selection of exotic foods; for example the Traiteur department sells Japanese sushi and Middle Eastern and Greek specialities.
◐ all year Mon-Tue, Thur-Sat 9-6, Wed 9.30-7

🔋 Map 4 D3
Steve Hatt
88-90 Essex Road, Islington, London N1 8LU
Tel. London (01) 226 3963
For details consult a London street guide.

This well-known traditional fishmonger, catering for both wholesale and retail customers, is now run by the third generation of the Hatt family. It has a very fast turnover and all its produce is guaranteed fresh. It has 2 of the biggest traditional smokehouses in London and is renowned for its smoked haddock, trout and mackerel. All types of wet fish from all over the world are on sale and, whenever possible,

are fresh rather than frozen. Specialities include Beluga caviar, whole turbot and jumbo halibut. A particular feature is the individual handwritten labels which are written daily with descriptions of the fish and their origins.
◐ all year Tue, Wed, Fri 7.30-5, Thur 7.30-1, Sat 7.30-5.30

☺ Map 4 E1
Hewitts Farm and Farm Market
Chelsfield, Orpington, Kent BR6 7QR
Tel. Knockholt (0959) 34271
From Orpington follow A224 southwards, after 2½ miles turn left to farm. Signposted.

This well-established and popular pick your own farm grows 45 different crops. These include apples, 30 varieties of pumpkins, 6 varieties of plums, quinces, kohlrabi, radicchio and squash. Hewitts also presses its own apple juice from the 41 varieties of apples grown and visitors are welcome to taste the result. They can also fish in the large lake which is well stocked with trout. For children there are plenty of other attractions including farm animals, helicopter rides and the crops express railway. The shop sells ready-picked produce as well as English wines, cider, juices, jams and other preserves, dairy produce, health foods and frozen foods.
☞ rod £2.00 per ½ hour, fish caught 75p each
◐ PYO: May-early Nov daily 9-6; shop: end May-early Nov daily 9-7.30; mid Nov-mid May daily 9-6
Facilities: ⬛ ⦿ 🚻 🚗 ☺
★ Oct apple festival with tasting of first juice of season, potato time with cookery demonstrations & baked potato ovens with 15 varieties of potato
⦿ teas served

🔋 Map 4 C3
Hobbs and Company
29 South Audley Street, London W1
Tel. London (01) 409 1058
For details consult a London street guide.

This popular delicatessan sells a range of homemade vegetarian products such as quiches — made from free-range eggs and wholemeal pastry — and at least 10 different salads a day. Cheese is imported directly from France and there is also a good range of farmhouse goats' cheese, both French and English. Customers can choose from a wide range of cured and cooked meats including Bressola and Italian and French salamis, Scotch smoked salmon, gravadlax and Beluga caviar. Fruit and vegetables are delivered twice a week from France and, in season, the shop also sells fresh truffles from Italy and France.
◐ all year Mon-Fri 9-7, Sat 9-5.30

🔋 Map 4 C3
Jeroboams
24 Bute Street, London SW7 3EX
Tel. London (01) 225 2232
For details consult a London street guide.

Managed by Juliet Harbutt, this is a small but very well stocked cheese and — as its name implies — wine shop. They specialise in unpasteurised cheeses both from France and Britain. Many of their French cheeses are supplied by M. Androuet of Paris and their farmhouse British cheeses are personally chosen by Juliet. They also sell olives, butter, clotted cream and, on Fridays and Saturdays, 'Pain Poilane' flown over specially from Paris.
◐ all year Mon-Fri 9-7, Sat 9-6
Facilities: ⚬
★ tutored wine & cheese tastings by appointment

287

MAP 4　　　**SOUTH EAST ENGLAND**

Map 4 C3
C Lidgate
110 Holland Park Avenue,
London W11 4UA
Tel. London (01) 727 8243
*For details consult a London
street guide.*
Founded in 1850 and still run by
the Lidgate family, this specialist
food shop stocks a wide range
of naturally reared, additive-
free meat and free-range
poultry. It also produces its own
homemade sausages, pies,
pâtés, sausage rolls, quiches,
raw milk cheeses and take-
away items.
● all year Mon-Fri 7-6, Sat 7-5,
closed Bank Hols
Facilities: ☕

Map 4 C3
Ken Lo's Kitchen Shop
14 Eccleston Street,
London SW1
Tel. London (01) 730 7734
*For details consult a London
street guide.*
This small shop is named after
the well-known Chinese cook
and writer, Ken Lo, and is just
round the corner from his
famous restaurant. The shop is
packed full of oriental
ingredients from China and
other eastern countries. There
is an excellent range of dried
and fresh herbs like coriander
and lemon grass, spices, sauces
and a selection of frozen
delicacies such as dim-sum, fish
balls, pancakes and fresh tofu. A
range of Chinese cooking
utensils and equipment is also
stocked.
● all year Mon-Sat 9.30-5

Map 4 C2
Matahari
328 Balham High Road,
London SW17 9RR
Tel. London (01) 767 3107
*For details consult a London
street guide.*

The Tooting branch was the
first in this chain of 4 shops
specialising in oriental
provisions. All the shops have a
comprehensive range of
oriental spices, several different
types of bean curd and a large
range of frozen sea food. Exotic
fruit, herbs and fresh
vegetables, like winter melons
and pea aubergines, are flown
in each Friday. The staff are
happy to advise customers on
cooking methods. Branches at
11-12 Hogarth Place, London
SW5, 102 Westbourne Grove,
London W2 and 8 Shrubbery
Road, London SW16.
● all year daily 10-8

Map 4 B2
**Natural Food Butchers
Shop**
90 Elm Road, Norbiton,
Kingston, Surrey KT2 6HU
Tel. London (01) 546 1556
*For details consult a London
street guide.*
Refurbished in the style of a
traditional butcher's shop with
old wooden counters and
sawdust on the floor, this
establishment sells a variety of
products supplied by the Real
Meat Company in Wiltshire. All
the meat is free from additives
or artificial substances and
comes from animals kept in a
natural environment in
compliance with the Animal
Welfare Code. Products include
most cuts of meat, poultry and
game as well as handmade
sausages in natural skins, pâtés,
pies, free-range eggs, chutneys,
mustards and jellies.
● all year Mon, Tue, Thur-Sat
9-5, Wed 9-12
Facilities: ▧

Map 4 C3
Neal's Yard Dairy
9 Neal's Yard,
London WC2H 9DD
Tel. London (01) 379 7646

*For details consult a London
street guide.*
Neal's Yard Dairy buys cheeses
direct from farms all over the
UK and Ireland and matures
them on the premises. They list
57 cheeses and usually have 30
to 40 varieties in stock
depending on the time of year.
The selection includes many
unusual cheeses not often seen
outside the area where they
were made, for example
Molland, Coleford Blue,
Llangloffan, Coolea and
Swaledale. The shop also sells
other dairy products such as
yoghurts, free-range Maran,
bantam and duck eggs and a
selection of butters.
● all year Mon-Wed 10-5.30,
Thur, Fri 10-6, Sat 10-5

Map 4 D4
Netherhouse Farm
Sewardstone Road, Chingford,
Essex E4 7RJ
Tel. London (01) 524 7217
*For details consult a London
street guide.*
This pick your own farm within
London offers soft fruit and a
few vegetables. The shop also
sells ready-picked vegetables,
local eggs, goats' cheese and
jam.
● end Jun-end Jul Tue-Fri 10-8,
Sat, Sun 9-5; Aug-end Sep Tue-
Fri 10-5, Sat, Sun 9-5
Facilities: ▧ 🚗 ♨

Map 4 C3
**New Covent Garden
Market**
Nine Elms Lane, London SW8
Tel. London (01) 720 2211
*For details consult a London
street guide.*
Covent Garden Market moved
across the river to this purpose-
built 60-acre site in 1974. It is
Britain's leading fruit, vegetable
and flower market with over

MAP 4

200 tenants and 3,000 employees. The range of produce is impressive — probably the best in Europe — with about 70% being imported.

◐ all year Mon-Fri 4-11; flowers only: Sat 4-9

Map 4 B3
Newens and Sons
288-290 Kew Road,
Kew Gardens, Richmond,
Surrey TW9 3DU
Tel. London (01) 940 2752

For details consult a London street guide.

This shop, which has been run by the same family since 1760, sells Maids of Honour cakes, still made to the original recipe. The cakes were first made for Henry VIII in the Palace at Richmond.

◐ all year Tue-Sat 10-6, Mon 9.30-1
Facilities: 🍽️ 👤 🚻

Map 4 C3
Paxton and Whitfield
93 Jermyn Street,
London SW1Y 6JE
Tel. London (01) 930 0250

For details consult a London street guide.

Established in 1797 this old-fashioned shop is now known the world over. It sells over 300 varieties of cheeses, specialising in farmhouse British cheeses. Customers are encouraged to taste before buying and the staff are on hand to give expert service and advice. Pies, pâtés, chutneys, exotic teas and coffees, biscuits and fruits are also sold. A specially chosen range of wines and ports is available to complement the cheeses.

◐ all year Mon-Fri 8.30-6, Sat 9-4, closed Bank Hol weekends
Facilities: 🚻

Map 4 C3
Richards
11 Brewer Street,
London W1R 3FL
Tel. London (01) 437 1358

For details consult a London street guide.

This fishmonger in the centre of Soho is one of London's most highly regarded fish shops. Well known for its huge variety of fresh fish it claims to sell anything that swims. The shop specialises in British-caught fish but also has a good selection of foreign fish such as sardines, tunny and snapper; samphire is on sale from May to September. There is an enormous variety of fresh shellfish including 6 varieties of prawns, oysters, venus clams, vongole, langoustines, cuttlefish and cockles in their shells. Smoked fish, both dyed and undyed, is also available.

◐ all year Tue-Thur 8-5, Fri 8-5.30, Sat 8-3

● **Paxton and Whitfield sell a vast range of English and continental cheeses**

MAP 4   SOUTH EAST ENGLAND

RESTAURANT RECIPE

♟ Map 4 C3

THE RITZ

Piccadilly, London W1V 9D6
Tel: London (01) 493 8181

For details consult a London street guide.

One of the most beautiful dining rooms in Europe, decorated in gilt and marble. First class ingredients are used in this historic hotel, with simple dishes such as Steak, Kidney and Oyster Pudding, cooked superbly.

● Mon-Sun Meals: 7.30-10.30, 12.30-2.30, 6.30-11
Price range £10-40 Set D £38.50
Seats 120
Cards: Access, Amex, Diners, Visa
Facilities: ♟

STEAK, KIDNEY AND OYSTER PUDDING

filling:
2lb chuck steak
1lb ox kidney
4oz onions chopped
3oz butter
1 pint beef consomme
¼ pint red wine
8oz mushrooms thickly sliced
1 bouquet garni
18 oysters
suet paste:
10oz self-raising flour
1 tsp baking powder
½ tsp salt
white pepper
¼ tsp thyme chopped
¼ tsp parsley chopped
5oz suet
water

Dice the steak, removing all the sinew and fat and seal in butter in a hot pan. Dice the ox kidney and blanch in boiling salted water, remove and allow to cool. Place all the ingredients for the filling, except the oysters, in a bowl to marinade overnight. Mix all the paste ingredients together well, except the water. Add the water slowly until the paste binds lightly together and then roll out without breaking. Butter a large pudding basin, line with the prepared paste, leaving ¼ of the paste to one side for the top. Fill with the marinaded pudding filling and add the oysters. Cover with the remaining paste. Cover with buttered paper and a double layer of muslin cloth and tie securely. Steam for 4-5 hours.

🍫 Map 4 C3
Rococo Chocolates
321 King's Road,
London SW3 5EA
Tel. London (01) 352 5857

For details consult a London street guide.

This little shop specialises in handmade English chocolates made from natural ingredients with no artificial colouring or additives. There are 3 ranges of chocolates: fresh cream truffles, the Swiss selection and English chocolates. Novelty chocolates are available at Christmas, Easter and for Valentine's Day.
● all year Mon-Sat 10-6.30

🌿 Map 4 B3
Royal Botanic Gardens
Kew, Richmond,
Surrey TW9 3AB
Tel. London (01) 940 1171

For details consult a London street guide.

● **Royal Botanic Gardens, Kew**

MAP 4

Amongst its many treasures Kew has a 17thC herb garden incorporating a vegetable area. Throughout the gardens visitors can see various tropical food plants growing in their natural habitats. These include banana, coconut, rice, cocoa, tea and coffee plants. A collection of old agricultural implements is on display in the basement of the Temperate House.

☞ adults 50p, children (under 10) free
◗ Apr-Oct Mon-Sat 9.30-6.30, Sun 9.30-8; Nov-Mar daily 9.30-4
Facilities: ♨ ⦿ & wc ⛲

🏛 Map 4 C3
The Science Museum
Exhibition Road,
South Kensington,
London SW7 2DD
Tel. London (01) 589 3456
For details consult a London street guide.

The Agricultural Gallery of the Science Museum provides a fascinating insight into agricultural methods of the past and present. Two displays show the contrast between old and new agricultural methods. There is a collection of old farm tools and machinery showing how the land was tilled and harvested 500 years ago. A combine harvester shows how reaping and threshing are done today.

☞ free
◗ Mon-Sat 10-6 Sun 2.30-6, closed May Bank Hol
Facilities: ♨ ⦿ & wc

🐀 Map 4 C3
See Woo Hong
18-20 Lisle Street,
London WC2H 7BE
Tel. London (01) 439 8325
For details consult a London street guide.

One of the largest Chinese supermarkets in London, See Woo Hong has been here in the centre of Chinatown for about 100 years. It stocks over 10,000 different items from rice and dim-sum to hair moss and dried scallops. There is an excellent selection of fresh fruit and vegetables including Pak Choi and Kai Lan which are similar to broccoli. Malay, Thai and Indonesian ingredients are also stocked and there are often new products for tasting.
◗ all year daily 10-9

🐀 Map 4 C3
Slater and Cooke
65-69 Brewer Street,
London W1R 3FB
Tel. London (01) 437 2026
For details consult a London street guide.

This butcher has a large range of sausages all made by hand on the premises. Popular varieties include Toulouse sausage with garlic and spices, Britannia sausage with pork, Park Lane with spices and Algerian merguez with lamb. The shop also sells all kinds of meat, venison and game in season, free-range poultry, haggis and hamburgers.
◗ all year Mon-Fri 7-5, Sat 7-3

🐀 Map 4 D3
Smithfield Market
West Smithfield,
London EC1 9AA
Tel. London (01) 236 8734
For details consult a London street guide.

There has been a meat market here for 1,000 years. The name Smithfield originated from Smoothfield as the market was situated on the first smooth piece of ground beyond the City walls. About 60 firms trade here and, on average, over

420,000lb of meat and poultry are sold each week. The market consists of 4 main buildings: the Victorian East and West Markets, the Poultry Market where game is also sold and the General Market which sells cooked meats, bacon and delicatessen items.
◗ all year Mon-Fri 5-12

🐀 Map 4 D3
Spitalfields Market
65 Brushfield Street,
London E1 6AA
Tel. London (01) 247 7331
For details consult a London street guide.

There has been a fruit and vegetable market in this area for over 600 years and Spitalfields itself was established in the early 17thC.
◗ all year Mon-Sat 4-11

😋 Map 4 E2
Viners Farm
High Street, Farnborough, Orpington, Kent BR6 7BU
Tel. Farnborough (0689) 57547
In village.

This pick your own farm offers a wide range of fruit and vegetables including mangetout, various apples and 3 types of strawberry. The shop also sells local honey, cream and free-range eggs.
◗ PYO: mid Jun-Sep daily 9-6.30; Jul-Aug daily 9-7.30; shop: all year daily 9-5.30
Facilities: ♨ wc 🚗 ⛲ 🏧

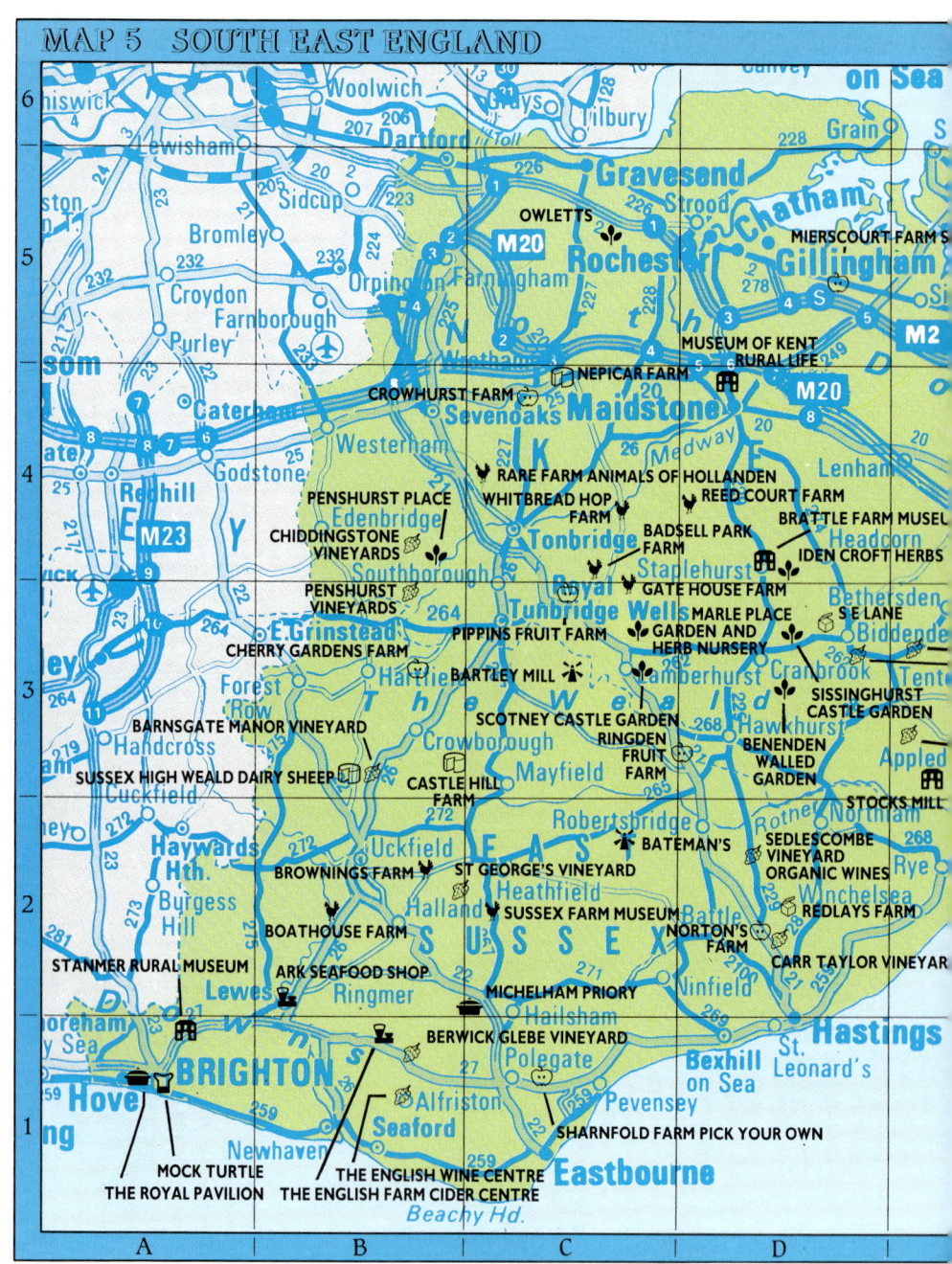

MAP 5 SOUTH EAST ENGLAND

Kent, known as the 'Garden of England', is famous for its cherries, hops and apples. It is studded with Pick Your Own farms, and many of these grow old fashioned apple trees offering varieties which are not usually for sale. Try St Edmund's Pippin — a golden russet with a taste of pears; Worcester Permain — famous for its brilliant red colour and strong strawberry taste; and Miller's Seedling — a Kentish apple with a sweet, light taste.

🦞 Map 5 B2

Ark Seafood Shop

51-52 Cliffe High Street, Lewes,
East Sussex BN7 2AN
Tel. Lewes (0273) 476912

In town centre.

A high quality fish and seafood shop stocking a wide range of fresh and frozen fish and

MES ESTUARY

Leysdown Herne Bay Birchington Margate Nth. Foreland
2231
Whitstable
OUR OAKS
PICK YOUR OWN
BRAMBLES ENGLISH WILDLIFE Sarre Broadstairs
Faversham THEOBOLDS BARN CIDER
Sturry Ramsgate
Stour
ST NICHOLAS OF ASH VINEYARD AND WINERY
Canterbury FIVE ACRES NURSERY
WHITE MILL FOLK MUSEUM
Wingham Sandwich
THREE CORNERS VINEYARD
Chilham Eastry
BADGERS HILL FARM SHOP STAPLE VINEYARD Deal
Barham Walmer
WYE COLLEGE AGRICULTURAL MUSEUM SUTTON COURT FARM
ELHAM VALLEY VINEYARDS
STELLING MINNIS WINDMILL Sth. Foreland
Hawkinge
SWANTON MILL Dover
Smee ROWLAND CONFECTIONERY
M20 Folkestone
Lympne Hythe HARBOURNE VINEYARD
Hamstreet BIDDENDEN VINEYARDS
Dymchurch WOODCHURCH WINDMILL
TENTERDEN VINEYARDS
New Romney
Lydd
Dungeness

EAST SUSSEX & KENT

F   G   H   I

---

shellfish. Particular specialities include home-smoked undyed cod, haddock, trout and homemade crab and smoked salmon pâtés. The shop also sells wines specially selected to complement fish, including its own label Ark Wine.

◑ all year Mon 8.30-12, 2-5, Tue-Sat 8.30-5, closed Bank Hols

🕐 Map 5 F4
Badgers Hill Farm Shop
Chilham, Canterbury,
Kent CT4 8BW
Tel. Canterbury (0227) 730573

In village. Signposted.

This pick your own farm offers a wide range of produce including 15 varieties of apples. The farm also makes its own

cider and visitors are welcome to look at the presses and other equipment. Its speciality is Pippin Cider made from Cox's apples. There is a collection of rare breed chickens and the shop sells their free-range eggs as well as locally made jams and honeys.

◑ all year Mon-Sat 9-6, Sun 10-6
Facilities: 🚐

293

MAP 5 SOUTH EAST ENGLAND

🍋 Map 5 C4
Badsell Park Farm
Crittenden Road, Matfield,
Tonbridge, Kent TN12 7EW
Tel. Paddock Wood (089283)
2549

*From Tunbridge Wells follow
A264 north eastwards, after 1
mile join B2015 for 3 miles, then
turn right into Crittenden Road
for ½ mile to farm. Signposted.*

The farmhouse on the 180-acre
Badsell Park estate dates back
to 1712 and was originally a
hunting lodge for the Earl of
Westmorland. After a period as
an iron foundry it was a hop
farm before becoming the
cereal and fruit farm it is today.
The farm has a number of trails,
an animal park and organises
tractor rides. A wide selection
of fruit is grown including pears,
tayberries, blackberries,
raspberries, strawberries and 7
varieties of apple. Other crops
are barley and sweet corn. The
shop also sells organic
vegetables, chutney, free-range
eggs, cider, cream, homemade
cakes, jam, fudge and honey.
The farm also offers pick your
own fruit and vegetables

● **Apple picking, Chilham,
Kent**

including Russet apples and late
strawberries.

☞ animal park: adults £1.20,
senior citizens & children
(under 16) 80p
● animal park: May-Nov daily
9-6; PYO: Jul-Sep daily 9-6
Facilities: ⦿ ⛛ ♿ wc 🚗 🛋 ⚲

🍷 Map 5 B3
Barnsgate Manor Vineyard
Herons Ghyll, Uckfield,
East Sussex TN22 4DB
Tel. Nutley (082571) 2854

*From Crowborough follow A26
southwards for 3 miles to Herons
Ghyll. Signposted.*

Set on the edge of Ashdown
Forest, this 22-acre vineyard is
run by the Pieroth family of
Bingen, West Germany — a
family with over 270 years of
experience in growing vines.
Visitors may tour the grounds
and buy both the vineyard's
own produce and a variety of
other wines from the shop.

☞ free
● all year daily 10-4, tours by
appointment
Facilities: wc 🚗 ⚲

🌿 Map 5 C3
Bartley Mill
Bells Yew Green, Nr Frant,
East Sussex TN3 8BH
Tel. Lamberhurst (0892) 890372

*From Tunbridge Wells follow
B2169 south eastwards, after 3
miles take the second right after
Bells Yew Green onto unclassified
road for ½ mile to mill on right.
Signposted.*

This farm has a variety of
attractions including a working
mill, trout lakes, a craft
workshop and a farm trail.
Visitors are welcome to explore
all these and may also buy flour
and organic farm produce in
the shop.

☞ adults £1.00, senior citizens
20p, children 50p
● all year daily 10-6
Facilities: 🍴 ⦿ wc 🚗 ⚲

🌿 Map 5 C2
Bateman's
Burwash, East Sussex
Tel. Burwash (0435) 882302

*From Heathfield follow A265
north eastwards, after 5½ miles
turn right onto unclassified road
for ½ mile to house on right.
Signposted.*

Formerly the home of the
author Rudyard Kipling
between 1902 and 1936 — and
where he wrote many of his
best known books and poems.
Visitors to this country house
are welcome to wander
through the herb garden and
see the working watermill in
the grounds. Flour milled there
is for sale.

☞ adults £2.30, children £1.20;
weekends & Bank Hols: adults
£2.60, children £1.30
● Apr-Oct Sat-Wed 11-6
Facilities: 🍴 ⦿ wc 🚗 ⚲

🌿 Map 5 D3
Benenden Walled Garden
Benenden, Cranbrook,
Kent TN17 4AE
Tel. Cranbrook (0580) 24079

*From Cranbrook follow A229
northwards, after 1 mile turn
right onto A262 for ½ mile then
turn right at Sissinghurst onto
unclassified road for 2 miles to
garden on right in grounds of
Benenden School. Signposted.*

This walled garden contains
over 2,000 varieties of culinary
herbs, gourmet vegetables and
oriental food plants. There is
also a large display of
ornamental, fragrant and
medicinal herbs. The shop sells
all the herbs and vegetables in
retail packs.

☞ adults £1.00, senior citizens
& disabled 75p, children free
● 25 Mar-19 Apr, 28 May-1 Jun,
10 Jul-13 Sep, 29 Oct-6 Nov daily
10-dusk, or by appointment
Facilities: 🍴 ⦿ ♿ wc 🚗 ⚲ 🛋

MAP 5

🍴 homemade cakes including speciality cider cake, scones, honey & jams served in tea room

---

🍷 **Map 5 B1**
Berwick Glebe Vineyard
Frensham Cottage, Berwick, East Sussex BN26 6SP
Tel. Alfriston (0323) 870361

From Alfriston follow unclassified road northwards, after 1½ miles turn left onto A27 for 200 yards, then turn right to vineyard.

This small 2-acre vineyard, situated at the foot of the South Downs, 90 feet above sea level, grows Reichensteiner and Müller-Thurgau vines on the double Guyot system. Visitors are welcome to tour the vineyard and taste the 2 quality wines produced here: Berwick Glebe, a dry white wine, and Alfriston Glebe, a medium dry wine made from 100% Müller-Thurgau grapes. Both of these are sold from the shop either by the bottle or case.

🎫 free
⬤ all year daily 11-6
Facilities: 🚗

🍷 **Map 5 D3**
Biddenden Vineyards
Little Whatmans, Biddenden, Ashford, Kent TN27 8DH
Tel. Cranbrook (0580) 291726

From Biddenden follow A262 southwards, after 1 mile turn right onto unclassified road for 1 mile, then turn left onto unclassified road for ½ mile to vineyard. Signposted.

Founded in 1969, this 18-acre vineyard is near the picturesque village of Biddenden and produces a number of interesting wines. The main types are Müller-Thurgau, Reichensteiner, Huxelrebe and Ortega, plus a rosé. It also makes cider and a speciality blend known as Monk's Delight, a mix of cider, honey and spices. Visitors may walk in the vineyards, see the winery and cider press and enjoy a free tasting. The shop sells the wines, cider and also homemade preserves.

🎫 free
⬤ May-Oct Mon-Fri 9-5, Sat 11-5, Sun 12-5; Nov-Apr Mon-Fri 9-5, Sat 11-2, Bank Hols 11-2
Facilities: 🍽 🚻 🚗 ♿

🐄 **Map 5 B2**
Boathouse Farm
Isfield, Nr Uckfield, East Sussex TN22 5TY
Tel. Isfield (082575) 302

From Lewes follow A26 northwards, after 5 miles turn left onto unclassified road for ½ mile to farm on right. Signposted.

This 220-acre organic farm using no pesticides, herbicides or artificial fertilizers, is virtually self-sufficient. It is a mixed farm with beef cattle, sheep, hens and 100 acres of arable land.

Twenty tonnes of potatoes are grown annually and all the feed for the animals is grown on the farm. Visitors may ramble on farm walks and see the flour mill in operation. The shop sells large freezer packs of lamb and beef, free-range eggs, potatoes, and stoneground organic flour.

🎫 free, tours 50p
⬤ all year daily 9-5, tours by appointment
Facilities: 🚗 ♿

● **Berwick Glebe Vineyard**

MAP 5   **SOUTH EAST ENGLAND**

Map 5 F5
Brambles English Wildlife
Wealden Forest, Herne
Common, Nr Canterbury, Kent
Tel. Canterbury (0227) 712379

*From Herne Bay follow A291
southwards for 2½ miles to
Herne Common. Signposted.*

Set in 20 acres of natural
woodland, this wildlife park
contains deer, owls, foxes and
rare breeds of farm animals.
Visitors can follow the nature
trail and also explore the large
walk-in rabbit enclosure. A
shop sells honey and gifts.

adults £1.50, children 75p
Easter-Oct daily 10-5
Facilities:

Map 5 D4
Brattle Farm Museum
Brattle Farm, Staplehurst,
Kent TN12 0HE
Tel. Staplehurst (0580) 891222

In village. Signposted.

This museum of agricultural
and domestic bygones is the
personal collection of farmer
Brian Thompson and his wife,
historian Anita. Housed in
Brattle Farm's old cow sheds
and oast house the exhibits are
divided into a number of
sections to cover all aspects of
rural life over the past 200
years.

● **An end-over-end butter churn**

adults £1.00, senior citizens
& children 50p
Easter-Oct Sun, Bank Hols
9.30-6.30
Facilities:

Map 5 B2
Brownings Farm
Blackboys, Uckfield,
East Sussex TN22 5HG
Tel. Framfield (082582) 338

*From Uckfield follow B2102
eastwards for 3 miles to
Blackboys. Signposted.*

This 100-acre beef and arable
farm on the edge of the High
Weald has a 1¼-mile farm trail
starting and finishing by the
farm buildings. Visitors may see
the daily running of the farm
from cattle grazing to crop
growing. A group of old farm
buildings has been converted
into craft workshops which are
also open to the public. The
shop sells the farm's own
potatoes, onions and leeks.

free
farm: all year daily dawn to
dusk; craft workshops: all year
Mon-Sat 9-5
Facilities:

Map 5 D2
Carr Taylor Vineyards
Westfield, Hastings,
East Sussex TN35 4SG
Tel. Hastings (0424) 752501

*From Hastings follow A21
northwards, after 3 miles turn
right onto A28 for 2 miles to
Westfield, then turn left onto
unclassified road for 1 mile to
vineyard. Signposted.*

Established in 1971, this 21-acre
vineyard grows a wide range of
French and German vines on
the high wire trellis system.
Visitors may follow the
vineyard and winery trail which
culminates in a free tasting of 2
wines. The shop sells the full
range of wines, including 7
whites and a rare English
sparkling wine, either by the

bottle or case. It also stocks
presentation gift packs, cider,
homemade wine mustard,
honey, preserves and petit
fours.

wine trail: adults £1.00,
senior citizens 75p, children
free
Apr-24 Dec daily 10-5,
4 Jan-Mar Mon-Fri 10-5
Facilities:

Map 5 B3
Castle Hill Farm
Rotherfield, Crowborough,
East Sussex TN6 3RR
Tel. Rotherfield (089285) 2207

*From Crowborough follow B2100
eastwards, after 2 miles turn
right onto unclassified road for 1
mile to farm. Signposted.*

This is one of the largest dairies
in south east England
producing an on-farm cheese
which is made traditionally
using the farm's own milk.
Unpasteurised milk from the
farm's Friesian herd is used to
produce 650lbs of full fat hard
cheese a week. Visitors may
tour the dairy, the cheese room
and the store house where the

MAP 5

cheeses are turned every day to help them mature evenly. Demonstrations are given each morning. The shop sells both a full fat hard cheese and a medium fat soft cheese in a variety of weights.

☞ free
◑ all year Mon-Fri 10.30-1 or by appointment
Facilities: 🚗

☺ Map 5 B3
Cherry Gardens Farm
Groombridge, Tunbridge Wells, Kent TN3 9NY
Tel. Groombridge (089276) 348

From Tunbridge Wells follow A264 westwards, after 3 miles turn left onto B2110 for 1½ miles, then turn left onto B2188 for 1 mile to farm.

Most fruit and vegetables are available here on a pick your own basis. Specialities include mangetout, peppers, aubergines and organic raspberries and strawberries. The shop also sells herbs, honey, cream, free-range eggs, jams and chutneys. A pets' paddock with Jersey cows, sheep, chickens, ducks and rabbits is available for children.
◑ May-Oct daily 9-6
Facilities: 🚾 🚗 ☺ ⚠

☞ Map 5 B4
Chiddingstone Vineyards
Vexour Farm, Chiddingstone, Kent TN8 7BB
Tel. Penshurst (0892) 870277

From Edenbridge follow B2027 eastwards, after 5 miles turn right onto unclassified road for 1 mile to vineyard on left.

This 12-acre vineyard, enthusiastically run by the Quirk family, produces quality French-style dry white wines. There are free tastings for visitors, who can also buy the wine by the case.

☞ free
◑ all year by appointment
Facilities: ♿ 🚗

☺ Map 5 C4
Crowhurst Farm
Crowhurst Lane, Borough Green, Sevenoaks, Kent TN15 8PE
Tel. Borough Green (0732) 882905

From Wrotham follow A227 southwards, after 1½ miles cross over A25 at Borough Green and continue into Quarry Hill Lane for ½ mile, then continue into Crowhurst Lane for ¼ mile to farm on left.

This pick your own farm offers strawberries, raspberries, plums, damsons, gages, apples and various vegetables. However, the speciality is undoubtedly the large range of cherries, with 18 varieties spread over 15 acres.
◑ mid Jun-Jul daily 9.30-8; Aug-Sep daily 9.30-6; Oct daily 9.30-5
Facilities: 🚾 🚗 ☺

☞ Map 5 F4
Elham Valley Vineyards
Breach, Barham, Nr Canterbury, Kent CT4 6LN
Tel. Canterbury (0227) 831266

From Barham follow B2065 southwards for 2 miles to vineyard. Signposted.

This 3-acre vineyard is in an area of outstanding natural beauty. Visitors may take a self-guided tour and see the whole wine production process, from the growing of 3,000 vines through harvesting, winemaking, bottling and labelling to tasting. The shop sells the wine by the bottle or case and also stocks local honey and herbs.

☞ adults £1.00, children free
◑ May-24 Dec Tue-Sun, Bank Hols 10-6
Facilities: 🚗 ☺

☚ Map 5 B1
The English Farm Cider Centre
Middle Farm, Firle, Lewes, East Sussex BN8 6LJ
Tel. Ripe (032183) 411/303

From Lewes follow A27 eastwards for 3½ miles to farm on left. Signposted.

This dairy and arable farm is the home of the English Farm Cider Centre and stocks over 100 varieties of cider from all over England. It also has one of the largest selections of farm produce in the country including milk, organic vegetables, 30 varieties of English cheese, English wine, meat, poultry, game, butter, yoghurt, cream and ice cream.
◑ farm & shop: all year daily 9-5
Facilities: 🍴 🚾 🚗 ☺
🍴 tea room serves homemade farmhouse cooking

☞ Map 5 B1
The English Wine Centre
Drusillas, Alfriston, East Sussex BN26 5QS
Tel. Alfriston (0323) 870532

In village.

The English Wine Centre has a small experimental vineyard with 10 varieties of vines and 3 different pruning systems in operation, and it makes 3 brands of English wine itself — Cuckmere, Sussex County and Wealden wines. The small wine

CUCKMERE English Table Wine

MAP 5　　　　　　　　**SOUTH EAST ENGLAND**

● **Homebaked bread from the Cottage Bakery, The English Wine Centre**

museum has collections of 18thC bottles and drinking vessels, early wine and cider-making equipment and corkscrews. The English Wine Off Licence sells the centre's own wines and over 30 other English wines. Wine can be tasted free of charge in the bar which always has several varieties of English wine available. The Cottage Bakery shop sells delicious homebaked bread and cakes all made from recipes over 50 years old and also stocks a range of local specialities including Sussex pies, Tipsy Sussex Squire flans, elderflower cordial, ciders, apple juices, pickles and local cheeses. Rare breeds of sheep and cattle can be seen in the farmyard area of the Zoo Park.

☞ off licence: free; tours: £2.25; zoo park: £2.50
● off licence, farm park & shop: Apr-Oct daily 10.30-5; Nov-23 Dec, Feb-Mar daily 10.30-4 or by appointment; tours: by appointment; museum, vine garden & cellars: by appointment
Facilities: 🍺🍴♿🚻🚗🍽⚱
★ 3-4 Sep 14th English wine & regional food festival
🍴 lunches & teas served in Thatched Barn Restaurant which specialises in Taste of

Sussex dishes like Sussex Pie, Tipsy Sussex Squire flans & local spicy sausages

---

🌱 Map 5 G4
Five Acres Nursery
Saunders Lane, Ash,
Canterbury, Kent CT3 2BX
Tel. Ash (0304) 812475
From Sandwich follow A257 westwards for 2 miles to Ash. Signposted.

Five Acres Nursery specialises in growing 150 varieties of herb plants which it supplies to garden centres throughout south east England. Its other speciality is Alpine plants, of which it has over 100 varieties.

☞ free
● all year by appointment
Facilities: 🚗

😊 Map 5 E5
Four Oaks Pick Your Own
Luddenham, Faversham, Kent
Tel. Faversham (0795) 536087
From Faversham follow A2 westwards, after 1½ miles turn right onto unclassified road for ½ mile to farm. Signposted.

Various soft fruits and vegetables are available at this pick your own farm including late strawberries, mangetout, sweet corn, Chinese leaves and

pumpkins. The shop also sells homemade ice cream.
● Jun-Nov daily 10-7
Facilities: 🚻🚗🍽

🍴 Map 5 C3
Gate House Farm
Brenchley, Tonbridge,
Kent TN12 7AD
Tel. Tonbridge (0892) 723723
From Lamberhurst follow A21, then B2162 northwards, after 2½ miles turn left at Horsmonden onto unclassified road for 1½ miles to Brenchley. Signposted.

This typical fruit farm is situated in a delightful Kentish village. Visitors are welcome to follow the farm trail, with the help of a trail leaflet, to see the fruits growing, the lake and conservation area. They grow a variety of soft fruits in season including strawberries, raspberries, red and blackcurrants and blackberries. Cherries and apples are also grown as well as 2½ acres of vines. Ready-picked soft fruit is for sale in season and also apple juice made from the farm's own apples.

☞ free
● trail: Jun-Oct daily 10-6
Facilities: 🚻🚗🍽

🍷 Map 5 E3
Harbourne Vineyard
High Halden, Tenterden, Kent
Tel. Wittersham (07977) 420
From Tenterden follow A28 northwards for 4 miles to vineyard.

Visitors are welcome to tour this vineyard which aims to use as little machinery and as few chemicals as possible. The grapes are pressed in basket hand presses, fermented, bottled and sold all on the premises. The wines produced are a medium dry white, a dry white and a rare English rosé. Visitors are welcome to taste all the wines and to buy them either by the bottle or case.

MAP 5

The shop also sells its own cider, apple wine, wine spices, honey, grapes, apples and potted grape vines.

☞ free

● all year by appointment

Facilities: 🚗

❦ Map 5 D4

Iden Croft Herbs

Frittenden Road, Staplehurst, Kent TN12 0DH

Tel. Staplehurst (0580) 891432

From Staplehurst follow A229 southwards, after ½ mile turn left onto unclassified road for ½ mile to garden. Signposted.

This 8½-acre herb farm has both traditional and informal gardens. Part of the farm is a commercial fresh-cut herb operation providing a large quantity of herbs for chefs, caterers and wholesale food markets. It also grows a variety of unusual salads, chicories, leaves and edible flowers which can be made up into packs provided they are ordered in advance. Visitors are welcome to follow a trail through the various beds and also visit the herb information centre and origanum collection. The shop sells herb plants — including pots of rocket, orache, purslaine and other delicious leaves — seeds, herb blends and gifts.

☞ free

● 31 Mar-Sep Mon-Sat 9-5, Sun 11-5; Oct-30 Mar Mon-Sat 9-5

Facilities: 🍴 🚻 🚗

🍴 teas served with local strawberries & cream, homemade cakes & local dairy ice cream

---

🎲 Map 5 D3

S E Lane

White House Farm, Biddenden, Ashford, Kent TN27 8LN

Tel. Biddenden (0580) 291289

From Biddenden follow A262 westwards, after 1½ miles turn right at Three Chimney's Inn onto unclassified road for ¼ mile to farm on left.

This dairy farm and shop, set in the heart of the Weald, has a herd of Jersey cows and produces its own cream, clotted cream, yoghurt, butter and dairy ice cream. Visitors are welcome to walk around and look at the animals, watch them being milked, inspect the small processing plant and taste the products. Specialities include untreated whole and skimmed Jersey milk and a range of 15 flavours of ice cream including brown bread, butterscotch, whisky and ginger, honey yoghurt, strawberry and blackcurrant made with fresh fruit. Everything is made on the premises using only natural ingredients and no artificial additives and is sold from the shop in tubs and cartons in a variety of sizes.

☞ free

● all year daily 8-6

Facilities: 🍴 🚻 🚗

❦ Map 5 C3

Marle Place Garden and Herb Nursery

Marle Place, Brenchley, Tonbridge, Kent TN12 7HS

Tel. Brenchley (089272) 2304

● **Marle Place Garden and Herb Nursery**

MAP 5

SOUTH EAST ENGLAND

From Lamberhurst follow A21 northwards, after 1 mile turn right onto B2162 for 2 miles, then turn left onto unclassified road for 1 mile to garden on left. Signposted.

Marle Place is a Grade II listed 17thC house with 10 acres of beautiful Wealden gardens. These include an Edwardian rockery with winding paths planted with herbs and a 'potager' kitchen garden. Visitors may also see a fine selection of fancy bantam chickens. The shop sells herb plants, homemade vinegars, dried herb and wildflower garlands and free-range duck, goose and bantam eggs.

☞ garden: adults £1.00, senior citizens & children (under 12) 50p; nursery: free

◑ nursery & herb rockery: Apr-1 Oct Mon-Fri 10-5; gardens: Apr-1 Oct Wed 10-5 or by appointment
Facilities: ▣🚗🍴

🏠 Map 5 C2
Michelham Priory
Upper Dicker, Hailsham, East Sussex BN27 3QS
Tel. Hailsham (0323) 844224

From Polegate follow A22 northwards, after 3 miles turn left onto unclassified road for 2 miles to Priory on right. Signposted.

● **Japanese-style rock garden at Mount Ephraim Gardens**

Michelham Priory was founded in 1229 by the Norman Lord of Pevensey and today offers visitors the chance to see a splendid Tudor estate complete with gardens and a watermill. The working kitchen is of particular interest with a great open hearth and a chimney divided into two. On one side is a smoke room for curing meat and bacon and on the other an 18thC spit-driving mechanism. The extensive gardens include a physic garden where 94 varieties of medicinal and culinary herbs are cultivated. The Fish Stews, where the canons originally stored their fish, is now a shop selling herb plants, homemade vinegars,

dried herbs, wildflower garlands and free-range duck, goose and bantam eggs.

☞ adults £2.00, senior citizens £1.80, children (5-16) £1.00

◑ 25 Mar-Oct daily 11-5.30
Facilities: ☕🍴♿▣🚗👥🏕
🍴 lunches & teas served in restaurant, own stoneground wholemeal flour used

---

☺ Map 5 D5
Mierscourt Farm Shop
Mierscourt Road, Rainham, Gillingham, Kent
Tel. Medway (0634) 370283

From Gillingham follow A2 eastwards, after 3 miles turn right at Rainham into Mierscourt Road for 1 mile to farm. Signposted.

This farm shop sells a wide range of local produce including apples, pears, plums and other soft fruit and vegetables. It also stocks skimmed milk, butter, yoghurt, ice cream, jams, preserves, mustards, honey, marmalade, eggs, bread and homemade cakes.

◑ all year Mon-Sat 8-6, Sun 9-6
Facilities: 🚗

🍀 Map 5 F5
Mount Ephraim Gardens
Hernhill, Nr Faversham, Kent
Tel. Canterbury (0227) 751496

● **The restored watermill, Michelham Priory**

MAP 5

From Faversham follow B2040 eastwards, after 2 miles turn left onto A299 for 1½ miles, then turn right onto unclassified road for 1 mile to Hernhill. Signposted.

Here are 7 acres of gardens which were laid out in 1912. Plums, pears and a number of rare apples are grown here and, at the beginning of the apple season and harvest, an Apple Sunday is held featuring their own apples and those of local producers. The Somerset cider press makes apple juice and visitors can watch demonstrations of the cider making and processing.

☞ adults £1.25, children 20p
◑ May-Jun, Aug-Sep daily 9-6
Facilities: ✦ ▥ ☎ ☺
★ Apple Sunday telephone for exact date
✦ teas served on Sundays — everything is homemade including jam made from the farm's own fruit

🏠 Map 5 D4
Museum of Kent Rural Life
Lock Lane, Sandling, Maidstone, Kent ME14 3AU
Tel. Maidstone (0622) 63936
From Maidstone follow A229 northwards for 1 mile to museum. Signposted.

● **A bee-keeper at work**

This museum has exhibits tracing the history of crops and livestock in Kent. As well as agricultural tools and equipment the museum has 'living' exhibits on its own 27 acres of market garden. These include crops, livestock, a herb garden, a hop field, orchards and an apiary. The shop sells organic produce and honey.

☞ adults 80p, senior citizens & children 40p
◑ 31 Mar-11 Oct Mon, Tue, Thur, Fri 10-5, Sat 12-5, Sun 12-6, or by appointment
Facilities: 🍽 ✦ & ▥ ☎ ☺
★ 25 Jun midsummer fair & good food festival; 10-11 Sep hop picking & drying; 9 Oct ploughing
✦ lunches & teas served using local produce

● **Kentish oasthouse**

● **Picking hops**

MAP 5   SOUTH EAST ENGLAND

⌂ Map 5 C4
Nepicar Farm
Wrotham Heath, Sevenoaks,
Kent TN15 7SR
Tel. Borough Green (0732)
883040

*From Wrotham follow A20 south
eastwards, after 1½ miles turn
right onto A25 for 1 mile to farm.
Signposted.*

The only farmhouse cheese-
maker in Kent, this dairy makes
Fetta and 2 varieties of sheep's
milk cheese. These are
Carolina, using a 12thC recipe,
and Cecilia, a full-fat hard
cheese matured in hops. Both
are made with vegetable
rennet only and are free from
all artificial flavourings and
colourings. The farm holds
regular sheep-milking
demonstrations between
March and September and
visitors are welcome to look
round the cheese rooms and
taste the produce. A shop sells
all the produce as well as meat,
game, free-range eggs,
homemade 100% pork
sausages, sheep's milk and
yoghurt.
☞ adults 50p, children 25p
◑ all year daily 9-5
Facilities: ▦ ⛟ ⛺

☺ Map 5 D2
Norton's Farm
Sedlescombe, Battle,
East Sussex TN33 0SG
Tel. Sedlescombe (042487) 471

*From Hastings follow A21
northwards for 3 miles to farm.
Signposted.*

This farm offers a wide range of
pick your own fruit and
vegetables and also has a farm
trail which takes visitors round
the more interesting areas.
They can see a variety of farm
animals including working Shire
horses. A museum housed in
an old barn contains many
historical agricultural
implements, some of which are

302

still used on the farm. The shop
also sells ready-picked produce.
◑ May-mid Jun, Oct-Nov daily
9-5; mid Jun-Sep daily 7-9 or
dusk
Facilities: ⛴ ⸙ ▦ ⛟ ⛺
⸙ Hungry Picker's Kitchen
serves morning coffee, salad
lunches & cream teas

🍃 Map 5 C5
Owletts
Cobham, Kent

*From Rochester follow A2
westwards, after 3 miles turn left
onto B2009 for 1½ miles to
house on right.*

Built in the reign of Charles II,
this friendly family-run house
has a kitchen garden laid out in
the traditional manner through
which visitors are welcome to
wander and admire the fruit
and vegetables.
☞ 60p
◑ Apr-Sep Wed, Thur 2-5
Facilities: ⛟
★ occasional flower festival,
write for details

🍃 Map 5 B4
Penshurst Place
Penshurst, Kent TN11 8DG
Tel. Penshurst (0892) 870307

*From Tonbridge follow A26
southwards, after 1½ miles turn
right onto B2176 for 4 miles to
house on right. Signposted.*

One of England's finest country
houses situated in an area of
great beauty. The Tudor
gardens have been restored
and include a kitchen garden,
an orchard of standard apple
trees and a nut garden of
coppiced cobnuts
underplanted with daffodils,
bluebells, tulips and other
spring flowers. The Farm
Museum, housed in an old
barn, includes a collection of
historic agricultural machinery
most of which was collected
from the barns of neighbouring
farmers. An exhibition of life on

the Penshurst Estate is
particularly interesting.
☞ house & grounds: adults
£2.75, senior citizens £2.00,
children (5-16) £1.50; grounds:
adults £2.00, senior citizens
£1.50, children £1.00
◑ Apr-2 Oct Tue-Sun, Bank
Hols grounds: 12.30-6; house:
1-5.30
Facilities: ⛴ ⸙ ▦ ⛟ ⛺ ⛽

⸙ Map 5 B3
Penshurst Vineyards
Grove Road, Penshurst,
Kent TN11 8DU
Tel. Penshurst (0892) 870255

*From Tunbridge Wells follow
A264 westwards, after 3 miles
turn right onto B2188 for 3 miles,
then turn left into Grove Road for
½ mile to vineyard on right.
Signposted.*

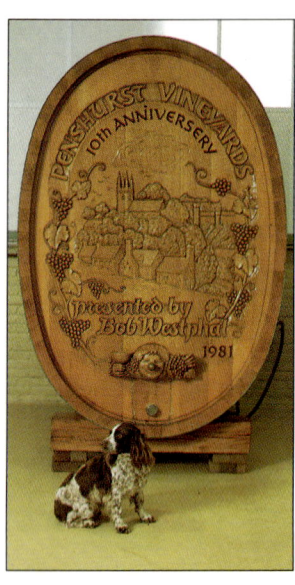

Penshurst is one of the most
modern wineries in England,
producing some 50,000 bottles
of wine each year. A variety of
grapes are grown and blended
to produce a characteristically
light and fruity wine. Visitors
are welcome to walk around
the estate, admire the mob of

MAP 5

● **Penshurst Vineyard and its wines**

🍴 coffee shop serves homebaked refreshments, light lunches & Kentish cream teas

---

🛍 Map 5 D2
Redlays Farm
Cottage Lane,
Westfield, Hastings,
East Sussex TN35 4RR
Tel. Sedlescombe (042487) 696

From Hastings follow A21 northwards, after 3 miles turn right onto A28 for 2 miles to Westfield, then turn left into Cottage Lane for 1 mile to farm.

This small dairy farm, with a herd of pedigree Ayrshire cows, produces traditional, additive-free dairy produce. Visitors may buy wholemilk fruit yoghurt containing hand-picked local fruit, as well as unpasteurised milk and unpasteurised double cream.

☞ free
● all year daily 8-8
Facilities: 🚗

🍴 Map 5 D4
Reed Court Farm
Marden, Tonbridge,
Kent TN12 9SX
Tel. Hunton (06272) 314

From Maidstone follow A229 southwards, after 5 miles turn right onto B2079 for 2 miles to farm.

This traditional 400-acre farm grows fruit, hops and corn as well as supporting beef cattle, sheep and pigs. Visitors may take the trail and learn about the day-to-day working of the farm.

☞ free
● Easter-Oct daily dawn-dusk
Facilities: 🚗 🛆

😊 Map 5 D3
Ringden Fruit Farm
Flimwell, Wadhurst,
East Sussex TN19 7QY
Tel. Flimwell (058087) 385

wallabies, black swans and flock of rare breed sheep and afterwards enjoy a free tasting. The shop sells the wine by the bottle or case and also stocks delicious apple wine and juice.
☞ free
● Mar-Dec daily 9-5; Jan-Feb Mon-Sat 9-5 (groups only)
Facilities: ♿ 🚻 🚗 🛆

😊 Map 5 C3
Pippins Fruit Farm
Maidstone Road,
Pembury, Tunbridge Wells,
Kent TN2 4AB
Tel. Pembury (089282) 4569

From Lamberhurst follow A21 northwards, after 5 miles turn right onto unclassified road for 1 mile through Pembury, then turn right onto unclassified road for ¼ mile to farm.

Over 50 varieties of apples and plums are grown on this pick your own farm, as well as the usual soft fruits. Visitors are welcome to taste and buy Pippins' Vintage Kent Cider which is made on the premises.
● Jun-Sep daily 9-6; Oct-May Fri, Sat, Sun 10-5, Mon-Thur 2-5
Facilities: 🚗

🐦 Map 5 C4
Rare Farm Animals of Hollanden
Mill Lane, Hildenborough, Nr Sevenoaks, Kent TN15 0SG
Tel. Sevenoaks (0732) 832276

From Sevenoaks follow A225 southwards, after 3 miles continue onto B245 for 1½ miles, then turn left into Mill Lane for 1 mile to farm on right. Signposted.

Set in one of the most picturesque parts of west Kent this centre keeps over 60 breeds of rare farm animals. Many of these sheep, cattle, pigs and poultry were once common throughout Britain but now survive only on dedicated farms such as this. There is a special pets' corner where children are welcome to meet and feed the animals. Visitors may also pick their own soft fruit and vegetables. The shop sells ready-picked farm produce, fresh cream and free-range eggs.
☞ adults £1.99, senior citizens & children £1.25
● farm park: Easter-16 Oct daily 10.30-5; farm shop & PYO: Easter-16 Oct daily 9-6
Facilities: 🍽 🍴 🚻 🚗 🛆 ⚠

MAP 5

SOUTH EAST ENGLAND

From Robertsbridge follow A21 northwards for 4 miles to farm. Signposted.

This farm shop offers 20 varieties of apples and 4 different sorts of pears as well as potatoes, eggs, tomatoes, strawberries, plums, cherries, cream and apple juice.

● all year daily 9-5
Facilities: 🚻 🚗 ♨

⛩ Map 5 G3
Rowland Confectionery
17 Old High Street, Folkestone, Kent CT20 1RL
Tel. Folkestone (0303) 54723

In town centre.

This sugar confectionery manufacturer has been making lettered rock since 1887. Visitors may watch the rock being made from start to finish and learn the secret of the writing through the middle. The shop sells a range of other sweets including old-fashioned humbugs.

● shop: all year Mon-Sat 9-6, Sun 9.30-5; factory: Mon, Tue, Thur-Sat 9-4

🏛 Map 5 A1
The Royal Pavilion
The Old Steine, Brighton, East Sussex BN1 1UE
Tel. Brighton (0273) 603005

In town centre.

The Prince Regent's fantastic seaside palace, complete with domes and minarets, was built by Nash in 1822. The magnificent Regency kitchen, which has been totally renovated, was the most attractive and up-to-date of its day and was one of the first to be situated close to the dining room. The huge tent-like copper canopies and the iron and copper palm tree columns bring the oriental flavour of the rest of the Pavilion into the kitchen. Visitors can see the impressive copper 'batterie de cuisine', the smokejack which is now powered by electricity, and the dressers with over 500 pieces of china on their shelves. Many great chefs worked here including Carême — the 'Chef of Kings and King of Chefs' — who came from France in 1817. Visitors can also see the Banqueting Room with its centre table laid with a wonderful collection of Regency candelabra and silver, an elegant Royal Worcester dinner service and Regency crystal.

🎟 adults £2.00, senior citizens £1.25, children (5-15) £1.00, family ticket (2 adults & up to 4 children) £5.00, family ticket (1 adult & up to 4 children) £3.00
● Jun-Oct daily 10-6; Nov-May daily 10-5
Facilities: 🍴 🔱 ♿ 🚻

● **The Nash view of the Great Kitchen of Brighton Royal Pavilion, 1826**

MAP 5

● **The Great Kitchen of the Royal Pavilion, Brighton**

🍇 **Map 5 B2**
St George's Vineyard
Waldron, Nr Heathfield,
East Sussex TN21 0RA
Tel. Horam (04353) 2156

From Heathfield follow A265 westwards, after 1 mile turn left at Cross in Hand onto unclassified road for 2 miles to Waldron. Signposted.

This 20-acre vineyard and winery produces and sells its own wine. It also specialises in traditional Sussex food including English wine sorbet, cheeses, honey, mustard, chocolates, home-smoked pâtés, trout and herbs. Visitors are welcome to walk around the vineyard, taste the wine and even adopt a vine, as well as view the wine exhibition.

☞ wine exhibition: free; vineyard walkabout & glass of wine: £1.25; audio vineyard tour & glass of wine: £1.75 — groups only
● 23 Apr-2 Oct daily 11-5; Nov-22 Apr Sat-Sun 1-4
Facilities: 🍽️ 🚻 🅿️ ♿
★ gourmet food fair — telephone for details
🍽️ quality food & wine, all Sussex produce, served all day 11-5. Five-course medieval banquets available

● **St George's Vineyard**

🍇 **Map 5 G4**
St Nicholas of Ash Vineyard and Winery
Moat Lane, Ash, Canterbury, Kent CT3 2DG
Tel. Ash (0304) 812670

From Sandwich follow A257 westwards for 2 miles to Ash. Signposted.

This family-run vineyard continues the long tradition of wine-growing in Kent. It grows Müller-Thurgau and Schönburger grapes, producing a fine white in the modern winery. Visitors are welcome to explore the vineyard on a self-guided tour or follow the vineyard trail which links 3 local vineyards. The shop sells the estate's wine and also apple wine made from east Kent apples.

☞ self-guided tour & tasting: £1.25
● all year daily 9-6
Facilities: 🍽️ 🚻 ♿ 🚾 ♿
★ open days: 7 Aug, 25 Sep, 4 Dec
🍽️ teas served with homebaked cakes & scones

🍀 **Map 5 C3**
Scotney Castle Garden
Lamberhurst, Tunbridge Wells, Kent TN3 8JN
Tel. Lamberhurst (0892) 890651

From Lamberhurst follow A21 southwards, after ½ mile turn left onto unclassified road for ½ mile to garden. Signposted.

Visitors can walk around the herb garden which has been planted in a large circular bed in the courtyard of the National Trust's ancient Scotney Castle. It is well stocked with a variety of herbs and is in a particularly attractive setting.

☞ adults £2.00, children £1.00
● Apr-13 Nov Wed-Fri 11-6, Sat, Sun & Bank Hol Mon 2-6 or sunset
Facilities: 🚾 🅿️ ♿

MAP 5   SOUTH EAST ENGLAND

♈ Map 5 A1

MOCK TURTLE
4 Pool Valley, Brighton,
East Sussex BN1 1NJ
Tel: Brighton (0273) 27380
In town centre.

A traditional English tea shop. All cakes and scones are homemade on the premises, including this aromatic Almond Cake.

◐ Tue-Sat 10-6, closed Sun, Mon, & 2 weeks in autumn
Price range cream tea £2.75
Seats 35

ALMOND CAKE
4oz butter
5oz caster sugar
3 eggs lightly whisked
3oz ground sweet almonds
¼oz ground bitter almonds
1½oz flour sifted
½ glass sherry

Heat oven to gas 4 (350F, 180C). Thoroughly cream the butter and sugar, beat in the eggs, fold in the ground almonds and flour and add the sherry carefully. Bake for approximately 50 minutes. When cooked leave in tin for about 15 minutes. Turn out and sprinkle with caster sugar.

🍇 Map 5 D2
Sedlescombe Vineyard Organic Wines
Nr Robertsbridge,
East Sussex TN32 5SA
Tel. Staplecross (058083) 715

From Robertsbridge follow A21 southwards, after 3 miles turn left onto B2089 for 2 miles, then turn right onto A229 for 1 mile to vineyard.

This was the first organic vineyard in Britain to produce wines in accordance with the Soil Association's standards. Vegetables and strawberries are grown in amongst the vines. Visitors may follow a self-guided trail and visit the winery to see the antique grape press which is still in use. The shop sells wine, organic fruit and vegetables.

☞ free
◐ May-Sep daily 10-6; Oct-Apr Sat-Sun 12-5
Facilities: ♿ 🚻 🚗 👶

😊 Map 5 C1
Sharnfold Farm Pick Your Own
Hailsham Road,
Stone Cross, Pevensey,
East Sussex BN24 5BU

From Pevensey follow A27 westwards, after 1½ miles turn right onto B2104 for ½ mile to farm on left. Signposted.

Most soft fruits and a good selection of vegetables are available on this pick your own farm. The shop also sells carrots, marrows, broad beans, mangetout and sweet corn.

◐ mid Jun-mid Aug daily 9.30-7; mid Aug-mid Sep daily 9.30-6
Facilities: 🚗 👶 🧺

♣ Map 5 D3
Sissinghurst Castle Garden
Nr Cranbrook, Kent
Tel. Cranbrook (0580) 712850

From Biddenden follow A262 westwards, after 3½ miles turn right onto unclassified road for ½ mile to castle. Signposted.

Sissinghurst Castle was the home of the writer Sir Harold Nicolson and his wife, author Vita Sackville-West, from 1930 until her death in 1962. They were both keen and inspired gardeners and Sissinghurst, now owned by the National Trust, attracts hundreds of thousands of visitors every year who come to admire their work. Vita's white garden is particularly famous; she was one of the first gardeners to use colour so boldly. The herb garden is charming and very comprehensive. Visitors are also welcome to wander through the orchards which, during the spring, are covered with bulbs. A small collection of herbs and plants from the gardens are for sale.

☞ adults £2.80, children £1.40; Sun: adults £3.40, children £1.70
◐ Apr-15 Oct Tue-Fri 1-6.30, Sat, Sun, Good Fri 10-6.30
Facilities: 🚌 🍴 🚻 🚗
🍴 restaurant serves snacks, lunches & teas specialising in local produce

● A Kentish hop garden

MAP 5

OAST CAKES

1 lb plain flour
¾ tsp salt
¾ tsp baking powder
4oz lard
3oz caster sugar
6oz currants
fat for frying

Sift the flour with the salt and baking powder, rub in the lard to a crumbly mixture and add the sugar and currants. Mix to a light dough with water and divide into small pieces. Roll out to ½-inch rounds. Fry in shallow fat until golden brown, turning once. Serve hot.

🏠 Map 5 A1
Stanmer Rural Museum
Stanmer Park, Nr Brighton,
East Sussex

From Brighton follow A27 north eastwards, after 3 miles turn left to park.

This museum of rural and domestic life is part of a 5,000-acre conservation area on the South Downs run voluntarily by the Stanmer Preservation Society. Exhibits include kitchen equipment and agricultural implements.

☞ free
◑ Easter-30 Oct Sun, Bank Hols 2.30-5

🦋 Map 5 G4
Staple Vineyard
Church Farm, Staple,
Canterbury, Kent CT3 1LN
Tel. Ash (0304) 812571

From Sandwich follow A257 westwards, after 3 miles turn left onto unclassified road for 1½ miles to Staple. Signposted.

This 7-acre vineyard and winery produces 40,000 bottles of wine a year. Visitors are welcome to follow the self-guided tour which includes an opportunity to taste the wines.

The shop sells wine by the bottle or case and also stocks herb plants, vegetables, dried flowers, a selection of homemade jams, chutneys and speciality mustards.

☞ adults £1.00, children free
◑ Easter-Sep Mon-Sat 11-5, Sun 12-4; Oct-Easter telephone for details
Facilities: 🚾 🚗 🍽

🪁 Map 5 F4
Stelling Minnis Windmill
Mill Lane, Stelling Minnis,
Canterbury, Kent CT4 6AF
Tel. Stelling Minnis (022787) 595

From Canterbury follow B2068 southwards, after 7 miles turn left onto unclassified road for 1 mile to Stelling Minnis. Signposted.

This historic flour mill has been restored to working condition. When not milling it is open to visitors who can see the machinery and the tools used for maintenance.

☞ adults 50p, children 25p
◑ Apr-Sep Sun, Bank Hols 2-5
Facilities: 🚗 🍽

🏠 Map 5 E3
Stocks Mill
The Stocks, Wittersham,
Tenterden, Kent TN30 7ER
Tel. Wittersham (07977) 309

From Tenterden follow B2082 southwards for 6 miles to The Stocks.

The tallest post mill in Kent, Stocks Mill has been restored by Kent County Council and now contains a small collection of farming and craft tools.

☞ adults 30p, children 10p
◑ Apr, May, Aug Bank Hols, 3 Jun-25 Sep Sun 2.30-5

🌱 Map 5 C2
Sussex Farm Museum
Horam Manor, Horam,
Nr Heathfield,
East Sussex TN21 0JB
Tel. Horam Road (04353) 3161

From Heathfield follow B2203 southwards for 3 miles to Horam. Signposted.

This working farm offers trails, guided tours, fishing and craft demonstrations. A rural life museum has exhibits on the chicken cramming industry of Heathfield, the story of a shepherd's pie, a dairy where visitors can watch butter-making demonstrations and a collection of hopping tools. It is also the home of the medieval Sussex spaghetti fork!

☞ adults £1.40, senior citizens £1.20, children 80p
◑ Apr-Oct Tue-Sun 10-5
Facilities: ☕ ♿ 🚾 🚗 🍽 ⛪
★ butter-making & corn grinding demonstrations throughout the year
🍴 teas served with homemade cakes

🏛 Map 5 B3
Sussex High Weald Dairy Sheep
Putlands Farm, Duddleswell,
East Sussex TN22 3BJ
Tel. Nutley (0825) 712647

From Uckfield follow A22 northwards, after 2 miles turn right onto B2026 for 1½ miles to farm. Signposted.

This sheep farm makes and sells a wide range of sheep's milk products. Visitors can see yoghurt and cheese being made and, in summer, watch sheep milking demonstrations. The shop sells 10 varieties of sheep's cheese including Sussex Slipcote, a full fat soft cheese made from a recipe from Shakespeare's day, Foresters hard ewe's milk cheese containing vegetarian rennet and Halloumi, a traditional

Cypriot cheese. The shop also sells milk, milk shakes, yoghurt and ice cream.

☞ telephone for details
◗ all year daily 8-6
Facilities: ☕ 🚗

☺ Map 5 G4
Sutton Court Farm
Sutton Court, Sutton by Dover, Kent CT15 5DF
Tel. Deal (0304) 375033
From Dover follow A258 northwards, after 5 miles turn left at Ringwould onto unclassified road for 2 miles, then turn left onto unclassified road for 1/4 mile to Sutton.

This farm offers pick your own strawberries.

◗ 20 Jun-Jul daily telephone for times
Facilities: 🚻 🚗 🥤

✈ Map 5 E3
Swanton Mill
Lower Mersham, Ashford, Kent
Tel. Aldington (023372) 223
From Ashford follow A20 south eastwards, after 3 miles turn right onto unclassified road for 2 miles to mill. Signposted.

This working watermill grinds organically grown wheat into wholemeal flour. A small milling museum is open to visitors who can also buy the stoneground flour.

☞ adults £1.00, children 50p
◗ Mar-Oct by appointment
Facilities: 🍴 🚻

🍴 teas served with homemade scones

🍷 Map 5 E3
Tenterden Vineyards
Spots Farm, Small Hythe, Tenterden, Kent TN30 7NG
Tel. Tenterden (05806) 3033
From Tenterden follow B2082 southwards for 2 miles to Small Hythe. Signposted.

This 18-acre vineyard and winery has some of the most modern equipment in Britain

---

including an automatic grape press, a bottling line and stainless steel fermentation tanks. Visitors may follow self-guided tours and also wander in the unusual herb garden where over 400 varieties of herbs and wild flowers are grown. There is a good selection of wines and apple juice, both of which can be tasted before buying. The shop sells herb plants, vines, local honey, preserves, herbal teas and dried herbs.

☞ adults £1.00, senior citizens 75p, children (under 16) free
◗ mid Mar-24 Dec daily 10-6 or dusk if earlier
Facilities: 🍷 🍴 🚻 🚗 🥤

🍴 tea rooms serve traditional cold lunches & teas with homemade cakes & scones

---

🍺 Map 5 G5
Theobolds Barn Cider
Heronsgate Farm, Stourmouth, Canterbury, Kent CT3 1HZ
Tel. Canterbury (0227) 722275
From Wingham follow B2046 northwards for 4 1/2 miles to farm on right.

This real Kentish cider is matured in oak rum barrels, the combination of oak wood and rum adding a unique flavour to the fully fermented drink. Its alcohol content is 9% proof which certainly makes it a delightfully heady mixture. Visitors to the family-run Heronsgate Farm, specialists in growing apples and pears, can sample the cider and pure apple juice and watch cider pressing demonstrations when in season. There is a farm shop with a wide range of fresh produce. Apples and pears can be bought by the pound, box, pallet or lorry load, cider comes in 1 litre bottles, 1/2 gallon flagons and 5 gallon barrels, and apple juice in 1 litre bottles. Also on sale are local cheeses, additive-free jams and pickles and local stoneground flour.

☞ free
◗ 9 Aug-23 Dec Tue-Sun 10-12.30, 1.30-5; 2 Jan-Jul Tue, Thur, Sat 10-12.30, 1.30-5
Facilities: 🚗

🍷 Map 5 G4
Three Corners Vineyard
Beacon Lane, Woodnesborough, Sandwich, Kent CT13 0PA
Tel. Ash (0304) 812025
From Sandwich follow A258 southwards, after 1/4 mile turn right onto unclassified road for 2 miles through Woodnesborough to vineyard on right. Signposted.

This 3 1/2-acre vineyard won the bronze medal for English Wine of the Year in 1987. It specialises in early ripening vines to produce slightly unusual dry white wines. These are Tricorne Siegerrebe, a dry white wine; Tricorne Trocken, a crisp dry white wine blended from Riechensteiner and Siegerrebe grapes; and Tricorne Mélange. Visitors are given a talk on the history of English wine, vine culture and the Three Corners Vineyard and may then follow the trail before enjoying a free tasting. The vineyard shop sells wines by the bottle, in a pack of 3, or by the case.

☞ adults £1.50, children £1.00
◗ Easter-Oct Mon-Sat 10.30-7, Sun 12.15-7
Facilities: 🚻 🚗

🌾 Map 5 C4
Whitbread Hop Farm
Beltring, Paddock Wood, Nr Tonbridge, Kent TN12 6PY
Tel. Maidstone (0622) 872068
From Tonbridge follow B2017 eastwards, after 5 miles turn left onto B2015 for 1 1/2 miles to Beltring. Signposted.

This is the farm which produces the hops for Whitbread's brewery. Set in 100 acres of beautiful Kent countryside it

MAP 5

● **Hop picking, September 1875**

has a number of attractions for visitors. They may see hops and cereals growing, make friends with the Shire horses, try their hand at coarse fishing, visit the pets' corner or follow the nature trail. There are also several museums, housed in the largest group of oasthouses in the world. These include a hop and a rural life museum, a collection of bottles and signs and even some live working craftsmen.

☞ adults £1.75, children 75p
● 29 Mar-23 Oct daily 10-5.30
Facilities: ⬛ ⑪ ⬛ 🚗 ⛺ ⚠

🏠 Map 5 G4
White Mill Folk Museum
Ash Road, Sandwich,
Kent CT13 9JB
Tel. Sandwich (0304) 612076
From Sandwich follow A257 westwards for $\frac{1}{2}$ mile to museum.

This 18thC windmill is complete with sails and original machinery. It is now a folk museum showing the life of the

miller and his family over a period of 100 years. The original farm buildings, including the miller's house, are currently being restored.

☞ adults 50p, senior citizens & children 25p
● Easter-mid Sep Sun, Bank Hols 2.30-5; Aug Wed, Sun, Bank Hols 2.30-5
Facilities: 🚾 🚗 ⛺

🏹 Map 5 E3
Woodchurch Windmill
Woodchurch, Ashford,
Kent TN26 3SH
Tel. Woodchurch (023386) 572
From Tenterden follow B2067 eastwards, after 4 miles turn left into Woodchurch.

Woodchurch Windmill has remained unused for over 60 years but now, after extensive restoration, its sails are turning again. Guided tours can be arranged.

☞ adults 40p, children 20p
● Easter-25 Sep Mon, Wed 2-4, Sun 2.30-4.30, or by appointment
Facilities: ⛺

🏠 Map 5 F4
Wye College Agricultural Museum
Wye College, Wye, Ashford,
Kent TN25 5AH
Tel. Wye (0233) 812401
From Ashford follow A28 northwards, after 3 miles turn right onto unclassified road for $2\frac{1}{2}$ miles through Wye to museum in village of Brook.

This museum contains a comprehensive collection of agricultural implements and artefacts housed in a 14thC barn. It includes a dairy, kitchen equipment and a wide variety of horse-powered farm machinery. An exhibit on the importance of hops to the region is held in a 19thC oast-house.

☞ free
● May-Jul, Sep Wed 2-5; Aug Wed, Sat 2-5
Facilities: 🚗

· CALENDAR OF EVENTS ·

APRIL

Easter Bun Ceremony
2 April
A hot cross bun is added to a collection hanging from the ceiling in The Widow's Son Inn, Bromley-by-Bow, London E3.

Butterworth Charity
2 April
A presentation of hot cross buns and coins is made to 'poor widows of the parish' at St Bartholomew-the-Great, London EC1.

Biddenden Dole
4 April
An ancient custom where cheese, tea and biscuits, with pictures of the two Biddenden maids on them, are distributed at The White House, Biddenden, Kent.

MAY

Blessing of the Nets and Mackerel Service
9 May — Rogation Day
Mackerel are brought ashore in nets and blessed in Brighton, East Sussex.

Blessing of the Sea
9 May — Rogation Day
An ancient Rogationtide custom in Hastings, East Sussex.

Festival of English Wines
28-30 May
Wine festival at Leeds Castle, Maidstone, Kent.

Surrey County Show
30 May
An annual agricultural show at Stoke Park, Guildford, Surrey.

JUNE

English Civil War Garrison
11-12 June
A Civil War re-enactment by the English Civil War Society including period cooking at Dover Castle, Dover, Kent.

Kent Good Food Festival
26 June
An opportunity to taste and buy quality food from small Kent producers at Museum of Kent Rural Life, Sandling, Nr Maidstone, Kent.

JULY

World Custard Pie Championship
2 July
Watch about 50 teams of 4 people throw custard pies at each other at Ditton Park Community Centre, Maidstone, Kent.

Kent County Show
14-16 July
An annual agricultural show with livestock and a food fair at Detling, Maidstone, Kent.

Royal Isle of Wight Show
21 July
An annual agricultural show with various country attractions at Cowes, Isle of Wight.

New Forest and Hampshire County Show
27-28 July
The area's biggest annual agricultural event at Brockenhurst, Hampshire.

Whitstable Oyster Festival
30 July-7 August
A week of festivities including cookery demonstrations and oyster tastings at various venues in Whitstable, Kent.

AUGUST

Great British Beer Festival
2-6 August
Annual beer festival at The Metropole, Brighton, East Sussex.

Garlic Festival
14 August
An annual festival with garlic orientated food, a garlic stripping contest, a garlic queen, stalls, sideshows and many other attractions at Arreton, Isle of Wight.

Whitbread's Country Fair
28-29 August
A country fair at Whitbread Hop Farm, Paddock Wood, Kent.

SEPTEMBER

English Vineyard Festival
3-4 September
The 14th festival at the English Wine Centre, Drusillas, Alfriston, East Sussex.

DECEMBER

Royal Smithfield Show
5-8 December
London's annual agricultural show at Earl's Court, London, SW5.

WALES

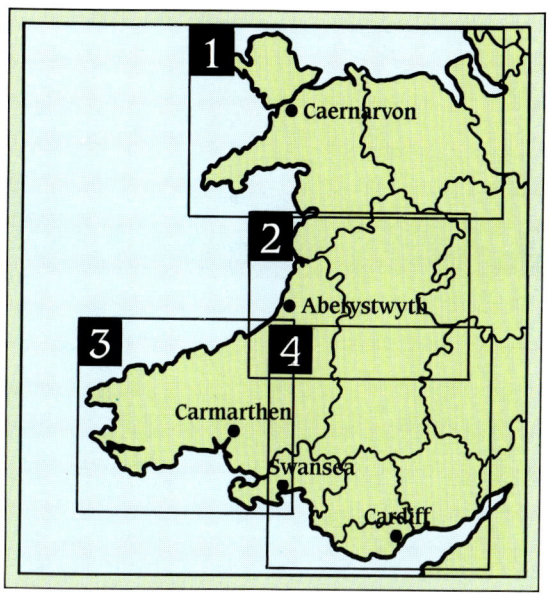

WALES

● **The Vale of Llangollen**

by Gilli Davies
WELSH FOOD SPECIALIST AND COOKERY WRITER

Food and drink play an important part in Wales' heritage. Lady Llanover wrote in 'Good Cookery', published in 1867, about a visitor, "Hospitality had greeted him and courtesy had taken him prisoner". In those days before easy transport in Wales, a remote farm might see very few visitors, but on arrival travellers would be sure to find a warm welcome and a table laden with farmhouse cheese, Welshcakes and local honey in their honour.

You can even eat as the Romans did on cockles, oysters and laver, an edible seaweed, from the Welsh coast, drink mead or wine produced from vines planted on the very soil where the Romans planted theirs.

The tradition of griddling on a bakestone links the Welsh with the Scots, the Irish and the Bretons in northern France. Pancakes are common diet in all these countries, but unique to Wales is the baking of a scone-like mixture for Welshcakes. Most households throughout the Principality have a tin of Welshcakes baked freshly at least once a week.

But if you would like to taste one hot off the griddle then visit Swansea Market where the bakestone is always warm and few shoppers can resist the temptation.

Baking has always been the strength of the Welsh diet; look out for bara brith — a rich tea-bread glazed with honey and served thickly-sliced and spread with salted Welsh butter. And there's Teisin lap, another fruit cake with a moist texture, which was particularly favoured by miners as it left no crumbs in their tuck box.

Caerphilly cheese was also popular with miners, with its mild flavour and soft texture encased in a firm crust. The acidity of Welsh soil suits cheeses like Caerphilly and there is evidence that as long ago as the 10thC a similar 'brined' cheese was made in Wales. The art of cheese-making almost died out during the wartime restrictions, but over the past 15 years there has been a resurgence of cheese-making in Wales.

The south west region of Wales is

paradise to cheese lovers. Over 30 cheeses are made in Dyfed — there are farmhouse Cheddars, and Caerphilly, Gouda type, Colby cheese, sheep's and goats' milk cheese, cream cheese, soft and hard cheeses — and many are made from unpasteurised milk to give them a fuller flavour.

Bordered on three sides by sea, Wales has strong fishing connections. Milford Haven dock is worth a visit early in the morning when as many as 50 local species of fish, such as lug, razorfish, pollack, bass and flounders are auctioned off, but go early — between 4 and 8am. Then there are the inland rivers and lakes for the keen angler. Search for the mysterious Torgoch in Lake Bala, a fish dating back to the Ice Age.

The smoking of fish — or indeed any food — has been practised in Wales for centuries and was a great means of preservation. Sides of pork, legs of lamb, mackerel, salmon and even Caerphilly cheese were tucked up the chimney in many a country house to see the family through the winter months.

Driving around in a car is quite a challenge; never judge a map with your thumbnail for most routes take longer, much longer, than anticipated. Few roads are straight, most go up or down or twist around the valleys. But wherever you go, you may be sure that the Welsh 'will keep a welcome'.

Gilli Davies

MAP 1 WALES

Map 1 C3
Anglesey Sea Zoo
The Oyster Hatchery,
Brynsiencyn,
Anglesey LL61 6TQ
Tel. Brynsiencyn (024873) 411
*From Menai Bridge follow A4080
south westwards, after 4 miles
turn left at Brynsiencyn onto
unclassified road for 1½ miles to
Sea Zoo. Signposted.*

This marine zoo features
everything from sea urchins to
giant conger eels. It is unique in
that the adjoining shop sells fish

More Welsh is spoken here than anywhere else in Wales
and it is curious to hear a 'foreign' tongue whilst still in Britain. Anglesey was known as the 'granary' of Wales as it once
supplied most of its grain. Locally milled wheat and oats are
still used in the amazing variety of Welsh cakes and biscuits
which you will find as you travel around the country. Bara-
bread appears in a variety of shapes, sizes and flavours.
There is bara tun-tin bread, bara fflat-batch loaf, bara planc
— cooked on a bakestone, bara sinsir — gingerbread, bara
ceirch — oatcakes, and bara brith — speckled bread, probably the best known of all.

Map

WALLASEY
MERSEYSIDE 551
Hoylake 553
BIRKENHEAD
ST. HELENS
M57
LIVERPOOL
Widnes
Runcorn

Prestatyn
Rhyl
548
5151
547
548
Colwyn
Bay
dudno
Abergele
55
St. Asaph
FELIN-Y-GORS FISHERIES
Llanfair
Talhaiarn
548
525
Holywell
55
Flint
Queensferry
The Wirral
Mersey
Ellesmere
Port
M53
561
562
562
M56
Frods
56

Denbigh
TY'N-Y-COED FARM TRAIL
541
541
538
540
550
550
541
540
C
H
Chester
51
54
51

Bylchau
543
Mold
Buckley
549
PENTRE MILL
494
anrwst
CLWYD
525
544
55
483
Broxton
534
Ruthin
550
Caergwrle
5104
541
Holt
WREXHAM ROAD FARM
tws-y-oed
543

foelas
5
Cerrigydrudion
494
525
525
TOMLINSON'S CHEESE SHOP
Wrexham
483
ERDDIG
528
525
41
Druid
5104
Ruabon
542
Corwen 5
539
539
525
ron-goch
Bala
494
Dee
UPPER MILLS TROUT FARM
Llangollen
5
Chirk
Ellesmere
495

Bala L.
BERWYN
2713
llyn
494
Llangynog
2970
L. Vyrnwy
Oswestry
Whittington
495
528
49
Wem
Burlton
W. Felton
5
Llanfyllin
490
495
Pant
Hadnall

E   F   G   H   I

---

from the tanks, allowing visitors to choose their own. The shop also sells shellfish, game, smoked fish, laverbread and gourmet food.

☞ adults £1.75, senior citizens £1.20, children (over 3) 90p
◑ 13 Feb–Oct daily 10–5
Facilities: ☕ 🍴 ♿ 🚻 🚗 ♨ ⚒
🍴 restaurant serves speciality seafood & salad platters

Map 1 C3
Bryntirion Open Farm
Dwyran, Anglesey LL61 6BQ
Tel. Brynsiencyn (024873) 232

From Newborough follow A4080 eastwards, after 2 miles turn right onto unclassified road for ¼ mile to farm on right.

Bryntirion Farm offers visitors the chance to experience first hand the pleasures and problems of running a modern organic farm. They are encouraged to come into close contact with the livestock and participate in everyday farm life. A museum exhibiting agricultural implements gives an insight into the rural life of the past.

☞ adults £1.20, children (over 3) 80p
◑ May–Oct daily 10.30–5, tours at 11, 2 & 4
Facilities: ☕ 🍴 🚻 🚗 ♨ ⚒

● **Ewe and lambs**

MAP 1   WALES

🛥 Map 1 H2
Erddig
Nr Wrexham, Clwyd LL13 0YT
Tel. Wrexham (0978) 355314

*From Wrexham follow A5152
south westwards, after 1 mile
turn left onto unclassified road
for 1½ miles, then turn left to
house. Signposted.*

This late 17thC country house,
owned by the National Trust,
has a complete range of
working service quarters
including kitchens, laundry,
bakehouse and scullery. The
kitchens are arranged to show
visitors how food was prepared
in a typical 19thC country
house. The gardens, too, have
been carefully thought out and
contain varieties of fruit known
to have been grown here in the
17thC. The shop sells fruit and
plants from the gardens as well
as the National Trust's own
range of biscuits and sweets.

☞ house & garden: adults
£2.50, children £1.00, family
ticket (2 adults & 2 children)
£5.00; garden: adults £1.00,
children 50p
● 31 Mar-16 Oct Sat-Thur 12-5

Facilities: 🪑 🍴 ♿ 🚗 🍽
🍴 light lunches & teas served in
licensed restaurant

● **Felin Isaf 17th century watermill**

✈ Map 1 E4
Felin Isaf Watermill
Glan Conwy, Clwyd LL28 5TE
Tel. Glan Conwy (049268) 646

*From Llandudno follow A470
southwards for 5 miles to mill on
right. Signposted.*

Felin Isaf consists of a series of
grade II listed buildings all
related to milling. Fully
renovated and now back in
working order, the mills
recently won awards for their
contribution to the
conservation of local
architecture. The larger of the 2

mills was built in 1740 and has 4
pairs of mill stones. Visitors may
examine the flour production
machinery and read the history
of flour milling in the area. The
site also has an oat kiln, used for
drying the grain before milling
and a miller's cottage. The shop
sells stoneground wholemeal
flour, freshly baked bread, bara
brith and Welsh cakes.

☞ adults £1.00, children 50p
● all year daily 10-dusk
Facilities: 🪑 ♿ 🚻 🚗 🍽 🏔

🎣 Map 1 F4
Felin-Y-Gors Fisheries
Trout Farm, St Asaph Road,
Bodelwyddan, Clwyd LL18 5UY
Tel. St Asaph (0745) 584044

*From St Asaph follow A55
westwards, after 2 miles turn left
onto unclassified road for ¼ mile
to fisheries. Signposted.*

Set in secluded wooded
surroundings, these lakes are
supplied with natural spring
water and stocked with prime
trout. Visitors may fish their
own and have their catch
cleaned, smoked and packed
free of charge. There are
regular tours as well as
demonstrations of gutting,
filleting and smoking. The shop
sells fresh rainbow trout,
home-reared chickens and
eggs.

☞ fishing: £12.50 per day,
£6.50 per ½ day, rod £2.50 per
day
● farm: all year daily 9-6; fishing:
Feb-Nov daily 9-10 or dusk
Facilities: 🚻 🚗 🍽

🐟 Map 1 D4
The Fish Shop
Pant Yr Afon, Penmaenmawr,
Gwynedd LL34 6BY
Tel. Penmaenmawr (0492)
623557

*From Conway follow A55
westwards for 4 miles to
Penmaenmawr.*

MAP 1

• **A good catch at a Welsh fish farm**

This fishmonger smokes his own fish such as salmon, cod, haddock and also chicken. He sells fresh fish and shellfish, much of it caught locally in the Menai Straits including monkfish, plaice, whiting, turbot, Dover sole, sea bass and sea trout. He also sells free-range poultry and local game — pheasant, partridge, mallard, geese from Anglesey and cuts of venison. He makes his own venison sausages and also smokes them.
◑ all year Tue, Thur, Fri 8-5, Mon, Sat 9-1, Wed 8-1

🐟 Map 1 E3
Glangors Salmon Ranch
Coed Llydan Bach,
Melin-Y-Coed, Llanrwst,
Gwynedd LL26 0SL
Tel. Llanrwst (0492) 641668
From Llanrwst follow A470 southwards, after 1 mile turn left onto unclassified road for ½ mile to Melin-y-Coed.
Based in the Snowdonia Park, with its breathtaking views, this salmon farm and smokery offers still-water fishing in totally tranquil surroundings. Visitors are invited to catch their own fish, watch the curing and smoking processes and even to have a go at smoking

their own freshly caught salmon. Specialities for sale include spiced and whisky salmon and the shop also sells trout, chicken, duck, cheese and prawns — all smoked on the premises.
☞ FYO: £27 per day
◑ smokery: all year daily 9-5; fishery: all year daily dawn-dusk
Facilities: ⬤ 🚗 🛏

🏠 Map 1 C3
Maes Mawr
Llanllyfni, Caernarvon,
Gwynedd LL54 6DG
Tel. Penygroes (0286) 881809
From Caernarvon follow A487 southwards for 7 miles to Llanllyfni.
This dairy goat farm makes traditional cheeses which have a unique and sophisticated flavour. Visitors are welcome to view the dairy and to taste and buy the range of cheeses produced from their unpasteurised goats' milk: Marianglas, a natural crust matured hard cheese; or 2 soft cheeses — one with chives rolled in paprika and one blended with mixed dried fruit and rolled in black pepper — both made in ¼lb rounds.
☞ free
◑ all year by appointment

🍷 Map 1 D1
HOTEL MAES-Y-NEUADD
Talsarnau,
Gwynedd LL47 6YA
Tel: Harlech (0766) 780200
From Harlech follow A496 northwards for 3 miles to hotel on right. Signposted.
A stone manor house standing in 8 acres. The dining room has Georgian-style panelling with silk wallpaper and boasts beautiful views. This gently spicy recipe for Welsh Lamb with Honey and Cider works particularly well with real Welsh lamb because it has very little fat.
◑ Mon-Sun D, Sun L, Mon-Sat L by prior arrangement
Meals: 12.30-2, 7.30-9, closed 3 Jan-4 Feb
Price range Sun L £8.75, Set D £15.50
Seats 32
Cards: Access, Visa
Facilities: 🍷⬤🚗

WELSH LAMB cooked in Honey and Cider
3lb leg Welsh lamb
ground ginger
3 tbsp honey
fresh rosemary
½ pint cider
cornflour

Heat oven to gas 7 (425F, 320C). Rub a little ground ginger into the skin of the lamb, place in a baking tin, coat with the honey and sprinkle with rosemary. Pour the cider around the meat and roast in the hot oven for 20 minutes, then lower the heat to gas 4 (350F, 180C) for 1 hour. Strain the juices, thicken with a little cornflour and serve with the joint, which should be pink.

MAP 1   WALES

✶ Map 1 G3
Pentre Mill
Loggerheads Country Park,
Loggerheads, Mold,
Clwyd CH7 5LH
Tel. Llanferres (035285) 586

*From Mold follow A494 south
westwards for 2 miles to
Loggerheads. Signposted.*

This working corn mill,
powered by water from the
River Alyn, is part of the
Loggerheads Country Park
which covers over 67 acres of
Clwyd countryside. The mill
was built in the 19thC and
visitors can read about its
history in the information
centre, follow guided tours and
watch milling demonstrations
in the mill itself. The nearby
'Leete', or water course, was
built by a Cornishman, John
Taylor, in 1823. It ran for 3 to 4
miles and provided enough
power to operate the water
wheels of several mines and
mills along the valley. It was a
well-known attraction in the
past and both the composer
Mendelssohn and Charles
Kingsley, author of 'The Water
Babies', visited it. Stoneground
flour is for sale.

☞ telephone for details
◑ telephone for details
Facilities: ⬛ 🍴 ♿ 🚾 🚍 ☕

🏠 Map 1 B4
Plas Dairy Farm
Llanfaelog, Nr Rhosneigr,
Anglesey LL63 5TU
Tel. Rhosneigr (0407) 810261

*From Rhosneigr follow A4080
eastwards for 1 mile to
Llanfaelog.*

This dairy farm milks its own
goats and cows and produces
soft cheeses, yoghurt and
cream. Visitors are welcome to
see the dairy by appointment
and to buy the farm's produce.

☞ free
◑ by appointment

LAVERBREAD

Traditional laverbread is sold
in a few bakeries. Do seek it
out, because it is difficult to
make at home.

● **Laverbread, made from
seaweed**

REGIONAL RECIPE

WELSH CINNAMON CAKE

4oz butter
4oz granulated sugar
2 egg yolks
$\frac{1}{2}$lb flour
$\frac{1}{2}$ tsp baking powder
1 heaped tsp cinnamon
apricot jam
3 egg whites
3 tbsp caster sugar

Heat oven to gas 4 (350F,
180C). Cream the butter and
sugar, beat in the egg yolks
and add the sifted flour,
baking powder and
cinnamon. Knead to a dough,
roll out to fit an 8$\frac{1}{2}$-inch tart
tin with a removable base
and bake for 20 minutes.
Heat a large tablespoon of
jam with a little water, sieve it
and brush thinly over the
cake. Beat the egg whites
until stiff, fold in the caster
sugar and beat again until
thick and creamy. Pile on to
the cake, swirling the top as
decoration and bake for 15
minutes, or until meringue is
set.

📇 Map 1 H2
Tomlinson's Cheese Shop
The Butcher Market, High
Street, Wrexham, Clwyd
Tel. Wrexham (0978) 265975

In town centre.

Mr Need has run Tomlinson's
Cheese Shop in Wrexham's
historic market building for 9
years. He sells all types of
cheeses, most of which are
English and Welsh farmhouse
varieties, with some from
smaller Welsh producers. He
also sells farmhouse butter and
free-range eggs.
◑ all year Mon, Tue, Thur-Sat
9-5.30

🏠 Map 1 C3
Ty'n Rhos Farm
Seion Llanddeiniolen,
Caernarvon,
Gwynedd LL55 3AE
Tel. Port Dinorwic (0248)
670489

*From Caernarvon follow B4366
north eastwards, after 3 miles
turn left onto unclassified road
for $\frac{1}{4}$ mile to farm. Signposted.*

This small farm set in beautiful
countryside makes its own
cheese once a week on a very

● **A cheese room**

MAP 1

● Honey fair at Aber Conway, 1873

small scale. Visitors are welcome to view the dairy and to taste the cheese.

☞ free
● by appointment
Facilities: 🚗 ♨

🌱 Map 1 H4
Ty'n-y-Coed Farm Trail
Ty'n-y-Coed, Northop, Mold, Clwyd CH7 6DG
Tel. Flint (03526) 61232
From Mold follow A5119 northwards, after 3 miles turn right into Starkey Lane for 1 mile to farm.

This traditional, family-run beef and sheep farm is set in the beautiful countryside of North Wales. Visitors may take a guided tour or walk the trail through the farm conservation area. There is also a pets' corner and a collection of farm curios. Beef and lamb in freezer packs are available by arrangement.

☞ adults £1.00, children (under 14) 60p

● Easter-Sep Sat, Sun 10-4; school hols daily 10-4
Facilities: 🚻 🚗 ♨

🎣 Map 1 G2
Upper Mills Trout Farm
Glyn Ceiriog, Clwyd LL20 7BY
Tel. Glyn Ceiriog (069172) 225
From Oswestry follow B4579 north westwards, after 8 miles turn right onto B4500 for ¼ mile, then turn left onto unclassified road for ¼ mile to Glyn Ceiriog.

This trout farm offers visitors the opportunity to fish their own trout in the River Ceiriog. The farm smokes its own trout and both these and fresh fish can be bought from their shop.

☞ fishing £5.00 per day, £3.00 per half day, in season
● all year daily 9-5
Facilities: 🚻 🚗 ♨

🍎 Map 1 H3
Wrexham Road Farm
Holt, Nr Wrexham, Clwyd LL13 9YU
Tel. Farndon (0829) 270304

From Holt follow A534 south westwards, after ¼ mile turn right to farm.

A pick your own farm and a shop offering most soft fruits and vegetables.

● Jul-Oct daily 9-7; Nov-Jun Sun-Thur 9-5, Fri 9-6, Sat 9-5.30
Facilities: 🚻 🚗 ♨

● A selection of Welsh cheeses

MAP 2 WALES

MID WALES

Mid Wales — known more poetically as the Heart of Wales — produces excellent lamb. One of the great traditional dishes is Cawl Cymreig — or Welsh Broth. Like many farmhouse recipes the ingredients change depending on what is in season but lamb or mutton is essential to give a rich, nourishing flavour. To quote an old Welsh proverb "This broth is as good to drink as to eat the meat".

🐾 Map 2 F3
Bacheldre Watermill
Churchstoke, Montgomery, Powys SY15 6TE
Tel. Churchstoke (05885) 489
From Montgomery follow B4385 south eastwards, after 3 miles turn right onto A489 for ½ mile,

then turn left onto unclassified road for ¼ mile to mill on right just after bridge. Signposted.
An 18thC watermill which has been restored to working order and now produces stoneground flour commercially. It is one of the last surviving examples of a

small operational country mill on the mid-Wales border. Visitors are welcome to tour the mill and a selection of stoneground flour and bran is for sale.

🐾 adults 60p, children 20p
◑ Easter-Sep Fri-Tue 1-6
Facilities: 🍽 🚻 WC ♿
🍽 teas served with homemade scones & cakes made from their own flour

〰 Map 2 B4
Cambrian Traditional Foods
Hafod Wen, Rhoslefain, Tywyn, Gwynedd LL36 9NH
Tel. Tywyn (0654) 710033

Map 2 C4

The Centre for Alternative Technology

Machynlleth, Powys SY20 9AZ
Tel. Machynlleth (0654) 2400

From Machynlleth follow A487 northwards, after 3½ miles turn right onto unclassified road for ½ mile to centre. Signposted.

Opened in 1975, the Centre for Alternative Technology is an attempt to show how technology can be used to lessen man's impact on the environment. Completely self-sufficient, it demonstrates new renewable technologies which save resources and cut waste and pollution. A 10-acre smallholding and vegetable garden are worked organically, providing the Centre with meat, eggs and vegetables. The farm also keeps free-range hens, goats, fish, bees, sheep and pigs. There is an interesting ecological gardening display which includes a large pond and shows how to make gardens more attractive to wildlife.

adults £2.20, senior citizens £1.20, children (5-16) 80p
all year daily 10-5
Facilities: 🍽️ ♿ 📷 🚗 ☕ 🏧
★ residential courses on organic gardening, vegetarian cookery
🍽️ wholefood vegetarian restaurant serving homemade organic food

Map 2 B4

Dorothy Bakery

37 High Street, Tywyn, Gwynedd LL36 9AY
Tel. Tywyn (0654) 710553

In town centre.

All the goods produced by this bakery are made in the traditional way. Local specialities include hand-moulded bread and Tywyn butter buns. A selection of homemade jams, savouries and delicatessen items is also available. Old fashioned sugar baskets and cakes can be made to customers' orders.
Apr-Oct Mon-Sat 7-5; Nov-Mar Mon, Tue, Thur-Sat 7-5, Wed 7-1
Facilities: 🚗

Map 2 C4

Felin Crewi Working Watermill

Felin Crewi, Penegoes, Machynlleth, Powys SY20 8NH
Tel. Machynlleth (0654) 3113

From Machynlleth follow A489 eastwards, after 1½ miles turn right to mill in Penegoes. Signposted.

Built in the late 1700s Felin Crewi corn mill was working until the 1940s but then fell into disrepair. It has now been restored to working order and retains much of its original character. A large mill, it is

From Tywyn follow A493 northwards, after 5 miles turn left at Rhoslefain onto unclassified road for ½ mile, then turn right to house.

One of the few traditional smokeries in Wales, this company smokes a wide range of products including salmon, trout, hams, fillet steak and duck breast and also sells nuts, cheese and free-range eggs. Visitors are welcome to tour the smokery and watch a demonstration of the smoking techniques.

free
all year, any reasonable time
Facilities: ♿ 🚻 🚗

● **Organic garden at The Centre for Alternative Technology**

MAP 2   WALES

driven by a water wheel and originally had 3 sets of stones which were used to grind wheat, barley and oats. Visitors may see the mill in operation as well as displays telling its history. The shop sells stoneground products, muesli, bara brith and Welsh country hampers.

☞ adults 85p, senior citizens 60p, children (under 14) 40p
◑ Easter-Sep daily 10.30-6; Oct-Mar Mon-Fri 9-1
Facilities: ☕ ⛽ ⛽ 👤 ♿ 🚻 🚗
🍴 teas & lunches served with homebaked scones, cakes, bara brith & vegetarian dishes

---

🌿 Map 2 D2
Gigrin Farm and Nature Trail
South Road, Rhayader, Powys LD6 5BL
Tel. Rhayader (0597) 810243
From Rhayader follow A470 southwards for ½ mile to farm. Signposted.

Visitors are welcome to wander unaccompanied round the 2-mile trail on this mixed farm. The trail goes through fields of cows and sheep, by a duck and trout pond and through a bird sanctuary where there are badger setts. Other farm animals include breeds of poultry, a donkey, goat, pony, blue-faced Leicester rams and lots of dogs and cats.

☞ adults £1.00, children 50p, family ticket (up to 4 people) £2.50
◑ Easter-Oct daily 10-6
Facilities: 🚻 🚗 🐕 ⛺

🦞 Map 2 E3
William Jones and Sons
1-3 High Street, Newtown, Powys SY16 2NX
Tel. Newtown (0686) 25509
In town centre.

This butcher specialises in local meat, particularly Welsh lamb.

His meat is butchered by both traditional and continental methods and he offers a comprehensive range of products, all cut and packed to customers' requirements. He has a range of 15 different homemade sausages and all his pies, burgers, pâtés and cooked meats are prepared on the premises.

◑ all year Mon-Fri 8-5.30, Sat 8-5.00

●**Fresh Welsh salmon**

🌿 Map 2 B5
Llwyn Onn Farm and Nature Walk
Llwyn Onn Uchaf, Barmouth, Meirionydd, Gwynedd LL42 1DX
Tel. Barmouth (0341) 280077
From Barmouth follow A496 eastwards, after 1¼ miles turn left onto unclassified road for 1½ miles to farm.

This small, old-fashioned mixed stock mountain farm keeps many rare breed farm animals. Visitors may take a conducted tour around the farm and buy free-range eggs and, occasionally, a free-range pig.

☞ £1.50
◑ 7 Jun-15 Sep Tue-Thur 9-1, May & Aug Bank Hols
Facilities: 🐕

EGG AND BACON PIE
1lb thin lean bacon rashers diced
6-8 eggs
¾lb puff pastry
salt & pepper
1 beaten egg

Heat the oven to gas 7 (425F, 220C). Roll out the pastry and use half to line a 7-inch pie plate. Spread half the bacon over the pastry base, break in the eggs, cover with the remaining bacon and season. Cover with the rest of the pastry, brush with egg and bake for 30 minutes, reducing heat after 10 minutes.

🏠 Map 2 B1
Mesen Fach Farm
Bethania, Nr Llanon, Dyfed SY23 5NL
Tel. Llangeitho (097423) 348

From Tregaron follow A485 north westwards, after 4 miles turn left onto B4577 for 4 miles, then turn left onto B4576 for 1 mile, then turn right onto unclassified road for 50 yards, then turn right onto unclassified road for ½ mile to farm on left.

This organic working farm, 6 miles from the Welsh coast, has dairy sheep, pigs and peacocks. Visitors are invited to watch the sheep-milking at 4pm and sample the famous handmade Acorn ewes' milk cheese produced using vegetarian rennet and pure salt. Sheep's milk cheese is available in truckles of 4 to 4½lb.

☞ adults £1.00, accompanied children 50p
◑ Apr-Sep daily 4-6

🐟 Map 2 E3
Nettesheim Fish Farm
Lake Mochdre, Newtown, Powys SY16 4JN
Tel. Newtown (0686) 25623

MAP 2

From Newtown follow A489 westwards, after 1 mile turn left at Theatr Hafren onto unclassified road for 4 miles to Lake Mochdre. Signposted.

Visitors are welcome to walk round this trout farm and try their hand at fishing. The shop sells fresh and home-smoked trout.

☞ farm: 50p; fishing: £10 per day up to 4 fish, £6.50 per ½-day up to 2 fish
● all year daily 10-6
Facilities: 🚻 🚗 🛝

WELSH LAMB

One of the best places to buy the local lamb, as well as beef and pork, is in Newtown at William Jones, 1-3 High Street. You can also buy endless different sausages here, including some good spicy varieties.

🏠 Map 2 B1
Porthrhiw Dairy Goats
Capel Betws Lleucu, Llwynygroes, Tregaron, Dyfed SY25 6SW
Tel. Llangeitho (097423) 387
From Tregaron follow A485 southwards, after 1 mile turn right onto B4342 for 3 miles, then turn left at Llangeitho onto unclassified road for 1½ miles to Capel Betws Lleucu.

This organic farm specialises in goats, sheep and pigs and also grows some fruit and vegetables. Soft and hard farmhouse cheeses are made on the premises and cheese-making demonstrations are given by arrangement. The shop sells yoghurt and free-range, organically reared kid-meat and pork.
☞ free
● all year by appointment
Facilities: 🚻 🚗 🛝

🏠 Map 2 B3
Rachel's Dairy
Brynllys, Borth, Dyfed SY24 5LZ
Tel. Borth (097081) 489
From Aberystwyth follow A487 north eastwards, after 4 miles turn left onto B4353 for 2 miles, then turn right after railway bridge onto unclassified road for ¼ mile, then turn left to farm. Signposted.

Rachel's Dairy has practised organic farming since 1948 and continues to produce natural, healthy foods. Visitors are welcome to come anytime, take the farm trail or simply visit the farm shop where they can buy the best in organic dairy products including cream, fruit yoghurt, butter and soft and hard cheeses.
☞ free
● all year any reasonable time
Facilities: 🍴 🚻 🚗

♥ Map 2 F5
Rhandregynwen
Four Crosses, Llanymynech, Powys SY22 6SN
Tel. Oswestry (0691) 830497
From Welshpool follow A483 northwards, after 6 miles turn right at Four Crosses onto unclassified road for 1 mile to farm on left.

This mixed farm has many rare breeds of animals but

specialises in goats — visitors can see the well-known Sandford herd. There is also an interesting antique dairy and a small farm museum with agricultural implements.
☞ adults £1.50, senior citizens & children (under 16) 75p
● Easter-Oct Fri-Sun, Bank Hols 10.30-5
Facilities: 🍴 🚻 🚗 🛝

♥ Map 2 B3
Trefrifawr Farm Trail
Trefrifawr, Aberdovey, Gwynedd LL35 0SL
Tel. Aberdovey (065472) 247
From Aberdovey follow A493 eastwards, after 1½ miles turn left onto unclassified road for 1 mile to farm. Signposted.

Visitors to this farm overlooking the Dyfi estuary can spend a day relaxing in the beautiful countryside and observing the day-to-day life on a hill farm. There is a wide variety of farm animals to see and spectacular views on the farm walk. The farm sells Welsh lamb both boned and rolled either in vacuum or freezer packs.
☞ adults 80p, children 40p
● May-Oct daily 10-6
Facilities: 🍴 🚻 🚗 🛝 /🅰
🍴 homemade Welsh cakes & bara brith

● **Welsh honey**

MAP 3 WALES

SOUTH WEST WALES

New Quay
TEIFI FARMHOUSE CHEESE
PANT-YR-HOLIAD GARDEN
Sarnau
Y FELIN
Cardigan
487
FELIN GERNOS DAIRY
484
475
NEVERN DAIRY
Newport
FELIN GERI MILL
Goodwick
CAWS CENARTH TRADITIONAL WELSH
Newcastle
487 CHEESE
Emlyn
484
Fishguard
Crymmych Arms
RHOS DDU FARM
CANOLFAN GIG
487
LLANGLOFFAN FARMHOUSE
CHEESE CENTRE
Mathry
Letterston
MOUNTPLEASANT GOAT FARM
Tufton
LLEITHYR FARM MUSEUM
LLYSYFRAN RESERVOIR AND
COUNTRY PARK
478
PANTYLLY
CHEESE
WILSONS OF TREFFGARNE
PEMBROKESHIRE FISH FARMS
CILOWEN UCHAF
Carmart
St.
David's
Newgale
40
SCOLTON MANOR MUSEUM
GREGORY'S DELICATESSEN
Whitland
40
LLAWHADEN FISH HATCHERY
487
Haverfordwest
St. Brides Bay
RIDGEWAY HONEY FARM
40
GLYNCOCH
FRUIT FARM
ears
Narberth
477
4115
LLANTEGLOS BREWERY
478
Laugharne
4076
EASTWOOD NATURE PARK
4066
Milford
Haven Neyland
4075
477
MARROS FREE RANGE EGG
Pendine
Dale
477
Pembroke
Dock
Tenby
Carmarthen Bay
Pembroke
4139
Manorbier
Caldy I.
St. Govan's Hd

A   B   C   D

Dyfed is an enormous county which bustles with small rural food industries. Follow handwritten signs down windy country lanes and discover a host of farmhouse cheeses, smokeries, restored flour mills, deer farms, herb gardens and trout and salmon fisheries. Wild salmon and salmon trout — sewin — are fished on the rivers Teifi and Tywyi from coracles — light boats which were once made from horse or ox hide, though nowadays tar-coated canvas is used. This type of boat existed before the Romans settled here and the method of fishing has hardly changed since.

☺ Map 3 B4
Canolfan Gig
Glyn Cynnil, Castle Morris,
Haverfordwest,
Dyfed SA62 5XA
Tel. St Nicholas (03485) 657

From Fishguard follow A487 south westwards for 4 miles to shop.

This farm shop and processing unit specialises in home-reared

📖 Map 3 D4

Caws Cenarth Traditional Welsh Cheese

Fferm Glyneithinog, Pontseli Boncath, Dyfed SA37 OLH
Tel. Newcastle Emlyn (0239) 710432

From Newcastle Emlyn follow unclassified road south westwards for 1½ miles to Penrherber, then turn right, then first left onto unclassified road for 1 mile to farm on right. Signposted.

This family cheese-making farm uses milk from its own herd of pedigree Friesians to produce handmade traditional Welsh Caerphilly. An old barn has been converted into a cheesery which has a special viewing room for visitors as well as displays of old cheese presses, posters and photographs. The farm uses only vegetable rennet and sea salt and avoids

● **Traditional Welsh cheeses**

● **A farm making traditional Welsh cheeses**

pork and lamb. Emphasis is on naturally bred animals using no hormones or growth promoters. The hams and bacon are cured on the premises. The shop also sells game, local fresh vegetables and free-range eggs.
◖ all year Mon 1-6, Tue-Fri 10-8, Sat 9-6, closed Bank Hols
Facilities: 🚗

MAP 3   **WALES**

all artificial colourings, flavourings and preservatives. Visitors may purchase the cheese in 10lb wheels, 14oz miniatures and in special presentation packs.

☞ free
◑ cheese-making: all year Tue-Thur mornings by appointment
Facilities: ⬛ 🚗 ⛺

🏠 Map 3 D3
Cilowen Uchaf
Login, Whitland,
Dyfed SA34 OTJ
Tel. Llanboidy (09946) 303
From Narberth follow A478 northwards, after 4 miles turn right at Llandissilio onto unclassified road for 3 miles, then turn right just past Login onto unclassified road towards Crosshands for 1 mile to farm. Signposted.

This cheese-producing farm is the only one in the UK to use milk from the rare breed of Red Poll cows. The herd is grazed on organic pastures which have not been sprayed with insecticides or herbicides. Llanboidy farmhouse cheese is still made in the traditional way by hand. Visitors may taste the cheeses and purchase wedges of any weight up to 5lb or wheels of 10lb. The shop also sells laverbread, made from seaweed.

☞ free
◑ all year daily 9-11, 4-7 or by appointment
Facilities: 🚗

♀ Map 3 B2
Eastwood Nature Park
Uzmaston, Haverfordwest, Pembrokeshire,
Dyfed SA62 4QA
Tel. Haverfordwest (0437) 66372
From Haverfordwest follow unclassified road south eastwards through Uzmaston, after 2 miles turn left to Park. Signposted.

One of the features of Eastwood Nature Park is the Cooper's Museum which shows the tools and equipment used in Llewellins Royal Prize Churn Works for over 200 years. The butter churns and moulds made there were at one time exported all over the world. The heritage farm has naturally reared farm animals and there are regular demonstrations of sheep-milking and cheese and yoghurt-making. The farm shop sells cheese, yoghurt, milk and garden produce.

☞ adults £1.50, senior citizens & children 75p
◑ May-Sep daily 10-6
Facilities: ⬛ 🍴 ⬛ 🚗 ⛺ 🏠
★ sheep-milking demonstrations

🐟 Map 3 D4
Felin Geri Mill
Cwm Coy, Newcastle Emlyn, Dyfed
Tel. Newcastle Emlyn (0239) 710810
From Newcastle Emlyn follow B4333 north westwards for 2 miles to Cwm Coy. Signposted.

Felin Geri is one of the few surviving watermills in Wales. Set in 40 acres, the picturesque mill has a fascinating and well-documented history. It now works all year round producing traditional stoneground wholemeal flour. Part of the flour is then separated and mixed to produce semolina which in turn is used to make shortbread and biscuits. Visitors can see all stages of the milling process exactly as it was 100 years ago. The surrounding grounds contain trout pools and many rare breeds of animals as well as a 2-mile trail. The shop sells wholemeal baked goods and organic produce.

☞ adults £2.00, senior citizens £1.50, children (over 5) £1.00

◑ Easter-Oct Mon-Fri 10-6, Sat, Sun 10.30-5.30 or by appointment
Facilities: ⬛ 🍴 ♿ ⬛ 🚗 ⛺ 🏠
★ 2nd annual food fair for country producers
🍴 lunches, teas & dinners served in mill's licensed restaurant — menu features mill's own lamb, bread & fish

---

🏠 Map 3 E4
Felin Gernos Dairy
Felin Gernos, Maesllyn,
Llandysul, Dyfed SA44 5NB
Tel. Rhydlewis (023975) 362
From Llandysul follow A486 northwards, after 4 miles turn left onto unclassified road for 1 mile through Maesllyn to farm. Signposted.

The Felin Gernos Dairy is a family business making traditional Welsh cheese. Visitors may taste and buy the dairy's own cheese as well as the produce from other local suppliers such as mustard, honey, waffles and butter.

☞ free
◑ all year Mon-Sat 9-6
Facilities: ⬛ ⬛ 🚗
★ demonstrations of cheese-making by arrangement
🍞 homemade bread, cakes, scones, cheese, fresh lemonade & locally made butter

---

😊 Map 3 D3
Glyncoch Fruit Farm
St Clears, Carmarthen,
Dyfed SA33 4AR
Tel. St Clears (0994) 230665
From St Clears follow A40 westwards for 1 mile to farm. Signposted.

A pick your own farm offering strawberries, raspberries, gooseberries, blackcurrants, loganberries and some vegetables.
◑ telephone for details
Facilities: 🍴 ⬛ 🚗 ⛺ 🏠
🍴 cream teas include freshly picked strawberries & raspberries

MAP 3

Map 3 C2
Gregory's Delicatessen
Market Square, Narberth, Dyfed
Tel. Narberth (0834) 861212

In town centre.

Gregory's claims to offer the finest selection of foodstuffs under one roof in Wales. They have assembled produce from all over Britain and Europe and are especially proud of their fine range of cheeses. They stock over 90 different varieties including many Welsh cheeses such as Llanboidy Farmhouse. They also specialise in cold meats — with over 50 salamis — fine wines and a large assortment of tea and coffee. Customers may order specially made-up hampers.

● all year Mon-Sat 9-5.30
Facilities: 🍽 🚻 wc
🍽 lunches & teas served in licensed coffee shop

Map 3 E3
Home Farm
Llanllawddog, Carmarthen, Dyfed SA32 7JE
Tel. Llanpumsaint (026784) 436

From Carmarthen follow A40 north eastwards, after 1 mile turn left onto A485 for 6 miles, then turn right onto unclassified road for ½ mile to farm. Signposted.

Visitors can fish their own trout — fly fishing only allowed — in a 2½-acre trout lake in the beautiful Llanllawddog valley. They can also watch the fish being fed at the adjacent fish farm and wander around the beechwood valley where there are plenty of glorious spots for a picnic. Trout is sold in the shop with a smokery planned for this season.

☞ farm: free; fly fishing: £10 per day, limit of 4 fish

● farm: Apr-Oct daily 10-6; Nov-Mar daily 10-4; fly fishing: mid Feb-6 Dec daily 9-9 or dusk
Facilities: wc 🚐

Map 3 B4
Llangloffan Farmhouse Cheese Centre
Llangloffan Farm, Castle Morris, Nr Mathry, Haverfordwest, Dyfed SA62 5ET
Tel. St Nicholas (03485) 241

From Fishguard follow A487 south westwards, after 5 miles turn left onto unclassified road towards Castle Morris for ½ mile to farm on right. Signposted.

Llangloffan Farm has won several awards for its naturally produced cheese. The milk comes from a champion pedigree Jersey herd which grazes on old leys fertilised organically with farmyard

manure and calcified seaweed. The cheese itself is made by hand using traditional equipment and contains no chemical residues or artificial additives. Visitors arriving at the farm between 10 and 12.30 will be able to watch the cheese-making process and later take the farm walk. They can visit the dairy with its original cheese-presses, moulds and curd knives. The shop sells cheese, which can be tasted, mustard, fudge and ice cream.

☞ adults £1.00, senior citizens 75p, children (5-14) 50p
● cheese-making: Apr-May,

● **Making the cheese, Llangloffan Farm**

● **The cheese room, Llangloffan Farm**

MAP 3　　　　　　　　**WALES**

Sep-Oct Mon, Wed, Thur,
Sat 10-12.30; Jun-Aug Mon-Sat
10-12.30; shop: all year Mon-Sat
9-5
Facilities: 🍵 🅦🅒 🚗 🛏 🏧
🍵 homemade bara brith,
scones & biscuits

🍺 Map 3 D2
Llanteglos Brewery
Llanteg, Nr Amroth,
Dyfed SA67 8PU
Tel. Llanteg (083483) 677
*From Tenby follow A478
northwards, after 4½ miles turn
right onto A477 for 5 miles to
Llanteg. Signposted.*

Llanteglos is Pembrokeshire's
only brewery producing real
ale. Visitors can tour the
brewery and enjoy a tasting in
the adjoining country club bar.
Beer is for sale in 4 pint jugs or
2 gallon boxes.

☞ telephone for details
● 31 Mar-Sep by appointment
Facilities: 🍵 🍴 ♿ 🅦🅒 🚗 🛏 🏧

🎣 Map 3 C3
Llawhaden Fish Hatchery
Old Mill, Llawhaden, Narberth,
Dyfed SA67 8DJ
Tel. Llawhaden (09914) 256
*From Haverfordwest follow A40
eastwards, after 7 miles turn left
at Canaston Bridge onto
unclassified road for 1½ miles
towards Llawhaden, then turn
right onto unclassified road for ½
mile to farm on left. Signposted.*

Set in the beautiful eastern
Cleddau valley this fish
hatchery invites visitors to take
a guided tour and watch the
feeding of the fish. The shop
sells fresh and smoked pink
rainbow trout and a variety of
homemade trout pâtés and
smoked cheeses.

☞ telephone for details
● Apr-Sep Tue-Sun, Bank Hols
10.30-1, 2-6; Oct-Mar Tue-Sat
10.30-1, 2-5
Facilities: ♿ 🚗 🛏

🏚 Map 3 A3
Lleithyr Farm Museum
Nr Whitesand Bay,
St David's, Pembrokeshire,
Dyfed SA62 6PR
Tel. St David's (0437) 720245
*From St David's follow
unclassified road northwards,
after ½ mile turn left onto B4583
for 1 mile, then turn right onto
unclassified road for ¼ mile, then
turn left onto unclassified road
for ¼ mile to farm on right.
Signposted.*

Lleithyr Farm Museum has
some interesting displays of
kitchen and household goods
including butter-making
utensils and farming
implements. There are also
some farm animals.

☞ adults £1.00, children (4-14)
50p
● May-Oct Tue-Sun, Bank Hols
10-5
Facilities: 🍴 ♿ 🅦🅒 🚗 🛏 🏧
🍴 teas served with homemade
Welsh cakes, bara brith & fruit
cakes

🎣 Map 3 C3
**Llysyfran Reservoir and
Country Park**
Clarbeston Road,
Haverfordwest, Dyfed
Tel. Maenclochag (09913) 273
*From Haverfordwest follow
B4329 north eastwards for 8
miles to park on right.
Signposted.*

This well-stocked reservoir
provides excellent fly and
worm fishing for brown and
rainbow trout. A 7½-mile
perimeter walk offers the
opportunity to see a wide
range of birds and wild animals.

☞ fishing by permit, telephone
for details
● all year daily 8-dusk
Facilities: 🍵 ♿ 🅦🅒 🚗 🛏

WELSH ONION CAKE
This recipe is ideal for using
Pembrokeshire potatoes and
onions.
1½lb potatoes peeled
¾lb onions peeled and sliced
4oz butter
salt & pepper
Heat the oven to gas 4 (350F,
180C). Slice the potatoes
paper-thin and put in a bowl
of cold water. Swish them
around to get rid of the
starchy juice, then pat dry.
Grease a shallow dish and put
in alternate layers of potatoes
and onions, seasoning each
layer and dotting with butter,
leaving about 1oz of butter to
cover the top. Cover with foil
and cook for 1½ hours,
removing the foil for the last
½ hour to brown. Either serve
the cake in its dish or turn out
onto a plate, flashing under a
grill to brown the other side.

🐔 Map 3 D2
Marros Free Range Eggs
Tal-Fan Farm, Marros, Pendine,
Dyfed SA33 4PN
Tel. Pendine (09945) 282
*From Pendine follow B4314
northwards, after ½ mile turn left
onto unclassified road for 1 mile
to Marros. Signposted.*

Overlooking Carmarthen Bay,
this is the largest free-range egg
farm in Wales. The hens' feed is
guaranteed free from artificial
yolk colourings, hormones and
preservatives. As well as eggs
the shop sells fresh oven-ready
chickens, chicken portions and
nuggets.

☞ free
● all year daily 9-6
Facilities: 🍵 🍴 ♿ 🅦🅒 🚗 🛏

GOATS' CHEESE
Farmers often keep small
herds of goats and there are
some delicious smallholders'
cheeses to be found.

MAP 3

● **Butter-making**

✱ Map 3 F3
Melin Maesdulais Watermill
Porthyrhyd, Carmarthen,
Dyfed SA32 8BT
Tel. Llanddarog (026786) 472

From Carmethen follow B4300 eastwards, after 5 miles turn right onto B4310 for 3 miles to Porthyrhyd. Signposted.

This water-powered mill produces a range of flours for bakeries and shops specialising in health foods. In addition to the 100% wholemeal, organic wholemeal, rye and bran flours there are a variety of products unique to Melin's. These include seed flour, seed and herb, seed and spice, garlic and chive, malted wholemeal, nut brown and muesli. Visitors to the mill can take a guided tour led by the miller.

☞ adults 80p, senior citizens 60p, children 40p
● Easter-Sep Wed-Sun 10-5.30; Mon, Tue flour sales only
Facilities: 🍽️ 🚻 🅿️ 🚗 😋

🏠 Map 3 D3
Mountpleasant Goat Farm
Mountpleasant, Pen-y-Bont,
Nr Trelech, Carmarthen,
Dyfed SA33 6PP
Tel. Madox (09948) 315

From Carmarthen follow A40 westwards, after 4 miles turn right onto B4298 for 4 miles, then turn right onto B4299 for 5 miles, then turn right onto unclassified road for 1 mile to Pen-y-Bont.

Pen-y-Bont goats' cheese is made to a traditional Wensleydale recipe which suits perfectly the properties of goats' milk. The flavour and texture of the cheese vary from month to month — depending on what the goats are eating. The lush grasses of early summer produce a sharp, crumbly cheese whilst the blackberries and the thistles of late summer produce a more moist and mellow cheese. They also make their own firm and creamy goats' milk yoghurt. They offer cheese-making demonstrations, guided tours of the farm and cheese-making and goat-keeping courses.

☞ cheese-making demonstrations £4.00 inc. lunch; tours £2.00; family ticket £5.00; courses £7.00 per day
● by appointment
Facilities: 🍽️ 🚻 🅿️ 🚗 😋

🏠 Map 3 C4
Nevern Dairy
Glasdir Farm, Nevern,
Newport, Dyfed SA42 0NQ
Tel. Newport (09913) 820354

From Newport follow A487 eastwards, after 2 miles turn left onto B4582 for ¾ mile to Nevern, then turn left onto unclassified road for ½ mile, then turn right onto unclassified road for 1 mile to farm on right. Signposted.

Nevern Dairy arranges tours and demonstrations to show visitors how traditional Cheddar cheese and butter are made. The shop sells cheese, butter, homemade cakes and free-range eggs.

☞ free

● Easter week, Spring Bank Hol week, Jul-Sep Sun-Fri 9-5; Oct-Jun Mon-Fri 9-5
Facilities: ♿ 🚻 🚗 😋

🏠 Map 3 E3
Pantyllyn Cheese
Pantyllyn, Blaenycoed,
Carmarthen, Dyfed SA33 6HB
Tel. Cynwyl Elfed (026787) 478

From Carmarthen follow A40 eastwards, after 1 mile turn left onto A484 for 7 miles, then turn left at Cynwyl Elfed onto unclassified road for ¾ mile, then turn left onto unclassified road for 1½ miles, then turn right to Blaenycoed. Signposted.

This is a small working dairy farm producing its own cheese by traditional methods. The dairy uses only unpasteurised milk, vegetarian rennet and a low sodium salt. Demonstrations are given and the cheese can be bought in small pieces or in whole rounds.

☞ demonstrations: adults £1.00, children free
● Easter-Sep Tue, Thur 10-5.30 or by appointment
Facilities: 🍽️ 🚗

🍦 Map 3 D4
Pant-yr-Holiad Garden
Rhydlewis, Llandysul,
Dyfed SA44 5ST
Tel. Rhydlewis (023975) 493

From Sarnau follow A487 eastwards, after 1 mile turn right onto B4334 for 2 miles, then turn right onto unclassified road for 2 miles to garden. Signposted.

This small balanced dairy farm with a herd of Jersey cows makes its own cream, butter and buttermilk. Visitors are welcome to watch demonstrations of butter-making and examine the machinery used. There is also a small nursery, herb garden and some rare breeds of poultry. All

MAP 3   WALES

produce can be bought at the farm.

☞ adults £1.00, children 50p
◗ Easter-Sep Wed, Sun, Bank Hols 2-5, demonstrations by appointment
Facilities: 🚾 🚗 👜

🎣 Map 3 C3
Pembrokeshire Fish Farms
Vicar's Mill, Llandissilio, Clynderwen, Dyfed SA66 7LS
Tel. Clynderwen (09912) 553

From Narberth follow A478 northwards, after 4 miles turn left at Llandissilio onto unclassified road for ½ mile to farm. Signposted.

This is one of the few fish farms where visitors are free to walk around unaccompanied. They can watch the day-to-day running of the farm, feed the fish and enjoy the picturesque setting. The shop sells fresh and smoked trout, sea rainbow trout, both whole and in fillets, fresh salmon and pâtés.

☞ adults 50p, senior citizens & children 30p
◗ all year daily 10-5
Facilities: 🚾 🚗

🐓 Map 3 D4
Rhos Ddu Farm
Crymych, Dyfed SA41 3RB
Tel. Crymych (023973) 220

From Crymych follow unclassified road eastwards towards Tegrin for 2 miles, then turn right onto unclassified foad for ½ mile to farm. Signposted.

Rhos Ddu is a working farm which encourages visitors to try their hand at farm life. They can feed chickens and baby calves, hand milk Daisy, the pet cow, and even join in machine-milking the herd of Friesians. A nature trail takes in the spectacular countryside including a hedgerow estimated to be 700 years old, natural waterfalls and badger setts. The shop is licensed to

sell untreated milk in 1 pint packs and also stocks fresh eggs and pure ice cream.

☞ adults £1.30, senior citizens & children 70p
◗ Easter, May, Jun, Sep daily 1-6; Jul-Aug daily 10-6; Oct-Apr by appointment
Facilities: 🍽️ 🚾 🚗 👜 ⛺
★ 10 Aug milk & butter day
🍽️ teas served with homemade scones, bread, butter, cheese & cream

● **An assortment of Welsh soups**

🍯 Map 3 C3
Ridgeway Honey Farm
Rock Cottage, Llawhaden, Nr Narberth, Dyfed SA67 8DG
Tel. Llawhaden (09914) 268

From Haverfordwest follow A40 eastwards, after 7 miles turn left at Canaston Bridge onto unclassified road for 1½ miles to Llawhaden. Signposted.

A working pottery and apiary, this farm organises tours to show visitors all stages of honey production and collection. The shop sells honey in glass jars, ceramic pots and by the comb.

☞ apiary: £5 for 2
◗ shop: Apr-Sep daily 10-5; Oct-Mar telephone for details; apiary: Mar-Sep by appointment with at least 4 days notice
Facilities: 🚾 🚗

🏠 Map 3 B3
Scolton Manor Museum
Spittal, Haverfordwest, Dyfed SA62 5QL
Tel. Clarbeston (043782) 328

From Haverfordwest follow B4329 northwards for 5 miles to museum on left. Signposted.

Set in a country park, Scolton Manor Museum tells the history of the county. An old village has been reconstructed with attention given to the details of the shop interiors. Visitors are also welcome to follow the nature trail in the park. The shop sells Welsh produce.

☞ adults 50p, senior citizens & children 25p
◗ May-Sep Tue-Sun, Bank Hols 10.30-6 or by appointment
Facilities: 🍽️ 🚾 🚗 👜 ⛺
🍽️ lunches & teas served including traditional wholemeal & vegetarian food

🧀 Map 3 E4
Teifi Farmhouse Cheese
Glynhynod Farm, Ffostrasol, Llandysul, Dyfed SA44 5JY
Tel. Rhydlewis (023975) 528

From Llandysul follow A486 northwards, after 4 miles turn left at Blwch y Groes onto unclassified road for 1 mile to farm on left. Signposted.

Glynhynod Dairy Farm, in the picturesque hills of West Wales, makes cheeses with unpasteurised milk using methods dating back 5 centuries. Their award winning cheese is free from any chemicals, colourings or artificial flavourings. Visitors to the farm can watch cheese and butter being made and sample the different varieties. The shop sells cheeses whole or in wedges as well as butter, milk and fresh eggs.

☞ demonstrations: adults £1.00, children (under 14) 50p
◗ shop: all year daily 9-8; demonstrations: all year daily 9.30-11.30 by appointment
Facilities: 🚾 🚗 👜

🎣 Map 3 F4
Teifi Valley Fish
Ty Mawr, Llanybydder, Dyfed SA40 9RE
Tel. Llanybydder (0570) 480789

MAP 3

From Lampeter follow A485 south westwards, after 5 miles turn left onto B4337 for 2 miles to farm.

Set in peaceful surroundings on the edge of the Brechfa Forest, this trout farm is fed with pure waters from the nearby spring. Visitors can fish their own, feed the fish and listen to talks on all aspects of freshwater fish. Fresh, frozen or smoked trout are on sale and also salmon and sea trout during the season from June to October.

☞ fishing permit: adults £2, senior citizens & children £1.00; rod & bait free; fish caught £1.38 per lb

◑ all year daily daylight hours
Facilities: 🚻 🚗 ⛺

🏠 Map 3 F5
Tyn Grug Farmhouse Cheese
Goetre Isaf, Derry Ormond, Bettws Bledrws, Dyfed
Tel. Llangybi (09745) 237

From Lampeter follow A485 northwards for 2 miles to farm. Signposted.

This organic dairy farm specialises in a cheese unique to the farm. Visitors may watch cheese-making demonstrations, view the cheese-maturing rooms and taste the product. The shop sells farmhouse cheese, organic cheese — 'Pencarreg' from Lampeter, fresh eggs and organic vegetables.

☞ demonstrations: adults £1.00, children 50p
◑ Apr-Oct Tue-Sat 10-5 or by appointment
Facilities: 🚻 🚗 ⛺

🌾 Map 3 B3
Wilsons of Treffgarne
Nant-y-Coy Mill, Treffgarne, Haverfordwest, Dyfed
Tel. Treffgarne (043787) 686

From Haverfordwest follow A40 northwards for 5 miles to mill. Signposted.

● **Welsh pancakes**

Nestling in the shadow of Treffgarne Gorge, this historic corn mill and adjacent farmhouse have been restored to their original 1844 condition. As well as a special display of over 150 jugs there are exhibits of cooking utensils, agricultural implements, a harp and other musical items. Designated an area of special interest to botanists and geologists, Nant-y-Coy is also a haven for otters. Visitors are welcome to take the picturesque rural walks and view the local waterfall. The shop sells honey, fudge, toffee and rock.

☞ adults 50p, senior citizens & children 25p
◑ May-Sep daily 10-5; Mar-Apr, Oct-Nov by appointment
Facilities: 🍴 🚻 🚗 ⛺
🍴 snack bar serves Welsh cakes, honey teas & local dishes

🌾 Map 3 C4
Y Felin
Mill House, St Dogmaels, Cardigan, Dyfed SA43 3DY
Tel. Cardigan (0239) 613999

From Cardigan follow B4546 westwards for 1 mile to St Dogmaels. Signposted.

This 17thC watermill, formerly part of the nearby abbey estate, fell into disuse in the 1930s but has now been restored by the current owners. Visitors to the 3-storey building may see the overshot water wheel, mill machinery and the kiln for roasting oats. They can also watch the complete milling process from cleaning through milling and grading to bagging. Stoneground wholemeal and specialised flours are for sale in 1.5 to 35Kg bags.

☞ adults 75p, children (5-16) 35p
◑ mill: Easter-Oct daily 10-5.30; Oct-Easter Sat, Sun 10-5.30 by appointment
Facilities: 🍴 🍴 🚻 🚗
🍴 tea room serves homemade scones, cakes, bread rolls & biscuits with local butter & cream; open Easter-Oct Mon-Fri 10.30-5.30, Sat, Sun 12.30-5.30

MAP 4 WALES

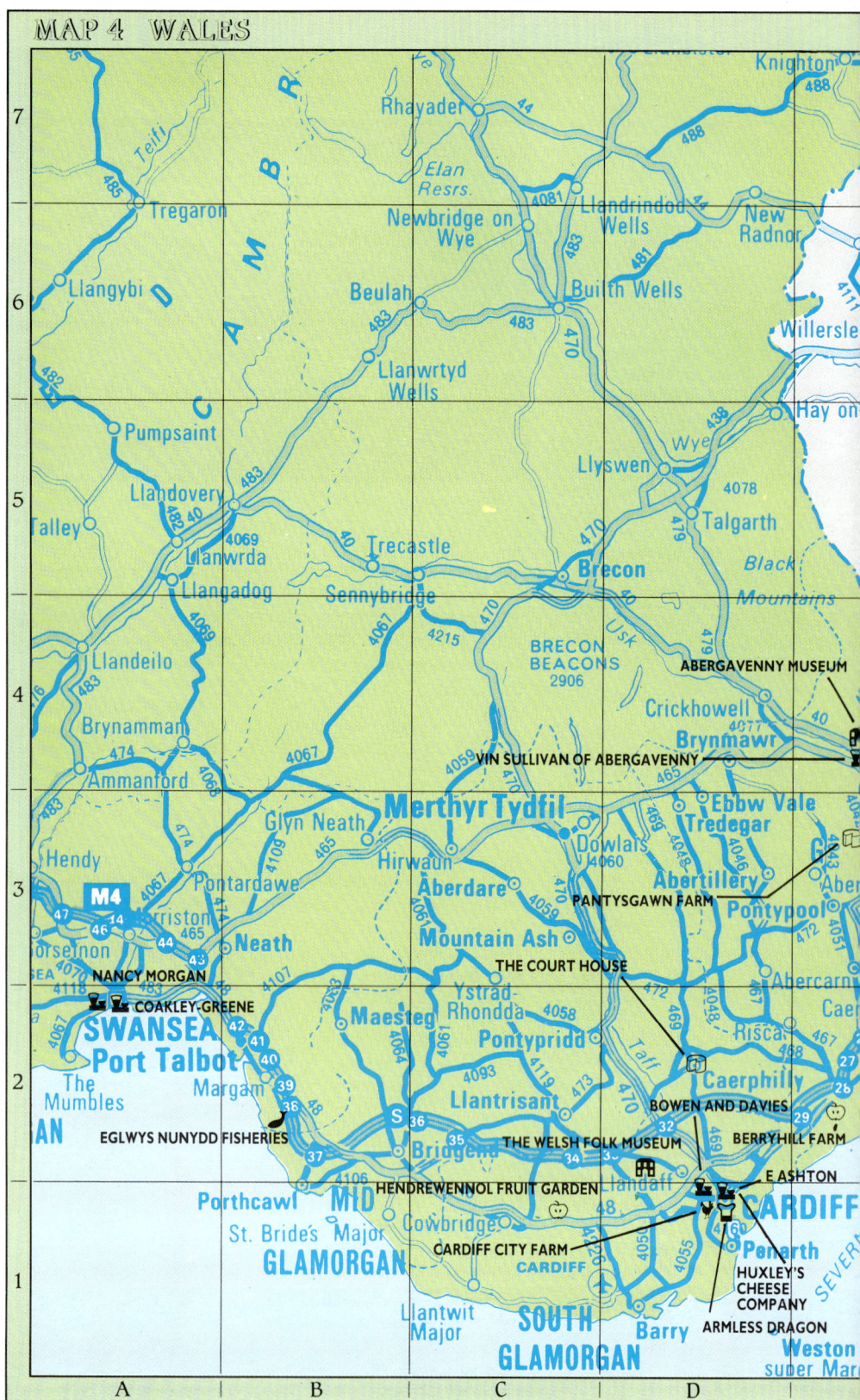

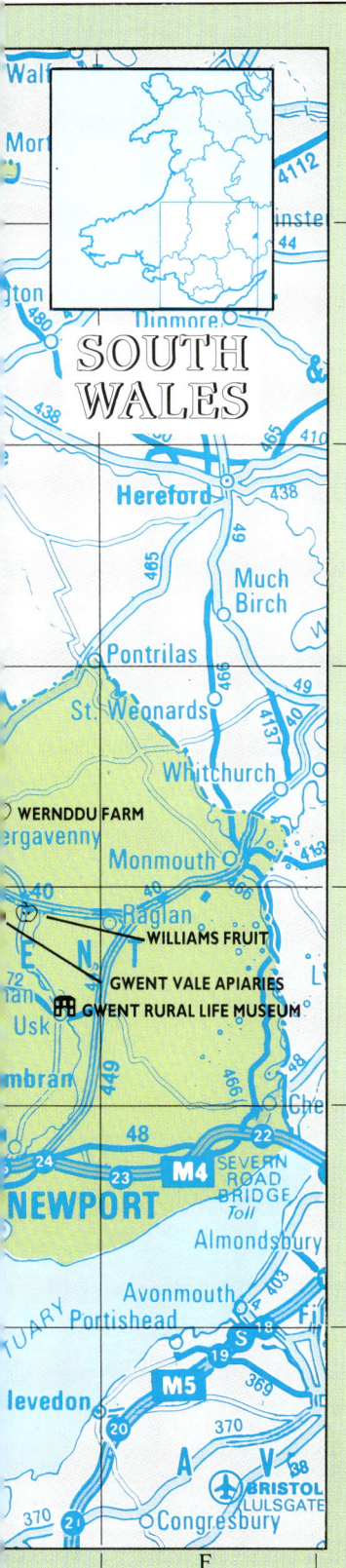

Fertile valleys lead down from the Brecon Beacons to the Bristol Channel. Pick your own fruit farms abound and salmon leap in the Usk. This is where Caerphilly cheese comes from; originally made from skimmed milk, it was a good country cheese which shepherds sold at market along with their lambs. It is still made in a brine-bath which gives it a light salty flavour. Don't be fooled by Glamorgan sausages — they are made from Caerphilly cheese and contain no meat at all. To sample all these, visit Swansea or Cardiff market and see the produce of South Wales at a glance.

Map 4 E4
Abergavenny Museum
The Castle, Castle Street,
Abergavenny, Gwent NP7 5EE
Tel. Abergavenny (0873) 4282

In town centre. Signposted.

The Abergavenny Museum traces the history of this busy market town from pre-historic times to the present day. A particularly interesting feature is a reconstructed Welsh Border kitchen of the 1890s, showing traditional furniture and cooking implements.

adults 60p, senior citizens & children 30p

Mar-Oct Mon-Sat 11-1, 2-5, Sun 2-5; Nov-Feb Mon-Sat 11-1, 2-4

Facilities:

Map 4 D1
E Ashton
Central Market, Cardiff,
South Glamorgan CF1 2AU
Tel. Cardiff (0222) 29201

In city centre.

One of the largest retailers of fish in the UK, employing 26 staff, this shop stocks over 100 kinds of sea, freshwater and shellfish as well as smoked fish. Unusual examples include octopus, carp, pike, spider crabs, goose-necked barnacles, cuttlefish, shark, squid, clams, tunny, langoustine and smoked eels. Game and poultry are also for sale.

all year Mon-Sat 8.15-5.30
Facilities:

Map 4 E2
Berryhill Farm
Coedkernew, Newport,
Gwent NP1 9UD
Tel. Newport (0633) 680

From Newport follow A48 south westwards, after 3 miles turn left onto unclassified road for 1/4 mile to farm on right. Signposted.

This pick your own farm offers a wide range of apples, soft fruit and vegetables including mangetout, asparagus, squash, pumpkins and newly planted sunberries. The shop also sells produce ready-picked, greenhouse tomatoes, cream and free-range hens' and duck eggs.

Jun-Jul daily 9.30-8; Aug Tue-Sun 9.30-7; Sep Tue-Sun 9.30-6; Oct Tue-Sun 9.30-5, Nov-Dec telephone for details
Facilities:
barbecues & teas with homemade cakes

● **Sorting the fish catch**

MAP 4　　　　WALES

🐾 Map 4 D1
Bowen and Davies
231 Cathedral Road, Cardiff,
South Glamorgan CF1 9PP
Tel. Cardiff (0222) 27180

*From Cardiff follow A4119
Cathedral Road north westwards
for ½ mile to shop.*

Bowen and Davies opened 2
years ago with the aim of
providing a personal, high
quality food service. It now sells
a wide range of additive and
preservative free foods. The
shop specialises in local
produce such as Welsh
farmhouse cheeses, fresh herbs
and pasta, smoked turkey, trout
and homemade pâtés.
Customers are welcome to
taste samples of any food and
may have individual hampers
made to order.
◗ all year Mon-Fri 8.30-6, Sat
8.30-5, closed Bank Hols

🌱 Map 4 D1
Cardiff City Farm
Sloper Road, Grangetown,
Cardiff,
South Glamorgan CF1 8AB
Tel. Cardiff (0222) 384360

*From Cardiff follow A4160
Penarth Road south westwards,
after 1½ miles turn right into
Sloper Road to farm. Signposted.*

The Cardiff City Farm Trust,
formed in 1978, has reclaimed 4
acres of derelict land to
establish a successful, working
farm on the edge of Cardiff.
The farm now boasts trees,
shrubs, a farmhouse study
centre, animal houses, barns,
greenhouses, gardens,
allotments, fish ponds, play
areas and ancillary buildings.
The Trust practises a policy of
organic gardening and
preservation. The herb garden
is based on a medieval design
and the vegetable sanctuary
cultivates varieties now
discontinued by EEC
regulations. The main fish pond

produces 300 fish a year for
local angling clubs to restock
lakes and rivers. Visitors are
welcome to tour the site and
become involved in farm
activities such as milking. The
shop sells free-range hens',
goose and duck eggs, goats'
milk and cheese, organically
grown vegetables, herbs and
plants.
☞ adults 50p, children (over 5)
20p
◗ all year daily 8-6, groups only
Facilities: 🍺 🍴 ♿ 🚻 🚗 🧺

🐾 Map 4 A2
Coakley-Greene
41c The Market, Oxford Street,
Swansea,
West Glamorgan SA1 3PF
Tel. Swansea (0792) 53416

In city centre.

Established in 1856, Coakley-
Greene now trade from the
modern retail market in
Swansea. This quality
fishmongers offers on average
45 varieties of fish and shellfish.
All fish is gutted, cleaned and
prepared ready for cooking and
the staff are happy to advise
customers on local recipes and
how to cook fish. Specialities
include sewin — salmon trout
— from the Welsh rivers
during the season, fresh

salmon, tunny, swordfish, red
snapper, red mullet, lobsters,
crabs, scallops, squid and
oysters. They are also licensed
game dealers and stock
pheasant, partridge, quail,
guineafowl, grouse, pigeon,
mallard and hare in season.
◗ all year Mon-Sat 8.30-5.30;
closed Bank Hols

🏠 Map 4 D2
The Court House
Cardiff Road, Caerphilly,
Mid Glamorgan CF8 1FN
Tel. Caerphilly (0222) 888120

In town centre.

The Court House is a
combination of pub, café,
restaurant and dairy. The dairy
produces up to 200lb of
Caerphilly cheese each week
and the cheese-making process
can be seen from the
restaurant, café and bar.
Demonstrations and talks may
be arranged.
☞ free
◗ cheese-making mornings: all
year by appointment
Facilities: 🍺 🍴 ♿ 🚻
🍴 lunches, teas & dinners
served in restaurant & café
include ploughman's lunches
with Caerphilly cheese, Welsh
& vegetarian dishes from à la
carte menu

● **Welsh water, beer and ale**

MAP 4

⌇ Map 4 B2
Eglwys Nunydd Fisheries
B S C Sports and Social Club,
Groes Margam, Port Talbot,
West Glamorgan
Tel. Port Talbot (0639) 871111 Ext
3368
*From Margam follow A4211
south eastwards, after ½ mile
turn right onto unclassified road
for ½ mile to reservoir on right.
Signposted.*

This fish farm on the Port
Talbot reservoir specialises in
rainbow and brown trout.
Visitors may catch their own or
buy fish from the shop.
☞ day fishing permits: adults
£5.00, children £2.00
● 3 Mar-Sep daily dawn-dusk
Facilities: 🚾 � 🍽

🏫 Map 4 E3
Gwent Rural Life Museum
The Malt Barn, New Market
Street, Usk,.Gwent NP5 1AU
Tel. Usk (02913) 3777
In town centre. Signposted.

Housed in an ancient malt barn
this museum contains a fine
selection of old-fashioned farm
implements and machinery.
The dairy collection includes a
great variety of butter and
cheese-making equipment and
also an early milking machine. In
the kitchen there is a genuine
cottage range, a bread oven and
a selection of cooking utensils.
Visitors are encouraged to
touch the objects and ask the
staff questions. The shop sells
Gwent honey.
☞ adults 80p, senior citizens &
children (5-16) 40p
● Apr-Sep Mon-Fri 10-12.30,
2-5, Sat, Sun 2-5; Mar, Oct
Mon-Fri 10-12.30, 2-5, Sun 2-5;
Nov-Feb Mon-Fri 10-12.30, 2-5
Facilities: 🚾 🍽

RESTAURANT RECIPE

🍴 Map 4 D1
ARMLESS DRAGON
97 Wyvern Road, Cathays,
Cardiff,
South Glamorgan CF2 4BG
Tel: Cardiff (0222) 382357
In city centre.
A friendly restaurant set in a
couple of converted houses
close to the centre of Cardiff.
● Mon-Sat Meals: 12-2.30,
7.30-10.30, closed Sat L
Price range £11-15
Seats 50
Cards: Access, Amex, Diners,
Visa

BLACKCURRANT FOOL
*1lb blackcurrants
pinch of semolina or rice flour
2oz sugar
½ pint double cream whipped
mint leaves*

Stew the blackcurrants until
soft, mix in the semolina or
rice flour to absorb the juices
– the mixture should be the
consistency of a wet cake
mixture. Leave to cool and
then add sugar to taste and
the cream. Garnish with mint
leaves.

---

⑤ Map 4 E3
Gwent Vale Apiaries
Bryn Y Pant Cottage,
Upper Llanover, Abergavenny,
Gwent NP7 9ES

*From Abergavenny follow A4042
southwards, after 4 miles turn
left onto unclassified road for ½
mile to cottage. Signposted.*

A working apiary where visitors
can watch demonstrations and
buy honey.
☞ free
● all year by appointment
Facilities: �

☺ Map 4 C1
**Hendrewennol Fruit
Garden**
Hendrewennol,
Heol-y-March, Bonvilston,
South Glamorgan CF5 6TS
Tel. Bonvilston (04468) 367
*From Cowbridge follow A48
eastwards, after 3 miles turn left
onto unclassified road for 1 mile,
then turn right onto unclassified
road for ½ mile, then turn right
to farm. Signposted.*

This pick your own farm offers
5 varieties of strawberries and
raspberries as well as tayberries
and red and blackcurrants.
● mid Jun-mid Aug daily 9-8
Facilities: 🚾 � 🍽

🧀 Map 4 D1
Huxley's Cheese Company
Luc Lacerre's Wine Warehouse,
37-39 Birchgrove Road,
Birchgrove, Cardiff,
South Glamorgan CF4 1RR
Tel. Cardiff (0222) 692295
In city centre.

Huxley's offer their own
handmade Cheddar cheeses as
well as a vast selection of other
cheeses from the rest of Wales
and from England, France,
Switzerland, Germany, Holland,
Italy, Spain and Scandinavia. The
staff are very knowledgeable
about all the produce and can
provide ready-made
cheeseboards with information
sheets.
● all year Mon-Fri 10-6, closed
Bank Hols
Facilities: ♿ 🚾 �
★ regular cheese tastings

🧀 Map 4 A2
Nancy Morgan
84 Bryn-y-Mor Road, Swansea,
West Glamorgan SA1 4JE
Tel. Swansea (0792) 460981
*From Swansea follow A4067 St
Helen's Road south westwards,
after ½ mile turn right onto Bryn-
y-Mor Road to shop.*

MAP 4   WALES

This family-run bakery business was founded 23 years ago and makes all its own produce from only the best quality ingredients and according to traditional recipes. Amongst the foods for sale are Welsh cakes, bara brith, bakestones — bread baked on a hot plate — stoneground brown and granary bread, savouries, fresh cream cakes and vegetarian cheese pasties. They make pancakes, hot cross buns, Christmas cakes and Yule logs. The family also have a small stall in Swansea Market — number 44G — which is open market hours.

◑ all year daily 8.30-6.30

Pantysgawn Farm
Map 4 E3
Mamhilad, Gwent NP4 8RG
Tel. Abergavenny (0873) 880844
From Abergavenny follow A4042 southwards, after 4½ miles turn

right onto unclassified road for ¾ mile, then turn right at Pencroesoped village shop onto unclassified road for 1 mile to farm.

The famous vegetarian soft goats' cheese made on this farm recently won the first 4 prizes at the Nantwich International Cheese Show. Here it can be tasted and bought in 4oz rounds in plain, herb, cracked black pepper and sweet pepper varieties. The shop also sells a complete range of Welsh farmhouse cheeses.

☞ free
◑ all year daily 9.30-5 by appointment
Facilities: 🚻 🚐 🍴

Vin Sullivan of Abergavenny
Map 4 E4
4 Frogmore Street, Abergavenny, Gwent NP7 5AE
Tel. Abergavenny (0873) 6989

In town centre. Signposted.

This shop stocks a huge range of sea food with over 100 different kinds of British and Mediterranean fish. It sells tropical delights from the Seychelles, fresh local poultry, a wide selection of game in season and delicatessen items. It also has a tank of live lobsters.
◑ all year Tue-Sat 9-5
Facilities: ♿

The Welsh Folk Museum
Map 4 D2
St Fagan's, Cardiff, South Glamorgan CF5 6XB
Tel. Cardiff (0222) 569441
From Cardiff follow A4161 westwards, after 1 mile turn right onto A48 for ¼ mile, then turn left onto unclassified road for 1½ miles, then turn right onto unclassified road to castle on left. Signposted.

● **The Welsh Folk Museum, St Fagan's, Cardiff**

MAP 4

This museum, with its buildings, manor house and parkland, represents the life and culture of a nation. Many historic buildings have been moved from all over Wales and re-erected at St Fagan's. Visitors can see a number of kitchens in farms and cottages, refurbished in correct period detail from the 15thC up to the present day. There is also a 17thC kitchen in St Fagan's Castle Manor House and a collection of kitchen equipment displayed in the Material Culture Gallery. The formal gardens around the Manor House include a herb garden. Visitors can also see the working 19thC cornmill and bakehouse and a collection of agricultural implements in the Agricultural Gallery. Stoneground flour from the mill and freshly baked bread and bara brith from the bakehouse are on sale in the shop along with Welsh honey and preserves.

☞ adults £2.00, senior citizens £1.50, children (5-16) £1.00
● Apr-Oct daily 10-5; Nov-Mar Mon-Sat 10-5
Facilities: 🍽 & ♿ 🚗 ⛺
★ 29 Apr-2 May Old May Day Fair, Sep Harvest Festival — both featuring local crafts, traditional cookery demonstrations & baking 🍽 licensed restaurant serves lunches & teas including local & regional specialities like cawl, bara brith & Welsh cakes

COCKLES

Swansea market is filled with cockle sellers. Soak the cockles in salt water, rinse to remove any grit and eat them plain with homemade bread and salty butter.

☺ Map 4 E4
Wernddu Farm
Old Ross Road, Abergavenny, Gwent NP7 8NG
Tel. Abergavenny (0873) 5289

● **Cleaning the fish catch**

From Abergavenny follow B4521 north eastwards, after 1½ miles turn right onto unclassified road for ¼ mile, then turn right to farm. Signposted.

Soft fruit, apples, plums and vegetables are on offer at this pick your own farm, while the shop also sells eggs, honey and fruit juices as well as ready-picked produce. Visitors may also see the herb garden.
● Jun, Sep daily 10-6; Jul daily 9-8; Aug daily 10-7
Facilities: 🍽 ♿ 🚗 ⛺ 🏔

REGIONAL RECIPE

SOUSED HERRINGS

3 herrings
pinch of mixed spices
1 tsp salt
¼ pint vinegar
¼ pint water

Heat oven to gas 4 (350F, 180 C). Clean, bone and roll the herrings. Place in a casserole dish with the mixed spices, water and vinegar. Cover and cook for an hour. Either serve hot in the vinegar sauce, or cold with a salad.

☺ Map 4 E3
Williams Fruit
Great Tyrmynach Farm, Raglan, Gwent NP5 2JP
Tel. Raglan (0291) 690470
From Usk follow B4598 northwards, for 5 miles to farm. Signposted.

Beginning with asparagus in late April, this pick your own farm offers a wide variety of soft fruit and vegetables throughout the season including mangetout, spinach, french beans, scallopini and a range of raspberries and strawberries. The shop sells produce ready-picked and also local Jersey cream, cheese, ice cream and cold drinks.
● Apr-mid Aug daily 9.30-7
Facilities: ♿ 🚗 ⛺ 🏔

· CALENDAR OF EVENTS ·

MARCH

Welsh Beekeeping Convention
26 March
An annual fair at Builth Wells, Powys.

AGRICULTURAL SHOWS

A number of annual agricultural shows are held in Wales — they are normally a good source of local produce. The following is a selection:

APRIL

Lleyn and District Agricultural Show
4 April at Nefyn, Pwllheli, Gwynedd.

MAY

Montgomery Agricultural Show
28 May at Feggy Leasowes, Welshpool, Powys.

JUNE

Aberystwyth Agricultural Show
11 June at Tanycastell Park, Rhydfein, Aberystwyth, Dyfed.

JULY

Royal Welsh Show
18-21 July at Llangelwedd, Builth Wells, Powys.

Cardigan Show
27 July at Cardigan, Dyfed.

Abergavenny and Border Counties Show
29 July at Abergavenny, Gwent.

AUGUST

Gower Show
4 August at Swansea Airport, Swansea, West Glamorgan.

North Wales Agricultural Show
4 August at Caernarvon, Gwynedd.

Brecon County Show
6 August at Brecon, Powys.

Anglesey Show
9-10 August at Mona, Nr Llangefni, Gwynedd.

United Counties Show
11-12 August at Carmarthen, Dyfed.

Pembrokeshire County Show
16-18 August at Withybush, Haverfordwest, Dyfed.

Denbighshire and Flint Show
18 August at Rhyl, Clwyd.

Monmouthshire Show
25 August at Vauxhall, Monmouth, Gwent.

NOVEMBER

Mid Wales Beer Festival
16-20 November
The 8th beer festival held in the freehouses of 'the smallest town in Britain', Llanwrtyd Wells in Powys, with a choice of about 30 different 'real' ales.

SCOTLAND

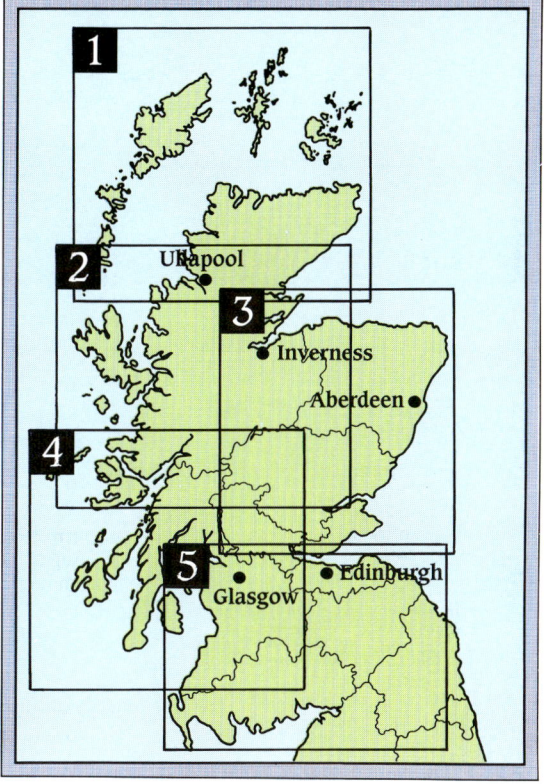

SCOTLAND

● **The Castle from the Vennel, Edinburgh**

by Catherine Brown
SCOTTISH FOOD SPECIALIST AND COOKERY WRITER

It's a mistake to believe the myths about Scottish food. There is much more to it than porridge-eating, haggis-bashing and whisky-drinking. Just as there is more than one Scottish biscuit; shortbread may be everywhere but you should not ignore bridies, crumpets or pancakes.

Those of you who have eaten quality Scottish produce will know what I mean — Angus beef, West Coast shellfish, Atlantic salmon, Highland grouse and Blairgowrie raspberries all appear on menus in the best restaurants in Paris, London and New York.

Nowhere in the whole of Scotland are you much more than fifty miles from the sea. As you leave Edinburgh's New Town on a clear day the air from the Firth of Forth beckons towards the salt-sprayed Fife fishing villages on the East coast, to old harbours, and to fishing boats coming in to land their catches.

Some of the best smoked fish in the world is here and in many other fishing towns and villages round the long Scottish coastline which stretches to more than three times the length of the French one.

The traditional cures, the Finnans, Smokies and Kippers, go back far into the past, to when nothing more sophisticated than an upturned barrel was fitted with racks for the fish, holes in the top to let the smoke out and a fire lit underneath.

Visiting Auchmithie, the home of Smokies, you notice the barrels perched precariously on flat ledges on the steep cliffs leading to the harbour. In the cliff-top fishing village you can even smell the smoke as it wafts through the streets. But more than anything there is the taste of the dark coppery fish, with their creamy insides, delicious with hot melted butter.

The Smokie, along with Finnan Haddock, are distinctive East Coast cures. But travel northwards again, leaving the red sandstone soils of Angus to grey-granite country, with

Aberdeen, Peterhead and Fraserburgh the largest fishing ports in the country.

To find the real Highlanders you must cross the country to the Atlantic west beyond Inverness; and to the islands. The Celtic peoples live by a milder air and a gentler rain from the Gulf Stream.

Originally a self-sufficient crofting country, it is home to the hardy mountain cattle which played such an important part in the development of Aberdeen Angus. People here have always turned to the sea, the pure cold water and rich feeding grounds, and are now farming fish. Oysters and salmon and other fish are hatched, grown and harvested in these unpolluted waters.

From wherever you stand on this rugged west coast there are patterns of islands beyond — Islay, Jura, Mull and Coll; Skye, Lewis, Harris, the Uists, Benbecula and Barra. All strangely different, all strongly influenced by the sea.

The Orkney islands off the North coast have better land and farmhouse cheese-making has developed, while beremeal, a distinctive northern type of barley, is ground and made into wonderful bannocks by local bakers; they have a strange earthy tang which goes best with some creamy farmhouse Orkney. No-one can leave without sampling the whisky. Single malts made from barley, peat and pure spring water are distilled throughout Scotland but some of the most famous come from the Highlands — with their fine characteristic taste and aroma.

Travel southwards back into the lowlands to Glasgow, a creative and spunky city. It is the melting pot for many different peoples with myriad food traditions — even the Pakistani community design their own tartan and eat their own version of haggis — curried of course — on Burns night.

Further south there are the lush green farmlands of the wetter west — Ayrshire, Dumfries and Galloway — the land of Ayrshire Dairy Cows, the land of cheese-making, the land of Burns.

His poems tell of an age when oatmeal reigned supreme, when the staple of the Scottish diet was porridge three times a day. When an 'honest, sonsie' haggis, 'warm-reeking rich' was elevated to 'chieftain o'the pudding race'.

Though over the years Scots have been tempted from these traditional foods, they are still an important part of the fabric of eating in Scotland. Many a Scot can be found on a cold winter's morning, making a bowl of warming porridge or frying a slice of haggis with some bacon and eggs.

MAP 1 SCOTLAND

MAP 1 SCOTLAND

7

SHETLA
ISLAND

WESTERN
ISLES

Butt of Lewis
Port of Ness

South

6
Borve
Barvas
Nth. Tolsta

St. Magnus
Bay
Muckle Roe
Papa Stour
Sandness

Shawbost
Carloway

Gt. Bernera
Miavaig
Garynahine
Stornoway
Broad Bay
Portnaguiran
Garrabost

MAIN

Brenish
Eye Peninsula
THE SHETLAND SMOKEHOUSE

Valla
Cu
971

West Burn

5
L. Langavat
Balallan

Scarp
Husinish
Amhuinnsuidhe
Lemreway
L. Seaforth

Taransay
Tarbert
Scalpay
Shianti

4
SOUTH HARRIS SEAFOODS
HARRIS MUSSELS

Rodel
C. Wrath

Port nan Long
North
Uist
Lochmaddy
MERMAID FISH SUPPLIES
Durness
Whiten Hd.

Sheigra
Kinlochbervie
Eriboll
Tongue
Bettyhill

3
Carnish
Ronay
Rhiconich
Laxford Bridge
B. HOPE
3040
L. Loyal
Syre

Benbecula
Wiay
Eddrachillis
Bay
Scourie
L. More

Creagorry
Kylestrome
Unapool
Altnaharra
L. Naver
B.
KLIBRECK
3154
L. Coire

Howmore
Drumbeg
Stoer

2
Inverkirkaig
Lochinver
Inchnadamph
B. MORE
ASSYNT
3273
Loch
Shin
L. Assynt
CANISP
2779
Black W

Reiff
Enard
Bay
SUMMER ISLES FOODS
Shinness
Brora

Ehboisdale
BRATAN BAGHASDAL
South Uist
Summer Is.
Achiltibuie
Oykel
Bridge 837
Lairg
Altassmore
Gol

Kilbride
Sd. of Barra
Eriskay
Strathkanaird
Bonar
Bridge
Ardgay
Clashmore

1
Barra
888
Ullapool
Carron
9
Kincardine
Edderton
Tain

Castlebay
Cove
Aultbea
Ardessie
AN
TEALLACH
3483
Loch
Broom
L.
Ewe
B. DEARG
3547
HIGHLAND

Melvaig
Poolewe

A   B   C   D

This is the remotest area of Britain. Until recent years the Islanders, in particular, were self-sufficient. Life was very hard and most of the time was spent in growing and catching food to ensure there was enough to eat throughout the long winters. Consequently nothing was wasted and every part of the animal was eaten. Old Shetland dishes include Krappit — fish heads stuffed with fish livers, and Hugga-Muggie — a version of haggis with the fish stomach, the 'muggie' — filled with meal and onions.

● **Cheese display**

🎵 Map 1 A2
Bratan Baghasdal
Lochboisdale Salmon and Mussel Farm,
Lochboisdale, South Uist,
Western Isles PA81 5TJ
Tel. Lochboisdale (08784) 549
In village.

Visitors to this salmon and mussel farm may see the rafts and sea-cages used in the breeding process and also feed the fish. The shop sells freshly caught salmon and mussels.
☞ free
◑ all year daily 8-6
Facilities: 🚗

MAP 1   SCOTLAND

Map 1 G6
Breckan Rabbits
Upper Breckan, Sanday,
Orkney KW17 2AZ
Tel. Sanday (08575) 421

On Sanday Island. Signposted.

This rabbit farm specialises in meat processing as well as fur and angora products. No artificial colouring, flavouring, preservatives or growth promoters are used and all rabbits are processed at an early age for maximum tenderness. Visitors may see the livestock, food processing unit and smokehouse and also the skin tanning and fur sewing in the craft workshop. A wide range of 'Orkney Fare' products are available including smoked rabbit pâté, smoked Orkney sausage made from rabbit and herbs, smoked rabbit and rabbit joints. Rabbit recipe books are on sale at £1.25.

free
all year daily 9-9
Facilities:

REGIONAL RECIPE

SHORTBREAD

1 lb plain flour
1 lb self-raising flour
1 lb butter
½ lb caster sugar
½ tsp salt

Heat oven to gas ½ (250F, 120C). Cream the butter and sugar together, then work in the sieved flours and salt - do not knead. Turn out onto a lightly floured board and press into 1 or 2 large rounds. Place on an ungreased baking tray, prick all over with a fork and bake for about 1 hour.

SHETLAND LAMB

Lamb from the Orkney Isles has an unusual flavour. They feed on the seaweed which gives the meat a slightly salty, crisp taste.

Map 1 B4
Harris Mussels
Quidinish, Isle of Harris,
Western Isles PA85 3JQ
Tel. Manish (085983) 311

From Tarbert follow A859 southwards, after 4 miles turn left onto C79 for 8 miles to Quidinish.

This mussel farm organises trips out to the beds where visitors can pick their own mussels. The shop also sells ready-picked mussels.

free
all year Mon-Sat 9-6 by appointment
Facilities:
lunches, teas & dinners include mussel dishes

Map 1 G5
Highland Park Distillery
Holm Road, Kirkwall,
Orkney KW15 1SU
Tel. Kirkwall (0856) 3107

In town centre. Signposted.

Highland Park is the most northerly whisky distillery in Scotland and produces a fine single malt whisky — Highland Park. Visitors are welcome to tour the distillery and to watch a 15 minute audio-visual presentation. Whisky is on sale in the shop including Famous Grouse which is blended from Highland Park.

free
Apr-Sep daily 10-4
Facilities:

Map 1 A3
Mermaid Fish Supplies
Clachan, North Uist,
Western Isles PA82 5ET
Tel. Locheport (08764) 209

From Lochmaddy follow A867 south westwards, after 9 miles turn right at Clachan Corner onto A865 for ¼ mile to farm. Signposted.

This fishery produces peat-smoked salmon from the Outer Hebrides — a distinctive Scottish taste. Visitors may watch demonstrations and learn how fresh fish is smoked. The shop also sells other fresh fish and shellfish.

free
all year Mon-Sat 9-6
Facilities:

Map 1 E5
Scoop Wholefoods
The Old Infant School,
King Harald Street, Lerwick,
Shetland ZE1 0DG

In town centre.

This friendly shop claims to be the most remote wholefood shop in Britain. As well as a very large range of produce it caters for people with special diets. It stocks locally grown organic vegetables when available.
all year Mon, Tue, Thur-Sat 10-4.30
Facilities:

Map 1 E5
The Shetland Smokehouse
Skeld, Shetland ZE2 9NS
Tel. Reawick (059586) 251

● **The stillroom of a Scottish whisky distillery**

MAP 1

● **Seafood display**

From Culswick follow B9071 eastwards, after 2 miles turn right onto unclassified road for 1½ miles to Skeld.

This beautifully located modern smokery produces smoked salmon, gravadlax, kippers, mackerel, whitefish, marinaded herring and smoked lamb. Visitors may watch demonstrations on the techniques of smoking fish, taste the produce and buy it from the shop.

☞ free
◑ all year Mon-Fri 9-5
Facilities: ♿ 📶 🚗 🍽 ⛰

🐟 Map 1 B4
South Harris Seafoods
Old Mill, Geocrab, Isle of Harris, Western Isles PA85 3HB
Tel. Manish (085983) 220

From Tarbert follow A859 southwards, after 4 miles turn left onto C79 for 5 miles to Geocrab.

Set on the Isle of Harris, this salmon hatchery has associations with Lord Leverhulme's attempt to industrialise the island back in the 1920s. It now cultivates both salmon and shellfish, such as mussels, crabs and lobsters, which it sells to the public —

either fresh or frozen — by arrangement.

☞ free
◑ all year Mon-Fri 9-5.30, Sat by appointment
Facilities: 📶 🚗

〰 Map 1 B2
Summer Isles Foods
The Smokehouse, Altandhu, Achiltibuie, Ullapool, Ross-shire, Highland IV26 2YG
Tel. Achiltibuie (085482) 353

From Achiltibuie follow unclassified road north westwards for 5 miles to Altandhu. Signposted.

Located in the heart of Scotland's salmon-producing region and overlooking the Summer Isles, the Achiltibuie Smokehouse is one of only 8 holders of the Scottish Salmon Smokers Association's Quality Approved seal. Visitors can watch the salmon being prepared from a viewing gallery which overlooks the processing plant and learn about the techniques of filleting, smoking and slicing from the detailed information panels. Products for sale in the shop include oak-smoked fish such as salmon, trout and eel, smoked fish pâtés, cheese and smoked meats and poultry including lamb, venison and sausages.

Also available are Highland biscuits and shortbread, soups, honey, mustards, preserves, marinaded herrings, prawns and lobsters in season.

☞ free
◑ Apr-Oct Mon-Sat 9.30-5.30; Nov-Mar Mon-Fri 9.30-5.30
Facilities: 🚗

🍴 Map 1 F2
BAYVIEW HOTEL
Russell Street, Lybster, Highland KW3 6AG
Tel: Lybster (05932) 346

In town centre.

◑ Mon-Fri Meals: 12.30-2, 7.30-10
Price range Set L £6.25-9
Set D £11.75
Seats 40
Cards: Access, Amex, Carte Blanche, Diners, Visa
Facilities: ♿ 📶 🚗 🍷 🎲

GLAZED LEG OF LAMB

*1 leg of lamb
2 tbsp butter
1 tbsp mustard
1 clove of garlic cut into slivers
½ pint meat stock
1 wine glass of port
1 tbsp redcurrant jelly
1 tbsp flour
salt & pepper*

Heat oven to gas 5 (375F, 190C). Make cuts in the fat of the lamb and insert the slivers of garlic. Mix the butter and mustard, spread over the meat and roast in oven for 1 hour. Drain off the fat and add 1 tbsp of flour, cook and then add the meat stock, port and redcurrant jelly. Bring to the boil, strain and pour over the lamb.

MAP 2 SCOTLAND

SOUTH
HIGHLANDS

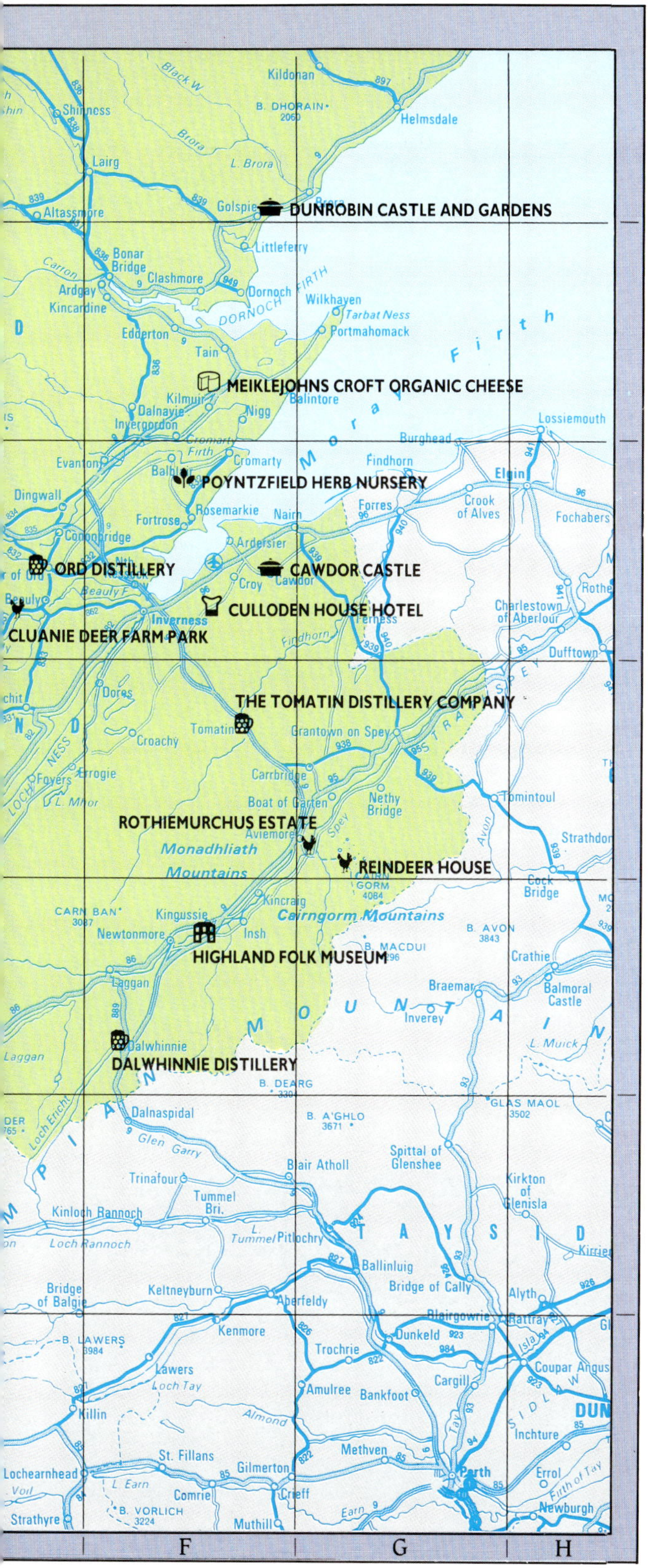

Sparsely populated, the Southern Highlands offer superb game, including grouse, capercaillie and deer. There are now a number of deer farms in this area and farmed venison has become a speciality. Jane Grigson suggests cooking it with local wild mushrooms; in early autumn the woods are thick with a variety of fungi, including chanterelles and cèpes. Look out for them when driving through the region.

🥘 Map 2 F5
Cawdor Castle
Cawdor, Nairn,
Highland IV12 5RD
Tel. Cawdor (06677) 615
In village. Signposted.

This 14thC castle is the traditional home of the Thanes of Cawdor. Visitors may take an extensive tour which includes the Old Kitchen and grounds. The Old Kitchen, which was in active use from 1640 to 1938, has a 19thC cooking range, an 18thC spit and a well dug straight into the old red sandstone rock on which the castle is constructed. There is also a large amount of kitchen equipment on display including a circular knife grinder, butter hands, a 'lazy Susan' and a bucket-yolk. Cawdor's grounds include a kitchen garden which dates from about 1600. The shop sells shortbread, baked in the castle kitchen, as well as Cawdor Castle Pure Speyside Malt whisky and miniatures of Thane of Cawdor Blend.

● **The old kitchen, Cawdor Castle**

Map labels

DUNROBIN CASTLE AND GARDENS
MEIKLEJOHNS CROFT ORGANIC CHEESE
POYNTZFIELD HERB NURSERY
ORD DISTILLERY
CAWDOR CASTLE
CULLODEN HOUSE HOTEL
CLUANIE DEER FARM PARK
THE TOMATIN DISTILLERY COMPANY
ROTHIEMURCHUS ESTATE
REINDEER HOUSE
HIGHLAND FOLK MUSEUM
DALWHINNIE DISTILLERY

MAP 2   SCOTLAND

☞ adults £2.20, senior citizens £1.80, children (5-15) £1.20, family ticket £6.50; grounds only: £1.20
◐ May-2 Oct daily 10-5.00
Facilities: ☕ 🍴 ♿ 🚾 🚗 ☺
🍴 lunches & tea include extensive variety of home baking, fresh wild salmon, salad bar & fresh fruit from vegetable garden; local speciality is Cock-a-Leekie soup

♟ Map 2 E5
Cluanie Deer Farm Park
By Beauly, Inverness-shire, Highland IV4 7AE
Tel. Beauly (0463) 782415
From Beauly follow A862 southwards, after 1 mile turn right onto A831 for 2 miles to farm on right. Signposted.
Cluanie Deer Farm Park is in the heart of the beautiful Scottish Highlands. Visitors may see the deer at close quarters including the spectacular stags. The farm also keeps cattle, sheep, pigs and goats, some of which are rare breeds and all of which can be seen from the nature trail. The shop sells a range of venison products including sausages and burgers as well as cuts of venison; also kid meat, free-range eggs and,

• Young Tamworth pigs, Cluanie Deer Farm Park

if ordered, beef and lamb.
☞ adults £1.50, children (3-16) £1.00
◐ mid May-Sep Thur-Tue 10-5
Facilities: ☕ ♿ 🚾 🚗 ☺ ♨

♟ Map 2 E5
Culligran Deer Farm
Culligran Estate,
Glen Strathfarrar, Struy,
Nr Beauly, Inverness-shire,
Highland IV4 7JX
Tel. Struy (046376) 285
From Beauly follow A862 southwards, after 1 mile turn right onto A831 for 8 miles, then turn right onto unclassified road for 1 mile to farm.
Situated amidst the beautiful Strathfarrar National Nature Reserve, this deer farm offers 1½-hour guided tours by Landrover. Visitors may see the the deer and wildlife at close quarters and even feed some of the animals. There is also

a salmon and trout lake where visitors are welcome to fish. Venison from a neighbouring farm is for sale.
☞ tours: adults £2.50, reductions for children
◐ tours: all year by appointment
Facilities: 🚗

🍶 Map 2 F3
Dalwhinnie Distillery
Dalwhinnie, Inverness-shire, Highland PH19 1AB
Tel. Dalwhinnie (05282) 264
In village.
The highest malt whisky distillery in Scotland, Dalwhinnie offers a free tour and tasting. The shop sells whisky and allied goods.
☞ free
◐ Easter-Oct daily 9.30-5, telephone to confirm
Facilities: ☕ 🚾

🏰 Map 2 F7
Dunrobin Castle and Gardens
Golspie, Sutherland, Highland KW10 6SF
Tel. Golspie (04083) 3177
From Golspie follow A9 north eastwards for 1 mile to castle. Signposted.

• Red deer stags, Cluanie Deer Farm Park

• Culligran Deer Farm

MAP 2

● **Exhibits at Dunrobin Castle**

Dunrobin Castle, home to the Sutherlands, is the most northerly of Scotland's great houses and also the largest with 189 rooms. It has a fascinating collection of furniture, pictures, objets d'art and family memorabilia which includes a collection of antique household equipment. Kitchen equipment is displayed and includes copper pots and pans, samovars, tea boilers and other paraphernalia. The Duke of Sutherland's Victorian fishing and picnic equipment is also on view.

☞ adults £2.00, senior citizens £1.30, children (5-16) £1.00, family £5.00
● 15 Jun-15 Sep Mon-Sat 10.30-5.30, Sun 1-5.30
Facilities: ▨ ▨ ▨ ▨

⚓ Map 2 D2
Great Glen Foods
Old Ferry Road,
North Ballachulish, Onich,
Fort William, Inverness-shire,
Highland PH33 6RZ
Tel. Onich (08553) 277

In village. Signposted.

Great Glen Foods makes 'Islay Tablet', a unique and traditional Scottish sweet. It is a low fat fudge, handmade from goats' milk and contains no artificial preservatives or colours.

Islay comes in 18 different flavours including whisky, Drambuie, rum, brandy and kirsch. The shop also sells other goats' milk products, preserves, marmalades, jellies, honeys, mustards, soups, herbs, teas, biscuits, shortbreads, cakes and special ice cream.
● Jan, Feb Mon-Fri 9.30-4.30; Mar-Jun, Sep-Dec Mon-Sat 9.30-5.30; Jul-Aug Mon-Sat 9.30-5.30, Sun 1-5.30;
Facilities: ▨

🏠 Map 2 F3
Highland Folk Museum
Duke Street,
Kingussie, Inverness-shire,
Highland PH21 1JG
Tel. Kingussie (05402) 307

In town centre. Signposted.

This folk museum is of particular interest to the food lover. There are regular demonstrations of traditional oatcake baking and a major exhibition on Highland cooking in which staff in period costume cook over an open fire. There are also displays on milk and grain processing.
☞ adults £1.25, senior citizens & children (4-17) 65p
● Apr-Oct Mon-Sat 10-6, Sun 2-6; Nov-Mar Mon-Fri 10-3
Facilities: ▨ ▨ ▨
★ Jun-Sep oatcake baking, telephone for details

❀ Map 2 C6
Inverewe Gardens
Poolewe, Ross-shire,
Highland IV22 2LQ
Tel. Poolewe (044586) 200

From Poolewe follow A832 northwards for 1 mile to gardens on left. Signposted.

These splendid gardens were created by Osgood MacKenzie between 1862 and 1922. One interesting feature is a walled garden where visitors can see a typical mixture of Scottish vegetables and fruits as well as flowers and herbaceous borders.
☞ adults £1.90, senior citizens & children 95p
● Apr-24 Oct daily telephone for details
Facilities: ▨ ▨ ▨ ▨ ▨ ▨

🏠 Map 2 F6
Meiklejohns Croft Organic Cheese
Lamington, Nr Invergordon,
Ross-shire, Highland IV18 0PE

From Evanton follow A9 north eastwards, after 11 miles turn left onto unclassified road towards Scotsburn for 1½ miles, then turn left onto unclassified road for ¼ mile to farm on left. Signposted.

This Highland cheesery makes both soft and hard cheeses by traditonal methods. The owner, Alisdair Hutchinson, uses only organically produced goats' and sheep's milk and all his cheeses carry the Soil Association symbol. Visitors are welcome to walk around the cheesery, see the animals and discuss cheese-making with Mr Hutchinson. They can also taste and buy the unique Strathrusdale goats' and Strathrorie sheep's cheeses.
☞ free
● all year daily 9.30-5
Facilities: ▨ ▨

MAP 2 **SCOTLAND**

RESTAURANT RECIPE

Map 2 F5
CULLODEN HOUSE HOTEL

Culloden, Nr Inverness,
Inverness-shire,
Highland IV1 2NZ
Tel: Inverness (0463) 790461

*From Inverness follow B9006
eastwards for 4 miles to
Culloden. Signposted.*

This country hotel has an
Adam-style dining room
dated 1772. The food
combines Scottish best with
new cooking trends and
includes much game and
seafood. The recipe for
Medallions of Venison
wrapped in pastry with wild
mushrooms makes a rich,
gamey meal out of local
produce.

● Mon-Sun Meals: 12.30-2,
7-9
Price range L £10-20,
Set D £23
Seats 45
Cards: Access, Amex, Diners,
Visa
Facilities: ♀ ♿ ⇔

MEDALLIONS OF VENISON wrapped in pastry with wild mushrooms

*1¼lb loin of venison boned
and trimmed
2lb puff pastry
1½lb wild mushrooms
1 egg
2oz butter
salt & pepper
2 pints game stock
¼ pint port*

Heat oven to gas 5 (385F,
190C). Cut the venison into
four pieces, season and sauté
to seal the meat. Slice 5oz of
the mushrooms and chop the
remainder. Melt the butter in
a small sauté pan, add the
chopped mushrooms, season
and cook. Place the venison
and mushrooms on the
rolled-out pastry and fold into
a parcel. Leave to rest in
fridge for 45 minutes. To
make the sauce, gently sauté
the sliced mushrooms in the
butter, add the port and game
stock and reduce to required
consistency. Egg wash the
puff pastry and place in oven
for 10-15 minutes. Garnish
with the sauce.

Map 2 E5
Ord Distillery
Muir of Ord, Ross-shire,
Highland IV6 7UJ
Tel. Muir of Ord (0463) 870421

*From Muir of Ord follow A832
north westwards, after ½ mile
turn left onto unclassified
Aultgowrie road for ½ mile to
distillery.*

Founded in 1838, Ord Distillery
is now part of United Distillers.
A highly modern, efficient
plant, it still produces a
traditional malt based on the
pure water from 2 nearby
lochs. Visitors may tour the
distillery, taste its products and
purchase the malt whisky,
including miniatures, on site.

☞ free
● all year Mon-Fri 9-12, 2-3
Facilities: ♿ ⇔

Map 2 F5
Poyntzfield Herb Nursery
Black Isle, by Dingwall,
Ross-shire, Highland IV7 8LX
Tel. Poyntzfield (03818) 352

*From Cromarty follow B9163
westwards for 5 miles to nursery.
Signposted.*

● **View from Mam Ratagan to Skye**

MAP 2

This nursery specialises in the cultivation of herb plants using organic and biodynamic methods. Amongst the 300 varieties for sale are plants native to Scotland and many rare and unusual species from around the world.

☞ free
● Mar-Oct Mon-Sat 1-5, Nov-Feb by appointment
Facilities: ⅚ 🚗

REGIONAL RECIPE

CHOCOLATE WHISKY CAKE

This is a rich dessert and should be eaten in small portions.

10oz plain chocolate
6oz butter
6oz sugar
3 egg yolks
2-3 drops angostura bitters
2-3 tbsp whisky
12-16 shortbread fingers
½ pint double cream stiffly whipped

Line the sides of a 7-inch loose-bottomed cake tin with shortbread fingers. Melt the chocolate in a basin over hot water. Beat the butter and sugar together until creamy, beat in the egg yolks, angostura and whisky and fold in the melted chocolate. Pour into the lined tin and chill overnight. Remove from the tin, fill the centre with the cream, cover with a layer of grated chocolate and serve in thin wedges.

♥ Map 2 G4
Reindeer House
Glenmore, Aviemore, Inverness-shire, Highland PH22 1QU
Tel. Aviemore (0479) 86228
From Aviemore follow B970 eastwards, after 2 miles turn right into ski road for 5 miles to Reindeer House on left. Signposted.

This 6,000-acre reindeer farm offers a chance for visitors to go behind the scenes. They can see these beautiful animals in their natural habitat and learn how the farm breeds them. Venison can be bought in season.

☞ tours: adults £1.50, children 75p
● all year daily tour at 11, telephone for details
Facilities: 🚻 🚗

♥ Map 2 G4
Rothiemurchus Estate
Dell of Rothiemurchus, by Aviemore, Inverness-shire, Highland PH22 1QH
Tel. Aviemore (0479) 810647
From Aviemore follow B970 eastwards for ½ mile to visitor centre on left. Signposted.

This privately-owned, 25,000-acre Highland estate is operated under a system of integrated management which aims to use the land to greatest advantage. Cattle, deer and trout are all reared. Visitors may take a tractor-trailer ride to see the red deer and Highland cattle in their natural habitat, as well as find out how fish are farmed and even try their hand at fishing in the beginner's loch. The shop sells Inverdruie smoked salmon, trout, venison, trout pâté, beef, and herb plants.

☞ fish farm: adults £1.00, children 50p; rod: £2-3
● all year daily 9-6, telephone for details of tours
Facilities: 🚌 🍴 ⅚ 🚻 🚗 ⛺ ⚠
🍴 lunches served including trout pâté with local oatcakes, local fish, venison & beef

---

🐟 Map 2 F4
The Tomatin Distillery Company
Tomatin, Inverness-shire, Highland IV13 7YT
Tel. Tomatin (08082) 234

In village. Signposted.
The Tomatin Distillery Company was established in 1897 — the height of the Victorian whisky boom. It is now the largest malt whisky distillery in the world, producing up to 5 million gallons of whisky a year. Its distinctive taste comes from the pure, soft water used, drawn from the Alt-na-Frith — Gaelic for 'free burn'. Visitors may take a tour of the distillery and buy both whisky and whisky products in the shop.

☞ free
● Apr-Sep Mon-Fri 9.30-4; Oct-Mar by appointment
Facilities: ⅚ 🚻 🚗

BLACK BUN

Black Bun was formerly eaten on Twelfth Night and is now served at Hogmanay. A rich cake, it contains a delicious filling of sultanas, currants, peel, almonds, spices and brandy in a crisp pastry case.

🏛 Map 2 D2
The West Highland Museum
Cameron Square, Fort William, Inverness-shire, Highland PH33 6AJ
Tel. Fort William (0397) 2169

In town centre. Signposted.
This museum records the history of West Highland life. Exhibits include a whisky still, a croft house interior with a herring cooking over the fire and a collection of traditional agricultural implements.

☞ adults 40p, children 20p
● Oct-May daily 10-1, 2-5; Jun, Sep daily 9.30-5.30; Jul, Aug daily 9.30-9
Facilities: 🚻

MAP 3 SCOTLAND

MAP 3 SCOTLAND

TUGNET ICE HOUSE
CASCADE
BRODIE CASTLE
STRATHISLA DISTILLERY
GLEN GRANT DISTILLERY
DARNAWAY FARM VISITOR CENTRE
LADYCROFT FARM MUSEUM
MILL OF TOWIE
WALKERS' SHORTBREAD SHOP
CARDHU DISTILLERY
BALNAKYLE DEER
THE GLENFIDDICH DISTILLERY
CRAGGANMORE DISTILLERY
GLENDRONACH DISTILLERY
OLD MILL VISITORS CENTRE
MONTGARRIE MILLS
OLD SEMEIL HERB GARDE
DEE VALLEY CONFECTIONERS
ROYAL LOCHNAGAR DISTILLERY
THE RETREAT
BLAIR ATHOLL MILL
BLAIR ATHOLL DISTILLERY
EDRADOUR DISTILLERY
GLENGOULANDIE DEER PARK
WILLIAM SADDLE AND SON
GLAMIS CASTLE
ANGUS FOLK MUSE
ARBROATH MUSEUM
DUNDEE
SCONE PALACE
GLENTURRET DISTILLERY
JOHN DEWAR AND SONS
DRUMMOND FISH FARM
THE COMRIE CHEESE SHOP
THE SCOTTISH DEER CENT
HILL OF TARVIT MANSION HOUSE
MONARCH DEER FARM
BALLINGALL FARM
THE FISH FARM
THE LODGE AND FISH FARM

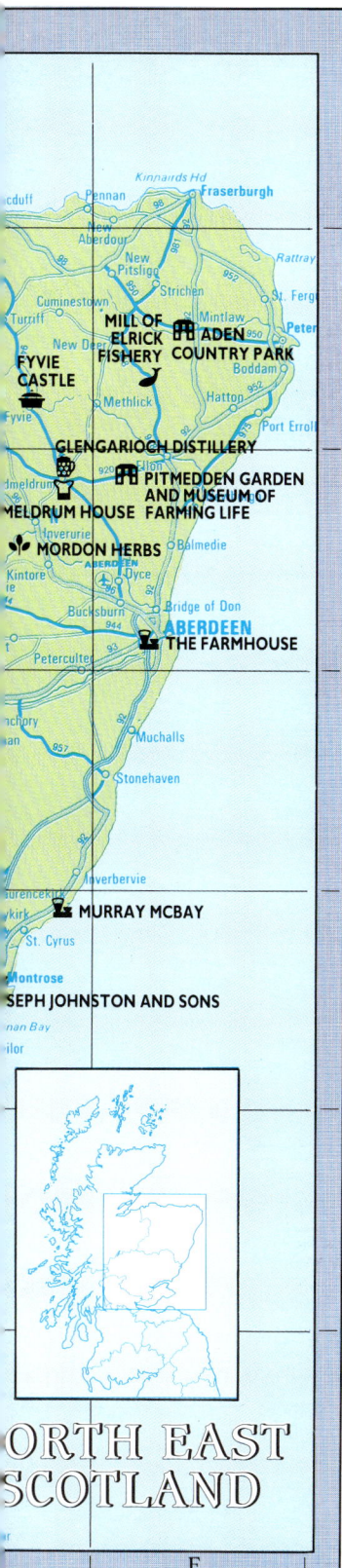

MILL OF ELRICK FISHERY

ADEN COUNTRY PARK

FYVIE CASTLE

GLENGARIOCH DISTILLERY

PITMEDDEN GARDEN AND MUSEUM OF FARMING LIFE

MELDRUM HOUSE

MORDON HERBS

ABERDEEN
THE FARMHOUSE

MURRAY MCBAY

SEPH JOHNSTON AND SONS

NORTH EAST SCOTLAND

F

Malt whisky has been made for centuries in the Highlands. In this area you can follow the only malt whisky trail in the world for 70 miles through the spectacular countryside of the Grampian Highlands as the sign-posted route takes you past 7 malt whisky distilleries. Malt covers a wide range of flavours from light to medium dry to sweet, with something to suit every palate.

Map 3 F6
Aden Country Park
Aden by Mintlaw,
Aberdeenshire,
Grampian AB4 8LD
Tel. Mintlaw (0771) 22857

From Mintlaw follow A950 westwards for 1 mile to park on left. Signposted.

The Aden estate was acquired by the Russell family in 1758 who built a mansion house, gasworks, ice house and a unique semicircular farmstead before financial difficulties forced them to sell up in 1937. After a period of disuse, the 230-acre estate was restored by the Banff and Buchan District Council and now houses an agricultural heritage centre. Visitors may watch audio-visual displays of farming over the past 200 years and see bread-making on an open fire. There are also displays of domestic equipment and agricultural implements. Outside, visitors may take advantage of free fishing on the River Ugie and also visit the 19thC exotic garden.

☞ free
◑ park: all year daily telephone for times; heritage centre: May-Sep daily 11-5; Apr, Oct Sat, Sun 12-5
Facilities: 🍽️ ⑂ WC 🚗 ⛺ ⚠️

◖ lunches, teas & dinners include selection of homebaked dishes

Map 3 D3
Angus Folk Museum
Kirk Wynd, Glamis, Angus,
Tayside DD8 1RT
Tel. Glamis (030784) 288

In village. Signposted.

This domestic, rural and agricultural museum is run by the National Trust for Scotland. Domestic exhibits are housed in six 18thC cottages and include a kitchen with a collection of cooking and other domestic items. Of particular interest are the branders, utensils used in the preparation of bannocks. A dairy, complete with earthenware pots and butter moulds, is set out to show how butter and cheese were made. Outside, the agricultural exhibits are on display in the yard and outbuildings. There are a number of large implements used in the cultivation of grain and root crops in Angus and a further display illustrates changes in the countryside over the last 200 years.

☞ adults £1.20. senior citizens & children 60p
◑ Easter, May-Sep daily 12-5
Facilities: WC 🚗 ⛺

● **North East of Scotland Agricultural Centre, Aden Country Park**

MAP 3   SCOTLAND

● **Traditional costume of an Arbroath fisherwoman**

🏠 Map 3 E3
Arbroath Museum
Signal Tower, Ladyloan,
Arbroath, Angus,
Tayside DD11 1PU
Tel. Arbroath (0241) 75598

In town centre.

This local town museum has interesting exhibits on the history of the fishing and preparation of Arbroath Smokies. Displays cover Smokie preparation from the last century until the present day and include fishing equipment and the traditional costumes of fishwives.

☞ free
● Apr-Jun, Sep, Oct Mon-Sat 10.30-1, 2-5; Jul, Aug Mon-Sat 10.30-1, 2-5, Sun 2-5; Nov-Mar Mon-Fri 2- 5, Sat 10.30-1, 2-5
Facilities: 🚻 🚗 👶

☺ Map 3 D1
Ballingall Farm
Leslie, Fife KY6 3HD
Tel. Glenrothes (0592) 742963

● **Arbroath Museum signal tower**

From Markinch follow A911 westwards, after 2 miles turn right at Leslie onto unclassified road towards Falkland Hill for 1 mile to farm. Signposted.

Five varieties of strawberries and 2 of raspberries are among the fruits available on this pick your own farm. A selection of vegetables is also for sale and all produce can be bought ready-picked from the shop. There is also a children's farm.
● Jul-Aug daily 10-8, Sep, Oct daily 12-5
Facilities: 🚻 🚗 👶 ⛰

🌷 Map 3 C6
Balnakyle Deer
Carron, by Aberlour, Banffshire,
Grampian IV34 7RE
Tel. Carron (03406) 279

From Charlestown of Aberlour follow A95 south westwards, after 2 miles turn right onto unclassified road for 1 mile, then turn left by distillery to farm. Signposted.

This red deer farm breeds animals for sale either live or as venison. Visitors may see the herd and buy all cuts of venison in various sizes, either fresh or frozen.

☞ family ticket £1.50
● all year Mon-Fri 12-8, Sat, Sun 9-7
Facilities: 🚗 👶

🍇 Map 3 C3
Blair Atholl Distillery
Pitlochry, Perthshire,
Tayside PH16 5LY
Tel. Pitlochry (0796) 2268

In town centre. Signposted.

Visitors to this malt whisky distillery are invited to take a free tour and tasting, view the audio-visual displays on the contribution of distilling to local farming and wander in the museum of old distilling artefacts. The shop sells a wide range of malt whiskies, souvenirs and whisky-based products.

☞ free
● Nov-Feb daily 10.30-3.30; Mar-Oct daily 9.30-5.30, telephone to confirm
Facilities: 🍽 ♿ 🚻 🚗

🌿 Map 3 B3
Blair Atholl Mill
Blair Atholl, Perthshire,
Tayside PH18 5SH
Tel. Blair Atholl (079681) 321

In village. Signposted.

Dating back to 1613, this mill fell out of use in 1929, but was restored in 1976 and is now once again a fully working watermill. Visitors may see the milling room, kiln drying floor, hopper room and water wheel. The shop sells baked goods and oatmeal and wholemeal flour

MAP 3

milled on the premises in 0.5 to 32Kg bags.

☞ adults 45p, children (over 5) 40p

● Apr-Oct Mon-Sat 10-5.30, Sun 12-5.30

Facilities: 🍲 ⑩ ⚹ 🚗

⑩ tea room in old granary serves lunches & teas including homebaked wholemeal scones, bread, shortcake, clootie dumplings, flapjacks & homemade soup

---

🍲 Map 3 C6

Brodie Castle

Forres, Morayshire, Grampian IV36 0TE
Tel. Brodie (03094) 371

From Forres follow A96 westwards, after 4½ miles turn right onto unclassified road for ½ mile to castle. Signposted.

Brodie Castle, built in 1567, is in the care of the National Trust for Scotland. It has a superb Victorian kitchen with fitted ranges, one original and the other, a handsome 1890's Eagle range, a replacement. The copper 'batterie de cuisine' has been rescued from disused pantries and outhouses where it had been discarded. The

tea room was the castle kitchen and, equipped with an Esse stove, was in use until 1979.

☞ adults £2.00, senior citizens & children £1.00

● Easter, May-Sep Mon-Sat 11-6, Sun 2-6

Facilities: 🍲 ⚹ 🚗 ♿ 🏛

★ 20 Aug Taste of Moray, all day food, craft & produce with Scottish music & entertainment

🍲 homemade sandwiches, cakes & shortbread

🍶 Map 3 C6

Cardhu Distillery

Knockando, Aberlour, Banffshire, Grampian IV35 7SB
Tel. Carron (03406) 204

From Rothes follow A941 southwards, after 2 miles turn right onto B9102 for 6 miles, then turn left onto unclassified road to distillery. Signposted.

Cardhu offers free guided tours round the distillery followed by free tastings. There is also a nature walk and shop which sells a range of malt whiskies and associated items.

☞ free

● 28 Mar-22 Oct daily 9.30-5

Facilities: 🍲 ⚹

☺ Map 3 D6

Cascade

Cranloch, Elgin, Morayshire, Grampian IV30 3QX
Tel. Lhanbryde (034384) 2378

From Elgin follow A96 eastwards, after 2½ miles turn right onto B9103 for 2½ miles to Cranloch.

This 4-acre croft grows and sells strawberries, raspberries, red and blackcurrants, gooseberries and herb plants in pots.

☞ free

● all year Mon, Wed-Sat daylight hours

Facilities: 🚗

🧀 Map 3 B2

The Comrie Cheese Shop

Drummond Street, Comrie, Perthshire, Tayside PH6 2DW
Tel. Comrie (0764) 70408

In town centre.

In the summer Charles and Grace Lacaille's cheese shop stocks about 100 cheeses including farmhouse, locally made and smoked varieties. They also specialise in other Scottish products including the full range of Moniack Castle products, Columba Cream liqueur, oatcakes, shortbread, goats' milk and malt whisky.

● Jan, Feb Thur-Sat 9-1, 2-5; Mar-Jun, Sep-Nov Mon, Tue, Thur-Sat 9-1, 2-5.30; Jul, Aug Mon-Sat 9-1, 2-5.30; Dec Mon, Tue, Thur-Sat 9-1, 2-5; closed 3rd Mon Feb-Jun, Sep-Nov

---

🍶 Map 3 C6

Cragganmore Distillery

Ballindalloch, Banffshire, Grampian AB3 9AB
Tel. Ballindalloch (08072) 202

From Grantown-on-Spey follow A95 north eastwards, after 12 miles turn left onto B9137 for 1 mile to distillery. Signposted.

Visitors are welcome to see the production of Cragganmore

● **The kitchen at Brodie Castle**

MAP 3   **SCOTLAND**

malt whisky at first hand by touring the distillery, tasting the product and looking around the visitor centre. The shop sells the famous 12-year-old Cragganmore malt whisky by the bottle and in miniatures.

☞ free
◗ all year Mon-Fri 10-4
Facilities: 🆆 🚗 ♨

♥ Map 3 C6
Darnaway Farm Visitor Centre
Tearie Brodie, by Forres, Moray, Grampian
Tel. Brodie (0309) 469

From Forres follow A96 westwards, after 3 miles turn left onto unclassified road for ¼ mile to farm on right. Signposted.

The Centre is part of the ancient estate of the Earl of Moray. Today it offers visitors the opportunity to walk round a Victorian farm and its modern counterpart, watch the afternoon milking of 240 cows from an elevated viewing walkway and see a display of old-fashioned farm implements. The shop sells milk and potatoes.

☞ adults £1.00, children (over 5) 50p
◗ Jun-20 Sep daily 10-5
Facilities: 🍽 ♿ 🆆 🚗 ♨ 🏔

☉ Map 3 D4 ·
Dee Valley Confectioners
Station Square, Ballater, Aberdeenshire, Grampian AB3 5QL
Tel. Ballater (0338) 55499

In town centre.

This confectionery factory has a special viewing area for visitors. They can watch as craftsmen make confectionery using methods that go back to the turn of the century. The shop sells a range of products including boiled sweets,

Edinburgh rock, toffee fudge, flavoured macaroons and chocolates.

☞ free
◗ factory: all year Mon-Thur 9-5; shop: all year Mon-Fri 9-5, Sat 9-4
Facilities: 🍽 🍴 ♿ 🆆 🚗

RESTAURANT RECIPE

♥ Map 3 E5
MELDRUM HOUSE
Oldmeldrum, Aberdeenshire, Grampian AB5 0AE
Tel: Oldmeldrum (06512) 2294

In village.

The ancient family home of proprietor Robin Duff where visitors are made to feel like guests.

◗ daily Meals: 12.30-1.30, 7-9.30, closed mid Dec-mid Mar
Price range Set D £15, £21; snacks from £1.50
Seats 60
Cards: Amex, Diners
Facilities: 🚗

SMOKIE PÂTÉ

for 8 people take:
2 Arbroath Smokies
½lb butter
½ pint fresh double cream
1 shot of whisky
1 tbsp lemon juice
pinch of nutmeg
black pepper

First clean the smokies, then melt most of the butter. Put smokies in liquidiser, blend, add remaining ingredients and blend again. Turn into container and top with remaining butter. Keep in fridge for 2 days before serving.

🍺 Map 3 C2
John Dewar and Sons
Inveralmond, Perth, Tayside PH1 3EG
Tel. Perth (0738) 21231

From Perth follow A9 northwards for 1½ miles to brewery at intersection with western bypass.

The House of Dewar has produced blended whisky since it was established by John Dewar in 1846. There are many varieties of whisky distilled in Scotland, but Dewar's are proud to proclaim that they produce 'the Scotch that never varies'. Modern methods of handling materials do not detract from the traditional skills of the distiller and blender — the blender's nose alone decides how 40 different whiskies are to be married. Guided tours are provided to show visitors how the whisky is blended, bottled and dispatched. Free tastings are also given. Standard, De Luxe and Malt whisky are for sale along with whisky marmalade.

☞ free
◗ all year Mon-Fri tours at 10.15, 2.15, closed Bank Hols
Facilities: 🆆 🚗

🐟 Map 3 B2
Drummond Fish Farm
Aberuchill, Comrie, Perthshire, Tayside PH6 2LD
Tel. Comrie (0764) 70500

From Comrie follow A85 westwards for 1½ miles to farm on left. Signposted.

On entering this fishery visitors are given a packet of food for the fish and a booklet to guide them on a comprehensive tour. Rods are available for fishing in a special well-stocked trout pool. The surrounding countryside is ideal for a family picnic. The shop sells trout fresh, frozen, filleted or smoked, as well as venison and pheasant.

MAP 3

☞ self guided tour: adults 70p, senior citizens & children 30p; fishing: £1.50, rod £2.00, fish caught £1 per lb
◐ farm: Apr-Sep daily 10-5; shop: all year daily 10-4
Facilities: [wc] [car] [🏺]

♨ Map 3 C3
Edradour Distillery
Pitlochry, Perthshire,
Tayside PH16 5JP
Tel. Pitlochry (0796) 2095

From Pitlochry follow A924 north eastwards, after 2 miles turn right onto unclassified road for ½ mile to distillery. Signposted.

Edradour is the smallest malt whisky distillery in Scotland. Hidden deep in the hills of Perthshire, it was established in 1825 by a group of local farmers and named after the burn that runs through it. The distillery remains virtually unchanged since Victorian times and a guided tour will show visitors the traditional distillers' art practised here as it has been for over 160 years. There is a video film and a small exhibition. The shop sells Edradour 10-year-old malt whisky and its associated blends, 8 and 10-year-old House of Lords and 5 and 12-year-old Clan Campbell. Edradour ceramic jugs, malt whisky fudge and marmalade are also on sale.

☞ free
◐ Apr-Oct daily 10-5 or by appointment
Facilities: [wc] [car]

▮ Map 3 F5
The Farmhouse
Chapel Street, Aberdeen,
Grampian AB1 1SQ
Tel. Aberdeen (0224) 640681

In city centre.

Entering the Farmhouse is like entering an Aladdin's cave of fine food. This delicatessen is stocked with food from around the world. It started when

farmers Alistair and Isabella Massie decided to open a shop to sell their produce. With their commitment to quality and imaginative and interesting produce, the shop soon became the Scottish centre for speciality foods. Its cheese counter boasts some 150 different cheeses with some fine local examples. There is also a large selection of fruit, vegetables and cold meats. Traditional Scottish fare is catered for with meat and vegetarian haggis, honeys, mustards, chutney and bottles of fruit wine made at Monaich Castle.
◐ all year Mon-Wed, Fri, Sat 8.45-5.30, Thur 8.45-7.30
★ instore promotions during year

◢ Map 3 C1
The Fish Farm
Crook of Devon, Kinross,
Tayside KY13 7UL
Tel. Kinross (05774) 297

From Kinross follow A977 westwards for 5 miles to Crook of Devon. Signposted.

Visitors can catch their own trout and have it served for supper at this fish farm and restaurant. Lines and bait can be hired and catching a fish is almost guaranteed. For the

non-fisherman there is the chance to watch the trout rise in the ponds and to feed them. Trout and salmon are smoked on the premises and are on sale, along with honey and eggs, at the Farm Food Bar.

☞ farm & adventure park: 70p; fishing: adults £4.00, children (under 16) £2.00
◐ Mar-Jun, Sep, Oct daily 10-6; Jul-Aug daily 10-8
Facilities: [🍴] [🍴] [♿] [wc] [car] [🏺] [⛲]
🍴 restaurant overlooking ponds serves lunches, teas & dinners including fresh trout & salmon — grilled, baked or smoked & served with salad

● **Fresh trout**

● **The Fish Farm, Crook of Devon**

MAP 3   SCOTLAND

Map 3 E6
Fyvie Castle
Turriff, Grampian AB5 8JS
Tel. Fyvie (06516) 266
In village. Signposted.

Fyvie Castle, in the care of the National Trust for Scotland, has an interesting Victorian kitchen which now houses a tea room.

☞ adults £2.00, children (under 18) £1.00
● May-Sep daily 11-6
Facilities: 🍵👶♿🚻🚌🏕
🍵 homemade cakes, scones & fruit pies

Map 3 D3
Glamis Castle
Glamis, Angus, Tayside DD8 1RJ
Tel. Glamis (030784) 242
From Glamis follow A928 northwards for 1 mile to castle on right. Signposted.

Glamis has a rich past — a Royal residence since 1372 it is also the legendary setting of Shakespeare's play Macbeth and the childhood home of HM The Queen Mother. The castle kitchens — now the tea rooms — date from the 17thC, with fittings from the early 19thC. There is an interesting array of historic cooking equipment and a magnificent copper 'batterie de cuisine'. The dining room table is laid for a dinner party —

a setting dominated by the large silver nef or centrepiece. In the Lower Hall of the 14thC tower house there is an old well, long since dried up but once the castle's only source of water. The great armorial china service, in King Malcolm's Room, was made for the family in the 18thC. There is a small shop in the form of a market produce stall.

☞ castle: adults £2.50, senior citizens £2.00, children (5-16) £1.20; grounds: £1.00
● Easter daily 1-5; May-3 Oct Sun-Fri 1-5; Nov-Apr by appointment
Facilities: 🍵🍴🚻🚌🏕⛩

Map 3 D6
Glen Grant Distillery
Rothes, Aberlour, Banffshire, Grampian
In village. Signposted.

Established in 1840, Glen Grant's 'Two Highlanders' label is well known throughout Britain and Europe. Visitors are welcomed in the reception centre, taken on a guided tour and offered a free dram. The shop sells whiskies and related items.

☞ free
● end Apr-early Oct Mon-Fri 10-4 by appointment
Facilities: 🚻🚌

Map 3 E6
Glendronach Distillery
Forgue by Huntly, Aberdeenshire, Grampian
Tel. Forgue (046682) 202
From Huntly follow A97 north eastwards, after 7 miles turn right onto B9001 for 2½ miles to distillery.

Free daily tours guide visitors round this traditional malt whisky distillery. Glendronach whisky can be tasted and bought.

☞ free
● tours: all year daily 10, 2
Facilities: 🚻🚌

Map 3 D6
The Glenfiddich Distillery
Dufftown, Banffshire, Grampian AB5 4DH
Tel. Dufftown (0340) 20373
From Dufftown follow A941 northwards for ½ mile to distillery. Signposted.

This famous whisky first ran from the stills on Christmas Day 1887 and the Grant family have owned and managed the operation ever since. The distillery is unique in two ways: it is the only one in the Highlands where the whisky is bottled on the premises and so it is possible to see the whole process, from barley to bottle. It is also the only malt to use a single source of Highland spring water — in this case water from the Robbie Dubh spring. An audio-visual presentation is available in the theatre in several languages while a shop sells the company's products in many shapes and sizes. There are free tastings at the end of the tour.

☞ free
● mid May-mid Oct Mon-Sat 9.30-4.30, Sun 12-4.30; mid Oct-mid May Mon-Fri 9.30-4.30
Facilities: 🚻🚌🏕

● **Glamis Castle**

MAP 3

• **The Glenfiddich Distillery**

• **A nosing session, Glenfiddich Distillery**

This deer park, set in an area of great natural beauty, offers visitors the chance to see red deer and rare wild animals in their natural environment. Also on view are some rare breeds of sheep, Highland cattle, geese and ducks. Trout fishing is available and the shop sells venison, salmon, pheasant and pigeon.

☞ car load £2.00
◑ Easter-Sep 9-2 hours before dusk
Facilities: 🚾 🚗 👶 ⛺

🍶 Map 3 B2
Glenturret Distillery
Crieff, Perthshire,
Tayside PH7 4HA
Tel. Crieff (0764) 2424
From Crieff follow A85 north westwards, after ¾ mile turn right onto unclassified road to distillery. Signposted.

This is the oldest single Highland malt distillery in Scotland. Glenturret has been producing whisky since 1775, although there was a break in production between 1921 and 1960. Visitors can take a guided tour, see the heritage centre, watch an audio-visual presentation and sample the whiskies at the tasting bar. The large shop sells a full range of malt whiskies along with whisky flavoured confectionery, marmalade, mustard and honey.

☞ guided tour: adults £1.25, children (12-17) 60p; heritage centre: adults 50p, children 25p; tasting bar: £1.50, VIP visit: £4.00
◑ Apr-Oct Mon-Fri 9.30-4.30, Sat 10-4; Mar, Nov-Dec Mon-Fri 9.30- 4.30; Jan-Feb shop only Mon-Fri 2-4
Facilities: 🚌 🍴 🚾 🚗 👶
🍴 Smugglers Restaurant serves traditional Scottish food including Glenturret-flavoured dishes

---

🍶 Map 3 E5
Glengarioch Distillery
Oldmeldrum, Inverrurie,
Aberdeenshire,
Grampian AB5 OER
Tel. Oldmeldrum (06512) 2706
In village.
Glengarioch is the nearest working malt whisky distillery to Aberdeen. Visitors can tour the distillery and see traditional floor maltings and kilning as well as the world famous waste energy scheme in which 10-acres of glasshouses are heated by waste produce. These produce 140 tonnes of tomatoes and 30,000 pot plants each year.

☞ adults £1.00
◑ all year by appointment
Facilities: 🚾 🚗 👶

🐾 Map 3 B3
Glengoulandie Deer Park
Glengoulandie, Foss,
by Pitlochry, Perthshire,
Tayside PH15 6NL
Tel. Kenmore (08873) 509
From Aberfeldy follow B846 westwards for 9 miles to park on left. Signposted.

MAP 3   **SCOTLAND**

Map 3 D2
Hill of Tarvit Mansion House
by Cupar, Fife KY15 5PB
Tel. Cupar (0334) 53127
From Cupar follow A916 southwards for 2 miles to house on left. Signposted.

This mansion house, in the care of the National Trust for Scotland, has an Edwardian kitchen fitted out and beautifully equipped exactly as it was when in use. Visitors can see a 'Simplex' coal range with basic dampers, brick flues and a firebox that would consume up

● **Hill of Tarvit Mansion House**

to 6 scuttles of coal a day. The copper 'batterie de cuisine', apart from the square kettle which is original, came from Lochinch. Also on display are some early aluminium stew pans. The pantry contains a selection of china and silver belonging to the Sharp collection and the servery has a steam-heated cupboard for keeping plates and made-up dishes hot during meals.

☞ adults £2.00, children £1.00
◐ Easter, Oct Sat-Sun 2-6; May-Sep daily 2-6
Facilities: ●● ⬛ 🚗 ♨ ⚠

Map 3 E3
Joseph Johnston and Sons
3 America Street, Montrose, Tayside DD10 8DR
Tel. Montrose (0674) 72666
In town centre.

Salmon fishers since 1827, Joseph Johnston offers locally netted sea trout and fresh salmon. They also sell whole sides of smoked salmon or sliced in packs.
● May-Aug Mon-Fri 8-5, Sat 8-12; Sep-Apr Mon-Fri 8-5, Sat 8-10
Facilities: 🚗

Map 3 C6
Ladycroft Farm Museum
Wester Elchies, Archiestown, Aberlour, Morayshire, Grampian AB3 9SL
Tel. Carron (03406) 274
From Rothes follow A941 southwards, after 2 miles turn right onto B9102 for 3 miles to Archiestown. Signposted.

This museum includes kitchen and dairy displays as well as farm implements and a craft shop. Outside, the farm keeps horses, goats and poultry. The shop sells free-range eggs, homemade shortbread and cake.
☞ adults 50p, children (5-15) 30p
● all year daily 10-dusk
Facilities: ●● ♿ ⬛ 🚗

● **The tiled kitchen at Hill of Tarvit Mansion House**

MAP 3

♪ Map 3 C1
The Lodge and Fish Farm
Loch Fitty,
Kingseat by Dunfermline, Fife
Tel. Dunfermline (0383) 723162
From Dunfermline follow B912 north eastwards for 2 miles to farm on left. Signposted.
This trout farm lies on the shore of the famous Loch Fitty. The loch is 1 mile long and famed for its hard-fighting trout. There are 2 types: the mature brown trout and the rainbow trout. Both are for sale in the shop.
☞ boat fishing: £16.80 per day for 3 people; bank fishing: £6.20 per day, rod £3.00 per day, telephone for evening prices
● Mar-Oct daily 9-dusk
Facilities: ♨ ◉ ⑩ ➹ ➻
iⓞi specialities include homemade soups, homebaking & grilled trout

♨ Map 3 E3
Murray McBay
Lobster Merchants,
Johnshaven,
Grampian DD10 0EZ
Tel. Inverberrie (0561) 62207
From Montrose follow A92 northwards for 8 miles to Johnshaven.
This shop specialises in the supply of live lobsters and other local shellfish such as scallops and prawns. The lobsters can be viewed as they swim around in their ponds.
● all year daily telephone for details
Facilities: ⑩ ➹

♪ Map 3 F6
Mill of Elrick Fishery
Mill of Elrick, Auchnagatt,
Aberdeenshire,
Grampian AB4 9US
Tel. Auchnagatt (03583) 628
From Ellon follow A948 northwards for 7 miles to Mill of Elrick.

Visitors are welcome to browse around this fishery feeding or catching the rainbow trout. With 2 separate lochs in which to fish, all standards are catered for, from experienced fly fishermen to children. Tuition and rod hire can also be arranged and there is a special fun fishery for children. The shop sells fresh and smoked rainbow trout.
☞ fish food: 50p; fishing:£10 per day & 4 fish, £6 per day & 2 fish, rod £1-£3.00 per day
● all year daily 8-dusk
Facilities: ♨ ◉ ⑩ ➹ ➻ ⋏

✶ Map 3 D6
Mill of Towie
Drummuir, by Keith, Banffshire,
Grampian AB5 3JE
Tel. Drummuir (054281) 307
From Keith follow B9014 southwards for 2½ miles to mill. Signposted.
This 16thC watermill has been restored to full working order and is now once again producing oatmeal. The miller offers tours and there are also farm animals to be seen and free fishing in the mill pond. There are displays relating to milling and agricultural implements, including a neep pluck and some turnip mashers. The shop sells oatmeal, honey from the mill's own bees, jams and ice cream.
☞ tour: adults 70p, senior citizens & children 30p
● all year daily 10-5
Facilities: ♨ iⓞi ◉ ⑩ ➹ ➻ ⋏
★ Burns Night supper; Valentines' dinner; Mothers' Day lunch; monthly musical evenings with buffet
iⓞi lunches, teas & dinners served in licensed restaurant in converted grain store include Scottish specialities such as cullen skink & haggis

♀ Map 3 C1
Monarch Deer Farm
Naemoor Road,
Crook of Devon, Nr Kinross,
Tayside KY13 7UH
Tel. Fossoway (05774) 310
From Kinross follow A977 westwards, after 5 miles turn right at Crook of Devon onto unclassified road for ¼ mile to farm on left. Signposted.
Established in 1981, this 100-acre deer farm has red and fallow deer as well as a large collection of rare breeds and other farm animals including Highland cattle, sheep, goats, pigs, donkeys and poultry. There is also a trout stream and fishing is available. The shop sells all cuts of venison as well as venison sausages and burgers.
☞ farm: adults £1.00, children 50p; tours: £1.50; rod £3 per day
● all year daily 9-dusk
Facilities: ♨ ◉ ⑩ ➹ ➻ ⋏

✶ Map 3 E5
Montgarrie Mills
Alford, Aberdeenshire,
Grampian AB3 8AP
Tel. Alford (0336) 2209
From Alford follow unclassified road northwards for 1 mile to Montgarrie.
There has been a mill on this site for some 250 years although the present water wheel dates from 1880. Local oats are cleaned, screened, dried, toasted and finally milled to produce 6 different 'cuts' of oatmeal, from superfine to rough and 'pinhead'. Any waste goes into animal feed. Montgarrie Mills make their own brand of 'Alford Oatcakes' and their traditional oatmeal can be used to make a range of Scottish recipes from porridge and steamed gingerbread to pan haggis.

MAP 3   SCOTLAND

☞ adults 80p, senior citizens & children (under 16) 50p
● tours: Apr-Oct Tue, Thur 2, 3.30 by appointment
Facilities: ⛟

✿ Map 3 E5
Mordon Herbs
Mill Farm, Kemnay, Inverurie, Grampian AB5 9NY
Tel. Kemnay (0467) 43167

From Inverarie follow B993 south westwards, after 4 miles turn right at Kemnay onto unclassified road for 2 miles to farm. Signposted.

This herb farm has its own spring water source so its potted herbs are guaranteed free from artificial chemicals and sprays. All the well-known favourites — parsley, marjoram, tarragon, mints, fennel, sage and thyme — can be supplied either as pot-grown herbs for planting or as sprigs, shrink-wrapped in trays. There is also a demonstration area where visitors can learn more about the care of herbs.

☞ free
● all year daily 9-5.30
Facilities: ⓦ ⛟

♨ Map 3 C5
Old Mill Visitors Centre
Tamnavulin-Glenlivet Distillery, Tomnavoulin, Ballindalloch, Banffshire, Grampian
Tel. Glenlivet (08073) 442

From Tomintoul follow B9008 north eastwards for 5 miles to Tomnavoulin. Signposted.

Visitors can take a guided tour of the Tamnavulin-Glenlivet distillery, which includes an audio-visual presentation explaining the traditional production process. Afterwards they may sample a free dram of Glayva 10-year-old whisky and buy a selection of other malts and blended Scotch whiskies.

☞ free
● 28 Mar-29 Oct daily telephone for details
Facilities: ♿ ⓦ ⛟ ☺

✿ Map 3 D5
Old Semeil Herb Garden
Strathdon, Aberdeenshire, Grampian AB3 8XJ
Tel. Strathdon (09752) 343

From Strathdon follow B973 eastwards, after 1½ miles turn right onto unclassified road for ½ mile to garden. Signposted.

Situated 1000 feet above sea level in the foothills of the Grampian Mountains, this organically cultivated herb garden contains more than 100 varieties of culinary herbs and medicinal plants. Operating under the Soil Association symbol, all chemical fertilisers and sprays are banned. The visitor can learn interesting facts about some of the lesser known herbs and their uses. For example, that fennel seed tea is said to aid slimming, or that sweet cicely, one of the herbs used to flavour Chartreuse, can be added to sweeten whipped cream or trifles. The shop sells a full range of hardy herb plants as well as compost, seeds, pots, booklets and herbal gifts.

☞ free
● May-Sep Mon-Wed, Fri-Sun 10-5
Facilities: ⛟

⌂ Map 3 F5
Pitmedden Garden and Museum of Farming Life
Ellon, Aberdeenshire, Grampian AB4 0PD
Tel. Udny (06513) 2352

From Ellon follow A920 westwards, after 5 miles turn left onto B900 for ¼ mile to garden. Signposted.

The Great Garden of Pitmedden was founded by the advocate Sir Alexander Seton in

● **Part of the Great Garden at Pitmedden**

MAP 3

• **The 'bothy', the farmhands' quarters, Pitmedden**

1675 and is now part of the National Trust for Scotland. The gardens comprise 4 parterres — each with 40,000 plants, 3 miles of boxwood hedges, apple trees and a recently added herb garden with over 100 species. The Museum of Farming Life, set up in 1980, includes displays of a farmhouse kitchen, a byre, a threshing mill and a wide range of dairy equipment and agricultural implements. Visitors may also see the rare breeds of sheep, hens and Highland cattle which are allowed to roam the fields. Apples from the garden are sold at the end of September.

☞ adults £1.60, senior citizens & children (5-17) 80p
◐ May-Sep daily 11-6
Facilities: ⌕ & ⓌⒸ 🚗 ♨
★ Sep working day at museum including baking, ploughing, threshing, crafts, music demonstrations
⌕ tea room serves Scottish specialities baked daily on premises, local honey, oatmeal & Scottish sweets

🏠 Map 3 D4
The Retreat
Glenesk, Brechin, Angus
Tayside DD9 7YT
Tel. Tarfside (03567) 236

From Edzell follow B966 northwards, after 1½ miles turn left onto unclassified road for 9 miles to Glenesk museum. Signposted.

This century-old shooting lodge is now the location for a folk museum, Highland home industries shop and tea room. There is an interesting display of historic kitchen equipment and a collection of agricultural implements.

☞ adults 50p, children (5-12) 30p
◐ Easter, Apr, May Sun 2-6, Jun-Sep daily 2-6
Facilities: ⌕ ⌕ ⓌⒸ 🚗 ♨
⌕ teas & high teas served with homemade rhubarb jam, home-baked shortbread & scones

🍴 Map 3 D4
Royal Lochnagar Distillery
Crathie, Ballater,
Aberdeenshire,
Grampian AB3 5TB
Tel. Ballater (0338) 4273
In village. Signposted.

This malt whisky distillery offers conducted tours rounded off by a free 'dram'. There is also a visitors centre, museum and shop selling the whisky and souvenirs such as Royal Lochnagar decanters and sweaters.

☞ free
◐ all year daily 9.30-4.30
Facilities: ⌕ ⓌⒸ 🚗

🍴 Map 3 D3
William Saddler and Sons
35 East High Street, Forfar,
Angus, Tayside DD8 2EL
Tel. Forfar (0307) 63282
In town centre.

This bakery produces the famous Forfar Bridies. The bakers guard the traditional Forfar Bridie recipe and denounce any Bridie made outside the boundaries of the town. The bakery also produces other traditional baked goods which can be sampled in the tea room.
◐ all year Mon-Sat 8-5.30, closed Bank Hols
Facilities: ⌕ ⓌⒸ
⌕ tea room serves famous Forfar Bridies

• **Royal Lochnagar Distillery**

MAP 3   **SCOTLAND**

⬥ Map 3 C2
Scone Palace
Perth, Perthshire,
Tayside PH2 6BD
Tel. Perth (0738) 52300
*From Perth follow A93
northwards, after 1½ miles turn
left for ¼ mile to palace.*
This is the original home of the
Stone of Scone or Destiny,
which was removed to the
Coronation Throne in the
Palace of Westminster in 1296
as a symbol of Edward I's
victories in Scotland. On display
in the baronial dining hall is the
magnificent modern silver
service commissioned from
Stuart Devlin, the silversmith,
to commemorate the wedding
of Lord and Lady Mansfield.
The 'old kitchen', with its old
range, is now a licensed
restaurant. The produce shop
specialises in the estate's game
and smoked Tay salmon but
also sells homemade bread,
fruit loaves, shortbread thistles,
chutney and marmalade.
☞ adults £2.50, children £2.00,
family ticket £9.00
◑ Easter- 10 Oct Mon-Sat 9.30-5,
Sun 1.30-5
Facilities: ⬤ ⬤ ⬤ ⬤ ⬤ /⬤
⬤ lunches, teas & dinners
served in licensed restaurant
specialising in estate's game,
salmon from River Tay & home
cooking

⬥ Map 3 D2
The Scottish Deer Centre
Over Rankeilour Farm,
Cupar, Fife
Tel. Ladybank (0337) 28369
*From Cupar follow A91
westwards for 3 miles to farm.
Signposted.*
Reediehill was Britain's first
deer farm and, as from April
1988, will be open to the public.
Visitors will be able to walk
through the farm and watch an
audio-visual exhibition
explaining man's changing

relationship with deer through
the ages. The shop offers a
tempting variety of venison
products from deer bred,
slaughtered and expertly hung
on the farm.
☞ adults £2.00, children £1.50
◑ farm: Apr-Oct daily 9-5.30;
shop: Apr-Jan daily 9-5.30
Facilities: ⬤ ⬤ ⬤ ⬤ ⬤ ⬤ /⬤
⬤ licensed farmhouse
restaurant serves lunches &
teas specialising in venison &
home-cooking, open all year

● **Red deer stag at The
Scottish Deer Centre**

⬥ Map 3 D6
Strathisla Distillery
Seafield Avenue, Keith,
Banffshire, Grampian AB5 3BS
Tel. Keith (05422) 7471
In town centre.
Strathisla Distillery, established
in 1786, is one of the oldest
operating distilleries in Scotland
and is housed in picturesque
old buildings. It offers visitors a
full tour, a video explaining the
production process and a
'dram' to finish up. However,
visitors cannot buy the
distillery's products on site.
☞ free
◑ mid May-mid Sep daily 9-4.30
Facilities: ⬤ ⬤ ⬤

⬥ Map 3 D7
Tugnet Ice House
Spey Bay, Fochabers, Moray,
Grampian
Tel. Forres (0309) 73701

*From Fochabers follow A96 north
westwards, after 1 mile turn
right onto B9104 for 5 miles to
museum. Signposted.*
This museum of commercial
salmon fishing is housed in the
largest ice house in Scotland.
Built around 1830, the ice house
is underground and contains a
collection of equipment relating
to the salmon industry.
Commercial salmon fishing has
been carried out from Tugnet
since at least the early 18thC
and the museum, with its
audio-visual display and
changing exhibitions, celebrates
this past.
☞ free
◑ Jun-Sep daily 10-4 or by
appointment
Facilities: ⬤ ⬤ ⬤ ⬤

⬥ Map 3 D6
Walkers' Shortbread Shop
Aberlour, Grampian AB3 9PB
Tel. Aberlour (03405) 555
In town centre. Signposted.
Walkers' shortbread factory is
still located in the village where
the clan established their first
bakery in 1898. The company
prides itself on using high
quality ingredients and
attributes its Queen's Award
for Industry in 1986 to this
concern. The shop sells
shortbread in all shapes and
sizes as well as fruitcakes,
oatcakes and gift selection
boxes.
◑ all year Mon-Thur 8.30-5.30,
Fri 8.30-4.30
Facilities: ⬤ ⬤

DUNDEE CAKE

Dundee Cake is a very rich
fruit cake which will keep for
months in a tin and makes an
excellent cake for
christenings, weddings or
Christmas. Walkers' of
Aberlour make an excellent
one.

MAP 3

● Scone Palace

● The dining room, Scone Palace

MAP 4   SCOTLAND

THE

7

Loch Shiel
861 Blaich
Ardmolich
Acharacle
Salen
Kilchoan
L. Sunart
861
Strontian
Corran
Onich
Nth. Ballachulish
Laroch
884

6
Coll
Arinagour
Tiree
Scarinish
Tobermory
Calgary
Dervaig
L. Frisa
Bonnavoulin
Salen Mull
Oskamull
Ulva
ISLAND
Staffa
B. MORE
3169
OF
Craignure
MULL
Lochbuie
L. Scridain
Iona
Fionnphort
Bunessan
849
Claggan
Lochaline
Lismore
SEA LIFE CENTRE
Portnacroish
828
OBAN DISTILLERY
Loch Etive
CRUACHAN
3689
Connel
Oban
Taynuilt
INVERAWE
SMOKEHOUSES
Kerrera
Firth of Lorn
Kilninver
Kilchrenan
819
Portsonachan
Seil
Easdale
Kilmelford
L Awe
Inveraray
816
Luing
Scarba
Ford
Furnace
Kilmartin

5

THE
WEST COAST

Colonsay
Scalasaig
ANDREW ABRAHAMS
Oronsay
BUNNAHABHAIN
DISTILLERY
Sanaigmore
JURA
PAPS OF
JURA 2571
Port Askaig
Feolin
Ferry
Bridgend
846
Ardlussa
Sound of Jura
Keillmore
Lagg
Kilberry
Tarbert
Crinan
Lochgilphead
83
Ardrishaig
Achahoish
Tighnabruaich
KILFINAN HOTEL
Kilfinan
8003
Colintraive
RITCHIE'S OF ROTHESAY
of Bute
Roth
Innella

4

Port Charlotte
ISLAY
846
Bowmore
BOWMORE DISTILLERY
Portnahaven
Port Ellen
Ardbeg
Mull of Oa
West
L Tarbert
Whitehouse
Clachan
Skipness
Lochranza
Gigha I
Tayinloan
Dippen
Glenbarr
Saddell
Kilchenzie
Machrihanish
Campbeltown
CAMPBELTOWN CREAMERY

3
Sound of
Kilchattan
Bute
BRODICK CASTLE
Pirnmill
Corrie
GOAT FELL
2866
Island of
Brodick
Arran
ARRAN PROVISIONS
Lamlash
Blackwaterfoot
AUCHAREOCH FARM
Dippin

2
NORTH
Rathlin I.
Mull of Kintyre
Southend

1
Portrush
Portstewart
Bushmills
Carrowreagh
Ballycastle
MOYLE
Coleraine
Ballycarton
Ballybogey
Armoy
ANTRIM
Ballymoney
Limavady
Crossgare
BALLYMONEY
Glenariffe
Cushendall
LIMAVADY
Garvagh
COLERAINE
Killagan Eork
Clogh
Carnlough
Dungiven
Kilrea
Glenarm
MOUNTAINS
Lendalfoot
Balla
GLEN APP FISHERIES

A   B   C   D

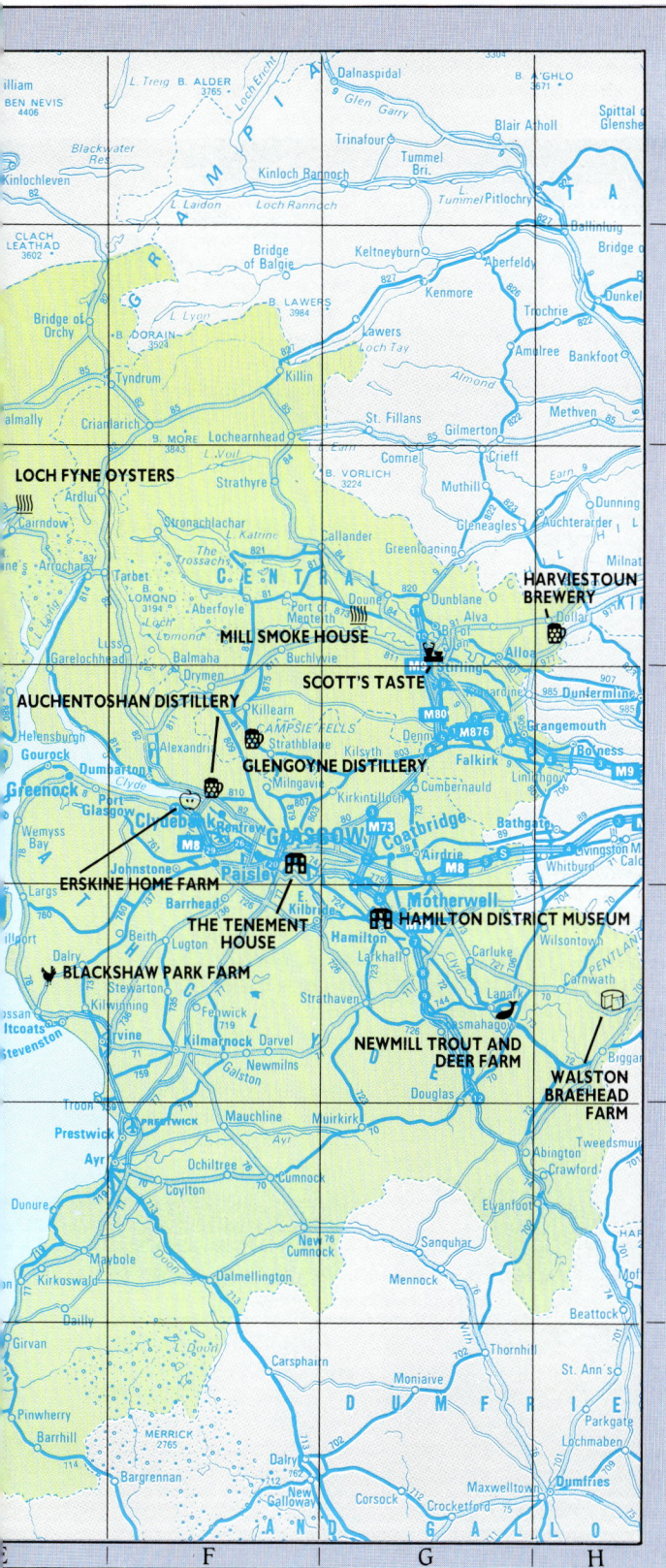

The West Coast of Scotland produces some of the finest fish and shellfish in the world. The clear, clean waters, warmed by currents from the Gulf Stream, are an ideal breeding ground. Lobster, oysters and salmon are not to be missed. Treat yourself to a locally smoked side of Scottish salmon; it's so good that it's exported the world over but it is probably best eaten with a slice of bread and butter by the side of a loch.

Map 4 B4
Andrew Abrahams
The Strand, Isle of Colonsay, Argyll, Strathclyde PA61 7YR
Tel. Colonsay (09512) 365

From Scalasaig follow A869 southwards for 3 miles to Garvard and The Strand.

Some of the finest oysters in the world are produced in Scottish waters and Andrew Abrahams has both an oyster and a honey farm. Visitors are welcome to see the smokehouse where oysters and other shellfish are smoked, and the honey extracting and bottling plant. He sells oysters from the farm, either fresh or smoked, and honey, either in jars or by the cut comb.

☞ free

◗ all year telephone for details

Map 4 E3
Arran Provisions
The Old Mill, Lamlash, Isle of Arran, Strathclyde A27 8JU
Tel. Lamlash (07706) 606

In village. Signposted.

This family business was founded in 1981 to produce speciality foods made by traditional methods. It now has a manufacturing plant on the Isle of Arran and exports goods worldwide. Customers may sample and buy a wide variety of products including mustard,

367

MAP 4   SCOTLAND

chutney, confectionery, preserves, honey, all sorts of jellies, mincemeat, ice cream, whisky, wine and soft drinks. Hampers can be made to order.
◑ Jul-Aug Mon-Sat 9-5; Apr-Jun, Sep, Oct Mon-Fri 9-1, 2-5
Facilities: 🚗 ⛺

🏠 **Map 4 D2**
Auchareoch Farm
Kilmory, Isle of Arran, Strathclyde KA27 8PH
Tel. Sliddery (077087) 336
From Dippin follow A841 westwards, after 7 miles turn right at Kilmory onto forestry road for 2½ miles to farm.
This sheep dairy farm, situated deep in a pine forest, produces a range of Isle of Arran ewes' milk cheese and yoghurt as well as Alice's Cheese — a soft cows' milk cheese. They are all made from pasteurised milk and vegetarian rennet with no other additives or preservatives. Visitors are welcome to look round the farm and to buy the cheeses.
☞ free
◑ Jun-Sep daily 12-5 by appointment
Facilities: 🚗

🐝 **Map 4 F4**
Auchentoshan Distillery
Dalmuir, Clydebank, Dunbartonshire, Strathclyde G81 4SG
Tel. Dintocher (0389) 78561
From Glasgow follow A82 north westwards, after 10 miles turn left onto A814 to distillery.
This is the nearest working malt distillery to the centre of Glasgow and visitors are welcome to tour the premises and try a dram. A unique feature is the triple distillation process which produces a very fine malt whisky. A wide range of products, including miniatures, can be bought in the shop.

☞ adults £1.00
◑ all year by appointment
Facilities: ♿ 🅆 🚗 ⛺

🌾 **Map 4 E3**
Blackshaw Park Farm
West Kilbride, Ayrshire, Strathclyde
Tel. Kilmarnock (0563) 34257
From Dalry follow B780 southwards, after 2½ miles turn right onto B781 for 1 mile to farm on left. Signposted.
This 300-acre working hill farm has spectacular views of the Firth of Clyde and the Mull of Kintyre. The farm specialises in beef cattle and sheep but also keeps a wide variety of other animals which can be seen from the trail. Visitors may watch daily demonstrations of milking, sheep-shearing, dipping and other typical farm chores. A small museum displays agricultural implements and farmhouse kitchen equipment. The shop sells many varieties of vegetables as well as homemade jams, jellies and chutneys.

● **Sheep-shearing, Blackshaw Park Farm**

adults £1.50, children (under 16) £1.00, car load £4.50
◑ Easter-Sep Wed-Mon 10.30-5
Facilities: 🍴 🍴 ♿ 🅆 🚗 ⛺ /𝕄
🍴 teas & light lunches served with homemade soups, pancakes & cakes

---

🐝 **Map 4 B3**
Bowmore Distillery
Bowmore, Isle of Islay, Argyll, Strathclyde
Tel. Bowmore (049681) 441
In village.
This working distillery, with beautiful views of Lochindad, has a number of distinctive features: visitors are invited to tour the premises and see the traditional floor malting of barley and a sophisticated in-house waste energy scheme before tasting the whisky produced. The visitor centre sells a selection of whiskies including miniatures.
☞ free
◑ by appointment
Facilities: 🅆 🚗 ⛺

🏰 **Map 4 D3**
Brodick Castle
Isle of Arran, Strathclyde KA27 8HY
Tel. Brodick (0770) 2202
From Brodick follow A841 northwards for 2 miles to castle on left. Signposted.
Brodick Castle, now owned by the National Trust for Scotland, is a typical Victorian Highland house. Its kitchen is equipped with a large Carron range with 2 fires, 3 ovens and an unusual water-driven roasting spit. There is also a separately fired bread oven and a charcoal stewing stove. The kitchen still has some of its original utensils including a copper 'batterie de cuisine' and pewterware engraved with the Hamilton crest. The display of porcelain and silver in the dining room is changed each year to highlight

MAP 4

• **The kitchen, Brodick Castle**

different aspects of the Beckford and Hamilton collections. A shop sells National Trust for Scotland products.

🎫 adults £2.10, children £1.05
◖ Easter-Sep daily 1-5
Facilities: 🚌 🍴 ⓌⒸ 🚗 ♿ /🏧

🍴 light lunches & afternoon teas served with homemade soups, homebaked bread & cakes

---

🦋 Map 4 C4
Bunnahabhain Distillery
Bunnahabhain, Port Askaig, Isle of Islay, Argyll, Strathclyde PA46 7RP
Tel. Port Askaig (049684) 646

From Port Askaig follow A846 south westwards, after ³/₄ mile turn right onto unclassified road for 4 miles to Bunnahabhain. Signposted.

This distillery is set in a remote and picturesque area on the Isle of Islay. Visitors are invited to tour the premises and taste the product. The shop sells whisky in bottles and miniatures.

🎫 free
◖ all year Mon-Fri 10-4
Facilities: 🚗 ♿ /🏧

🏨 Map 4 D2
Campbeltown Creamery
Witchburn Road, Campbeltown, Argyll, Strathclyde PA28 6JU
Tel. Campbeltown (0586) 52244

In town centre.

The cheese made here was voted Supreme Champion at the Royal Highland Show in 1985 and 1987 and Overall Champion at the Scottish Cheese Show in 1984 and 1986. The plant is modern, producing over 3,000 tonnes of Campbeltown Scottish Cheddar a year using milk from the Kintyre peninsula and the island of Gigha. Visitors may take a guided tour, enjoy tastings and buy both mild and mature cheeses from the shop.

🎫 free
◖ Jun-Aug Tue, Fri 9-11 or by appointment
Facilities: ⓌⒸ 🚗

🍎 Map 4 F4
Erskine Home Farm
Bishopton, Renfrewshire, Strathclyde PA7 5PN
Tel. Bishopton (0505) 862305

From Renfrew follow A8 westwards, after 5 miles turn right onto B815 for 1 mile to farm on left. Signposted.

• **The cheese-making plant at Campbeltown Creamery**

MAP 4   SCOTLAND

This pick your own farm offers 4 varieties of strawberries. They are also available ready-picked.

● Jul Mon-Fri 10-8, Sat, Sun 10-5
Facilities: 🚻 🚗 🍴

〰 Map 4 E1
Glen App Fisheries
Finnarts Bay Salmon Farm, Glen App, Ballantrae, Ayrshire, Strathclyde KA26 OPG
Tel. Cairn Ryan (05812) 271
From Ballantrae follow A77 southwards for 9 miles to fisheries. Signposted.

This fish farm breeds and smokes its own fish and specialises in salmon. Visitors may tour the premises and watch the smoking process. The shop sells fresh and smoked salmon and trout, as well as smoked cheese and pâté.

☞ free
● shop & smokery: all year daily 8-7; salmon farm: by appointment
Facilities: 🚗 🍴

🍷 Map 4 F4
Glengoyne Distillery
Dumgoyne, Stirlingshire, Central GL3 9LB
Tel. Killearn (0360) 2150254
From Strathblane follow A81 north westwards for 3 miles to distillery. Signposted.

Dating from 1836, this distillery has been owned by Lang Brothers since 1876. Visitors are welcome to take a short tour and buy Glengoyne 10 and 17-year-old malt whisky from the shop.

☞ free
● Apr-Oct Mon-Fri 10.30-3.15; tours: 10.30, 11.15, 12.00, 2.00, 3.15; no production mid Jul-Aug
Facilities: 🚻 🚗

RESTAURANT RECIPE

🍴 Map 4 D4
KILFINAN HOTEL
Kilfinan, Strathclyde PA21 2AP
Tel: Kilfinan (070082) 201
In village.

This restored coaching inn is delightfully situated in an extremely rural location and offers a warm welcome, log fires and good Scottish cuisine, including a large selection of fish and this rich recipe for a Salmon Mousseline.

● Mon-Sun Meals: 12-2, 7.30-9.30
Price range £8.50-16
Set D £15
Seats 22
Cards: Access, Amex, Visa
Facilities: 🍷🍴♿🚗

MOUSSELINE OF SALMON with a prawn sauce

1lb fresh salmon filleted
4oz smoked salmon
3 egg whites
½ pint double cream
juice of 1 lemon
salt & black pepper
carrots peeled and cut into fine strips
courgettes peeled and cut into fine strips

prawn sauce:
shells of 6 jumbo prawns
2 bayleaves
¼ pint white wine
1 measure brandy
6 black peppercorns
1 onion quartered
2 tomatoes quartered
parsley stalks
2 pints water
2 tbsp tomato purée
double cream

Heat oven to gas 5 (375F, 190C). Purée the fresh and smoked salmon in a blender with all the mousseline ingredients except the cream, carrots and courgettes. When smooth add the cream until absorbed. Butter six ramekins and line with alternate strips of carrot and courgette, allowing ³/₄- inch over the top of the dish. Place mousseline in the dishes and overlap the carrot and courgette strips. Place in a water basin, cover with tin foil and cook in the oven for 15-20 minutes. Put all the sauce ingredients in a pan except the cream, bring to the boil and then simmer until reduced by half. Strain and finish with double cream, reducing again to a smooth consistency.

🏛 Map 4 G3
Hamilton District Museum
129 Muir Street, Hamilton, Strathclyde ML3 6BJ
Tel. Hamilton (0698) 283981
In town centre.

This museum is housed in a 17thC coaching inn originally known as the Hamilton Arms but later referred to simply as 'the best inn in the town' — and once even described as the best inn in the country. It now contains a reconstructed Victorian kitchen and an exhibition of agricultural implements. Cheese-making and dairying equipment are on display in the restored 18thC stable.

☞ free
● all year Mon, Tue, Thur, Fri 10-5, Wed, Sat 10-12, 1-5
Facilities: 🚻 🚗

🍷 Map 4 H5
Harviestoun Brewery
Dollar, Clackmannanshire, Central
Tel. Dollar (02594) 2141
From Dollar follow B913 southwards for ½ mile to brewery. Signposted.

MAP 4

Housed in a 200-year-old stone brewery, Harviestoun brews ale by the traditional full mash method. Visitors are welcome to tour the premises and taste the product. Beer is for sale by the pint, flagon or polypin.

☞ free

◖ all year Mon-Sat 8.30-5
Facilities: ♿ 🚾 🚗 ♨

〰 Map 4 E6
Inverawe Smokehouses
Inverawe, Taynuilt, Argyll,
Strathclyde PA35 1HU
Tel. Taynuilt (08662) 446

From Taynuilt follow A85 eastwards, after 2 miles turn left at the Bridge of Awe onto unclassified road for 2½ miles to Inverawe. Signposted.

This family business welcomes visitors to its old, traditional smokery and to fish in the river and lakes. The shop sells the many products smoked on the premises including salmon, trout, venison, eel, cod's roe, kippers and a range of pâtés and cheeses. Fishing is also available both in the river and the 3 lochs.

☞ adults 15p

◖ smokery: all year Mon-Fri 9-5; fishing: Apr-Oct daily telephone for details
Facilities: 🍽 🚾 🚗 ♨ ⛺

〰 Map 4 E5
Loch Fyne Oysters
Ardkinglas, Cairndow, Argyll,
Strathclyde
Tel. Cairndow (04996) 217

From Cairndow follow A83 northwards for 1 mile to farm. Signposted.

Loch Fyne Oysters deals not only in fresh oysters but also Dublin Bay prawns or langoustines, salmon — both wild and farmed — trout and herrings. A good deal of the produce, including salmon and kippers, is smoked on the premises and the process can be seen by visitors. The

● **Loch Fyne Oysters**

business prides itself on the freshness and quality of the produce. The oysters have a Grade 1 rating from the Health Authority which means they need not be passed through sterile water tanks. The salmon and langoustines are of the highest possible quality and the oak-smoked kippers are undyed.

☞ free

◖ Jun-Sep daily 9-5; Oct-May Mon-Fri 9-5
Facilities: 🍽 ♿ 🚾 ♨
🍽 seafood snacks available

OYSTERS
Oysters from the Loch Fyne fishery can now grace any table in Britain within 36 hours. But if in the area why not buy them direct from the source at Loch Fyne.

〰 Map 4 G5
Mill Smoke House
Cessintully Mill, Thornhill,
Stirling, Central FK8 3QE
Tel. Thornhill (078685) 348

From Stirling follow A84 north westwards, after 5 miles turn left onto A873 for 3 miles, then turn left onto unclassified road for ½ mile to smokehouse. Signposted.

This small smokehouse

specialises in chicken, trout, wild and farmed salmon, kippers, eels and trout pâté. The emphasis is on local produce — even the chips and sawdust used for smoking are supplied by local coopers who remake whisky barrels from America into barrels for ageing and storing Scotch whisky.

☞ free

◖ all year daily by appointment
Facilities: 🚗

🎣 Map 4 G3
Newmill Trout and Deer Farm
Cleghorn, Lanark,
Strathclyde ML11 7SL
Tel. Lanark (0555) 870730

From Lanark follow A706 north eastwards for 2½ miles to farm. Signposted.

This trout and deer farm prides itself on keeping the fish and animals in the most natural conditions possible. No artificial or chemical additives are used either in the feed or processing of the meat. Visitors may catch their own trout in the fishery, with rod and bait provided, or feed the fish and watch casting demonstrations. The shop sells a wide range of trout, salmon, venison, game, rabbit, hare and Scottish cheeses — all smoked

MAP 4   SCOTLAND

● **Highland food display**

in a specially constructed smokehouse.
☞ free, fishing & rod telephone for details
● all year daily telephone for details
Facilities: 🍺 ⬥ ♿ wc 🚗 👶 🏔
🍽 licensed restaurant features farm's own produce & local game

---

🏠 Map 4 D6
Oban Distillery
Stafford Street, Oban, Argyll, Strathclyde PA34 5NH
Tel. Oban (0631) 62110

In town centre. Signposted.

This is the only malt whisky distillery along this stretch of the west coast. Visitors may watch an audio-visual presentation on whisky production, tour the plant and then taste the various products. The shop sells different ages of malt whisky and whisky-based food and drink specialities.
☞ free
● Oct-Mar Mon-Fri 9-12.30, 1.45-5; Apr-Sep daily 9.30-5, telephone to confirm details
Facilities: 🍺 wc

REGIONAL RECIPE

GRAVADLAX

Marinaded salmon with dill is one of the easiest ways to prepare salmon at home. The trick lies in cutting very thin serving portions.

1 fresh salmon or 2 large pieces of fresh salmon
olive oil
salt
sugar
crushed peppercorns
bunch of fresh dill

Scrape the scales from the fish and cut in half lengthways. Remove the backbone and any small bones. Moisten the flesh with oil and rub in a mixture of equal quantities of salt and sugar and some crushed peppercorns. Place skin side down on a bed of fresh dill, cover with more dill, add the second piece of salmon, skin side up, and cover with remaining dill. Place a plate with a small weight on top and keep in the fridge for 2-4 days. Slice thinly to serve.

〰 Map 4 E4
Ritchie's of Rothesay
37 Watergate, Rothesay, Isle of Bute, Strathclyde PA20 9AD
Tel. Rothesay (0700) 3012

In town centre.

This smokehouse uses no dyes in the curing and smoking of local fish, including Loch Fyne kippers, wild Scotch salmon, haddock and rainbow trout. These can be bought from the shop in addition to fresh fish.
☞ free
● all year Mon-Sat 9-5
Facilities: 🚗

🦐 Map 4 G5
Scott's Taste
19 The Arcade, King Street, Stirling, Central
Tel. Stirling (0786) 63793

In town centre.

This specialist food shop stocks a very wide range of quality goods from all over the world. Of particular note are the Moniack Castle range of Highland wines including Silver Birch, Elderflower, Bilberry and

MAP 4

Meadowsweet, as well as mead and sloe gin and a large selection of farmhouse cheeses. Other products sold include port, whisky, sherry, shortbread, biscuits, meat, confectionery and homemade salads.

◑ all year Mon-Sat 9-5.30
Facilities: 🍵

★ occasional cheese & wine tastings, telephone for details

🏨 Map 4 D6
Sea Life Centre
Barcaldine, Connel, Argyll, Strathclyde PA37 1SE
Tel. Ledaig (063172) 386

From Connel follow A828 northwards for 6 miles to Centre. Signposted.

Situated on the shores of Loch Creran, the Sea Life Centre is a huge marine aquarium with the largest display of marine creatures in Britain. Here, modern technology and materials give visitors a fascinating and memorable experience. They can see all the species of fish that are familiar on the fishmonger's slab actually swimming around — cod, plaice, lemon sole, turbot, octopus, lobsters and, in a specially constructed aquarium, they can actually stand in the middle of a shoal of herring. A fish farming display shows the stages of rearing salmon, turbot and halibut. Children and adults can handle rockpool creatures like starfish and hermit crabs in the living 'touch' pools.

☞ adults £2.10, senior citizens £1.40, children (4-16) £1.25
◑ 28 Mar-Jun, Sep, Oct daily 9-6; Jul-Aug daily 9-7
Facilities: 🍵 🍴 ♿ 🚻 🚗 ♨ ⛰
🍴 licensed restaurant serves A Taste of Scotland lunches & teas, specialising in seafood & homebaked fare including salmon pie, seafood pie & seafood lasagne

● **The Tenement House**

🏨 Map 4 F4

The Tenement House

145 Buccleuch Street, Garnet Hill, Glasgow, Strathclyde
Tel. Glasgow (041) 3330183

In city centre. Signposted.

Tenement House was the home of Agnes Toward, an ordinary Glasgow citizen, from 1911 to 1965. It is one of 56 similar flats in a massive Victorian tenement development and is now owned by the National Trust for Scotland which was also responsible for its restoration. It contains all the original fittings and much of the furniture and furnishings belonging to Miss Toward. The kitchen is typical of the period and has a large black range with a coal bunker, a sink with brass taps, fitted shelves and a bed in the recess behind the door. It is furnished and equipped exactly as it would have been in the early 20thC.

☞ adults £1.10, senior citizens & children 55p
◑ Apr-Oct daily 2-5, Nov-Mar Sat, Sun 2-4

🗓 Map 4 H3
Walston Braehead Farm
by Carnwath, Lanarkshire, Strathclyde
Tel. Dunsyre (089981) 257

From Carnwath follow A721 eastwards, after 3 miles turn left onto unclassified Walston Road for ½ mile to farm.

This mixed hill farm has a sheep dairy producing handmade cheeses: Lanark Blue is made from ewes' milk to an ancient recipe and is similar to Roquefort; Dunsyre Blue is reputedly Scotland's only blue cheese made from cows' milk. Visitors can see the cheese-making and buy the cheeses from the farm.

☞ free
◑ all year by appointment
Facilities: 🚻 🚗

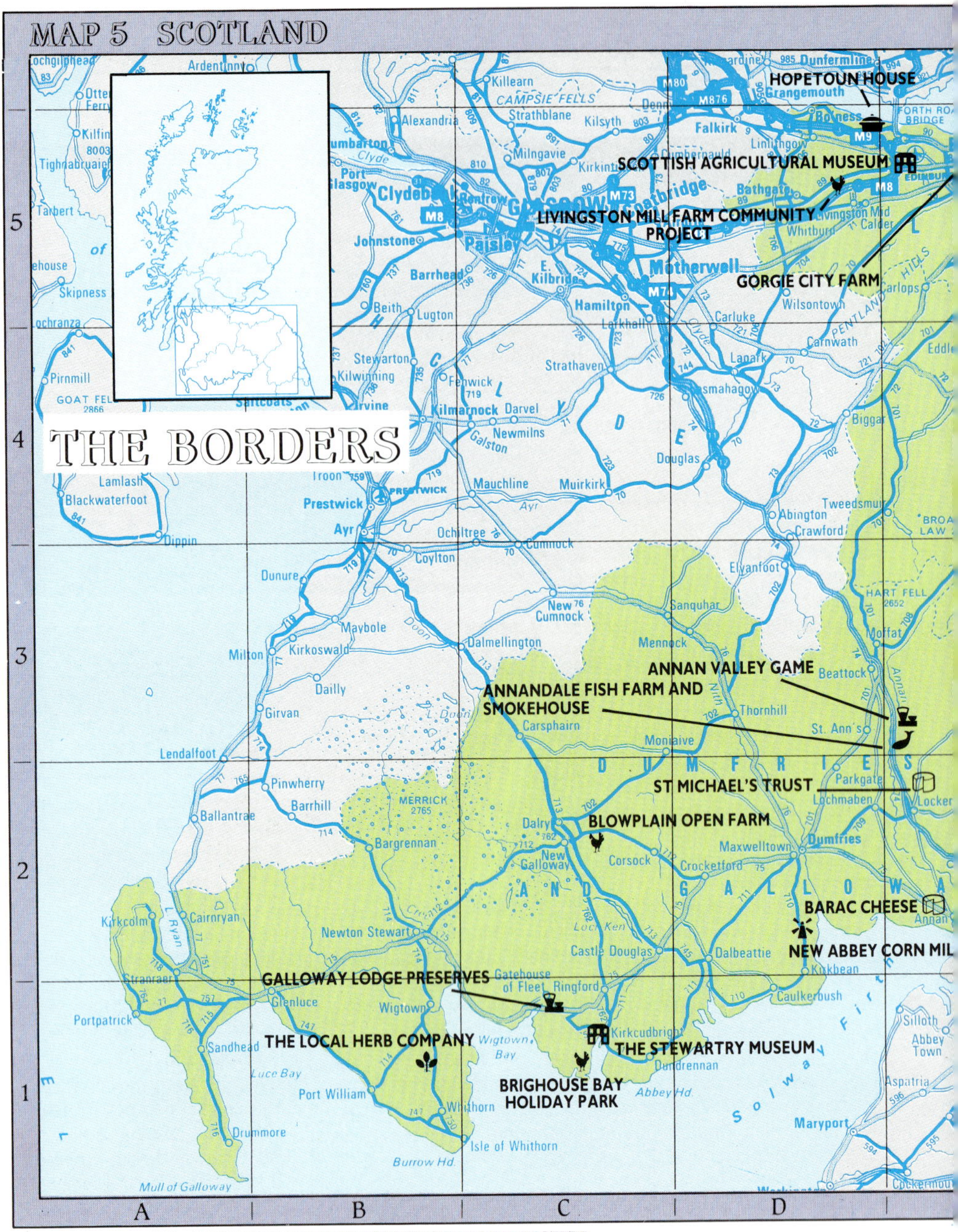
MAP 5 SCOTLAND
THE BORDERS
HOPETOUN HOUSE
SCOTTISH AGRICULTURAL MUSEUM
LIVINGSTON MILL FARM COMMUNITY PROJECT
GORGIE CITY FARM
ANNAN VALLEY GAME
ANNANDALE FISH FARM AND SMOKEHOUSE
ST MICHAEL'S TRUST
BLOWPLAIN OPEN FARM
BARAC CHEESE
NEW ABBEY CORN MIL
GALLOWAY LODGE PRESERVES
THE LOCAL HERB COMPANY
THE STEWARTRY MUSEUM
BRIGHOUSE BAY HOLIDAY PARK
Glasgow
Paisley
Motherwell
Hamilton
Falkirk
Ayr
Prestwick
Kilmarnock
Dumfries
Newton Stewart
Castle Douglas
Kirkcudbright
Stranraer
Girvan
Moffat
A
B
C
D
1
2
3
4
5

The rich, low-lying hills of the Borders are the most intensely farmed in Scotland. Recently cheese-making has been revived and this area offers some newly developed farmhouse cheeses such as Bonchester and Barac. For some reason the Borders produce more varieties of sweets than anywhere else in Scotland. There are cinnamon flavoured Hawick Balls, Jeddart Snails with a mild peppermint taste, Soor Plooms from Peebles, Coltart's Candy, Berwick Cockles, shaped like a cockle shell, and amber and gold-striped Moffat Toffee which has a distinctive flavour.

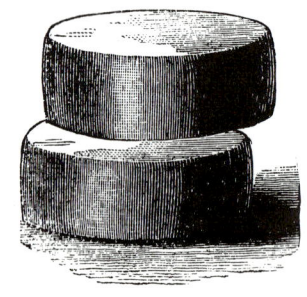

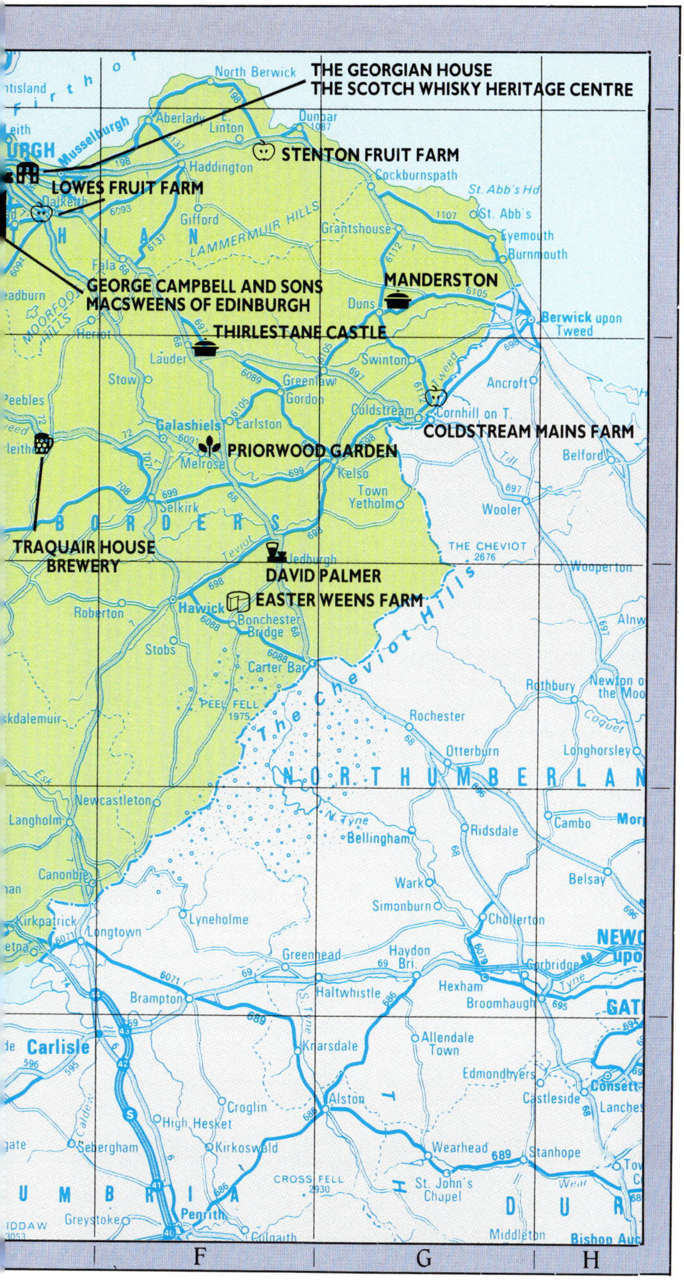

Annandale Fish Farm and Smokehouse

Johnstone Bridge, Lockerbie,
Dumfries and Galloway
DG11 1HD
Tel. Johnstone Bridge (05764)
392

From Moffat follow A701 southwards, after 1 mile turn left onto A74 for 6 miles to Johnstone Bridge. Signposted.

Specialising in trout and salmon netted from the mouth of the River Annan at Solway, this fish farm uses traditional smoking methods. The shop sells fresh and smoked salmon and trout.

🐟 free
◗ all year daily 9-5
Facilities: 🚗 😋

🏠 Map 5 E2
Barac Cheese

Windyknowe, Annan,
Dumfries and Galloway
DG12 5LN
Tel. Annan (04612) 4691

From Annan follow B722 northwards, after 2 miles turn left onto unclassified road for 1/4 mile to Windyknowe. Signposted.

This sheep farm overlooking the Solway and the Lakeland hills developed a new cheese, Barac, in 1980. Barac is a hard, traditional farmhouse cheese made from Friesland sheep's milk and allowed to mature for at least 3 months. It has a mellow, almost malty flavour. Visitors may watch demonstrations of cheese-making at 10am and sheep-milking at 4pm and of course taste the produce. The shop sells Barac in a variety of weights.

🐑 adults 25p, children (under 5) free
◗ all year daily cheese-making 10am, milking 4pm
Facilities: 📶 🚗 😋

🏚 Map 5 E3
Annan Valley Game

Jocksthorn, Wamphray, Moffat,
Dumfries and Galloway
DG10 9NF

Tel. Johnstone Bridge (05764)
331

From Moffat follow A701 southwards, after 1 mile turn left onto A74 for 5 miles to Jocksthorn. Signposted.

This game dealer processes all its own game and also manufactures handmade pies. The shop sells all kinds of fish and game including fresh venison, venison sausages and burgers, smoked salmon and game pies.

◗ all year daily any reasonable time

Facilities: 📶 🚗

Map labels:

THE GEORGIAN HOUSE
THE SCOTCH WHISKY HERITAGE CENTRE
STENTON FRUIT FARM
LOWES FRUIT FARM
GEORGE CAMPBELL AND SONS
MACSWEENS OF EDINBURGH
THIRLESTANE CASTLE
MANDERSTON
PRIORWOOD GARDEN
COLDSTREAM MAINS FARM
TRAQUAIR HOUSE BREWERY
DAVID PALMER
EASTER WEENS FARM

MAP 5   SCOTLAND

Map 5 C2
Blowplain Open Farm
Blowplain, Balmaclellan,
Castle Douglas,
Dumfries and Galloway
DG7 3PY
Tel. New Galloway (06442) 206
*From New Galloway follow A712
eastwards, after 1 1/2 miles turn
right onto unclassified road for
1 1/2 miles to farm. Signposted.*
This small working hill farm
allows visitors to see animals in
their natural environment. The
farm rears cattle, sheep, pigs
and a selection of farmyard
birds including ducks, geese,
hens, peacocks and guinea fowl.
Visitors may take a farm trail
tour and are welcome to feed
the farmyard birds.
adults £1.00, children (over
5) 50p
Apr-Oct Sun, Mon, Wed-Fri,
tours at 2pm
Facilities:

Map 5 C1
**Brighouse Bay Holiday
Park**
Borgue, Kirkcudbright,
Dumfries and Galloway
DG6 4TS
Tel. Borgue (05577) 267
*From Kirkcudbright follow A755
westwards, after 1/2 mile turn left
onto B727 for 4 miles, then turn
left onto unclassified road for 2
miles to park. Signposted.*
These 2 adjacent farms, one a
dairy farm and the other mixed,
cover some 640 acres in total.
Visitors may take a tractor-
trailer tour round both farms
which includes a lecture on
local farm history, a visit to the
modern dairy unit during
milking and an opportunity to
see bulls being prepared for
shows.
adults £1.25, children 85p
Easter-Oct 2.45 by
appointment
Facilities:

REGIONAL RECIPE

TROUT PUDDING

*8oz trout cooked
4 tbsp rice cooked
2 tbsp milk
1 tbsp white wine
1 tsp fresh herbs
1 tsp anchovy essence
salt & pepper
nutmeg*

Flake the trout and mix
thoroughly with all the other
ingredients. Turn into a
buttered ovenproof dish or
mould, cover with buttered
foil and steam for 30 minutes
or bake in a water bath in a
medium oven. Turn out and
serve with a fresh tomato
sauce.

Map 5 E5
**George Campbell and
Sons**
18 Stafford Street, Edinburgh,
Lothian EH3 7BE
Tel. Edinburgh (031) 2257507
In city centre.
Established in 1872 and still run
by the Campbell family, this
specialist food shop selling fish,
poultry and game was granted a
Royal Warrant in 1968. Another
branch has opened at 168 South
Street, Perth.

---

all year Tue-Fri 8-5, Mon, Sat
8-1
Facilities:

Map 5 G4
Coldstream Mains Farm
Coldstream, Berwickshire,
Borders TD12 4ES
Tel. Coldstream (0890) 2613
*From Coldstream follow A6112
northwards for 1 mile to farm.
Signposted.*
A 754-acre fruit farm with 21 1/2
acres given over to pick your
own. Fruit for picking includes
strawberries, raspberries, red
and blackcurrants and
gooseberries. The shop sells
ready-picked broccoli.
end Jun-Aug daily 10-8
Facilities:
mid Jul-early Aug light
refreshments including
homebaked cakes

Map 5 F3
Easter Weens Farm
Bonchester Bridge,
Nr Hawick, Roxburghshire,
Borders TD9 8JQ
Tel. Bonchester Bridge (045086)
635
*From Bonchester Bridge follow
B6357 north eastwards for 1/2
mile to farm. Signposted.*

● **Some of the herd of dairy cows at Easter Weens Farm**

MAP 5

● **The Georgian House's 18th century kitchen with its open fire range**

This dairy farm makes Bonchester cheese using unpasteurised whole milk from its herd of pedigree Jersey cows. The award-winning product is made using traditional methods and has a distinctive flavour somewhere between Camembert and Stilton and can be bought from the farm. Visitors can pick soft fruit in the summer.

🐾 free
● cheese sales: Apr-Dec Mon-Sat 8-8; PYO: mid Jul-mid Aug daily 1-5

🔬 Map 5 C1
Galloway Lodge Preserves
24-28 High Street,
Gatehouse-of-Fleet,
Dumfries and Galloway
DG7 2HP
Tel. Gatehouse (05574) 357
In town centre.

Galloway Lodge Preserves specialises in marmalades, chutney, mustards and traditional Scottish confectionery. The range of mustards and marmalades is particularly large with many actually produced in Gatehouse-of-Fleet. The shop also sells shortbread and craft products.
● all year daily 9-5
Facilities: 🚗

🏛 Map 5 E5
The Georgian House
7 Charlotte Square, Edinburgh,
Lothian EH2 4DU
Tel. Edinburgh (031) 2252160
In city centre.

Designed by Robert Adam in 1791 and formerly the home of the 18th chief of Clan Lamont, 7 Charlotte Square then passed into the hands of the 4th Marquess of Bute before being purchased by the National Trust for Scotland in 1973. The top 2 floors are now the official residence of the Moderator of the Church of Scotland while the rest of the house has been restored as a Georgian museum. The fine 18thC kitchen has an open fire range and a comprehensive 'batterie de cuisine', and the dining room table is fully set with a Wedgwood service and Old Sheffield Plate cutlery. The parlour has Spode and Minton china and visitors may also tour the wine cellar. The shop sells sweets, tinned haggis and biscuits.

🐾 adults £1.60, senior citizens & children 80p
● Apr-Oct Mon-Sat 10-4.30, Sun 2-4.30; Nov Sat 10-4, Sun 2-4

377

MAP 5

SCOTLAND

Gorgie City Farm

Map 5 E5

51 Gorgie Road,
Tynecastle Lane, Edinburgh,
Lothian EH11 2LA
Tel. Edinburgh (031) 3374202

From Edinburgh follow A71 south westwards for 1 mile to farm. Signposted.

Gorgie City Farm occupies a 2½-acre site in the heart of the city of Edinburgh. The farm, on what was once derelict ground, now aims to show city dwellers the relationship between farming and food. There is a wide range of crops and animals including sheep, goats, pigs, cows and poultry. The shop sells eggs, vegetables, homemade jams and bread.

☞ free
◐ all year daily 9-4.30
Facilities: ⬛ ⬛ ⬛ ⬛ ⬛ ⬛

● **A corner of Gorgie City Farm**

SELKIRK BANNOCK

Selkirk Bannocks, a kind of enriched bread with added fruit and butter, originated in the bakery in Selkirk owned by Robbie Douglas. Now bannocks may be bought throughout the region.

Hopetoun House

Map 5 D5

South Queensferry,
Lothian EH30 9SL
Tel. Edinburgh (031) 3312451

From Edinburgh follow A90 westwards, after 7 miles turn left onto A904 for 2 miles, then turn right onto unclassified road for 1 mile to house. Signposted.

Hopetoun House, built in the early 18thC and situated on the banks of the Forth, is Scotland's greatest William Adam mansion. The house contains a number of interesting rooms including a servery and a dining room set for dessert. In the grounds visitors can see a herd of fallow deer and the flock of rare black St Kilda sheep.

☞ adults £2.50, senior citizens £1.50, children £1.00
◐ Easter, 30 Apr-18 Sep daily 11-5.30
Facilities: ⬛ ⬛ ⬛ ⬛ ⬛ ⬛
★ Scottish gala evenings with Scottish food & entertainment

Livingston Mill Farm Community Project

Map 5 D5

Millfield, Livingston Village,
Lothian EH54 7AR
Tel. Livingston (0506) 414957

From Livingston follow A705 westwards, after 2 miles turn left onto B7015 for 100 yards to farm on right.

Livingston Mill Farm Community Project is a voluntary organisation set up in 1981 to develop educational and recreational activities on the outskirts of Livingston. The original farm, part of the Rosebery estates, was worked by the Buchanan family for over 160 years until the land was needed for the new town. The byre, pens and paddock house a range of traditional farm animals. The mill, built about 1770, was operated until the 1940s and the machinery is still

intact, including 3 pairs of stones for shelling and grinding. The museum illustrates life in the area before the advent of the new town with much of the collection gathered from local farms.

☞ adults £1.00, senior citizens & children 50p
◐ Easter-Sep daily 10-5; Oct-Easter 1st w/end in month 10-5 or by appointment; closed Jan.
Facilities: ⬛ ⬛ ⬛ ⬛ ⬛ ⬛

The Local Herb Company

Map 5 B1

Culnoag Cottage,
by Sorbie, Wigtownshire,
Dumfries and Galloway
DG8 8AN
Tel. Sorbie (098885) 249/303

From Whithorn follow A746 northwards, after 5 miles turn left onto B7052 for 1 mile, then turn left onto unclassified road for 1 mile to nursery on right. Signposted.

This small friendly nursery offers a wide range of herb plants, many of which can be seen growing in their natural habitat. The shop also sells some attractive local products such as lavender bags and pot-pourris.

☞ free
◐ May-Sep Thur-Sun 2.30-6 or by appointment
Facilities: ⬛

Lowes Fruit Farm

Map 5 E5

Camp End, Dalkeith,
Lothian EH22 2HJ
Tel. Edinburgh (031) 6602128

From Dalkeith follow A68 north westwards for 1 mile to farm. Signposted.

Brambles and tayberries are among the varieties of fruit and vegetables available at this pick your own farm. The shop also sells ready-picked strawberries and raspberries and local cheese.

MAP 5

🌙 end Jun-Sep daily telephone for details
Facilities: ♨ 🅆 🚗 🍴 ⚠

🍲 Map 5 E5
Macsweens of Edinburgh
130 Bruntsfield Place,
Edinburgh, Lothian EH10 4ES
Tel. Edinburgh (031) 2291216
In city centre.

For more than 30 years this Scottish family firm has specialised in the production of traditional natural-skinned haggis. They have a special recipe which contains only the best local-milled oatmeal. They have also kept up with changing eating patterns and produced a vegetarian version. The shop sells haggis in a number of sizes as well as other regional foods such as Scottish meats, black pudding, mealy pudding, game, smoked trout and salmon and gift packs of shortbread.
🌙 all year Mon, Tue, Thur, Fri 7.30-5.30, Wed 7.30-1, Sat 7-4.30
Facilities: 🅆

🍲 Map 5 G5
Manderston
Duns, Berwickshire,
Borders TD11 3PP
Tel. Duns (0361) 83450

From Duns follow A6105 eastwards for 1½ miles to house on left. Signposted.

This has been described as the finest Edwardian house in Britain. It has a superb example of sophisticated 'below stairs' domestic arrangements with some fascinating equipment. The huge Edwardian kitchen has an island cooking range, made by G. Drouet in Paris, with an underfloor flue connected to a chimney in the boiler house at the opposite end of the house. This provided heat to 4 ovens of varying temperatures and a hot plate. Food was equally well organised with produce stored in 6 separate larders, one each for ice, pastry, raw meat, cooked meat, game and fish. Even the cows had luxurious surroundings, with a dairy created by Italian and French craftsmen in marble quarried from 7 different countries. The dairy court is copied from an ancient Roman cloister complete with a fountain. The present owner is Adrian Palmer, so it is appropriate that Manderston also houses Britain's first privately-owned Biscuit Tin Museum, displaying tins made by Huntley and Palmer over the last 100 years.

The shop sells jams, honey, fudge and haggis.
🎫 adults £2.20, children £1.00
🌙 12 May-25 Sep, Thur, Sun, Whitsun & Aug Bank Hols 2-5.30 or by appointment
Facilities: ♨ 🍴 🅆 🚗 🍵
🍴 cream teas served

🏚 Map 5 D2
New Abbey Corn Mill
Old Mill House, New Abbey,
Dumfries,
Dumfries and Galloway
Tel. Dumfries (0387) 85260
From Dumfries follow A710 southwards for 7 miles to New Abbey. Signposted.

This working mill is a typical late 18thC lowland-type of water-powered grain mill. Although these mills could formerly be found all over the area very few remain working today. Visitors can see the mill in operation and follow the milling process, from the arrival of the newly threshed grain through drying in the kiln to the separation of husks from kernels and their grinding into oatmeal.
🎫 adults 50p, children 25p
🌙 Apr-Sep Mon, Tue, Fri, Sat 9.30-7, Wed 9.30-12, Sun 2-7; Oct-Mar Mon, Tue, Fri, Sat 9.30-4, Wed 9.30-12, Sun 2-4
Facilities: 🅆 🚗 🍵

🍲 Map 5 F4
David Palmer
3 High Street, Jedburgh,
Borders
Tel. Jedburgh (0835) 63276
In town centre.

This butcher was the Scottish champion haggis maker in 1984-86. As well as their superb haggis, visitors may buy beef, pork, lamb and homecooked meats and pies. There is also a branch at 39 Market Place in the centre of Selkirk.
🌙 all year Mon-Wed, Fri, Sat 7-5.30, Thur 7-12

● **Interior of the New Abbey Corn Mill**

MAP 5   SCOTLAND

● **The Herb Garden at Priorwood**

❧ Map 5 F4
Priorwood Garden
Melrose, Borders TD6 9PX
Tel. Melrose (089682) 2965

In town centre. Signposted.

The orchards in this National Trust for Scotland property were originally planted by the monks of Melrose Abbey. Today there are over 30 different varieties of apples grown and visitors may walk through the orchards seeing apples from all ages. For example the Pomme d'Api was first grown by the Romans while apples like Old Pearmain and Oslin were cultivated by monks from the 11th to the 16thC. Visitors can see how apple trees are trained, visit the herb garden and see orchards growing other fruit such as pears, plums, greengages, damsons, cherries and a medlar. The shop sells herb plants and a range of apple products including juice, jams, jellies and chutneys.

☞ free
● Apr, 5 Nov-24 Dec Mon-Sat 10-1, 2-5.30; May-Jun, Oct Mon-Sat 10-5.30, Sun 1.30-5.30; Jul-Sep Mon-Sat 10-6, Sun 1.30-5.30
Facilities: 🚗 ♨

🗗 Map 5 E2
St Michael's Trust
Dryfesdale, Lockerbie,
Dumfries and Galloway
DG11 2RH
Tel. Lockerbie (05762) 3386

From Lockerbie follow B723 northwards for 2 miles to farm.

This dairy, based in a Georgian house in its own grounds, produces goats' milk and cheese. Visitors may see the small dairy herd of goats and watch cheese-making demonstrations. The shop sells cheese and milk as well as information about the benefits of goat products for sufferers from eczema and allergies.

☞ free
● all year daily by appointment
Facilities: ♿ 🚻 🚗

�' Map 5 E5
The Scotch Whisky Heritage Centre
358 Castlehill, The Royal Mile,
Edinburgh, Lothian EH1 2NE
Tel. Edinburgh (031) 5544355

In city centre.

Opening in May 1988. Visitors will step into the heather-scented landscape of the Scottish highlands and islands, and learn some of the mystique of the Scotch Whisky industry. They will discover a fascinating working model of a distillery and then, in an electric barrel car, ride through a crofter's cottage, search for an illicit still in the highland hills and follow the trade's progress through history including its periods of prohibition and its boom years in the 19thC.

☞ adults £2.50, children (under 16) £1.25
● May-Oct daily 9-7, Nov-Mar daily 9-5

🏠 Map 5 E5
Scottish Agricultural Museum
Royal Highland Showground,

Ingliston, Edinburgh, Lothian
Tel. Edinburgh (031) 3332674

From Edinburgh follow A8 westwards, after 7 miles turn right into Edinburgh airport slip road, then turn left and left again to museum. Signposted.

This museum, specialising in the history of Scottish food production, is the best of its type in the country. Its large collection of 18th and 19thC farm machinery and implements show how Scotland was in the forefront of the agricultural revolution. Day-to-day life is conjured up through a display of domestic implements for food processing and preparation. There are also fully furnished room settings and an audio-visual presentation.

☞ free
● May-Sep Mon-Fri 10-5, Sun 12-5
Facilities: 🍴 ♿ 🚻 🚗 ♨

🕑 Map 5 F5
Stenton Fruit Farm
Ruchlaw Mains, Stenton,
Lothian EH42 1TD
Tel. Stenton (03685) 321

From East Linton follow unclassified road southwards for 2 miles to farm. Signposted.

A pick your own farm selling strawberries, gooseberries, raspberries, red and blackcurrants, brambles and tayberries. The shop also sells local potatoes, eggs, tomatoes and honey.
● Jul-Aug daily 10-9
Facilities: 🚻 🚗 ♨ ⛰

🏠 Map 5 C1
The Stewartry Museum
St Mary Street, Kirkcudbright,
Dumfries and Galloway
Tel. Kirkcudbright (0557) 30797

In town centre.

This museum of local history provides an interesting picture of Scottish life in times past. It houses a collection of domestic

MAP 5

and agricultural implements outlining methods of food production and processing.

☞ adults 50p, children 25p
◑ Easter-Jun, Sep-Oct Mon-Sat 11- 4; Jul-Aug Mon-Sat 11-5
Facilities: 🚻 ♨

🛏 Map 5 F4
Thirlestane Castle
Lauder, Berwickshire, Borders TD2 6RU
Tel. Lauder (05782) 430

From Lauder follow A68 south eastwards, after ¼ mile turn left onto unclassified road for ¼ mile to castle. Signposted.

Thirlestane Castle is an interesting combination of Scottish and English architectural traditions. Its foundations go back to the 13thC but its present form is the result of the prosperity brought to the Scottish aristocracy after the accession of the Stuart dynasty to the English throne in the 17thC. This makes an interesting contrast to some of the exhibits in the Border Country Life Museum which depict the life of ordinary people. There is special emphasis on the history of food production in the Scottish Borders through the ages and a display showing life below stairs in the kitchen.

☞ adults £2.00, senior citizens & children £1.50, family ticket £5.00, season ticket £5.00
◑ castle & museum: Easter Sun & Mon 2-5; May, Jun, Sep Wed, Thur, Sun 2-5; Jul-Aug Sun-Fri 2-5
Facilities: 🍴 🚻 🚗 ♨ /🏛

🎰 Map 5 E4
Traquair House Brewery
Innerleithen, Peebleshire, Borders EH44 6PW

From Innerleithen follow B709 southwards for ½ mile to house on right. Signposted.

Two hundred years ago almost every large country house

● The dining room, Traquair House

● Traquair House

● The Brewhouse, Traquair House

produced its own ale. Today Traquair House is the sole survivor of this tradition. The house was a traditional Jacobite stronghold and both Mary Queen of Scots and Bonnie Prince Charlie visited here. Today the brewery is housed in 2 rooms and brewing takes place every 2 to 3 weeks. Production is limited by the size of the equipment, some of which was purchased in 1739.

Visitors may take a tour of both the house and brewery, taste the beer and stroll through the extensive grounds.

☞ Sep-Jun: adults £2.00, children £1.00; Jul-Aug: adults £2.50
◑ 13 Apr-Jun, 14 Sep-18 Oct daily 1.30-5.30; Jul-14 Sep daily 10.30-5.30
Facilities: 🍴 🍴 🚻 🚗 ♨

· CALENDAR OF EVENTS ·

JUNE

Borders Country Fair
4-5 June
An annual country fair at Coldstream, Berwickshire.

JULY

Eyemouth Herring Queen Festival
9-16 July
A colourful custom culminating with the Fishermen's Service at the Parish Church at Eyemouth, Borders.

Scottish Game Fair
22-24 July
An annual fair organised by the Scottish Landowners' Federation and the Country Landowners' Association at Floors Castle, Kelso, Borders.

NOVEMBER

Scottish Agricultural Winter Fair
30 November-1 December
An annual fair at Ingliston Showground, Edinburgh.

AGRICULTURAL SHOWS

A number of annual agricultural shows are held in Scotland — they are normally a good source of local produce. The following is a selection:

MAY

Catrine Show
14 May at Catrine, Ayrshire.

JUNE

International Horticultural Show
1-2 June at the Scottish Exhibition and Conference Centre, Glasgow, Strathclyde.

Royal Highland Show
19-22 June at Ingliston Showground, Edinburgh.

JULY

Doune and Dunblane Agricultural Show
2 July at Dunblane, Central.

Deeside Agricultural Show
23 July at Banchory, Grampian.

Angus Show
27 July at Arbroath, Angus, Tayside.

Border Union Agricultural Show
29-30 July at Kelso, Borders.

AUGUST

Dumfries and Lockerbie Show
6 August at Dumfries,.

Orkney Show
13 August at Kirkwall, Orkney.

ACKNOWLEDGEMENTS

The publishers would like to thank the following, both individuals and organisations, for their help, advice and co-operation:

ASSISTANT EDITORS Denise Carter, Merlo Michell, Sarah Toynbee, Richard O'Brien, David Ward.

PICTURE RESEARCHER Jane Williams.

CONTRIBUTORS Sharon Barclay, Mark Bryant, Janice Harrison, Nicola Hill, Charlie Hurt, Diane Leah, David Prout, Anne Satchell, John Vaughan.

ORGANISATIONS British Beekeepers Association, British Sheep Dairying Association, British Trout Association, CAMRA, COSIRA, Cumbria Tourist Board, Dyfed County Council, East Anglia Tourist Board, East Midlands Tourist Board, English Heritage, English Tourist Board, Farm Holiday Bureau, Farm Shops & PYO Association, Farm Wildlife Advisory Group, Heart of England Tourist Board, Herb Society, Historic Houses Association, National Association of Cider Makers, National Council for the Conservation of Plants and Gardens, National Farmers Union England & Wales, National Farmers Union Scotland, National Federation of City Farms, National Trust England & Wales, National Trust for Scotland, Northumbria Tourist Board, North West Tourist Board, Rare Breeds Survival Trust, Scotch Whisky Association, Scottish Tourist Board, Society for the Protection of Ancient Buildings, Soil Association, South East England Tourist Board, Southern Tourist Board, Thames & Chilterns Tourist Board, Wales Tourist Board, West Country Tourist Board, Yorkshire & Humberside Tourist Board.

The publishers would also like to thank the following for their kind help in supplying photographs used in this book:

Angus District Libraries and Museums page **354** *left and right*; Britain on View **21, 27, 39, 41, 131, 284, 294, 344, 371**; Cheddar Gorge Cheese **216** *above and below*; Cromer Museum **162**; The Geffrye Museum, London **285**; Highlands and Islands Development Board **343, 345, 350, 372**; Jarrold Colour Publications **49, 59, 146** *left*, **147, 158, 364** *above and below*, **381** *above and below right and left*; Jordans' Holme Mills **8, 10, 11, 173**; Mansell Collection **18, 46, 113, 134, 150, 186, 188, 198, 254, 258, 281, 286, 306, 309, 312, 319** *above*, **340, 363**; Museum of Cider, Hereford, **125, 126, 128**; Museum of Kent Rural Life **301** *left, above right and left*; National Trust **50, 51, 55, 207, 237, 238, 244, 279**; National Trust for Scotland **355, 360** *above and below*, **362, 363** *above*, **369** *left*, **373, 377, 380**; Robert Opie Collection **144, 145**; Puffin Fisheries, Isle of Wight **269**; Welsh Development Agency **315, 317, 318** *left and right*, **319** *below*, **322, 323, 329, 330, 331, 333, 334, 337**.

Maps prepared by the cartographic staff of George Philip Cartographic Services Ltd. Maps are based upon the Ordnance Survey maps, with the permission of the Controller of H M Stationery Office, Crown copyright reserved.